KEYWORDS FOR INDIA

Also available from Bloomsbury

CONTEMPORARY CRITICAL DISCOURSE STUDIES
edited by Christopher Hart and Piotr Cap

KEY TERMS IN SECOND LANGUAGE ACQUISITION
by Bill VanPatten and Alessandro G. Benati

LANGUAGE, MEANING, AND USE IN INDIAN PHILOSOPHY
by Malcolm Keating

POLITICAL METAPHOR ANALYSIS
by Andreas Musolff

RETERRITORIALIZING LINGUISTIC LANDSCAPES
edited by David Malinowski and Stefania Tufi

THE BLOOMSBURY RESEARCH HANDBOOK OF INDIAN AESTHETICS
AND THE PHILOSOPHY OF ART
edited by Arindam Chakrabarti

THE BLOOMSBURY RESEARCH HANDBOOK OF INDIAN
PHILOSOPHY OF LANGUAGE
edited by Alessandro Graheli

KEYWORDS FOR INDIA

A CONCEPTUAL LEXICON FOR THE TWENTY-FIRST CENTURY

Edited by
Rukmini Bhaya Nair and Peter Ronald deSouza

BLOOMSBURY ACADEMIC
LONDON • NEW YORK • OXFORD • NEW DELHI • SYDNEY

BLOOMSBURY ACADEMIC
Bloomsbury Publishing Plc
50 Bedford Square, London, WC1B 3DP, UK
1385 Broadway, New York, NY 10018, USA

BLOOMSBURY, BLOOMSBURY ACADEMIC and the Diana logo are trademarks of
Bloomsbury Publishing Plc

First published in Great Britain 2020

Copyright © Rukmini Bhaya Nair, Peter Ronald deSouza and Contributors, 2020

Rukmini Bhaya Nair and Peter Ronald DeSouza have asserted their right under the Copyright, Designs and Patents Act, 1988, to be identified as Editors of this work.

For legal purposes the Acknowledgements on p. xiii constitute an extension of this copyright page.

Cover design: Mir Suhail with Rukmini Bhaya Nair
Cover image: Woman Writing a Love Letter/Indian Sculpture, 11th Century © akg-images

All rights reserved. No part of this publication may be reproduced or transmitted in any form or by any means, electronic or mechanical, including photocopying, recording, or any information storage or retrieval system, without prior permission in writing from the publishers.

Bloomsbury Publishing Plc does not have any control over, or responsibility for, any third-party websites referred to or in this book. All internet addresses given in this book were correct at the time of going to press. The author and publisher regret any inconvenience caused if addresses have changed or sites have ceased to exist, but can accept no responsibility for any such changes.

A catalogue record for this book is available from the British Library.

A catalog record for this book is available from the Library of Congress.

ISBN: HB: 978-1-3500-3924-7
PB: 978-1-3500-3923-0
ePDF: 978-1-3500-3927-8
eBook: 978-1-3500-3925-4

Typeset by Deanta Global Publishing services, Chennai, India

To find out more about our authors and books visit www.bloomsbury.com and sign up for our newsletters.

CONTENTS

Advisory board members	xii
Acknowledgements	xiii
Diacritic character table	xv

Introduction *by* Rukmini Bhaya Nair — 1

1 Classical heritages: Databases of memory — 19

Atma (ātmā) *by* TRS Sharma	19
Ahimsa (ahinsā/hinsā/satya/asatya/śānti) *by* Gangeya Mukherji	20
Artha (artha) *by* Mohini Mullick	22
Aryan (āryan)/Dravidian *by* Lakshmi Subramaniam	23
Asmita (asmitā) *by* Sanjay Palshikar	24
Bhava (bhāva) *by* TRS Sharma	26
Bhakti (bhakti) *by* TRS Sharma	27
Caste *by* Surinder S. Jodhka	28
Colonialism/postcolonialism *by* Ulka Anjaria	30
Darshana (darśana) *by* Sanjit Chakraborty	33
Dharma (dharma) *by* Bijoy Boruah	35
Dhyana (Dhyāna) *by* Bijoy Boruah	37
Golden Temple *by* Ronki Ram	38
Guru (guru) *by* Sanjit Chakraborty	39
Haj *by* Maidul Islam	41
Heritage sites *by* A. G. K. Menon	42
Hinduism *by* Shashi Tharoor	43
Indian Ocean *by* Sanjay Chaturvedi	45
Itihasa (itihāsa) *by* Sibesh Bhattacharya	47
Janmapatri (janmapatrī) *by* Rama Kant Agnihotri	48
Kama and Kamasutra (kāma and kāmasūtra) *by* Gurcharan Das	49
Mahabharata (mahābhārata) *by* Sibaji Bandyopadhyay	51
Mantra, Tantra, Yantra (mantra, tantra, yantra) *by* Ranjit Nair	54
Manuvadi (manuvādī) *by* Sasheej Hegde	55
Maya (māyā) *by* Mohini Mullick	56
Moksha/Nirvana (mōkṣa/nirvāṇa) *by* Ranjit Nair	58
Mussalman (musalmān) *by* Taslima Nasrin	59
Orientalism *by* Ulka Anjaria	60

Contents

Parsi (pārsī) *by* Keki Daruwala	62
Pir/Murid (pīr/murīd) *by* S. Imtiaz Hasnain and Masood Ali Beg	64
Purana (purāṇa) *by* B. N. Patnaik	65
Kismat/Takdir (qismat/takadīr) *by* Shivangini Tandon and S. Imtiaz Hasnain	66
Ramayana (rāmāyaṇa) *by* Paula Richman	68
Sati/Jauhar (satī/jauhar) *by* Malashri Lal	70
Sufi (sūfī) *by* S. Imtiaz Hasnain and Masood Ali Beg	72
Zero *by* Iwan Pranoto and Ranjit Nair	73

2 Contemporary aesthetic modes: Reimaginings — 75

Alankara (alaṅkāra) *by* Harsha V. Dehejia	75
Beauty parlour *by* Katyayani Dalmia	76
Bharatnatyam (bharatanāṭyam) *by* Leela Samson	77
Bhoot (bhūta) *by* Brahma Prakash	79
Bollywood *by* Ravi Vasudevan	80
Foto (phōṭō) *by* B. N. Goswamy	82
Gana (gānā) *by* Antony Arul Valan	83
Gorapan (gōrāpan) *by* Katyayani Dalmia	84
Gym *by* Santosh Desai	86
Hero/Heroine *by* Irwin Allan Sealy	87
Ishq/Pyar (iśq/pyār) *by* Shivangini Tandon	89
Jatra (jātrā) *by* Roma Chatterji	90
Leela (līlā) *by* Leela Samson	91
Naach (nāc) *by* Brahma Prakash	92
Nakhra (nakhrā) *by* Brahma Prakash	93
Padma Awards *by* Vibha Puri Das	94
Qawwāli (qavvālī) *by* Yousuf Saeed	95
Raga (rāga) *by* Tista Bagchi	97
Ramlila (rāmlīlā) *by* Sudha Gopalakrishnan	98
Rangoli (raṅgōlī) *by* Sudha Gopalakrishnan	100
Rasa (rasa) *by* Hemachandran Karah	102
Sahitya (sāhitya) *by* B. N. Patnaik	103
Saree (sāṛī) *by* Gopika Nath	105
Saundarya (saundarya) *by* Harsha V. Dehejia	107
Selfie *by* Seema Khanwalkar	109
Shamiyana (śāmiyānā) *by* Ira Pande	110
South Indian films *by* Uma Vangal	112
Taj Mahal *by* Timeri N. Murari	113
Tamasha (tamāśā) *by* Arjun Ghosh	114
Vaastu (vāstu) *by* Rajat Subhra Banerjee	116
Yoga (yōga) *by* Ranjit Nair	117

3	Economic mantras, media and technological change	121
	Aadhaar (ādhār) *by* Vijayanka Nair	121
	Aspatre/Haspatal (aspatre/haspatāl) *by* Kavery Nambisan	122
	Benami *by* Paranjoy Guha Thakurta	124
	Black economy *by* Arun Kumar	125
	Breaking news *by* Pamela Philipose	126
	Climate change *by* Navroz K. Dubash	127
	Computer/laptop/mobile *by* Souvik Mukherjee	129
	Corporate social responsibility *by* Arun M. Kumar	131
	Cyberbhakt *by* Thomas Abraham	132
	Demonetization *by* C. Rammanohar Reddy	133
	Development *by* Pulapre Balakrishnan	135
	Digital India *by* Sandeep Mertia	136
	Green Revolution *by* Aditya Dasgupta	138
	Human development *by* A. K. Shiva Kumar	140
	Indian Railways *by* Vijaya Singh	141
	Inflation *by* Dipak Dasgupta	142
	Inheritance systems *by* Bina Agarwal	144
	Jhuggi, Jhopri, Slum, Chawl (jhuggī, jhōpḍi, Slum, cāl) *by* Darryl D'monte	145
	Jobless growth *by* Montek S. Ahluwalia	147
	Land grabbing *by* Varsha Bhagat-Ganguly	149
	LPG *by* Pulapre Balakrishnan	151
	Mai Baap Sarkaar (maiṁ bāp sarkār) *by* Parikshit Ghosh and Debraj Ray	153
	Mall *by* C. Ramachandraiah	155
	Mandi/E-chaupal (maṇḍī/E-caupāl) *by* Jeemol Unni	156
	Microfinance *by* H. S. Shylendra	157
	Middle class *by* Pavan K. Varma	159
	Nasbandi (nasbandī) *by* Poonam Muttreja	160
	NREGA (naregā) *by* Reetika Khera	161
	Outsourcing *by* Souvik Mukherjee	163
	Policy paralysis *by* Vipul Mudgal	165
	Pollution *by* Shahzad Gani and Pallavi Pant	167
	Public private partnership *by* Bibek Debroy	168
	Public health *by* Poonam Muttreja	169
	Refugee *by* Paula Banerjee	171
	Reserve Bank of India *by* Raghavendra Lal Das	172
	Sensex *by* Hoshang Netarwala	174
	Social media *by* P. Vigneswara Ilavarasan	176
	Start-up *by* Souvik Mukherjee	178
	Tax *by* Saba Sharma	179

Contents

4 Intimacies: Culture and material culture — 181

Azan (azān) *by* Hilal Ahmed	181
Badh (baḍh) *by* Punam Tripathi	182
Balti and Lota (bālṭī and lota) *by* Shivani Chopra	183
Behenji (bahanjī) *by* Ajoy Bose	184
Bhadralok (bhadralōk) *by* Supriya Chaudhuri	185
Bhailo/Bhaiya/Ghanti/Paklo *by* Rochelle Pinto	187
Bhukamp (bhūkamp) *by* Punam Tripathi	188
Chappal (cappal) *by* Gopika Nath	189
Choolah (cūl'hā) *by* Shahzad Gani and Pallavi Pant	190
Coolie *by* Harish Trivedi	191
Cricket *by* Boria Majumdar	192
Cycle-wala (sā'ikilwālā) *by* Jean Drèze	193
Danda/Lathi/Lathi Charge (ḍaṇḍā/lāṭhī/lāṭhī Charge) *by* Manindra Thakur	194
Female foeticide *by* Ravinder Kaur	196
Food *by* Jasmine Anand	197
Godmen *by* Akshaya Mukul	200
Godrej almirah (godrej ālmirah) *by* Dipti Kulkarni	202
Haram/Halal (harām/halāl) *by* Amir Ali	203
Izzat/Sharam/Honour Killing (izzat/śaram) *by* Shivangini Tandon	205
Jagannath/Juggernaut (jagannāth/juggernaut) *by* Jatindra Kumar Nayak	206
Jagran/Kirtan/Bhajan (jāgaraṇ/kīrtan/bhajan) *by* Jaskiran K. Mathur	207
Jharoo/Teel Jharoo/Eerkali Chool (jhāḍū/teel jhāḍū/eerkali chool) *by* Susan Visvanathan	208
Jootha (jūṭhā) *by* Rama Kant Agnihotri	209
Kabbadi, Gili Danda, Jallikatta (kabaḍḍī, gillī ḍaṇḍā, jallīkaṭṭū) *by* Souvik Naha	210
Kai (kāī) *by* Vanamala Viswanatha	212
Kayaka (kayaka) *by* N. Manu Chakravarthy	213
Khadi (khādī) *by* Tridip Suhrud	214
Lakshman Rekha (lakṣmaṇ rēkhā) *by* Rukmini Bhaya Nair	215
Mada, Nall (mād, nāl) *by* Alito Siqueira and Asawari Nayak	217
Mela (mēlā) *by* Chandan Gowda	217
Missed call *by* Satish Padmanabhan	219
Prakriti/Sanskriti (prakr̥ti/sanskr̥ti) *by* Ranjeeta Dutta	220
Ramzan (ramzān) *by* Hilal Ahmed	221
Shamshan (śamśāna) *by* Ipshita Chanda	222
Sogadu (sogāṛū) *by* N. Manu Chakravarthy	224
Susegad (sussegād) *by* Alito Siqueira and Asawari Nayak	224
Stamp paper *by* Ramanjit Kaur Johal	225
Street children *by* Harsh Mander	227
Street vendors *by* Ritajyoti Bandyopadhyay	228
Temple entry *by* Dipti Kulkarni	230

	Tribal customary law *by* Melvil Pereira	231
	Zanana (zanānā) *by* Nazima Parveen	231
5	**Emancipatory imaginaries**	**233**
	Adivasi (ādivāsī) *by* Virginius Xaxa	233
	Ambedkarite *by* V. Geetha	235
	Amir Gharib (amīr/gharīb) *by* S. Imtiaz Hasnain and Masood Ali Beg	237
	Anganwadi (āṅganavāḍī) *by* Sarojini Ganju Thakur	239
	AYUSH (āyūṣ) *by* Madhulika Banerjee	241
	Bhaichara (bhā'īcārā) *by* Satish Aikant	245
	Chandrayaan (candrayāṇ) *by* Gopal N. Raj	247
	Dalit (dalit) *by* Gopal Guru	248
	Democracy *by* Peter Ronald deSouza	249
	Disability *by* Annie Koshi	251
	Dowry (dahēj) *by* N. Jayaram	252
	Gandhian *by* Sudarsan Padmanabhan	253
	Gaon (gānv) *by* Jitender Parsad	255
	Hijra (hijḍā)/LGBT *by* Ashley Tellis	257
	Janta (jantā)/public *by* Rama Kant Agnihotri	258
	Love marriage *by* Rajni Palriwala	259
	Maa (māṁ) *by* Geetanjali Shree	262
	Madrasa (madrasā) *by* Mohd. Sanjeer Alam	264
	Modernity *by* Kavita Panjabi	266
	Mohalla (mōhallā) *by* Nazima Parveen	269
	Nehruvian *by* Madhavan Palat	271
	Parivar/Samaj/Biradri (parivār/samāj/birādarī) *by* Nilanjan Mukhopadhyay	272
	Patriarchy *by* Uma Chakravarti	274
	Police reforms *by* Prakash Singh	276
	RTI *by* The MKSS Collective	278
	Shakti (śakti) *by* Vrinda Dalmiya	280
	Scientific temper *by* Ranjit Nair	281
	Self-respect *by* V. Geetha	282
	Seva (sēvā) *by* Tridip Suhrud	284
	Sarva Shiksha Abhiyan (sarva śikṣā abhiyān) *by* Vimala Ramachandran	286
	Sudhar (sudhār) *by* Tridip Suhrud	287
	Sukh-dukh (sukh-dukh) *by* Aditi Mukherjee	288
	Swaraj (svarāj) *by* Dunu Roy	289
	Virangana (vīrāṅgaṇā) *by* Usha Mudiganti	292
	Visva-Bharati (viśva-bhāratī) *by* Partha Ghose	293
	Vote bank *by* Manisha Madhava	295
	Yojana (yōjanā)/Planning *by* Nalini Nayak and Pulin B. Nayak	296

Contents

6   Language and self-reflection — **299**

Adda (aḍḍā) *by* Manas Ray	299
Adjust *by* Santosh Desai	301
Akshara (akṣara) *by* Aditi Mukherjee	302
Baat-cheet (bātcīt) *by* Rama Kant Agnihotri	303
Bhasha (bhāṣā) *by* Karthika Sathyanathan and Rajesh Kumar	303
Eighth Schedule *by* Om Prakash	305
Endangered languages *by* Jatindra Kumar Nayak	307
English *by* K. Narayana Chandran	308
File *by* Shiv Visvanathan	310
Firangi/Angrez (phiraṅgī/aṅgrēz) *by* Gilian Wright	311
Gaali (gālī) *by* Praveen Singh	312
Hello-ji (hēlō jī) *by* Maidul Islam	314
Indian writing in English (IWE) *by* G. J. V. Prasad	315
Jugaad (jugāḍ) *by* Lallan Baghel	316
Karpu *by* Antony Arul Valan	318
Katha, Kahani, Qissa, Dastaan (kathā, kahānī, kis'sā, dāstān) *by* Mahmood Farooqui	320
Khari Boli (khaḍī bōlī) *by* Abhay Kumar Dubey	321
Kolaveri (kōlāverī) *by* Fahima Ayub Khan	323
Languages and linguistic states *by* Rama Kant Agnihotri	324
Matlabi (matlabī) *by* Shiv Visvanathan	326
Nara (nārā) *by* Navprit Kaur	327
Neta (nētā) *by* Manish Thakur	328
Pravachan (pravacan) *by* Rama Kant Agnihotri	330
Settled *by* Shiv Visvanathan	331
Shruti and Smriti (śruti and smr̥ti) *by* Praveen Singh	332
Thalaivar (talaivar) *by* Sudarsan Padmanabhan	334
Tension *by* Anushka Rajesh Patel and Merdijana Kovacevic	335
Three language formula *by* Jatindra Kumar Nayak	337
Time-pass *by* Vanamala Viswanatha	338
Translation *by* Rita Kothari	339
VIP *by* Shiv Visvanathan	340

7   Politics and the political — **343**

AFSPA and other draconian laws *by* Ujjwal Kumar Singh	343
Atrocity *by* Chandraiah Gopani	345
Ayodhya (ayōdhyā) *by* A. K. Verma	346
Babu/Sarkar/Revenue Officer (bābū/sarkār/revenue officer) *by* Tabish Khair	348
Border *by* Yogesh Snehi	350
Bureaucracy *by* Aakar Patel	351
Chunav (cunāv)/election *by* Mona Mehta	353
Coalition dharma *by* E. Sridharan	355

Communal violence *by* Harsh Mander	356
Corruption *by* C. Rammanohar Reddy	358
Desivad (dēsīvād) *by* Bhalchandra Nemade	360
Dharna/Rail Roko/Bandh/Hartal/Gherao (dharnā/rēl rōkō/bandh/ haṛtāl/ghērāv) *by* Samir Kumar Das	361
DM/BDO *by* Ashok Thakur	363
Dominant caste *by* Ghanshyam Shah	365
Emergency *by* Suhas Palshikar	366
Fatwa (fatvā) *by* Irfanullah Farooqi	368
Ghar Wapsi (ghar vāpsī) *by* Rudolf C. Heredia	370
Hindu Rashtra (hindū rāṣṭra) *by* Pralay Kanungo	372
Human rights *by* Savita Bhakhry	374
IAS, IFS *by* Yogendra Kumar	375
Insurgency/terrorist/jihādī/militant *by* Sanjoy Hazarika	377
Jumla (jumlā) *by* Mona Mehta	379
Lal Batti (lāl battī) *by* Manish Thakur	381
Lok Adalat (lōk adālat) *by* Siddharth Peter De Souza	383
Minorities *by* Peter Ronald deSouza	385
Nagar Palika (nagar pālikā) *by* George Mathew	386
National, anti-national *by* Kaisser Rana	387
Naxalite (nakslā'iṭ) *by* Bela Bhatia	388
Northeast India *by* Pradip Phanjoubam	390
Panchayati Raj (pañcāyatī rāj) *by* George Mathew	392
Partition *by* Salil Misra	394
Patwari (paṭvārī) *by* Ramana Murthy V. Rupakula	395
Peasant movements *by* Muzaffar Assadi	397
Political parties *by* Ashutosh Kumar	399
Rajya Sabha, Lok Sabha (rājya sabhā, lōk sabhā) *by* Valerian Rodrigues	400
Rape *by* Mary E. John	402
SAARC *by* Rahul Tripathi	403
Sarkar (sarkār) *by* Chandan Sinha and Neilabh Sinha	404
Schedule *by* Justice Suhrud Dave	405
Secular *by* Rajeev Bhargava	406
Subaltern *by* Shail Mayaram	408
Thana (thānā) *by* Santana Khanikar	409
UPSC *by* Maruthi Prasad Tangirala	411
Violence *by* Neera Chandhoke	413
Epilogue *by* Peter Ronald deSouza	**415**
Notes on contributors	421
Index	441

ADVISORY BOARD MEMBERS

Arjun Appadurai (Anthropology, NYU)
Upendra Baxi (Law and Development, Warwick)
Akeel Bilgrami (Philosophy, Columbia)
Zoya Hasan (Political Science, JNU)
Sudhir Kakar (Psychology, Goa)
Sunil Khilhani (Intellectual History, King's College London)
Ashis Nandy (Psychology, CSDS)
Deepak Nayyar (Economics, CSDS)
Bhikhu Parikh (Politics, House of Lords)
K. Satchidananan (Literature, Sahitya Akademi)
Romila Thapar (History, JNU)

ACKNOWLEDGEMENTS

We have many beautiful words in the Indian languages that we can draw upon to thank the large number of people who have helped us take this project from conception to creation. This book has grown from the germ of an idea to a volume with over two hundred contributors – each one of whom has, ironically for a keywords volume, left us speechless. Their combined wit, wisdom and, above all, generosity of spirit has been an object lesson in the power of words to constitute communities. In Konkani, the phrase 'dev borem korum', literally translated, means 'may god do good to you'. One of the editors of this book believes this benefic phrase works for both believers and non-believers; the other is more sceptical but both are equally and profoundly grateful. We want to say to all who have helped us 'dev borem korum'. We thank you for your marvellous contributions, your patience and most of all for your belief in the viability and worth of what we set out to do.

It would be impossible for us to list all those who have made this book possible, so we will mention only those who, at various stages in the life of the book, were involved in tying up stubborn loose ends, foremost among them Gorki Bora and Banasmita Bora. Without them this book might have remained a great tangle of loose ends. Ekta Khemchandani, Nonita Oberoi, Shikha Vats, Priyanka Sharma, Priyanka Verma, Dipti Kulkarni, Manaswita Bharadwaja, Sanchita Sharma and Nivida Chandra all helped give the project a form. Their assistance, across digital space and different time zones, was truly outstanding. It is noteworthy, too, that they were all women, reminding us that in India, women's names encompass every virtue, such as Ekta (unity), Shikha (peak or high point), Sanchita (collection, a gathering), Dipti (lustrous, shining), Manaswita (mind aspiring, intelligent). The women who helped us were all these things and more: they drew up lists of contributors, prepared Excel monitoring sheets, sent endless reminders, intrepidly helped us convert long biographies and entries into brief bio notes and svelte slim-fit essays and dealt with the disappointments of regret in rishi fashion but celebrated acceptance with Bollywood fervour. Dev Borem Korum to the women who assisted us; they richly deserve every blessing.

Then they were those who were our genies, appearing magically when the going got rough, such as Ramakant Agnihotri, Hoshang Merchant, Antony Arul Valan, Chandrika Pandey, Amit Bhaya and Satish Padmanabhan. All of them made this project happen. Dev Borem Korum to them.

The detailed comments made by the two anonymous reviewers for the book proposal much before it fully came into being were enormously helpful and helped shape our vision for the book. That they were both based in the United States and that both frankly admitted that they were not South Asia specialists was a great bonus because the perspectives offered seemed so clear-eyed and unbiased. One of them wrote at the time with great prescience: 'Such a volume – with the right contributors and a strong editorial hand – could be extraordinary. It is hard to imagine that it could even pretend to cover the topic adequately. But it could be an interesting spur to conversation, debate, and more research.' The reviewer was wise. To 'even pretend to covering the topic adequately' would be a farce when the topic in question

Acknowledgements

happened to be India. It would be like trying to pour the sea into a pail or *balti* (one of the material culture keywords in our volume). However, we feel that as far as our contributors go, we have more than fulfilled expectations. The flaws in the text are surely our own and can never be theirs. We are not so sure about those 'strong editorial hand(s)', though. Despite genuine doubts on this front, however, we shall keep our fingers crossed about the 'extraordinariness' of this book and the promise that it will yield fine conversations and research in the years to come. Meanwhile, Dev Borem Korum to both reviewers.

We would be remiss not to record our gratitude to several institutions where several formal and informal brainstorming, sessions took place, vivacious suggestions were received on what words to include and sage advice given on how to avoid the hegemonic trap of the globally dominant languages. The Indian Institute of Advanced Study, Shimla, hosted one such meeting, as did the Nehru Memorial Museum and Library which supported a fellowship for one of the editors. Their support was invaluable. The IIT Delhi and the CSDS Delhi, our respective home institutions, enabled us to host small informal meetings with groups of potential contributors, many of who contributed substantially to our project. We value their support. Our publishers, Bloomsbury, and our editors, Gurdeep Mattu, Andrew Wardell and Becky Holland, deserve our thanks for believing in this marathon project and urging it to the finish line. Given the fact that India's verbal zest is infinite, we have already started preparing for next year's race, such is the energy that we have drawn from our engagement with this volume.

Finally, to our families who offered unsolicited advice and who, for affective reasons, gave us unstinting support, we are truly grateful. Dev Borem Korum.

Rukmini Bhaya Nair and Peter Ronald deSouza
Delhi, 1 June 2019

DIACRITIC CHARACTERS BASED ON THE INDIC SYLLABARY

Vowels		Consonants		Special Character and Nukta	
अ	a	क	ka	क़	qa
आ	ā	ख	kha	ख़	ḥa
इ	i	ग	ga	ग़	ġa
ई	ī	घ	gha	ज़	za
उ	u	च	ca	फ़	fa
ऊ	ū	छ	cha	ड़	ṛa
ऋ	ṛ	ज	ja	ढ़	ṛha
ए	e	झ	jha	क्ष	ksh
ऐ	ai	ट	ṭa	ज्ञ	jña
ओ	ō	ठ	ṭha	त्	t
औ	au	ड	ḍa	द्व	dva
अं	aṅ	ढ	ḍha	त्र	tra
अः	aḥ	ण	ṇa	श्र	śra
		त	ta	र्प	rpa
		थ	tha	द्	ṭra
		द	da		
		ध	dha		
		न	na		
		प	pa		
		फ	pha		
		ब	ba		
		भ	bha		
		म	ma		
		य	ya		
		र	ra		
		ल	la		
		व	va		
		श	śa		
		ष	ṣa		
		स	sa		
		ह	ha		

Note: This diacritic table does not correspond to the standard IPA chart. Rather, it comports with the syllabic system of writing used in most Indian languages. Also known as the International Alphabet of Sanskrit Transliteration (IAST), this is the most familiar system of transcription in India. However, since modern Indian languages, such as Hindi, no longer use the mid central vowel 'schwa' at the end of most words, we have deleted this phoneme derived from the Sanskrit from our entries so that they are closer to current pronunciation: for example, 'Dalit' rather than 'Dalita'. Further, many of the words in our lexicon have long been familiar to the Indian public in the Roman script, even if not quite accurate in terms of their phonological representation: 'dharma' or 'kahani', for instance. Given this complex orthographic scenario, we have provided the familiar 'demotic' version followed by the IAST transcription in the case of each of our keywords but then reverted to the more usual form for ease of reading. The stylistic choice made in this volume to have diacritic marks on capital letters is also slightly unusual. Finally, despite the careful attention that we have attempted to pay to these issues of transcription, errors and idiosyncratic uses remain. For these, we apologise most sincerely.

INTRODUCTION

Prolegomenon: homologies

There are times in history when patterns of memory shift, geography is reconfigured and language unpredictably mutates. Raymond Williams' iconic *Keywords: A Vocabulary of Culture and Society* (1976) seems, in fact, to have been written in response to just such a realization that he had been witness to a transformative break in hitherto familiar cognitive habits. In the opening paragraphs of his Introduction, he recounts this anecdote about how his book came to be:

> In 1945, after the ending of the wars with Germany and Japan, I was released from the Army to return to Cambridge University … but in the movements of war I had lost touch with all my university friends. Then, after many strange days, I met a man I had worked with in the first year of the war … He too had just come out of the Army. We talked eagerly, but not about the past. We were too much preoccupied with this new and strange world around us. Then we both said, in effect simultaneously: 'the fact is, they just don't speak the same language'. (p. 11)

Such an acute feeling of suddenly inhabiting a 'new' world, where the language of thought has changed so radically that the state of mind individuals seem to share most in common is simply the perception of estrangement, can also afflict us in times of peace. At the uncertain beginning of the present millennium, in the midst of a communications revolution so profound that it has redefined even that ancient and atavistic word 'war' in terms of cyber fortifications and breaches thereof, it is no surprise that we are subject to bewildering psychological dislocations similar to those described by Williams. In short, we are forced to recognize certain homologies or 'family resemblances' (Wittgenstein, 1953) that seem to exist across cultures and between times, when the linguistic signposts we have long relied on no longer help predict future directions, prompting a *sphota* moment out of Bhartrhari (sixth century BCE) or that dramatic shock of recognition that Aristotle (first century BCE) called *anagnorisis*. At such times, a civilization reviews its discontents, its loss of bearings.

How, then, do societies reorient? How do they use the habitus of the familiar to engage with the unknown in times of unusual social perturbation? In this volume, we ask this question with respect to India, a civilization space distinguished by its diehard pluralisms as well as its mnemonic continuities of language, culture, religion and belief. Nothing in India is ever conceptually singular and, by the same paradoxical token, all concepts are remarkably singular. We have so much to remember that to forget efficiently is a homological trick the subcontinent has mastered for ages. Our linguistic wealth is exhaustive but it is also exhausting. It is in this context that the Indian lesson in verbal stress busting could be critical in a world bending and cracking under the burden of information overload and social media tribalisms. How does one reflexively engage with conceptual hubbub, with language medleys coming at one from all sides that persistently threaten to crowd out a sense of inner peace, of foundational certainties? It is, after all, no accident that India has presented itself and the world, over time, with various routes towards simultaneously expressing spiritual dispassion and earthly engagement. From dharma to yoga to Sufism to the reams of sophisticated linguistic theories it has produced to explain our place in the world as creatures committed to symbolic thought, India seems to have acknowledged that verbal cacophony and calm of mind are inseparable. Spend an hour at any street-side chai stall, taking in the no-holds-barred conversation while the hot, sweet comfort of tea repairs you from within, and this hypothesis should be amply confirmed.

Another commonplace but powerful strategy that Indians may also have an inside edge on is the rehearsal of synonymy. Indian schoolchildren in large swathes of the country memorize multiple words for concepts like the 'moon' or 'spring' or 'water,' even today, as an integral part of their classroom routines – a tradition that could date back to the *Nāmaliṅgānuśāsanam*, popularly known as the *Amarakośa* (rough translation: 'collection of immortal words', a bit like Roget's *Thesaurus* but of a much earlier origin, somewhere between the fourth and seventh century CE). Such embedded and commonplace iterations in Indian word space have been little remarked on, but it seems to me incontestable that they constitutes a long-standing investment in verbal banking, a widespread network of small-scale semantic savings accounts to rely on in times of need. Keeping this background in mind, our current preoccupation with keywords seems not to derive only from Williams' extraordinary achievement but also from inherited procedures of memorialization on the subcontinent.

To reiterate, focussing on 'keywords' as cultural enchiridions is a time-tested strategy in India that could offer a partial answer to what might be called the 'reorientation problem' that India and the world are up against today. While it is undeniable that speed at which we communicate and the speech in which we communicate is astonishingly febrile at present, our mutable bodies, our affective inclinations and our attachments to verbal and visual simplicities appear somehow curiously untouched by all this linguistic canoodling. We remain quite as nasty and violent towards each other as we ever were. Our words are not our bonds. Yet, it could be precisely for this reason that our keywords volume matters. By its very structure, its generic design, a keywords book is as much about antonyms and antagonisms as it is about synonyms and sweet accord. It brings disagreements – even disagreeableness – into the open. It forces us to examine old linguistic wounds and scrutinize the roles of the new language band aids we've invented to cover them up. In this sense, India is a fascinating exemplar. However, the implications of the language quarrels and categories we suggest here seem universal. The basic methodology of a 'keywords' volume directs our attention towards a disturbingly obvious question: can the culling of 259 keywords over hundreds of others, especially in a country almost the size of Western Europe and arguably far more culturally diverse, and then presenting them globally in English, a language of immense elite power, in any way a justified procedure? Does this not reinforce rather than remedy old language hegemonies? In any case, to what extent can any 'keyword' truly be declared part of a global cultural vocabulary and to what extent does it remain specific, born out of particular local circumstances?

Queries such these are hardy perennials in every garden variety of academic enquiry as well as popular debate. Our contention in this book is that they are valuable for that very reason. Consider, for instance, the subtitle of the present volume, *Keywords for India*, which seems to suggest that words such as 'dharma', 'caste' or 'Bollywood' possess meaning primarily in the sub-continental context; they are keywords 'for India'. Yet, we know that these words have long been part of a worldwide diaspora of the imagination. They have immigrated not just into the parts of the world where English dominates but also have found conceptual niches in languages as different as Portuguese, Indonesian and Russian. In this respect, they are keywords *from*, as much as *for*, India. Their global relevance might, as a consequence, have been severely underestimated.

One had only to consider commonplace words in the world lexicon such as *avatar, guru, karma, kismet, mantra, nirvana, pundit* or *yoga* to grasp that these do not just constitute what we have long characterized as an 'alternative' mythos but rather make up an integral part of the linguistic atlas of the world, multiplying opportunities for theoretical problem-solving, concept formation and critical self-reflection in various arenas of the humanities and social sciences. The import of this volume is that it seeks to provide, via a constellation of words such as those mentioned above, a discourse mapping of the present that pertains to India, certainly, but also to a global world desperately in need of new vocabularies. As it happens, this is a time in world history when major social movements ranging from Dalit mobilisation in India to the Me-Too protests in the United States to dispossessed 'refugee' voices from Syria to South Sudan have at their disposal new technological tools to promote a fresh awareness of 'what it means to be human'. Coincidentally, these vital 'free speech' cultures have also been accompanied in the present century by a deep geographical disruption that has a uniquely Indian aspect. The influential global suggestion that the early twenty-first century should usher in a new epoch to be called 'the Age of the Anthropocene' is, of course, well known, since it has now become blindingly clear that human inventions and interventions have had a severe effect on the wellbeing of the planet. Our 2020 lexicon appears in a diachronic era in which the entire geological division of time is itself being hotly contested, but what has gone unremarked is the part that India plays in this project of grand epochal renaming, not only because it is a steadfast supporter of environmental accords but also in terms of its pre-history. It turns out that the last phase of the Holocene epoch in which we now live, spread over the last 4500 years, has recently been renamed the 'Meghalayan', after a small state in India's extreme northeast known as Meghalaya or 'the abode of clouds' on account of the fact that in its caves are perfectly preserved the climate records of that remote age of extreme drought and hence likely large human migrations. Perhaps the word 'Meghalayan' is, in this sense, a key contribution to a global understanding of shared world prehistories, perhaps not; but at a time when data is increasingly being stored in 'clouds' of infinite extension, we must surely wonder at the cross-cultural serendipities of conceptual lexicons such as this one. In this regard, ours is an intervention within a series of encounters that the Indian subcontinent has long held with the future. Far from calling a halt to a process of documentation and debate, this volume marks what we expect will be a significant step forward in maintaining that 'argumentative' spirit held to be central to India's being (Sen, 2005).

In curating these varied 'talking points' describing the Indian ethos in the second decade of a new millennium, it is our hope that at its learned and animated best, as well as at its unruly and unscholarly worst, our volume constitutes an adventure of ideas; that it will foster an understanding of 'culture' from a set of perspectives that counterbalance but also encompass and engage with forms of possible western ethnocentrism in an increasingly interconnected, verbally syncopated virtual world. Thus, while its scholarship may be 'India-centric', this book does not shy away from the challenge of contributing to a vigorous global debate on the very idea of 'culture'. This introduction begins by offering five preliminary reasons as to why we are emboldened in this ambition.

Initiation: forms of the collective

We should begin by acknowledging that our enterprise is uniquely a collaborative one in that it involves not only a distinguished editorial board but also an impressive host of over 200 contributors, mostly based in India, many of whom have already contributed significantly to a study of the more than 250 topics on which we requested them to write. Indeed, I'd suggest that there are one or more subjects for PhD theses or book monographs embedded in each of these keywords, not to mention fodder for much self-directed humour, irreverence and delight.

A second feature of this book is that it contains several words intimately familiar to Indians at large (*anganwadi, chappal, danda*) that may nevertheless be unavailable even to scholars of South Asia domiciled in the west, simply because they are not necessarily part of their lived experience. These words fall into three categories not, to my knowledge, included in previous 'keywords' volumes: one, material culture words that are part of the everyday vocabulary of Indian citizens such as *chulha* and *balti*; two, acronyms such as RTI and BDO; and three, 'borrowings', usually from the English, such as *public* and *beauty parlour*, where the usage is so different from the original and so attuned to the Indian cultural scene that entire meditations on the semantics of contextual interpretation are called for. So far, most keyword volumes have focussed almost entirely on grand narrative (see Browning 2000, on this point), high-culture terms such as 'nation', 'bureaucracy' or 'nature' that populated the pioneering Williams volume. This meant, in effect, that the little narratives of lived experience went almost unnoticed in the design of these works. One of the strategies of 'reorientation' that the present volume adopts is to include quotidian material culture words cheek-by-jowl with the great philosophical abstractions that have stereotypically been associated with Indian thought. It is quite possible that our book does no more here than reflect the democratization of culture and knowledge brought about by the explosion in e-interactions over the past decades. Nevertheless, I was surprised by and grateful for the enthusiastic support that this hybrid approach received from all quarters, not least from my wonderful co-editor, Peter deSouza, then Director of the Indian Institute of Advanced Study – which brings me to a third aspect of our sub-continental language inheritance.

A certain wry skepticism, an attitude of mind, seems to be shared by all Indians about the 'meaning of meaning', to borrow C. K Ogden and I. A. Richards immortal 1923 book title. In a culture so linguistically heterogeneous, no Indian can afford to take words for granted. India is routinely referenced as a 'subcontinent', but I have always thought of it as linguistically *in*continent, spilling over with puns and unexpected language contretemps. For example, in a casual conversation during a flight, I once dared laud the robust quality of our modern Indian democracy. It had, I proclaimed, survived extraordinary travails since its formal birth in 1947 when India became an independent nation state. There could be few rivals when it came to such a triumphant achievement. The Uttar Pradesh politician beside me would, however, have none of this maudlin sentiment. He punctured my ballooning thought at once with a bilingual pun: *hamare yahan*, he said, *ham to ise kahte hain 'de more kursi'* (translation: 'in our part of the world, though, we call it *de-more-kursi* or 'give me that chair!', where *more* is a local variant of the Hindi possessive *mereko*, and *kursi* or 'chair' is understood to be a metonym for political power and corrupt influence). From the accretion of small incidents of this sort in our collective memory banks, it can be asserted with some degree of confidence, I believe, that not even the most sacred of words, such as 'democracy', is immune to the multilingual forces of satire in India.

Our joint effort in this book offers reliable evidence of such manifold ironies of language throughout. It is also, I believe, why even the supposedly most straight-laced of Indian scholars generously supported the move to let words of the upstart variety ('beauty parlour' or 'gym') share a terrain with superior and time-tested concepts ('maya' or 'shakti') in this lexicon. If we were for a moment to think of language in terms of the pervasive Indian metaphor of caste, we may see in this book a concerted attempt to challenge accepted norms of verbal conduct, a sort of structural move towards the breaking-down of oppressive conceptual barriers. A related, optimistic surmise: if ever Indians sense a threat to their democratic freedoms, they know they can draw on oceans of language so deep and buoyant that the ship of *swaraj* will not sink. We might recall here that for Gandhi, Tagore, Ambedkar, Azad, Sarojini Naidu and so many others during the movement of independence from colonial rule, the concepts *swaraj* (self-rule, freedom) and *shiksha* (education) were inseparable. Yet, as Gandhi wrote wryly then, 'The real difficulty is that people have no idea of what education truly is.' Insofar as the keywords in this volume succeed in offering us some lessons in the exercise of freedoms of speech and the ethics of open conversations, they could constitute a contribution to a no-holds-barred Gandhian exploration of what 'education truly is'.

Fourth, it cannot be sufficiently stressed that this conceptual lexicon is interdisciplinary in a manner quite hard to imagine in the 'developed world' where most disciplines support a critical mass of scholars. Despite its approximately one thousand universities, India does not yet possess all that many experts in any discipline and is unevenly 'professionalized'. Yet, this is perhaps as much an advantage as a disadvantage, since it means that scholars are less likely to remain in disciplinary silos. Crosstalk across disciplines is the norm, not the exception in India. Although our volume is excitingly unique in that it brings together, probably for the first time, over two hundred voices speaking on subjects of concern to Indians, it is also emblematic. The panoply of contributions to this book includes insights from activists, anthropologists, economists, educationalists, engineers, environmentalists, doctors, historians, journalists, lawyers, linguists, literary theorists, novelists, performers, politicians, political theorists, philosophers, psychologists, scientists, sociologists, teachers, translators and still others who do not see their professional identities as paramount. It is hard to imagine such a collective effort emanating from conventional 'Western academia'. I would even go so far as to claim that this is a cultural 'style' of intellectual cooperation that India would do well to retain, sustain and perhaps export.

Fifth, by evolving loose thematic categories that take cognisance of this exuberant will to converse across disciplinary boundaries, we have here for the first time a 'keywords' book written in English that is not regimented entirely according to the Roman alphabet – a difficulty that Williams also wrestled with, confessing that a strict alphabetic order failed to capture the 'clustering' between words that he wanted. Our volume has attempted to cut this Gordian knot via a sort of blended editorial solution. In it, our keywords are sorted into seven broad sections but retain ordering by alphabet within each. If one were being fanciful, one might suggest that if the 'magic pentagram' of *culture, democracy, art, class* and *industry* provided the structure for Williams' book, ours, I realized once I'd intuitively come up with the general classification below, seemed to call up memories of T. E Lawrence's marvellously asymmetric *Seven Pillars of Wisdom* (1926) written in an autobiographical (and far from un-empathetic) mode as he led his wild charges against Turks and Arabs and assorted 'others'. Our categories, at a glance, are:

1. Classical Heritages: Databases Of Memory
2. Contemporary Aesthetic Modes: Reimaginings
3. Economic Mantras, Media and Technological Change
4. Intimacies: Culture and Material Culture
5. Emancipatory Imaginaries
6. Language and Self-Reflection
7. Politics and the Political

Unregimented categories such as these, it goes without saying, leave their flanks open to attack. For example, the choice of the word 'lexicon' as the container for our collective semantic speculations is in itself a risky one. Williams himself was infinitely more cautious. He humbly described the words he had assembled as a 'vocabulary', going to great lengths to distinguish his keywords volume from a dictionary and, in particular, the OED. Williams underscored the fact that, unlike the makers of the OED, he was interested in the historical and cultural connotations of words. He did not, however, consider 'lexicon' as part of his title for one moment. Yet to me, lexicon seemed an obvious choice since the word 'lexis' refers specifically to 'the stock of words in a language' – not to pronunciation or even to grammar and vocabulary but to *words*. Our asymmetrical sorting into 'sections' allows for a host of broad discourse associations. Ideas about inherited memories in the first chapter, shared cultural aesthetics in the second, notions of economic power and technological change in the third, the intimacies of everyday experience in the fourth, the nature of freedom in the fifth, the language of thought in the sixth and the structures of political power in the seventh hardly ever stay within their assigned boundaries. They spill incorrigibly spill over. For example, the keyword 'dharma' in our first chapter, is retooled as a political concept in the widely used collocation 'coalition dharma' which occurs as an entry in our seventh and final chapter; similarly, the words 'Hinduism' and 'Hindutva' jostle for conceptual space in the volume, demonstrating once again that subtleties of language are key to interpreting the ideological and philosophical currents of thought on the subcontinent.

The point has already been made that this lexicon selects unevenly and often 'unfairly' from the huge stock of interrelated words generated in the subcontinent. Likewise, we took a tactical decision to mainly invite scholars based in India because of our emphasis on 'lived experience'. In the end, though, we left even this boundary fluid. There are contributors to this volume who are not Indian citizens and never have been. This is because we strongly believe that intellectual property rights belong, in the last resort, to a universal commons. An American scholar who studies Bhartṛhari or Kabir in Chicago has as much ownership of these texts as an Indian who pores Borges or Kierkegaard in Chennai. Several of our contributors, moreover, confidently live out lives in more than one continent, sometimes three or four. This constitutes an impressive range of habitations, but every contributor to the book shared with Peter and myself, I think, an implicit premise. Our project ruled out *comprehensiveness*; *comprehension* of divergent perspectives seemed to us a more sustainable goal. As a group, we shared only an intuitive, emotional, sometimes over-determined and stereotypic and sometimes under-determined and chaotic, engagement with the multidimensional space of the Indian *bhāṣhā*s. Words performed their functions within this contentious cultural matrix. Ethically and psychologically, this meant that we had constantly to remind ourselves to take no one's participation in our provisional collective for granted – from which it followed that every contributor 'owned' and still owns his or her entry even as it belongs to our keywords 'commons'. In this work, we have implicitly attempted, I think, to prevent a tragedy of this great commons (Hardin, 1968) by working together in the full knowledge that we did not always hold with each others' views. Not just asymmetry and disputation but frequent misunderstandings are therefore part of the book's schema, which is not unsurprising given that it emerges from one of the world's most linguistically, ethnically, religiously, economically and socially diverse places. Moreover, 65 per cent of India's population is less than thirty-five years of age. This generation is trying to imagine itself in the mirror of an urbanized India at a moment when the country emerges as the fifth largest world economy – but there's no denying that this not always trustworthy looking glass is still, by and large, framed by a set of ornate, stereotypic images that celebrate a 'village' India immortalized by writers from Kipling to Raja Rao, not to mention the mainstream as well as regional Indian cinema. Such an uneasy lack of fit is apparent throughout the book. Thinking in terms of the histories of the future that *Keywords for India* might predict, it seems probable therefore that it is this e-savvy demographic, including large cohorts of sub-continental immigrants, who could make substantive decisions as to which of our keywords will last and which disappear into cloud-cuckoo land. Many of them have written for us in this volume and may down the road reconfigure the whole idea of what a 'keyword' is – or could be.

Lexis: forms of the keyword

What is a keyword? In a rough first reckoning, it might be characterized as encapsulated and enduring thought, part of an architecture of concepts that cultures tend stubbornly to uphold. At the same time, because culture building is, unavoidably, a work in progress, new keywords are constantly on offer, especially in times of technological transformation that have already impacted our ancient, slow-moving evolutionary modes of communication. Worth noting, though, is the fact that a naturalistic metaphor remains core to e-interpretations of the meta-term 'keyword'.

Online, 'keywords' are routinely referred to as 'seeds' or potential kernels that generates rich series of 'search queries', fresh hypotheses, communicative interchanges and conceptual experimentation. Changing metaphors, but staying in the domain of nature still, the best keywords are believed to be those with 'long tails', such as that, let's say, flaunted by the peacock, India's national bird. Such a tail is memorable, marked, exquisite; its heavy weight keeps the peacock close to the ground, assists directional navigation – and yet does not prevent flight. Long-tail keywords, that is, are those where the basic keyword attracts more precise, longer phrases, so that word searches on the web become more accurate. Consider the Indian keyword *azan* that heads up Chapter 4 of the book. The entry for it is unpretentious, down-to-earth. Yet this word, as the entry shows, could attract a host of phrases such as '*azan* for Sunnis' versus '*azan* for Shias', 'the significance of *azan* in Indonesia', 'the muezzin's role in *azan*', 'the historical spread of *azan*' or even 'the use of loudspeakers in *azan*'. All these 'long tail' permutations indicate that *azan* is a highly productive keyword with global outreach.

Such an evolutionary dynamic that supports the creation of new tools for meaning-making is underscored in an essay on 'linguistic diversity' by Shaylih Muehlmann (2004). Intriguingly, for a technical piece by a cultural anthropologist interested in environmental conflict, Muelhmann invokes Raymond Williams' work, arguing that:

> Raymond Williams' *Keywords: A vocabulary of culture and society* (1976) provides a useful framework for understanding the complexity of meanings. Williams' notion of a 'keyword' is one whose complexity is the result of ... three effects: a keyword connect areas that are generally kept separate, masks radical semantic variation by its continuous verbal identity; and often expresses a contradiction (p. 140).

Ideally a keyword is an 'Open Sesame': it throws open a myriad windows and doors that might admittedly slam shut on occasion, yet can lead to sudden breathtaking insights and reveal unexpected cultural verandahs and courtyards, vistas and walkways. Games of historical hopscotch and geographical *gilli danda* are commonplace in any keyword space. Extrapolating from Muehlmann's reading of Willams, a 'keyword', as I see it, links conceptual lexicons; it is a spur to interdisciplinary and cross-cultural cooperation; it reflects kinetic processes of continuity and change, structure and variation in language. In addition, it possesses a linguistic design robust and capacious enough to make room for differences of perspective and competing grammatical explanations. With this background in mind, the general format specified for entries in our volume appears below: with suitable modifications and stringent criticism once this book appears in print, it could just provide a general template for writing keyword entries on cultural topics, no matter which culture(s) claim our allegiance.

- A keyword entry should be between 300 (minimum) to 3000 (maximum) words. This flexibility is required because the word *sarkar* (government) may, for example, merit a much longer entry than the word *samosa* (a popular snack). Most entries should ideally include the following information:
- The origins of the word, its etymological past and its possible cognates in other languages
- Common current usage, that is, examples of the ordinary uses of the word in conversations, newspapers, jokes and so on, as well as possible anecdotal perspectives
- The general significance and association of the word, its importance in philosophical, literary, legal and/or psychological terms
- Statistical side-lights or other unusual 'facts' about the word, e.g. the entry on the word *akshara* might note that the phoneme 'r' is held to be the most ubiquitous across Indian syllabaries

- Contribution of the word to the cultural context to which it belongs, for example, 'India' and its possible future as part of a wider world lexicon of ideas
- A couple of references at the end of each entry

Needless to say, given the large number of participants in our project and the disinclination of Indians to ever march in step, the format outlined above was never followed to the letter and often not in spirit either! At the same time, as a collective, it gave a degree of coherence to our efforts to capture the 'meme-tic' quality of a keyword. In this connection, it is tempting to connect the notion of a 'keyword' to the idea of the 'meme', first adumbrated by Richard Dawkins (1976). Now popularized as the 'internet meme' by netizens across the globe, one way to think of a keyword is as a 'viral' meme.

Daniel Dennett (1995), explicating Dawkins, writes that the meme is a 'new kind of replicator'. This is the "meme" which obeys the laws of natural selection. Just as genes propagate themselves in the gene-pool by leaping from body to body via sperms or eggs, so memes propagate themselves by leaping from brain to brain by a process which can, in a broad sense be called imitation.' Ten examples of memes that Dennett cites are: *arch, vendetta, wheel, clothes, alphabet, calendar, the Odyssey, chess, calculus* and *impressionism*. As I have argued elsewhere (Nair, 2011, 2012, 2014), there can also be niche intra-memes that circulate mainly, if not exclusively, within cultures. As long-tail 'peacocks', such keywords possess cosmopolitan, bio-diverse, potential. Should the right historical circumstances come about, they can take flight across international barriers and enchant audiences across the world.

Perhaps such a time is now, with our selection of Indian keywords. Ten specifically Indian memes might include, for example, the *Hindu/Arabic numeral system* which includes the 'zero', long acknowledged as an 'Indian invention' in world mathematics; the idea of *ahimsa* or non-violent action; the *Taj Mahal*; the *sari*; *hot pickles*; the aesthetics of '*rasa*' theory; the epics Ramayana and Mahabharata; the notion of reincarnation or *avatara*; *yoga*; Mughal miniature paintings and so on. In this first pass at a conceptual lexicon 'for' and 'from' India, we have begun by including some of these memes in our book.

Memes obviously possess great symbolic value. The difficulty lies, of course, in having to reassess the strength and endurance of key memes in an e-age when regular info-bombardments are the order of the day. All those over-simple indices of discrimination between true and fake knowledge that we had earlier used, such as resort to scholarly authority, seem to have become outmoded in such a world. It is now commonplace to remark that cell phones and other apparently non-threatening devices have humbled old-fashioned scholarship to the extent that the world's information base can now, so to speak, be held in the palm of one's proletarian hand. Infinities of holes have, as a direct consequence of such technological legerdemain, been drilled in the wall between academia and media, between cloistered expertise and popular understanding, between fact and opinion, and even between humans and machines, revealing to us that sticking one's finger in the dyke to bravely save the citadels of knowledge is no longer an option – if ever it was. At its most useful, a keywords volume such as this should encourage the articulation of bold, yet untested sets of ideas around the geopolitics of 'walls' and other hitherto sacred barriers (see also Nair, 1997, 2002a). After all, encyclopaedic entries these days seem to require 'updates' almost before the last word is keyed in. Collaboration at such a time of instant communication is not an option; it is a prerequisite to the dissemination of resilient memes. This 'Indian keywords' book as a concept repository is potentially such a cross-cultural meme.

Genealogy: forms of the book

Like its cousins, the dictionary, the thesaurus and the encyclopaedia, a lexicon is a very particular genre of book. A dictionary concentrates on as straightforward an explanation of meaning as possible, on grammar and on pronunciation; a thesaurus on synonymy and antonymy; an encyclopaedia, which often runs into multiple volumes, on whole fields of human knowledge. A lexicon, however, should not be confused with these lookalikes. Its focus is on semantics, usage and the interconnections between words and their corresponding concepts. Put simply, our project valorises 'lexis' or the power of words to organize our lives and give social and political meaning to our actions – intellectually, individually and institutionally. As Foucault (1969) pronounced long ago, even before Williams,

> The book is not the simple object that one hold in one's hands; and it cannot remain within the little parallelepiped that contains it. Its unity is variable and reflexive. (p. 23)

A 'unity variable and reflexive' is a fine description of the imaginative task that we have set ourselves in this volume. Once we recognize the inevitable dissonances between the great unifying questions such as 'what is a science? what is an oeuvre? what is a theory? ... what is a text?' and so on (p. 5), Foucault appears to argue, it seems easier to surmount academic barriers and enter a 'complex field of discourse' (p. 23). Judgements as to whether a lexicon, as a species of book, ought to be comprehensive, definitive and authoritative versus focussed, suggestive, open-ended; if it should adopt a 'nativist' as opposed to a 'cosmopolitan' stance; if it must perforce commit itself to explaining, let's say, the etymological connections or breaks between old, 'pure' Sanskrit-based lexical resources and the new 'hybrid' language pluralisms', appear less crucial. We can relax into a conversational mode, where history is not a weighty burden but a sort of therapeutic digging, an archaeology that may be patchy and discontinuous but never fails to reveal a vast subterranean genealogy of inter-texts. It is this putative inter-textual genealogy to which I next turn.

Returning to Williams' inspirational *Keywords*, we recognize that in the present era of communicative unrest, Williams' mode of singular scholarship, tucked away in a Cambridge college, appears a nostalgic dream. Nor is irony absent – for, as scientists currently debate whether it is time that we moved on from the era of the Meghalayan Holocene to that of the incorrigibly inventive but environmentally polluting and self-destructive 'Anthropocene', they seem to be in favour of fixing the date for this apocalyptic change at the exact moment that Williams presciently identified in his keywords book: namely, 1945, the end of the Second World War. Some texts, it appears, are never exhausted; rather they carry forward into new millennia and global scenarios the inherited wisdom of their local traditions. By bringing together some concepts that inform the 'cultural unconscious' of the subcontinent we take a step in this book, as Williams did in post-war Europe, in the direction of forging critical tools that might be put to use in cultural and cognitive studies, broadly defined.

Introduction

It has often been suggested that the postcolonial discourse of the humanities produced on the Indian subcontinent functioned largely with interpretative categories borrowed from a canonical western tradition with little appreciation of the underlying universalist assumptions that might problematize such endeavours. Alternatively, attempts to read 'Western' texts from the perspective of Sanskrit poetics have not necessarily resulted in more than a few idiosyncratic readings with the constant dangers of an ill-conceived and naive nativism lurking in the background. The present volume shows that the Sanskrit language, like its cousins Latin and Greek, is a rich source for the lexicalization of critical terms in different Indian languages. However, it also reveals that we can by no means assume that Sanskrit is a primary source. In other words, even 'Sanskrit' can be read as just another theoretical category, which can only be rescued from a splendid isolation if it engages with a host of other critical terms thrown up by the complex discourses of contemporary India. One of the liveliest debates with contributors to this book was in fact on how the word 'Sanskrit' was to be transcribed. Should the hypercorrect form *saṃskṛt* be used or was the vastly more familiar Romanized transliteration 'Sanskrit' to be preferred? In the end, we settled for a commonsensical 'hybrid' solution, once again. As Indians would put it, we 'adjusted'. Our entry on the key pair of words 'Prakriti/Sanskriti' indicates upfront the 'classic' pronunciation for these words but, for the rest, we stick to 'Sanskrit'. More generally, we have consciously refrained in *Keywords for India* from trying to force our keywords in into a cohesive 'nationalist' idiom, led by Sanskrit or any other hegemonic linguistic force.

A quick look at our tesselated Index will show that, as 'long-tail' verbal species, each of our keywords belongs both to a local context and a cosmopolitan assemblage. Each, we claim, contains within it possibilities of structural stability as well as conceptual variability; has the capacity to arouse uproarious Hanuman laughter while being as serious as a Buddha; possesses a strong aesthetic resonance in conjunction with intellectual and ethical clout; and, finally, has the potential to offer succour in times of crisis, to be a talisman, a meme, an enchiridion. Our lexicon, in short, makes up in ambition what it lacks in its necessary incompleteness. As it attempts to open up a gateway to the dauntingly large number of intellectual possibilities that the Indian subcontinent has to offer at the beginning of a fraught new millennium haunted by old memories, it is simultaneously in search of new, invigorating myths. This is the sort of inclusiveness of the imagination, the ache for wholeness that is a constant affective refrain in this book, as it once was in William's courageous one-man show.

Williams' *Keywords* belonged, as we know, within a tradition of literary commentary that included, for example, Matthew Arnold's notion of cultural 'touchstones' adumbrated in his influential *Culture and Anarchy* (1869). Like Williams, Arnold held that linguistic, artistic and literary touchstones were especially important when a society was in historical turmoil – caught between two worlds, 'one dead and the other powerless to be born'. Then, twelve years after Williams' ground breaking work, E. D. Hirsch undertook a similar exercise with his American dictionary *Cultural Literacy* (1988), which can partly be read as a plea for a common cultural curriculum in US schools. Arnold's and Hirsch's works have, however, been criticized for their conservative appeal to highbrow culture, where the 'canon' to be taught and transmitted is already well established. What is singularly attractive about William's venture, on the other hand, is that it was clearly prompted by a deep sense of cultural disorientation. It is this vivid consternation, this perplexity that also seems to me absent from the admirably fluent *New Keywords: A Revised Vocabulary of Culture and Society* (2005) edited by Tony Bennett, Lawrence Grossberg and Meghan Morris. In this volume, the editors add several new important keywords like 'alternative', diaspora', 'fundamentalism' and 'narrative' to Williams' original list of 130 words. This 'revised vocabulary' of about 140 entries, however, crucially eliminates some words that Williams included. One of the most striking of these omissions is the word 'violence' – the single, stark entry that Williams had entered under the letter 'V'. In *New Keywords*, 'violence' is replaced by the words 'virtual' and 'value' – impressive words, without a doubt, but can they counterbalance the engrained and haunting notion of 'violence' in cultures? Perhaps the editors would argue, convincingly enough, that since they'd now included words like 'holocaust', which cannot be discussed without a proper understanding of what violence is, the word violence no longer had special status. Discussions like this, concerning losing the long genealogy of 'violence' to the historically specific 'holocaust', raise an issue that is pertinent to our present project and also make *New Keywords* a distinguished predecessor.

In our book, a hard lesson we learnt from earlier books, not to mention our everyday experience of being Indian citizens, was not to jettison words like 'violence' (Sen, 2006). This is just too pervasive a word to be left out of a sub-continental or even a world keywords lexicon. So, we chose to retain 'violence' as an epistemic concept in our book while also trying to draw attention to its simulacra. We have included, almost instinctively, the various cruel guises of violence in historically inherited, culturally particular words such as 'sati'; in the entries on physical locations such as 'slums'; in political settings when a dread acronym like AFSPA (the Armed Forces Special Powers Act) is strategically deployed; in cases where the old French-English word 'atrocity' acquires a new set of meanings in the Indian context; and not least, in relation to its moral other, the embedded idea of 'ahimsa' or non-violence in India's composite culture. That is, in almost every section of our lexicon, the concept of violence runs like a binding thread, as do many other concepts such as 'dharma' in the ethical domain and 'economics' in the social. Ours is a book that begins with *atma*, the enduring Sanskrit word for 'soul', and ends the English word 'violence' – in which simple, fated conjunction some might read the entire narrative of the subcontinent and, possibly, the human race.

Turning now to the far from non-violent colonial and postcolonial legacy of this volume, we owe much to the mammoth, truly astonishing *Hobson-Jobson: A Glossary of Colloquial Anglo-Indian Words and Phrases, and of Kindred Terms, Etymological, Historical, Geographical and Discursive* by Henry Yule and A. C. Burnell (1886) and to its grandchild, the *Hanklyn-Janklin* by Nigel Hankin, billed as a 'rumble tumble guide to some of words customs and quiddities Indian and Indo-British' (2003). Our volume appears, again, to be a hybrid in this respect, since it is as much in this line of quirky descent as it is in consonance with other more recent academic volumes such as *The Future of Knowledge and Culture: A Dictionary for the 21st Century* by Vinay Lal and Ashis Nandy (2005); *Keywords for Modern India* by Craig Jeffrey and John Harriss (2014) and *Key Concepts for Modern Indian Studies* edited by Gita Dharampal-Frick, Monika Kirloskar-Steinbach, Rachel Dwyer and Jahnavi Phalke (2015). Evidently, it is 'keywords season' with more such books appearing each year. Our text should ideally be read in conjunction with these other works, for it could be that the current search for genuine keywords has a common motive: they are a response to a sort of post-traumatic stress in civil societies the world over (see Nair, 2009). Keywords books remind us that we may need old-fashioned 'talking cures' (Freud, 1930) to alleviate the widespread stress of being compelled to dress in full communicative regalia at all times and being under constant pressure to upgrade our images online everyday. This lexicon therefore invests in the idea of conceptual conversations that are not 'for' anyone or anything in a narrow sense but will stimulate fresh, perhaps directionless, enquiries, contributing to what K. C Bhattacharya has felicitously called 'Swaraj in Ideas' or independent thought. Our goal for this book is that it starts up the sorts of polyphonic conversations that we may want to live for but not necessarily die for.

Conversations: forms of the unpredictable

Speaking of conversation, polyphonic or otherwise, the fact is that one can ever quite know what's coming next in a conversation, unless it is entirely staged. This feature gives every talk situation its stimulating interpretive ambiguity and interactive enchantment. It also could be the elementary appeal of our own lexicon, which presents a narrative in media res, the present being visibly remade back and forth in its pages. Taking a theoretical cue at this point from specific research by ethno-methodologists (see Sacks, Schegloff and Jefferson, 1974; Nair, 2003) who have made it their business to study the structure of conversation in every minute detail, we find that the elaborate 'turn-taking' mechanisms characteristic of human colloquy have inbuilt resources for what is known as 'repair'. That is, a participant in any conversation anywhere on the globe at any given moment, is evolutionarily primed to attend to the cues she get from others as well as from her own 'feedback loops' to constantly mend her utterances. As Alan Turing once brilliantly argued in his thought experiment comparing humans and machines in *Mind* (1950), an open-ended conversation may be the best measure we have of the fallible yet flexible computational power of human language.

Members of the human species seem instinctively recognize that incoming information in ordinary talk is processed under conditions of radical epistemic uncertainty. Ordinary, everyday conversations alert us, that is, to the pervasive, yet enjoyable and mutual presence of imperfection in our conceptual universes. Indians, in particular, are a nation of indefatigable talkers. We could argue that this makes us self-reflexively aware of the hidden snares of linguistic relativism (see Whorf, 1956), sensitising us to human infirmity in the form of conversations that are ever in need of 'repair'. Inherent in any such exercise are the curative possibilities of crosstalk between all sorts of non-homogenous cultural formations from college undergraduates to ordinary citizens exploring new territories of the mind to scholars of South Asia seeking to refresh their scholarly memories. Most of all, we have in mind casual readers across the plurality of India's twenty-nine 'linguistic states' who will dip into our book without inhibition or fear of being overawed. In the long run, our preliminary effort might even spur an interest in local 'Lexicon Start ups' across the regions of India, while Departments that teach South Asian Studies in the United States, UK, Europe and Asia might also decide to be part of our 'joint venture'. However, even if such naive optimism is entirely unwarranted, we will still have begun an open-ended conversation. To my mind, this lexicon marks a transitive moment when the millennials of the selfie generation encounter their alien forebears where pre-history confronts post-truth. Cohabitations are not always legitimate in it: material culture and ancient culture are profiled side by side and consumerist appetites for glossy international brands confront a gnawing hunger for the imagined certitudes and scriptural benedictions of the past. Our lexicon offers a handy travellers' guide into this treacherous but exciting terrain.

This hybrid text, as I've underlined, is both 'for' and 'from' India; if it is pedagogic, it is aimed mainly at self-education, in an India still trying to sort out the influence of its colonial past. An example: Indian society, across castes, classes and religious affiliations, acknowledges that it is obsessed with astrology in everyday life. Elaborate astrological charts or *janmapatri* are drawn up to indicate portents at birth and are matched for marriages. Even state sessions of the legislature may choose to wait for an appropriately 'auspicious' moment for new governments to be sworn in. Yet the odd thing is, colonial hangover or not, there are still no serious anthropological theses examining the phenomenon and few respectable academics will go anywhere near the subject! It was really hard to find any colleagues brave enough to discuss the topic, let alone do an entry on it. That a scholar did agree to do an entry on *janmapatri* in the end is a tribute to the collective trust we established during the making of this volume. But there will be others who ask why we were so foolish as to include 'astrology' in this postcolonial, purportedly progressive text. Containing within it these seeds of a potent instability, of fractious theoretical discord as well as ideological mockery, this book at its most basic is about the necessary fragilities of form: forms of community, lexis, grammar, genre, gender, translation and conversational polyphony, amongst others (see Nair, 1992, 2002b, 2003a,b, 2013).

A quasi-biographical note at this point: this Indian Keywords initiative was first given shape at the Nehru Memorial Museum and Library (NMML) during a fellowship I was awarded there in 2010. It was then followed by a workshop convened by my fellow editor, Peter deSouza, and attended by more than thirty scholars from all over India at the Indian Institute of Advanced Study (IIAS) in 2013. At this seminar, experts from across India in a variety of disciplines commented animatedly – and not always approvingly – on my list of 'keywords'. During our discussions, a number of useful methodological 'how' questions, on which I took rough notes, came up repeatedly. I list about a dozen below.

1. Recording the contemporary moment: how is this achieved through 'keywords'?
2. According 'respect' to words: how does this happen?
3. How does one locate the universal in the local and the specific?
4. How have our ideas of 'progress' changed?
5. How do we record the changes in tradition/modernity over the last 150 years?
6. What is the place of memory and what is the relevance of classical lexicons today?
7. How can regional representation be meaningfully achieved in such project?
8. How to deploy humour and include taboo concepts in such a lexicon?
9. How might visual and auditory categories be captured in the lexicon? Will diacritical marks be included?
10. How does this work go about finding its audience?
11. How might the collaborative status of this work be highlighted?
12. How is the future relevance of this lexicon to be gauged?

It is because the grounds for debate round this book appeared so fertile that it seemed to us timely and appropriate to embark on the present keywords project – a twenty-first century biography, so to speak, of that imaginary yeti-like being, kindly dubbed the 'speaking Indian' in the annals of orientalism.

Postscript: Homo phoneticus indicus

'Homo phoneticus indicus' J. E. B Grey wrote in 1959, 'was no mere cross-sectioned larynx under an empty cranium; on the contrary, the whole man, head, heart and belly, produced voice.' Just six years later, in 1965, perhaps India's most famous contemporary woman poet, Kamala Das declared, 'I am Indian, very brown, born in Malabar, I speak three languages, write in two, dream in one.' Teasingly, Das maintained a decorous silence about the language she 'dreamt in' until, in one of her last interviews, she divulged that it was English! Such are the contradictions of the language scenario in India.

One way to characterize our volume is to view it as a record of the creative, often painful production of 'voice' in an India where no single identity is sufficient. In last two or three decades alone, 'Indians' have been depicted as lustful, corrupt and divisive (Khushwant Singh, writer, in *We Indians*, 1991); inclusive, tolerant, multilingual (Sunil Khilnani, historian, in *The Idea of India,* 1997); entrepreneurial, energetic, materialistic, bureaucratic (Pavan Verma, diplomat, in *Being Indian,* 2004); argumentative, intellectual, syncretic (Amartya Sen, economist, in *The Argumentative Indian*, 2005); undemocratic, indulging in family-oriented sexual fantasists (Sudhir Kakar, psychologist, in *The Indian People*, 2007); wise and enduring in the acceptance of their own traditions (Mark Tully, non-fiction writer and journalist, in *Non Stop India*, 2011); political, democratic and yet dynastic (Patrick French, historian, in *India: A Portrait*, 2011). All of which readings prompt us to unrealistically demand: *Will the real Indian please stand up and be counted?* In this book, we invite our unknown readers to encounter 'the Indian within' them by negotiating its winding labyrinths. For me, personally, the emancipatory possibilities that this 'Indian' maze of words have offered have been literally amazing. I end then with the personal that, as feminist theory has taught us, is always political. Kamala Das's poetry has given us a glimpse into India's non-trivial language politics. Here now, to complete the triad, is an oblique glance in the direction of two other women, makers of our 'mother-tongues': my mother and the anonymous woman on the cover of this book.

When my mother, Angela Soares, born into a Goan Christian family, married my Bengali father, she moved into a culturally unknown sphere, that of the Bengali *bhadralok* (a keyword in the present lexicon). A formal meeting was arranged between the new bride and the august male head of the household. Three staccato questions were then asked of her, which later became family lore. These were the following: 'what is your staple diet?' (my mother said she had a hysterical urge to answer 'oats'), 'do you wear a gown?'(my mother silently shook her heard at this) and 'what is your native language?' (this last question had my mother stumped; English was the language she knew best because of her historical placement but it was certainly not her native tongue). Diet, clothing, language, moral dilemmas, self-questioning: these basic intersections in the story of my mother's life seem to me also to run through this joint work of ours, giving it at once the feel of experiential familiarity and cognitive distance.

Moving back more than a millennium to the woman from the eleventh century Khajuraho carving depicted on the cover of this book, she embodies like my mother, as I see it, those tantalizing 'keyword' qualities that I've tried to inadequately enumerate in this introduction. I first came across her many decades ago when I was in college and was instantly awestruck by her cool. Even then, I noticed that there was an unusual fit between her lower and upper half. Look closely. No 'real' woman could ever stand at that angle and yet her asymmetric posture spoke. It illuminated a realm beyond fact. It boldly spoke 'the truth' about cultural continuities and ruptures. In a society where women are still objectified as bodies on whom all sorts of unbearable tortures can be inflicted without pause and, at the same time, worshipped as pure, untouchable goddesses, here was a woman who calmly took her the buxom, unclad beauty for granted, absorbed in the task of writing and composition even as a child (her own?) tugs at her for attention. To me, this image represents the emacipation that the words in our book can, at their best, offer us all.

Rukmini Bhaya Nair

References

Arnold, M. *Culture and Anarchy*. New York: Macmillan and Co., 1869.
Bhattacharya, K. C. 'Swaraj in Ideas'. *Visvabharati Quarterly* 8 (Calcutta), 1931.
Browning, Gary K. *Lyotard and the End of Grand Narratives*. Cardiff: University of Wales Press, 2000.
Das, Kamala. *Summer in Calcutta: Fifty Poems*. New Delhi: Rajinder Paul, 1965.
Dawkins, Richard. *The Selfish Gene*. New York: Oxford University Press, 1976.
Dennett, Daniel C. 'Darwin's Dangerous Idea'. *The Sciences* 35, no. 3 (1995): 34–40.
Dharampal-Frick, Gita, Monika Kirloskar-Steinbach, Rachel Dwyer and Jahanvi Phalkey, eds. *Key Concepts in Modern Indian Studies*. Delhi: Oxford University Press, 2015.
Foucault, Michel. *The Archaeology of Knowledge*. Paris: Éditions Gallimard, 1969.
French, Patrick. *India: A Portrait*. Delhi: Allen Lane, 2011.
Freud, Sigmund. *Civilization and Its Discontents*. New York: WW Norton & Company, 1989 (First published, 1930).
Gandhi, Mahatma K. *True Education*. Ahmedabad: Navajivan Publishing House, 1962.
Grey, J. E. B. 'Homo Phoneticus Indicus'. *Bulletin of the School of Oriental and African Studies* (London), 1959.
Hankin, Nigel. *Hanklyn-Janklin*. New Delhi: India Research Press, 2003.
Hardin, Garrett. 'The Tragedy of the Commons'. *Science* 162, no. 3859 (1968): 1243–8.
Hirsch, E. D. *Cultural Literacy: What Every American Needs To Know*. New York: Vintage, 1988.
Jeffrey, Craig and John Harriss. *Keywords for Modern India*. Delhi: Oxford University Press, 2014.
Kakar, Sudhir. *Indian Identity*. Delhi: Penguin Books, 2007.
Khilnani, Sunil. *The Idea of India*. London: Hamish Hamilton, 1997.
Lal, Vinay and Ashis Nandy. *The Future of Knowledge and Culture: A Dictionary for the 21st Century*. New Delhi: Penguin Global, 2005.
Lawrence, Thomas Edward. *Seven Pillars of Wisdom*. London: Penguin UK, 2000.
Muehlmann, S. 'Conservation and Contestation: In the Crossfire over "Diversity"'. *Proceedings of the Twelfth Annual Symposium about Language and Society–Austin*, 2004.
Nair, Rukmini Bhaya. 'Gender, Genre and Generative Grammar: Deconstructing the Matrimonial Column'. In *Text and Context: Essays in Contextualised Stylistics*, edited by M. J. Toolan, 227–54. London: Routledge, 1992.
Nair, Rukmini Bhaya. *Lying on the Postcolonial Couch: The Idea of Indifference*. Minneapolis: University of Minnesota Press and Delhi: Oxford University Press, 2002a.

Nair, Rukmini Bhaya. *Translation, Text and Theory: The Paradigm of India*. New Delhi, India, Thousand Oaks, USA; and London, UK: Sage, 2002b.

Nair, Rukmini Bhaya. *Narrative Gravity: Conversation, Cognition, Culture*. London and New York: Rutledge, 2003a.

Nair, Rukmini Bhaya. 'Sappho's Daughters: Postcoloniality and the Polysemous Semantics of Gender'. *The Journal of Literary Semantics* 32, no. 2 (2003b): 113–35.

Nair, Rukmini Bhaya. *Poetry in a Time of Terror: Essays in the Postcolonial Preternatural*. New Delhi and New York: Oxford University Press, 2009.

Nair, Rukmini Bhaya. 'The Nature of Narrative: Schemes, Genes, Memes, Dreams and Screams!'. In *Religious Narrative, Cognition and Culture: Image and Word in the Mind of Narrative*, edited by A. W. Geertz and J. S. Jensen, 117–46. London: Equinox Series in Religion, Cognition and Culture, 2011.

Nair, Rukmini Bhaya. 'Philological Angst: Or How the Narrative of Census, Caste and Race in India Still Informs the Discourse of the 21st Century'. In *WortMachtStamm: Rassismus und Determinismus in der Philologie 18./19 Jh*, edited by M. Messling and O. Ette, 55–87. Munich: Wilhelm Fink, 2012.

Nair, Rukmini Bhaya. *Mad Girl's Love Song*. New Delhi: Harper Collins, 2013.

Nair, Rukmini Bhaya. 'Narrative as a Mode of Explanation: Evolution and Emergence'. In *Modes of Explanation: Affordances for Action and Prediction*, edited by A. Garber and M. Lissack, 151–9. New York: Palgrave Macmillan, 2014.

Nair, Rukmini Bhaya, R. Bajaj and A. Meattle. *Technobrat: Culture in a Cybernetic Classroom*. Delhi: Harper Collins, 1997.

Ogden, C. K. and I. A. Richards. *The Meaning of Meaning: A Study of the Influence of Language upon Thought and of the Science of Symbolism*. New York: Harcourt, Brace & Company, 1946 (First published, 1923).

Sacks, H., E. A. Schegloff and G. Jefferson. 'A Simplest Systematics for the Organization of Turn-Taking for Conversation'. *Language* 50, no. 4, Part 1 (1974).

Sen, A. *The Argumentative Indian: Writings on Indian History, Culture and Identity*. London: Macmillan, 2005.

Sen, A. *Identity and Violence: The Illusion of Destiny*. London: Penguin Books, 2006.

Singh, K. *We Indians*. Delhi: Orient Paperbacks, 1982.

Tully, M. *India: The Road Ahead*. London: Rider and Co., 2011.

Turing, A. 'Computing Machinery and Intelligence'. *Mind* 59, no. 236 (1950): 433–60.

Varma, P. K. *Being Indian: Inside the Real India*. New Delhi: Viking Books, 2004.

Whorf, B. L. *Language, Thought and Reality*, edited by J. B. Carroll. Cambridge: MIT Press, 1956.

Williams, R. *Keywords: A Vocabulary of Culture and Society*. New York: Oxford University Press, 1976.

Wittgenstein, L. *Philosophical Investigations*. Chichester: John Wiley & Sons, 2009 (First published, 1953).

Yule, H. and A. C. Burnell. *Hobson-Jobson – A Glossary of Anglo-Indian Colloquial Words and Phrases*. London: John Murray, 1886.

CHAPTER 1
CLASSICAL HERITAGES: DATABASES OF MEMORY

ATMA (ĀTMĀ)

TRS Sharma

Usually translated as 'soul', this everyday yet metaphysical word has a complex and ancient etymology. In terms of possible cognates, we have the Anglo-Saxon *aefm* meaning 'breath or soul'; the Old High German *aatum* and Modern German *atem* for 'breath' and, more generally, the foundational principle of life and sensation. In many Indian languages today, the word *atma* functions as both an independent term and as a primary or base word that readily lends itself to prefixes and suffixes that make compound words.

As an independent base word, the word atma constitutes an abstract concept yielding several meanings. It is multi-ordinal and can mean any number of things depending upon the context: breath, self and soul, spirit and essence are the main contenders in this respect. Historically, the word atma often appears to shuttle between two prominent schools of thought in ancient Indian metaphysics, namely, the pluralists (the *nyaaya vaisheshika* school) and the monists (the *vedantic* school). Its meanings thereby proliferate, enriching the vocabulary and cultures of several Indian languages.

Vedic thought (*c.* 1500–2000 BCE) often postulated God as one reality without any second, a universal being (*sat*) or Brahman, an ultimate reality that comprises the atma of the entire universe. The problem, however, is: how is this abstract notion of atma realized? Here both *Vedanta* and some Buddhist schools agree that the atma can be realized only via the route of negation: 'not this, nor this' (*neti, neti*).

In this somewhat frustrating, if logically sound, context, the *Kaṭho Upanishad* (iii 3.3) provides us with a vivid metaphor to comprehend the mystery that atma constituted in the Vedic canon. It visualizes the atma or soul as riding in a chariot, the body being the chariot, the intellect the chariot driver, the mind the reins and the senses horses. This famous metaphor presents atma as a human experiencer endowed with body, mind and intellect as well as the senses.

Following this brief excursus into atma as a singular base word, we turn now to the play of affixes. As mooted earlier, atma is an all-weather term, lending itself easily to the use of both prefixes and suffixes. With prefixes, we have already mentioned *antaraatman* (the soul within); and then there is *paramaatman* (the supreme soul, usually translated as 'God'). It is also important to note that such uses are not in the least esoteric but are part of ordinary parlance in many Indian languages. When it comes to suffixes, the base word atma lends itself even more easily to the formation of compound words. A few of these are listed here: *aatmajnaanam* (self-knowledge), *aatmatattvam* (the true nature of the soul), *aatmadarshana* (to behold oneself), *aatmanivedanam* (offering oneself) and so on (see V. S. Apte for a fuller list of these highly generative compound terms).

References

Apte, V. S. *Sanskrit-English Dictionary*. Delhi: Motilal Banarsidaas, 1970.
Chinmayananda, Swami, ed. *Kathopanishad*. Madras: Chinmaya Publications, 1976.

AHIMSA (AHINSĀ/HINSĀ/SATYA/ASATYA/ŚĀNTI)

Gangeya Mukherji

This cluster of related concepts forms the spine that holds up an ethical system developed over a long period on the Indian subcontinent. Today, these words are commonplace in the domain of both secular and religious discourse.

To begin with the concepts of *ahimsa* and *satya*, these appear on the etymological plane to exist in a manifestive relationship. Of the two, satya (truth) is the more fundamental quality derived from the root *sat*, which translates to 'that which exists' or 'that which is virtuous'. Accordingly, satya may be defined as 'that which generates welfare'. The manifestations of satya, by convention, included the virtues of equality or non-discrimination, self-restraint, clarity, equanimity, renunciation, forgiveness, mercy and, prominently, ahimsa. The public concept of satya, currently in common use as truthfulness, or rather fact-based truthfulness, is conveyed in the secondary meaning of *vachic satya*, meaning uttered truth.

The etymological root of ahimsa derives from the Sanskrit root *hims*, which refers to physical injury, including of the fatal kind, and thus leads to a more nuanced and accurate interpretation of *a-hinsā* as physical non-injury. Beginning with the *Rig Veda* (*c.* 1500 BCE), the Brahmanic tradition profusely categorized and explained the pair of words hinsā and ahimsa. Over time, the main sense of this coupled concept came to be defined in Brahmanic, Jain and Buddhist epistemology primarily in terms of killing and non-killing, even though an astonishingly detailed classification and discussion concerning these terms exists in the texts of all three traditions. The range of definitions conveying both the variety of perspective and the philosophical and literary significance associated with the two terms illustrates their profound and continuing significance in the discourse of the time. The *Jabaladarshana Upanishad*, or instance, describes physical, mental and linguistic hinsā in terms of the actions committed in contravention to Vedic admonition. According to the Jain tradition, hinsā primarily entails hurting the life principle, although any action undertaken without passion and attachment and adhering to scriptural norms is exempt from the sin of hinsā even if it causes bodily hurt or loss of life. Texts in Jainism also regard internal purification, detachment and renunciation as amounting to ahimsa. Buddhist texts in Pali refer to *vihimsa* (injury) and *avihamsa* (non-injury), mainly in terms of mental violence, rather than hinsā-ahimsa, whereas the Pali phrase *panatipata veramani* is used to state the injunction against the killing of living beings.

Śānti, on the other hand, is a mental state. It obeys no explicit injunction to kill or not kill but has, rather, been etymologically described in Sanskrit as the quenching of passion and anger, and the faculty of transcending pain and bliss, and being content with that which one possesses or does not possess. In its later and more current sense of peace, śānti is a quality or condition which facilitates a deep inner calm.

Discussions on the subject of war and violence only further underline the complexity of the question of ahimsa, most crucially regarding its desirability and viability in matters of state. As mentioned above, even avowedly pacifist Jain and Buddhist principles state exceptions to the norm of ahimsa under particular conditions, approximating to the classic position of the *Bhagavad Gita* in the epic Mahabharata regarding war, and even extending to justification of retributive violence, instantiated, for instance, in the first-century *Mahaparinirvana Sutra* of Mahayana Buddhism, the third-century *Uttaradhyayana Sutra* and the eighth-century *Brihatkalpa Bhasya* in the Jain canon.

Non-violence and public truth, notwithstanding their elevated textual position as ethical touchstones, nevertheless, remained quite as elusive as practicable public ideals in Indian history as in the rest of the world. At the beginning of the twentieth century, M. K. Gandhi insisted that satya and ahimsa were fundamental to the moral order of society and the only way to individually achieve the highest of human goals: śānti in life and thereafter the liberation of the soul (*mokṣha*). The substantial debate on ahimsa among theoreticians during the Indian national movement witnessed effective critique, by Gandhi and Rabindranath Tagore especially, of the violence of extremism or revolutionary terrorism animatedly presented by thinker-activists such as M. N. Roy. Counter-critiques centred around Gandhi's allegedly ambivalent attitude towards the relationship of non-violence, religion and state formation, Tagore's ambiguous position on social change and also the analyses of the innate violence rather than peaceability of the Hindu tradition. In this connection, it is worth noting how strenuously Gandhi rejected the notion of the separation of public and private morality, as he did the notion that the working of politics broadly, and government generally, required an essential element of untruth, highlighted by Kautilya's *Arthashastra* in ancient India and in ancient Rome as *arcana imperii* or the mystery of government. Thus, the Gandhian idea of society and politics has today come to be acknowledged as a particularly Indian achievement.

In modern India, undiminished and even growing public fascination with muscular nationalism and protest has, on the one hand, fostered scant respect for civic law and, on the other, contributed to the acceptability of both Naxalism and majority vigilantism. However, it must be simultaneously noted that the ideals of transparent government and honest democracy have drawn abiding inspiration from the enduring concepts of satya and ahimsa. The robust and long-standing debates around these concepts guided the highest traditions of the Indian freedom movement and the early years of the Indian state and remain values that individuals across units of governance and society can still actively draw on as they work towards justice and reform as well as against the untrammelled exercise of political and legal privilege.

References

Houben, Jan E. M. and Karel R. Van Kooij, eds. *Violence Denied: Violence, Non-Violence and the Rationalization of Violence in South Asian Cultural History*. Leiden: E. J. Brill, 1999.

Tahtinen, Unto. *Ahimsa: Non-Violence in Indian Tradition*. Ahmedabad: Navjivan Publishing House, 1976.

ARTHA (ARTHA)

Mohini Mullick

One of the most intriguing concepts in the Indian philosophical arsenal, *artha* is primarily known as one of the four *purusarthas* (goals of human life), as defined in the *Dharmashastras* (texts relating to *dharma* [duty]).

Interestingly, the word artha forms part of the very word purusartha. In many Indian languages today, it is actually a word the meaning of which is 'meaning', a point adumbrated a couple of paragraphs later here. More traditionally, the meaning of artha was suggestive of the fact that all human lives have/ought to have certain purposes, whether or not these purposes are hierarchically arranged. When unpacked, artha in its original sense refers to the entire range of the material purposes of human life – but primarily to the acquisition of wealth and well-being. One might conclude from this that it is near tautological in the Indian tradition to consider the garnering of wealth as the goal of human life. Yet, this is clearly not the case. The author of the canonical *Arthashastra* may, understandably, demur but most commentators agree that the other goals of *kama* (love and desire), dharma and *mokṣha* (liberation) are in fact superior to the goal of material aspiration and aggrandizement. So, it goes to the everlasting credit of ancient Indian thinkers that they refused to shy away from the realities of human psychology.

In popular as well as traditional belief, the social arrangements envisaged in the *varnashramadharma* (stages of life) give due respect to the householder or provider, who must necessarily pursue artha before he (the unmarked subject here is almost inevitably male) withdraws into a life of contemplation. A king or ruler's primary purushartha is also artha, since he is responsible for the welfare of his people, which includes their security. In modern parlance, we may say that in the classical notion of artha, economics and politics belong broadly to the same register at the conceptual level. Whether there is perhaps a lesson to take away from this piece of ancient wisdom remains a moot point.

What then is the relation between these two senses, political and economic – not to mention a third to which we will advert below – of artha? Clearly, the common element is the other-directedness of the term, as both goal and as material gain. Indeed, the third and most salient use of artha, as the meaning of a word/any articulation in language, seems to confirm this hypothesis. For an object is indeed the object (goal) of the word. More graphically, one might say that the word takes aim at an object: the word 'dog', for example, directs attention to an object outside of oneself. This very connotation of artha as meaning has deep implications for Indian epistemology and, of course, for the philosophy of language today.

The major work in Indian classical literature on the topic is clearly the *Arthashastra* of Kautilya (*c*. second century BCE to third century CE). In this work, Kautilya argues for the primacy of artha as a goal of individual life, of the life of the state and of society at large, all of which revolve around the idea of material well-being/welfare. For him, artha is the root of dharma and its fruit is kama. When pursued in the right manner, therefore, the achievement of artha is the foundation of universal success in life or *sarvarthasiddhi*.

Given modern moral and religious sensibilities in contemporary India and across the world, where it is often appropriate to speak in politically correct terms of shunning material values while pursuing them vigorously in practice, artha may as a concept appear to be relegated to the textbooks of economics or as an ordinary word just meaning 'meaning'. It is, however, one of the richest notions that Indian thought has produced, insinuating itself not only in the economic and the political realms but also pervading linguistic theory and indeed the very fabric of Indian society.

References

Olivelle, P. and D. R. Davis, eds. *The Oxford History of Hinduism: Hindu Law: A New History of Dharmasastra*. Oxford: Oxford University Press, 2017.
Rangarajan, L. N. *Kautilya: The Arthashastra*. New York: Penguin Classics, 1992.

ARYAN (ĀRYAN)/DRAVIDIAN

Lakshmi Subramaniam

The pair words 'Aryan' and 'Dravidian' are normally associated with the people and languages of the Indian subcontinent. Since the 'discovery' of Sanskrit and the Vedas by orientalist scholars like William Jones in the eighteenth century, the categories Aryan and Dravidian have constituted the staple of controversy. Most of these heated debates concern the 'original homeland' of the Indo-European-speaking peoples, the 'peopling' of the Indian subcontinent and the interactions between language groups and communities.

The label 'Indo-Aryan', roughly synonymous with 'Indo-European', is a language label that should not be confused with a racial label, according to Romila Thapar. It encompasses the complex historical experience of migration and settlement by Indo-European language groups who deployed the Sanskrit language for the ritual and poetry of the Vedic culture dating to the period approximately between the middle of the second millennium BCE and 600 BCE. Referred to in the *Rig Veda* as *Arya Varna* (a self-designating epithet) and *Dasa Varna* (an 'other' designating term, which is sometimes translated as 'slave colour' or race and sometimes as 'original' inhabitants), thus underline, according to some scholars, a racial interpretation of the term Aryan. As Thapar argues, however, there were elements of mediation in all such encounters: the Indo-Aryan speakers negotiated with local inhabitants and the marks of these negotiations are evident in language practices across the subcontinent. Referring to a linguistic study of Vedic Sanskrit words, where a number of terms associated with agriculture come from proto-Dravidian or Austro-Asiatic words, she expressly rejects the association of race exclusively with language and points out the dangers of overstating the racial distinction between the Aryas (newcomers adhering to Vedic culture) and Dasas (the indigenous peoples).

Thapar's analysis is largely a response to nineteenth-century European scholarship on race and language as well as a critique of nationalist Indian claims that Aryans were indigenous to the subcontinent. A turning point in this history was that of burgeoning Orientalist scholarship and William Jones's startling observations on the similarities between Sanskrit and the other classical languages of Europe. This prompted Jones to suggest that there must have been an early proto-group of people, who spoke the *ur*-languages from which Indo-European languages evolved. For a short time during the eighteenth century, India was envisaged as the original homeland of the Indo-European language peoples and as the cradle of human race. However, following Max Müller, many nineteenth-century scholars argued that the Aryans originated in Central Asia, with one branch migrating to Europe and the other to India. These settlers were the pioneers of the Vedic civilization and poetry. They were perpetually engaged in conflict as they subordinated the original inhabitants through the second millennium BCE and introduced their new Indo-European language(s). Vedic poetic expression in Sanskrit referred to Dasas as *Dasyus*, counterposing them with Aryas and thereby initiating a preliminary understanding of the occupational division in society that eventually solidified around notions of caste and fixed taboos against intermarriage between the allegedly fair-skinned Aryas and dark-skinned Dasas. Max Mueller often associated language with race but primarily as a device to differentiate Aryans (peoples who spoke Sanskrit and maintained caste rules) from non-Aryans (who spoke a number of different languages). In this pervasive narrative, the latter peoples were seen to inhabit the region south of the Vindhyas, especially the peninsula, and were speakers of languages such as Tamil, Malayalam, Kannada, Telugu, Kodagu, Toda and so on. Of these 'Southern' languages, Tamil was estimated to possess the most extensive literature, to stand out as the most original and, in its 'pure' state, as having very little resemblance to Sanskrit.

The Dravidian proof is associated with Madras orientalists like F. W. Ellis and the missionary-linguist Robert Caldwell whose scholarly endeavours with local collaborators established a 'Dravidian' family of languages that enjoyed a historical unity and had non-Sanskritic origins. New linguistic analysis suggests that the Dravidian family (consisting of eighty language varieties) is almost 4,500 years old and certainly in evidence before the beginning of the Indo-European/Āryan migrations. Whether or not these speakers were associated with the Indus Valley civilization is hard to establish, however.

References

Thapar, Romila. *The Aryan Recasting Constructs*. Delhi: Three Essays Collective, 2008.
Trautmann, Thomas. *Conversations in Colonial South India: The Dravidian Proof in Colonial Madras*. Berkeley: University of California Press, 2006.

ASMITA (ASMITĀ)

Sanjay Palshikar

Asmita connotes the interrelated ideas of a sense of identity, of pride and the sense of being distinct. A word of Sanskrit origin, and now a recognizable part of the political discourse in some regions – such as, for example, Gujarat – the entry of the word asmita into some of the modern Indian languages seems to have been late. Molesworth's *Marathi-English Dictionary* (1857) does not include it, and in Gujarati, asmita was brought into use only by K. M. Munshi in the early twentieth century. In Bengali (or Bangla), the poet Sudhin Datta (1901–1960) used the word to signify 'the sense of specific existence', but unlike in present-day Gujarat, the word gained little currency then. The present popularity of the word may have partly to do with its invocation, first by Chimanbhai Patel during his second term as the chief minister of Gujarat and later by Narendra Modi. Though they belonged to different political parties, they both projected Gujarat's *vikas* (development) through vigorously pursued mega projects as their declared goal. Within this political rhetoric, whoever opposed these projects was seen as being against the asmita (the pride, the distinctive identity) of Gujarat. In the neighbouring state of Maharashtra, Shiv Sena leaders often speak of the asmita of Maharashtra, though they do not have a monopoly over it.

Asmita, in modern India, is thus prominently used in assertions of regional identity. This is in stark contrast to its ancient Sanskrit usage. In Patanjali's *Yōgasutra*, asmita implies a false identification of the self with the body or the bodily senses, leading to suffering. The modern sense of the word, in contrast, is wholly positive even when it is not overtly political as in the case of the well-known women's organization Asmita, a resource centre for women engaged in women's issues through research, advocacy and counselling. In this case, asmita underscores a positive women's identity and has no obvious connotations of glory or pride, as in the case of regional identity. The Asmita theatre group in the north is another example of a usage not related to regional identity. But, whatever the specific meanings and allusions, possessing asmita in its modern sense is supposed to be good.

It should also be pointed out that states other than Maharashtra and Gujarat, where asmita is not used or is used less frequently, are hardly lacking in the politics of regional identity. N. T. Rama Rao routed Congress in the 1983 Assembly Elections in Andhra Pradesh and came to power riding the wave of Telugu *atma gauravam* or Telugu self-respect. *Garva* (pride) or *gourava* (glory) is also not unknown in Bangla, and, as in *Garv se kaho hum Hindu hain* ('Say with pride that you are Hindu'), garva has also been part of the Hindu majoritarian aggressiveness. In this sense, both asmita and garva are deployed to express pride in one's collective identity and often have strong nationalist overtones.

The regional/religious assertiveness expressed through the word asmita was recognized, countered and appropriated by Dalit writers in Maharashtra quite some time ago when they launched the literary magazine called *Asmitadarsha* (or, reflection of Dalit identity). In Gujarat in 2016, when several Dalit groups marched in protest against atrocities on Dalits by cow vigilante groups, they, too, spoke of asmita. This notion of asmita can be translated as self-respect, unlike the asmita of the Gujarati elite which is all about the glory and pride of Gujarat.

New-age guru Sri Sri Ravi Shankar has declared that not being one with existence and having a separate identity, recognizing that 'I am different from others' is asmita: 'What [do] people think of me? What do I want from them? How do I take advantage of them? Do they think I am good or bad? All these things about "me, me, I, I" are called asmita.' Now, such a version of asmita is supposed to 'eat you up', causing suffering. But does it? Obviously, India's political leaders, fired by the idea of asmita, do not seem worried about its consequences even as they confer honours on the guru; the guru, likewise, is probably not addressing his wise counsel to them. We must therefore ask: whose asmita causes suffering to whom? This may be a hard question to come to grips with, but what is not in doubt is the power and generative capacity of the word asmita in contemporary India.

Acknowledgement

The author would like to acknowledge the contributions of Probal Dasgupta, Prachi Gurjarpadhye, Tridip Suhrud, Rita Kothari, V. Rajagopal, Velchery, Navin Rao, Rakesh Pande and Vasanth Kannabiran to this entry.

References

Kothari, R. and A. Kothari. *K.M. Munshi*. Delhi: Penguin-Random House, 2017.
Suhrud, T. 'Modi and Gujarati "Asmita"'. *Economic and Political Weekly* 43, no. 1 (5 January 2008).

BHAVA (BHĀVA)

TRS Sharma

Bhava derives from the root 'bhoo', which means 'to be, become, what occurs'. The cognate *bhaavana* means to 'become', but adds up to something along the lines of 'forming in the mind', to notions of conception or imagination. This gradually perhaps made way for the concept of emotion to appear and 'embody'.

Talking about emotions (bhavas), aren't they known to be notorious in messing up one's moral life? Can we ever trust them? Besides, emotions haven't fared well in their conceptual history in the West either. Part of the reason is that the discourse on emotion has always been made within the rhetoric of rationality, and emotion and reason have always been looked upon as opposing forces in man. As if to add more substance to the subversive power of emotions, there is a basic composite concept formulated in Sanskrit called *arishadvarga*. This concept constitutes six hardcore, inimical emotions – the negative 'affects' if you will – such as *kama* (desire), *krodha* (anger), *lobha* (greed), *moha* (infatuation), *māda* (arrogance) and *maatsarya* (jealousy), all of which figure in the great Indian epic narratives and cause a great deal of havoc and cataclysmic changes in the lives of heroic men and women. They are paradigmatic and universal, though the way they manifest in psychosocial life is often culture-specific. However, we need 'to interpret emotions functionally in the sense of what they do', not what they are, suggests Owen Lynch.

The next question that arises is: do any of these raw emotions occur in its pristine form? It is most unlikely for each raw emotion gets laced with elements from other emotions – say, anger gets mixed with jealousy, or with greed, which when thwarted, explodes. Can we, then, ever experience each of these emotions in its pristine purity, unmixed with traces of other emotions so that we can objectify it, evaluate it? Yes, we can, says Bharata's *Natyashastra*: each emotion can be recreated on the stage so that the audience can experience its singular, nascent purity as *rasa* (aesthetic flavour or essence) through *abhinaya*. Abhinaya develops a new vocabulary and syntax through body language (gestures through eye and fingers, bearing and postures), drawing vastly on the 'corporeal semantics' peculiar to a culture and its semiotics.

Recent cognitive studies, however, offer a different perspective altogether and suggest that emotions can also act as moral sensors and reinforce one's ethical values. The classic example that one can cite is the exemplary dialogues between Arjuna and Krishna in the Mahabharata war as depicted in the *Bhagavad Gita*. Arjuna is not convinced that a cosmic design is at work in the war he is obliged to fight. He sees only specific things, his own kinsmen ready to kill and be killed. While he is convinced of the just cause of war, he is horrified at its consequences. He develops a sudden revulsion for the war, for the horrendous killing involved, even though he is raised as a warrior. His *svabhaava* (inner nature/impulse) which believes in human values is at war with his *svadharma* (his duty as a warrior), which will not baulk at killing his own kinsmen when at war. The complex emotive state that Arjuna undergoes is an aporetic event in the epic and is characterized by great ethical disturbance.

References

Lynch, Owen. *Divine Passions*. New Delhi: Oxford University Press, 1990.
Sharma, T. R. S. *Toward an Alternative Critical Discourse*. Shimla: Indian Institute of Advanced Study, 2000.

BHAKTI (BHAKTI)

TRS Sharma

The term *bhakti* derives from the root word *bhaj*, which means 'to share, adore, worship'. It assumes a specific form as devotion to a personal god, a Shiva or Krishna, mythical figures perhaps, and acquires additional meaning as 'partaking of god'. In a broader perspective, the term signified a form of religion which absorbs the spiritual notions of the Vedas, the Upanishads and the *Bhagavad Gita* and grew rapidly as a popular movement in South India. The idea of devotion to a personal god showed great potential for an upsurge, initiating poetry, songs and even classical music. This movement first occurs in Tamilakam (Tamil macro region comprising modern-day Tamil Nadu and Kerala), say, in the sixth century CE, and spreads in the adjoining territories soon after.

The loving hymns that the saints sang to a Shiva or Krishna construct situations wherein a personal relationship develops with the chosen god, the saint eventually longing for a physical union. The iconic and sensory details in these hymns/poems are often charged with incandescent sexuality, which sublimates in rapture leading to mystic experience. Here is Andal (of eighth-century Tamilakam) pleading with the passing clouds to tell Krishna to stay with her 'for one day / enter me / so as to wipe away / the saffron paste / adorning my breasts'. And, in what is today Karnataka, there is Akka Mahadevi (twelfth century), unique in many ways among the female saints, whose passionate pleadings with Shiva stand out: 'Look at / love's marvelous / ways: / if you shoot an arrow / plant it / till no feather shows; / if you hug / a body, bones / must crunch and crumble; / weld, / the welding must vanish. / Love is then / our lord's love' (trans. A. K. Ramanujan, 142).

Like the metaphysical poet George Herbert and Gerard Manley Hopkins of nineteenth-century England, the Indian saint-poet often gets into an argumentative mode with his or her personal god but much more cantankerously than his or her British counterparts. The example of Sundarar, the eighth-century Tamil saint, stands out unique among such saint-poets of India. He has two wives to support and gets into a querulous debate with his intimate god Shiva: 'you have a woman as half yourself; / the Lady Ganga lives on your spreading matted hair; / you know well the problems / of supporting two good women' (trans. Indira Peterson). This is in one sense 'confessional' poetry and in another sense an apodictic theatre in its totality – an internal theatre wherein Shiva hypostatizes into a character with whom the devotee engages in a constant apostrophization. There are of course saint-poets of North India, such as Kabir, Meera and the blind poet Surdas, but none of them could be as demanding, as querulous and as argumentative as Sundarar! But then this kind of devotion to a god has its own risks: bhakti for the saint is both agony and ecstasy, more agony perhaps – it is internal theatre wherein she or he is the chief actor.

The principal *rasa* (emotion in its essence) evoked in the context of bhakti is quite often *shrngaara*, which is one among the eight rasas mentioned by Bharata. But, this form of shrngaara comes with many faces, subsidiaries: it can be *naayaka–naayikaa bhava*, that is, hero–heroine relation, or *daasya bhava*, that is, the devotee as serving the master. It is even argued, as by Rupa Goswami, the Bengali saint-poet, that shrngaara is the one basic rasa which subsumes all other rasas as its subsidiaries, because the devotee in her or his dialogic relationship with god experiences almost all the rasas as auxiliaries to the main shrngaara.

Bhakti, in short, is a Tamil innovation developed within a Tamil context – an innovation on what Tamil had taken from Sanskrit and for which no Sanskrit parallel movement existed during this time or earlier. It was a movement in a civilizational process which flourished for nearly ten centuries, spreading, say, into neighbouring Karnataka by the twelfth century, and then moving on to Maharashtra and Gujarat, and, in the East to Odisha, Bengal and Assam, eventually encompassing the entire subcontinent by the sixteenth century.

References

Peterson, Indira, trans. *Poems to Siva: The Hymns of the Tamil Saints*. Delhi: Motilal Banarsidass, 1991.
Ramanujan, A. K., trans. *Speaking of Shiva*. London: Penguin Books, 1973.

CASTE

Surinder S. Jodhka

Caste is almost universally viewed as a peculiar system of social hierarchy and inequality, practised by the Hindus, who mostly live in India or South Asia or have their origin in the subcontinent. Implicit in this view is the assumption that caste has its origin in the religious faith of the Hindus, a part and parcel of their belief system. Further, its spatial aspect is also closely intertwined in this view. Though not all Indians are Hindus, this dominant view would assert, implicitly or explicitly, that the foundational values of Indian culture are quintessentially drawn from Hindu religious philosophy. The Muslims, the Christians, the Sikhs or even the Buddhists and Jains of Indian origin have either converted out of Hinduism (such as the Indian Muslims or the Indian Christians) or their faith systems are branches and varieties of the broader Hindu family. The presence of caste-like hierarchical divisions among the non-Hindu communities of India or those of other faith systems of Indian origin is thus cited as an obvious evidence of their Hindu ancestry. Drawn mostly from orientalist and colonial writings on India's past and enthusiastically endorsed and accepted by native 'reformers', including some of the mainstream nationalist leaders, this framing of Indian tradition with caste and

Hinduism at its centre has come to acquire the status of common sense and is widely accepted as an obvious fact. However, this view has also been seriously contested by a wide range of scholarship.

Paradoxically, the word 'caste' does not belong to any of the Indian languages. Nor does it have a literal equivalent in any of the Indian languages. It is presumed to have its etymological origin in the Latin word *castus*, which literally means 'chaste' or 'pure'. The Portuguese seafarers, who arrived on the west coast of India for trade in the fifteenth century, were the first to use it in the Indian context. Drawing its meaning closely from Latin, for the Portuguese also the word *casta* meant 'race' or 'lineage', which they presumably used for rigid divisions in their own society. The term would have perhaps compared well with the segregated community life of the local people they encountered on the coast.

The British colonizers, who soon followed the Portuguese, took the idea of caste very seriously, and as they expanded their interests and presence in the region, they developed elaborate accounts of Indian society and culture. Drawing actively from Indological and orientalist writing emanating from different parts of Europe, they too came to believe that Indians were obsessed with religion, which was primarily Hinduism.

Given this presumed centrality of religion in the life of the 'native', Hindu religious texts were to provide the foundational logic for all social and cultural practices in the region. Colonial anthropology also worked with the assumption that despite diversities of language and habits, Hinduism provided a sense of unity to the entire region. Another critical assumption of this theorization of India was of its being stuck in time, in its tradition, never capable of changing on its own. The textually constructed framing of caste began to acquire a life of its own when the colonial census, introduced in 1872, used it for enumerating groups and communities and assign them concrete status in the presumed hierarchical system.

The canonical text that provided the normative codifications of caste was the *Manusmriti*, presumably authored by Manu in ancient times. Following the textual dictum enunciated by Manu, caste was a neatly segregated system of social divisions where social groups were assigned occupational monopolies in an order of hierarchy. This order of hierarchy was largely based on an assigned degree of purity to a given occupation. The dialectics of purity and pollution produced a unique system of inequality which was inherently legitimate, embedded in local culture and remained unchanged. Given that the everyday practice of caste was reproduced through a neat hierarchy of occupations and a mutually exclusive division of social groups, the mundane materiality of occupational (economic) life was reducible to religious belief.

This framing soon became hegemonic and over a period of time, a social anthropology of caste evolved. The terms that were to translate caste into local lexicon were those of *varna* and *jati*. While varna provided a normative model of hierarchy, jatis were concrete groupings, which divided each varna into innumerable social units. The idea of varna as spelt out in the *Manusmriti* divided the Hindus into four mutually exclusive categories – the Brahmin (priest), the Kshatriya (warrior), the Vaishya (trader) and the Shudra (peasant/artisan/labourer). Beyond the four varnas was the *achhoot* (the untouchable). These four or five categories occupied specific positions in the status hierarchy, with the Brahmins at the top, followed by the other three varnas in the same order as mentioned above and the achhoots occupying a position at the very bottom. The jatis were groupings of kinship communities that maintained their symbolic border by strictly following rules of exogamy and endogamy in marriage practices. They were further divided into subgroups, which had localized names and systems of classifications. Jatis and their subunits numbered in the hundreds in every linguistic region and in the thousands across the entire subcontinent. Besides occupational divisions and hierarchies of ritual status, the caste system also had other features. Even when different caste groups lived together in a village, their localities were clearly segregated and those at the bottom, the untouchables, were forced to stay away from the main settlement of the village. Caste collectives also had clearly codified rules regarding sharing of food and social interaction and avoidance in everyday social life.

Notions of ascriptive hierarchy, social segregation and the practice of untouchability had indeed been a reality of life in most (though not all) regions of India from much before the Portuguese and British colonizers arrived. These notions were also supported by local religious and traditional belief systems. The term caste, defined as status and ascriptive hierarchies, also captures these differences and inequalities quite adequately. However, to reduce it to a singular pan-Indian reality that emanates exclusively from religious ideology is simply wrong and is not supported by any evidence.

Also, caste was not codified uniformly everywhere. Every region in the subcontinent has had a different set of caste-like communities. Even when notions of hierarchy and pollution have been common, the normative systems guiding social interactions among individuals and groups have varied across regions. For example, the four- or fivefold notion of varna has not even been a fact of life everywhere. Most of the southern regions did not have Kshatriya and/or Vaishya varnas. Similarly, even though hierarchy and untouchability existed, the Brahmins did not enjoy any kind of privilege or high status in the Punjab.

Viewed from this perspective, caste would inevitably appear as an evolving system, actively intersecting with regional ecologies, the dynamics of local economic process and the regimes of power. Thus, to assume that the process of modernization/urbanization or the introduction of a democratic political system that ought to erase caste is founded on simplistic notions and flawed assumptions. Such assumptions also inhibit us from exploring the contemporary realities of caste. It is only through the alternative perspective suggested above that we can make sense of the persistence of caste even when its traditional 'eco-system' is significantly weakened or altered. Caste survives as a resource, positive and/or negative, a kind of social capital that reproduces inequalities in different spheres of life in contemporary India.

References

Dirks, N. B. *Castes of Mind: Colonialism and the Making of Modern India*. Princeton: Princeton University Press, 2001.
Jodhka, S. S. *Caste in Contemporary India*, 2nd edn. New Delhi: Routledge, 2018.

COLONIALISM/POSTCOLONIALISM

Ulka Anjaria

Colonialism, the political and economic rule of a foreign power over a people different from them, has existed in many forms throughout human history. But, when placed in tension with the concept of postcolonialism, the term takes on a particular meaning, namely colonialism as understood through the lens of postcolonial theory. From this perspective, colonialism is not only political and economic domination but also ideological domination, founded in the collection of knowledge, a form of colonialism that was epitomized by British rule over India in the nineteenth century. This specific form of colonialism uses new developments in modern science, technology and disciplinary regimes, which together constitute a new discourse, to cast the colony as a space of backwardness, in need of political rule, as needing to catch up to modernity. Here, colonial rule penetrates to all aspects of society, including religion, architecture, literature, sports and even personal self-care. The elite classes of the colonized society are invited to participate in the project of remaking their own society in the model of the colonizer in order to usher their people into modernity. The political and economic aspects of colonialism are thus understood as part of a larger imperative to instil modern values in the minds of the colonized.

This ideological project is premised on the philosophical concept of the binary and of historicism; both of which structure thought and produce an irreducible 'Other' on the one hand and an idea of progress through empty homogeneous time on the other. The binary is a means of understanding the world based on what it is not. So, while Britain imagines itself as great, civilized, modern, historical, rational, masculine and ethical, it necessarily imagines the colonized as lowly, barbaric, backward, fantastical, irrational, feminine and violent. Nineteenth-century evolutionism combined with social science suggested that the colonized could one day attain the characteristics of British civilization, but that would require significant pedagogical investment on the part of the colonizer. Once colonialism is articulated this way – in Britain represented by the Anglicist view as opposed to the Orientalist one – its value becomes self-evident.

Postcolonialism, then, without the hyphen, is not a temporal indicator of a time after colonialism but an optics that renders visible the role of colonial discourse in colonial rule. Postcolonialism exposes projects such as cricket in India, the reform of the vernaculars, the rise of the novel and even the birth of nationalism as individual parts of the larger process of rule by discourse, even when they espoused an anti-colonial politics. It works by denaturalizing precisely what had become accepted or intuitive about colonial rule, by showing how colonial rule did not transform an India that already existed but *created* an India *to be transformed* through the power of representation in consolidating power. For instance, the British instituted a census in India that claimed to be merely recording the diversity of religions but in fact created religions as discrete categories in ways that had never really existed. Likewise, in their valorization of literary realism, they denigrated Indian literature as being fantastical and irrational and thus encouraged the invention of new literary modes that would better subscribe to the idea of modern literature. In these examples, the act of classifying becomes not an innocent or ideologically free enterprise but an act of world-making, *creating* a world that then becomes susceptible to colonial rule.

Moreover, postcolonialism highlights the continuity of the colonial and post-independence periods by showing how the nation-state was largely continuous with colonialism. In India, this is apparent not only in the continuity of laws between colonial and post-independence times (laws in favour of the strict division between private and public space, for instance) but also in the way the nation quickly formed its own discourse in which some people were considered outsiders or Others to the national project. The nation rules by rendering its various others – Muslims, Dalits, Adivasis, women, queer people and so on – as outside of the nationalist project. The nation-state inherits colonial classifications to describe and differentiate these groups in order to rule them.

Some forms of postcolonial thought have been influenced by poststructuralist theory, especially in the writings of the influential scholars Gayatri Chakravorty Spivak and Homi Bhabha, pioneers in the field who broke away from Edward Said's idea, advanced in *Orientalism*, of colonial discourse as all-powerful. Both these critics emphasized postcolonial theory as a deconstructive practice, which unravelled the very assumptions of colonial discourse, showing it to be not universal but based in a very specific set of circumstances that were highly contingent and precarious. This approach advances colonialism as a fundamentally weak discourse, whose constant assertions of its own authority might be read as indices of its own precariousness, even in the eyes of the colonizers themselves. Resistance, then, is not so much in powerful counter-assertions or in the misplaced idealism of the nationalist movement, but in attending to the weakness in colonial discourse itself, and indeed in noting the precarity of *all* linguistic assertions. This version of postcolonial theory focuses on moments of stuttering, word repetition or insistence as indices of language's *inability* to communicate effectively, of language's fundamentally *indexical* or self-referential quality.

Gender critique is also an important component of postcolonial theory, as it points to the way in which women served both colonial and nationalist discourses, leaving the actual agency of women outside of both discourses. Beginning with the British intent to adjudicate on the religious validity of the practice of *sati*, all the way to contemporary conversations on 'love jihad' and the role of women in public space, postcolonial theory shows how women become the bodies on which colonial and national regimes inscribe their validity. A postcolonial critique is thus necessarily gendered, not only recentering women as agents in oppositional histories but also showing how gender can unravel the entire discourse of colonialism or nationalism.

These versions of postcolonial theory have been influential in the academe. They have compelled many English departments to see literary study as potentially bearing the traces of colonial history and open it to its postcolonial Other. It has compelled anthropologists to question the power dynamics with which the anthropologist goes into the field as well as what counts as valid knowledge. In history, postcolonial theory has led scholars away from a simple valorization of nationalism to the margins of the nation, to those groups doubly othered, both by colonial rule and by nationalist rule. While the impact of postcolonial theory is less felt in the sciences and in the harder social sciences, such as economics, it has been one of the most influential interventions in the academe in the last forty years.

With economic liberalization, the rise of a new middle class and the power of global capital and technology in India in the first decades of the 2000s, it is possible to say that postcolonialism has entered a new phase, which we might variously call neoliberalism, or neocolonialism, or simply the contemporary. While the spectres of colonial rule continue in forms such as the persistent silence around Partition and the continuing crisis of secularism, they are supplemented by new concerns and aspirations, a new pragmatism around the use of English (rather than English only as a colonial legacy), a scepticism around cosmopolitanism and new forms of desire unleashed by the consumer economy – new concerns that cannot quite be accounted for through a postcolonial lens. While the continuing validity of the term will remain a matter of scholarly contention, the impact of the term in rethinking Indian modernity in a range of fields cannot be denied.

References

Bhabha, Homi K. *The Location of Culture*. London and New York: Routledge, 1994.
Loomba, Ania. *Colonialism/Postcolonialism*. London and New York: Routledge, 1998.

DARSHANA (DARŚANA)

Sanjit Chakraborty

Darshana, in the sense of true philosophical knowledge is first quoted in the *Vaiśeṣika Sūtra* (first century CE) to mean the perfect vision of everything. Etymologically, darshana evolves from the Sanskrit term *Dṛś*, that is, vision. The contemporary use of the term darshana finds its new dimension in the writings of Haribhardra (eighteenth century CE), who considers different philosophical schools in the cord of darshana in his text *Ṣaḍ-darśana-samuccaya*. Later, eminent Vedāntin Mādhava in fourteenth century CE popularized and expatiated the meaning of *darshana* in *Sarvadarśana Saṅgraha*. The purport of the term darshana is imbedded in the notion of Indianness that caters to an influential uniqueness in Hinduism, Jainism (*Samyak darshana* or liberation consists in right vision) and Mahayana Buddhism (Nagarjuna's dictum *tattva-darśana*, that is, the true reality, and Vasubandhu's use of *darshana marga*, that is, the conduit of seeing).

Darshanas or the schools of Indian philosophy are orthodox (*Āstika*) and heterodox (*Nāstika*). The *Āstikas* (Mīmāṁsa and Vedānta) have their direct cradles in the Vedic texts. Sāṅkhya, Yōga, Nyāya and Vaiśeṣika quest for the non-reliant ground; these schools have faith in the doctrine of humanistic thought that celebrates reasoning and experience. *Nāstikas* (Cārvāka, Buddhism and Jainism) defy the authority of the Vedas and are the non-believers of God.

Sāṅkhya is the oldest philosophy school in India. The sage Kapila propounded this school by maintaining the dynamic uniformity of the manifold world and objects that are unconscious. Sāṅkhya's aesthetic mode brings about the ultimate subtle material cause of the world as Prakriti which remains uncaused (*an unwarranted regressus ad infinitum*) and productive. The evolution of Prakriti is a manifestation, where the imbalance of the substratum (gunas – *sattva*, *rajas* and *tamas*) transmits conscious mind to unconscious objects and in the whole process Purusa, the second transcendental reality, stands as an inactive cum inert perceiver. Sāṅkhya believes in the unity of Purusa and Prakriti, which leads to the creation as well as liberation of the empirical self (*Jīva*). The apparent conjecture of Purusa and Prakriti is annihilated through transmigration for the sake of the emancipation of self.

Yōga, the theistic Sāṅkhya, engrafts God as the efficient cause of the world, while the material cause is doubtlessly Prakriti. Patānjali, the author of *Yōga Sūtra*, synthesizes *Mokshya* (salvation) as attainable through practicing meditation or yōga. Vyāsa's *Yōga-Bhāsya* (400 CE), a commentary, defines *yōga* as a method of knowing oneself and obtaining a kind of discriminative knowledge that can flatten even the potentiality of all afflictions. The eight limbs of *Yōga* in its fourfold stage (Samadhi, Sadhana, Vibhuti and Kaivalya padas) do not only restrain the mind of the yogi but also provide an abiding devotion to the transcendental consciousness (*Vivakjñānya*).

Vaiśeṣika, the second oldest philosophy, upholds a theoretical understanding of the universe as a search for true knowledge of reality instead of the transcendental self and so on. Vaiśeṣika doctrine considers atoms as undying and consistent particles of the world, and all worldly events have their own natural evolution maintained by the science of categories (*padārtha*). Kaṇāda's *Vaiśeṣika Sūtra* and Praśastapāda's commentary (600 CE) are the foremost classical texts suggesting that the cause lies in the material effects, while knowledge of particularity (*Viśeṣa*) demarcates one eternal substance from the other. Liberation means understanding the true knowledge of reality and an accomplishment of happiness (*pravṛtti*) and cessation of the negative action (*nivṛtti*).

Nyāya epistemologically refers to the methodology of argumentation. Gautama (200 BCE), the profounder of this darshana, was concerned about two different doctrines – logic and ontology safeguarded by Vaiśeṣika's epistemology in *Nyāya Sūtra*. Nyāya amplifies the nature of valid knowledge (*pramā*) through the instruments of valid knowledge (*pramāna*), such as perception, inference, comparison and testimony. Nyāya believes in the substantial mode of self as the intrinsic cause of cognition. The pre-existence and transmigration processes endorse the self that can attain liberation when the law of karma and false knowledge are nullified.

Mīmāṁsa, also known as *Pūrva Mīmāṁsa* or *Karma Mīmāṁsa*, enshrines the prior analysis of the Vedic knowledge from the aspects of action, rituals, ceremonies (yajña) and critical reflection. In Jaimini's *Mīmāṁsa Sūtra*, the Vedas are regarded as external, authorless and infallible knowledge and the attainment of the 'highest good' is possible through *dharma* (virtue or duties) and *dharmin* (the categories that possessed dharma) as prescribed by Vedas that give value to the human acts, an intense rationalistic appeal in conjunction with performing yajña and duties or non-duties. The continuation of ethical activities and understanding the Vedic verdicts are a theme in philosophy of language, which involves learning the exact meaning of *dharma* and proper way of conducing yajña.

Vedānta literarily means the zenith of Vedas and depends on the *Prasthānatrayi*, which are the Upaniṣads (*Śruti prasthāna* or wisdom), the Bhagavad Gita (*Smṛti prasthāna* or practice) and the Brahma Sūtras (*Nyāya prasthāna* or logic). All the major schools of Vedānta advocate that Brahma is the supreme and static material cause of the world. The metaphysical stance of Vedānta centres rounds the triangular structure of the world (*Jagat*), self (*Jivātman*) and ultimate reality (*Brahma*). Advaita defines Brahma as *Sat-cit-ānanda*, that is, existence, consciousness and bliss constitute the non-dualistic essence (svarūpa) of Brahma instead of his attributes (gunas); whereas other schools of Vedānta preserve *Sat-cit-ānanda* as Svarūpa and gunas together executing the concept of *Brahmasvarūpa-Svagata-bheda*. According to Advaita, liberation consists in purest realization where knowledge (*jñāna*) of absolute identity between the self and the ultimate Brahma is attainable, while other schools of Vedānta regards devotion (*bhakti*) and action (*karma*) manifested by knowledge as ways to achieve salvation.

Buddhism, the founder of this non-theistic creed is Gautama Buddha (sixth century BCE), whose philosophy later becomes a religious text *Tripiṭakas*. The essence of Buddhism lies in its Four Noble Truths (*catyāri ārya satyāni*), an anti-speculative outlook that directs an individual towards enlightenment through the paths of suffering and its causes and the way of its cessation or ultimate liberation (*nirvaṇa*) is made possible through *aṣṭāṅgika mārga*. Buddha's ethical philosophy rests on conditional-based existent objects (*pratītyasamutpāda*), the law of karma, momentariness (*kṣaṇika-vāda*) and the non-existence of the soul (*nairātmavāda*) that are concerned about the metaphysical cum epistemological basis of philosophical quests.

Jainism, propounded by Mahāvīra (500 BCE), is derived from the word *Jina*, a conqueror who subdues passions to attain liberation by practicing the tenets of non-violence, asceticism, veganism, meditation and liberation. This doctrine rests on three tenets: common-sense realism, the relativity of judgements (syādvāda) and pluralism or many-sided realities (anekāntavāda). Liberation in Jainism is made possible through *Ratnatraya*, that is, Samyak darshana (right faith/view), Samyak jñāna (right knowledge) and Samyak charita (right conduct).

Cārvāka is a *cāru-vāka* or sweet-speech materialistic doctrine that professes perception as the only *pramana*. They are also called *Bhutacaitanyavadin*, that is, consciousness is merely a by-product of the four material elements (earth, water, fire and air) from which the world is formed; whereas, the soul is a myth like God, an unnecessary creator. The ethical values of the Vedas or other schools have been despised by Cārvāka. Liberation takes place with physical death, and the logical upshot of Cārvāka metaphysics and epistemology persuades them to enjoy all material pleasures in life since the possibility of rebirth is absurd and illogical.

References

Chatterjee, Satischandra and Dhirendramohan Datta, *An Introduction to Indian Philosophy*. Calcutta: University of Calcutta, 1984.
Radhakrishnan, Sarvepalli and Charles A. Moore. *A Sourcebook in Indian Philosophy*. Princeton: Princeton University Press, 1973.

DHARMA (DHARMA)

Bijoy Boruah

Dharma is a term that has no direct English translation, because it is an all-embracing concept and is perhaps unique to Indian thought. The term is diffused in having different shades of meaning in a variety of respects: cosmological, sociological, religious, ethical, legal and also the functional essence of things. Etymologically, the term is derived from the Sanskrit root *dhṛ*, meaning 'to uphold, support, maintain, sustain, or to hold together'.

The cosmic connotation of dharma is fundamental to its nature, and it is in this sense that this concept provides a broad metaphysical grounding to various other senses of it. The cosmological-metaphysical meaning of dharma can be found in the Vedic texts, especially *Rig Veda*, according to which, that which upholds the created universe, supports and sustains it, without which the universe falls apart, is dharma. Dharma, as it is used to refer to the functional essence of things or the essential nature of things (e.g. the nature of the Sun is to emit sunshine, of fire to produce heat and so on), would seem to make the concept purely descriptive. But as soon as the essential nature of a human individual or society, the dharma of an individual or a community, is under consideration, the term takes a normative turn in implying a variety of imperatives, injunctions and other principles of human action.

Indeed, the normative connotation of dharma is overwhelming, so much so that in all the ancient Indian traditions – Buddhism, Jainism and Hinduism – it is meant to be an embodiment of the ethics of life. Jaimini's *Mimamsa Sutra* defines dharma as *codana lakshana*, that is, as a set of imperatives, or injunctive sentences of the Vedas, which command the human agent to act. Kanada's *Vaisheshika Sutra* characterizes dharma as that from which results prosperity and the highest good. In Mahayana Buddhism, dharma refers to both the teachings of the Buddha – the Four Noble Truths and the Noble Eightfold path – and the realization of enlightenment. For all the traditions of Indian thought, there is a list of virtues that is more or less common to the various formulations of dharma. This list includes non-injury, truthfulness, honesty, cleanliness, control of the senses, charity, self-restraint, love, forbearance, fortitude, modesty, forgiving disposition, serenity and meditative temper. What we have here is more a theory of virtue rather than a mere ethics of imperatives.

In the theory of the goals of human pursuit known as *purushartha*, which mentions the fourfold classification of the goals of life, dharma (righteousness or moral values) figures as one of these goals, the other goals being *artha* (pursuit of wealth, economic prosperity), *kama* (desire fulfilment) and *moksha* (ultimate liberation). It is obvious that the pursuit of wealth for livelihood and the fulfilment of physical desires are basic to human existence. But what makes the human life of desire and wealth distinctively *human* is the way these two basic pursuits are regulated by righteous behaviour and moral values. That regulative principle of life is dharma, which plays its vital role in preventing the life of material prosperity and pleasure from turning into individual deterioration and social chaos and leads to a balanced mode of life conducive to true happiness. It is in this sense that dharma is said to be the foremost of the four categories in the scheme of life. In this respect, dharma parallels Hegel's idea of *sittlichkeit* or the actual ethical order that regulates human conduct at the levels of the individual, family, civil life and the state.

The relation between dharma and moksha is rather problematic. Is dharma necessary for attaining moksha? While on the one hand dharma is advanced as a means to moksha, on the other hand dharma is also considered to be a hindrance to moksha. Moksha is somewhat of an outsider in the fourfold categorial scheme, because ultimate liberation is supposedly other-worldly (requiring renunciation of the life of artha and kama) whereas the life of dharma refers to worldly human existence. It is usually said that dharma helps one in getting *svarga* (heaven) but not moksha. Dharma as well as *a-dharma* are equally the causes of bondage and rebirth, whereas ultimate liberation requires going beyond the cycle of birth altogether. However, the idea of 'action with renunciation of desire for the fruit of action' (*nishkama karma*) or 'craving free, dharma-driven action' is proposed as a compromise between the two conflicting concepts. Ultimate liberation may come unsolicited if one lives the life of *anasakti* or action with detachment.

References

Olivelle, P. and D. R. Davis, eds. *The Oxford History of Hinduism: Hindu Law: A New History of Dharmasastra*. Oxford: Oxford University Press, 2017.

Srivastava, D. C. and B. H. Boruah, eds. *Dharma and Ethics: The Indian Ideal of Human Perfection*. New Delhi: Decent Books, 2010.

DHYANA (DHYĀNA)

Bijoy Boruah

Dhyana as a concept and a practice originated in the Vedic and Upanishadic era. In Hinduism, it refers to self-directed yogic awareness, by which the yogi realizes the *atma* (self) and finally oneness with the ultimate reality (*brahman*). Etymologically, the concept dhyaana is derived from its root *dhi*, which in the early Vedic text refers to 'imaginative vision'. However, the general meaning of the concept is contemplative and concentrated meditation, coupled with the metaphysical and soteriological implication of aiming at ultimate self-knowledge and self-liberation.

The unique meaning of this concept in Indian thought is best grasped by reference to its place and role in the philosophy and practice of yoga, which is distinctively Indian. Patanjali's *Yoga Sutra* provides the context and comprehensive background of the essential nature of *dhyaana*. Given the pervasive Indian belief that ignorance, born of attachment, is the cause of suffering in the life cycle of action and reaction (*samsara*), the core project of Patanjali's *Yoga Sutra* is to outline the process of attaining freedom from attachment and ignorance. The second chapter of the *Sutra* features the eight limbs of yoga, which are the means of achieving discriminative discernment: *yama* (abstention), *niyama* (observance), *asana* (posture), *pranayama* (breath control), *pratyahara* (disengagement of the sense), *dhaaranaa* (concentration), *dhyaana* (meditation) and *samaadhi* (absorption). Thus, the concept of *dhyaana*, the seventh limb of the eightfold path of yoga, is best understood as part of the soteriology and praxis of yoga philosophy enunciated in Patanjali's *Yoga Sutra*. It is to be properly understood as a state organically connected with a complete process of enlightenment.

This process of consecutive stages of internalization can be divided into two categories. While the first five limbs are ways of outer practices, that is, of internalizing attention away from external and bodily influences, the last three are inner practices, that is, purely mental and internal in orientation. The first five limbs constitute 'external yoga', whereas the triad of the last three limbs constitute 'internal yoga'. Understanding the nature of the triad of dhaaranaa-dhyaana-samaadhi is important to articulate the meaning of dhyaana. All the three are directly related to meditation. Indeed, they *are* meditation. Dhaaranaa involves fixing the mind in one place. However, the concentration here is not fixed on a single spot as an object of meditation. It is the 'one-pointedness' of the mind on one image, a singular attention on a single object of meditation, in an unbroken flow of consciousness free from any distraction that characterizes dhyaana. So the process of 'internalization' is progressively more concentrated and focused, with the mental flow as uninterrupted as it can be, in this state. Naturally, the occurrence of a state of uninterrupted mental flow singularly fixed on a single object or image is prone to culminate in samaadhi, the ultimate goal of a true yogi. The mind is so fully absorbed in the object of meditation that there is no self-consciousness at all, no reflective attitude. Dhyaana is therefore the penultimate stage in a very intensely concentrated continuum of contemplative process, which is initiated in full earnestness at the stage of dhaaranaa.

References

Iyengar, B. K. S. *Light on the Yoga Sutras of Patanjali*. London: HarperCollins, 2002.
Srivastava, D. C. and B. H. Boruah, eds. *Dharma and Ethics: The Indian Ideal of Human Perfection*. New Delhi: Decent Books, 2010.

GOLDEN TEMPLE

Ronki Ram

The Golden Temple at Amritsar, originally called Harimandir Sahib (Temple of God) and Darbar Sahib, is a revered site for millions of people, irrespective of caste, creed or even race, across the Indian subcontinent and the Indian diaspora. It is the only temple of *nirankar* (non-anthropomorphic god), which is accessible from all four directions: east, west, north and south. The temple is symbolic of equality among members of the four *varna*s. It is built at a level lower than the surrounding land (unlike European churches) to further emphasize the values of egalitarianism and humility. An enthralling three-storeyed structure surrounded by various historic buildings, of which the four-storeyed Akal Takht (supreme religious authority of Sikhism) is especially noteworthy. On an average, over one hundred thousand people visit the Golden Temple daily.

The city of Amritsar was envisioned by Guru Amar Das and benefitted from contributions by both Guru Ram Das and Guru Arjan Dev. Amritsar is to the Sikhs what Benares is to the Hindus and Mecca is to the Muslims. As desired by Guru Amar Das, the city was established by Bhai Jetha (later on Guru Ram Das, the fourth Nanak) and Baba Budha in 1570 CE on land which was acquired by the earlier gurus on grant or payment from the *zamindar*s (prominent landlords) of the surrounding villages. Originally, Amritsar was known as Chak Guru/Guru Ka Chak/Chak Ram Das/Ram Das Pura. After his accession to *gurgaddi* (seat of guru), Guru Ram Das shifted to Guru Ka Chak along with his family. To make this newly established religious town socially inclusive and financially self-sustainable, Guru Ram Das invited fifty-two types of artisans and professionals, irrespective of faith, to settle there thus creating the microcosm of an urban township. To further meet the daily needs of this growing township, a market (Guru Bazaar) was then added. In 1577 CE, Guru Ram Das was instrumental in the creations of two holy *sarovar*s (tanks or pools), which eventually become known as Santokh Sar (Pool of Contentment) and Amrit Sar or Amrit Sarovar (Pool of Nectar). It was only after the completion of the temple and the filling of its sarovar with water that the city was named Amrit Sar.

Hazrat Sai Mian Mir, a famous Sufi pir of Lahore, laid the foundation stone of Harimandir Sahib in 1588 CE at the request of Guru Arjan Dev who designed the architecture of the temple as well as supervised its construction. After the completion of the Harimandir Sahib, Guru Arjan Dev took on the mammoth task of compiling the writings of his predecessors, his own as well as those of venerated spiritual figures from other faiths; critically, the latter category included those from the 'untouchable' castes. The purpose was to emphasize the oneness of God as well as equality among all. He completed this task in August 1604 CE with the assistance of Bhai Gurdas as scribe. The Sri Guru Granth Sahib is written in the same language, commonly spoken by the people of that region. Further, it has the distinct and unique status of retaining its original wording and prose structure till this very day.

Harimandir Sahib came to be known popularly as the Golden Temple during the reign of Maharaja Ranjit Singh (1799–1839) after he granted rupees 5 lakhs (half a million) for gold plating it. During the British rule, between 1883 and the 1920s, the temple became a centre of the Singh Sabha Movement. When control of the Harimandir Sahib was regained from the British government–Mahant combine, M. K. Gandhi sent a complimentary telegram to the Sikhs at Amritsar: 'First battle of India's freedom won. Congratulations.' In the early 1980s, the temple once again entered a phase of conflict between the Indian government led by the late Indira Gandhi, some Sikh groups and a militant movement spearheaded by Jarnail Singh Bhindranwale. In 1984, the Indian Army entered the precincts of the Golden Temple damaging several historic buildings and the library, a repository for thousands of rare and original manuscripts.

The Golden Temple is not only spiritually the most significant shrine in Sikhism but has also evolved to become a rallying centre of the Sikhs and gives direction to the Sikh *panth* (society). The enchanting words of Guru Arjan Dev capture the eternal celestial beauty of the Golden Temple: *Dithe sab thav nahi tudh jehia* ('I have seen all places, there is not another like thee' (Sri Guru Granth Sahib, p. 1362)).

References

Kaur, Manjit. 'The Harimindir'. In *The City of Amritsar: An Introduction*, edited by Fauja Singh, 25–41. Patiala: Punjabi University, 2000.
Shan, Harnam Singh. *So Said Guru Arjan Dev*. Chandigarh: Government of Punjab, 2006.
Singh, Khushwant. *A History of the Sikhs, Vol. 1: 1469–1839*, 2nd edn. New Delhi: Oxford University Press, 2004.

GURU (GURU)

Sanjit Chakraborty

The conception of the word *guru* in Indian cultures goes back to the Upanishadic era, especially in the *Mundakopanishad*, where Brahma (the creator of the world) taught the *Brahma Vidya* (the foundation of all knowledge or the speculative discussion about ultimate reality) to his eldest son, Atharvan. Later, Artharvan transmitted the Brahma Vidya to Angiras who shared the absolute knowledge with Satyavaha, a successor of Sage Bharadwaja. Satyavaha narrated to Bharadwaja, who finally imparted the knowledge (both the higher and lower levels) to Angiras. A significance that one could find here is the use of the Upanishadic term *paraparam* (*Mundakopanishad*, 1.2). The term not only indicates that the foundation of all knowledge has two different folds – *para* (transcendent) and *apar* (mundane) – but also that the term paraparam tinges to the transmission progression of the knowledge from guru (enlightened master) to his *shisya* (dedicated disciple). The proper way of learning Brahma Vidya depends on the *gurupasadana*, that is, only guru can condescend to expose wisdom to the devoted disciples.

The criterion of a guru is clearly mentioned by Upanishads which say that a guru must be an enlightened person (*jnani*) who learned the Vedas carefully and dedicated himself to the contemplation of Brahman. The guru would be a man of wisdom who has not only seen the truth but also has the capability to teach in an appropriate way to his disciples. The guru possesses wisdom, equanimity, self-control, empathy and a desire to help others, who strive for the complete recasting of the oneness as versed in the *shruti* (canonical, unquestionable) and *smṛti* (supplementary, liable to change) texts.

A shisya (*adhikarin*) must have the proclivity to know the absolute knowledge and have a reverent interest in learning the truth, channelized by self-control, thought, intellectual apprehension and reasoning. Both, the guru and the shisya, need to tread the inner path guided by *sravana* (hearing), *manana* (contemplation) and *niddidhyasana* (meditation). Our mind is a curvature line of the harvest field (wisdom), which could be controlled by the consort of spiritual life, faith in Brahma, knowledge about Brahma and finally self-realization. These procedures ought to be guided by the gurus, the most fortunate seekers who attained the illumination of Brahma Vidya by guru *parampara* (uninterrupted succession).

A guru seeks the eternal knowledge in the immutable absolute being by attaining consciousness of the difference between all non-eternal appearances and the absolute Being. Besides, a dedicated disciple for the sake of knowledge of the absolute Being needs to approach a spiritual preceptor who is rooted in the consciousness of Brahma. The radiance of absolute knowledge is a quest where the guru is regarded as one part (*purvarūpam*) and other complement part (*uttararūpam*) is rigidly the shisya; and their union (*sandhi*) escorts towards the production of knowledge through the recitation of the Vedas. The seeker must be a son/daughter or a worthy pupil.

This Sanskrit term guru that originated from the Vedas has an overall Indian root and its use is not bounded only by Hinduism but also has linkages to Buddhism, Jainism, Sikhism, Baul and so on. These different religions infuse guru–shishya parampara, where knowledge is passed through successors, through either one's heirs or pupils. In neo-Indian tradition of the Bauls of Northern India, the guru, or the Arabic *murshid*, is the person who shows the *sahaj* (simple) way to segregate worldly turmoil and teach the seeker (*baul*) to merge his or her mind to his or her inner mind, where the eternal and all-pervading Truth resides.

Archaeological and epigraphical evidence point out that in ancient and medieval India, pupils studied and practiced the śāstras in the *gurukul* (the house or the teaching place of gurus), which was considered an auspicious place.

Most cultures, such as the English, French, German, Polish, Russian, Portuguese and Spanish, are habituated to the use the word guru in the sense of sage and spiritual leader. However, in contemporary India, the etymological meaning of the term guru transmits to different concepts, such as a teacher of *tantra* (esoteric traditions), yōga, music, game, arts, etc. It has no significant connection with the term guru as promoted in the Hindu śāstras. Most of them never practiced the sacred knowledge of the Vedas and are falsely considered as an authority on God or a direct incarnation or prophet of God. They demean the revered term guru whom the Upanishads placed as high as God. These fraud gurus and their followers engage in mundane rejoices. Now in Indian languages, such as Bengali, Hindi, Gujarati, Telugu and Malayalam, the term guru ironically indicates an extremely sly personality who can manage anything for her or his self-interest.

References

Aurobindo, Sri. *The Upanishads, Part One*. Pondicherry: Sri Aurobindo Ashram, 1981.
Tagore, Rabindranath. *The Religion of Man*. Visva-Bharati: Visva-Bharati University Press, 1931.

HAJ

Maidul Islam

Haj or *hajj* (visitation of the holy places of Mecca) is generally regarded as one of the five fundamental pillars or central tenets of Islam. The others being *iman* (the confession of faith by belief in Allah as the sole God and that Muhammad is the prophet of Allah), *ṣalat* (the five daily prayers), *ṣawm* (fasting in the month of Ramadan) and *zakat* (stipulated alms-giving). It is an annual pilgrimage to Mecca during the Islamic lunar calendar month of Dhu al-Hijjah. The focus of haj is not the city of Mecca but the Great Mosque where the holiest shrine of Islam, the *Ka'bah* (house of Allah, originally rebuilt by Prophet Ibrahim) is situated. In this respect, it is the only tenet of Islam that cannot be accomplished in the comfort of one's own home. It is obligatory for all adult Muslims to perform haj at least once in their lifetime, if they are physically and financially able. Also, the *haji*s (haj pilgrims) must be able to financially support their dependants while they are away for the pilgrimage. Muslim women are allowed to take part in haj, provided she is accompanied by a male chaperon (*mahram*) with whom she is legally unable to marry. For unmarried women, either her father or brother and for married and older women, either their husbands or sons generally accompany them during the pilgrimage. According to the new rules of 2014, a woman over the age of forty five may travel without a Mahram with an organized group by submitting a 'no objection letter' from her husband, son or brother. India has followed this rule from 2018. Haj symbolizes the unity of the *ummah* (community of Islamic believers) as it provides a shared space where Muslim pilgrims come in contact with each other – overcoming differences in class, gender, age, language, nationality, culture and race.

The haj pilgrimage started with Prophet Muhammad's first and only haj in March 632 CE, the last time he visited Mecca before going back to Medina. This 'farewell pilgrimage', according to the Islamic tradition, is important for two reasons. First, it laid down the performative act of haj along with establishing the key rites and rituals that Muslims have been following for centuries. Second, Muhammad's sermon at the end of that haj summarized his teachings that Muslims often cite. Haj comprises of several rituals including the core ritual of *tawf*, which involves circling of the *Ka'bah* seven times in the anti-clockwise direction, attempts to touch or kiss the 'black stone' in the wall of the shrine, drink water from the Zamzam stream that flows through the basement of the Great Mosque, passing seven times between the nearby peaks of as-Safa and Marwa, quoting passages from the Qur'an (the obligatory ritual of *sa'yee*), the mass procession to Mount Arafat on the ninth day of Dhu al-Hijjah and the sacrifice of an animal (generally sheep, camel or other cattle) on Mount Mina on the tenth day of Dhu al-Hijjah. Finally, the haj ends with throwing seven stones for each of the three pillars symbolizing Satan (the ritual of *ramyee*), which the pilgrims pass on their way back to Mecca.

Men who have completed the pilgrimage to Mecca generally adopt an honourific title of *haji* (*hajjah* for women) to precede their name. Muslims believe that the proper performance of haj with sincere intention (*niyah*) absolves the pilgrim from all previous sins. In North India, there is an interesting anecdotal perspective on the word, which is colloquially used in everyday humour: *Sau chuhe khake billi chali haj ko* ('After eating 100 rats the cat now goes to the pilgrimage'). The appropriate metaphorical expression of such a literal translation is that 'after committing all the sins one goes for pious salvation'.

The Saudi Arabian government, headed by the Saudi royal family, currently oversees haj. Indians constitute the second largest national group performing the haj after Saudi Arabia; in 2019, two lakh Indian Muslims have performed haj.

References

Horrie, Chris and Chippindale, Peter. *What Is Islam? A Comprehensive Introduction (1990)*, Revised and Updated Edition. London: Virgin Books, 2007.
Sardar, Ziauddin. *Mecca: The Sacred City*. London: Bloomsbury, 2014.

HERITAGE SITES

A. G. K. Menon

The diversity of heritage sites in India reflects the country's diverse social and cultural history. Many still evoke a sense of ownership among its contemporary legatees and are technically defined as 'living' heritage sites. 'Heritage site' is a contested term, often used to define and assert present-day identities of its stakeholders and often to settle old historical scores. Thus, heritage sites in India are defined both by their tangible and intangible associational values, and it is difficult to define their cultural significance or deal with them in a standardized manner.

The continued cultural relevance of heritage sites creates problems for modern-day governance. Indian heritage protection laws are derived from colonial sensibilities, which have since the Second World War morphed into universal guidelines adopted by the Archaeological Survey of India (ASI) and their counterparts in the states, which are the 'official' guardians of heritage sites in India. The problematic genealogy of their conservation practices is further reinforced by their aspirational intent to modernize and remain in conformity with international norms.

Many anomalies arise from these circumstances. For one, colonial exigencies restricted the contemporary definition of 'official' heritage sites to only about ten thousand all over the country. This has meant that the hundreds of thousands of remnants of a fecund cultural past are left outside the official purview and have been either lost through attrition or have become victims of contemporary development priorities. Many, however, are cared for by its present-day users, who continue to practice indigenous systems of repair and rebuilding, guided by traditional craftsmen, but these systems of repair are often at variance with international norms that dominate the official imagination and practice.

Another anomaly is that the 'official' focus has been on individual buildings and not on heritage sites comprising culturally identifiable neighbourhoods, historical cities and even the larger cultural landscape which continues to evoke equally strong emotional affinities among different sections of society. In terms of conservation, the coalescing of the temporal characteristics of cultural heritage with its ethno-geography presents undefined challenges to protecting heritage sites in India: its authenticity is circumscribed both by the history and the geography of the site. It resurrects the relevance of the cyclical view of time in the definitions of heritage and introduces the concept of *jeernodharan* (renovation) in the lexicon of Indian conservation practice.

Thus, two approaches of dealing with heritage sites coexist in India, one modern and aligned to precepts of conservation promoted by universal knowledge systems and the other rooted in indigenous sensibilities but also dealing with modern circumstances. Seen in this light, the issue of conserving heritage sites in India includes its development to meet the needs of its contemporary stakeholders. These questions are being foregrounded because government policymakers are recognizing the economic potential of heritage sites as tourist destinations. These initiatives have in the past largely been directed towards attracting foreign tourists and the needs of high-end tourism infrastructure. But the fact is that, in India, pilgrimage tourism and even domestic tourism for recreation is by far the larger component of the tourism pie and has therefore shifted the focus towards upgrading urban infrastructure and urban environment within which many of the heritage sites exist and thereby improve the quality of life in cities and towns. This offers fertile ground to examine the unfolding discourse on the nature of appropriate urban development and heritage conservation strategies for the country: to what extent should the baggage of tradition be respected or discarded?

References

Mallik A., S. Chaudhury, T. B. Dinesh and Chaluvaraju. 'An Intellectual Journey in History: Preserving Indian Cultural Heritage'. In *New Trends in Image Analysis and Processing – ICIAP 2013. ICIAP 2013. Lecture Notes in Computer Science, vol 8158*, edited by A. Petrosino, L. Maddalena and P. Pala. Berlin, Heidelberg: Springer, 2013.

HINDUISM

Shashi Tharoor

The name 'Hindu' itself denotes something less, and more, than a set of theological beliefs. In many languages, French and Persian among them, the word for 'Indian' is 'Hindu'. Originally, Hindu simply meant the people beyond the River Sindhu, or Indus. But the Indus is now in Islamic Pakistan, and to make matters worse, the word 'Hindu' did not exist in any Indian language till its use by foreigners gave Indians a term for self-definition. In other words, Hindus call themselves by a label that they didn't invent in any of their own languages but adopted cheerfully when others began to refer to them by that word. (Of course, many prefer a different term altogether, *Sanatana Dharma* [eternal faith].) 'Hinduism' is thus the name that foreigners first applied to what they saw as the indigenous religion of India. It embraces an eclectic range of doctrines and practices, from pantheism to agnosticism and from faith in reincarnation to belief in the caste system. But, none of these constitutes an obligatory credo for a Hindu. The religion has no compulsory dogmas.

Hinduism is predicated on the idea that the eternal wisdom of the ages and of divinity cannot be confined to a single sacred book; we have many, and we can delve into each to find our own truth (or truths). Hindus can claim adherence to a religion without an established church or priestly papacy, a religion whose rituals and customs one is free to reject, a religion that does not oblige the adherent to demonstrate her or his faith by any visible sign, by subsuming her or his identity in any collectivity, not even by a specific day or time or frequency of worship. (There is no Hindu pope, no Hindu Vatican, no Hindu catechism, not even a Hindu Sunday.) Hinduism offers a veritable smorgasbord of options to the worshipper – of divinities to adore and to pray to, of rituals to observe (or not), of customs and practices to honour (or not), of fasts to keep (or not). Hinduism allows each believer to stretch her or his imagination to a personal notion of the creative godhead. The Hindu texts uniquely operate from a platform of scepticism, not the springboard of certitude. Indeed, not even what one might think of as the most basic tenet of any religion – a belief in the existence of God – is a prerequisite in Hinduism: agnosticism is a key principle of more than one major school of Hindu philosophy.

Most faiths prioritize one identity, one narrative and one holy book. Hinduism recognizes that everyone has multiple identities, accepts diverse narratives and respects several sacred books, as Sarvepalli Radhakrishnan notes. Hinduism, in other words, incorporates almost all forms of belief and worship within it; there is no need to choose some or reject others.

If Hinduism as a set of spiritual ideas is unusually liberal, undogmatic and flexible, Hindu society has not always lived up to the freedom enshrined in the faith. The prevalence of the caste system, with social hierarchies linked to occupation and widespread discrimination against 'lower' castes, has provoked reformers for centuries; most of its worst practices, such as denial of temple entry to outcastes, were outlawed in the twentieth century. Constitutionally mandated affirmative-action programmes are dramatically reversing many caste-imposed disabilities once and for all. But this is not a new phenomenon; Hinduism has been reforming and reinventing itself for millennia, starting with the challenges posed to it by Buddhism and Jainism with their emphasis on ethics over rituals, then by Islam with its egalitarianism and iconoclasm and finally by colonial Christianity with its association with modernity. Hinduism responded through repeated reinvention of itself and absorption of ideas from its critics as well as through a typically Hindu proliferation of forms of the faith. The early idea of a formless God (*nirguna brahman*) and the complications of too abstruse a philosophy gave way to that of the *saguna brahman* with millions of manifestations of the divine, including as a woman with eight arms riding a tiger, a pot-bellied figure with an elephant's head and a muscular figure with a monkey's head and tail, all reflective of different aspects of the godhead and embodying wonderful stories about themselves. A period of stagnation led to the vigorous philosophical preaching of Adi Shankara at the cusp of the ninth century and his propagation of the faith through the establishment of religious centres across the subcontinent; its popularization by Ramanuja and dozens of sages who brought worship from priestly Sanskrit into the vernacular; its spreading through verse and song in the mystic Bhakti movement; the rejection of idolatry by sects like the Brahmo Samāja and the Arya Samāja; and the flourishing of gurus and 'godmen' to guide some believers to the Absolute. All changed the manner in which Hinduism was practiced and all are valid ways of being Hindu.

In the twenty-first century, Hinduism has many of the attributes of a universal religion – a religion that is personal and individualistic, privileges the individual and does not subordinate one to a collectivity; a religion that grants and respects complete freedom to the believer to find her or his own answers to the true meaning of life; a religion that offers a wide range of choices in religious practice, even with regard to the nature and form of the formless god; a religion that places great emphasis on one's mind and values one's capacity for reflection, intellectual enquiry and self-study; a religion that distances itself from dogma and holy writ that is minimally prescriptive and yet offers an abundance of options, spiritual and philosophical texts and social and cultural practices to choose from. Each Hindu must seek and find her or his own truth.

In a world where resistance to authority is growing, Hinduism imposes no authorities; in a world of networked individuals, Hinduism proposes no institutional hierarchies; in a world of open-source information sharing, Hinduism accepts all paths as equally valid; in a world of rapid transformations and accelerating change, Hinduism is adaptable and flexible – which is why it has survived for nearly four thousand years.

References

Radhakrishnan, S. *The Hindu View of Life*. London: George Allen & Unwin, 1927.
Tharoor, S. *Why I Am a Hindu*. New Delhi: Aleph Books, 2018.

INDIAN OCEAN

Sanjay Chaturvedi

In India's world view and deeper layers of socio-spatial consciousness, one finds the enduring vision/self-image as Bharatavarsha, located on the southern petal of Jambudvipa, described in sacred Indian texts as a four-petalled lotus floating at the centre of seven concentric oceans separating six regions (*varshas*), each endowed with its own mountains and river systems. Bharatvarsha has the Himalayas, mighty rivers and seas surrounding its triangular shape. The maritime facet of India's sacred geographies of pilgrimage is graphically revealed at places like *triveni* of Kanyakumari (the virgin Goddess) at the southernmost tip of India (duplication of the riverine triveni at Prayag but with a difference) with waves coming in from the Arabian Sea to the west, the Bay of Bengal to the east and the Indian Ocean to the south.

The Indian Ocean (Hind Mahasagar) – the only ocean on the planet named after a country – is an embayed ocean covering approximately 74 million square kilometres, nearly 20 per cent of the world's total ocean area with almost 70,000 kilometres of coastline, and inhabited by close to 40 per cent of humanity. Endowed with 7,500 km of coastline, 1,200 islands and 2.4 million square kilometres of exclusive economic zones (EEZs), India has a major stake in a cooperative and peaceful maritime regional order. Contrary to the Atlantic and the Pacific as 'open' oceans, the Indian Ocean can only be accessed through several 'choke points', including the Straits of Hormuz and the Straits of Malacca. As the fastest-growing economy in the world, critically dependent on maritime trade, India no doubt has a major stake in securing these sea lines of communication (SLOCs), but interconnectedness between the Indian Ocean as a 'space of flows' and the Indian civilization is much deeper and older.

Before the Vasco da Gama period (i.e. before 1497–8), the Indian Ocean acted as a 'crucible' for what John Hobson has termed as 'oriental globalization', involving Chinese, South Asian and Middle Eastern trade. What Fernand Braudel would call *longue durée*, or the long-term rhythms of long-distance maritime trade, facilitated the diffusion of religious and cultural systems such as Hinduism, Buddhism and Islam across the Indian subcontinent. It was during the rule of the Pallava dynasty in South India, from the mid-sixth to the mid-eighth centuries, that trade between India and Southeast Asia brought the Bay of Bengal littorals in a closer embrace. The period that witnessed the rise and fall of the Chola empire in South India (ninth to thirteenth centuries) also saw the zenith of premodern commerce in the Bay of Bengal, which would be known as 'Chola Sea' or 'Chola Lake'. Whereas in the Arabian Sea, a seaborne network of commercial, social and cultural relationships in the seventeenth century – connecting the 'trade on the coast' with the 'trade in the interior' – connected India to the Middle East and East Africa. Such recollections, memories and imaginaries serve as a critical resource for India's cultural and economic diplomacy today and facilitate India's Look East policy.

Deploying geohistorical perspectives, the Indian Ocean could be imaginatively approached as a critical social science laboratory by those interested in a non-Eurocentric international relations and critical geopolitics to expose the limits of the 'area studies' approach. Narrow state-centric understandings of 'maritime order' could be tempered with the realization that the history of human mobility – ably assisted by regularly reversing monsoon winds – in the Indian Ocean is much older than that of Westphalian territoriality. Sugata Bose would rather describe Indian Ocean historically as 'interregional arena' with fuzzy inside–outside distinction. Whereas Andrew Phillips and J. C. Sherman have persuasively demonstrated how, historically, in highly 'heterogeneous Indian Ocean International System', polity diversity proved constitutive rather than subversive of 'order'.

No longer neglected, the Indian Ocean today is central to Indian statecraft, foreign policy and diplomacy, as recently articulated through the vision of SAGAR (Security and Growth for all in the Region). The numerous challenges faced by India and others in the Indian Ocean region today (e.g. maritime security and safety, ecological unsustainability, climate change, migration) will continue to demand proactive policy engagement, international cooperation and critical theoretical reflection.

References

Barendse, R. J. *The Arabian Seas: The Indian Ocean World of the Seventeenth Century*. New Delhi: Vision Books, 2002.

Chaturvedi, Sanjay. 'Mapping the Maritime Order from International Relations' Theoretical Perspectives'. In *Whither Indian Ocean Maritime Order? Contributions to a Seminar on Narendra Modi's SAGAR Speech*, edited by Yogendra Kumar, 33–70. New Delhi: Knowledge World, 2017.

ITIHASA (ITIHĀSA)

Sibesh Bhattacharya

Several terms that generally signified accounts of the past were current in ancient India. *Gatha, narasamsi, akhyana* (variant *Akhyayika*), *itihasa, purana, vamsa, carita, vamsanucarita* and *itivritta* are some of the more frequently occurring ones. Among all of them, itihasa, either singly or in association with purana, was the most prominent and one of the oldest. In fact, the term occurs as early as in the *Atharva Veda*. Kautilya makes itihasa a compulsory subject of study for a prince training for kingship. The Buddhist work *Milindapanha* counted itihasa as an important branch of knowledge. There was an *itihasika* school of interpreting the Vedas. Although itihasa compositions did not fully conform to the present-day notions of history, in their intent and purpose if not in methodology, they did serve as history. In a general sense, they can thus be regarded as 'historical compositions'.

Itihasa obviously has family resemblance with history, for it was thought of as an account of the past. Itihasa, however, is a far older concept than history. A primary point of difference between itihasa and history is that the former is more explicitly didactic; it teaches by example. Itihasa's interest is only in what is exemplary and of didactic value and not in the whole past. Etymologically, itihasa means 'this is what it was'. The word itihasa invokes the past more imaginatively than history. The word 'history' originally (Greek *historia*) meant 'investigation'. The term history, to begin with, thus had no direct association with the past; investigation could be of many other things. By picking up the word historia for the title of his construction of the past, Herodotus underlined right at the birth of the discipline its empirical methodology. The seeds of difference in outlook between itihasa and history and the divergent paths they took lie here.

The term itihasa gained wide penetration, popularity and longevity. On that score too, it can rival history. Practically in all modern Indian languages, east, west, north, south, itihasa is used as the equivalent of history. Notable exceptions are Tamil and Malayalam. Both use caritra or its variations; Malayalam also uses *puravritta*. These terms have been derived from the ancient *carita, itivritta* and so on. In modern Indian languages, however, the term itihasa has lost much of its ancient character; today, it connotes the Western idea of history.

The ancient Indian 'historical compositions', though referred to for the first time in the sacred Vedic literature, might have originated as a secular enterprise. While the predominant concern of the Vedic literature is the divine, it is man and not gods that was at the centre of these historical compositions. However, they soon got incorporated into the Vedic ritual tradition and acquired a moral content.

Itihasa and purana were very intimately related; they were frequently spoken together and quite often as a compound. Together, they were given the status of the 'fifth Veda' attesting to their prestige and importance. In the beginning, the two terms might have just been synonyms; their themes may have been identical. Later, they seem to have somewhat diverged. Purana became a distinct set of works with five ascribed features, the *panchalakshana*. Their thematic sweep became truly universal, spanning the 'creation–dissolution' dyad of the cosmos in recurring cycles, including the intervening human history in each cycle. Their traditional number was eighteen, all said to have been composed by the redoubtable Veda Vyasa, the author of the Mahabharata. However, confusion about the difference between Itihasa and Purana persisted right up to medieval times; Sankaracharya, Medhatithi and Sayanacharya gave diametrically opposite interpretations about their contents. Though not always to the same cosmic proportions, the scope of itihasa too expanded to include all aspects of human life. According to Kautilya, Itihasa came to include episodic narratives (itivritta, akhyayika, udaharana) on the one hand and the societal (dharmasastra, arthasastra) and even the cosmic (purana) on the other. The Mahabharata is a prime example of Itihasa literature, that is what it preferred to call itself. A worthwhile lesson in the scheme of itihasa is the one which guides man in the pursuit of the ends of human lives, the *purusarthas*. Since what is ephemeral is really not valuable; guided by dharma, man ought to try reaching gradually to what is permanent and changeless. To exemplify that value is the goal of itihasa. It is in this sense that the Mahabharata calls itself itihasa. Itihasa, therefore, is not empirical; it selects and abstracts. The Mahabharata further suggests that the term itihasa was employed in two different ways. First, as narration of a background event to explain the significance of a later event – the way Ganga narrated the itihasa of drowning her newly born babies. Second, and the predominant one, the usage of itihasa was to illustrate a point pertaining to dharma by narrating a story.

From the point of view of itihasa, history's insistence on minute recording of the past tends to make it preoccupied with the ephemeral. Itihasa would approve Descartes's opinion that history seems to encourage keeping alive the memory of past injustice and keenness to avenge. Itihasa, on the other hand, places the highest emphasis on justice.

References

Dowson, John. *A Classical Dictionary of Hindu Mythology and Religion*. New Delhi: Rupa, fourteenth impression, 2004.
Thapar, Romila. 'Puranic Lineages and Archaeological Cultures'. In *Ancient Indian Social History: Some Interpretations*. New Delhi: Orient Longmans, 1978.

JANMAPATRI (JANMAPATRĪ)

Rama Kant Agnihotri

Janmapatri or *janampatri* or *patri* or *tip* or *teva*, or the casting of horoscopes, is central to the lives of substantial sections of the Indian population. While many hold strong views against the 'superstitious' stranglehold of this practice, in critical life situations, they often admit to being 'forced' by their family or friends to consult an astrologer. 'What, after all, do you lose?', they are asked. Nor is this a question voiced by those close to one alone. It is a question that Indian society at large asks of its members: in an uncertain world, why not trust the starry and immutable predictions of a janmapatri?

Words like janmapatri and its cousins across the various regions of India generally refer to a rolled long handwritten document that is taken to a family astrologer on occasions such as birth, marriage, the advent of sickness, job search, examination results, the filing of candidature to elections or making choices among political parties, buying property, making a major investment, starting a business and setting up a factory. There is no aspect of human life and its knotty conundrums that a janmapatri cannot address. This document, the janmapatri, ideally cast at birth, contains the *kundali*, or horoscope of the individual, and is said to be unique to this person and this person alone since according to the astrologers, it captures the relationship of the individual to the universe in terms of her or his name, *rashi* (equivalent of the Western moon sign), time and place of birth. At that moment, it is claimed that each of the planets, the sun, the moon and the constellations of the zodiac constitute a particular configuration that enables an astrologer to see the past, present and future of the particular individual. The astrologer claims to map the position of the *navgrahas*, the nine 'planets' (the sun, the moon, Mercury, Venus, Mars, Jupiter and Saturn as well as the two eclipse nodes, Rahu and Ketu) against the background of twelve houses mapped across the 360 degree zodiac, each house being associated with the constellation identifying it. It is on this basis that a horoscope is made, capturing such a mapping of the heavens at the time of birth; an astrologer tries to predict a person's personality traits and makes major predictions about the life of an individual by correlating the planetary positions at the time of birth. If a prediction has to be made about any crisis points in the life of an individual, it is based on these principles of identifying the houses and the nature of planetary motions, whether forward or retrograde.

Irrespective of the vociferous and long-standing debates about whether astrology is or is not a science, the astrologers who make the janmapatri and the vast populations who regularly consult them believe that the planetary combinations at the moment of birth actually determine what will happen in the life of an individual. It is on account of this compelling and widespread belief system that is woven into the very fabric of social practice in India that the 'common man' as well as those who occupy high stations rush to the pundit whose role, in common parlance, often encompasses the role of an astrologer, when they face decision points in their lives.

There is no denying, then, that the janmapatri is central to Indian social life. At the moment of finalizing a matrimonial alliance, for instance, the janmapatri acquires untold significance. Both familial parties in such a case visit their family astrologer to ensure whether a match is suitable or not in terms of the kundalis of the boy and the girl. Many *grah* (planetary) locations and the predicative and predictive personality features of the two (usually referred to as the boy and girl) must match in order for an astrologer to declare a match suitable. All these associations, partially understood by ordinary people, make the mystique of visiting an astrologer all the more exciting; he is always held in some kind of awe. If you wish to find the auspicious moment to do something, you once again consult a reliable astrologer. For example, to ascertain the suitable date and timing for say marriage, or buying property or even filing political nominations, people regularly visit astrologers to ask for a *shubh muhuurat*, the most auspicious moment when that particular task must be done. Today, the undying popularity of astrology in India is attested by its move into the digital universe where one may witness any number of online 'Vedic astrology' sites on YouTube and elsewhere.

KAMA AND KAMASUTRA (KĀMA AND KĀMASŪTRA)

Gurcharan Das

Kama is a masculine Sanskrit noun, which means both 'desire' and 'pleasure'. It can refer to a desire for anything, but like the English word 'desire', kama has come to generally refer to erotic desire. In the earliest Vedic texts, kama was conceived as a cosmic and human energy, animating life and holding it in place. Although a primal, biological drive, kama is best understood primarily as a product of culture. Reflecting the erotic and the ascetic aspects of human nature, its history is the story of a struggle between 'kama optimists' and 'kama pessimists'. In the clash between the two, the 'kama realists' emerged, who offered a compromise in the dharma texts by confining sex to marriage.

Unlike the Judeo-Christian tradition, where in the beginning was light (when God said 'Let there be light' in the Book of Genesis), in the *Rig Veda* (c. 1500 BCE) it was kama in the beginning: the cosmos was created from the seed of desire in the mind of the One (10.129). Because kama is a 'life force', the source of action, creation and procreation, the ancients elevated it not only to an elegant god, Kama, but also to one of the four aims of human life. In contrast, desire was associated with 'original sin', guilt and shame in the former tradition.

We tend to blame the Victorians for today's prudishness of the Indian middle class, but lurking deep within the Indian psyche is deep pessimism about kama's prospects. More than 2,500 years ago, in the forests of north India, ancient yogis, renouncers and the Buddha were struck by the unsatisfactory nature of kama. The yogis sought ways to quiet this endless, futile striving. Their goal was *chittavrittinirodha*, 'to still the fluctuations in the mind', says Patanjali, in his classic text on yōga. And the great ascetic god, Shiva, burned the god Kama in frustration when the latter disturbed his thousand-year meditation. Hence, desire exists *ananga*, 'bodiless', in the human mind.

The answer of the *Bhagavad Gita* to this conundrum involving kama is to learn to act without desire. But how is this possible when 'man is desire' according to the *Brihadaranyaka Upanishad*, the earliest of the Upanishads: 'You are what your deep, driving desire is. / As you desire is, so is your will / As your will is, so is your deed. / As your deed is, so is your destiny' (4.4.5). The Mahabharata proclaims that desire is the essence of life. Opposed to the pessimists were kama optimists, who flowered in the courtly culture in the first millennium CE, especially during the Age of the Guptas, culminating in Sanskrit love poetry and the erotic text of manners, the *Kāmasūtra*, which is not a sex manual but a charming, surprisingly modern guide to the art of living. Addressed to both men and women, it teaches good manners: 'The best alliance plays the game / so that both sides taste one another's happiness / and treat one another / as unique individuals' (*Kāmasūtra* 3.1.23). The hero of the *Kamasutra* is the *nagaraka*, 'a cultivated man-about-town', who regards kama as one of the legitimate aims of life in which sexual pleasure exists for its own sake and not only for procreation. Towards the end of the book, it offers the best advice: 'If you are kissed, / kiss back'.

The optimists focused on *līlā* (the playfulness of mischievous gods), and one in particular, Krishna danced the *raslila* with forty thousand women for an entire Brahma night that lasted 4.5 billion human years. Even the devotional love of god took a romantic turn in Jayadeva's *Gita Govinda*, where Radha, a married woman, longs to unite with Krishna, her divine, adulterous lover.

Kama optimists argued that, in human beings, instinctual desire travels from our senses to our imagination, whence it creates a fantasy around a specific individual. These fantasies are the source of intense pleasure, and despite all the constraints, men and women find a way to communicate their fantasies, and this gives rise to erotic love. Ancient society worried about this charming human inclination and instituted monogamy via marriage for the sake of social harmony. This turning point to 'kama realism', from polygamy to monogamy, is narrated vividly in the Mahabharata when Shvetaketu is appalled that his father is not in the least bit concerned that his wife sleeps with a different man every night.

The beguiling world of kama is full of paradoxes, as is inherent in the following sentence: 'I desire only what I don't have; once I attain it, kama dies.' The mythology of god Kama posits five stages of desire from birth to death, represented by five flower arrows that Kama shoots from his bow made of sugar cane and a string made of bees. Kama is a lack of something that I do not possess and lovers long to unite in order to fill this deficiency. The extreme pleasure associated with kama is possibly a recompense for the loneliness of the human condition. But how can something that is missing compensate for loneliness or perish once attained? How can it be a goal of life?

Kama is ubiquitous and indestructible. *Kamagita* (song of desire), embedded deep inside the Mahabharata, reminds us that when one controls one desire, another pops up (XIV 13.9). If one gives up the desire for wealth and gives away one's money, a new craving emerges – a desire for reputation; if one renounces the world and becomes an ascetic, one is driven by a desire for heaven (*mokṣha*), 'liberation' from the human condition. One may grow old, but the thirst of kama does not cease, as King Yayati learns in the Mahabharata.

The underlying premise of the four aims of life is that we live for a while and then we die. It matters to us that our lives have meaning. Accordingly, kama is also one of the sources for a meaningful life. We are constantly reminded about *dharma*, 'our duty to others'. However, the thought escapes us that kama is a 'duty to ourselves' for living a fulfilling life. But how do we nurture desire without harming others or oneself? The dilemma often is whether to betray the other or oneself.

References

Das, Gurcharan. *Kama: The Riddle of Desire*. Delhi: Penguin Random House, 2018.
Iyengar, B. K. S. *Light on the Yoga Sutras of Patanjali*. London: HarperCollins, 2002.
Miller, Barbara Stoler, ed. and trans. *Love Song of the Dark Lord: Jayadeva's Gitagovinda*. New York: Columbia University Press, 1977.

MAHABHARATA (MAHĀBHĀRATA)

Sibaji Bandyopadhyay

The Mahabharata stubbornly defies every attempt at straight-jacketing. Not only does the picturesque epithet 'jungle' fit the Mahabharata perfectly, the colossal work continually escapes forces aiming to tame it. The authorship of the Mahabharata is attributed to Vyasa, the sage. But, internal evidences make it patent that the word 'author' – a word usually used as shorthand for some regular 'organizing principle' – makes no sense as far the work is concerned. As it is, the Mahabharata was composed over centuries: roughly between fourth century BCE and fourth century CE. Besides carrying inputs from several contributors, the chronicle has within it traces of earlier stories which have faded from public memory due to the intrusion of newer ones. The Mahabharata, as we know it today, is best comparable to a towering edifice which has undergone the tortuous process of being built, partly demolished and being rebuilt over and over again.

It is also next to impossible to specify the genre into which the Mahabharata can be satisfactorily slotted. Even if one accepts the charitable view that the notion of genre is broad enough to signify a cluster of typical features, the Western term 'epic' does not quite fit the bill. The difficulty of zeroing in on a single label is further exacerbated by the fact that the Mahabharata on its own describes itself in ways more than one: *kavya* or 'poetry', *purana* or 'lore', *akhyana* or 'narrative', *itihasa* or 'thus it was'. Of these, itihasa, which resonates as it does with the word 'history', the etymology of which, in Greek can be successively traced back to historia or 'learning acquired by investigation', historein or 'inquire', histor or the 'wise', has a unique significance for the Mahabharata.

The itihasa is itihasa, a compendium of historia, precisely because it presents an ensemble of 'histors' of various shades. The wise enquirers of the Indian past are more or less unanimous that the itihasa is both indirectly and directly coloured by the great ideological churning which took place in the eastern Gangetic plains in 500 BCE. Daring to re-evaluate all received values, the stirring challenged age-old Brahmanical practices as well as the apparatus of belief associated with them. Coalescing into a full-blown uprising, known collectively as the Sramana Movement, its message rapidly reached the west, the heartland of hoary Brahmanism, where it succeeded in forcing the priestly class to partly modify some of the Vedic assumptions to which it had steadfastly clung to thus far. The Mahabharata bears the imprints of this massive shake-up – a structural readjustment whose historic relevance is yet to be exhausted. Simultaneously, it speaks of residues that remain unaccounted for by the act of assimilation/absorption/neutralization undertaken by the priestly class under siege. Emanating from the *nastika* or Veda-denying Sramana sects, such as the Jain, Buddhist and Lokayata, the unprocessed remnants function as irrepressible irritants which resist the smooth running of the moral economy grounded on the postulates of the *astika* or Veda-espousing camps. And, to make the matter even graver, on occasions, the blockades by themselves constitute the bone of contention. On the whole, these interruptions, minor or major in scale, prevent the Mahabharata's discursive field from becoming foreclosed or frozen into a self-sufficient wholesome entity.

Containing multitudes and consistent in happily contradicting itself, the Mahabharata raises a host of ethical problems without resolving them to the full. It is this intrinsic incompleteness, the daring to fish out truths entrapped in the mire of falsehoods without getting trapped by false holistic truths, which keeps the Mahabharata alive, perennially contemporary. Over and above this, self-reflexive by temperament, the Mahabharata arrogates to itself the term 'fifth Veda'. In contra opposition to the four canonical Vedas sealed and reserved for the upper classes, the fifth intends to address everybody. The dual longing to be multi-perspectival as well as all-inclusive is what renders to this itihāsa magical quality. Non-linear in progression, the text faces no trouble in moving in and out of the core narrative whenever or wherever it wills. The main plot does develop at a steady pace; but, with countless subsidiary episodes both criss-crossing and enveloping it, the plot gets increasingly caught up in an intricate pattern of pauses. At best thinly connected with the primary storyline, which anyway is rather convoluted, the overgrowth of secondary tales further complicates the Mahabharata. Not being held by any still Archimedean point, the focus of the text keeps shifting. Its manner of enunciation too enhances the fuzziness stemming from continual deferral and decentring.

The Mahabharata maintains an astonishing degree of rigour while portraying characters. Not one of Mahabharata's principal protagonists is rounded or a mere cardboard piece. Instead, each of them, be he a good guy or a rotten one, be she docile or rebellious, is a bundle of contradictions. It is well-nigh impossible to psychologize them in terms of any fixed set of parameters.

The difficulties pertaining to the untangling of the knots peculiar to the Mahabharata – some of which have been listed above – are compounded by the different versions of the Sanskrit text doing the rounds along the length and breadth of the country. At the same moment, there exist instances of unified compilations set up by premodern editors upon which they built their commentaries. Of them the most pre-eminent is the seventeenth-century scholar Nilakantha – to arrive at the 'best' possible reading of the tome 'he had compared many copies of the Mahabharata, collected from different parts of India', as Sukthankar notes.

At the Eleventh International Congress of Orientalists held in Paris in 1897, Maurice Winternitz, the Austrian expert on ancient India, floated the idea of construing an ideal edition of the Mahabharata. Following the founding of the Bhandarkar Oriental Research Institute in 1917, the painstaking task of producing the Mahabharata's critical edition started on a war footing after V. S. Sukthankar assumed charge of overseeing the programme in 1925. Treating the Nilakantha version as the vulgate or the commonly accepted reading, Sukthankar and his associates initiated a search for manuscripts far wider in scope than that of the seventeenth-century compiler. Spreading out in all directions, researchers collected 1,259 manuscripts – some truncated, some nearly complete – in total. Of them about eight hundred were collated. The gathered material was put under two headings: 'N' or Northern Recension and 'S' or Southern Recension. While the N-manuscripts comprised the Sanskrit text copied in Sarada (or Kashmiri), Nepali, Maithili, Bengali and Devanagari letters; the S-manuscripts did so in those of Telugu, Grantha (or Tamil) and Malayalam. The objective was to compare and contrast the five N-recensions and the three S-recensions between themselves and then to determine to what extent the two sets of recensions mutually corroborated each other. Once this was finished with, they proceeded to select the verses which would feature in the Critical Edition on the basis of the formula $N = S$. Snipping them away with meticulous care, the Critical Edition succeeded in reducing the total number of 'official' verses to around seventy-five thousand from the unwieldy one hundred thousand. Undeniably, it is the most reliable testimony of the manuscript tradition. That, however, does not mean that the Critical Edition had recovered the 'original' Vyasa's Mahabharata transmitted orally over centuries; for, even the oldest of the written parchments belonged to the fifteenth century CE. In spite of the Critical Edition's Himalayan effort to make sojourns into the mess called the Mahabharata motorable, the itihasa is still as jungle-like, as baffling as it was before.

The main plot of the Mahabharata revolves around animosity between two groups of cousins, the Kauravas and the Pandavas, which leads to a devastating, all-consuming war. The finale to the eighteen-day war is provided by a calculated terroristic attack. The terror strike spells out a grammar with such precision and breadth that it can, with minimal tinkering, accommodate the daily ferocities we encounter today. Yet, despite depicting blood-curling scenes in graphic details, the Mahabharata does not abide by the codes vital to 'epics' in general – it stands apart by *not* celebrating the winning party or masculine vigour. The glory of the itihasa lies in the fact that it inaugurated a discourse on discursive tussles between champions of war and proponents of peace. The residual excess which distinguishes the Mahabharata is its valorization of non-violence over violence.

Utterly confident of its staying power, the Mahabharata declares, 'Some bards have already sung this itihasa; and some again are teaching it to others; others will no doubt do the same hereafter on earth.' All said and done, this may not be an empty boast.

References

Bandyopadhyay, Sibaji. *Three Essays on the Mahābhārata: Exercises in Literary Hermeneutics.* Hyderabad: Orient BlackSwan, 2016, reprint, 2017.

Bhate, Saroja. 'Methodology of the Critical Edition of the *Mahābhārata*'. In *Mahābhārata Now: Narration, Aesthetics, Ethics*, edited by Arindam Chakrabarti and Sibaji Bandyopadhyay. New Delhi and London: Routledge, 2014.

MANTRA, TANTRA, YANTRA (MANTRA, TANTRA, YANTRA)

Ranjit Nair

Mantra in popular parlance has come to mean a mystic utterance conveyed by a guru to a disciple. The word is a compound of *manas*, which is mind as an internal organ, with an ending which denotes instrumentality, and the suffix *tra*, which could be interpreted to mean taking across (*tarayati*) as well as saving (*trayati*), making for a polysemy that allows the word mantra to denote sacred text or speech, a prayer or eulogy, a hymn from the Vedas or a votive formula in a ritual setting. Contending interpretations of the meaning of mantras were advanced by Kautsa who held that the mantras were meaningless (*anarthakah mantrah*) and were elements of rituals, and this view was countered by Yaska in *Nirukta*, perhaps the earliest work on etymology in any tradition. Mantras appear in the *samhitas*, *brahmanas* and *aranyakas*, which are the ritual sections of the Vedas. The debate between the ritualists and interpreters was important for the ancient grammatical tradition, leading to debates over key questions such as whether meaning was attached to words or sentences, with Yaska championing the former.

Perhaps the most famous of all mantras is the diphthong *aum* (often written as *om*), which is regarded as a compound of three vowels interpreted to stand for three states of awareness – waking, sleep and dreamless sleep. The Gayatri Mantra consists of a whole hymn recited in the morning, while facing and addressing the Sun.

An early derivative of mantra was *mantri*, which meant 'thinker, adviser, counsellor' in the Vedas and was also understood to mean 'one who consents or agrees'. This is what was expected of a minister to a king, to counsel as well as execute. The word *mandarin*, used across East Asia, is an adaptation of *mantrin*.

Tantra is also expansively polysemous, applying to 'a loom, the warp, the leading, principal or essential part, main point, characteristic feature, model, type, system, framework'. Its root signifies stretching or extending, applicable to bodies. Recalling the Cartesian definition of matter as *res extensa*, the word tantra applies to the body as the word mantra does to the mind. As practiced, *tantrik* schools taught various methods of bodily control, some of which were abhorrent to traditional thinkers. Shankara's relentless campaign to purge tantra on account of its fixation on the body bore fruit, although the titillating features of the tantra ensured that it was pursued in secret as well as openly in places where the reformer's writ did not hold sway.

Yantra, the last of the triad of words noted in this entry, relates to *yana* (path), making it an instrument to control motion or to direct an object along a path, which could range from the fetters, thongs and reins used by a horseman to surgical instruments in the hands of a surgeon, especially a blunt-edged one. Yantra came to mean instrument or apparatus, machine or engine. Massive masonry-built astronomical observatories, known as *jantar mantar*s, set up by Raja Sawai Mansingh contained various yantra, such as the gnomon and the sundial. Despite the Raja's efforts, however, the word yantra could not shake off its application to mystical diagrams and amulets allegedly endowed with occult powers.

References

Khanna, Madhu. *Yantra: The Tantric Symbol of Cosmic Unity*. Rochester: Inner Traditions, 2003.
Pontillo, Tiziana and Maria Piera Candotti. *Signless Signification in Ancient India and Beyond*. London: Anthem Press, 2014.

MANUVADI (MANUVĀDĪ)

Sasheej Hegde

How does the critique of caste appear today? What form(s) does it take, and what concepts underwrite the terms deployed in this work of critique? And, moreover, by no means secondary, what attitude towards both that form and its conceptual repertoire can and should one adopt? This will largely constitute the order of our entry into the keyword 'Manuvadi'. Unlike, say, other keywords of the Indic sociopolitical landscape, such as *praja* or *sēvā* or *niti*, or even *jati*, whose meanings are, as it were, adrift, the term Manuvadi remains by and large docked to its conditions of emergence.

Let me therefore begin by gesturing at aspects of its emergence. The term Manuvadi may be contextualized to its North Indian Hindi-speaking landscape of an anti-Brahminism transforming into political non-Brahminism by the early decades of the twentieth century – incidentally, a development not limited to North India but also obtaining across western India and southern India as well and soon thereafter forming the basis of a distinctively Dalit articulation that waxed and waned while resurfacing again in our contemporary times with the Bahujan Samāj Party within the shifting regional configurations of modern India. Consequently, the term Manuvadi, as both noun and adverb, cannot be taken to be exclusive to the Dalit critique of caste. In fact, even as the term did not quite obtain in such a fashion, its concept and referent found expression in the hostility to Brahmins expressed by Dayananda Sarasvati and the entire Arya Samāj network of the late nineteenth and twentieth centuries in North India as well as in the articulations of the Indian socialists of the twentieth century like Acharya Narendra Deva and soon thereafter Rammanohar Lohia.

However, it must be stated that certain things remained constant in B. R. Ambedkar's thinking about caste throughout his writing life, namely, Brahminism's centrality to the development of caste relations and the quasi-juridical basis of caste regulation as epitomized by the *Manusmriti*. In fact, this latter text (whose composition Ambedkar dates to 170–150 BCE and whose public burning in December 1927 he oversaw as part of the extended set of events that was the Mahad Satyagraha in Maharashtra) was taken as the prime symbol of Brahmin domination by various caste radicals of the twentieth century – and thus the association of *Manusmriti* with Manuvadi as both noun and adverb – with the text's ban on education for women and untouchables and the prescribed ill treatment of the *Shudra* castes being repeatedly challenged as symbols of Hindu cruelty and despotism. Indeed, as part of the enlarged space of political non-Brahminism, Manuvadi – not quite the word but the politics it translates into – predates the Dalit critique, without of course changing the meanings of the word (and its associated politics) as taken to signify the interpenetration of caste power with Brahmanical authority.

Now, of course, this challenge to caste power and Brahmanical authority has a longer genealogy than as suggested above – although Manuvadi as a distinctively early-twentieth-century importation cannot be discounted – marking the contours of dissent within 'Hinduism' in historical terms. To be sure, practices associated with what may be termed a 'Brahmanical' imaginary – specifically for those traditions that accept a special mediating role for ritual experts referred as Brahmins and feature major textual formations in Sanskrit (and by no means limited to the *Manusmriti*) – are clearly delineated as different from (say) antinomian yogic practices in other Sanskrit sources. This also means that the Brahmanical traditions were diverse and decentralized, hardly taking a centralized institutional form. Indeed, as the religious studies scholar Leela Prasad has eloquently demonstrated, the authoritative texts associated with Brahmanical Hindu tradition obtain in diverse ways, functioning largely as 'imagined texts' where 'injunctions' and 'actions' come together in an imagined representation of the normative that is 'constructed by each individual – or by a community – commingling memory and experience with learning and teaching'.

Doubtless, there is more to Brahmanical traditions than the fact of caste exclusion. The force of this recognition notwithstanding, it must yet be admitted that there has always obtained, across sociopolitical spaces in India, a salience ascribed to caste; and, what is more, this salience has been institutionalized through cultural mediations of the kind that renders Brahmins as 'always already' and 'distinct pre-possessors' of social and cultural power. Understanding caste and Hinduism historically, then, requires that we open up to the 'thresholds and limits' that attach to Manuvadi (the key integuments of which I have outlined in our foregoing paragraphs).

References

Rao, Anupama. *The Caste Question: Dalits and the Politics of Modern India*. Berkeley: University of California Press, 2009.
Rocher, Ludo. *Studies in Hindu Law and Dharmasastras*. New York: Anthem Press, 2012.

MAYA (MĀYĀ)

Mohini Mullick

Maya, it can truly be said, is a uniquely Indian notion. Thus, although it has often been rendered in the English language as 'illusion', the gloss just does not begin to approach the complexities of the concept of maya. Maya is associated primarily with the philosophical school of Vedanta, whose main expositor was the Adi Sankara. Maya also plays a role in Buddhism, but for reasons dwelt on below, it takes on somewhat different connotations here. The term Vedanta suggests that the system referred to is not only an interpretation of the truths of the Vedas but also an elucidation of the very goals of all existence that the Vedas only began to reveal. The Upanishads, as part of the larger corpus known as *sruti*, constituted the disquisitions into the *jnanamarg* (the way through knowledge), as opposed to the *karma marg* (the way through action/practice) to the attainment of these goals. The final goal is, of course, *mokṣha* (broadly, 'liberation').

'Liberation from what?' one may ask. The answer is as follows: this phenomenal existence which is but a manifestation of maya, an apparent 'limiting adjunct' of the Ultimate Reality that is described as Brahman. Unfathomable, inscrutable and variegated (*anirvacaniya*), it gives rise to the realm of *nama-rupa* (name and form) which dissolves for each individual at the moment of realization that all is Brahman. Though there is questioning on this subject, there is finally no answer to why the Absolute needs to seemingly create an imperfect world. The closest one gets to an 'explanation' is that the cosmic principle of *avidya* (ignorance) leads to the error of imagining a created world of nature and of all life. In Samkhya, the oldest of the 'schools' of Indian thought, *prakriti* (nature) plays the role of maya. The *Bhagavad Gita*, based as it is on Samkhya, also refers to prakriti as the field (*ksetra*) of worldly action.

Advaita writings are replete with images of the 'seeing' of silver where only the conch shell exists, recoiling from the 'snake' when a rope is all that lies ahead. These metaphors have limited heuristic value however, for, unlike the snake and the silver, maya is neither real (*sat*) nor unreal (*asat*).

In Buddhism, maya is linked even more closely to cosmic ignorance which results in the cycle of suffering and rebirth (*samsara*). To exit this cycle is to attain *nirvaṇa* (the blowing out of existence). Denying the reality of a Brahman or any Ultimate Reality, there is no positive goal such as mokṣha for the Buddhist life. The realization of the truths of suffering, its causes traceable to ignorance, and also its cure finally set the individual free of maya. As Buddhism has evolved, nirvaṇa has been viewed more as a state of enlightenment in this very world resulting from the recognition of the ephemeral nature of causal relations, of contingency in the interdependence of events. Interestingly, Buddha's mother was named Maya. Thus, maya also denotes the principle of fecundity, of primeval potentiality which gives birth to the world, samsara.

The notion of maya has been a powerful conceptual force in the historical Indian imagination: it survives today in popular folklore as the *jagat* (world) of *moha* (attachment), *ichha* (desire) and *ahamkara* (ego). If there is truth in the observation that human life comes at a low premium in India, then surely this is so because of a deep cultural investment in the notion of maya. Vivekananda, Aurobindo and S. Radhakrishnan, to mention only some of the prominent early philosophers of colonial India, were deeply influenced by the prevailing paradigms of Western thought. Even more poignantly, they felt an urgent need to respond to criticism of Indian thought, emanating from the West. Thus, Schelling's claim of an etymological affinity between maya and *magia* (magic) in his *Philosophy of Mythology* demanded rebuttal. In the academia, maya is today explicated in the English language in altered tropes. The image of maya as the realm of nama-rupa gives way to a world described in terms of space-time and causality and as the bearer of only relative existence (as opposed to Absolute Reality) by

Vivekananda. Plato, Bradley and Kant are invoked by various academics to lend substance to this construct. More recently, keeping step with the philosophical concerns and locutions of the day, even the godman Rajneesh argued that this phenomenal existence is neither meaningful nor meaningless. Finally, in a silent revolution, religion, a notion unknown to ancient India, becomes the prime instrument for the final renting of maya's veil.

References

Goudriaan, T. *Maya: Divine and Human*. New Delhi: Motilal Banarsidass, 2008.
Mullick, M. and M. S. Santanam, eds. *Classical Indian Thought and the English Language: Perspectives and Problems*. New Delhi: Indian Council of Philosophical Research and D. K. Printworld, 2015.

MOKSHA/NIRVANA (MŌKṢA/NIRVĀṆA)

Ranjit Nair

Among the four *purusharthas* (human ends), *mokṣha* appears last. Scholarly opinion is divided as to whether mokṣha was a later inclusion, with some maintaining that it can be found in the Vedas in the 500–1000 BCE and others noting that its rise to prominence occurred towards the end of the first millennium BCE and the first century CE. Questions have been raised about the possible mapping of the purusharthas onto the four *varnashramas*, namely *brahmacharya*, *grhastha*, *vanaprastha* and *sannyasa*. These contentious issues cannot be resolved without detailed scholarship relying on the commentaries that steadily accrete around the key texts.

Mokṣha and mukti are derived from the Sanskrit root muc, meaning 'to release, to free'. On the other hand, nirvaṇa, which is the term preferred by the Bauddhas and the Jainas, means 'blowing out'. This is connected to the idea of metempsychosis with the atman (soul), compared to a lamp which can light other lamps, the passage from one birth to another until its final cessation. With the doctrine of the atman so dearly beloved in the Vedanta, being denied by the Bauddhas, it is puzzling that metempsychosis is considered at all. The Buddha was aware of the apparent dissonance between the idea of the ever-changing world, or samsara, and the anatman doctrine. The resolution lies in the recognition of the composite nature of the individual or self and the restitution of the elements to its respective realms. The recognition of impermanence is the root to the final dissolution. As the Madhyamika philosopher Nagarjuna put it some five centuries after the Buddha, 'Samsara is nirvāṇa'.

Mokṣha is invariably perceived in the literature as the telos of every activity, prompting twentieth-century interpreters to dismiss it as a literary conceit devoid of serious content. This is an instance of a feature of Indian civilization, which looks odd to the outsider. It is patronizing to think that the laity is philosophically untutored and hence prone to bringing into every action of theirs the lofty aim of mokṣha. The idea of nishkama karma (disinterested action) advocated in the Bhagavad Gita, is an instance where mokṣha is applied to all sorts of karmas. The laity had access to the Gita in a variety of forms, textual as well as in performative arts.

There were, inevitably, disagreements about the route to mokṣha and nirvaṇa, as eschatology depended on the ontologies and epistemologies that were adopted. For the Jainas, the soul needs to get rid of its worldly defilements in order to attain mokṣha or nirvaṇa. In the mainstream Vedantic traditions, mokṣha meant enlightenment, getting rid of false notions and being able to see the world as an artifice that stood in the way of comprehending the unity of the self (atman) and the essence of the world (brahman). The Bauddha position on this topic is rather similar, emphasizing the cessation of all desire in the state of nirvaṇa.

The Vivekacudamani (The Crest Jewel of Discrimination) attributed to Shankara avers that among the ingredients for mokṣha the most weighty is bhakti (devotion). The verse goes on to define bhakti as svasvarupanusandhanam (the search for one's own self). The result of the search is to find that one's own self was identical to the self of all, as advaita (non-dualism) holds. Mokṣha, like several core concepts of the tradition, was amenable to multiple interpretations. Through Gaudapada, the teacher of Shankara's own teacher Govinda, the Bauddha and Vedantic conceptions of mokṣha came together, which was of course bitterly resented by his detractors who called him a crypto-Buddhist and much worse.

Folk belief in mokṣha as the final liberation of the self from becoming embodied time and again is widespread among the pious. They get drawn into weird cults resulting in the loss of lives, as reported recently with a family of eleven, who hanged themselves in the wee hours of 1 July 2018 in their home in Burari, a census town in North Delhi, after much careful preparation and for no ostensible reason other than conviction.

References

Bhatt, S. R. 'The Concept of Moksha – An Analysis'. *Philosophy and Phenomenological Research* 36, no. 4 (June 1976): 564–70.
Press Trust of India. '"Burari Deaths Not Suicide but Accident": Forensic Lab Report'. [online] *NDTV. com*, 2019. Available at: https://www.google.com/amp/s/www.ndtv.com/delhi-news/delhis-burari-deaths-not-suicide-but-an-accident-psychological-autopsy-report-1916739%3famp=1&akamai-rum=off (accessed 26 May 2019).

MUSSALMAN (MUSALMĀN)

Taslima Nasrin

The Mussalman or Muslims of the Indian subcontinent live in different situations in each of the countries. They are a majority in Pakistan and Bangladesh and a minority in India. Pakistan is founded on the basis of religion, so the Muslims there tend to be rigid (hardliners). Bangladesh fought a war against Pakistan with the aim of becoming a secular state, but, a few years after Independence in 1971, the process of making Bangladesh a Muslim country was set in motion. In India, Hindu fundamentalism is on the rise. Hindu fundamentalists are very hostile to Muslims. Many claim that fundamentalists are created because of the pollution of politics by Muslims (to get the Muslim vote?). The behaviours of Hindu and Muslim fundamentalists are exactly the same.

India's Hindutva followers believe that India's Muslims do not love the country. And that they must therefore have this love beaten into them. Those who are not thieves, dacoits and rioters are harassed in the streets only because they are Muslims. Such feelings of hate are not good for the well-being of any country. Seventeen crores (170 million) India's citizens are Muslims. Oppressing them, insulting them and lynching them to death because they have eaten beef will not be able to erase such a large population. Policy should not ghettoize Muslims, but rather it should aim at bringing them into the mainstream; it should not confine them to the masjids and madrassas but bring them into modern colleges and universities. Just as there are bad elements in all religions, there are also good ones. Being hated can turn those good into bad. Beating up and chasing Muslims out of India are not going to solve all of India's problems. India's greatness lies exactly in the fact of having survived as one country made up of many peoples, religions, languages and cultures.

On the Indian subcontinent, sentiments of distrust and hate between Hindus and Muslims alternate between being dormant and being exhibited monstrously. One cannot forget the great Calcutta killings of 1946, the Noakhali riots of 1946, the Malabar rebellion of 1921, the Nagpur riots of 1927, the Nellie massacre of 1983, the Ranchi-Hatia riots of 1967, the Gujarat riots of 1969, the Bhiwandi riots of 1984, the Meerut riots of 1987, the Bhagalpur riots of 1989, the Hyderabad riots of the 1990s, the Bombay riots of the 1990s, the Gujarat riots of 2002 and, in the last few years, the Canning riots of 2013, the Muzaffarnagar riots of 2013 and Kaliachak riots of 2016. In all these riots, people from both Hindu and Muslim communities were killed. India was partitioned ostensibly to promote peace between Hindus and Muslims and to avoid riots and deaths. However, when Hindus from one side and Muslims from the other were crossing over in trains, a total of about ten lakh were murdered at each other's hands. Sometimes it seems that perhaps Hindus and Muslims will never be able to live side by side as friends and relatives. Although there have been no Hindu–Muslim riots in Bangladesh and Pakistan, oppression of the minorities by the majority continues unabated, and fear has led the minorities to emigrate or convert to the majority religion. All minorities are feeling endangered in the subcontinent.

There have been some unprecedented incidents in the midst of all these Hindu–Muslim riots, turbulence and jealousy. There have been incidents where Muslim youths did not hesitate even for a moment to break their religious fasts in order to help Hindus in their hour of need. Similarly, in Bangladesh, Hindu (ISKCON) and Buddhist temples feed the Muslim poor (*iftar* dinners) during the holy month of Ramadan. If all communities were to practice humanity, friendship between them would prosper. All religions would be known as humanitarian religions. This is what being civilized means. There is no greater religion than the religion of humanity. Once humanity disappears, what remains of religion is merely singing the praises of the Lord to escape from hell or to go to heaven.

References

Nasrin, Taslima. *Shame: A Novel* (translated from the Bengali novel Lajja). New York: Prometheus Books, 1997.
Nasrin, Taslima. *Split: A Life*. London: Penguin Hamish Hamilton, 2018.

ORIENTALISM

Ulka Anjaria

The origin of the term Orientalism goes back to Western representations of the non-Western world, specifically the Middle East and India. Representations included painting, travel writing and other genres. Orientalism also referred to an academic body of knowledge interested in non-Western cultures and languages. William Jones was perhaps the most well-known Orientalist, who, in the eighteenth century, developed the theory of a common origin to Indo-European languages after extensive study of Middle Eastern and South Asian languages. As British rule was rationalized and bureaucratized in the late nineteenth century, the debate between Anglicists and Orientalists heightened, with the former pointing out India's backwardness in relation to Western civilization as a justification for colonial rule and the latter suggesting that Indian religion and spirituality had something to teach a disillusioned and secularized Europe.

The publication of Edward Said's path-breaking *Orientalism* in 1978 changed the meaning of this term and made it central to what was later called postcolonial theory. Using Foucault's idea of the episteme or regime of truth, Said argued that Orientalism was not only a branch of learning and a form of representation but also a discourse that included many different forms, genres and even political positions (from Flaubert to Marx). This discourse did not merely describe the non-Western world but also created a non-Western world that would be subject to colonial rule. Representation, in particular seemingly non-ideological forms of representation such as literature, art and travel narrative, was central to this endeavour, precisely because it appeared to be apolitical and to merely represent experiences. But, as Said brilliantly shows, this vast diversity of writings operated on a finite number of tropes, which, in their very reproducibility and translatability across genres, turned the idea of an 'Orient' open for British rule into a self-evident reality.

This idea not only of Orientalism specifically but also of colonial discourse as the prerequisite for colonial rule radically changed the study of colonialism and might be said to have given impetus to the metropolitan brand of postcolonial theory already anticipated by anti-colonial thinkers such as Frantz Fanon, Aimé Césaire and others. Following *Orientalism*, the study of colonial discourse became the primary work of postcolonial theory, showing how different texts and forms of representation, from Victorian novels to Linnaean classificatory schemes, to botany, to English literary study itself, were part of this massive discursive formation that made colonial rule not only possible but also desirable. The geographic specificity of Said's work was expanded to include other Orientalisms, such as American orientalism, Ottoman orientalism, Zionist orientalism and so on.

At the same time, some postcolonial theorists felt that Said's representation of an all-encompassing discourse that, in Foucauldian terms, had no outside presented colonial rule as more powerful than it actually was. Scholars such as Homi Bhabha pointed to the precarity of colonial rule founded in the precarity of language itself. Other scholars felt that Said did not pay enough attention to resistance to colonial rule, suggesting that not only nationalist leaders but also the nation's margins, such as women, Muslims, Dalits and others, were able to contest Orientalism from the outside. Others, especially Marxist scholars, argued that in focussing on ideological domination, Said did not pay enough attention to the material basis of empire. Even Said himself retreated from what was taken to be an analysis of colonial power as all-encompassing and unassailable. It is probably fair to say that the strength and the persistence of these critiques has rendered the idea of Orientalism less relevant to contemporary scholarship on colonialism, even though it radically reshaped the field when it was first forwarded.

References

Said, Edward W. *Orientalism*. London: Penguin, 1978.
Said, Edward W. 'Orientalism Reconsidered'. *Cultural Critique*, no. 1 (Autumn 1985): 89–107.

PARSI (PĀRSĪ)

Keki Daruwala

Parsi are a bit of an enigma to the rest of mankind: a harmless comical race to the movie scriptwriter; great patronizers – *aapri Ranee* (Elizabeth), *aapro Ratan* (Tata); superb skirmishers when it comes to fighting among themselves; and equally superb litigants – a law court hath no fury like a Parsi plaintiff. To the surprising regret of the rest of mankind, they are also a diminishing race, perched on the precipice of premature extinction. (Parsi love alliteration, incidentally.)

Parsi are Zarthustis, followers of possibly the oldest prophet, Zoroaster, the man who invented monotheism, heaven, hell, the day of judgement and dug an unbridgeable chasm between good and evil. Parsi fled Persia after enduring Muslim/Arab persecution for about two centuries and reached Diu, on India's western coast, a thousand years ago. A syrupy sentimental story – invented and documented in *Qisseh-i-Sanjan* (1599), by its author the Parsi priest Behman Kaikobad Sanjana – has it that the incoming Parsi were shown a full pot of milk, denoting that the place was full up and could not accommodate more. The Parsi priest placed jaggery in the milk pot, meaning that the Parsi will live there like sugar in milk. The conditions laid out to them in turn were 'forsake weapons, adopt the Gujarati language and attire and celebrate weddings after sundown'.

This piece is not about Cyrus the Great or about Herodotus and Queen Tomyris. This is about Parsi from the province 'Pars' in Iran, who refused to convert to Islam despite state coercion and torture, sailed to India and found sanctuary in Gujarat, in the tenth century or thereabouts, landing first at Diu where they stayed for nineteen years before shifting to Sanjan, where the first sacred fire was 'enthroned'. Once the Khiljis conquered Gujarat and the Tughlaks followed, they wiped out Hindu temples and Parsi fire temples. Alaf Khan, a Tughlak general, massacred the Parsi in Sanjan after suffering a reverse the previous day. Parsi fled Sanjan and moved into Navsari, Surat and Udwada. Where the Parsi went so did their sacred fires, housed in Atash Behrams (Big Fire Temples) and their *dokhma*s (bleak roofless towers), vulture fringed, where they disposed of their dead.

Meanwhile, Parsi had taken to farming and planting orchards. The Dutch arrived in Surat, and many Parsi shifted there. Mughal monetization, the setting up of the Dutch East India Company in Surat in 1602 changed Parsi outlook. It paved the way for seafarers of the seventeenth and eighteenth centuries, who traded with the Far East and China in silks, cotton and opium. Parsi who traded with China became known as 'Merchant princes' – Banajis, Camas, Readymoneys and Jamshetji Jejeebhoy. (The last named has been dealt with shabbily by an Indian novelist recently.) By 1805, sixteen Parsi firms and two Parsi–China agencies were flourishing. They exchanged cloth and opium for tea, silk, silver and ceramics. They ploughed back much of their money into charities. For instance, Jamshetji's wife gave away money of rupees 155,800 from her personal wealth in 1841 to build the Mahim Causeway joining Bandra island with Mahim. Jemshetji's name heads 126 charities, including Sir JJ School of Art, JJ School of Architecture, JJ School of Applied Art, high schools and many dharamshalas for the destitute. He even bought grazing grounds for cattle herders, because the British were charging a grazing tax. And of course Jamshetji Tata put up India's first steel mill, as also the Taj Hotel.

Before Independence, while most Parsi were pro-British, though they never went as far as appropriating Winston Churchill with an 'apro bulldog' attitude, we had our pioneers in Dadabhai Naoroji (1825–1917), who was Congress president in 1886, 1893 and 1906. He was known for his unfavourable views on the British economic policy in India. In his famous book *Poverty and Un-British Rule in India*, he noted that India was being unfairly taxed and the wealth of the country was being drained. Bhikaiji Cama is famous for unfurling the Indian flag in Stuttgart. She was never allowed by the British to come back to India till she was almost on her death bed.

Beside this, the community was backed by a resurgent spirit of enterprise (now absent). The women developed their own Parsi cuisine, of which *dhansak* (Parsi delicacy; goat meat cooked with lentils and vegetables) is just a miniscule part. Parsi became the advance guard of puppetry, astrology and theatre. The Parsi theatre, with its rumbustious jokes (semi-ribald), was favourite in Gujarat and Bombay and was the inspiration behind the Marathi theatre. Today, they boast of novelists like the brothers Rohinton and Cyrus Mistry and poets like Gieve Patel, Adil Jussawalla and Kersy Katrak. Gieve is also a playwright and painter with his paintings displayed at the Smithsonian. In art they have made a mark, not just with opening the Cawasji Jahangir Gallery but with painters like Jahangir Sabhawala, portrait painter Bhiwandiwala and others. In films, Parsi can unscroll a long list of luminaries, starting from Sohrab Modi and ending with Ronnie Screwwala. Sohrab Modi acted as king Porus in the film *Sikander* but never got his due from the community because he married the Muslim actress Mehtab. It would also be important to remember Farrokh Bulsara and apro Freddy Mercury.

General Sam Manekshaw who headed the army when the Pakistani forces were defeated, resisted going to war till he and the army were fully prepared, is now a legend. The air force and navy have had Parsi chiefs, some of whom have won the Param Vir Chakra.

One should not forget the Parsi of other countries, Frene Ginwala of the African National Congress (ANC) who drafted South Africa's Constitution and was the first Speaker, Justice Dorab Patel of Pakistan who gave a dissenting note in the trial of Zulfiqar Bhutto and Jamshed Marker, Pakistan's ace diplomat.

Today, the community is lacking in enterprise, chutzpah and aspiration. Few Parsi are getting into covenanted services. And the physical diminishing of the population adds to the despair. The population decline in the community has been precipitous, from 114,890 in 1941, to 57,264 in the 2011 census. In 2013, the community recorded 174 births against 756 deaths. Such depressing statistics leave very little hope for the community's future in India. Ninety-five per cent Parsi live in two states, Maharashtra and Gujarat. Inbreeding, delayed marriage, non-marriage and the falling fertility levels are responsible for the decline. With government help, a Jiyo Parsi scheme was ushered in through a dedicated organization called PARZOR (Parsi Zoroastrian) led by Dr Shernaz Cama.

References

Desai, Ashok V. 'The Origins of Parsi Enterprise'. *The Indian Economic & Social History Review* 5, no. 4 (1968): 307–17.

Hinnells, John and Alan Williams, eds. *Parsis in India and the Diaspora*. Oxford: Routledge, 2007.

PIR/MURID (PĪR/MURĪD)

S. Imtiaz Hasnain and Masood Ali Beg

Pir is a Persian word which literally means 'old person' or 'elder', both in terms of age (e.g. *pir-o-jawan*, 'old and young') as well as being wise, knowledgeable and experienced. Pir is also a title used for a Sufi master or spiritual guide. Other equivalent terms include the Persian *sarkar* (lord or master) and the Arabic *shaikh* or *hazrat*. In its most general sense, sheikhin also refers to a tribal, religious or organizational leader. As titles, however, pir and sheikh are honourifically conferred on someone who is in possession of spiritual knowledge. In Urdu-Hindi speech contexts, pir is also commonly used as an adjective, for example, *pir baba* or *pir sahib*, to give salutation to a Sufi master or an honoured person.

In Sufism, the pir's role is to guide and instruct his disciple in the Sufi path. This is done by imparting general lessons known as *subahs*. Bosworth and Nizami note that, as a religious and spiritual head in the Sufi order called *tarīqa'*, the pirs are seen as a mediator or connecting link between man and God, as one who 'has already followed the path [*saluk*] to God and has acquired spiritual powers [*wilaya*]' and is, thus, 'qualified to encourage and direct the aspiring novice [*murīd*] on the Sufi path' in search of truth. In this sense, *murshid*, another Arabic word connoting 'teacher' or 'master' (originating from *rashad* 'straight road') is also used precisely in relation to the role of spiritual guide.

While in mystic parlance pir is commonly used for a spiritual guide, its usage in Indo-Muslim context provides a range of creative dimensions, producing a variety of senses when prefixed with different terms. Bosworth and Nizami enlist a typology of usages of pir with clearly identifiable functions.

Since Sufism grew as an integral part of Islamic tradition, it drew its inspiration from the same Holy Qur'an and the practices and preachings of Prophet Muhammad. One aspect of this inspiration is reflected in its attempt to systematically establish sainthood, which can be construed as a parallel to prophethood. Also, in their endeavour to further elaborate 'distinctively mystical ways of reading and interpreting the Qur'an', the Sufis struggled to find 'new ways and venues' to gather around to learn from Sūīi exegesis. Pir, shaikh and murshid thus emerged as a converging point for learning. These are titles for a senior Sūīi spiritual master who instructs and guides his *murīd* ('disciple') on the Sūfi path and thus wields institutional authority in Sufi order.

The word murīd has its roots in Arabic and means 'committed one' or 'aspirant seeker'. It refers to someone with a strong 'will power'. As seeker of guidance, he inculcates a Sufi order or tariqa' ('spiritual path') of blind submission to the murshid or 'inspired guide' for spiritual realization. The murshid, reputed for the spiritual acumen and wide experience, facilitates in bringing about the hierarchical relationship between teacher and student, murshid–murīd. In Sufi tradition, this relationship is transactional in nature where murīd, with all respect and humility, takes the 'oath of allegiance', known as a *baī'at* or *bay'ah*, to surrender himself to the supervision of the murshid or pir who takes him under his guardianship to lead and guide him to the path of Sufism. This marks the beginning of an 'inward' (*batin*) journey of the murīd, who is constantly guided to refrain from arrogance and pride, to control his greed, cravings and other weaknesses, to correct his character and achieve purity.

In the musical tradition in the context of *dargah* (shrine built over the grave of a pir), one may also find hierarchical and assumed subservient position between the pir and the *qawwals* (singers of the Sufi devotional songs known as *qawwalis*) bounded by sacredness. The power of the pir derives its strength from 'their closeness to God, demonstrated by their austerity, enactment of miracles and broad learning', which the qawwals accentuate and eulogize in their songs.

References

Bosworth, C. E. and K. A. Nizami. *Pīr* in *The Encyclopaedia of Islam*, vol. 8, edited by C. E. Bosworth, E. Van Donzel, W. P. Heinrichs and G. Lecomte. Leiden: E.J. Brill, 1995.

Kalra, Virinder, S. *Sacred and Secular Musics: A Postcolonial Approach*. London, New Delhi, New York and Sydney: Bloomsbury, 2015.

PURANA (PURĀṆA)

B. N. Patnaik

Purana constitutes an important genre of Sanskrit literature. Ancient Indian scholarship distinguishes between puraṇa and *itihasa*. *Srimad Bhagavata*, *Vishnu Puraṇa* and *Vamana Puraṇa* are categorized as puranas and Ramayana and Mahabharata are categorized as itihasas. Both puranas and itihasas are long narratives written in verse, and both have a dialogic structure in that there is a narrator who tells a story to a hearer or a group of hearers. The story has a narrative-dramatic structure – the dramatic is embedded in the narrative.

The distinction between a puraṇa and an itihasa is that the former tells of events that are very ancient, whereas the latter tells of happenings in the not-so-distant past. Some of the major vernacular languages of India have a rich repertoire of puranas; the distinction between puranas and itihasas is not maintained here because from the point of view of these compositions, all happenings in the puranas and itihasas are located in the very distant past. The vernacular puranas are not translations of the Sanskrit puranas but retellings. A retelling retains the basic story and even the structure of the original but modifies the details so as to give the story a distinctly local flavour and express the poet's philosophy of life and of the world.

There are eighteen Sanskrit puranas, which have been organized into three categories: *satvik*, *rajasic* and *tamasic*. Each category contains six puranas. *Srimad Bhagavata* and *Vishnu Puraṇa* are among the satvik puranas, *Vamana* and *Brahmanda* are among the rajasic puranas and *Agni* and *Shiva* are among the tamasic puranas. This categorization may be merely sectarian, reflecting the prevalent power structure at the time of classification, where the Vaishnavas (followers of god Vishnu) had supremacy over the Saivites (followers of god Shiva). From another point of view, those puranas that deal with spiritual concerns rather than material concerns were more highly valued and called satvik. Thus, *Srimad Bhagavata* is generally rated most highly among the puranas.

There are said to be five major themes that a puraṇa was supposed to deal with: creation of the universe; its dissolution and recreation; genealogy of gods, sages and demons; creation of humans and the rule of the Manus (lord of the epochs); and histories of the kings of the solar and lunar dynasties. But, not all puranas actually deal with these either adequately or systematically. All puranas, however, certainly deal with *jaya* (victory). Events lead to a terrible, conclusive war, mostly among gods and demons, and the gods win, signifying the victory of good over evil and the restoration of cosmic balance, upset by the dominance of negative forces. In cosmic time and universal space, this engagement goes on, but the victory of the gods over demons in a particular puraṇa brings closure to that narrative. In the war, both gods and demons use trickery and other unethical means; thus, there is no real *dharmayuddha* (virtuous war) in puranic literature. Victory establishes the supremacy of one culture and belief system over another. A *mahapurana* (great puraṇa) like *Srimad Bhagavata* is indeed a major and even the defining cultural narrative of a people.

Puranas bring knowledge and wisdom embodied in the Vedas and the Upanishads to the common man. The *Bhagavad Gita* presents insights of the Upanishads in an accessible form, but it is not a puraṇa, because a puraṇa must be a story, a narrative. One can surmise that since the dissemination of knowledge took take place in the oral mode, verse became the chosen vehicle for narration. Puranas are didactic compositions, providing instruction about values to be cherished, ethical practices to be followed and knowledge to make sense of one's world and one's place in it. They offer to the listener solace, escape from the grim realities of life and spiritual satisfaction. This is the real *phala sruti* (benefit of reading/chanting rituals).

References

Dowson, John. *A Classical Dictionary of Hindu Mythology and Religion*. New Delhi: Rupa, fourteenth impression, 2004.
Mittal, Sushil and Gene Thursby, eds. *The Hindu World*. New York: Routledge, 2004.

KISMAT/TAKDIR (QISMAT/TAKADĪR)

Shivangini Tandon and S. Imtiaz Hasnain

The term *kismat* is derived from the Arabic root *qisma*, which literally means 'sharing out, distribution and allotment'. In the early Arabic poetry of the first century AH (i.e. 622 CE–719 CE), it came to mean 'portion or lot' and was later specifically used to refer to the share of good or bad happenings in the life of each individual. The *Encyclopedia of Islam* defines kismat as fate or destiny, and in Persian and Turkish poetry, words like *falak* and *gardun* were used to describe this concept of destiny. In Ottoman usage, the variant *kismet* was also a technical term of the *kassdmlik*, the official department of state responsible for the division of estates between the various heirs. Though in Quran it is used only in terms of division or apportionment, in terms of the usual usage in Islamic theology and philosophy, it means determinism and predestination. In popular Islamic thought, kismat is seen as the fatalistic acceptance of what God has preordained as one's lot. What is written (*maktub*), what is decided (*maqdur*) and what is my lot (kismat) are part of common discourse that suggests an unquestioning acquiescence of fatalism and a willing denial of freewill.

There are four major types of beliefs about destiny in the Indian subcontinent:

1. 'Universal' script: Whatever happens, happens exactly as it should and it couldn't have been otherwise. In other words, it was predestined to happen this way.
2. 'Soul Specific' script: Whatever happens, happens as a result of your 'fate' or 'destiny' (*nasib* or qismat). That means the journey of your life was written before your birth or at your birth, and you have no choice of changing the same.

3. 'Accounting' script: Whatever happens, happens as a result of your past 'deeds' (*karma*). This means, things happen to you depending upon your good or bad deeds in your previous birth or births. Some say that deeds of current life are settled in the current life itself.
4. 'Happy Ending' Script: Whatever happens, happens for good (*bhagya*). There is a 'higher purpose' behind every event.

An interesting aspect of kismat is that it brings with it a strange sense of ambivalence. Sometimes, in the hands of the motivated preachers of religion, kismat becomes a convenient tool, quite akin to the proverbial opium of the masses. Kismat here starts acting as a 'safety valve' making people believe that whatever abysmally low existence or negative circumstances they are going through are all pre-decided by their fate and so they can do little to change it. Alternatively, kismat is also often used as an excuse by those who oppress the weak. By making the latter believe that their oppression is their fate, the oppressors successfully crush any possibility of revolt on their part. Interestingly, the great poet Allama Iqbal in his *Kulliat-i-Iqbal* has also made use of this discourse of kismat to contextualize the dehumanizing tendencies and the capitalist mindset perpetuated during the period of the Industrial Revolution around the eighteenth century, where he sees fate as dominating over one's hard work and creative endeavours.

God has complete mastery over all creation, an integral part of Islamic belief. Such belief and usage find prominent mention in songs and stories in Hindi. However, this was not always so, as we have seen in the case of Iqbal.

The word 'takdir' stems from the three-letter root *qa-da-ra* with the basic meaning of 'to measure'. Takdir basically means to make something according to a measure/standard. When something is given with no consideration of measure, it carries a sense of plenitude. On the other hand, if it is done with careful measuring, it has an implication of shortage and therefore very important in cultural representation. Some derivatives of takdir include *miqdar* (a model, pattern or a standard), *jaza' qadrahu* ('He transgressed his limits') and *qadrun* (measurement in volume, size, weight, etc.). Since, to make something exactly according to a set standard, and specific measurements, one needs the ability, prowess and control, the last word 'qadrun' means to have power and be in control. For instance, in the following phrases derivatives of taqdir refer to power in so many different ways: *qaddartu 'alashshai* ('I had the power needed to change the thing according to my standard'), *qadir* ('One who has power and control'), *aqdir* ('One who shapes things according to set standards') and *qadr* (value, standard, guiding proportion also, to assess and respect). It is perhaps in this trajectory that the aforementioned usage of taqdir to redeem oneself from 'one's lot' may have arisen.

To conclude, the relentless use of statements terming the cause of events as destiny, etc., is a result of our conditioning and causes hindrance in the growth of our rational, creative thinking and scientific reasoning. It is, therefore, absolutely essential to keep our rational faculties intact along with our belief in kismat/takdir and not reduce them to mere superstitious beliefs or notions.

References

Adamec, Ludwig W. *Historical Dictionary of Islam*, 2nd edn. Lanham: Scarecrow Press, 2009.

Raghavendra, M. K. *Seduced by the Familiar: Narration and Meaning in Indian Popular Cinema.* New Delhi: Oxford University Press, 2015.

RAMAYANA (RĀMĀYAṆA)

Paula Richman

Ramayana has been used in two ways. Most specifically, Ramayana is the title of the Sanskrit seven-*kanda* (book) narrative whose composition is traditionally attributed to Valmiki. Hindu tradition views the title as composed of 'Rama' and '*ayana*' (going), meaning 'the journey of Rama'. Valmiki's text is the earliest, extant, full, literary telling of the story of Rama and Sita. Most scholars date *Rāmāyaṇa*'s middle five kandas to approximately the last centuries BCE. Pious devotees assume that Valmiki composed the whole text, but philologists argue that a later hand composed the first and last kandas, due to the differing styles and representations of Rama and his enemy, Ravana. More generally, 'The Rāmāyaṇa' is widely used to refer to all tellings of the story.

Valmiki's text contains the core story of Rama and Sita summarized here. To uphold the honour of his father, King Dasaratha, Prince Rama agrees to an exile into the forest accompanied by his wife, Sita and brother, Lakshmana. Shurpanakha, a *rakshasi* (demoness), falls in love with Rama, who spurns her offer of marriage. When she persists, Lakshmana disfigures her, after which she flees to the court of her brother Ravana, king of the rakshasas, and persuades him to desire and abduct Sita, thus revenging his sister's dishonour. Disguised as a mendicant holy man, Ravana approaches Sita and carries her off to his island kingdom of Lanka. Rama allies with the forest dwellers. The court minister of the forest dwellers, Hanuman, discovers and visits the imprisoned Sita in Ravana's palace garden. After building a causeway across the sea, Rama's army attacks Ravana. Valiant warriors on both sides die, and eventually Rama slays Ravana, and Sita is freed. After an ordeal by fire in which Sita proves her purity, the couple returns home, where Rama is crowned and rules wisely. Valmiki's last kanda portrays Rama banishing a pregnant Sita to the forest, where Valmiki shelters here in his ashram while she raises her two sons. This synopsis does scant justice, however, to the diverse ways that this core story has been reinterpreted and transformed over many centuries in India.

Using 'Ramayana' to refer to multiple individual texts leads to confusion since the many individual texts, dramatizations and oral narratives differ from each other in genre, language, region, religious affiliation, usage in humour and proverbs, political comments and contemporizing. Improving on Camille Bulcke's earlier distinction between *ramkatha* (the core story) and 'Ramayaṇa' (i.e. texts that instantiate the story), in 1991, A. K. Ramanujan argued that each rendition should be termed a 'telling' with its own history and social context, rather than viewing Valmiki's work as the original text and later ones as divergent derivatives (1991). The phrase, 'the Ramayana tradition' best describes the capacious diversity of the many tellings and the ways in which the story developed and can be encountered in various genres composed over the centuries on the Indian subcontinent.

Valmiki's *Rāmāyaṇa* is an epic composed in Sanskrit that portrays Rama primarily as a valiant hero in battle and a lawful king. However, many post-Valmiki Hindu renditions of the story are devotional texts in regional literary languages of India. Kamban composed one of the earliest of these bhakti texts, the twelfth-century Tamil *Irāmāvatāram* (The Descent of Rama) which circulated in what today are Tamil Nadu and Kerala. The sixteenth-century Hindi *Rāmcaritmānas* (The Lake of Deeds of Ram) by Tulsidas is widely recited, read and enacted by devotees across northern and central India. This text also provides the basis for *Ram-lila*s (dramas that enact and praise the salvific deeds of Rama) that take place in cities as well as villages across northern and central India.

Furthermore, striking diversity occurs in characterization over time. Many orthodox Hindus see Rama as the best of men while some cultural critics today deem him cruel to women. Some have praised Sita (and others have condemned her) for her unwavering devotion to her husband even after he banished her; others have identified her as a pioneering single parent. Commentators have condemned Shurpanakha for her lack of modesty, while activists against assault on women see her as a victim of male violence. Various scholars have interpreted the narrative illustrating the consequences of adhering to and deviating from dharma and most would agree that the story prompts reflection variously on the nature and rewards of virtuous male and female behaviour, the demeritorious consequences of passions and desires and the legitimacy (or not) of the interconnected hierarchic social and political orders.

An egregious misperception of the Indian Ramayana tradition's diversity is the reductive notion that it consists only of Hindu texts. *Dasaratha Jātaka*, a story of one of the Buddha's previous lives, depicts him as Rama learning of his father's death while in exile and giving a discourse on the impermanence of existence. Prakrit and Kannada poetry include a lineage of Jain tellings in which Lakshmana kills Ravana and Rama becomes a Jain monk. Muslim rulers served as patrons of illustrated renditions of the story, such as the Persian summary-translation under Emperor Akbar. A folksong also circulates among Muslim Mappilas in rural Kerala which portrays Ravana as a sultan and Shurpanakha as a begum. In a different vein, some Tamil atheists (most prominently E. V. Ramasami [1879–1973]) identify Lanka as an ancient Dravidian kingdom and see Ravana as the ancestor of the Tamil people.

Phrases from the Ramayana tradition appear frequently in today's Indian discourse with a humour and relevance distinctive among national epics. In several Indian languages, a simpleton is described as one who listens to the story of Rama and Sita all night and then asks how Sita is related to Rama. The Tamil saying, 'He is an ascetic like Ravana' indicates that a person has taken the disguise of an ascetic for nefarious purposes. The Assamese/Ahomiya proverb, 'That Rama is no more, that Ayodhya is no more', expresses a longing for a past golden age.

Some Hindus idealize the era of Rama's reign as the standard for good Indian governance. In fact, Rama's rule (*Ram rajya*) can be defined from two perspectives. On one hand, it is defined as a time when the king ruled dharmically and his subjects adhered to their *dharma* (codes for conduct prescribed in accord with one's *varna/jati* ['caste'], sex and stage of life), thereby maintaining order and harmony in society. This conservative vision privileges the sociopolitical status quo. On the other hand, during Rama's reign, no social or natural disasters are said to have occurred: children never die before their parents, no one is robbed or murdered and people live long and prosperous lives. Further, disease, poverty, floods and droughts are absent from the kingdom. This utopian lens depicts Rama as actively righting wrongs to ensure that his subjects suffer no poverty, hunger or disease.

The Ramayana tradition has been invoked by people adhering to a range of ideologies. Some used Rama-rajya as an indigenous notion of governance, as opposed to political notions derived from the West: to promote hand-spun, hand-woven, khadi cloth, M. K. Gandhi invoked a Sita who worked at a golden spinning wheel, C. Rajagopalachari urged Indians to treat government ministers with the same respect rendered to Rama and Swami Karpatri preached restoration of Rama's reign in opposition to a secular state. In the late twentieth century, the Bharatiya Janata Party used an image of Rama with his bow drawn to symbolize their campaign to gain control over the Babri Masjid (Ramjanmabhoomi) site.

References

Goldman, Robert P., gen. ed. *The Rāmāyaṇa of Vālmīki: An Epic of Ancient India*, 7 vols, Princeton Library of Asian Translations. Princeton: Princeton University Press, 1984–2017.

Lutgendorf, Philip. *The Life of a Text: Performing the Rāmcaritmānas of Tulsidas*. Berkeley: University of California Press, 1991.

Ramanujan, A. K. 'Three Hundred Rāmāyaṇas: Five Examples and Three Thoughts on Translation'. In *Many Rāmāyaṇas: The Diversity of a Narrative Tradition in South Asia*, edited by Paula Richman, 22–49. Berkeley: University of California Press, and New Delhi: Oxford University Press, 1991.

Richman, Paula., comp. and ed. *Ramayana Stories in Modern South India: An Anthology*. Bloomington: Indiana University Press, 2008.

SATI/JAUHAR (SATĪ/JAUHAR)

Malashri Lal

The originary sources of customary practices such as *sati* and *jauhar* reside in myths and folklore. As an easy differential, one can say that sati is an individual act of self-immolation committed by a Hindu woman who burns herself on the funeral pyre of her husband, whereas jauhar refers to mass self-immolation of women, mainly of the Rajput clan in medieval India, who feared a sexually violent captivity by Muslim victors at war with their kingdom. In both cases, the practice alludes to the dread of widowhood and the conviction that death is preferable for a woman than living without her husband and 'protector'. In this patriarchal practice, women were complicit in the arrangements and even glorified the terms of such self-sacrifice.

Sati has a longer history than jauhar. The word 'sati' comes from the Sanskrit word *sat* (truth) and it is said that the first wife of Shiva, also called Sati, gives the name to this practice. This claim is questionable. Sati is said to have immolated herself in the *yagya* (sacred fire) at her father's home as a protest because her husband Shiva had not been invited to the holy ritual. In frenzied anger, Shiva bore the corpse of Sati on his shoulder and threatened to destroy the universe. He could only be stopped when Vishnu's divine instrument cut Sati's body into 108 parts which fell to the ground in various places, each being turned into a *saktipeeth* temple.

Ancient Hindu scriptures make no reference to sati as a funeral practice. According to the historian Anant Sadashiv Altekar, there is no mention of sati in the period of Brahmana literature (*c.* 1500–700 BCE). The later *Grhya Sutras* (600–300 BCE) describe a number of rituals but not sati. The Mahabharata mentions a few instances of sati, such as Madri, wife of Pandu, while the Ramayana mentions none. According to John Hawley, the first archaeological evidence in the form of sati stones commemorating performance of sati appear around 700 CE. Accounts of sati as a practice start appearing in the tales of thirteenth-fourteenth-century travellers such as Marco Polo and extend to popular accounts such as those of the seventeenth-century merchant Jean-Baptiste Tavernier and physician Francois Bernier, giving leads to the Mughal period. During British times, anecdotal eyewitness accounts narrate pathetic attempts by women to escape the ordeal, the best known among these being the ones narrated by the social reformer Rammohan Roy, who saw his sister-in-law consumed by the flames in 1811, and Fanny Parkes, wife of a British administrator, who reported an episode in Allahabad in 1828.

Bengal and Rajasthan were the prime areas for sati. Largely through the efforts of Rammohan Roy and the social reformers, sati was banned first in Bengal, then in all jurisdictions of British India on 4 December 1829 by Governor General Lord William Bentinck. Despite this, practice seems to have continued covertly into modern times. Roop Kanwar's death on the pyre in Rajasthan in 1987 and the adulation from some quarters propelled debates about woman's volition in committing sati. Taking strong exception to the practice, The Commission of Sati (Prevention) Act, which 'prohibits glorification of this action' in any form, was passed by the Parliament in 1988.

Jauhar is a more localized practice in the history of Rajasthan and is largely related to the period of Turk dominance to which some Ranas (local kings) offered resistance. The origin of the term is shrouded in mystery. According to G. S. L. Devra, the death chamber created for the women was called *yamgraha* (Yama, being the god of death), which subsequently changed to 'Jamaghar' in local dialect and then to 'Jauhar'. Jauhar is also mentioned in Lieutenant Colonel James Todd's *Annals and Antiquities of Rajasthan*, compiled in 1829 from eclectic sources (as the narrative traditions in the state were largely oral or scripted in courtly form). The famous jauhar performed by Rani Padmini of Chittor is told through ballads and heroic tales extolling the act. The recent controversy over Sanjay Leela Bhansali's film depiction of this jauhar in *Padmavat* has stirred discussions on historicity, customary practice and oral traditions. Though local inhabitants show the architectural evidence of jauhar in the chambers of Chittor fort, historians question the existence of Padmini who is said to be the literary creation of Malik Muhammed Jayasi in a poem written in 1540, two hundred years after the purported episode. History shows that Ala-ud-Din Khalji attacked Chittor and other forts in the area in 1303 and the custom of jauhar did exist. Several were committed in Rajasthan, prominent among them being in Ranthambhor in 1301, and in Gagron in 1423, when it was overtaken by Sultan Hoshang Shah of Malwa. In all these instances, women refused to yield to the Muslim marauders and plunged into the fire pit. However, it has to be noted that many such women were not Rajputs. In parallel with jauhar is the saka tradition followed by Rajput men who wore saffron clothes, garlanded each other with tulsi and rode bravely into a battlefield of certain death.

Sati and jauhar are now punishable offences under Indian law, but reverence for the women who committed such acts is still seen at sati temples and in jauharkunds.

References

Sharma, A. *Sati: Historical and Phenomenological Essays*. Delhi: Motilal Banarsidass, 1988.
Sreenivasan, R. *The Many Lives of a Rajput Queen: Heroic Pasts in India, c. 1500–1900*. Washington DC: University of Washington Press, 2007.

SUFI (SŪFĪ)

S. Imtiaz Hasnain and Masood Ali Beg

A *Sufi* is a person with piety and chastity of heart and mind (*ikhlaas* or *mukhlis*), one who is impervious to worldly desires and worldly wealth. According to Adamec, Sufi is 'a member (*nutasawwif*) of one of the Sufi orders, a devotee of a mystical "path" (*tarīqa*') or discipline that consists of graded esoteric teachings leading through a series of initiations to the status of an adept'. The original Sufis were basically mystics – people who followed a pious form of Islam and who believed that a direct, personal experience of God could be achieved through meditation. A Sufi, therefore, is a member of the mystical, ascetic branch of Islam, abstaining from worldly pleasures, living frugally and concentrating all of your energy on spiritual development. Sufism emphasizes personal experience with the divine rather than focussing on the teachings of human religious scholars.

There has been considerable discussion regarding the origin of the Arabic word *suf*, which gave rise to Sufi. First, from the word *ahl al-suffa*, a group of Prophet's companions who took part in the emigration (*hijra*) to Medina. Second, from *saff*, lines where people are standing during a prayer. The first saff in a prayer is an honourable place that will be rewarded by a first place before God in the next world. It is also believed that the Sufis will be rewarded by such an honour, because they are considered God's lovers in this world. Third, *safu* (purity), thereby meaning a person who is pure. A Sufi is so called because this term refers to somebody who purifies his heart by way of long and harsh training. Fourth, from the Greek word *sophos* (wisdom). This designation comes from the fact that a Sufi is known as a person of wisdom (*ahl al-hikma*). Fifth, from the Arabic word *suf* meaning 'wool', which was commonly used to make Sufi robes. These robes were made of coarse wool and have come to symbolize penitence and renunciation of worldly vanities, a main characteristic of Sufism. Sixth, from *Sufah*, the name of a tribe of Arabs who in the 'time of ignorance' separated themselves from the world and engaged themselves exclusively in the service of Makkah Temple. All of these six different opinions have a plausible connection with the Sufi tradition in the course of history.

A discussion on the origin of the term Sufi cannot be separated from the context of the several stages of Sufi development. This can be seen in the term ahl al-suffa, for instance, which bears an early stage of development in Sufism, characterized by their ascetic life (*zuhd*). This ahl al-Suffa, according to Arberry, was the first ascetic community in Islamic history, since *tasawwuf* referred only to Islamic mysticism. Nicholson would rather call them 'quietist' and characterize them as a God-fearing people. In this sense, Jullandri describes them as a society based on justice and a sense of responsibility to God and who mirrored a happy fusion between *shari'a* (Islamic law) and tariqa'. However, they were horrified by a new situation when Mu'awiya, the first caliph of the Umayyad dynasty, came to power. In fact, the Umayyad rulers were aristocratic masters of their subjects. Political murder and bribery were frequently practiced. By then, the ideal of creating a just society, for which the Prophet and his companions had worked, had been completely forgotten. As a result, the ensuing political struggle for power between the Umayyad and the parties of the day, such as the Kharijites and Shi'a, led some people to be despondent and choose for a life of seclusion. They had no courage to fight against the Umayyad rulers and avoided the political drama. Thus, these remaining God-fearing people were among the ascetics (*zuhhad*) who were later called the Sufis. In the later stages of development, the Sufis were identified by their wearing wool garments. It was possible, then, that the word Sufi actually referred to people who wore such garments. From a linguistic point of view, tasawwuf means 'wearing of wool', just as *taqammus* means 'wearing a *qamis*' (a kind of shirt). In line with this view, Arberry mentions that towards the end of the eighth century CE, pious Muslims who remained faithful through all trials and temptations began to form little groups for mutual encouragement and the pursuit of common aims. They took to wearing wool to proclaim their other-worldliness and were therefore popularly referred to as Sufis.

References

Adamec, Ludwig W. *Historical Dictionary of Islam*. Lanham, Toronto, Plymouth: The Scarecrow Press, Inc., 2009.
Arberry, A. J. *Sufism: An Account of the Mystics of Islam*. New York: Routledge, 2008.

ZERO

Iwan Pranoto and Ranjit Nair

That India invented nothing was a familiar colonial trope. In a precise sense, this was true. India did invent nothing in the form of an honest to goodness number – śūnya – that represented the idea of nothing.

In the first millennium, people in both India Intra Gangem and India Extra Gangem knew and used the zero. One of the earliest representations of zero as a number can be seen in Kedukan Bukit inscription (seventh century CE), discovered in Palembang, Sumatra, Indonesia. Written in the southern Indian script Pallava, derived from the Tamil-Brahmi, it shows the zero symbol with exactly the same modern base-10 place value system. Similarly, an inscription on a stele that adorned a seventh century temple in Sambor in Cambodia, where the writing is in ancient Khmer, supports the idea that zero was transmitted from India. In India, the Chaturbhuja temple in Gwalior, dated the mid-ninth century CE, also records the zero. Recently, Marcus du Sautoy and his collaborators have claimed to have pushed back the date of the appearance of zero even further to the third or fourth century CE on the Indian subcontinent by carbon-dating a manuscript discovered in 1881 which is with University of Oxford's Bodleian Libraries. This mss consisted of seventy leaves of birch bark discovered in Bakhshali near Peshawar. Written in the Sarada script, the Sanskrit text has hundreds of zeroes represented by dots.

European scholars, in contrast, came to this number system only after an Italian mathematician, Fibonacci de Pisa (c. 1170–1250), introduced it in the twelfth century. Since then, Western mathematicians and philosophers have been effusive about this foundational Indian contribution. Pierre-Simon Laplace (1749–1827) wrote thus:

> It is India which gave us the ingenious method of expressing all numbers by means of ten symbols, each symbol receiving a value of position as well as an absolute value, a profound and important idea which appears so simple to us now that we ignore its true

merit. But its very simplicity, the great ease which it lent to all computation, puts our arithmetic in the first rank of useful inventions and we appreciate the grandeur of this achievement the more, when we remember that it escaped the genius of Archimedes and Apollonius, two of the greatest men produced by antiquity.

In our own times, we have Laurent Lafforgue, a Fields Medalist, proclaim: 'The invention of zero is the most important in the whole history of mathematics. The bulk of literature on mathematics could not have been written without zero.' This is no exaggeration.

The honours for the gift of zero are not even shared, although often contested. The Sumerians left a blank space, later marked by a couple of parallel wedges, which the successor civilization of the Babylonians took over, but no calculations were enabled thereby, as indeed was the case with the glyph that the Mayan civilization of Central America, circa 345 CE, employed. There were clear indications of the need for a zero, but the mathematical imagination in these two civilizations, widely separated in space and time, did not result in the invention.

It has been suggested that the philosophy of śūnyata was responsible for the evolution of the zero in India. Śūnyavåda or the doctrine of emptiness was advanced by the Mahayana Buddhist school Mādhyamika whose principal exponent was Nāgārjuna. Gautama Buddha's cryptic statement that all is empty – sarvam śūnyam – could simplistically be construed as nihilism or the philosophy of the void, but 'emptiness' for Nāgārjuna referred, rather, to the lack of an absolute essence. Concepts (vikalpa) did not correspond to entities in their own right; they made sense relationally. There could be no better example of this than the number zero, whose value depended on where is it located in the string of symbols that represented a number.

In the mathematical literature that survives, Brahmagupta's treatise Brāhmasphuṭasiddhānta (628 CE) is the earliest surviving work which sets out the properties of zero as a number within a decimal positioning system. Brahmagupta comments on his illustrious predecessor Âryabhata, who used letters rather than numerals in his work. While the work, Âryabhatiyam's understanding of the decimal place value system in which zero figured, is implicit, there are no numeral signs employed.

The Paninian linguistic zero 'lopa', which appears in the monumental Ashtadhyayi, functions as a drop rule. Pingala, regarded as the younger brother of Panini (or his leading commentator, Patanjali), wrote a work on prosody entitled Chhandasastra, which was nimble-footed in its use of the binary system of arithmetic consisting of 0 and 1, which anticipated the digital era by more than two millennia!

The case of the zero exemplifies the powerful role that 'soft power diplomacy' played in the past. Indian and East Asian scholars might take their cue from this in order to shape the knowledge collaborations of the twenty-first century. Yes, India invented nothing and that turned out to be an enormous contribution to world civilization.

References

Joseph, G. G. *The Crest of the Peacock; Non-European Roots of Mathematics*, 3rd edn. Princeton: Princeton University Press, 2010.
Sarvanandin, *Lokavibhāga* 458 CE in *Lok Vibhag* (1962) Ac. 6785, Digital Library of India.

CHAPTER 2
CONTEMPORARY AESTHETIC MODES: REIMAGININGS

ALANKARA (ALAṄKĀRA)

Harsha V. Dehejia

We in India adorn with a passion and a purpose, a dedication and a meaning – whether it is adorning our house or our bodies, our *havelis* or palaces, our shrines or temples. Adornment is to beautify but, even more, it is a metaphor of another reality and equally a visual prayer. At one level, adornment is beautification but, on another, it is a statement of a world view where the beautiful is cherished as a value and as a *purushartha* (object of human pursuit). In our world view, adornment spreads and bestows auspiciousness around it and therefore it is *mangalmaya* (fortunate). By its very presence (*sannidhya*), the adorned object – be it a deity or a woman, the threshold of a home, the palace or a haveli or the *rangamandapa* (main hall) of a temple – makes everything around it resonate with a certain radiance, tremble with energy and exude a joyous affirmation of life.

The first order of adornment (*alankara*) is our speech. The Rig Veda gives exalted speech a pride of place. Beautiful speech is poetry, and the aesthetics of poetry identify two types of *alankara* – *shabdalamkara* or ornamentation through words and *arthalamkara* or ornamentation through meaning. Words, through their sound and texture, rhythm and cadence, add beauty to poetry. Meaning adds a certain depth, and the highest adornment is through what is called *rasa-dhvani* or suggested emotional states and situations.

Adornments are an attribute mainly of *prakriti* (matter), and the woman is the highest representation of prakriti. Traditionally, a nayika adorns herself with sixteen adornments which include *vastra* (clothes), *mahavar* (red dye to the cheeks), *keshbandhan* (coiffure), *pancha angarag* (the five colours to the body), *bhushan* (ornaments), *shauch* (cleansing bath), *pushaphar* (flower garlands), *dantaranjan* (cleaning of teeth), *misi* (fragrant paste for the teeth), *lali* (red colour to the lips) and *bindi* (the mark on the forehead). Understood this way, a woman's adornment is the total beautification of her body which enhances her sensuality and makes her ready for the many pleasures of romantic love. Also, the adornments are drawn from the world around her and this, therefore, establishes a bond between her and nature.

The adornment of a woman, especially when she is romantic, is a rite of love for to adorn is not just to beautify but also to celebrate the sanctity and beauty of love. When she offers her adornment to her beloved, it becomes an act of devotion both to love and to the beloved. Very often, the beloved will complete her adornment by putting a flower in her hair or applying a *tilak* (mark) to her forehead. However, there is another more nuanced meaning to this – when a *nayak* (hīōo) participates in his beloved's adornment and the man and woman come together in this act of adornment, it is a moment of perfection of love, of *purnatva* (fullness). It is the coming together of purusha and prakriti, of one becoming the other.

Adornments are a part of our visual arts as well, thus paintings and sculptures feature ornamentation like decorated pillars or arched spaces, sinuous lines and trees in bloom and ornate *pranay mandapa*s with havelis. Colours are an important part of the grammar of adornment; different colours not only add beauty to the painting but also evoke different emotions. For instance, red is the colour of fertility and yellow is the colour of young love and auspiciousness. We adorn our deities with distinct colours: *ghanashyam* or blue is the colour of Krishna, *neel* or green that of Shiva, white of Saraswati and black of Kali.

Ornaments, or jewellery, both made of gold and precious stones and even of flowers, are an important part of adornment for, both, our gods and humans, where every part of the body from the tresses to the toes is enhanced with a special ornament. The gifting of ornaments to a temple is considered a pious act. Music, both vocal and instrumental, is ornamented with beautiful phrases.

Alankara is an important part of the Indian aesthetic tradition. It answers both to *akanksha* (expectation) and *auchitya* (appropriateness).

References

Dehejia, H. V. and M. R. Paranjape, eds. *Saundarya: The Perception and Practice of Beauty in India.* New Delhi: Samvad India Foundation, 2003.

Dehejia, V. *The Body Adorned: Sacred and Profane in Indian Art.* New York: Columbia University Press, 2009.

BEAUTY PARLOUR

Katyayani Dalmia

Across India's sprawling metropolises, provincial cities and small towns, beauty parlours are spaces of aspiration for clients and beauty workers alike. In varied global contexts, beauty 'salons', 'shops' or 'parlours' are analysed as ambiguously political – as spaces of both reproduction and transformation, perpetuating social norms through ideals of beauty, but also affording possibilities for political change in fostering unique forms of sociality. If in many geographical and cultural milieus, parlours make evident the political possibilities of segregated space – segregations of gender, and sometimes of community, as seen in the American context where racially demarcated spaces were put to productive political use by black men and women in barber/beauty shops – in India, salons are vibrant spaces of both separation and proximity. Single-gender parlours exist along with mixed parlours that bring individuals from diverse caste, religious, gender and class backgrounds into intimate bodily contact unusual in light of the social and corporeal distance observed between them in other spaces of everyday urban life.

From eponymous outlets of national and international beauty brands (Lakme, L'Oreal, Toni and Guy, VLCC, Jawed Habib) to neighbourhood 'Divya' and 'Alice' parlours, the beauty industry in India is booming, employing 3.4 million individuals in 2013 and forecast to absorb 12.1 million workers in 2022, across the organized and informal sectors.[1] Beauty services, such as facials and bleaches for 'fair' and 'bright' complexions, waxing, hair straightening and setting and bridal and party make-up, materialize associations between appearance and social status. Yet, parlours encapsulate desires for social acceptance and mobility not simply for customers but also for beauty workers, offering entry into modern, professional and even corporate worlds for those without access to educational degrees, in a country where urban mobility is usually premised on these.

Demographically, individuals from across the caste and religious gamut work in parlours, ranging from members of 'upper castes' to those who are associated with handling hair, nails and the bodily 'dirt' of pedicures and facials in conventional caste schemes, for instance, in North India, Hajjam/Salmani among Muslim and Nau-Thakur among Hindu barber castes.[2] Parlours, as well as their more upscale kin in big cities – spas – are popularly imagined as emblems of modern life. Yet they retain the unstated connection between work and caste identity, as evident in the prevalence of stereotypes that it is 'lower' or Dalit castes who tend to take up parlour work and in jokes that spa/parlour beauticians and hairdressers encounter about working in a *nai-ki-dukaan* (barber shop). As such, parlours capture some of the key contradictions that make up urban Indian life.

References

Ahmed, S. M. Faizan. "Making Beautiful: Male Workers in Beauty Parlors." *Men and Masculinities* 9, no. 2 (2006): 162–85.

Zande, Archana. "Nhavi Women in Pune City: Renegotiating New Opportunities for Livelihood," in *Land, Lasons and Livelihoods: Indian Women's Perspectives,* edited by Bina Fernandez, et al. Palgrave Macmillan, 2016.

BHARATNATYAM (BHARATANĀṬYAM)

Leela Samson

Bharatnatyam generally refers to a dance art practiced by a community of women called *devadasis* (literally, 'in the service of the Lord'), who performed in the temples of South India during the Chola dynasty in the eleventh and twelfth centuries. This dance, practiced inside the temple precinct, then referred to as *sadir*, was ritualistic in nature. It was considered auspicious for a dancer to perform before the deity every day, on all festive occasions and during religious processions, as part of her duties. The word *sadir* means 'beauty'; it also refers to dance that was

---

[1] Source: KPMG report on 'Beauty and Wellness for India', cited in Verma, Tarishi (2017).
[2] North Indian language terms for barber castes sourced from the author's field work in Lucknow (2014–15) as well as from Ahmed 2006 for Bihar and Delhi (see references) and Nadeem Hasnain's *The Other Lucknow* for UP (2016, Vani Prakashan).

performed in the courts of kings. However, the custodians of this dance form, barring a few, did not call their art *sadir*. Dr B. M. Sundaram, a scholar, writer and raconteur on music and dance, makes a case for the fact that the term 'Bharatnatyam' existed from the twelfth century and extensively quoted from different writers and composers over the centuries to prove this.

Much earlier though, in the Sangam period of Tamilakam – spanning from the third century BCE to the third century CE – a literary work called the *Akananuru* mentions a dancer who performs, accompanied by a *nattuvanar* who plays the cymbals and a mridangist who plays the drum standing behind the dancer. At this period, it was perhaps called *nadanam – nadai-an-am* – which, in Tamil, means 'stylistic dance'.

Today, dancers and scholars attribute the change of reference to this dance art from sadir to bharatnatyam to E. Krishna Iyer and to Rukmini Devi, both social reformists who rallied for an end to the 'exclusivity' that the dance afforded one community. The name bharatnatyam existed much earlier and 'renaming' it was not on their initiative. However, in 1977, Rukmini Devi did say, 'So far as I know, I was the first person, when I began to dance in the early 1930s to give the (new) name to the dance and since then the word Bharatanātyam has become acceptable.' The truth is that her first public performance, which happened in January 1935, was called 'bharatnatyam'. Rukmini Devi's extreme commitment to the art brought in radical change. The learning of dance by girls from all strata of society soon became a reality. She created pedagogy for teaching and upholding the highest standards in the dance. This was momentous and came at an appropriate moment in history causing all manner of change to be attributed to her, sometimes falsely. She simply used the term bharatnatyam to describe the form because it had now been taken out of the context of the temple. Dr V. Raghavan also used the word bharatnatyam for the first time in 1933, in an article captioned 'Bharatanātyam Classical Dance – The South Indian Nautch'.

Bharatnatyam has been variously described as a synonym for *bhāva* (emotion), *raga* (melodic framework) and *tala* (rhythm) as represented in the splitting of the word 'bharata' into 'bha', 'ra' and 'ta'. This seems to be a romantic idea and one of convenience rather than of reality. Most others attribute the name to Bharatamuni, the sage Bharata, who is the author of the bible on Indian dramaturgy – the *Natyashastra*. This too is unfounded. It is questionable whether Bharata refers to one man or to several like him, possibly his disciples, who wrote this voluminous treatise over what seems like several decades. Others simply understand the term to be a reference to India, also referred to as 'Bharat', thereby meaning 'the dance of India'. However, there are so many other dance forms – classical, theatrical, folk, tribal, martial, ritualistic and ceremonial; are they not all Indian? All three of the above interpretations seem to be simplistic justifications. The names given to our dance forms evolved over time and were consciously given. These terms for the forms of dance they represent are secular and inclusive; they do not beg classification or eternity. Like all spoken language or languages of communication like dance, they change over time. Tradition is that which transits the passage of time.

References

Rukmini Devi. 'The Spiritual Background of Bharata Natyam'. In *Classical and Folk Dances of India*. Bombay: Marg Publications, 1963.

Vatsyayan, Kapila. *Bharata, the Nāṭyaśāstra*. New Delhi: Sahitya Akademi, 1996.

BHOOT (BHŪTA)

Brahma Prakash

The term *bhoot* is familiar to almost every child in contemporary India, an intrinsic part of India's folklore and its life-worlds. Although, it refers nowadays to 'ghost' in popular usage, this was not always the case. The word also stands for 'spirit', 'free elements' and for the 'primordial forces'. In the broader cultural context of primitive and indigenous societies, the bhoot is used for being and the existence of life, its very make-up. It finds expression both in old Vedic texts and in the popular beliefs of the common people. While in the *shastra* (textual) traditions, it stands for certain quality of being, for the common people it manifests through figures and figurations and has a changeable usage, often depending on region, culture, class and caste hierarchies. In 'Bhootaradhne' ritual of Karnataka, the communities worship the spirits of heroic men and women, who have sacrificed their lives for the community. In this regard, H. S. Shivaprakash observes that 'the deities considered benevolent by lower castes and tribal communities are identified as demons by upper caste Hindus'. In the case of another Southern community, the Tulu, these spirits are regarded as god. While there is a lot of worship around bhoot and *bhutakhela* (play of the spirits) in North India as well, they are primarily worshipped in these diverse manifestations by only subaltern communities.

Terms related to the idea of the bhoot include ojha and bhagat. These terms are used to refer to the person commonly referred to in the west as the 'shaman'. The ojha and bhagat are ritual priests and are also often play the roles of 'mediums' or the people who communicate between the deity and the worshippers and between ghosts or spirits and the people disturbed by them or who want to speak to them. Though ojha and bhagat perhaps had a more prominent role to play in the social, cultural and political structures of indigenous societies in the past, their influence is hardly to be discounted in many pockets of twenty-first-century India. For instance, they primarily work as healers in rural areas and prepare medicines from herbs locally available and at times perform rituals. Additionally, they also offer pronouncements of justice, and advice, at various levels. This is because of an entrenched belief in many cultures across the subcontinent that good and bad fortune in everyday life is caused by spirit forces. They are looked up to for suggestions on ways to come out of social or personal crises, and their role is often underestimated. In fact, it may well rival that of the better-known 'gurus', 'god-men' and spiritual leaders who are so commonly associated with 'Indian thought' across the world.

References

Ishii, Miho. 'Wild Sacredness and the Poiesis of Transactional Networks: Relational Divinity and Spirit Possession in the Būta Ritual of South India'. *Asian Ethnology* 74, no. 1 (2015): 101–2.

Shivaprakash, H. S. *Incredible India: Traditional Theatres*. New Delhi: Wisdom Books, 2007.

BOLLYWOOD

Ravi Vasudevan

In the early 2000s, a number of public figures including cricket icon Sunil Gavaskar, movie *mogul* Subhash Ghai and film star Shah Rukh Khan expressed irritation that Mumbai's film industry was being referred to as Bollywood. Their irritation stemmed, it seems, from the implication that Hindi cinema was an imitation of the American behemoth. Mumbai was not the only one involved in this imprecation. Suddenly, Hollywood variants proliferated in South Asia. For instance, Kollywood for Tamil Nadu's Kodambakkam-based cinema and, perhaps, more facetiously, Lollywood for Lahore's film output.

Nationalist anxieties have abated since; there are no longer any strident refutations. We may now step back and note certain transformations associated with the new name. Bollywood, as a term, probably dates back to the mid-1990s. Scholarship has argued that its timing converges with that of India's globalization, following from the liberalizing initiatives of the early 1990s. The Indian film industry was always known for its informal, non-accountable and sometimes outright criminal networks of finance. Now, in line with economic liberalization, the growing call was to create 'transparent' corporate practices. For the first time, long-standing demands by the film trade – for the government to recognize it as industry and, thus, make it eligible for loans from nationalized banks – were granted in 1998.

By the early 2000s, the Federation of Indian Chambers of Commerce and Industry (FICCI) developed a film cell and supported an annual business entertainment conference called FRAMES (Film Radio Audio-Visual Music Events Shows) to monitor and help develop the entertainment industry. In a new consumer economy which involved malls, urban gentrification, satellite broadcasting and the incipient pleasures of the internet (Web 2.0 was yet to come), the cinema provided a key cultural resource. The mall-multiplex, in particular, came to be a key feature in the refiguring of the urban, with cinema as one of the attractions to draw the consumer into a globalizing economy. So-called Bollywood cinema would also be crucially transnational in its bid for audiences, involving diaspora populations, but also trying for a crossover appeal. By the early 2000s, foreign returns were regularly calculated, especially from markets in the UK, the United States, Europe and Australia. Today, industry watchers tend to be all-inclusive, with a special interest in China and the Middle East as significant territories.

As the FRAMES conference indicates, cinema is now part of an extended commodity network involving different media – from music and internet sites to television content and ringtones – many points of exhibition and systems of distribution and delivery – from cinema theatres to satellite premiere to video on demand, internet downloads and mobile devices. Bollywood, as a contemporary media constellation, is in this sense defined by media convergence and proliferation, tipping over into other industries, notably music and fashion. The transnational terms of these innovations are not all one-way – India presenting market and outsourcing opportunities for major Hollywood production houses. Thus, Reliance Entertainment has not only provided Hollywood with digital resources for special effects in its studios in a Navi Mumbai Special Economic Zone but has also acquired Hollywood property as a major stakeholder in Steven Spielberg's Dreamworks.

A key discourse in the fallout of such corporatization is the claim that the film business would now be more transparent in its financial practices, supplanting earlier kinship, social and financial networks. However, corporate transparency has never quite won through, if it does anywhere, and informal arrangements and payments continue to define the film industry.

Film historians were the foremost sceptics in challenging the new nomenclature. Some observed that both media industry and shoddy scholarship were now reading Bollywood back into the very origins of Indian cinema, for example, by referring to pioneer D. G. Phalke's mythological films in the 1910s or the Indo-German *Light of Asia/Prem Sanyas* (Franz Osten, 1925) as Bollywood films. If such anachronism deserves withering put down, a second critique of the term and its limits is less persuasive. Focused on contemporary transformation, the critics argue that while some companies and even a certain aesthetic and narrative ideology are part of contemporary Bollywood as a force of transmedia globalization and nationalist hegemony, others are not. The reference to the new normal was the high-end diaspora themed films such as *Dilwale Dulhania Le Jayenge* (Brave of Heart Wins the Bride – Aditya Chopra, 1995), *Pardes* (Foreign Land – Subhash Ghai, 1997), *Kuch Kuch Hota Hai* (Something Is Happening – Karan Johar, 1998) and *Kal Ho Na Ho* (Whether Or Not There's a Tomorrow – Nikhil Advani, 2004). Critics assumed that such a repertoire meant that Bollywood primarily drew on the family social film to address the Indian diaspora and indeed to mobilize diaspora investment. In this rendering, Bollywood, as cinema, was anything which deployed codes of melodramatic storytelling centred on the family addressing the global nation and deploying spectacular song/dance sequences; anything else lay outside Bollywood.

In fact, such views were echoed in the industry. For example, a significant figure of the early 2000s, Ram Gopal Varma, a maker of edgy films in a variety of genres – road movie, gangster film, horror – would position himself as an antagonist of the sentimental family socials of Karan Johar. However, Varma himself struck deals with 20th Century Fox, was financed by Singapore-based NRI corporate firm, K Sera Sera, and made a bid for the US market through Cinemaya Media. If we understand Bollywood to mean a new, transmedia business form interfacing with global flows of capital, then Varma was not outside Bollywood.

It is impossible to understand contemporary cinema without the multiplex and the idea of the multiplex film. Along with blockbuster movies, multiplex theatres would also feature more modestly scaled films catering to a niche audience. This has meant that, as cinema, contemporary Bollywood is composed of a rich field of practices and, to use industrial parlance, the phenomenon of product differentiation. Even Yash Raj and Dharma studios diversified beyond the family social into action, comedy and even films with an indie feel. Thus, Yash Raj would produce films such as the urban dystopian thriller, *Titli* (Butterfly – Vikas Behal, 2014), the mode retro of *Detective Byomkesh Bakshi* (Dibakar Banerjee, 2015) and distribute films such as the very fine Macbeth adaptation, *Maqbool* (Vishal Bharadwaj, 2004), and the quirky road movie, *Piku* (Shoojit Sircar, 2015). Karan Johar's Dharma Productions pulled off a careful character study by Irrfan Khan in *The Lunchbox* (Ritesh Batra, 2014), a modest international success at film festivals and in the art house circuit. The financial position is perhaps best captured in the way the irreverent Anurag Kashyap *(Dev D, 2009; The Gangs of Wasseypur, 2012; Raman Raghav 2.0, 2016; Mukkabaaz, 2018)* draws on the new Bollywood economy, perhaps, most dramatically, with Reliance Entertainment buying up 50 per cent stake in Phantom Films – the company started by independent-minded film-makers Anurag Kashyap, Vikramaditya Motwane, Vikas Behal and Madhu Mantena. None of this invalidates the innovation and creativity of these film-makers, but, perhaps, we should note that however recent and abused a term Bollywood is, it is composed of a complex range of practices along with the bid to produce India as a 'brand equity'.

References

Govil, Nitin. *Orienting Hollywood: A Century of Film Culture between Los Angeles and Bombay*. New York: New York University Press, 2015.

Rajadhyaksha, Ashish. 'The "Bollywoodization" of Indian Cinema: Cultural Nationalism in a Global Arena'. *Inter-Asian Cultural Studies* 4, no. 1 (2003).

FOTO (PHŌṬŌ)

B. N. Goswamy

Who, from among the millions who use the term, cares – one is entitled to wonder – where the word comes from or for the fact that photography is, as the dictionary says, 'the process or art of producing pictures by means of the chemical action of light on a sensitive film on a basis of paper, glass, metal etc.'? For the common person here, the *aam aadmi* in other words, a 'foto' is a 'foto' – in routine usage, simply a picture, a likeness, a facsimile – nothing more nor less. The ease with which the term – as a version of the original word 'photo', which in turn descends of course from 'photograph' – has entered every person's vocabulary is truly astonishing. Less than two hundred years ago, the word did not even exist in India and now everyone uses it as if it has been part of their language since *srishti* (creation) began. One knows that elsewhere, as in England for instance, the word 'photo' was used, from quite early on, as a colloquial abbreviation of 'photograph'. However, here, with us, it is different, for it has come to stand for *any* picture or likeness at all, the virtual equivalent of *taswir* (the Persian as also the Urdu word that serves to describe 'painting, limning; a picture, image, effigy, likeness, sketch, drawing').

Consider the range of uses; when someone here says, 'I bought a large phōṭō of Guru Nanak today', it almost certainly means he or she bought a print, some oleograph, a 'calendar-picture', for hanging in his or her home or placing it in the family 'worship room'. It does not even cross his or her mind that no photograph of the Guru Nanak – a great guru belonging to the sixteenth century – could possibly have existed, ever. Similarly, when children in the village used to gather around a 'byscope', peering at images with eyes glued to large glazed holes, the vendor – of what in Germany used to be called *guckkasten* – kept belting out information for the benefit of his young 'customers', that they were looking now at the foto of a *baaraman kidhoban* – buxom laundress who weighs nothing short of twelve maunds (which equals 400 kilograms) – now of the *shehar* (city) of London, regardless of whether the objects he was showing were coloured lithographs or faded engravings. It was a show of fotos.

It is a bit unsettling, perhaps, the universal use of this word overriding, subverting, mocking, all other words for any kind of likeness, but it is here to stay. Tamilians use it with as much ease, or thoughtlessness, as Gujaratis do; you hear it from Assam to Punjab, Kashmir to Jharkhand. Anything drawn, painted, limned, that even remotely suggests a likeness, or an imagined likeness, is now a foto. A friend used to be very fond of a quietly romantic Urdu couplet and would often recite it – *Dilke aaeeney mein hai taswir-iyaar/jab zaraa garden jhukaai, dekh li* (The image of my beloved is there, shining in the mirror of my heart/Any time that I long to gaze at it, I just have to bend my neck). He was, I know, quite upset when a poetaster ruined it for him when he used the same thought for a cheeky song in a recent film. In a sequence, a skimpily dressed dancer sang it, to the accompaniment of lewd movements and the sound of wolf-whistles – *Meri phōṭō ko seeney se yaar/ chipka ley saiyyan* Fevicol *sey* ('Come, my lover, hasten! Take my phōṭō and paste it on your chest with Fevicol', where the last mentioned is a popular adhesive paste). It is all there in this word – the looseness of understanding, layering, anachronism and even adhesion.

References

Goswamy, B. N. *Essence of Indian Art*. San Francisco: Mapin Pub., 1986.
Jain, Nishtha. *City of Photos* [Motion Picture]. India: Raintree Films, 2004.

GANA (GĀNĀ)

Antony Arul Valan

Today, Tamil *gana/paattu* (song) rings loud and clear beyond its historical confines. It is an art form that is breaking the monolithic view that the culture of Chennai is its 'classical' traditions. Along with *thappaattam* and *parayattam*, gana is being recognized as an art form that is an important constituent of the Tamil cultural landscape. But what is gana?

Chennai-based playwright, Thomas Manuel, says gana is 'a collection of rhythms, beats and sensibilities native to the dalits of Chennai'. S. Anand calls it 'a rap-like musical idiom of the Dalits in Chennai' and explains how the form has 'moved from the slums and burial grounds where the genre was spawned to cinema, commercial gigs and recorded tapes. From an instant improvisational form, the genre has become a distinct marketable commodity.' A. Mangai calls them 'the more urban version of Dalit music' and states that they are from, what is known as, the 'Black Town of Chennai' (*karuppar nagaram*).

Academic research has traced the evolution of the art form to the songs of the *siddhar*s of ancient Tamilakam and then, more recently, to the Tamil Muslim mystic Gunankudi Masthan Sahib – whose compositions in the early nineteenth century are still sung by gana singers today – and Samuel Vedanayagam Pillai, popularly known as the first Tamil novelist. However, in the words of V. Ramakrishnan, '[gana] reached Chennai through migrants who came in search of work'; he concedes, despite this, that it is difficult to explain its origins.

Gana singers have sung in Chennai for at least two centuries, with their voices muffled by the politics of nation-building that could only accommodate the songs of the affluent sections of the city. With the advent of recording devices, a few gana singers made the effort to tape their compositions and record it for posterity. When these were heard outside of the slums, a few Tamil film-makers in the early 1990s took gana to the silver screen, which eventually led to its adoption in college campuses. At least one report in the early 2000s rues the loss of the 'angst and melancholy' that characterized the genre, as the shift to college campuses involved, primarily, 'themes of fun and romance'. Soon, in the movement from small pockets of the city to the screen and campuses, the genre came to be known as a repertoire that reeks of misogyny and sexual innuendos.

According to a popular exponent of the art form, 'Marana Gana' Viji – who makes it clear that he does not prefer to sing sexually explicit songs and those that demean women – 'gānā is not a music form that tries to infuse self-confidence ... It stems out of pain ... It is not a form that can be learnt, like carnatic ... It is a form that is about living and experiencing our life.' He lists five types of gana: *attu gana* – when the singer takes a tune from a popular film song and adds his or her own lyrics to it and sings it; *all gana* – when the tune, beats and lyrics are all composed by the singer; *jigil gana* – when the lyrics are centred around intoxication and intoxicants; *deepa gana* – when the song and tune have been composed by singers of yore (these ballads at times run for several hours); and *marana gana* – when the song is about the philosophy of death (it could be handed down from the past or composed by the singer).

The year 2016 marked the formation of the South Indian Gana Singers Association. And 2018 has brought a new form of life to the genre with the establishment of 'Casteless Collective', a first-of-a-kind band of gana artists who have been brought together by the Ambedkarite film-maker, Pa Ranjith. Their debut performance on 6 January 2018 was attended by over four thousand people, and it 'created ripples on the internet'. The band performs compositions against caste discrimination, raps on Ambedkar's life and gushes about the 'small joys' that living poor in Chennai affords them. In fact, there is also a lesbian gana in the repertoire of the Casteless Collective. (This should be seen in the context of a singer in a 'classical' genre being relegated to the margins by the powers, because of her sexuality.) Though the Collective clearly states that this is an attempt at political mobilization around the art form, the impact this assertion will have on the perception of the cultural fabric of the city and indeed the state and its people is heartening.

References

Govindarajan, Vinita. 'The Casteless Collective: A Music Band's Debut Has Caught the Attention of Chennai and the Internet'. *Scroll.in*, 11 January 2018.
Hindu Tamil. The '"Danga Maari" Marana Gana Viji Interview Part 01'. Available at: https://www.youtube.com/watch?v=M8UgeIiJiqg (accessed 1 June 2018).

GORAPAN (GŌRĀPAN)

Katyayani Dalmia

Gorapan – a light skin tone – is a highly coveted aspect of appearance in South Asia. In many languages of the subcontinent, one simply has to say 'good', 'clear' or 'clean' colour to indicate fair skin – *nalla niram* in Tamil and Malayalam, *accha* or *saaf rang* in Urdu and Hindi, *rong porishkar* in Bengali. Apart from the ubiquitous mention that it finds in matrimonial classifieds, the most obvious indication of the social obsession with complexion is demonstrated by the flourishing use of skin-lightening creams by women and men alike, in a context where beauty, as well as 'smartness' of appearance, is imaginatively linked to light skin. While the first fairness cream in India, Afghan Snow, made its appearance a century ago – in 1919 – currently, the most widely used brand is Hindustan Unilever's Fair and Lovely, launched in

1975 and accounting for 34.7 per cent of India's entire skin-care market in 2014. Whiteners and lighteners comprised almost half the value of the Indian facial-care market in 2014 (30 billion out of 66 billion rupees or 454.55 million out of 1 billion dollars), with the latter expected to grow to a 130 billion rupee (1.96 billion dollar) market by 2019.[1]

In the first attempt to define 'colourism', African-American feminist, Alice Walker, describes it as the 'prejudicial or preferential treatment of *same-race people* based solely on their color' (emphasis added, Walker, 1983). As such, colourism is distinct from racism in that it is a mode of discrimination that is seen as operating as much *within*, as *between*, races or communities. In the Indian context, skin colour has a complex relationship with community categories; late-nineteenth and early-twentieth-century colonial anthropology read caste as a form of race, understanding 'superior' physical features such as a 'finer' nose and a lighter complexion as corresponding to 'higher' caste positions (Dirks, 2001). Indian sociology, subsequently, debunked this position, with G. S. Ghurye observing in the 1930s that 'the physical type of the population is mixed, and does not conform in its gradation to the scale of social precedence of the various castes' (Ghurye, 2004). More recently, Dalit activists have argued for conceiving casteism as akin to racism but on grounds very different from colonial census commissioners and ethnographers; the focus of the comparison is no longer external bodily features but an analysis of both racism and casteism as oppression based on descent (see Reddy 2005).

Beyond statistics on commodities and the century-long caste/race debate, the complex meanings and significance of skin colour in Indian social life is illustrated by the ways in which it is discussed within everyday contexts of family, friendship and work, in its subtle use in sizing up strangers as well as its importance in assessments of loved ones and the self – in how it is evoked in jokes, banter and abuse alike and its centrality in the most serious of all businesses: marriage. If the consequences of dark skin are particularly deleterious for women, affecting their marital prospects much more than men, they are common across genders in terms of associations between skin tone and status. Stereotypical connections between skin colour and caste identity burst forth in everyday interactions. It is as common for a fair-skinned Dalit to be greeted with surprise on her skin colour ('you don't look like an SC!') as it is for a dark-skinned Brahmin to be told that she looks '*chamar*-type' (like a chamar – an 'untouchable' caste, associated with leather work in North India). A common adage in Uttar Pradesh expresses this idea – *Kariya brahman aur gor* chamar, *inse sada rehna hoshiyar* (this translates: A dark-skinned Brahmin and a fair chamar, never trust either), expressing the concern that in each of these cases, there is an incongruity between caste and colour that renders the individual suspect.

Associations between colour and caste, however, are flexible; in urban contexts where caste identities are less publicly known, individuals use skin colour – in combination with other aspects of appearance such as manners, speech, dress and diet – to try and guess each others' 'background'. Yet, at the same time, as they employ the upper caste/fair skin, lower caste/dark skin stereotype in these mundane practices of guesswork, people also readily offer examples of Brahmins 'dark as the bottom of an iron cooking plate' or Dalits 'fair as milk'. Gorapan, then, is a mobile category, in three senses of the term – first, in how it is associated with groups;

---

[1] All figures are from Deshpande and Chaturvedi (2017) (see references).

second, in how it is understood to be inherited or acquired; and third, in the course of an individual's life. Fair skin connotes status in terms of class, caste and sometimes religion – for instance, Shia Muslims in the Awadh area and upper- or middle-class Muslims, more broadly, are imagined as fair. Regional variations are significant and in some cases, certain elite castes – for example, *Kayasths* in Uttar Pradesh – are also stereotyped as dark-skinned. Skin tone is understood to be inherited genetically but in popular emic theories, its inheritance is also seen as affected by the diet of the mother during pregnancy and the season in which a child is born. Lastly, a rich and dynamic language around skin tone – colour 'opens', meaning that a person has become lighter and 'brighter'; colour is 'suppressed' or 'lost', meaning that a person has become darker – attests to a mobile conceptualization of complexion. This understanding of colour, however, is also asymmetrical in so far as dark skin – that is, skin that is darker than the in-between shades of 'dusky' and 'wheatish' – is seen as more fixed than skin, which is fair or *gora*.

References

Deshpande, Rohit and Saloni Chaturvedi, 'Fair & Lovely vs. Dark Is Beautiful'. *Harvard Business School Case 516-079*, March 2016. Revised March 2017.
Dirks, Nicholas. *Castes of Mind*. Princeton: Princeton University Press, 2001.
Ghurye, G. S. *Caste and Race in India*. Mumbai: Popular Prakashan, 2004.
Reddy, Deepa. 'The Ethnicity of Caste', *Anthropological Quarterly*, 78, no. 3 (2005): 543–84.
Walker, Alice. "If the Present Looks Like the Past, What does the Future Look Like?" in *In search of our Mothers' Gardens*, 290–312. San Diego: Harcourt Brace, 1983.

GYM

Santosh Desai

Like its cousin, the beauty parlour, the gym is now an ubiquitous part of the urban landscape. In towns, big and small, well-equipped gyms dot the landscape. Staffed by people of robust musculature and lithe frames, the gym is a little piece of urban infrastructure that gathers a very particular set of people in its fold. The young and fit, who want to push their body to higher level of performances; the unfit, across the age spectrum, who see it is as a place of possible redemption; the marriage hopefuls, who wish to whip their frames into some approximation of svelteness before their big day; the reluctant, going through the motions, there because of unwise resolutions and persistent relatives; the addicted, who treat exercise as a fix they must have, all different varieties, congregate to the new temple of the body – the gym.

After all, the body is, in many ways, experienced as the primary site of change today. Viewed increasingly as a defining asset of the self, the body becomes an object to be cherished and developed. The idea that one's physical self is mutable, and, that too, in ways that are under one's direct control, has been gaining ground. The shaping, sculpting, building, adorning and grooming of the body has become a profitable and growing industry that cuts across age and gender differences. The gym is the foundational site of this movement, a place where the manufactured body comes into being and, literally, takes shape. The new grows out of the old, a harder overlay of sinewed muscle.

The gym, as a place, becomes a new kind of meeting ground. Amidst grunts of effort and panting exertions, a community is born. The idea of physical fitness includes elements of health and beauty, of getting the body fit and 'in shape'. The idea of 'working out' imagines labour in a new way – one that is both purposive and self-directed. The output of this labour is enhanced input to the self. There is a grim sense of determination in the users of a gym, a sense of having to overcome obstacles in order to reach the goal one has set for oneself. One's body becomes an opponent, to be taught discipline and be beaten into shape.

The gym varies dramatically from its country cousin, the *akhara*, where the wrestling arena is a mud pit, the wrestlers wear rudimentary slabs of cloth and live in a world of oil massages and ghee. The rules that surround wrestling are hierarchical and austere. There is a moral pursuit inherent in the act of training at an akhara, one that fears the sapping effects of modernity. The gym, on the other hand, lives in an entirely different cultural universe of sophisticated machines and specialized equipment, of gear, protein shakes and personal trainers. If the akhara's main concerns are with the retention of an uncontaminated form of masculinity, the gym is part of the modern market discourse where the body is prepared as a site that consumes as well as offers itself for consumption. The idea of 'fitness' captures the desire to 'fit' and align with the external context, physical and otherwise. The body becomes equipped to be deployed in ways that are necessary through the act of frequenting a gym.

The gym of today has come a long way from its roots. The gymnasium, in its earlier avatar, fulfilled a similar purpose but in a very different way. There was an air of industrial purpose in these warehouses of the physical. Only those needing to bolster their physical selves for some purpose frequented the gym; the gym was a specialized space for people like athletes, bodybuilders and soldiers. Today, the world of the gym is one of air-conditioned sleekness, where men and women go as part of a lifestyle, and 'going gymming' is a routine, everyday event.

References

Alter, J. S. *Moral Materialism: Sex and Masculinity in Modern India*. London: Penguin Books, 2011.
Alter, J. S. *The Wrestler's Body: Identity and Ideology in North India*. Oakland: University of California Press, 1992.

HERO/HEROINE

Irwin Allan Sealy

The word 'hero' is used to denote someone who is a 'protector, defender, one who safeguards'. It is derived from the Proto-Indo-European word *ser-* (which means, 'to watch over, to protect'). The Indic equivalents of the term are *veer* and *surma*, both of which may carry the defensive sense of 'hero' as well as valour in warfare (i.e. an offensive sense as well).

The word could also simply denote the protagonist of a literary work or other artefact (*nayak*). In this context, the word could connote strength, as in the case of Ram who draws the bow when no other can; or majesty, as in the case of Akbar who rules a greater empire than any; and bravery, which extends even to a commoner who risks his or her life to save his or her country or a defenceless child. Of course, physical prowess alone will not do – Ram is strength and serenity; also implied is maturity – the boy Krishna must outgrow his prankishness and mischief. In Indic literatures, therefore, a hero may be deified, but a god may not be reduced to a 'hiroo'; a villain may have heroic qualities, but she or he would misuse them.

The word hero can also be used to denote an icon. In this sense, it primarily confines itself to the filmic world, denoting the protagonist and connoting brawn (e.g. Salman Khan), though puckish good looks (e.g. Shah Rukh Khan) can outclass muscle. Youth is essential, but gravitas, a greying Amitabh Bachchan, for instance, will do. At the same time, one blessed with a comic sense and immaculate timing can be 'Hero No. 1' – Govinda, whose swart, chubby face can meet any challenge from the above roster and make later hatchet-faced men look ashen and polar and un-Indian; equally possibly, a villain might steal the show, as did Sanjay Dutt in the film *Khalnayak*.

The word hero could also be used to refer to a sturdy thing. For instance, a bestselling bicycle, a popular motorcycle, a stalwart scooter – the Chetak, riding on its association with the hero Rana Pratap's heroic horse (see story 'Chetak Ki Virta'). A simple banyan or singlet cut to show muscle, advertised by a brawny film star, such as Salman Khan, can stretch to meet the word hero. There is also sometimes added a cautionary sense to the word hero. For instance, when the common utterance, *'Hero mat ban'* ('Do not try to be a hero'), reveals a depth of irony not ordinarily associated with the Indic mind.

If we turn to the feminine form of the word, 'heroine', we notice that it is not frequently used in parlance. It has not penetrated the lexicon to the same degree as the word hero has. However, it has found considerable use in the film world. Prominent historical queens from the subcontinent, such as Razia Sultana or Jodhabai, may be described as 'heroines' for their celluloid depiction but not for their historical value as icons of power or capability, for which purpose a local language equivalent would be pressed into use. Among politicians, J. Jayalalithaa from the state of Tamil Nadu might qualify on the grounds of her past in the film industry; otherwise, even an astute practitioner such as Indira Gandhi would require a descriptive term rather than the term heroine. A commoner, such as the anti-AFSPA activist Irom Sharmila, who displays resolution and iron will might be described as a heroine. Virtue, by itself, would not merit inclusion, and godliness would immediately disqualify the applicant; thus, even if Sita were viewed in her role as a protagonist in an epic drama, the word heroine would not apply (except in say a Ramlila performance). This is because usage of the term can seem faintly sacrilegious.

References

Kumari, N. Vijaya and D. Shanmugam. 'Postcolonial Politics in Irwin Allan Sealy's Hero: A Fable'. *Notions* 7, no. 4 (2016).
Sealy, I. A. *Hero: A Fable*. New York: Viking Press, 1990.

ISHQ/PYAR (IŚQ/PYĀR)

Shivangini Tandon

The terms *ishq* and *pyar* can both be translated into English as 'love', though they have their distinct trajectories of historical development. The terms have both secular and sacred connotations describing feelings of attachment, eroticism, romance and emotional desire, among others, between lover and the beloved – *pir* and *murid* and the creator and the created. Scholars like Francesca Orsini have tried to map the history of love in South Asia where it can be defined both in terms of affect and sociality. The intention here is to make the point that both ishq and pyar originated in very different sociocultural, literary and philosophical settings. Therefore, there is a need to highlight the plurality of these idioms of love which get manifested in the Indian literary discourse (through poetry, prose, drama, etc.) and have multiple synonyms in the Indian vernacular tradition – *prem, srngara,* ishq, *kāma, sneha, mohabbat* and so on. The main characteristic feature that distinguishes the notion of pyar and iśq from each other is the following: while the former describes any form of attachment in relationships without necessarily being erotic, the latter is marked by its intensity and eroticism.

Iśq is an Arabic word meaning love or passion, also widely used in other languages of the Muslim world. Traditional Persian lexicographers considered the Persian *esq* and Arabic *isq* to derive from the Arabic verbal root *asaq* – 'to stick, to cleave to'. They connected the origin of the root to *asaqa* – a kind of ivy, because it twines around and cleaves to trees. Iśq developed a unique literary tradition and entered South Asia in the eleventh century with the Ghaznavids. In its most common classical interpretation, iśq refers to the irresistible urge to obtain possession of the beloved (*ma'shuq*), expressing a want or desire that the lover (*ashiq*) must fulfil in order to reach the stage of perfection (*kamal*). The word iśq also has a distinctive discursive place in the Indo-Persian literary culture and in the classical Persian tradition; it is somewhat similar to mohabbat. Some scholars define it as a form of attachment that is marked by sensual love. However, Sufis generally relate this word with the divine and divide it into two: *Iśq-e Haqiqi* or real love or the love of god and *Iśq-e Majazi* or profane love or love for god's creation, that is, love of a man or a woman.

The distinction between spiritual and profane love is also suggested in the *qissa*, a genre of story-writing that developed in India during the medieval and early modern periods, which invokes the trope of iśq as challenging the normative boundaries. At the same time, Sufis have read these stories as representing the love of the human soul for God. Such romance stories like that of Hir–Ranjha, Laila–Majnu and Ratansen–Padmawati also reflect a conflict between iśq and ethics or between the code of iśq and that of family honour.

Pyar has been derived from the Sanskrit word *priya* or *priyakara*. It is used to describe almost all kinds of love, whether it is towards one's lover, parent, children or friends. Its other synonyms in the various Indian languages are prem, sneha, *dosti* and *mitrai*. This word is part of the Indo-Persian vocabulary and borrows a great deal from the Indian vernacular tradition. Scholars like Orsini have analysed the notion of pyar as a significant emotion or *bhāva* which can manifest itself in terms of relationship between the servant and the master (*dasya bhāva*), erotic love (*madhurya bhāva*), that of the friend (*sakhya bhāva*) and that of the mother and the child (*vatsalya bhāva*).

Keywords for India

In this modern age, this multiple vocabulary of love reflects a unique cultural and linguistic synthesis in India. Whether it was expressed as courtly, romantic or devotional love, the emotion it encompassed within itself stood for dedication, attachment and affection.

References

Meisami, Julie S. *Medieval Persian Court Poetry*. New York: Princeton University Press, 1987.
Orsini, Francesca, ed. *Love in South Asia: A Cultural History*. Cambridge: Cambridge University Press, 2007.

JATRA (JĀTRĀ)

Roma Chatterji

The Bangla word *jatra* or *yatra* in Sanskrit, literally journey, refers to troupes of itinerant players and, by extension, to the theatrical form as well. Its historical origins are difficult to establish, though there are apocryphal stories that trace it to the movement of ecstatic Krishna devotion initiated by Sri Chaitanya in the sixteenth century. In fact, Sri Chaitanya is said to have performed in musical dramas about the life of the god Krishna and the discovery of an incomplete manuscript of a play on Krishna's sport with the *gopis* (cowherd girls) in the twentieth century is used to give credence to this story. Whatever its history may be, jatra, unlike many other forms of folk theatre, continues to attract audiences in both rural and urban Bengal.

The reason for this may be due to its flexible and open-ended structure that allows it to absorb novel elements from the ever-changing performative environment. Thus, not only has it absorbed techniques of proscenium theatre that came to Bengal in the colonial period, but it has also allowed itself to become a vehicle for the expression of new political ideas, at first, through the Indian Peoples Theatre Movement in pre-independence Bengal and then, later, in the 1960s when the Marxist playwright and actor, Utpal Dutta, decided to use jatra to reinvent a form of political theatre in Bengal. Techniques such as the use of frontality, direct address to the audience, breaks in narrative continuity and song and dance through the use of allegorical figures, such as *Bibek* (conscience) and *Niyati* (fate) that add a moral dimension to the story, make it an attractive vehicle for political activism. Another aspect of the jatra that is extremely important, though not often written about, is its ability to impact other performance styles, especially in rural Bengal. As jatra troupes travel across the countryside with their *palas* (plays), they become a source of new ideas that are then taken up for exploration in other forms of performance. Jatra, because of its popularity, perhaps, but also because of its open-ended structure that allows for the accretion of elements from elsewhere, is a dominant influence on diverse forms of folk theatre and dance.

Hypostasis, or the use of figural types to represent ethical perspectives as well as alternative historical paths, is a technique that has enabled the jatra mode of narrative enactment to retain its relevance in the contemporary performative environment and to take on complex political themes. Thus, in vernacular renditions of the 9/11 strike on the World Trade Centre, Bibek and Niyati are subtly used to portray Osama Bin Laden, a complex persona in whom demonic and saintly aspects coexist, poised on the edge of time, whose actions will actualize one or the other aspects of his personality and, in the process, shape the course of history as well. By portraying Bin Laden as an archetype, the event becomes a singularity in the Deleuzean sense, not so much an event in 'real' time that can be shaped into a linear narrative but rather a virtuality in which contrary signs are co-present. After all, the turbaned and bearded face that has become the global signifier of the 'demonic' other also denotes the 'saintly' figure of the *pir*.

References

Chatterji, R. *Writing Identities: Folklore and Performative Arts of Purulia, Bengal.* New Delhi: Indira Gandhi National Centre for the Arts, 2009.
Skoda, U. and B. Lettman, eds. *India and Its Visual Cultures: Community, Class and Gender in a Symbolic Landscape.* New Delhi: Sage India, 2018.

LEELA (LĪLĀ)

Leela Samson

Līlā or *leela*, like many Sanskrit words, can neither be literally nor sensitively translated into English. It can only be loosely translated as 'divine play'. The word also alludes to beauty, charm, to a yogini and to a divine drama or play.

Līlā is a variant of the female given name 'Leila', derived from the Semitic word for 'night'. Over time, it has come to mean 'dark beauty' or 'dark-haired beauty'. In Spanish, *līlā* is the word for the colour 'lilac'. In German, it means 'purple'. The word has different meanings. It could mean play, sport, spontaneity or drama, but most importantly, it usually focuses in one way or another on the effortless or playful relation between the Absolute – or Brahman – and the contingent world. The concept of līlā is common to both non-dualist and dualist philosophical schools, but it has a markedly different significance in each. According to the philosophy of the sixteenth-century theologian Shree Vallabhacharya, 'Play or *leela* is the spontaneous activity generated from curiosity.' The word līlā also exists in almost all Indian languages. For example, in Tamil, it is *leelai* or *kali*, that which is toxic, seductive, ecstatic dance – as in after drinking *kallu* or toddy. This is not unlike *unmaatha taandavam*, the dance of extreme ecstasy.

Detailing occurrences of līlā from Indian traditions would help differentiate the various shades of its meaning. In the Krishna bhakti tradition, rasa līlā is considered to be one of the highest and the most esoteric of Krishna's pastimes. In this tradition, romantic love between human beings in the material world is seen as merely a diminished, illusionary reflection of the soul's original, ecstatic love for Krishna in the spiritual world. Just as a child plays at will with its own reflection in a mirror, with the help of *yogamaya* (i.e. power to create, sustain and withdraw the world), Krishna sports with the *gopis* (cowherds) of Vrindavan, who are like shadows of His own form. The rasa līlā is also an *uttsava*, a celebration. People believe that our souls were once blissfully one with the universal spirit. There was no doubt, no pain and no fear in that state. Then, for līlā, the Lord separated the soul from Himself and sent it 'to play' in the universe. Enlightened souls of numerous sages and saints sought various ways of getting back to that blissful state of oneness with the universe. These sages and saints became gopis of Vraj in order to experience what they could not as sages. In this form, they saw how easy it was to achieve bliss. Leaving behind their preconceptions and prejudices, they gradually became free of everything that stopped them from enjoying their oneness with the universal spirit. In His lilas, the Lord is said to have cleansed them and removed the many layers of attachment and maya (illusions) that enveloped them.

In *chirharan* līlā, the Lord removes the *dvaita* (duality) from the minds of the gopis. He steals their garments while they bathe in the river, hides them atop a tree and then asks them to lift their arms in supplication, that is, to forget the physical and experience abandonment.

In the *Gita Govinda*, a Sanskrit poem written by Jayadeva, Radha is none other than Krishna, the very fount of his *lilasakti* or creative power. She transmutes his glory into the zenith of blissful happiness, in which alone he takes pleasure. Līlā is also the playfulness in God, in nature, in man. But playfulness is not trivial. Whether in life or in the dance of life, how do you reconcile 'depth' with 'playfulness'? It is indeed paradoxical.

References

Misra, Ram Shanker. *The Integral Advaitism of Sri Aurobindo*. Delhi: Motilal Banarsidass Publishers Pvt Ltd, 1998.
Sax, William Sturman, ed. *The Gods at Play: Lila in South Asia*. New York: Oxford University Press, 1995.

NAACH (NĀC)

Brahma Prakash

It is believed that the origin of the Hindi term *naach* is the Prakrit term *nachacha*. In its current usage, naach stands for a dance tradition in North India. This connotation, however, is very new and limited, beginning with the colonial period. In common parlance, otherwise, the term would represent a performing arts genre that is very close to *natya*, the broad genre of performing art which includes dance, music, stories and so on. Dance and music are intrinsic to the performance of naach. Naach is gender-neutral and can be performed by men, women and transgenders. In some regions of North India, performers are called *nacha* or *nachar*. Based on the style and movement pattern, a naach can be *mornaacha* (peacock dance), *patangnaach* (kite dance), *kaharwanaach* (palanquin dance), *launda naach* (the dance of female impersonators) or any of the other myriad forms and styles.

The utterance of the term and its related cultural practices have varied presence from region to region. In Bengal, it is called *nachni*, while in Bihar it is naach, and in Madhya Pradesh and Chhattisgarh, it is called *naacha*. The tradition was also deeply caste-based, and before Independence, there were many caste-specific variants of the naach, such as rautnaach, chamaruanaach, dhobiyanaacha and gondnaach, referring to various communities. Performers largely came from the lower castes or Dalits. And, of late, there has been assertion of naach from the community point of view. *Nacchi se bacchi* ('Daughter of a dancer') is a popular slogan used by an Adivasi activist in Jharkhand, as a way of reclaiming the word from the world of stigma and prejudices it has come to represent.

During the colonial period, the word was written in its anglicized form as 'nautch'. Nautch has very rich and complex histories in relation to the postcolonial discourse. Historian Pran Neville gives several accounts of the encounters where the English and the dancers came together but often on unequal terms. The term 'naach' saw its resurgence in Colonial India subsequent to the government banning various art forms. It appears that it is under the encounter of colonial culture, which also tried to individuate cultural practices, that the use of nautch became restricted only to dance. And, today, many naach traditions are vulnerable to extinction in the absence of patronage, which began to be dismantled by the colonial power.

References

Jassal, Smita Tewari. *Unearthing Gender: Folksongs of North India.* Durham: Duke University Press, 2012.
Raheja, Gloria Goodwin and Ann Grodzins Gold. *Listen to the Heron's Words: Reimagining Gender and Kinship in North India.* Berkeley: University of California Press, 1994.

NAKHRA (NAKHRĀ)

Brahma Prakash

Nakhra is a term of affection. It carries a sense of pretension. It stands for a playful love and hate relationship in a familial situation. A baby can do nakhra to get more love from its mother. Similarly, lovers do nakhra if they not receive the desired attention and therefore these are also acts of desire. Nakhra has dramatic pretensions with elements of dobbing, whispering and pleading. The person may not be angry but she or he will show that she or he is angry as something due has not accorded to her or him. *Ruthna* (sulking) is closely related to nakhra. It was believed that courtesans would do nakhra to seduce men in power. From that perspective, nakhra is a feminine act with sexual undertones for economic and political ends. One who does a lot of nakhra is called nakhrali or nakhreaj.

However, in general, nakhra is a flirtatious act or attitude. The idea is to give oneself air. It is closely related to the mannerism referred to as blandishment and coquetry. Nakharā is social behaviour as well as an artistic and playful act. In many performing art traditions in India, expressions of sensuality are called nakhra. For example, nakhra plays an important role in ghazal and khyal singing and the dance tradition of kathak. It is an art, an aesthetic of pretence in which one party negotiates with the other in the form of coquetries. Facial expressions play a vital role in the act of nakhra.

Reference

Manuel, Peter. 'A Historical Survey of the Urdu Gazal-Song in India.' *Asian Music* (1988): 93–113.

PADMA AWARDS

Vibha Puri Das

Padma, a synonym for the flower lotus, enjoys salience in various strands of Indian mythology; it connotes beauty and purity, rising above the ordinary. Padma is an ancient and beloved analogy for the cosmos and for aspiration to perfection. While Padma awards do not form part of the constitutional frame notified on 26 January 1950, as they were instituted in 1954, the two share their roots, wellsprings and rationale.

The Padma awards, as in the other national symbols, generate pride in the nation-state of a longing to adhere to a notion of 'Indianness' and a sense of belonging to a wider and larger entity. In today's lexicon, when nationalism tends to be conflated with militarism, when development seems synonymous with exclusive enclaves of privilege, when environment sensitivity are conversely creating more and more ecological refugees, entities which evoke national pride remind one of the need to nurture the roots of nation-building that were based on not speaking to primordial emotions of otherness.

The categories of Padma awards are the Bharat Ratna, Padma Vibhushan, Padma Bhushan and Padma Shree. The granting of awards has had its share of controversy – with the granting of the award to some eminent scholar, musician or public personage or the omission of a deserved grant. However, the return of the award, on the few occasions that it has happened, has invited considerable public interest and discussion about bringing the phrase award-*wapsi* (return of the award) into common lexicon.

The frames visible from the vantage point of the Padma award include a differentiation between a monarchy bestowing awards as patronage and the political republic, instituting state recognition of distinguished service in diverse fields. This constitutes a mutuality in as much as the state is a partner in recognizing the excellence – arguably, it is the state that privileges those aspects of excellence it awards, not individual excellence alone, that demand recognition: Svarāja as in self-rule. At a second remote is the frame of the 'Righteous Republic' where the dharma underpinnings of the republic find sustenance and growth through individual's aspiration to fulfilment of its evolutionary raison d'etre. Gandhi's conception of connection between self-realization (atma darshan) and politics (rajya prakaran) posited that inner change within individual leads to outer changes in society. Another frame looks at the power and beauty accompanying the sthitaprajna, 'the man of steady mind or steady wisdom' who strives to attain inner svarāja and perhaps seated in padma asana: svarāja as in swadharma.

Ethical and ennobling aspirations reflected in the Directive Principles of State Policy of the Indian Constitution find resonance in choice and designation of the Padma awards. Anything that helps India rid itself of debilitating poverty of the masses takes the country towards Svarāja. 'For the state to have a moral vision of the Human good rooted in truth, and not as a subjective legitimizing device'. The argument that without svarāja as self-rule, svarāja as self-government could degenerate into state oppression even in so-called liberal societies seems particularly prescient today while we celebrate Padma awards even as we hurtle towards greater disparity, greater voicelessness of the marginalized and bigger threat to civil liberties through technological invasion.

Most Padma awards have been conferred on living personalities but the Bharat Ratna has with attendant controversy been bestowed posthumously also. The most recent posthumous Bharat Ratna was given to founder of Banaras Hindu University, Madan Mohan Malaviya. One Bharat Ratna conferred posthumously on freedom fighter Subhash Chandra Bose was declined by his family on the ground that it may be interpreted as a slight to his memory.

References

Gandhi, M. K. *Hind Swaraj and Other Writings*, edited by Anthony J. Parel. Cambridge and New York: Cambridge University Press, 1997.
Thapar, Romila. *The Past as Present: Forging Contemporary Identities through History*. New Delhi: Aleph Book Company, 2014.

QAWWĀLĪ (QAVVĀLI)

Yousuf Saeed

Qawwālī (from Arabic *qaul* meaning to speak, a statement) is a vocal musical form performed in Sūfī shrines and secular spaces, including trendy concerts, in much of South Asia by a group of singers called *qawwal*s. They use both mystical and secular poetry, in languages ranging from Urdu and Hindi to Persian, Arabic and Punjabi. Although North India's classical or Hindustani music grammar (*raga*s, *tala*s) form the basis of a qawwālī rendition, one may also find in them influences of folk and light music tunes.

According to popular belief, qawwali was developed by the fourteenth-century Delhi poet – Amir Khusrau – to be performed for the Sufis of Chishti order such as Nizamuddin Aulia (d.1325). However, historical evidence suggests that musical forms named *qaul* and qawwali may have existed in Arabia and the Persianate world, at least a couple of centuries before Amir Khusrau. For instance, Ali Al-Hujweri, an eleventh-century Sūfī *shaikh* buried in Lahore, has written about qawwals reciting poetry in the *sama* gatherings of Sufis in Arabia, Central Asia and India. Many musical forms, instruments and styles arrived in India from central Asia via musicians and artists between the twelfth and fourteenth centuries, helping in the evolution of newer forms through their synthesis with Indian musical forms under the patronage of various rulers. Amir Khusrau was active, then, as a talented court poet and composer in Delhi and a close confidante of the Sūfī Nizamuddin Aulia, composing *ghazal*s and setting them to music for his patron kings of the Delhi sultanate using both Central Asian and Indian music. Present-day qawwali compositions like *Man kunto maula* and *Chhaap tilak sab cheeni*, attributed to Khusrau, are some of the basic songs performed by qawwals all over South Asia.

The training and repertoire of qawwali music have been passed down via oral transmission, in the families of present qawwals, with hardly any written documents. Today's qawwali is usually a long-duration group song (a composition may last anywhere from fifteen minutes to one hour or more) with an accompaniment of harmoniums, *dhol* (barrel drum), *tabla* and hand clapping. Some gramophone records from the early twentieth century contain short-duration (three- to four-minute) renditions called *kawali* (*Bhairabi Kawali, Pahadi Kawali* and so on) by well-known solo vocalists like Gauhar Jan and Peare *sahib*. These sound like fast tempo renditions of the classical *thumri* or *chhota khayal* and should not necessarily be considered a precursor to the twentieth-century qawwali, since terms like qawwal and *kalawant* were used, even during Mughal times, to mean a singer or vocalist in general.

Before exploring the popular or secular usage of qawwali in South Asia, it is important to highlight its importance in the traditional Sūfī *sama* (audition) itself. While one finds unending debates in the Islamic world, especially among the orthodox scholars about the illicit nature of music, Sufis liberally argue in favour of the practice of sama to enhance their spiritual experiences, often citing examples of the Prophet Muhammad himself who listened to, or did not object to, singing. Those who disapprove of the sama and music in Islam complain of its ability to lead listeners astray, especially towards the 'sinful' practices of music, dance, wine and lust. For most Sufis, however, the sensuous elements of music, such as rhythm and tone, are not as important as its lyrics are. Hence, for many early Sufis, sama meant listening to the recitation of thought-provoking or philosophical verses, often without the accompaniment of musical instruments – anything that could trigger a spiritual ecstasy. The *mehfils* (gatherings) of sama are usually exclusive. For instance, women are discouraged from participating or listening in many gatherings, although they may listen from nearby enclosures. In some Sūfī orders, the listener is allowed to move his or her body in whirling or dancing, whereas some orders or hospices discourage body movement.

The poetry recited in a qawwali is not necessarily always religious, sacred or spiritual, nor are any specific poets preferred. While there are many non-sacred romantic verses in the repertoire of a qawwal, besides the main song or ghazal that forms the backbone of a qawwali, the artists also occasionally insert a *girah* (knot) or an interlude couplet which thematically befits the main ghazal but may be very different musically or even from a different language.

While many traditional qawwals in India and Pakistan, especially those associated with specific shrines, come from a certain family tradition, *gharana* or caste, some also learn anew to perform in secular spaces or for record companies. Early gramophone records (for instance, advertised in 1941 by Twin Record Company) provide us names of artists like Abdur Razzaq qawwal, Kallan Khan qawwal, Wali Mohammad qawwal and Shaikh Lal qawwal, among others. Hundreds of qawwali records were being produced annually in the early twentieth century, besides inexpensive song books of qawwali lyrics, suggesting a vibrant popular culture of record-listening at homes and in public. In India's early cinema, many situations were used as backdrop for a qawwali, not necessarily all associated with a Muslim identity or a mystical/sacred context. One of the most prolific playback singers to give voice to cinema qawwalis through much of the twentieth century is the legendary Muhammad Rafi.

We do not know when, or by whom, the qawwali *muqablas* (competitions) between two facing groups (usually men and women) were introduced in cinema or otherwise. Such a tradition is unlikely to have existed at the Sūfī shrines, although poetry and music competitions were common in most royal courts in India. Competitive *mushairas* (soirees) of Urdu poetry were also frequent in public spaces. Many Bombay films have depicted such competitions, usually between the lead male and female protagonists. *Nakli Nawab* (1962), *Mere Mehboob* (1963), *Ghazal* (1964) and *Dayar-e-Madina* (1975) are such films that feature poetic rivalries, which often lead to the romantic union of the two protagonists. The naive mehfils of mushaira that were hallmarks of *adab* (literature) and *aadab* (etiquette) were catapulted to a more complex level of musicality, emotions and flirtation via these qawwali muqablas.

Gramophone records gave way to a culture of audiotapes and cassettes in 1960s, making the listening of recordings more affordable. People could easily make copies of recordings and also record live sessions. Some qawwals who gained fame through their appearance in Bombay cinema as well as their records/cassettes in 1960s to 1970s were Ismail Azad, Yusuf Azad, Rashida Khatoon and Shakila Bano Bhopali. In the 1980s, qawwals like Aziz Nazan, Shankar-Shambhu and Habeeb Painter and Pakistan's Sabri brothers also made themselves household names with their popular compositions. The rise of Pakistan's Nusrat Fateh Ali Khan saw a new phase in the popularity and appreciation of qawwali worldwide. Sūfī music and Sufism itself became trendy, with a much larger audience purchasing music or going to the concerts. Many musicians, including the late Nusrat, added Western or synthesized music to their performances, popularizing the art. Sūfī music, comprising of high-pitched *alaps*, *tans*, phrases of poetry from the well-known Sūfī poets and high-energy rhythmic beats, remains an integral part of Bombay film culture today. Although the Indian music industry today may be in the doldrums due to online piracy, qawwalis and Sūfī songs are some of the most-accessed types of music being downloaded and shared via social media the world over.

References

Qureshi, Regula Burckhardt. *Sufi Music of India and Pakistan: Sound, Context and Meaning in Qawwali*. Chicago: University of Chicago Press, 1986.
Saeed, Yousuf. 'The Debate on Amir Khusrau's "Inventions" in Hindustani Music'. *The Journal of Indian Musicological Society* 39 (2008): 220–32.

RAGA (RĀGA)

Tista Bagchi

A polysemous word of Sanskrit origin, *raga* originally meant 'colour, tinge' (from the verb-root *ranj*, meaning '(to) dye, (to) colour') and is historically related to the Persian-origin word *rang* (colour) used in several modern Indian languages; additional figurative meanings that have also become salient in these are 'passion, love, anger'. Although the term 'ragahas' entered the domain of nomenclature for musical and sartorial events and (sub-)brands in recent decades (for instance, *Morning Raga*, a 2004 film directed by Mahesh Dattani), historically and culturally it denotes a special category of scale-based patterning, sometimes called a 'melodic framework', in both the Hindustani and the Carnatic systems of Indian classical music (often with folk origins).

There is much greater scope of nuanced expression within the basic structure of a given raga than the common English translation 'mode' can capture. Paradoxically, the raga is grammatically more restricted: each raga comes with its own melodic and enharmonic constraints. Instead, the much later schemata of *thāt* specifications (as especially codified by the musicologist Vishnu Narayan Bhatkhande), a major figure in modernist pedagogy in Hindustani classical music, Bakhle notes, are better analogues to modes in Western classical music. The ragathus has no direct counterpart in Western musical traditions although, as Powers notes, note groups akin to ragas – and closer to the modes of Western classical music – are found in certain obsolescent musical traditions of Kashmir and West Asia.

Ragas are both sung by classical Indian vocalists and performed instrumentally by solo or accompanying instrumentalists. Most ragas have been grouped according to the appropriate times of day to perform them, for example, Bhairav/Bhairon and Todi(dawn), Bilawal and Asavari (morning to early afternoon), Multani (late afternoon), Purvi (sunset) and Bihag and Bageshri (night). *Raga-malika* (literally, 'garland of ragas', compositions that weave many ragas) representations abound in miniature Indian art as well.

While mentions of the term raga are found in Upanishadic and eighth-century texts, the first clearly musicological text focussing on the tonal details of different ragas is the *Raga-Tarangini*, a treatise on ragas ascribed to Lochana Sharma (aka Lochana-Pandita or Lochana-Kavi) and dated to *c.* 1150 CE. The work describes (in a mix of Sanskrit and contemporaneous Maithili) the different tonal characteristics of then-recognized ragas, such as Purva and Mukhari (which are no longer ordinarily performed).

In largely pre-Islamic categorization, ragas have further been differentiated from *raginis*, which are conceived as the more numerous female 'wives' of a smaller number of seasonally appropriate 'masculine' ragas, a distinction no longer salient. Furthermore, certain ragas are ascribed to poets/musicians such as Amir Khusrau (who is credited with inventing the khayal genre in which ragas are sung) and Tansen (ascribed to be the inventor of ragas Miyan ki Malhar and Miyan ki Kanara).

References

Bakhle, Janaki. *Two Men and Music: Nationalism and the Making of an Indian Classical Tradition.* New York: Oxford University Press, 2005.
Powers, Harold. 'Asian Ethnomusicology Lecture Series: South and West Asian Musical Traditions'. Hosted by the Department of Music and delivered at the Humanities Institute, University of Chicago in 1992.

RAMLILA (RĀMLĪLĀ)

Sudha Gopalakrishnan

The epic Rāmāyana, the story of Rama, has had a long oral history in India for more than two millennia. It was first composed by the poet Valmiki around the second century BCE. The epic poem has a sacred significance in India and in many cultures of the South and Southeast Asia. It has stirred the imagination of poets, writers, musicians, painters, ballad singers and dancers from all over the world, who have transformed the story into multiple creative expressions and is regarded as one of the symbols of cultural interaction in Asia.

Contemporary Aesthetic Modes

The term Ramlila combines two words: Ram and Līlā. Ram refers to the hīōo of Rāmāyana, who is revered in India as the incarnation of the god Vishnu, who took birth as the prince of Ayōdhyā and defeated the demon king Ravana. *Līlā*, in Sanskrit, has a specific contextual meaning in the domain of the sacred, which recognizes the human world as the spontaneous, joyous and playful creation of god. The world is illusionary in nature and is simply a construct of the mind. In a manner of speaking, the closest translation that one could make is that Ramlila is 'Ram's playful exploits'. In this sense, Ramlila is an enactment of the līlā of God for the sake of humans and is therefore the play of the God Rama. Ramlila is the performance of the Rāmāyana and, more specifically, of the *Ramcharitmanas* (or simply *Manas* as it is popularly known), an adaptation of the text composed by Tulsidas, in Hindi, in the sixteenth century.

The sway and the still-active presence of the Rama narrative across India and many parts of Asia have no parallels anywhere in the world. In India and elsewhere, it is believed that watching and playing Ramlila have a spiritual significance. There are several versions and adaptations of the performance in India, mostly based on local versions of the story and styles of performance. Performances in different regions adapt them to their own regional variations and include local versions, devotional songs and performative styles, and this heterogeneity is perhaps the most significant syntactical feature of the language of this performance.

The basis of many Ramlila performances in North India is the *Manas*. A class of reciters called *Ramayani*s narrate the entire text of the *Manas*, and each day's performance is a dramatization of the recited text. Fundamentally, Ramlila draws its narrative and performative power from the oral reservoir of the text and it is astounding to see the charged atmosphere and collective energy when the audience become participants in the recitation of the epic during the performance. It is perhaps this practice of ritualized public reading that led to the development of Ramlila as a performance.

Performed during the time of the festival of Dussehra, for a period ranging from nine to over thirty days, the līlā ground is considered sacred during the performance. The Ramlila of each region has its own dramatic conventions through which the story progresses day by day. In many cases, there are no strict divisions between the character and the audience, as the audience moves along with the performers through the shifting spaces, participating in the sequence of events including the wedding, banishment, kidnapping and war. The main characters (*svarupa*s) – Ram, Lakshman, Sita, Bharat and Shatrugan – are usually played by boys between the ages of 6 to 12 years and are revered as the representatives of Gods themselves. The make-up of the svarupas resembles temple traditions of decorating (*sringar*) the idols. Masks are used for characters such as Ravana, with ten joined heads. Ramlila masks are made of paper mache, metal and cloth.

Effigies used in the Ramlila are of enormous proportions, sometimes extending up to 50 feet in height. Largely, the effigies are made of Ravana, his brother Kumbhkarna and Meghnad. As a symbolic representation of the victory of good over evil, it is a common practice across India to burn the effigies on the last day of Dusshera, which marks the end of the annual cycle of Ramlila.

There are several varieties of Ramlila, different and dynamic ways of performing this story, with almost every town in North India having its own Ramlila ground. For example, the *jhanki līlā* (vision, view) is a spectacle with no narrative that presents a static visual enthroned on a chariot, usually one or more of the incarnations (*svarup*) of the God represented. It is the spectator who ascribes the meaning to the vision and the appeal of the tableaux (jhanki), to its spectators, arises from the special religious significance of the occasion. Another variety of the performance, called *tulsi* lilais, is more prevalent and is usually a grand show with stage props and splendid costumes, theatrical dialogues and processions which feature the story in a vivid manner. The Ramnagar Ramlila, perhaps the most well-known līlā representation that happens in Banaras, across the river Ganga, is a splendid ceremonial drama lasting for a month during the Dussehra time, which combines the narration of the text, tableaux and dialogue.

It is difficult to trace the exact origin of Ramlila, but it is said that Tulsidas, himself, may have imagined his poem as a performance, for a wider appeal. Story goes that a disciple of Tulsidas choreographed a performance of the scene of the reunion of Ram and Bharat, after fourteen years of Ram's exile into the forest. The play, staged at Nati Imli near Ramnagar, is still performed every year at the same site and draws many spectators, including the king of Ramnagar.

The sponsorship of Ramlila saw a major shift after independence, with the crumbling of royal/feudal systems. It became a community-based art, supported by the local communities. Performances usually held in the afternoon were replaced by elaborate night shows over consecutive evenings. In recent decades, wealthy and business families have come forward to sponsor private performances, and troupes (*mandalis*) have also sprung up in urban centres such as Mumbai, Delhi and Calcutta raising the popularity of the art across India. In 2005, UNESCO proclaimed Ramlila as a 'Masterpiece of the Oral and Intangible Heritage of Humanity'.

References

Kapur, Anuradha. *Actors, Pilgrims, Kings and Gods: The Ramlila of Ramnagar*. Calcutta: Seagull, 1990.
Lutgendorf, Philip. *The Life of a Text: Performing the Ramcharitmanas of Tulsidas*. Berkeley: University of California Press, 1991.

RANGOLI (RAṄGŌLĪ)

Sudha Gopalakrishnan

Creating intricate designs on the ground with rice paste and other natural colouring materials, intimately linked to worship and festive celebrations, is a common tradition across India. As we move from region to region, we see that these ornate patterns are almost solely crafted by women. What is striking is the variety and sophistication of this artistic practice across regions, communities and individuals.

The designs drawn on the floor are known by several names in India and are linked to diverse semantic references, some explicit and some others linked to concomitant attributes of different expressive ideas. In the northern parts of India, it is *rangoli*, derived from the Hindi word *rang* meaning colour. West Bengal has named its floor design *alpana*, in all probability drawn from *alimpana*, which means to plaster, coat or, by extension of the idea, to draw or paint on a surface. In Tamil Nadu, the word *kolam* means simply a design or form. The Telugu *muggu*, also, means a pattern. There are several other expressions of drawings made on the ground, in other places of India, such as *mandana* (the same Sanskrit word means decoration) in Rajasthan, *aripana* (perhaps from *alpana*?) in Bihar and *kalamezhuttu* (three-dimensional drawing of the goddess on floor; the sacred space is called *kalam*) in Kerala.

The patterns made on the floor by women are linked to a set of practices across India, practices that may overlap with other regions but also have distinctive features of their own. The art of floor painting is so diverse in usage, purpose and artistic features that it cannot be reduced to a singular set of signs and symbols. There are traditional designs associated with each occasion – ritual, festivity or any happy celebration. In many cases, the craft is used in connection with a festival, ritual or celebratory occasion. Alpana in West Bengal is associated with festive occasions such as Saraswati *Puja* and Deepavali. Muggu is drawn at home during occasions such as Sankranti, during the month of Dhanu. The crafting of kalamezhuttu has a highly ritualistic character and is associated with specific ceremonies and rituals, whereas pookkalam is a necessary feature during Onam celebrations in Kerala. In many areas, making floor diagrams is a daily customary routine, such as in the kolam of Tamil Nadu.

In spite of variations across India, the crafting of a floor diagram has a common set of rules. When the ground is made ready and the surface prepared, according to the place and occasion, the artist lays down the contours with initial strokes, making vertical, horizontal, diagonal and circular shapes according to the design. With combinations of colours placed onto this basic form, the picture magically comes alive, whether simple or intricate.

Rich in symbolic significance, intricate in patterns and vibrant in colours, rangolis represent the collective memory and artistic imagination of the women. The idea associated with the word has a propitiatory significance, as an offering and a vow directed towards the well-being of home, family and the community. It is also an assertion to keep alive a tradition handed down from mother to daughter for generations, not through any conscious method of teaching but through a shared involvement and nurturing.

The floor designs, in cases such as rangoli, alpana and kalamezhuttuis, are also thought to acts as spells to invoke a deity, ward off evil and spread welfare and peace in communities. They are also prayers to the deity of one's choice (*ishtadevata*) asking to fulfil a wish or seek blessings. It is significant that these are ephemeral drawings and are erased or destroyed once the deity has been invoked, prayer is addressed and the ritual action completed.

Some of the more prominent designs drawn on the floor are swastika, spiral, circle, lotus, full pitcher, flowers, leaves and the figures of animals and birds. While kolam uses only rice paste and has a geometric configuration, many other varieties are vibrantly colour-based. They use pigments and colours drawn from nature. Some of these include rice flour, turmeric and *kumkum*, dried and powdered leaves, charcoal and burned soil. The artists have expertise in mixing natural ingredients together to get variations in colours. For example, a mixture of turmeric and lime gives a dark red colour, while black is derived from burning charcoal.

The colours, the patterns and their symbolism, the practice and regional variations of rangoli, reflect India's rich heritage as a land of festivals and colour. However, it is also important to recognize that while we club these traditions together as India's common heritage, they are not actually homogeneous. There are several regional variations of floor decorations; for instance, floor decorations such as *hase* in Karnataka, aripana in Bihar, mandana in Rajasthan, *aipan* in Uttarakhand and *chowkpujan* in Uttar Pradesh do not have identical features. There is a wide range of social situations, where some of these forms are more conventional, some are put to use in a contemporary context and some others are constantly in a state of change, both in function and form. For example, currently, rangoli has adapted to more unconventional settings and has become part of any formal or informal occasion, including an office function, an evening dinner party or simply welcoming a special guest. Tourism departments and their allied institutions have popularized the art, and sometimes the designs also get replicated in fabric. The word rangoli, along with the craft that portrays it, is not likely to disappear any time soon. The forms may vary and the contexts may change, but the artistic skill and exquisite designs of rangoli, quintessentially Indian, are here to stay.

References

Gajjar, Irene. *Ancient Indian Art and the West*. D.B. Bombay: Taraporevala Sons, 1971.
Gode, P. K. 'History of Rangavalli Art between c. A.D. 50 and 1900'. *Studies in Indian Cultural History* 3 (1969): 87–102.

RASA (RASA)

Hemachandran Karah

I grew up relishing a special kind of salad called *pachadi* prepared exclusively on a Telugu New Year's Day. The pachadi was sweet, salty, bitter, astringent, pungent and sour, all at the same time. In helping us children figure out such an admixture of tastes, an elder never failed to remind us that life is as much an assortment of leads, likeable and otherwise. Pachadi and other lay creations are a reminder that the idea of taste is not a mere culinary affair in Indian imagination. Instead, it is embedded within a long-standing aesthetic persuasion called *rasa*. Appreciation of beauty, drama, poetry, music, dance and all things that make an emotional universe owe something or the other to the framework of rasa. Broadly, one may translate rasa as essence, flavour, taste and aesthetic relish. Contemporary English-educated audience may associate taste with an unforgiving moral judgement. Such a scepticism may have some validity. All the same, within the Indian cultural milieu, rasa emerges primarily as a spectrum of fleeting emotions, rendered stable by one's propensity for savouring them selectively. For example, most Indian filmgoers are aware of ephemeral emotions that their favourite heroes, heroines, villains, lyrical compositions and dialogues with a punch are capable of generating in them. No less importantly, they may also savour a particular emotion, heroic pride for example, in pursuing a dearly espoused political orientation.

Classical dramaturgist Bharatha who lived nearly two thousand years ago recognizes such moments of savouring, where flickering emotions transform into stable entities with a potential for transcendental vision. In *Natyasastra*, his treatise on drama, Bharatha describes at least eight stable emotions linked to rasa. They include the erotic (*sringaara*), the comic (*haasya*), the tragic (*karuna*), the furious (*raudra*), the heroic (*vira*), the terrible (*bhayaanaka*), the odious (*bibhatsa*) and the marvellous (*adbhuta*). Tenth-century philosopher Abhinava Guptha adds one more to this list which he calls the bliss (*santa*). Bharatha does not treat all the eight rasas as watertight sentiments. Instead, he recognizes them as emotional phenomena that animate in sync with a theatrical performance and yet live beyond. Bharatha also enlists a host of transitory emotions that go with an eightfold emotional cluster. A long lineage of critics until the present finds Bharatha's insights on aesthetic relish transformative and technically astute.

Bharatha's thesis on tastes is still tied to and dependent upon one's capacity to peruse the formal properties of a piece of art. It does not account for tastes that thrive everywhere and yet nowhere. The wherewithal of taste, its beginning, and end if any, catchment area, its spiritual hold on personhood and voices of those who breathe life into it, and the rest, require closer attention to the problem of subjectivity. Bhatta Nayaka, who lived during the tenth century, takes us exactly in that direction. Valmiki's Sita cannot remain the same across epochs, Nayaka would argue. For example, a contemporary teenager may relate to Sita for her fierce independence one moment, feminine charm in others and an unexplainable inner compulsion in others. Citing these instances, Nayaka would merrily declare – 'We should treat subjectivity not as a mere interior universe, but as a lived world that one may choose to inhabit and animate. Does that sound radical and completely in sync with the current reception theory? Yes it will.'

In sum, as a modality of aesthetic response, rasa resides somewhere between logical analysis and appreciation flavoured by intuition. As an object of taste, rasa is, and will remain, driven by subjectivity. Also, due to an element of savouring and meditation, rasa may also prompt a transcendental vision. This is useful in a real-time political situation. For example, disabled people may better understand the import of their social exclusion by unearthing certain cultivated tastes that work against them. At the same time, a meditation on a particular emotion such as bhayaanaka may aid them in making sense of vulnerabilities that do not spare anyone, including habitual oppressors. The point is this – human conditions such as vulnerability require an idiosyncratic and a universal purview. The framework of rasa can ably serve both pathways.

References

Schwartz, S. L. *Rasa: Performing the Divine in India*. New York: Columbia University Press, 2004.
Vatsyayan, Kapila. *Bharata, the Nāṭyaśāstra*. New Delhi: Sahitya Akademi, 1996.

SAHITYA (SĀHITYA)

B. N. Patnaik

Sahitya is a category term generally used for a body of linguistic art works, in the written form, such as poetry, drama, stories and novels, essays, biographies, autobiographies and travelogues. 'Literature', in its narrow sense, is its equivalent term. In its broad-sense usage, literature includes writing on themes such as development, environment, endangered languages, etc. At present, the word sahitya is not used to refer to writings on these themes. Here, literature is used in its narrow sense. Poetry, drama and fiction constitute the core of sahitya/literature.

Overgeneralizing a bit, these are instances of imaginative writing as against essays, biographies, travelogues and journalistic reporting, which deal with the real and the conventional attitude is to treat these as the poor cousins of poetry, drama and fiction – works of art. With respect to imaginative literature, one does not raise questions of validity – John Keats's 'beauty is truth, truth beauty' ('Ode on a Grecian Urn') is not contested because ugliness is truth too. No issues are raised when William Shakespeare describes life as 'full of sound and fury, signifying nothing' (*Macbeth*). There is no contestation of a cloud becoming a messenger for the lover to his beloved in Kalidasa's *Meghaduta* on the same ground. One willingly suspects one's disbelief here, accepting that the parameters of reality change in these works. In essays, travelogues and news stories, which are more 'realistic' genres, one expects strong rootedness in reality.

However, 'Art, Truth and Politics', Harold Pinter's Nobel Prize acceptance speech, which deals insightfully with issues of eternal human concern such as the nature of reality, unreality and truth in art and political life, can hardly not be called sahitya. The same holds true for Alexievich Svetlana's 'Voices of Chernobyl', which, as a deeply moving and perceptive account of a human-made disaster, transcends its specific context and its genre as journalism. Thus, a very basic characteristic of great sahitya turns out to be its universality and sometimes, its author's too, as in the case of the Mahābhārata, as multiple innovatively different versions are created across centuries. Generations of readers relate to great literature in manifold ways.

However, a great literary work is not about content alone; it is about language and style as well – 'what oft was thought but ne'er so well expressed' (Alexander Pope, 'An Essay on Criticism'). 'Gather me into the artifice of eternity' ('Sailing to Byzantium') is how W. B. Yeats articulates the desire for eternal existence. Eduardo Galeano captures the grace and beauty of Pele's game, by saying, watching him was like living moments 'so worthy of immorality that they make us believe immortality exists'. Immortality takes a different form in William Blake's expression – 'hold infinity in the palm of your hand'. Creativity is manifest in terms of rich metaphors which connect thoughts, feelings and objects never connected before – the reader perceives things in a new way. Ambiguity and indirectness are the essence of literary expression because of their suggestive power. The ambiguity of Maria's situation and the resulting confusion of interaction in the sanatorium are rendered into a profound tragedy of insensitivity and miscommunication in Gabriel Garcia Marquez's story, 'I Only Came to Use the Phone'. Instead of directly saying that one cannot destroy others without destroying oneself, Albert Camus, mixing facts and imagination, creates his Caligula, in his play *Caligula*, who embodies this vision. Exploring ways of creative expression, which sometimes takes the form of metaphor, the *Bhagavad Gita*, in the eleventh chapter, tries to describe the infinite in terms of the finite, the formless in terms of form.

The relationship between the world of literature and the real world is not always as transparent as in George Orwell's *Animal Farm*. It is often more complex. Much worthwhile literature is not a mirror of reality but an aesthetically appealing construction of it. The world of art is created from an understanding of the real world and to that extent it not exactly real; yet, ironically, this 'created' world of literature, with its economy of structure and intensification of thought, feeling and experience, enriches our knowledge of and sensitivity towards the real world. There is no point in looking for Meursault, Camus's 'outsider' in the real world, but this character helps us understand indifference as an attitude and disconnection with the world as a way of life and the situation of the loners in a world that mistrusts them. One must not hope to find Sita in the real world, but the Sita of *Uttara Kanda* of Valmiki's *Rāmāyana* helps us understand the tragedy of ignoring the limits of tolerance and willingly suppressing the natural voice of protest.

Great writers explore, in depth and sensitivity, the range of human experiences and the human situation as (s)he negotiates the world. Literary works of significance provide their readers intellectual and aesthetic pleasure, while illuminating and sensitizing them to the human predicament. Other things like helping them escape from their reality, educating and inspiring them to struggle and not give up, etc., are bonuses.

References

Albert, Edwary. *History of English Literature*. Delhi: Oxford University Press, 2017.
Kundera, Milan. *The Art of the Novel*. London: Faber and Faber, 2005.

SAREE (SĀṚĪ)

Gopika Nath

A *saree* is a 5.5–9-yard, unstitched garment, traditionally worn by women from India, Nepal, Bangladesh and Sri Lanka. The saree is a derivative of the Sanskrit word *shati* (pronounced 'shaatee') – meaning a strip of cloth – and from *shadi* ('shaadee') or *sadi* ('saadee') in Pali. It evolved over time to become the saree ('saaree') in contemporary usage. It could also have been derived from the Prakrit word *sattika*, meaning women's attire, found in Buddhist and Jain literature, or from the south-west Dravidian sāṛīri, pronounced as *sire* (Kannada).

Saree is the generic term used for the unstitched garment worn across the subcontinent. In different Indian languages, it can be referred to by other names. For instance, in Tamil, the saree is called *pudvai, selai* or *adai*; in Malayalam, it is *sela, pudava* or *tuni*; in Odia, saadi, sardhi, luga, kapta; in Marathi, saadi, *sardhi, shallu*; in Gujarati, saadi, *saalu, lugadu* or *cira*.

The saree can be traced back to the Indus Valley Civilization. It evolved from a three-piece ensemble – costumes belonging to the Vedic and post-Vedic period (1500 BCE to 350 BCE), generally consisted of three articles of clothing for men and women alike. These were not cut and sewn garments but rectangular pieces of beautifully crafted textiles. The *antariya* or lower garment (resembling the dhoti), fabric passing through legs, covering them loosely and then flowing into long, decorative pleats in front of the legs. The *uttariya* was like a mantle; it covered the upper part of the body, worn over shoulders or head. It could be worn across the back, resting on shoulders, to fall freely on the forearms. Sometimes, women took two uttariyas, one draped on the head and the other across the arms. They did not cover their breasts but married women wore a chest band, known as *stanmasuka* or *stanapatta*, which is similar to the mammillare or strophum worn by the Roman women. This three-piece ensemble or *poshak* (generic term for costume), is mentioned in Sanskrit literature and Buddhist Pali literature of the sixth century BCE. The antariya evolved into the skirt, known as *ghagra* and *lehenga*, the uttariya became the *dupatta* and the stanapatta developed into the *choli* and the uttariya and antariya merged to form a single garment known as the saree.[1] Sculptures belonging to the Maurya–Sunga period (324–78 BCE) reveal that antariya was always tied below the navel, emphasizing the curves of the female form.

Today, there are more than eighty recorded ways to wear a saree (Boulanger, 1997) which offer special insights into the ethnology of Indians and Southeast Asians and the archaeology of the periods in which it developed. The most commonly worn style, called the Nivi style, has the saree wrapped around the waist, with the loose end of the drape worn over the shoulder, baring the midriff. In ancient Indian traditions and according to the *Natyasastra* (ancient treatise on dance and costumes), the navel of the 'Supreme Being' is considered to be the source of life and creativity, hence explaining the need to bare the midriff when draping the saree. Other texts such as the *Dharmasastras* state that women should be dressed in such a manner that the navel is never visible.

With the advent of Western fashion trends, the more cumbersome and tricky-to-wear saree has been overshadowed by trousers, dresses and gowns. It has led to the advent of the ready-made or pre-stitched saree, which is easily available on popular online portals, apart from stores. Some designers have also devised the saree-gown – a single garment worn like a full-length dress, with pleats in the front and a faux *palla* draped over the left shoulder in the traditional *Nivi* style but without the midriff showing.

There was a time when wearing a saree signified maturity into womanhood and learning to drape and carry one's saree well was an attribute of elegance. For the Nair community, a woman receiving the *mundum neriyathum* from a man signifies marriage itself – *pudavakoda*. Especially, in North India, the saree is no longer worn every day by most. Instead, it is becoming synonymous with formal wear to an extent that wearing one could be overdressing. This decline in the draping of the saree and consequent impact on handloom production and livelihood of weavers has led to various social media events such as the hundred saree pact and others, which encourage women to wear a hundred saris and post pictures of themselves on social media.

Ancient literature, such as the Sanskrit novel *Kadambari* (seventh century CE) written by Banabhatta and his son Bhushanabhatta and the Tamil epic poem *Silappadikaram* (100 to 300 CE) by Ilango Adigal (pseudonym of one of many Jain and Buddhist authors in Tamil poetry), describes women in exquisite drapery or saree.

The saree has also been important in Hindu mythology. Draupadi's *Vastraharan* is an iconic scene from the epic, Mahābhārata (fourth century CE), symbolic of the violation of dharma, its restoration by divine grace and a woman's self-respect, faith and grit in the face of adversity. The ideal of self-respect as unending where there is faith is epitomized by the never-ending piece of fabric that clothed Draupadi. Draupadi's vastraharan is not seen as her humiliation but as her friendship with the male God, Krishna, her ally in the assertion of Dharma, who offered her a garment without end and thereby, endless grace.

---

[1] Sources also indicate that when the Aryans came into the plains of the North Indian rivers, they brought with them the word *vastra* for the first time. Though a Sanskrit word originally meaning a garment or cloth, for them it was a piece of treated leather made into wearable clothing. Moving southwards, they started wearing cotton weaves, in the manner of the Indus Valley inhabitants. This style of wearing a length of cloth around the waist, especially for women, and the cloth itself came to be known as *neevi*, an early precursor to the three-piece ensemble that morphed into the sari.

Although the saree evolved from the Indus Valley Civilization, after independence it became an emblem of national unity and identity in India, especially with Pakistan disowning it, because it was perceived as a Hindu dress, and Fatima Jinnah, the 'Mother of the Nation', referred to the saree as 'unpatriotic', consequently causing a loss in its popularity in Pakistan. So, the saree is a signifier of power and politics. India's Italian-born leader of the Congress Party, Sonia Gandhi, is never seen in anything but a saree. This becomes a signifier of power and politics in a fictional biography, entitled *The Red Sari*, which is the 'story of a woman who gets into power in spite of herself'.

Before we conclude, a word about Indo-Greek influences on the sartorial styles of the two civilizations. The connection between India and Greece precedes the arrival of Alexander the Great in 326 BCE by over a century due to the arrival of Cyprus the Great, of Persia, on a mission to conquer India in 558–535 BCE and that of his successor Darius in 518 BCE. A number of mercenaries serving in Darius's army chose to settle and formed small settlements, following their customs and speaking their own language. One such colony was at Nyasa in Swat Valley. There was fusion of art and religion within the borders of the Hellenistic kingdoms, especially in these north-west peripheries. The foundations of Hellenism in Gandhara were laid during the Indo-Greek period, in the second century BCE. A late first or early second century CE Gandhara frieze near Swat, now in the Victoria and Albert Museum collection, shows men and women wearing flowing robes. The men drape a skirt above the knees with front pleats, a portion of the fabric going around the waist, thrown across to the left shoulder and over it, leaving the torso bare. The women wear long, flowing gowns, fitted at the breast and down to their ankles. They drape a long and wide uttariya across the shoulders from the back, pulled downwards around the hips, almost like a saree pallu would be pulled out from behind the body, towards the left shoulder. The apparently soft and thin fabric of their garb begins its drape from the front of the left arm, loosened at the forearm, circling the body from behind, returning to the left forearm. The similarity between the garments preceding the sāṛīri and the drape of these figures raises poignant questions about who influenced whom.

References

Boulanger, Chantal. *Saris: An Illustrated Guide to the Indian Art of Draping*. New York: Shakti Press International, 1997.
Lynton, Linda. *The Sari: Styles, Patterns, History, Techniques*. New York: W. W. Norton, 2002.

SAUNDARYA (SAUNDARYA)

Harsha V. Dehejia

In a civilization like ours, the creation of the beautiful is a way of life, where both the *raja* (king) and the *praja* (populace) surround themselves with sensually rich and evocatively beautiful objects, where the creation of beautiful objects does not always need a *prayojana* (reason) and where the presence of the beautiful ushers *saubhhagya* (the auspicious).

In the Vedas, the beautiful was an integral part of *rta* (the cosmic order) and it was not to be understood separately from it. The hymn to Dawn is one, among many, example of the Vedic concept of the beautiful and how it is a part of rta. Once the religious *sampradays* (traditions or religious systems) began to be formed, the beautiful was mainly applied to the divine and it could not be understood on its own. The gods were therefore beautiful. However, as the first millennium was about to begin, little springs of speculation of the concept of the beautiful began to be formed, as we began our attempts to understand what is beautiful in the tradition. The beautiful was sensually pleasing and therefore *prakriti pradhan*, but it was Bharata's *Natyashastra* and the concept of rasa that made the beautiful also *bhāva pradhan* (emotionally driven). Contemplation of the *sundar* (beautiful) leads to *saundarya* or beauty and therefore a simple definition of saundarya is the subjective experience of what is objectively, sensually pleasing that leads to a state of *vishranti* (rest) and *ananda* (bliss).

Etymologically derived from *su nara*, the adjectival sundar or its variations such as *supratik* in the Vedas are applied initially to natural phenomena. In the *kavya* literature, the adjective sundar referred mainly to sensual or material beauty, without any suggestion of metaphysical, moral, ethical or spiritual excellence, as morality and spirituality were subsumed under the overarching term *dharma* and sundar was to be understood under the rubric of *kāma*.

The popular phrase *satyam, shivam, sundaram* is a much later addition in the Indian tradition and was probably imported into Sanskrit through English only in the nineteenth century. The concept of sundaram being tied to shivam, however, does appear in the bhakti literature, for beauty for the devout can only be in *ishvara* (god). Equally, Abhinava Gupta equates rasa with *brahma nanda* and that makes the connection of beauty with *sat* (the true essence or that which is unchangeable, Sanskrit). It was, therefore, not difficult to translate the English phrase beauty, truth, goodness into Sanskrit and make it a part of Sanskrit parlance.

The word sundar refers to what is secular and sensuous and is one of many in the family of words denoting sensual beauty and is replete in the *kavya* literature rather than in the *shastras*. Other poetic words for beauty in the *kavya* literature being *pramoda, caru, subhaga, mugdha, lavanya* and *lalita*, among many others. A survey of *kavya* literature suggests that while for the Indian poet the woman was the repository of beauty, yet since the *sharira* (body) was in a homologous relationship with *samsara* (universe), the attribute of feminine beauty always resonated with the world around. Poets, thus, used phrases such as *gajagamini, mriganayani, sulochana* and so on while describing feminine beauty. This relationship between the human and the world around was an assertion of a living resonance between the human world and that of nature – as between a woman and a tree – and the beautiful was best represented and understood in this context.

While the sundar is available to all, saundarya is the preserve of the *rasika* or the committed aesthete who initiates a contemplative analysis of what is sundar and uses not only the *pramana* of perception but also of inference to create an inner, subjective, restful realization characterized by vishranti and ananda which gives us an intuition of some transcendent beauty. Saundarya is therefore a philosophical concept and is best underpinned by the epistemology of Kashmir Shaivism. An important part of that philosophic system is *pratyabhijna* (repeated cognitions) to move the sundar to saundarya.

Saundarya is half received and half perceived and is context- and culture-dependent. In making this statement, there is also the assertion that the epistemic reality of sundar is never in doubt, for if sundar were to be purely subjective without any objective basis, no philosophical discourse could take place as it would eliminate the objective sundar. While what is naturally beautiful is a part of our cosmic reality, the aesthetic discourse on the beautiful is reserved for what is created by humankind or what is commonly called art as, in saundarya, we also celebrate human creativity.

In subsuming sundar and saundarya under the rubric of kāma, we are ensuring that it is one of the *purushartha*s and therefore an important part of noble and gracious living and thinking.

References

Dehejia, H. V. *The Advaita of Art*. New Delhi: Motilal Banarasidass Publishers, 1996.
Dehejia, H. V. and M. R. Paranjape, eds. *Saundarya: The Perception and Practice of Beauty in India*. New Delhi: Samvad India Foundation, 2003.

SELFIE

Seema Khanwalkar

According to the Oxford Dictionary, the term 'selfie' was first used on Flickr in 2004. A selfie is defined as 'a photograph that one has taken of oneself, typically with a smartphone or a webcam, and uploaded to any social media website'. Oxford Dictionaries named 'selfie' as its word of the year, in 2013. There are references to selfies in a few Indian languages; however, most Indian languages do not have an equivalent translation or a word for selfie. For instance, while Hindi has *swachitra/chayachitra*, Tamil has *cuyapatam* and Telugu has *sviyachitra*, Bangla has *selaphi*, Urdu, Malayalam and Gujarati use the same word – selfie – and Assamese, Kannada and Odia have no word for it. Most of these languages seem to have incorporated the word as a natural part of modern vocabulary.

However, the selfie is far from being a modern phenomenon; it dates back to 1839, when photographic self-portraits were part of the experiments of the time. The first such photograph was taken in 1839 by an amateur chemist and photography enthusiast from Philadelphia named Robert Cornelius. Cornelius had set his camera up at the back of the family store in Philadelphia. He took the image by removing the lens cap and then running into frame where he sat for a minute before covering up the lens again. On the back of the photograph, he wrote, 'The first light picture ever taken. 1839.' The two words are decades apart, but they both stem from the same timeless delight to document oneself. 'There is a primal human urge to stand outside of ourselves and look at ourselves', says Clide Thomson, a technology writer; according to Frédéric della Faille, 'it is much more a moment and a story, than a photo. It is not about being beautiful.' The selfie, in India, has found its way into the rural landscape as well. You know you are living in a tech-savvy world – craving constant communication – when a person chooses to broadcast a selfie over a bottle of chilled cola on a hot summer afternoon. Telecom companies launched a 10-rupee recharge pack that became a massive hit – so much so that Indian villagers now buy the recharge pack far more often than they do colas or candies.

The selfie imagination has fired a young Indian designer – Adriti, whose quirky Tumblr blog, called 'Selfie Gods', transformed the old Indian God paintings with the modern-day smartphone and selfie stick. According to Dr Pamela Rutledge, a media psychologist, humans are hard wired to respond to faces; we are engaged when we see faces. This is what prompted creators of smartphone applications to add the front-facing camera, despite reservations.

The selfie phenomenon stands in a Janus-like situation (caught at a crossroads), between empowerment and alienation. Amitabh Bachchan, an icon of Indian Cinema, posted recently that he was disgusted when some youth took selfies when he was attending a friend's funeral – 'The selfie culture tends to deprive youth of social stimulation, becoming more and more engulfed in the virtual and technological world of the media.' Taking selfies in hospitals, of people on ventilators or during surgeries is considered stony-hearted; it is considered an indicator of low self-esteem or extreme narcissism, in this case. The number of instances of youth dying while taking daredevil selfies corroborates this view. It is also said to encourage social withdrawal and alienation.

The selfie, however, is here to stay, as it gets transported to newer creative genres, thanks to technology, art and imagination. It remains to be seen how much the people mature to its use and empowering potential.

References

Wortham, Jenna. 'My Selfie, Myself'. *The New York Times, Sunday Review*, 19 October 2013.
Yun, Daniel. 'Selfie, A New Sense of Self'. blogpost on *After The Rain*, posted on 14 December 2013. Available at: https://danielyunhx.com/2013/12/14/selfie-a-new-sense-of-self/ (accessed December 2018).

SHAMIYANA (ŚĀMIYĀNA)

Ira Pande

Also spelt as *shamiyana*, the word takes its name from the Persian *shamiyan* – a cloth canopy stretched overhead to provide shade from the sun. *Shamiyanas* arrived in India with the Mughals who were known for the richly decorated cloth canopies they favoured. Miniature paintings of Mughal court scenes usually include a canopy over the imperial throne, when the ruler is seated. The word probably entered the lingua franca through Urdu – a language that grew up in the bazaars and cantonments of Delhi and North India – that was later adopted by local languages such as colloquial Hindi and Marathi. Over time, it became synonymous for a lavish cloth tent shelter that comprised a canopied structure and removable cloth walls. The latter were strung on bamboo poles, threaded within stitched channels in the cloth panels.

The shamiyana is used on ceremonial occasions, such as a royal visit, to mimic a court. This is probably why it was adopted by the East India Company's parvenus, to raise their standing among the hoi polloi, on their tax-collecting tours. Later, it became a standard practice to rig up a shamiyana for any outdoor festivity, even a cricket match played by the *gora sahib*s (white sirs). The beautiful floral panels of the Mughal shamianas gave way to less refined panels and, often, the shamiyana was a plain white tent or awning. This latter form travelled to England to emerge as the marquee at county cricket matches and other such domestic celebrations. Till today, marquees and outdoor tents outside India remain plain-white tented structures.

In India, however, the shamiyana continued to grow and evolve even after the royal courts of India died out. The side panels (*kanaat*, in Hindi) are a popular and inexpensive way to demarcate a temporary inclusion of public space. For instance, in the pre-run to the busy Diwali sales of sweets, the local *halwai* (confectioner) will rig up a few kanaats (with untidy and soiled, gaudy panels, hired from the nearby 'tent house' supplier) to accommodate the spill over from his smaller kitchen. These generally have geometric designs in bright colours and serve to provide a festive air to squalid surroundings. Village weddings, temple festivals and school sports days are other examples of scenarios that demand this kind of use.

The *puja pandal* (also now strangely known as the *pujo pandle*) is a genre by itself. The pandal is a variation of the shamiyana and takes its name from the famous puja festival in October when the country goes into an overdrive of spending and indulgence. Created by the nimble bamboo engineers of Bengal, these enormous structures are strung over bamboo scaffoldings that may take weeks to rig up. Lit with chandeliers, paintings and embellishments that highlight the theme behind it, these pandals attract thousands of viewers over the week-long celebration.

However, the most impressive version in India, today, is the wedding shamiyana that has breached the scale of lavishness seen in the heyday of princely India. No wedding, however modest, is ever held without a shamiyana to accommodate the guests who come to celebrate the occasion. It could be considered a minor industry in itself, supporting, as it does, a vast network of artisans and craftspeople who are part of the process of making it. Of late, such shamianas offer temperature-controlled interiors with giant mist-making fans and portable air conditioners to cool humid interiors and gas-fired heaters and braziers to warm the guests in winter. Swathes of bright chiffon and silk are strung to brighten the interiors and carpets cushion the floor.

The final word is provided by the Government of India (under Finance Act of 1997, Clause 77A, Section 65) – 'A Pandaal or Shamiyana means a place specially prepared or arranged for organising an official, social or business function.'

References

Dayal, Lala Deen. 'Exterior of Darbar Shamiana'. *RCS Photograph Collection, Queen Mary Collection, Album 12* (2004).
'Definition of SHAMIANA'. *Merriam-webster.com*. Available at: https://www.merriam-webster.com/dictionary/shamiana (accessed 25 May 2019).

SOUTH INDIAN FILMS

Uma Vangal

The term 'South Indian cinema' refers to the four Southern Indian film industries – Telugu, Tamil, Malayalam and Kannada. Industries in each of these languages are widely referred to by Hollywood-centric derivative names: Tollywood (for Telugu cinema), Kollywood (for Tamil cinema), Sandalwood (for Kannada cinema) and Mollywood (for Malayalam cinema). The origins of South Indian cinema can be traced back to films from studios in the Madras Presidency, as opposed to Hindi and Bengali cinema. These film industries are as old as any Indian cinema and are the dominant players in many ways. While lacking Bollywood's brand name, the South Indian film industry is far more dynamic, producing nearly half of the total films in India. Of the 1986 films released in 2018, 868 were from the south (Tamil 189, Telugu 242, Mollywood 173 and Kannada 264, as against Bollywood's 305).

Characterized by melodramatic storytelling and performance, high-decibel delivery of alliterative and emotive dialogues, extensively choreographed song sequences featuring numerous dancers and artists and elaborate costumes, south Indian films are often caricatured as loud and crude. However, these films are hugely popular within India and its diaspora. The exposure to global cinema makes the film-literate audiences here discerning enough to be unforgiving when undervalued. Be it the first southern talkie *Kalidas*, which was released in 1931; or the famous drum dance in *Chandralekha* (1948) that propelled the south onto the national stage; or, more recently, the films *Bahubali 1* (2015) and *Bahubali 2* (2017), which stormed the box office across the country and the world, south Indian films have constantly made Western critics sit up and take notice. If Telugu cinema can boast of legions of viewers in India and abroad, and its spectacular stunts, hyperbolic dialogue and performances and big screen entertainment, Tamil films are known to have revived film-making in Sri Lanka, Malaysia, Singapore and Canada and also for its experiments with genres such as the noir, gangster and science fiction in the last two decades. If Malayalam cinema has now heralded a New Age cinema in content and treatment, spearheaded by a young breed of storytellers, Kannada cinema, a pioneer in the New Wave Cinema of the 1970s, has seen a revival and is catching up with the other industries in terms of the number of productions.

The South Indian film industry is respected for its disciplined work ethic. Bound scripts, strict schedules, production plans, call sheets, with all crew and technicians respecting timelines and deadlines are a hallmark of the four industries. In all areas of film-making, such as in production, post-production, distribution and exhibition, South Indian films have led from the front with cutting-edge technology, with some of the finest post-production facilities in Asia available at Chennai and Hyderabad, and effective management of resources. The industry also boasts of many globally recognized names, such as Adoor Gopalakrishnan, Girsh Kasaravalli, G. Aravindan, K. Viswanath, Vetrimaraan, Mani Ratnam, Rajamouli, Sivaji Ganesan, MGR, NTR, ANR, Rajkumar, Prem Nazir, Rajinikanth, Kamal Haasan, Chiranjeevi and Sridevi.

The politics of the region are also seamlessly played out in films of this industry, often propelling actors into politics and power (M. G. Ramachandran aka MGR, Jayalalithaa and N. T. Rama Rao aka NTR are cases in point). In Tamil Nadu, in particular, the Dravidian movement consciously used films to propagate political ideology, just as it happened with Soviet cinema. In recent times, Hindi remakes of South Indian films have found huge success at the box office.

References

Pandian, M. S. S. *The Image Trap: M.G. Ramachandran in Film and Politics*. New Delhi: SAGE Publications, 1992.

Velayutham, Selvaraj. *Tamil Cinema: The Cultural Politics of India's Other Film Industry*. New Delhi: Routledge, 2008.

TAJ MAHAL

Timeri N. Murari

The Taj Mahal is named after the woman whose sarcophagus lies in the centre of the tomb, directly beneath the peak of the dome – Mumtaz Mahal. The Mughal emperor Shah Jahan's sarcophagus lies beside hers. He christened Arjumand, the wife he loved deeply, Mumtaz Mahal – the jewel of the palace. The Taj Mahal remains one of the Seven Wonders of the World, along with Petra in Jordon and the Statue of Liberty in New York.

These two words – Taj Mahal – which possess mystery and meaning, have defined India for centuries. If Taj Mahal did not exist in the world's vocabulary, India would, perhaps, not exist in its vocabulary either. The words had the power to cross global boundaries, unlike anything else that this ancient culture has created – temples, palaces, forts or even the great prehistoric civilizations.

For the majority of the world that does not know what it represents, the Taj Mahal has a meaning. It conjures up the ultimate sense of splendour, something beyond ethereal and their imaginations and yet, when the world hears the words, it understands that it defines ultimate beauty. People will not have ever seen it, probably only have a vague sense of its location, if that, but will identify, by its evocation, that it is the yardstick of aesthetic perfection. Added potency to the words is the knowledge that within the beauty lies a powerful love story and one cannot deny the power of love to seduce any individual's imagination.

The Taj Mahal appears frequently in national and international news media as presidents (Obama), prime ministers (Netanyahu), princesses (Diana), the list of powerful people, make the pilgrimage to Agra to pose on the same marble bench in front of the tomb. It is a must-see, must-do for every tourist (seven to eight million annually at the last count) visiting India, alongside Indians, themselves, who have never seen it before. We should be grateful that its serenity stilled the destructive impulses in humans. Four centuries of conquests and wars have raged around the Taj Mahal and though the Persian and other invaders did plunder the tomb of its silver doors and inlaid precious stones, they left it relatively unharmed. They were awed by its beauty, soothed by its icy calm and stole only what they thought was precious. It even survived the destructive impulses of our British overlords – the Marquis of Hastings and Lord Bentinck. Both of them wanted to break up the tomb and sell the marble to dealers in Calcutta. Fortunately for the Taj Mahal, the marble prices in London dropped as the British had discovered porcelain for their bathrooms. It was the viceroy – Lord Curzon – who not only saved the Taj Mahal but also carried out much-needed repairs after centuries of neglect.

Keywords for India

The overuse of those two words to define the country and evoke that beauty has, however, coarsened its meaning over the years. There must be hundreds of restaurants in the UK, Europe and other cities in the world, with the name Taj Mahal, not so much to celebrate the magnificence of this tomb but to announce to passers-by that Indian food (chicken *tikkas*) are served within. Worse happened to the words Taj Mahal when a real estate tycoon built a monstrously ugly building, filled it with kitsch that reflected the height of his bad taste, in Atlantic City and christened this definition of over-the-top awfulness, the Taj Mahal Casino. Despite his ignorance, he reached out for something that was, for him, the sublime idea of beauty, splendour and magnificence.

References

Murari, Timeri N. *Taj: A Story of Mughal India*. New Delhi: Aleph Books India, 2017.
Taj Mahal-Official Website of Taj Mahal, Government of Uttar Pradesh (India)'. Tajmahal.gov.in. Available at: https://www.tajmahal.gov.in/index.html (accessed 25 May 2019).

TAMASHA (TAMĀŚĀ)

Arjun Ghosh

The word *tamasha* is of Persian origin and can variously mean 'fun', 'play', 'entertainment' or 'spectacle'. By the twentieth century, the word spread to other parts of the world. In the Indian subcontinent, it has taken on additional meanings of 'commotion', 'chaos', 'excitement' or a 'large participative spectacle'. Tamasha also assumes a part of its meaning from a popular performance form that is prevalent in Maharashtra.

The most retweeted tweet, using the term tamasha in January 2018, interpreted the unprecedented press conference by four senior judges of the Supreme Court of India as a tamasha which was carried out in a state of mind that lacked 'calm … without thinking twice' – and a mistake which they would 'regret'. In an interview, eminent singer Ghulam Ali lamented that *ghazal* singing is being altered to suit commercial interests and styles and that unmindful of the traditions, contemporary ghazal had become a tamasha. In these instances, tamasha is seen as standing for a corruption of acceptable practices, a deformity that does not belong to the social mainstream.

On the other hand, a news story describing a new restaurant for a club associated with the Indian parliament is headlined, 'chefs stirring up a little tamasha'. The restaurant aimed to move away from the 'same pedestrian desi staple' to a cuisine that is cooked up at French cooktops, with fire guns, siphons and pipettes. Thus, a cultural shift from the ordinary or the mundane is described as sharing the excitement of tamasha.

In Maharashtra, tamasha is one of the most popular forms of rural theatre in India. Over four hundred tamasha troupes criss-cross the state putting together a variety entertainment involving songs, dances, music and narratives. These are performances by itinerant troupes which set up stage in open spaces and perform before large audiences numbering thousands.

The form came to Maharashtra through Mogul armies which, during its long years of campaign, camped in the area. Singing girls and dancers were brought in from the north to entertain the soldiers. Soon local musicians, percussionists and actors joined them to produce what today is tamasha – an escapist entertainment for a predominantly male audience.

In the seventeenth century, tamasha was patronized by the *Peshwas*. The court patronage receded in the nineteenth century, during British occupation. The tamasha survived under the patronage of the landlords. It was during this time that tamasha assumed vulgarity. During the Peshwa period, the *lavni* entered tamasha. A lavni is a narrative song that expresses love and vigour. It is accompanied by dancing with gyrations and lustful expressions. Till the nineteenth century, the female characters were performed by boys – the *nachya*. The absence of women also granted a licence to the performers to play up the lustful rendition before the largely male audience. When female dancers were introduced in the nineteenth century, such renditions bordering on vulgarity continued. As a result, the audiences looked upon the female performers as little more than prostitutes.

In an increasingly casteist India, the understanding of tamasha as vulgar is often seen in consonance with the incidence of the performers of tamasha who have been largely from the lower castes – the *Mahars*, the *Mangs* and the *Kolhaties*. This has caused the tamasha to be repeatedly censured by conservative opinion. Since the mid-twentieth century, the popularity of the tamasha has caused it to be appropriated for political and mass campaigning. Tamasha performances by the left-wing Indian Peoples' Theatre Association tried to cull out a more sanitized version of the form. In the 1950s, the central government initiated a programme of social reformation through drama. Balwant Gargi decried the attempt by social playwrights to substitute the 'lewd' language of tamasha with sanitized humour as one that was 'driven by bigotry' and 'taking the very guts out of the tamasha' for 'what is vulgar for the middle class is not vulgar for the commoner'.

Its association with the world of Bollywood lends to tamasha the association of glitz, glamour and sleaze. In the 1950s, as cinema grew in popularity, tamasha song and dance sequences influenced the Marathi cinema. But the cinema, in turn, returned to the tamasha with the audiences demanding film songs to be repeated on the stage. The performances compulsively exude energy to ensure that the spectators are not bored. The compere often shared light-hearted and provocative jokes with the audience to keep the focus on the bawdy aspects of the dances. During performances, often audience members would offer money to the dancers, both as requests to perform a particular number and to repeat raunchy gyrations.

The tamasha is also an extremely versatile performance form which can be performed at virtually any open space. This allows the form to be accessible to working-class districts and to the peasantry. Many of the songs of the tamasha operate in the second person with a constant reference to a figure among the audience. This, along with the tone of interaction, makes for a participative body of spectators. Thus, tamasha also carries with it a sense of a participative entertainment, a fun play, a lavish spectacle.

The word tamasha has leant itself to the titles of multiple enterprises – a chain of restaurants, a magazine for children and certainly to numerous theatre groups both in India and other countries. In each such usage, the word picks up a connotation that is distinctly subcontinental. For instance, a book by Himika Ganguly, which takes the reader through multiple encounters of a young woman with prospective suitors, is titled *The Great Indian Matrimonial Tamasha*. The narrative of the book relies on a dramatic dialogue between the woman and her various suitors in the matchmaking game where the conversations do anything but arrive at a meeting of the minds. In this instance, 'tamasha' indicates a show, a play which is make-belief and not always attaining its objective. When the Congress Party boycotted the midnight launch of the Goods and Services Tax in the parliament, it sought to discredit the event by calling it a tamasha. In both this case, 'tamasha' refers to a gathering of large numbers of people to watch a carefully orchestrated spectacle.

References

Gargi, Balwant. *Folk Theatre of India*. Delhi: Rupa & Co., 1991.
Pandit, Maya. 'Tamasha'. In *The Oxford Companion to Indian Theatre*, edited by Ananda Lal, 466–7. New Delhi: Oxford University Press, 2004.

VAASTU (VĀSTU)

Rajat Subhra Banerjee

Vaastu, or Vaastu Shastra, is a traditional Indian system of architecture. Vaastu Vidya, or the philosophy and design of buildings, was prevalent in various parts of India in the distant past, starting, most probably, from the Indus Valley Civilization. Temples were probably the first elements of building that were guided by Vaastu Shastra, though later it embraced all other forms of buildings and also town planning. Unfortunately, most of the ancient texts on Vaastu Shastra are lost in the mists of history. Only bits and pieces have survived, resulting in large gaps in the true understanding of this ancient philosophy.

These aforementioned gaps have led to a wide variety of interpretations for Vaastu today. People have merrily gone for a sort of fill-in-the-blanks exercise to come up with their own versions of Vaastu. I am no Vaastu expert by any means, but as a professional architect, I have met, over the years, many such 'specialists'. From these esteemed practitioners of an ancient philosophy, I have picked up the bits and pieces of Vaastu (along with a great many 'blanks'), as it is widely practiced in India, and especially Eastern India, at present.

Let us consider the example of a single residential unit. In Vaastu, as loosely practiced in Kolkata and other parts of Eastern India, the house is roughly divided into four quarters – Earth (Bhumi) – south-west, Water (Jal) – north-east, Air (Vayu) – north-west and Fire (Agni) – south-east. The planning of a house depends mainly on these four factors. There are, of course, several other considerations, but for the moment we'll stick to these basic issues.

Very simplistically, to begin with the Fire Zone (Agni Kon), this is associated as a general rule, with the kitchen, where a fire is lit everyday in a typical Indian household. This kitchen is to be placed in the south-east corner of the house. From the climatology point of view, the south-east corner is the ideal position of the master bedroom, but Vaastu deems otherwise.

The Water Zone (Jal Kon), once again, is associated with the bathrooms and overhead tanks, which are then placed in the north-east. The Air Zone (Vayu Kon) is, in its turn, believed to imply airiness and piety, thus balconies and puja rooms are preferred in the north-west to make the breeze flow and saintliness glow. Everything else is in the Earth Zone (Bhumi Kon) and tends to be crammed into the south-western section of the house.

There is, however, an alternative way of looking into these four entities. Hindu philosophy is full of allusions. What if these four entities represent the four stages of life or 'varnashrama'? A few thousand years ago, a man (yes, we'll be completely patriarchal here and restrict ourselves to men) would be expected to live to the ripe old age of 60, so we can divide his live into four quarters, each spanning roughly fifteen years. For the first fifteen years, a man is a child. This is the Water (Jal) period and one most important property of water is that it has no shape of its own; it assumes the shape of whichever container it is kept in. Similarly, a child starts with a more or less blank slate. Thus, the environment (or container) for the first fifteen years or so shapes his character. The next fifteen years, roughly from the age of fifteen to thirty, is one where the male patriarch is assumed to be at his physical peak. A fire now burns strongly within him. This is the period where he achieves whatever he'll achieve in his life (or so it was thought in that ancient Vedic Age), perhaps as a soldier of fortune or a farmer or a priest. So this is the Fire (Agni) period. Thereafter, comes the period between roughly the ages of thirty and forty-five, when a man settles down with his family in a house that he has built for himself on his own land, resting on the laurels gained during his previous fifteen years. This is the grounded Earth (Bhumi) period. Finally, there is a period where Air (Vayu) dominates, as the male figure in our story gradually ages and becomes vacant – more gas and less substance, until one fine day his soul departs into the ether forever.

Transposing the above temporal sequence in the spatial structure of a residential building, the child should ideally be housed in the north-east (Jal Kon), the young man in the south-east (Agni Kon), the middle-aged man in the south-west (Bhumi Kon) and the old and infirm in the north-west (Vayu Kon). Bathrooms, kitchens and balconies can be fitted in suitable niches within. As an architect, I feel reasonably certain that houses designed on these premises could turn out to be far more comfortable than houses having the kitchen, say, in the south-east corner – at least in Indian conditions. But the vaastu pandits are loathe to accept this interpretation, even as India continues to move into the twenty-first century and beyond.

References

Fazeli, Hengameh and Ali Goodarzi. 'The Principles of Vastu as a Traditional Architectural Belief System from an Environmental Perspective'. *WIT Transactions on Ecology and the Environment* 128 (2010): 97–108.
Birtchnell, Thomas. 'Vastu Compliance: The Gentrification of India's Sacred Spaces and the Mobilities of Ideas'. *Journal of Ethnic and Migration Studies* 42, no. 14 (2016): 2345–59.

YOGA (YŌGA)

Ranjit Nair

The earliest appearance in any visual record of yoga is on a steatite seal that has come to be known as the Pashupati seal from the Indus Valley civilization, thought to have perished by human or natural agencies around 2000 BC. The seal depicts a man seated in a yogic posture with animals surrounding him. Until the script is deciphered, there is little that can be conclusively established about the figure. Suffice it to say that yoga in embryonic form seems to manifest in this great civilization of antiquity.

In the Indian tradition, yoga was not just calisthenics but also stood for a philosophy which was counted among the 'orthodox' Hindu darsanas, of which there were six, by the reckoning of the celebrated eighth-century philosopher Shankara, who is credited with having revitalized Hindu philosophy and practice. Each darshana has a philosophical work as the starting point and yoga's was the Yoga Sutras of Patanjali which dates to back to the second century BCE. Patanjali summarizes yoga in the pithy epigram *yogaschittivrtiinirodhana* which, literally translated, means 'yoga is the inhibition of the diversions of consciousness'.

Yoga was paired with the Samkhya school of philosophy within the cohort of the six schools. The Samkhya or 'Enumeration' was based on a dualist conception of mind and body. To a considerable extent, yoga was to Samkhya as practice was to theory. Samkhya seems to have been the dominant philosophical tradition when the Bhagavad Gita was composed as the latter text maintains that there is no knowledge equal to that of Samkhya. The practitioner of yoga turned the senses inward, *avrtta cakhshu amrtatvam icchan*, 'with eyes turned inward, desiring immortality'.

The Bhagavad Gita, which nestles within the epic Mahābhārata, proclaims *yoga:karmasu kaushala*, meaning 'yoga is skill in works'. In his commentary on this sloka, Shankara explains skill as the ability to undertake works while keeping at bay the attachments which come with it. This is rephrased as *nishkama karma* or 'work undertaken without the desire for reward'.

As a system of meditation, the yoga appears across the spectrum of Indian philosophical traditions, both Vedic and non-Vedic. In each of them, the practice of yoga was an indispensable for emancipation from the everyday world, variously known as *mōkṣa*, *nirvāṇna* and *kaivalya* in the canon of each school. As part of the search for the knowledge that liberates, each tradition had its own account of yoga, consistent with its metaphysics and epistemology. Among the criteria of knowledge, the Yoga Sutra also lists yogic perception or *pratyaksha* that included a notion of perception transcending the senses, which was interpreted by different schools based on their own distinctive philosophical tenets. These differences are to be observed, for example, in the 'concept-free' (*nirvikalpaka*) *pratyaksha* of the northern Buddhist schools of Mahayana Buddhism and its offshoots to the Advaita Vedanta's state of supreme felicity which involved the recognition that the individual *atman* or self is in fact the *atman* of all being embodied in the *mahavakya* 'Tattvamasi' or 'that thou art' adumbrated by the Upanishads.

Later, yoga fascinated the modern West, with yoga groups emerging a century ago, in the wake of the exertion of scholar-monks like Swami Vivekananda who took it overseas. It caught the attention of the West in the first quarter of the twentieth century at a popular level as an exotic form of calisthenics and its breathing exercises or *pranayama* (literally 'control of the breath') were recommended by doctors as a method of oxygen intake which had positive impacts on health and well-being. In the sixties, the Beatles took to meditation, visiting Maharishi Mahesh Yogi in his ashram in Haridwar, making yoga a part of popular culture in the West. Several savants followed, including Buddhists, thus making yoga widely accessible. Yoga was commercialized, with some practitioners patenting their versions of yoga to make it part of consumerist culture. Yoga became a brand, with accessories such as yoga mats.

The hatha yoga, which involved physical exercises that could be strenuous, was popularized, even as warnings were issued by public health authorities that its contortions of bodily organs could cause injury.

In the contemporary world, yoga won recognition by UNESCO as recognized as living intangible cultural heritage by UNESCO. The Indian prime minister Modi suggested that 21 June be declared as the International Yoga Day, which found favour with the UN General Assembly and won them over with an overwhelming majority. Yoga is seen as a prime example of India's 'soft power' and there are tens of millions of people practicing it, proclaiming its aesthetic and mental value and teaching it across the world.

References

Burley, M. *Classical Samkhya and Yoga – An Indian Metaphysics of Experience*. New Delhi: Routledge, 2012.

Iyengar, B. K. S. *Light on the Yoga Sutras of Patanjali*. London: HarperCollins, 2002.

CHAPTER 3
ECONOMIC MANTRAS, MEDIA AND TECHNOLOGICAL CHANGE

AADHAAR (ĀDHĀR)

Vijayanka Nair

Across the length and breadth of India, the word 'Aadhaar' – which means 'foundation' or 'support' in many Indian languages – is now arguably synonymous with a government-issued twelve-digit unique biometric ID. In under a decade, the central government has issued an Aadhaar number to nearly every resident of India. Aadhaars are linked to individual iris scans, fingerprints, facial photographs and select demographics in a Central Identities Data Repository (CIDR). Instituted in 2009, the Unique Identification Authority of India (UIDAI) now presides over the world's largest biometrics-based identity verification system. Its unparalleled experiment is being watched closely across the world; indeed, Aadhaar is setting a global precedent for the possibilities and limits of national biometrics-enabled governance.

Aadhaar was heralded as a solution to a plethora of socio-economic problems. In postcolonial India, people have used a slew of papers to prove identity – common among them were ration cards, voter ID cards, driving licences, passports and Permanent Account Number (PAN) cards. Even as there were several IDs to choose from, not everyone had equal access to them. IDs beget IDs. Those who had none to begin with were thus continually denied recognition. The government's 'pro-poor' identification scheme would, most notably, make known to the government those who needed benefits, subsidies and services the most.

By allowing for 'anytime, anywhere' identification, the Aadhaar scheme also promised to staunch leakages in the government welfare delivery mechanisms and stymie corruption. The 'who are you?' question was thus also closely linked to the question 'are you who you say you are?' The UIDAI database would insure the weeding out of ghost, fake and duplicate identities from databases that the government already possessed.

What would unlock 'unique' identity would be a person's biological features. The UIDAI would collect minimal demographic information and rely on biometrics to verify the person's identity. After creating a total archive of the population, the only thing that the UIDAI would do would be to prove that you are who you say you are. This it would do in a Yes/No format, by connecting to the CIDR. The UIDAI's prerogative was to provide basic but universal identity verification across the country. It steered clear of guaranteeing rights, benefits or subsidies. Aadhaar would, however, supposedly ease the path to access all of these.

Early on, the UIDAI decided that it would need to draft government institutions to work on this massive national programme. Many government bodies served as 'registrars' for the programme. Both public and private players were enlisted to gather biometric and demographic data. The UIDAI was at the helm of affairs and succeeded in issuing IDs to nearly a billion people with extraordinary alacrity. By any yardstick, issuing the ID was a logistical success. The avowed central tenet of the UIDAI is that technology has the potential to empower the citizen. The UIDAI would mend ailing government structures through its 'scalable' open-source technologies. That was its promise.

Presented as a mere 'technical' intervention, however, Aadhaar soon descended into a contentious national landscape. Some have argued that the bullish pursuit of this programme meant ignoring, in many instances, the legal, economic and sociopolitical implications of the programme. The biggest question that Aadhaar raises relates to privacy and national security. Aadhaar is seen by its opponents as a tool to build a surveillance state and a means to destabilize the current hard-won balance of power between the state and the citizen. In turn, concerns are also being raised about malevolent actors compromising the database.

Aadhaar is founded on the principle that a technologically powered identity database can help 'leapfrog' India's development. It offers speed, efficiency and transparency. The making of Aadhaar is also a remaking of the idea of the citizen, then. Aadhaar is envisioned as the ubiquitous signifier of individual identity, with applications in healthcare, banking, education and, more broadly, as the basis of consumption. The all-consuming citizen and the all-seeing state appear to come together in the 'unique' Indian experiment that is Aadhaar.

References

Khera, R., ed. *Dissent on Aadhaar: Big Data Meets Big Brother*. Orient BlackSwan, 2019.
Nilekani, N., Viral Shah and Aparna Ranjan, *Rebooting India: Realizing a Billion Aspirations*. New Delhi: Penguin Books India, 2015.
Rao, Ursula and Vijayanka Nair, eds. 'Aadhaar: Governing with Biometrics, Special Section, South Asia.' *Journal of South Asian Studies* 42, no. 3 (2019): 469–611.

ASPATRE/HASPATAL (ASPATRE/HASPATĀL)

Kavery Nambisan

'When is the *aspatre* open?' is a question I'm often asked.

An enclosed passage measuring nine paces in length and three in width is a rough and ready portion of our home where I treat our village folk. There is an examination couch, a table and chair and two grey stone shelves built into the wall for the tablets, salves, splints and injections.

Aspatre is the South Indian equivalent of the *haspatal* or *aspatāl* in Hindi-speaking regions. They are lingual variations of the word 'hospital' which came to us through our British colonizers. The 'hospice' which cares for the terminally or chronically ill has been in existence since the eleventh century CE. The word itself is derived from the Latin *hospes*, which is the etymological root of 'host' and 'hospitality'.

Old age, injury and disease lie in wait for every healthy one of us. Places of refuge for the sick perhaps predate history. We have the *dharmshala*, *ashram*, *chaori* or a temple courtyard where travellers and pilgrims take shelter, and an ailing destitute will be offered safety and food. In South Indian languages, such shelters are known as the *chavadi*, *chatra* or *satram*. The meaning is derived from chatra or umbrella, meaning a place of shelter; or it may be a place where four roads meet.

In ancient Greece, Aesculapius, the God of Healing, resided in an oracle that spoke through the temple priest and advised the sick about diet, abstinence and penance. Patient details were inscribed on temple walls and were some of the earliest case records. From early Christian era till well after the Middle Ages, disease and suffering were attributed to a sinful life. The monks and priests had as much authority over this business as a doctor. In rural areas such as ours, it is still common to seek out the 'voice of god' that will speak to the sufferer through an exorcist or priest who then might incite the caring family to beat the evil spirits of disease away with sticks and brooms.

The hospital as we know it now, in its coldly professional, regimented form, offers the cure of disease. Cure has relegated care to the backseat and with that, the hospice and its corollaries more or less bowed out.

My idea of a hospital, haspatal, aspatre is a place where care and cure combine to heal the patient. The treatment corner of our home being called an aspatre is somewhat apt. My personal and professional zones have jostled for at least nine-tenths of my career. From single-room hospital accommodation to double-room, bedsit, flat or bungalow, I am never far from the sounds of stretcher, wheel chair, ambulance sirens, the shouting ayah or the wailing mourners. Ejected from slumber by an ever-conscientious husband, I curse, slip some clothes over my nightwear, grab the hide-all white coat and tear out of home and in through a side entrance of the hospital to a waiting patient. In Bihar, if the intercom did not jangle me out of slumber, it was an AK 47 which has an eerie resemblance to crackers.

If Susruta operated under a tree, as we are told to believe, it was good thinking: sanitary, well-lit, peaceful. The only spectators permitted to see the supersurgeon at work were potential patients. The barber-surgeons of Europe worked from cubby-hole chambers, showing off their expertise to curious passers-by. In 1834, Dr Ephraim McDowell of Kentucky operated on a woman for an ovarian tumour on the kitchen table, with her reading the Bible and the neighbours outside the door ready to lynch him if he failed. Surgery is very different now, but there is a lot that can be done outside the comforting space of a hospital.

Suffering cries for love. The gentle word, the soft touch, the preserving of dignity. Some of us will leave this world within the impersonal confines of a medical ward or an intensive care unit (ICU). As I wind down professionally, I do more and more of less and less. I try to erase the creases of suffering a tiny little bit, in my aspatre.

References

Kapoor, Bimla. 'Model of Holistic Care in Hospice Set Up in India'. *Nursing Journal of India*, October 2003. Available at: https://web.archive.org/web/20080119011430/http:/findarticles.com/p/articles/mi_qa4036/is_200308/ai_n9246448 (accessed December 2018).

Saunders, Dame Cicely M. and Robert Kastenbaum. *Hospice Care on the International Scene*. New York City: Springer Publishing Company, 1997.

BENAMI

Paranjoy Guha Thakurta

The word 'benami' is of Urdu origin, which literally translates as 'without a name'. In contemporary India, the word has been most frequently used to signify ownership and transfer of property (usually immovable) in the names of those who are not the real owners of the property but acting on behalf of, or at the behest of, others who are the real owners of the property – in legal parlance, the 'beneficial owners'.

Thus, typically, wealthy individuals transfer ownership of land and real estate in the names of their faithful retainers to avoid and evade payment of taxes. For example, the infamous Hyderabad-based Byrraju Ramalinga Raju, who set up the Satyam group of companies which was embroiled in a major financial scandal, made vehicle drivers and gardeners directors of companies that owned valuable properties although they were paid low salaries. The 'real' owners of these firms were Raju and his associates.

In 1973, the Law Commission of India recommended the enactment of a law to check benami transactions. In May 1988, the Indian parliament enacted the Benami Transactions (Prohibition) Act. The act defined a benami transaction as one in which property is transferred from one person for a consideration that is paid for by another person. Curiously, the rules that were required to make the law operational were not framed for nearly twenty-three years!

In 2011, the United Progressive Alliance government led by Manmohan Singh introduced a bill to amend the law ostensibly to make it more effective. But no offender was prosecuted. In July 2016, a little over a year after Narendra Modi became prime minister, the law was amended yet again. In its current avatar, the act gives the government the right to confiscate and recover the benami property without paying any compensation to its 'owner'. The new law has put in place mechanisms for appeals and an adjudicating authority.

The benamidar (in whose name the property is shown as standing), the beneficiary (who has actually paid the consideration) and the persons who are found to be 'abetting and inducing' benami transactions are prosecutable and may face rigorous imprisonment up to seven years besides being liable to pay a fine up to 25 per cent of the 'fair market value' of the property. Those furnishing false information to the law-enforcing authorities are also liable to be prosecuted, imprisoned and fined.

The amended law has been projected as a means to put the fear of prison in those who are rich and corrupt. But it has not been effective in the least thus far.

Paranjoy Guha Thakurta is an independent journalist, author, publisher, documentary film-maker and consultant.

References

'The Benami Transactions (Prohibition) Amendment Act, 2016'. www.egazette.nic.in/writereaddata/2016/171245.pdf (Retrieved 6 November 2019).

BLACK ECONOMY

Arun Kumar

The black economy is the key problem confronting Indian society today. It impacts every aspect of the nation's life, yet few analysts incorporate it in their analysis. There are many misunderstandings about it, such as it is all cash, or it is a parallel or an informal activity, or that all the black money is held abroad. The problem is black income generation and not black money held as cash; the distinction is between flows and stocks. By definition, the black economy is linked to illegality in society and it originates in both legal and illegal activities. While the entire income from the illegalities is black, the generation of black income from legal activities can be done by over- and under-invoicing.

Black economy is measured relative to the white economy. It has grown from 4–5 per cent of the gross domestic product (GDP) in 1955–56 to 62 per cent in 2012–13. While this adds to the measured GDP, it has been shown that the black economy lowers the rate of growth below the potential due to the inefficiencies it creates. Further, it leads to the failure of macro and micro policies, higher levels of inflation, higher deficit in the budget due to taxes not being collected and lower investment rates due to flight of capital. It leads to shortage of foreign exchange due to manipulation of exports and imports, failure of policies for education and health, aggravated poverty and inequality, environmental damage and lop-sided urbanization. It also impacts work ethic and leads to higher levels of criminalization. Justice is greatly delayed, and the corrupt take advantage of it to escape. The sense of social injustice in society increases leading to greater alienation. Politics and elections are closely linked to the black economy.

India has taken many steps to control the black economy over the past seventy years, but with little success, because it is a political problem and not a technical or an economic one. Tax rates have been lowered from 97.5 per cent in 1971 to the present level of 30 per cent, but the black economy has only grown. A large number of controls were removed from the statue books (e.g. Monopolistic and Restrictive Trade Practice [MRTP] and Foreign Exchange Regulation Act [FERA]) after 1991, but that did not impede the growth of the black economy. At 62 per cent, illegality is widespread and that is only possible if the instrumentality of the state is involved in its generation. It has been argued that the black economy is run by the triad of corrupt businessmen, the political class and the executive. Unless the triad is dismantled, the black economy cannot be checked. The need is for political movements to bring about accountability at all levels. There are no short-term solutions to the problem. Demonetization was a technical step which failed to curb the black economy, because it did not impact the triad at all.

References

Kumar, A. *The Black Economy in India*. New Delhi: Penguin India, 1999.
National Institute of Public Finance and Policy (NIPFP). *Aspects of Black Economy in India*. New Delhi: NIPFP, 1985.

Keywords for India

BREAKING NEWS

Pamela Philipose

The phrase 'Breaking News' holds up a mirror to the mediatization of contemporary Indian society and although it may be made up of two English words, they have made a seamless transition into local patois. While the term has an older provenance in the West, in India it began to be deployed widely only after the arrival of commercial television news production in the country, following the economic liberalization in 1991. Among the various media transformations that the post-liberalization era witnessed was the ending of the near monopoly on the generation of news that had been exercised by the state-owned broadcaster, Doordarshan. What followed was a sustained proliferation of news channels in a scenario that the media academic Nalin Mehta memorably described as 'an epidemic of fraud'.

Sunetra Sen Narayan notes that currently there are around four hundred channels in the country which 'do news' in some form of the other. The battle to gain and, more important, retain eyeballs amidst a volatile viewership and an intense competition for the advertising rupee led to television channels resorting to an assortment of strategies in their bid to survive. The use of the 'Breaking News' device is one such strategy. It is meant to function as a hook to keep that fickle viewer with a remote in hand constantly interested in the fare being offered so that the channel can gain those crucial brownie points, known in industry jargon as television rating points (TRPs)

The device is particularly important for twenty-four-hour news channels that have now become a distinctly significant part of the country's social and political landscape. If the first twenty-four-hour news channel in India made its appearance only in 1998, courtesy Rupert Murdoch and his Hong Kong-based Satellite TV Asian Region (Star TV network), over the next fifteen years there were to be over a hundred of such entities, all of them broadcasting news in a dozen languages around the clock.

What has complicated this avalanche of news unleashed by news channels is the arrival of social media and the smartphone. Social media sites have now emerged as important cogs in the machinery of news creation, both in terms of creating and breaking news. In fact, they have changed the way the newsroom functions. In an earlier era, the life of the story ended when the last edition of the newspaper went to bed or after the final television news bulletin of the day was broadcast. Social media has disrupted this pattern, making news generation an unending cycle of disparate events. Earlier, attention was focused on getting a complete and exclusive story ready by the end of the day; today, the emphasis is more on providing details of stories as they unravel. In such a fluid context, a device such as 'Breaking News', even as it keeps the interest of audiences alive, also provides a thread of connectivity between discrete parts of the story.

A recent blurb put out by the Hindi news channel, that defines itself as *sabse tez* ('fastest of all'), tells this story well: 'Aaj Tak, India's most watched news channel, is available as an app. The app brings to you Live TV, latest Hindi news, breaking news alerts (*taaza* Hindi *khabar*) … Download the Aaj Tak app on your Smartphone and watch Aaj Tak news channel Live.' But the very success of this device could be its undoing. The diminishing returns of crying wolf could mean that its inherent promise of delivering information of paramount public interest could become exposed for what, ultimately, it sometimes is: mere advertisement without substance, a purveyor of fake tidings and even sleaze. Often, breaking news is neither 'breaking' nor, strictly speaking, 'news', just the illusion of a busy news scenario. Despite this, the prospect of the veil being lifted from over the magic words 'Breaking News' is not upon us any time soon. There is still a lot of juice in this lemon, as most television news editors would maintain, and they will continue to squeeze it for some time yet.

The attractiveness of this peg for both news producers and viewers alike testifies ultimately to its compelling nature, catering as it does to inordinate appetite for news among ordinary Indians who are still prepared to spare time and attention for the electric lure of being 'in the loop'; that magical possibility of gaining a 'sneak peek' into what lies in the womb of the future.

References

Mehta, Nalin. *Behind a Billion Screens: What Television Tells Us about Modern India*, 14. New Delhi: Harper Collins, 2015.
Narayan, Sunetra Sen. *Globalization and Television: A Study of the Indian Experience 1900–2019*, 89. New Delhi: Oxford University Press, 2014.

CLIMATE CHANGE

Navroz K. Dubash

'Climate change' is a thoroughly un-Indian word. It originates in international discourse around a global-scale physical phenomenon. Indeed, there is little any single country can do alone to address climate change, other than prepare to bear its impacts. In many ways, climate change only makes sense as a global construct. However, because the sources of many of these gases – the burning of fossil fuels – are so essential to economic activity, each country has had to craft a narrative, political and policy response appropriate to its own context. Climate change, therefore, also takes on a national sheen. In this process, over the years, a distinctly Indian, if nascent, narrative around climate change has emerged.

For close to a quarter century, from the start of global negotiations in 1990 to about 2005, the use of climate change in India has been closely paired with the diplomatic challenge of 'negotiations'. Constructed as a problem created by the industrialized world, due to their profligate consumption and consequent high emissions, the issue was one of ensuring adequate consideration of 'equity' in climate discussions. Influenced by a distinctively Indian 'environmentalism of the poor' focused on access to and control over resources, equity applied across countries included consideration of a country's past emissions and its standard of development as the basis for a fair allocation of responsibility for action. Legally, the convoluted but evocative phrase 'common but differentiated responsibility' enshrined in the United Nations (UN) Framework Convention on Climate Change effectively signalled the need to treat the Global North and South differently with regard to climate obligations. India's diplomatic aim, successfully managed for two decades, was to avoid contamination of India's development discourse by climate change considerations.

Global political shifts have played an important role in dissolving this barrier. In geopolitical terms, by the late 2000s, the developing world, led by China, had experienced a decade of high growth, while the industrialized world struggled with low growth rates and a major financial crisis. Due to this, developing countries, including India, were accounting for an increasing share of annual emissions, even though these emissions remained low in per capita terms. Developing countries, it was argued, needed to step up and do more to address climate change. India, with one eye on a seat at the global high table, could not afford to refuse outright.

Formulating a domestic response in terms of 'co-benefits' provided one way to square the circle. The technocratic, yet surprisingly subversive term, 'co-benefits', crystallizes an understanding that the pursuit of developmental objectives could also simultaneously lead to global climate mitigation benefits. For example, better urban public transport makes for livable cities but also reduces emissions; climate and development need not always be in conflict.

Used as a framing concept in India's National Action Plan on Climate Change, 'co-benefits' was intended as a defensive measure to allow India to continue to prioritize development. But puncturing the strict binary between climate and development also complicated matters. If India gained developmentally from some climate actions, then why should rich countries always have to take the lead, and why should they pay entirely for India's mitigation efforts, as India had demanded? This discussion settled into a useful decision rule for policy: India should prioritize areas with co-benefits but also be alert to areas where climate mitigation and development are at odds.

Building on this understanding, climate change took on a new meaning as a policy construct, spawning a proliferating apparatus of policies and bureaucratic appendages. The National Action Plan seeded eight National Missions in areas as diverse as renewable energy and Himalayan states. A further extension to action plans in each state followed. On occasion, linkage to the high-profile climate issue enabled enterprising bureaucrats to strategically advance agendas, with substantial results, as in the case of accelerating adoption of energy-efficiency measures. More frequently, formal institutionalization driven by a pressure to demonstrate action to a global audience preceded adequate conceptualization, and many of these efforts struggled with the idea of how to 'mainstream' climate change into development.

Consequently, climate policy in India has been driven rather more by global imperatives than by citizen concerns about actual impacts, despite India's exposure to monsoon instability, declining crop yields, more violent weather and the like. Thus, a rare 2009 parliamentary debate on climate change focused almost exclusively on whether India risked surrendering its right to development under global pressure, with little mention of climate impacts. However, this may be gradually changing. A survey of (English-language) Indian newspaper articles on the subject in 2009–10 found that only 10 per cent of the articles were focused on science or impacts, while global and Indian climate politics dominated coverage; a larger survey spanning 2010–17 found that impacts occupied 25 per cent of the coverage.

Given the ample causes for concern, why are Indians not more alarmed about climate impacts? In the west, climate concerns are increasingly driven by the prospect of catastrophic climate change. In India, existential climate concerns may simply be crowded out by others that are more immediate and apparent, such as malnutrition, air and water pollution, and urban liveability. Under these conditions, climate change is unlikely to successfully seize a large share of an already overtaxed public imagination. Instead, it may receive indirect attention for its multiplying effects on immediate development challenges, such as food and water security.

Indeed, even the somewhat clumsy terminology for climate change in Hindi, *jal-vaayu parivartan* (water-air changes) invites an attention to a more localized and immediate perspective on the problem, one focused on lived experiences. Apple cultivators in Himachal Pradesh, for example, note changes in growing and ripening seasons for their fruit, with entire regions turning barren. But, even while the implications of climate change in the aggregate are existential, attributing any particular impact to climate change is scientifically challenging. Thus, while floods in Uttarakhand are emblematic of the sorts of damage climate change could cause through high rainfall events, the specific impacts are also likely driven by flawed local land-use policies. It is hard to develop a popular imagination around such heavily caveated narratives.

For all these reasons, climate change remains an arms-length concept in India. The idea and the language have been embraced rather more by the bureaucratic than the public imagination, driven by global conversations. The pathway to deeper Indian public engagement with climate change is less likely to pass through alarm about a future existential crisis and more likely to rest in deeper exercises in translation that tie the global more firmly to local experiences and concerns.

References

Dubash, Navroz K., ed. *India in a Warming World: Integrating Climate Change and Development.* New Delhi: Oxford University Press, 2019.
Dubash, Navroz K., Radhika Khosla, Ulka Kelkar and Sharachchandra Lele. 'India and Climate Change: Evolving Ideas and Increasing Policy Engagement'. *Annual Review of Environment and Resources* 43 (2018): 395–424.

COMPUTER/LAPTOP/MOBILE

Souvik Mukherjee

Computers may not have arrived in colonial India but the Indian Statistical Institute built the first analog computer in the 1950s, and this was followed by an indigenously built digital computer by Tata Institute of Fundamental Research (TIFR). Despite the relatively early beginnings of computing technology, the word 'computer' took its time to appear in common parlance in Indian society. As late as 1984, with the New Computer Policy and the liberalization of telecom services, the scenario saw a sea change in the rapid spread of both computing and mobile technology. The word 'computer' does not appear in Hindi–English dictionaries, such as *The Practical Hindi–English Dictionary* (1970) or even the *Siksarthi Hindi–Angrejhi Sabdakosa* (1989). The Bengali dictionary *Samsad Bengali–English dictionary* (2000) lists the Bengali equivalent of the word as *pariganaka*, which it translates to 'a reckoner, a computer, an enumerator'. This connects to the meaning of computing as enumerating or counting and not so much to the current meaning associated with the computer.

Although portable computers (now called 'laptops') date back to 1984, the appearance of laptops in the lives of Indians took over a decade. The case today is very different. Mobile phones are an integral part of the communications systems in India today. From banking, governance, finance, rural development to the swankiest fashion advertisements, 'mobile' is an integral part of the vocabulary of the major Indian languages. As Dinesh Sharma notes, 'Computers are no more the preserve of scientists, academicians, and businesses … [Mobile phones] are empowering citizens in many ways and even boosting the incomes of the poor. … enabling them to access agriculture-related information to supporting their fight against corruption in government departments.'

Associated with computers, laptops and mobile phones, there are a host of new entrants to the vocabulary of Indian languages and to the general culture of information and communication.

For example, computer-related terms such as 'hard disk', 'hard/soft copy', 'router', 'PC', 'desktop/laptop', 'Windows', 'Office', 'cybercafe', 'hacking' and 'crash' are some of the words that are part of the common usage in urban India – their usage corresponding to their global connotations. To these, one can add local words that have now been appropriated into computerese: the Hindi word *juġāṛa* is a case in point. Padmini Ray Murray and Chris Hand define the concept of ju'gāṛa as 'an indigenous form of hacking that differs from its Western counterpart in its ubiquity, precipitated by economic constraints and lack of resources'. Other less common, but arguably equally interesting, appropriations are words like the compound construction *cybermohalla*, defined by 'Sarai' as follows: 'the Cybermohalla (Cyber Neighbourhood) Project is a community of young practitioners who share each other's thoughts, ideas and creative energies in media labs located in working class areas of Delhi.' There are other such compound constructions in academic circles – such as *digi-naka* (digital crossroads) – that are less permanent in public memory. Another local modification, perhaps region-specific and temporary, is *lappie* for laptop.

Unlike the German *handi*, Indian languages have retained 'mobile phone' in the original English. Together with the technology, the terms such as 'smartphone', 'selfie', 'SIM card' and '3G/4G' have become part of the common parlance. A rather peculiar pan-Indian usage is 'missed call', which denotes someone making a blank call and disconnecting before the call is received, expecting the person on the other side to call back. For both computers and mobile phones, 'social media' is one key inclusion in the vocabulary of Indian languages as well as Indian English. 'Twitter' and its verb form 'tweeting' is now to be found in newspapers, political discourses and general conversations. Likewise, 'Facebook', 'blog', 'Skype' and 'WhatsApp' have also entered the dictionaries as verbs. Similarly, 'gamer' is another such inclusion that has entered the vocabulary recently from the videogame-playing subculture into mainstream discourse. We note that videogame scholar Adrienne Shaw, during a visit to India on a research project, asked the question, 'How do you say gamer in Hindi? How do you say it in Urdu, for that matter, in Gujarati, in Marathi, or in Punjabi?' And, she concluded that although Indian languages have multiple words for 'play', 'gamer' in its videogaming connotation has become a new word in the Indian lexicons. Another borrowing from computer games, particularly, the massively multiplayer online roleplaying games (MMORPGs), is the word 'troll'. Trolls are those who bully others on social media and disrupt conversations. Here, one mustn't forget related words from other sectors, such as industry and finance. 'IT' is perhaps the commonest acronym today to denote a profession in India; 'outsourcing', 'start-ups', 'BPOs', etc., are other common entrants into the vocabulary.

From the virtual absence of the computer in public discourse in the 1970s to the current IT-centric urban scenario, there has been a huge leap in computing discourse. Computer- and mobile-related words have entered the vocabulary of the Indian populace and are now fundamental parts of Indian culture and society.

References

Sarai. 'Cybermohalla Book Box: Sarai', 2003. Available at: http://sarai.net/cybermohalla-book-box/ (accessed December 2018).
Sharma, Dinesh C., *The Outsourcer: The Story of India's IT Revolution*. Cambridge: MIT Press, 2015.

CORPORATE SOCIAL RESPONSIBILITY

Arun M. Kumar

No serious business leader would contest the contention that corporations have responsibilities to society that go well beyond the goods or services they provide to their customers and clients, the welfare of their employees and the returns they deliver to their shareholders. Indeed, it is now well accepted that a company's long-term success is indeed impacted by its record on social responsibility, stewardship of the environment and ethical behaviour. This was not always the case. In the early years of industrialization, enterprise owners restricted their concerns to their own profits. Their engagement with society more broadly was left to their charitable impulses based on personal preferences.

Today, companies often establish organizational units and specific initiatives to address their 'corporate social responsibility', often abbreviated as CSR. These efforts seek to assert and fulfil the responsibilities a company feels towards advancing social well-being. In recent years, spurred by increasing consciousness of environmental sustainability, CSR efforts have particularly embraced a responsibility towards the environment.

CSR is a manifestation of 'corporate citizenship'. A citizen has responsibilities to fellow citizens, often realized through obligations to her or his city, state and country. In much the same way, corporations, which are indeed 'legal persons' in most jurisdictions, are expected to shoulder the responsibilities of citizenship. Visionary corporate leaders had taken on the mantle of such responsibilities long before CSR became a trend or was seen as an imperative. In India, Jamsetji Tata and his successors, as early as the end of the nineteenth century, envisioned regulated working hours for workers and a well laid-out city with facilities for healthcare, education and other amenities for workers and their families.

Around the world, CSR is seen as an important activity. The United Nations Industrial Development Organization (UNIDO) refines CSR as 'a management concept whereby companies integrate social and environmental concerns in their business operations and interactions with their stakeholders'. Inherent in CSR is the concept of a 'triple bottom line', a balance of economic, environmental and social imperatives. This balance is often seen, for instance by the European Commission, as critical for competitiveness, sustainability and innovation. CSR is seen to bring benefits in terms of cost savings, access to capital, customer relationships and human resource management.

The CSR movement is transitioning from its reliance on purely voluntary activity to the greater use of laws. India has emerged as one of the leading countries to make CSR mandatory by the passage of the Companies Act, 2013. This law mandates a CSR expenditure of 2 per cent of the average net profits for companies of a certain size and profitability. KPMG's *India CSR Reporting Survey 2017* noted that overall CSR spending in India was rising with education and health attracting most of the funding.

Beyond CSR is the millennials-inspired view that a corporation must have a higher purpose that captures the value it adds to society. People today want to be engaged in work that contributes to societal advancement and want to see the direct link their work has to social good. Laying bricks may be tedious, but constructing a cathedral makes the same work inspiring.

References

Gupta, Radha and Dil Pazir. 'Emerging Trends of Corporate Social Responsibility in India: An Overview'. *The Journal of Rural and Agricultural Research* (2012): 49.

Mitra, Rahul. 'Framing the Corporate Responsibility-Reputation Linkage: The Case of Tata Motors in India'. *Public Relations Review* 37, no. 4 (2011): 392–8.

CYBERBHAKT

Thomas Abraham

Cyberbhakt is a portmanteau word linking *bhakt* (devotee) and cyberspace. The term has both an earlier and a current meaning. Its current usage, dating to the period during and after the 2014 LōkaSabhā elections, describes ardent followers of the Bharatiya Janata Party (BJP), the Rashtriya Swayamsevak Sangh (RSS) and like-minded Hindu nationalist groups, which have taken to social media to aggressively promote their cause and attack their perceived ideological foes. The author of popular fiction Chetan Bhagat was an early popularizer of the term, and in a *Times of India* article in 2015 he had described the word as 'a cyber species often referred to as "bhakts". The term is used to refer to owners of right wing user accounts who tend to be aggressive fans of all things Hindu.'

For around two decades prior to that, the term was largely used to describe devotees who visited Hindu temple websites and participated in rituals online. One of the earliest reported media usages of this term was in an article in *India Today* in 1998, which commented, 'Gods have always been in heaven; now they are in cyberspace too.' Another study described the phenomenon of *cyberbhakti* and *cyberseva* as new internet-mediated forms of religiosity. These earlier forms of cyberbhakti had no overt political edge but created the context for the birth of online Hindu nationalism. The journalist Sagarika Ghose is credited with coining the term 'Internet Hindus' to describe the growth of a new, more militant avatar of the cyberbhakt. The coinage was made, appropriately enough, in a tweet in 2010, where Ghose commented, 'Internet Hindus are like swarms of bees. They come swarming after you at any mention of Modi, Muslims or Pakistan!'

Ghose's description captures some of the issues dear to the cyberbhakt's heart: a devotion to the BJP, Narendra Modi and Hindu nationalism, combined with a deep animosity to Pakistan and Muslims in general. The phenomenon of the political cyberbhakt is linked to the growth of the BJP's information technology (IT) cell, which guides the party's social media operations by feeding supporters a steady stream of tweets and WhatsApp messages to rebroadcast. However, these online activists are not just retweeters and forwarders of messages, they are also often influential professionals who juggle their day-to-day lives with bouts of online cyber activism in support of the BJP, Narendra Modi and other Hindu nationalist causes.

Cyberbhakts tend not to use the term to describe themselves. Also, Pakistan and Muslims are not the only target of the cyberbhakt's ire. Equally prominent in the bhakt's pantheon of enemies are 'anti-nationals', 'liberals' and 'secularists', the Congress Party, 'leftists', 'naxalites' and journalists who are seen as insufficiently supportive of the BJP and right-wing causes.

Liberal voices on the internet, particularly women, can get bombarded with abusive messages from nationalist cyberbhakts. Often, the cyberbhakt's chosen terms of abuse are corruptions of regular words. Thus, secular becomes 'sickular', 'Lutyens' (referring to the New Delhi that Edward Lutyens designed and seen as home to an entrenched liberal elite) becomes 'Lootyens'. Certain terms combine two or more cyberbhakt themes: thus, the anger against Muslims and the anger against the Congress for supposedly supporting Muslims more than Hindus in India has produced the term 'Khangress' (substituting the Muslim Khan for the first syllable of Congress). Other terms of invective such as 'pressitute' (an amalgam of press and prostitute) and 'libtard' (liberal and retard) are borrowed from global, particularly US, right-wing discourse.

The style of argument of the cyberbhakt is largely based on *ad hominem* attacks. Another form of argument that figures prominently in the cyberbhakt's rhetorical arsenal is commonly known as 'whataboutery' or deflecting attacks on an issue by pointing to similar acts by other parties. This form of argument is both logically and ethically untenable, since a wrong by one party does not justify a wrong by another party.

The cyberbhakts of the Hindu nationalist right are, of course, not the only Indian political voices in cyberspace. The Congress and other parties opposed to right-wing Hindu nationalism, as well as journalists and public intellectuals opposed to the BJP's vision of India, are active on Twitter and other social media platforms and have coined terms such as 'feku' to describe Narendra Modi and 'andh bhakt' to describe what they see as the cyberbhakts' blind devotion to their chosen cause. However, these other political forces do not seem to have the ability to relentlessly attack their opponents in the way the BJP and its supporters can.

References

Bhagat, Chetan. 'Anatomy of an Internet Troll: How Social Media Birthed a Strange New Phenomenon in India, the Bhakts'. *Times of India*, 11 July 2015. Available at: https://blogs.timesofindia.indiatimes.com/The-underage-optimist/anatomy-of-an-internet-troll-how-social-media-birthed-a-strange-new-phenomenon-in-india-the-bhakts/ (accessed December 2018).

Zavos, J., P. Kanungo, D. S. Reddy, M. Warrier and R. Williams, *Public Hinduisms*. New Delhi: Sage Publications, 2012.

DEMONETIZATION

C. Rammanohar Reddy

Until late 2016, 'demonetization' was a term almost completely unknown in India outside a small circle of economists and economic policymakers. This changed on 8 November 2016, when the Government of India decided to withdraw all 500 and 1000 rupees currency notes from circulation and replace them with a new series of 500 rupees and a new currency of 2000 rupees. The word 'demonetization' then became a permanent fixture in the Indian lexicon. In English, the term was 'demonetization', in Hindi the more direct *notebandi*. There was also the development of short forms and alliterations such as 'DeMo' and 'NaMo's DeMo' (Mr Narendra Modi's demonetization).

According to the dictionary, 'demonetization' comes from the French word 'demonetizer', which has its roots in the Latin *moneta* (for money) combined with the prefix *de* (reversal). In plain language, it means depriving a currency of its value as legal tender.

Demonetization is not a common occurrence, but it is also not a rare one. It is an extreme measure used in extreme situations. A well-known example is the demonetization of the German Mark in the 1930s due to hyperinflation. More recently, Brazil did the same in the 1990s, when its Real was replaced by the New Real, also during a time of high inflation. Yet another kind of demonetization was in the early 2000s when the Euro replaced the national currencies of the member states of the European Union.

The Indian experience with demonetization, however, is different. It is of the kind that has been used now and then to fight black money, black marketing, smuggling and other illegal activities. This it does by delegalizing high-value denomination notes, which are seen as the preferred form of holding illegal cash. A few countries – Myanmar, North Korea and Russia – have gone this route in the past couple of decades, though with mixed success. In the case of India in 2016, demonetization was a decision taken to achieve two main objectives: destroy 'black money' and end counterfeiting. Later, other objectives were formally and informally added: improving tax compliance, the promotion of digital payments and the 'formalization' of the economy.

Demonetization was not new to India in 2016. It had been carried out before twice – in 1946 and 1978. What was different in 2016 was the scale of demonetization, which explains the huge impact the process had on people's lives and which was also why it entered everyday language. In the earlier two demonetization events, the high-value notes that were demonetized accounted for less than 10 per cent of the cash in circulation. The impact on commerce and on people's ability to conduct daily transactions was therefore negligible. In 2016, the two currency notes that were demonetized accounted for as much as 86 per cent of the value of the currency in circulation. The impact was immediate and huge on production, trade and the everyday lives of households. The daily routine of production, distribution and consumption was severely disrupted at all levels, most of all among the disadvantaged.

The demonetized currency notes could be deposited in banks or exchanged for new notes and there were weekly limits on the transactions. But, since the scale of replacement was huge and adequate preparations had not been made to stock new currency notes, citizens faced many difficulties. They were denied complete access to their bank deposits. Everyone had to wait for hours in long lines for rationed amounts of cash. To make matters worse, the rules and regulations were frequently changed, sometimes reversing existing rules, and this caused both confusion and more dislocation.

It was not only the media which debated the pros and cons of demonetization. No public or private conversation could avoid speaking about the nitty-gritty of demonetization, its objectives, outcomes and many outlandish rumours. The suddenness, the lack of preparation, the ambiguity about whether its objectives could be met and the fact that its impact was felt every day for weeks on end naturally made it the subject of intense public discussion. Many of these conversations would be held when people stood in long lines to deposit or withdraw money from banks and at ATMs.

The upheaval, confusion and (until then) the unknown nature of the process of demonetization had another kind of impact as well. On social media, in particular, it became the subject of satire and saw immense humour as people found this to be one way of coping with the bewilderment. A large volume of jokes, puns and cartoons cropped up, all poking fun at everyone from the prime minister and the governor of the Reserve Bank of India downwards.

While it was a process that was carried out in the months of November and December in 2016, its short-term impact continued to be felt till early 2017. There was medium-term impact as well, experienced in the form of a slowdown in economic growth that has contunied into 2019–20. There was the promise of a beneficial impact in the long term through better tax compliance, less generation of black money and a less cash-intensive economy. If that does happen, it would be ascribed to that process whose name was difficult to roll over the tongue and yet had become permanently implanted in public consciousness.

References

Ghosh, Jayati, C. P. Chandrasekhar and Prabhat Patnaik. *Demonetisation Decoded: A Critique of India's Currency Experiment*. New Delhi: Routledge, 2017.
Reddy, Rammanohar C. *Demonetisation and Black Money*. Hyderabad: Orient BlackSwan, 2017.

DEVELOPMENT

Pulapre Balakrishnan

The term 'development' has come to mean different things to different people. After close to four decades of uncritical usage, including by the United Nations Organization (UNO), it was to be upended by the Colombian anthropologist Arturo Escobar, who used the historical experience of Latin America to reveal some of the outcomes in areas where public policy was pursued in the name of development. A feature of this was the decimation of the natural environment and thus an assault on the lives of the people whose lives depended upon it. Overall, it represented a subjugation to the interests of metropolitan capital of the native Americans. The title of Escobar's book, *Encountering Development*, suggests that development was not a happy experience for Latin America's subalterns.

In some ways, the Indian experience has features close to that subcontinent's. India's own indigenous populations have been driven to the margins of their own land. Dams and highways, pylons and mines have been eating into their homelands from the 1950s, when a concerted effort had been launched by the government of a newly independent India. Unlike in Latin America, however, it was not loaded against all of India's subalterns. Very likely, the life of the Indian peasantry improved in this period, though far too slowly, as agriculture benefitted from early economic planning in the country. However, this was not the experience of the tribals, whose exclusion may not have remained unchanged, but their lives may have worsened as the pace of denudation of the forests and extraction of minerals quickened. It is indeed a measure of 'progressive' politics in India that the lives of the tribals seldom figure in the discourse on Indian democracy.

Explicit use of the term 'development' in public policy in India is relatively more recent. Scepticism about the justification given to the policies of the Government of India in the name of development peaked with the 'Narmada Bachao Andolan', an agitation to prevent the construction of a gigantic dam which would drown whole villages. The agitation received worldwide attention and led to the cancellation of World Bank aid for the project. The project was not called off, however.

Is the idea of development flawed in its very conception as some appear to suggest? Certainly not. Amartya Sen has conceived of development as the 'expansion of freedom', a scheme in which an individual considers herself free if she is able to undertake the functionings she values. This formulation ensures that we don't use planners' preferences when designing development but go only by the aspirations of individuals. The central task of development now becomes one of building the capabilities of individuals.

Though advance, Sen's idea of development is anthropocentric. It must yet deal with the fact that, in the Anthropocene, human activity has depleted the earth's endowments, affecting its regenerative processes. This threatens the conditions of life for humans. While political agencies such as the UNO have identified the importance of sustainable development, the challenge is to devise an acceptable scheme that reconciles the goal of equitable human development across generations with the constraint of a finite natural resource endowment.

References

Escobar, A. *Encountering Development: The Making and Unmaking of the Third World*. Princeton: Princeton University Press, 1995.
Sen, A. *Development as Freedom*. New York: Anchor Books, 2000.

DIGITAL INDIA

Sandeep Mertia

If we search for contenders for global buzzwords and grand narratives of the twenty-first century, we will find the digital revolution somewhere near the top of the stack. Between old and new powerful claims, such as the world becoming flat and robots taking over humanity, the digital has transformed almost all spheres of contemporary life in materially, historically and culturally specific ways. Moving away from the charismatic dissonance of simultaneous constructions of utopias and dystopias of the digital revolution(s), this entry hopes to touch upon some possibilities for studying the many meanings of the digital in India's sociotechnical context.

India's relationship with the digital is constitutive of our contemporary social imaginaries of development, governance, entrepreneurship, entertainment, philanthropy and even academic discourse. We can perhaps begin to understand the confluence of performative and substantive complexity of this relationship through Prime Minister Narendra Modi's 'Digital India' programme that was launched in 2014 to 'transform India into a digitally empowered society and knowledge economy'.

What is so transformative and impactful about the phrase 'Digital India'? A few years ago, 'Digital India' was the name of something as seemingly mundane as a central ministerial board constituted to legislate the digitization of cable television systems in India. There has been a fundamental shift in the political and social currency of the word 'digital' in India in the last decade or so. Most commentators try to explain this shift through the growing ubiquity of the internet. While there is some value in this explanation, as of 2019, more than half the Indian population still does not have access to broadband internet. E-governance programmes have been a talking point for at least two decades now. 'Digital India', though charged with familiar pursuits of modernization and technocratic efficiency in its official use, is now enmeshed with internet cultures and digitally connected life worlds of social media (Facebook, WhatsApp, Twitter, etc.): Bollywood, pornography, politics, sports, business and e-commerce and what have you. From the evolution of National Informatics Centre's (NIC's) quaint web-design templates to the Twitter handles of government agencies tweeting communal bile – the boundaries of official work/affective labour, authentic/virtual, public/private, etc., which have never been perfectly stable, are now blurred beyond recognition.

Interestingly, the vast majority of the population that is yet to 'use' the internet on an everyday basis also experience and participate in this transformation. We do not need working internet connections in every village or a smartphone with every citizen to have a dominant imagination of Digital India. When people regularly see full-page newspaper ads about free 4G internet, receive audio-recorded calls and messages asking them to vote for a political party or observe the infrastructural changes due to cell phone towers and their signal problems, among other things, they experience fragments of the sociotechnical change that the phrase 'Digital India' promises. Mobile repair shops selling pirate media through SD memory cards and USB sticks, middle-class couples sharing an iPad device, rural youth using one Facebook account as a group, the now world-famous 'good morning' deluge from Indians on WhatsApp, etc., are all markers of differences and generative potentials that are often missed in the big picture views of technological development.

Needless to say, this picture of Digital India is far from stable. India has consistently been one of the fastest-growing internet and mobile markets in the world, and the non/usage statistics and patterns are undergoing rapid change. However, neither history nor technology move in a linear fashion. Today's seemingly draconian technocracy of Aadhaar and IndiaStack, blanket internet shutdowns, toxic masculinity and bigoted trolling online and fantastic imaginaries of cashlessness and smart cities, among other things, are far from expressions of a homogenous digital culture or politics.

Digital India cannot be summed up by counting the existing or predicting the future number of internet users and the emerging markets for the next billion users. Nor can we explain collective desires for digital media by rational rhetoric of infrastructural modernization. The fact that global internet companies refuse to host their servers in India, suspending the sovereign control of the state over media content, or the irony that so-called unicorn start-ups that make claims of contributing to Digital India are actually registered as companies in places like Singapore or funded by businesses based in China, demand fresh ethnographic attention. At a different level, the subalterns who can't speak are not simply equivalent with the digital subalterns who get excluded from welfare services by a poorly designed, leaky biometric database system. The collisions of long-standing social and political tensions of speech, claim-making, identity and governance, with digital technologies, open new questions not only about the emergent database society but also about the historical evolution of myriad paper-based systems and governmentality.

Keywords for India

Like most things Indian, Digital India also comes with some amnesias. India's tryst with the digital, technically speaking, dates back to at least the late colonial era, when the need for electronic computers to calculate large-scale sample survey data was first expressed by the statistician P. C. Mahalanobis. Over the next few decades, institutions like the Indian Statistical Institute, Tata Institute of Fundamental Research and Indian Institutes of Technology imported the first modern computers. This strand of the history of statistics and computing along with most of the pre-liberalization developments in electronics and telecom, though loaded with bold assertions of national planning and techno-scientific progress, seems to have little bearing on the contemporary imagination of the digital in India.

It is largely the post-liberalization boom in information technology (IT) and business process outsourcing (BPO) that is seen as a marker of India's emergence as a software superpower and inauguration of all things digital in the popular political and business discourse. The dominant narrative of IT outsourcing, amplified by the lack of academic focus on the history of technology in India, has led to conceptual and empirical silences around open-source software and open data, Right to Information (RTI) and hacker movements, which are all sites of creative debates on social relations of technology.

Understanding 'Digital India', thus, is not just about exploring or measuring the effects of digital media and technologies on Indian society. The substantive questions concerning Digital India, as this entry has tried to outline, are distributed across multiple disciplines, histories and materialiaties and can only be approached with non-essentialist ways of inquiry. At a time when many leading theorists in the world are absorbed in re/thinking what it means to be human in an increasingly technologized world, paying attention to Digital India – its flickering screens and circuits of transformation – is key for alterity and entropy in networks obsessed with predictability and autopoiesis.

References

Saith, Ashwini, M. Vijayabaskar and V. Gayathri, eds. *ICTs and Indian Social Change: Diffusion, Poverty, Governance*. New Delhi: SAGE Publications, 2008.
Thomas, Pradip N. *Digital India: Understanding Information, Communication and Social Change*. New Delhi: SAGE Publications, 2012.

GREEN REVOLUTION

Aditya Dasgupta

The phrase 'green revolution' refers to a period of global agricultural transformation due to the spread of high-yielding variety (HYV) crops. HYV crops were highly productive cultivars first developed by Norman Borlaug and scientists working in Mexico during the 1950s. Under irrigated conditions, the new HYV crops could achieve yields more than double that of traditional varieties. HYV crops swept across the developing world between the 1960s and 1980s, ending food shortages.

The green revolution, or *harit kranti*, as it is known in Hindi, reached India in 1966–67, when HYV crops first saw widespread dissemination. HYV crops were disseminated by the Indian government as part of 'new agricultural strategy' designed to boost food production, against a backdrop of droughts, food shortages and growing tensions with the United States (upon which India depended for food aid). Aided by a network of domestic agricultural research centres, well-known scientists, such as M. S. Swaminathan, international foundations and agricultural extension bureaucracy, the green revolution was tremendously successful in boosting agricultural productivity between the 1960s and 1980s, ended the threat of famines and made India food self-sufficient.

However, as a form of technological change or 'creative destruction', the green revolution had several disruptive economic, political and ecological consequences which continue to shape India even today. In districts impacted by the green revolution, agricultural productivity increased rapidly, producing an increasingly wealthy class of land-owning farmers. However, the economic benefits of the green revolution were distributed extremely unevenly, amplifying inequality. Because the cultivation of HYV crops depended on controlled irrigation, the green revolution was concentrated in regions with potential for irrigation, such as Punjab, Haryana and western Uttar Pradesh, while the arid regions of the country were left out. Within villages, the green revolution benefitted farmers with larger landholdings, who possessed the economies of scale needed to cultivate the input-intensive crops, while those with smaller landholdings as well as landless labourers were excluded.

Early observers feared that the growing rural inequality due to the green revolution could fuel support for left-wing extremism among the rural poor. In fact, the primary political effect of the green revolution was to mobilize the prospering middle peasantry and cultivating caste groups, who began to seek greater political power as well as subsidies and price supports for the agricultural sector. Opposition movements, such as the Janata Party, found great success in catering to these rising rural groups. In this way, the green revolution played a key role in the long-run decline of the Congress Party and the rise of agrarian and regional opposition parties supported by rural and cultivating caste groups.

By increasing the political power of rural groups, the green revolution also gave rise to a regime of extensive subsidization of the agricultural sector. Over the long run, this has contributed to an ecological crisis. Heavily subsidized electricity, along with extensive reliance on groundwater irrigation, has led to rapid depletion of aquifers. Heavily subsidized and extensive application of toxic pesticides has had detrimental impacts on biodiversity and human health. Moreover, excess reliance on a few varieties of crops has, some argue, increased susceptibility to weather shocks.

References

Dasgupta, Aditya. 'Technological Change and Political Turnover: The Democratizing Effects of the Green Revolution in India'. *American Political Science Review* 112, no. 4 (2018): 918–38.

Shiva, Vandana. *The Violence of the Green Revolution: Third World Agriculture, Ecology, and Politics*. Kentucky: University Press of Kentucky, 2016.

HUMAN DEVELOPMENT

A. K. Shiva Kumar

The origins of the term 'human development' can be traced to the writings of the Indian economist, philosopher and Nobel laureate Amartya Sen, who conceptualizes development as an enhancement of human capabilities rather than, narrowly, as an expansion of incomes or growth in gross domestic product (GDP) per capita. A person's capability translates into a set of valuable 'beings and doings' including the capability to lead a long and healthy life, to be educated and to enjoy a decent standard of living. Sen's approach has strong conceptual connections with Aristotle's understanding of human flourishing and with Karl Marx's foundational concern with 'replacing the domination of circumstances and chance over individuals by the domination of individuals over chance and circumstances'. Human development is about overcoming the sense of helplessness and powerlessness that characterizes the lives of many ordinary people.

Human development is a process of enlarging people's choices, which include political freedoms, guaranteed human rights and self-respect. Of what use is wealth to a woman married to the richest landlord if she cannot access healthcare facilities in the village in case of a medical emergency or if there is no decent school for her children. In other words, income and wealth have no intrinsic value. They are means which have only instrumental significance. And the conversion of income into well-being is not automatic and is often mediated by several factors, including the public provision of social services and by considerations of class, caste and gender.

There is an important policy lesson: countries need not become rich first before improving the lives of people. It is indeed possible to improve the lives of people even at relatively low levels of income.

Human development is a concern with the poverty of opportunities, not merely with the poverty of incomes. Just as life is multidimensional, poverty too has many faces. Poverty is much more than just earning low and insufficient incomes. It also about poor health and education, deprivation in knowledge and communication, inability to exercise human and political rights and the absence of dignity, confidence and self-respect. It follows that human development is a concern with equality of opportunities, not merely with equality of incomes. In the ultimate analysis, human development is a concern with social justice and the dignity of human lives.

References

Sen, Amartya. 'Development as Capability Expansion'. In *Handbook of Human Development: Concepts, Measures, and Policies*, edited by S. Fukuda-Parr and A. K. Shiva Kumar. New Delhi: Oxford University Press, 1989, reprint, 2009.

Sen, Amartya. *Development as Freedom*. Oxford: Oxford University Press, 1999.

INDIAN RAILWAYS

Vijaya Singh

Bhartiya Rail or the Indian Railways, owned by the Ministry of Railways, is the fourth largest rail network in the world. It first became operational on 16 April 1853 between Bombay and Thane. Since then, the rail network in India has grown from a mere 33 kilometres to 67,368 kilometres in 2017. It is divided into 17 zones, has 7,349 stations and runs a total of 11,000 trains every day, 7,000 of these are passenger trains carrying 13 million passengers per day.

This massive technological force has played an important role in shaping the destiny of the subcontinent as a geographical, social and cultural entity right from 1848, when the Marquis of Dalhousie, then governor general, first undertook the project of introducing the railways. Promoted and celebrated by the British as the harbinger of social change, the railways were to usher in nothing short of a sociocultural revolution in India. Caste and religion, it was assumed, would crumble and dissipate in the face of railway travel as would social taboos and superstitions. Paradoxically, the railways ended up reinforcing the strict divisions of race, caste and gender. Indians were not allowed to travel with the British, and upper-caste men made sure that purdah carriages were introduced for 'respectable' women travellers. Not to mention the class structure visible in the hierarchy of rail coaches arranged as first class, second class, third class and unreserved.

Indian nationalist leaders like Dadabhai Naroji, R. C. Dutt and M. K. Gandhi, on the other hand, viewed the railways as an exploitative force consolidating the hold of the British over the subcontinent. To that extent, they opposed the railways as an extravagant adventure at the cost of the Indian people and their resources.

Framed within this binary of social change, industrial progress and colonial thuggery, the railways played an ambiguous role in the development of India as a modern nation. If development is measured in terms of connectivity, volume of freight conveyed and passengers transported, then the Indian Railways has indeed played a consequential role in connecting people and places. Viewed from the other end, however, development also meant a violent tearing away at the socio-economic fabric of a vastly diverse society, whose forests, land, resources and manpower the railways made use of in propelling its engine of progress.

As the traditional forms of travel by foot, by horse, by bullock cart and *palkis* (palanquins) gave way to railway travel, railway stations, rail tracks and trains rumbling past villages, towns and cities became a familiar site across the subcontinent. Railways created a new pattern of social and geographical movement, leading to urbanization, creation of national markets and integrated labour markets. All this movement of people and goods across the length and breadth of the subcontinent naturally created a field of popular culture, literature and cinema around it. Writers, poets, folk singers, artists and film-makers started incorporating the railways as a site of artistic creation. Similarly, in the Bombay film industry of the early twentieth century, film-makers such as Homi Wadia, Himanshu Rai, C. M. Luhar, Ramesh Saigal and others used the railways to underscore themes of speed, displacement, encounters with technology, new people, new worlds, new ways of being and perception.

As the railways steadily became a greater part of everyday life in the twentieth century, they became sites for articulating aspirations, disappointments and struggles of a generation coming to terms with a rapidly changing world. Songs were created around the image of the moving train, which had already become a metaphor for a range of sentiments, emotions and feelings The train was especially conducive to staging desires that could not be accommodated openly. In the hit film *Solva Saala* (1958), Dev Anand sings the now-classic song *Hai apna dil toh awara, na jane kis pe aayega* for Waheeda Rehman, making it the anthem of love for young people all over the country. Not to mention the latest song, from the comparatively recent Hindi film *Masaan* (2015), *Tu kisi rail si guzarti hai, mein kisi pul sa thartharata hun*, coupling the terror and desire of inter-caste love in a neoliberal regime.

References

Bear, Laura, *Lines of the Nation: Indian Railway Workers, Bureaucracy, and the Intimate Historical Self*. New York: Columbia University Press, 2007.
Kerr, Ian J. *27 Down: New Departures in Indian Railway Studies*. New Delhi: Orient Longman, 2007.

INFLATION

Dipak Dasgupta

When prices rise for common consumer articles, it is known as inflation. Originally, in the nineteenth century, inflation was a term applied by economists to an increase in the general price level, suggesting 'too much supply of paper money chasing too few goods'. Nowadays, it is more commonly defined as an increase in prices of a basket of representative consumer goods and suggestive that such price increase can happen for more than monetary reasons alone. The translation of this term in Hindi/Bengali is *mudrasphiti*, with the more popular Hindi equivalent being *mhangai*.

In India, inflation is most commonly associated with increases in prices of food and other essential items such as fuel, bus and train fares, clothing, housing, schooling and health, all of which make living expenses a higher burden for households and the poor and reduces their purchasing power. Inflation is, therefore, a dreaded economic phenomenon for most households in India. Double-digit inflation in India is viewed as a crisis.

Governments in India are highly sensitive to inflation, because voters frequently punish incumbent political parties in power in times of high inflation, as it is perceived as a sign of their economic mismanagement. Onions and tomatoes, seasonal items with high volatility in prices, are particularly sensitive in the Indian context given their ubiquitous use in cooking; onion price spikes are thought to have contributed to the fall of at least two central governments. Persistent inflation above threshold levels is also commonly associated with resulting bouts of tighter monetary and credit policies by the Reserve Bank of India (RBI), in order to reduce the 'excess demand' and inflationary expectations thought to be the root causes. The result is a cycle of high-inflation episodes, followed by tighter demand management policies and subsequent slower growth and loss of jobs.

However, it is not clear if 'excess demand' is the main cause of periodically high and persistent inflation. Episodes of food inflation in India are frequently caused by fairly regular, if unexpected, monsoon failures in India that are tied to the global El Niño weather phenomenon. Transmission of speculative bouts of global commodity price cycles and spikes in global food and oil price rises – when all commodity prices shoot up – are also common. In addition, the effort of governments to raise minimum statutory prices (MSPs) of food grains and pro-cyclical public procurement to benefit farmers also unwittingly lead to sharply higher inflation. A fall in the exchange rate of the rupee can also cause pressures on domestic prices. When these factors happen to unfortunately coincide, as it did in the 1970s and more recently in 2009–13, persistent double-digit inflation is the result.

Traders (and futures markets) are also often blamed for hoarding and speculating in times of sudden food price spikes – a long-standing charge against the general class/caste of wholesale food traders (Aratdars and Mahajans) in India since the time of famines, which is deeply etched in the social memory of all Indians. However, there have been no famines since the last one in 1965 in Bihar and Eastern India, and this is thought to be because of the key ameliorative role played by large-scale public procurement, storage and distribution of food and the long-standing food ration public distribution system (PDS). Although disputed, evidence suggests that pro-cyclical speculative behaviour and futures markets activity have indeed been associated with sudden food price spikes in a India and globally, suggestive of collusive behaviour. State governments frequently invoke the Essential Commodities Act in an attempt to stop hoarding of stocks by food traders. Raids are conducted in full public view and traders are sometimes pictured arrested to convey the message of an active government working for the welfare of their citizens against food inflation, although these are just cosmetic measures. Another similar ineffective and inconsistent approach has been the sporadic use of sudden export and import bans, typically after the horse of inflation has already bolted.

Clearly, managing inflation remains an Achilles heel of economic management in India, as is true in much of the world. Indeed, given the many factors at work, and the usual inconsistencies in government policymaking, it is something of a miracle that inflation has nevertheless, on the whole, been held in check in India – not deviating too far, for too long, above a safe 'comfort' level of about 5 per cent annually. That speaks generally well of the institutions charged with economic management in India, such as the RBI and the Finance Ministry, of eventually getting things right – even if they blunder a bit – or, more accurately, the underlying power of competitive democratic pressures by citizens on elected governments, and the supply responsiveness of Indian farmers.

References

Dasgupta, D., R. N. Dubey and R. Satish. 'Domestic Wheat Price Formation and Food Inflation in India', *Working Paper, Department of Economic Affairs, Ministry of Finance, Government of India*, 2011.

Sharma, Naresh Kumar and Motilal Bicchal. 'The Properties of Inflation Expectations: Evidence for India'. *EconomiA* 19, no. 1 (January–April 2018): 74–89.

INHERITANCE SYSTEMS

Bina Agarwal

Inheritance systems embody mechanisms for the transmission of private property. They identify which class of heirs are entitled to a person's property and the basis of that entitlement.

In most countries, all citizens are governed by a single inheritance system. In India, however, inheritance systems differ not only by religion but also by type of property and region. Hindus, Muslims, Christians and Parsis are governed by different 'personal laws'. Hindu inheritance systems also distinguish between 'separate property' and 'joint family property'. The latter is principally ancestral property in which a community of interests and rights are recognized, held jointly by a group of members who become 'coparceners' by birth. Historically, as defined by the twelfth-century legal treatises – *Mitaksara* and *Dayabhaga* – coparcenary rights could be held only by males, up to a maximum depth of four generations. In separate property, an individual had absolute rights of ownership and disposal, but coparcenary property was subject to strong restrictions.

Over time, Hindu law has evolved, moving away from earlier systems which recognized only men as primary heirs to systems incorporating modern ideas which recognize the rights of women. The Hindu Succession Act of 1956 was a major, albeit partial, step in this direction but the 2005 Hindu Succession Amendment Act (HSAA) brought full equality, giving daughters the same rights as sons in both separate and joint family property, including agricultural land, a key property for rural livelihoods. Daughters are now recognized as coparceners on birth and can ask for partition of joint family property.

Christians and Parsis in India are governed by inheritance systems that are built on the secular Indian Succession Act of 1925, and sons and daughters enjoy equal rights. Muslims are still governed by the Muslim Personal Law (Shariat) Application Act of 1937. Under this law, women get smaller shares than men, but contrary to the Shariat, women are also discriminated against in relation to agricultural land, which was excluded from the purview of the Act. Post-1947, Tamil Nadu and Andhra Pradesh amended the Shariat Act to include agricultural land, but an all-India amendment is still awaited. Similarly, tribal communities are governed by discriminatory customs and need gender-equal codification of inheritance rights.

There is a long-standing debate on whether a single personal law – a uniform civil code – should apply to all Indian citizens, irrespective of religion. However, the debate has focused largely on marriage rather than inheritance. It is doubtful that a uniform gender-equal inheritance law, applicable to all, is even feasible. Such a convergence would require changes in all the personal laws and would need consensus on at least five substantive points of difference. First, Hindu law retains the concept of coparcenary joint family property. No other personal law has an equivalent. Second, Muslim personal law under the Shariat has very specific rules of succession. Women's shares are less than men's generically, and these shares can change in the presence or absence of particular categories of other heirs. No other inheritance law has such a complex architecture of rules. And this is spelt out in the Quran, leaving little room for interpretation in a gender-equal direction. Third, personal laws differ on the right to will. Hindus, Christians and Parsis face no restrictions, but Muslim law restricts wills to one-third of property, with Sunni and Shia differences on who can get such property and with whose consent. Fourth, Hindu law itself varies by state: for example, in 1976, Kerala abolished joint family property altogether, while the HSAA retained it, and matrilineal Hindus have their own rules. Fifth, cultural ideas differ about who deserves to inherit: Hindus emphasize *sapinda* ('shared body particles' in *Mitakshara*; 'religious efficacy' in *Dayabhaga*); other communities focus on blood and marital ties, proximity of residence, being looked after in old age, and so on. Given such divergence, the idea that we can amalgamate different personal laws into a new uniform law is unrealistic. An alternative would be to create a separate secular law, based on constitutional principles of gender equality, which either supersedes existing inheritance laws or which people can 'opt for' on reaching adulthood.

Laws, however, are only one determinant of inheritance. Their implementation is mediated by social norms and perceptions. For example, rural women rarely inherit agricultural land. Pressure from families and the absence of a national social security system compel many women to give up their claims in favour of brothers, for maintaining family harmony and ensuring future support. The ongoing digitization of land records could formally entrench the inequalities that result from these social pressures. In urban areas, where the family home is usually the main immovable property, women's claims are even less recognized, and unlike land, which is divisible, it is also difficult to divide a house.

There are, however, important regional differences in how women's inheritance claims are perceived and implemented. There is less resistance to women's rights in immovable property in South India than in North India. An important factor underlying these regional differences are social norms defining marriage patterns and post-marital relationships with daughters. In South India, marriages within the village and with extended kin are allowed. In such cases, land inherited by daughters can remain within the effective oversight of the extended family. Moreover, parents in need can seek financial help from married daughters. Property given to daughters can thus bring future benefits. In Northern India, however, in-village and within-kin marriages are banned, as is accepting financial help from married daughters. Here, land given to a daughter is seen as benefiting only her marital family, with no possible advantage to the parents. Resistance to daughters' claims are, therefore, greatest here and least in South India. Other regions have a mixed pattern. It is not surprising then that even in terms of law, the first states to partially reform inheritance systems in favour of women – among *both* Hindus and Muslims – were all located in South and West India, and none in North India.

References

Agarwal, Bina. 'Bargaining, Gender Equality and Legal Change'. In *Redefining Family Law in India*, edited by A. Parashar and A. Dhande 306–54. London: Routledge, 2008.
Agarwal, Bina. *A Filed of One's Own: Gender and Land Rights in South Asia*. Cambridge: Cambridge University Press, 1994.

JHUGGI, JHOPRI, SLUM, CHAWL (JHUGGĪ, JHŌPḌI, SLUM, CĀL)

Darryl D'Monte

To describe a *jhuggi-jhopdi*, single or hyphenated, as a hut or rudimentary dwelling, made of mud and corrugated iron sheets or other scavenged materials and located in a poor area of city, does not do justice to the panoply of meanings that it evokes.

It earlier referred to the abode of fakirs, sadhus and others of their ilk – very tiny dwellings. The building materials have changed, with the widespread use of blue plastic sheets to ward off the monsoons, especially in Mumbai, which has the world's largest urban population living in jhopdis.

Mumbai figures prominently when it comes to such housing, with around 60 per cent, the majority, of its 14 million population living in jhopdis. Among Marathi speakers, no one calls them jhuggis. The collective term is a slum, a word that originated in the depressed East End of London in the nineteenth century to denote a humble dwelling in a back alley. It is widely used today in India, even in official parlance, as in Mumbai's Slum Rehabilitation Authority (SRA). There are also squatter settlements, implying illegality.

The Marathi for a slum cluster is *jhopadpatti*. Dharavi, with seven hundred thousand people, is reckoned to be the third largest slum in the world. In North India, the term used is *basti* or even 'colony'. The term 'colony' is not inappropriate: colonial powers promoted city centres, isolating migrants who left their villages in search of work. Colonialists treated these as temporary workers, but later their families joined them and they could only live in slums away from the city centres. Dharavi used to be a village, referred to as a *Koliwada* or fisherfolks' colony. In 1887, the British expelled all tanneries, other polluting industries and the poor natives to what was then the northern fringe of the city. This settlement did not receive any investment in terms of roads, sanitation, public services or housing.

The existence of slums of this kind is a highly politicized issue. The middle class treats these informal settlements as an eyesore, even though they benefit from the services – such as maids and drivers – that these colonies provide. There have been periodic drives to evict such slum dwellers, which reached a climax during the national emergency in the mid-1970s. Near Turkman Gate in Delhi, Sanjay Gandhi ordered a demolition of slums in 1976 and when dwellers resisted, the police opened fire, killing an estimated six people and injuring many more. These drives also often included forced sterilization of slum dwellers. An estimated seventy thousand people were displaced from slums and commercial properties in large tracts of old Delhi in the twenty-one months of the emergency. In 1981, Chief Minister A. R. Antulay evicted pavement dwellers – the lowest rung in the 'housing' ladder – in Mumbai, and this action eventually went up to the Supreme Court, which ruled that housing wasn't a fundamental right, but slum dwellers had to be given alternate accommodation if their land was to be acquired for public purposes.

Slums continue to loom large in planners' lexicon. Thus, there are Orwellian 'resettlement colonies', 'unauthorized colonies' or – even more creatively – 'regularized-unauthorized colonies'. The earlier policy of removing or relocating slums has now ceded ground to in situ upgradation. This has found full fruition in the Maharashtra government's highly controversial Slum Rehabilitation Authority (SRA), under which, if a majority of slum dwellers at a particular site agree, a builder rehouses them in a separate tenement building there. In return, he earns building rights for a swanky high-rise cheek by jowl, which he uses to cross-subsidize their rehabilitation. Needless to add, the slum dwellers are given a raw deal with shabby tenements, cannot cope with monthly maintenance charges and often sell off their property and return to their shanties.

The world was introduced to Mumbai's jhopdis through the Oscar-winning film, *Slumdog Millionaire* (2008). At the very opening, the lead character, 5-year-old Jamal, dives through excrement in a makeshift pit latrine in his slum to get the autograph of Amitabh Bachchan.

When riots between Hindus and Muslims break out in the slum, Jamal and his brother flee and eventually Jamal, now 18, lands up in Dharavi. He competes, improbably, for the quiz show *Kaun Banega Crorepati* (Who Wants to be a Millionaire) and when he has one question left, is tortured by the police, who don't believe that a 'slumdog' can answer such tough questions.

A *cāla*, a corruption of *chal* in Marathi, is an early form of working-class collective housing typical of Mumbai, with *kholi*s (single rooms) along a balcony with a shared toilet at the end. A cāla is several steps up the social ladder from the humble jhopdi. These were five-storeyed elongated structures first built to house mill workers who migrated *en masse* around 1900 to Mumbai from their villages down the Konkan coast. Chawls were affordable and provided security to mill hands who shared the same social background. While chawls are no longer being built, they still survive as an anachronism in Mumbai, with its burgeoning skyscraper apartment complexes.

This unique form of housing has also bred crime. 'Dons' like Rama Naik and Arun Gawli both came from chawls in Byculla. Chawls flourished after the notorious Dawood Ibrahim fled from India, infiltrated the official mill union and engaged in fierce internecine warfare. One victim was the millowner Sunit Khatau, who wanted to 'persuade' his workers to sell his lucrative Byculla mill land and was shot dead by a rival criminal gang.

Chawls loom large in Mumbai's popular culture. Perhaps the most memorable of literary works that features the cāla is the one by the bilingual novelist Kiran Nagarkar. His *Ravan & Eddie* begins with the eponymous Hindu baby falling out of his cāla balcony and being saved from certain death by his Catholic neighbour's family below. As the *New York Review of Books* put it, 'If you grow up in the crowded Mumbai chawls, you get to participate in your neighbours' lives, whether you like it or not.'

References

Bhan, Gautam. *In the Public's Interest: Evictions, Citizenship and Inequality in Contemporary Delhi*. New Delhi: Orient BlackSwan, 2016.
Soofi, Mayank Austen. 'Life in an Illegal Colony', *LiveMint*, 26 November 2016. Available at: http://origin-alpha.livemint.com/Leisure/yJi2UuW8ZcW92Ta34n3mBI/Life-in-an-illegal-colony.html (accessed May 2018).

JOBLESS GROWTH

Montek S. Ahluwalia

Jobless growth is a relatively recent phrase, coined in the 1990s by Nick Perna to describe the then unusual phenomenon of the US economy recovering from the output recession of 1991 but with no increase in employment. Until then, recoveries had been accompanied by rehiring of labour in the trough of the recession, as employers began to anticipate that the economy was set to turn around. That this did not happen in 1991 led to a lively discussion of what factors might have been at work, with most economists focussing on the role of productivity increases and some on globalization and the relocation of labour-intensive industries to low-wage economies. The phrase gained wider currency in the aftermath of the financial crisis of 2008. This time, much of the blame was put, at least in the public discourse, on the effect of globalization.

Jobless growth was not much talked about in India until relatively recently. There were doubts about whether growth leads to an improvement in welfare, but the focus was primarily on whether it reduced poverty. GDP growth accelerated sharply in India in the mid-2000s, but sceptics argued that it did not help the poor because there were structural reasons why the benefits were inequitably distributed so that they did not 'trickle down'. This issue was finally settled only in 2013, when data from the National Sample Survey (NSS) household consumer survey for 2011–12 finally became available and established that between 2004–5 (when the last household survey was carried out) and 2011–12, the percentage of the population below the official poverty line fell from 37.2 per cent to 21.9 per cent and for the first time the absolute numbers below the poverty line declined from 407.1 million in 2004–5 to 269.3 million in 2011–12. Earlier, the percentages in poverty had fallen, but because of the growth in total population the absolute numbers below the poverty line had actually risen.

More recently, the criticism has shifted from whether growth reduced poverty to asking if it was creating enough jobs, and complaints about 'jobless growth' began entering the politico-economic debate. The only official data on employment comes from the NSS household surveys on employment which are conducted every five years. The last such survey was in 2011–12, and the next one, for 2017–18, is currently in the field and data will become available only by 2019. These surveys have consistently shown that open unemployment in India is relatively low. The NSS survey for 2011–12, for example, shows open unemployment to be only 3.2 per cent on the conventional definition. If a stricter definition is adopted, which allows for underemployment, the figure goes up to 7 per cent.

Whatever definition we choose, the surveys do not suggest that the rate of unemployment is increasing. However, it would be wrong to conclude from this that unemployment is not a problem. The fact is that the poor in India are too poor to stay out of employment, especially since there is no unemployment insurance payment on which they can rely. Therefore, they take any job they can find, usually in the informal sector, at low wages and with almost no social security benefits. They show up in the surveys as being 'employed', but a large proportion of those employed are dissatisfied with the jobs they are engaged in.

The problem of jobless growth in India is, therefore, best described not just as the insufficient number of jobs created – that may be true – but also as the low quality of jobs being created. The quality of jobs falls greatly below what the young, and increasingly better educated and more aspirational, new entrants to the labour force have come to expect. Just as the demand for quality jobs is rising, the supply of these jobs is shrinking.

The latest data shows that between 2004–5 and 2011–12, the organized sector created 58 million jobs, but almost 80 per cent of these new jobs were 'informal jobs', that is, contractual jobs which have much less job security and are often also lower paid than permanent employees in the same company doing the same work. The reasons for this phenomenon may have something to do with the rigidity of our labour laws. Economists have long argued that it is not easy to lay off workers in the organized sector, and for that reason, employers tend to: (a) adopt more labour-saving technology to reduce the need to hire labour than is economically justified; and (b) resort to 'contract labour' which can be hired and laid off more easily. These employees are technically employees of the labour contractor but are not eligible for full benefits.

Technology also contributes to an anti-employment bias. One reason is that new technology is evolved largely in industrialized countries, where wage costs are high and there is a natural incentive to develop technologies that replace labour. Furthermore, companies engaged in a global value chain often cannot avoid the new technology because they have to meet certain product quality standards, which can only be met if the new technology is adopted.

There is today a global concern that new technologies, especially artificial intelligence, 3D printing, etc., are set to produce massive job losses as many existing jobs will no longer be needed. It is difficult to separate hype from reality. In any case, the processes will unfold only slowly. However, it is important to recognize that while technological change often disrupts existing ways of doing businesses, leading to layoffs in the sector directly affected, these job losses are offset by job gains elsewhere.

To summarize, whether growth is indeed jobless requires going beyond the effect it has on a particular sector and calls for a careful measurement of other direct and indirect effects. Some growth processes may be more job creating than others, but locking production processes into outdated technology that makes it difficult for us to join global value streams is not in our interest. Equally, globalization is blamed for shifting jobs out of industrialized countries to developing countries. For the same reason, we should welcome it and not join the anti-globalization campaigns of luddites and protectionists in industrialized countries. However, we have to be cognizant of the fact that rapidly changing technology will create some disruption. We need to manage the transition better, and this calls for three measures that need to be taken up. First, we must do what we can to help the individuals affected by programmes of reskilling and encouraging them to get into other self-employed businesses. Second, we need to build in as much flexibility as needed in the economy to allow it to adjust and adopt new technology. Third, we need to reshape our systems of education and skilling to give the economy the skills it needs to function in the ever-changing world. It is well known that employers regard almost 40 per cent of those ostensibly graduating from relevant skilled courses as unemployable, and this situation has to change.

References

Bhattacharya, B. B. and S. Sakthivel. 'Economic Reforms and Jobless Growth in India in the 1990s', 2007. www.iegindia.org/upload/pdf/wp245.pdf (Retrieved 6 November 2019).

Planning Commission. *Press Note on Poverty Estimates, 2011-12*. No. id: 5421, 2013.

LAND GRABBING

Varsha Bhagat-Ganguly

Land grabbing, which refers to large-scale land acquisitions and land transformations, is a global phenomenon. Maria Cristina Rulli points out that as a term, land grabbing has been used more intensely only after 2008, initially in response to increase in food prices across the globe and gradually as a way/form, process and an outcome that has created challenges for the land users. The trend of land grabbing is studied mainly from the perspective of development paradigm and land governance. In the case of India, a shift in landownership from Adivasis or traditional landholders to private enterprises, mainly to bolster economic growth in the neoliberal era has been discussed in the literature with respect to role of the state. The direct involvement of the state and its agencies in evicting individuals and entire communities from territories targeted for economic development has made the state a land grabber, Pedlowski argues. In many countries, the issue of land grabbing is highly sensitive because of the perceived threat to national sovereignty and the impression that it represents a new wave of imperialism.

The following are some of the ways of land grabbing: owning the land, land on lease for a long period (from the government or otherwise), possession of the land. It can occur legally or illegally, as it is a way of control. As such, there is no exclusive land law that controls/curbs land grabbing nor is there any law under which land grabbing is punishable. In fact, in many cases, land grabbing is legitimate, for example, land on long-term lease based on contract and facilitation by the state for purchasing land on a large scale vis-à-vis land acquisition by the state and paying compensation for the same. While understanding land grabbing as a phenomenon, the size, people involved, control, legality and eventual usage need to be taken into consideration. Having a systematic database or precise information on the extent of land grabbing is one of the major constraints in problematizing the concept of land grabbing. Rapid pace of the phenomenon, lack of transparency with data and standard criterion for classifying land acquisitions make land grabbing data imprecise, Maria Cristina Rulli notes, leading to its authenticity being questioned.

Land grabbing is in a way a control, that is, a group of land users need to obey a specific set of rules for land use and the purpose of land use cannot be changed. The perspective from which a land deal is viewed plays an important role in how the benefits of those land deals are defined and whether they have been realized. As Kyle F. Davis observes, land deals are more likely to result in some economic and political benefits; however, losing access to land can carry with it a variety of economic, social, nutritional and cultural consequences. Sometimes land grabbing can lead to grave consequences, such as monoculture plantation or cash crops, which threatens human health, food security and national sovereignty. Land grabbing could also be a control in terms of land as a resource and a property, which is directly linked to finance and land valuation. Large-scale land acquisitions for economic ventures imply large-scale capital; this has higher likelihood of controlling resource-use orientation/purpose and is instrumental in climate change. In economic terms, capital is closely linked to land valuation, speculation, financial crisis and commodification at the expense of small and marginal land users/farmers.

Another aspect of land grabbing is that it is closely linked to water grabbing across the globe. In some cases, private enterprises are in search of water sources and land is a medium to acquire water; for agriculture, irrigation is directly linked with water grabbing. Maria Cristina Rulli observes that a few major environmental and social issues are emerging due to land and water grabbing, such as high levels of malnourishment and increase in biofuel production in countries where land grabbing is on large scale.

In India, the term 'land grabber' was used in early 1970s in the context of misuse of power by a sitting minister in the state of Punjab. In the case of the state of Haryana, the term land grabber was used when the state began launching its development projects in urban areas. In 1979, 'riots as a cover for land grabbing' was mentioned in the context of organized gangsterism of the Rashtriya Swayamsevak Sangh (RSS) in Jamshedpur. Influx of industries had led to phenomenal pressure on land as well as land speculation, especially on the fringe areas of the city. Riots began occurring and persons involved in land disputes began to be killed in these riots. Thus, the term land grabbing has also been used to denote criminal activity or misuse of power for legitimizing land possession or ownership.

D. Roy has studied land grabbing from the perspective of development as well as citizenship in democratic developmental state, based on case studies of resistance by peasants – Tata Nano project, Singur and Sanand and Nirma Cement Factory, Mahuva. This brings out the state's role as a facilitator in large-scale land acquisitions, peasants' resistance and dealing with resistance, that is, repression of peasants in Singur, inviting Tata Industries in Sanand, while as a facilitator for Nirma Cement Company in Mahuva. The peasants have expressed their resistance on streets, engagements with the administrative machinery and in the courts. The judicial interpretations and actions in these cases have been with regard to public purpose, technical expertise and environmental concerns; however, they have not yet examined in any detail the interconnections between the various ways in which land grabbing occurs and the role of the state.

References

Cristina Rulli, Maria. 'Global Land and Water Grabbing'. In *Proceedings of the National Academy of Sciences of the United States of America*, 892–7, January 2013.
Davis, Kyle F. Paolo, D'Odorico and Maria Cristina Rulli, 'Land Grabbing: A Preliminary Quantification of Economic Impacts on Rural Livelihoods'. *Population and Environment* 36, no. 2 (2014): 180–92.
Roy, D. 'Resistance to Land Grabs and Peasants' Practices of Citizenship in Democratic Development States: Case Studies from India'. *Future Agriculture*, 17–19 October 2012. Available at: https://www.yumpu.com/en/document/view/31435538/resistance-to-land-grabs-and-peasants-contested-global- (accessed 25 August 2017).

LPG

Pulapre Balakrishnan

The widely recognized initials 'LPG', which stands for 'Liberalization, Privatization and Globalization', describes the economic policy regime launched in India in 1991. Used mainly by critics of the move, the abbreviation was not meant as praise! Enthusiasts of the economic policy shift would rather use the term 'reforms' to describe it. The policy changes launched in 1991 and continued over the next quarter century have very likely not seen their culmination yet.

Liberalization refers to the move towards an economy with less governmental control. It is central to the dismantling of a state-controlled economic model based on the proposition that market forces should be given the lead in determining the course of the economy. In India, its support comes from sections who feel that the country has not progressed much in the years since 1947, due to the suppression of the private sector through regulation. The collapse of the former Soviet Union in the 1990s gave this view a fillip. Even though India did not share much of the features of that country, the collapse made it difficult to continue with any form of state control. It is altogether a different matter that a tiny constituency for less control had been present in the economy for close to four decades by then, most prominently represented by the writings of the economist B. R. Shenoy, who had penned a note of dissent on the Second Five-Year Plan document in the mid-1950s. Liberalization itself had two aspects, according to whether it had been focused on the internal economy or the external sector, even though such a strict demarcation is not always conceptually appropriate. In 1991, the principal reform of the policy regime, aimed at the domestic economy, was de-licencing or elimination of the requirement for a licence to invest. On the external front, it had taken the form of lowering of import tariff, albeit in phases. For an idea of how radical the change has been, it may be noted that by now the average tariff is lower than that of South Korea. Together, these moves constituted the trade and industrial policy reforms. They were intended to leave India an open economy. Thus, liberalization was the culmination of a movement initiated in the 1950s by a small section of India's business and intellectual circles.

Privatization strictly refers to the sale of assets in government-owned entities. In any case, privatization in the strict sense outlined above was not so central to the Indian agenda. The extent of privatization in India since 1991 has been negligible, sales of assets being confined to a glorified bakery and a second-rung hotel. However, now after twenty-five years, the movement has quickened a bit with the government signalling its openness to some big-ticket privatization, such as that of Air India, a public sector undertaking that shows little sign of improvement of its finances. However, while privatization in the sense of sale of public assets has not proceeded on anything like the scale claimed by critics of the changing policy regime, privatization in the sense of dismantling government monopoly has proceeded apace. The action has been particularly strong in the social sectors, such as health and education, and in the services, where telecom and airlines are the most prominent examples. While in the case of health provision it has often taken the form of very high fees, in higher education it has mostly taken the form of high fees without great improvement in quality. The latter has also been accompanied by an authoritarian culture in the new educational institutions, which has led one long-time observer to term the outcome as 'liberalisation without liberalism'.

Finally, globalization. Globalization itself has been deconstructed as both a trend and a project. The trend, it is pointed out, has been in existence for at least half a millennium. But the project, it is said, is quite recent and can be seen as an opportunity for global capital to secure for itself a free access to both the world market and profitable sites of production. The collapse of the Soviet Union was leveraged politically to clinch the argument for globalization, the implication invariably drawn from the event being, that closed economies were no longer a credible arrangement. It is not clear how the architects of the economic reforms launched in 1991 viewed globalization, though they appeared to have taken the pragmatic view that India is best not kept out of global trading arrangements, such as the World Trade Organization (WTO). Now twenty-five years later, two developments since India's greater integration with the world economy may be seen, both somewhat unexpected. First, the fears of a collapse of the Indian economy due to the greater prowess of Western economies has not materialized.

Second, and entirely unexpectedly, the West has not come out much stronger. Not only has the global financial crisis left the United States insecure, there has also occurred within its polity a serious backlash triggered by the loss of manufacturing jobs. The election of Donald Trump and the uncertainty that it presages is a reflection of this. Global corporations are now hesitant to push for globalization it seems, and India's position appears stronger today than it did when the debate over accession to WTO rules had spilled out into the streets.

References

Ahluwalia, Montek S., Deepak Nayyar, Prabhat Patnaik, Anjan Chakrabarti, T. Sabri Öncü, Atul Sood, Rajiv Kumar, Pulapre Balakrishnan, Chirashree Das Gupta, Surajit Mazumdar, R. Nagaraj, Shantanu De Roy, A. V. Rajwade and Aseem Shrivastava, *Quarter Century of Liberalisation in India: Essays from Economic & Political Weekly*. New Delhi: Oxford University Press, 2018.

Chandra, Ramesh. *Globalisation, Liberalisation, Privatisation and Indian Polity: Trade and Commerce*, vol. 5. Gyan Publishing House, 2004.

MAI BAAP SARKAAR (MAIṀ BĀP SARKĀR)

Parikshit Ghosh and Debraj Ray

The term *mai baap* literally means 'mother–father', and the term *sarakāra* means 'government'. In its modern use, the term sarkār has Persian roots: *sar* (meaning 'chief') and *kar* (an agent or doer). A sarkār was also a high official in the colonial or Mughal administrations, such as a landlord or a rent collector. Interchangeable with such feudal gems as *huzoor* (lord) or *malik* (master), this usage connotes servility and submission – on the part of the governed. Stir in the mai baap, and you might be forgiven for perceiving the Indian government not as an accountable and elected institution but as a divinely ordained body that disburses patronage on the basis of loyalty and whimsy. In 1947, newly independent India became a 'sovereign, democratic republic'. The Preamble of the Indian Constitution strongly echoes Lincoln's idea of a government 'of the people, for the people, and by the people'. And yet the whiff of paternalistic hauteur has never entirely left Indian government. It is reflected in the electoral success of dynastic families, the notion of hereditary rather than competitive leadership in political parties and the condescending attitude of many government officials.

There are other senses in which the term 'mai baap' may be deployed. Libertarians use mai baap to assail state meddling in free markets and private enterprise. Such meddling is presumasly to be traced back to Nehru's Soviet-style planning to control production which took a more stultifying form under his daughter Indira, whose *licence raj* was eventually dismantled by the Narasimha Rao government in 1991. Indira also coined the phrase *garibi hatao* – or 'banish poverty' – which served as a rhetorical springboard for a plethora of welfare schemes, including subsidies for food, fuel, fertilizer, electricity, transportation and housing. Meanwhile, garibi hatao is not infrequently confused with *garib hatao* ('banish the poor'), especially when politicians or visiting heads of state need to be shown a shiny clean city. Mai bap sarkaar carries a darker and more insidious charge, sometimes levelled by the economic Right. Perhaps political parties, especially the Centre-Left Congress, have developed a vested interest in preserving mass poverty since it allows them to win votes with the promise of handouts. Mai bap sarkaar allegedly suffers from the Munchausen syndrome by proxy; the premarket journalist Shekhar Gupta called it 'povertarianism'. So it is that economists such as Jagdish Bhagwati advocate the business-friendly Gujarat model over the welfare-focused Kerala model favoured by Amartya Sen. The ultimate liberation from mai baap, according to this viewpoint, is a restriction of scarce government resources to growth-friendly expenditures, such as infrastructure and fiscal breaks, and an eschewal of directly redistributive policies. On the other hand, Sen would consider such steps to be the actions of a deadbeat dad. When it comes to the basics – health, education, infrastructure, employment and insurance – we cannot but agree.

More recently, Arun Shourie labelled the supposedly fiscally conservative Bharatiya Janata Party (BJP) government under Prime Minister Narendra Modi as 'Congress plus cow'. Various subsidies on fertilizer, electricity, food and transportation will still take you up to 4 per cent of gross domestic product (GDP), while 'foregone revenues' accruing from tax exemptions and the like will hit you up for another 6 per cent. With the Union budget hovering around 13 per cent of GDP, these are remarkable numbers. In addition, much of this expenditure is regressive and whimsical. The rich consume more of many subsidized goods and use political connections or ju'gāṛa to corner benefits like land allotments and tax breaks.

Quick and visible benefits do proliferate in government policy. But, where mai baap negligence truly manifests itself is in the long and arduous task of human capacity building. The government reserves half of its jobs for disadvantaged groups and spends nearly one-eighth of its budget on food subsidies. Yet direct public expenditure on health and education is around 1.2 per cent and 3.8 per cent of GDP, respectively, well below the international average. Just under 40 per cent of our children are stunted, and about half the children in Class V cannot function at the Class II level. All in all, mai-baap largesse is far from transparent, programmatic, progressive policy. One might argue that apart from the basic rights to education, health, old-age security and gainful employment, the poor are best served by transparent, unconditional transfers. Indeed, the government's own *Economic Survey of 2017–18* proposed replacing many of the myriad schemes with a Universal Basic Income. Perhaps the best notion of a mai bap sarkaar is one that doesn't exist yet: do what good parents do – provide an allowance. And provide strong foundations for education, health, fundamental insurance and the vagaries of old age. And keep your hands off the rest: that's like handing out candy and toys to make up for lack of parental engagement.

What we have now is speed parenting at best. That makes for an unhappy family whose tragedy, as Tolstoy said, is interestingly unique. It is wise to remember that in contrast to trends in the US and other Western democracies, electoral data from India generally shows an anti-incumbency bias. And thus, the excesses of mai baap – as practiced today – are fortunately tempered by the occasional tantrums of their *betas* (sons) and *betis* (daughters).

MALL

C. Ramachandraiah

The mall is a ubiquitous part of urban vocabulary in Indian metros. It has become a symbol of aspiration and success today. Malls have encapsulated the imagination of the nation as a gateway to first-world experience in a developing country.

A mall can be understood as 'a large enclosed shopping area from which traffic is excluded'. Also known as shopping centres or shopping arcade, the mall is a complex of shops housed in one or more buildings that are connected using walkways for easy convenience. Charles Durant and J. W. Spencer built the first shopping mall of India, Spencer Plaza, in late nineteenth century in Anna Salai, Chennai. The current model of the mall owes its origin to Victor Green, who promoted the concept in the United States in the 1950s. Today, a shopping mall is made up of one or multiple buildings that house various retail stores. The retails sector in India has been dominated by unorganized traders, primarily in the form of *kirana* (grocer) and small shops. With the advent of globalization and foreign direct investment (FDI) in retail, there has been a growth in organized retail, giving rise to their presence in malls.

Until 2002, only three shopping malls existed in India – Ansal's Plaza in Delhi, Crossroads in Mumbai and Spencer Plaza in Chennai. After 2003, India saw phenomenal growth in the number of malls. By 2008, there were 225 operational malls which more than doubled to 570 by May 2013. Chains of multiplexes like PVR, Carnival Cinemas, Cinepolis and Inox have been linked to malls to provide entertainment. Similarly, eating joints like McDonalds, Subway and Ohris have found their way into malls. The presence of such varied stores lends the mall the feel of a composite place providing 'wholesome' experience.

Malls attract people from the middle and upper classes of the urban society. In rural India and small towns, traditionally, bazaars or *haat*s (markets) in India occupy the same position. Bazaars offer a wide variety of goods and services. It was a space of shopping as well as a melting pot for socialization. While some bazaars were permanent, some would be set up on a weekly basis. Festive seasons would bring out the colours and flavours, while adding to the merriment of occasion. Over a period of time, bazaars catering to specific clientele/purposes have also emerged. 'Market Yard' is a place in towns/cities where transactions of farm produce (from chillies to onions to fruits) take place in large quantities. In a way, then, bazaars in villages and towns encapsulate much of what the air-conditioned mall offers the urban dweller.

Malls also offer a safe space for musing. It offers scope for 'limitless imagination'. From high-end brands to world-class entertainment experience, malls offer respite from mundane hassles by catering to shopping and entertainment needs under one roof. Some of the reasons for the success of the mall culture in India are the ease of access to global brands, glamorous setting, promise of good quality, good infrastructure and public utilities and safety for women from harassment, as compared to traditional shopping areas.

References

Freidberg, Susanne. 'Supermarkets and Imperial Knowledge'. *Cultural Geographies* 14, no. 3 (2007): 321–42.

Voyce, M. 'Shopping Malls in India: New Social "Dividing Practices"'. *Economic and Political Weekly* 42, no. 22 (2–8 June 2007): 2055–62.

MANDI/E-CHAUPAL (MAṆḌĪ/E-CAUPĀL)

Jeemol Unni

The word *mandi* in Hindi refers to the marketplace. Mandis are named after the products they sell. So, a market selling vegetables (*sabzi*) is referred to as a sabzi mandi. The mandi often gets extended into a local fair with other sellers occupying nearby spaces and selling street food, trinkets and setting up entertainment stalls for children. Such mandis or fairs are also called *haat* or bazaar in rural areas in India.

I often visited the sabzi and fish mandi in South Kolkata, Calcutta, as a child. My father sat in the car, while my mother and I went into the sabzi mandi. It was always exciting to see and feel the brisk activity, the colours and the smells of the mandi. We visited various vegetable stalls where my mother chose vegetables as per her South Indian taste. When we reached the fish mandi, she would not let me enter because it was wet and messy, always a lot noisier and more confused than the rest of the mandi. She did not want me hanging on to her saree *pallu* while she negotiated the mess and confusion. I was asked to stand at the entrance and watch the activities from a distance.

A classic Urdu short story titled 'Aanandi' by Ghulam Abbas became more famous when it was made into a Bollywood movie titled *Mandi* (1983). The film told the story of a Madame of a brothel and her flourishing industry, frequently visited by politicians and elite, situated in the central hub of the city of Hyderabad. The film depicts a flourishing market, mandi. Various trades around the brothel do brisk business, such as flower sellers, 'paan' (betel leaf) sellers, tea and snack stalls, pimps, 'dalals' or brokers of various hues. The Madame is ousted by another younger stronger woman; she moves out with an old trusted helper. As she leaves the city, the helper notices a Shiv Lingam on the ground and the Madame notices a young sex worker running towards her. Madame soon sets up another brothel on the outskirts of the city and a mandi grows and flourishes around it. This film depicts the embeddedness of economy around the mandi and the holding within it of so many invisibilized lives.

However, it has to be noted that the mandi is seeing a decline today. Not due to any crackdown on illegalities but due to the establishment and spread of large grocery stores, such as Reliance Fresh, that offer the same fare in air-conditioned spaces and advertise attractive discounts. Mandis are likely to disappear from urban cities, though they may continue to flourish in rural areas. Another modern predator of the sabzi mandi is the swell of online retail stores that provide fruits and vegetables at the door step, such as Big Basket.

However, technological advancement and the internet are also playing their part in modernizing the mandi. This brings us to the second keyword in this context, 'E-chaupal'. This word is an extension of a market that is technology-driven. The Hindi word *chaupal* refers to a meeting place in the village. It generally depicts the central square with a large tree under which the village elders meet in the evening and children play all day. It does not necessarily mean a marketplace. The E-chaupal was invented by ITC Limited to integrate agricultural markets through the internet. It allows farmers to procure agricultural products and get access to information via the internet. The company has installed computers with internet facility in villages to facilitate agricultural marketing and dissemination of information to the farmers.

E-chaupal or other versions of this innovation portend a great future for the sabzi mandi in this era of digital technology. The Government of India has started the E-National Agricultural Market, which is an electronic trading portal. The idea was to create an integrated market throughout the country for agricultural products. Of course, it will no longer be called E-chaupal. The hope only is that it does not lose its relevance and become yet another digital tool in the long line of tools being so successfully marketed across the country.

References

Annamalai, K. and S. Rao. *ITC's E-Choupal and Profitable Rural Transformation*. Washington DC: World Resources Institute, 2003.
Kumar, Richa. 'Mandi Traders and the Dabba: Online Commodity Futures Markets in India'. *Economic and Political Weekly* 45, no. 31 (2010): 63–70.

MICROFINANCE

H. S. Shylendra

No phenomenon in the recent past has, perhaps, gained such unprecedented fame and infamy at the same time as microfinance. What has been its defining feature? The women's movement? Poverty lending? Social banking? Or the non-profit sector gone adrift? The answer may lie partly in all these factors without an aggregate picture emerging with ease.

The Indian microfinance movement, which shares several commonalities with its global counterpart, still stands out for its uniqueness reflected in its sheer size and diversity among other things. The movement, which began gaining prominence as an innovative attempt extending credit to the poor since the 1990s, is estimated to have reached more than 130 million members by 2017. The diversity of the base catered to reflects two distinct delivery models: (a) the MFI (Microfinance Institution) model and (b) the SHG (self-help group) and bank linkage model. The latter is a home-grown innovation supported by the state.

Microfinance, which currently focuses on purveying diverse financial services to the poor, owes its emergence to several local and external factors coming together in an opportune manner. Civil society, too, made some sporadic attempts by way of forming a women's bank and experimenting with informal groups. A major boost came from global advocacy led by many donors and multilateral agencies like the World Bank and the United Nations Organization (UNO) which projected microfinance as a panacea for poverty eradication and women's empowerment. The growing role of NGOs and the attempted withdrawal of banks from rural lending, under the guise of reforms, gave a further fillip to microfinance. The groups' working, based on the principles of peer monitoring and joint liability, was conceptualized as being a perfect substitute for physical collateral capable of reducing transaction costs in disbursing small risky loans.

The terms 'microfinance' and 'microcredit', often used interchangeably, are imports from the Western narrative. Though both terms have essentially come to mean provision of small credit without traditional collateral to the poor, especially women, certain implicit differences regarding the nature and approach of delivery are also conveyed by these terms. Those who prefer the term microfinance emphasize offering diverse financial services like credit, savings and insurance as an improved strategy. Microfinance even tends to get associated with a certain approach that advocates commercial orientation by microfinance agencies with links to the larger financial system. Incidentally, at the grass roots the members largely tend to use words of local parlance like *karza*, *saala*, *bachat*, *mandal* and *sangha* to refer to microfinance and its groups. Such a gap in terminology is reflective, in a way, of certain fissures that exist over microfinance practices between the community and the elite in the sector.

What have been the major outcomes of microfinance promoted with so much hope and hype? Anyone reviewing the available assessments on microfinance in India is bound to encounter rather mixed results, ranging from the dramatic to the dismal, constraining any sweeping conclusions. No doubt there have been some spectacular results, at least with regard to outreach and institutional changes. The SHG-bank linkage model alone reached close to 100 million households through 8.5 million SHGs spread across the country by 2017. SHGs have become ubiquitous with their presence felt while conducting regular meetings and pursuing a wide range of activities besides savings and credit in almost all villages. The humongous growth of SHGs has, in turn, spawned another layer of institutions called SHG federations or collectives owned by SHG women. Achievements of the MFI model are no less impressive. Initiated by civil society, the model now has diverse players, including NGOs, cooperatives, for-profit companies and small finance banks. At one point, over 1,500 NGOs were involved in microlending in India with the help of donor and borrowed funds. Faced with severe fund crunch and regulatory constraints, the model has since seen a great churning and transformation, especially involving NGOs. Many NGOs have metamorphosed into for-profit commercial companies and banks over the years. With fund flow easing, as a result of the change, the for-profit entities have seen massive growth both in rural and urban areas with the total client base reaching nearly 40 million borrowers.

But, with profits and self-sustainability becoming their main goal, many MFIs almost went berserk in terms of charging very high interest rates and adopting coercive recovery methods. The result was widespread resentment and even protests against MFIs in many quarters. The culmination was the allegation of borrower suicides and a clampdown on MFIs by the Andhra Pradesh state government in 2010 which branded them as moneylenders practising usury. What ensued was a crisis wherein almost the entire MFI sector came to a halt in the country before slowly recovering itself, though losing some of its sheen. Restoring credibility has meant new norms of regulation for MFIs with a clear thrust on consumer protection and social performance.

As regards the socio-economic impact of microfinance, results are mixed at best. Micro-level studies indicate several positive impacts, including the unleashing of women's agencies.

This has allowed women members to access savings and credit, undergo training, interact with outsiders, become office-bearers and explore collective ventures. Some of them have even managed to become local political leaders, raising their own and their group's profiles. The negatives reported include exclusion of very poor from the groups and increased burden on women owing to group norms and expectations. Microfinance groups seem to have replicated existing social and cultural hierarchies in their practices, including in their names, and precluding any radical changes in status.

Although macro results are scarce, the available proxy indicators indicate that microfinance impacts have not been transformational. Moneylenders and informal agencies continue to thrive as per official surveys. Microfinance loans, despite their huge numbers, account for less than 2 per cent of the total bank credit in the country; so much for the claim of the movement as having proved the poor as bankable! Boasting the largest presence of microfinance, India does not figure high in human development and gender empowerment indices. Unless other viable alternatives emerge, microfinancing is likely to continue under some name or form.

References

Basu, Priya and Pradeep Srivastava. 'Exploring Possibilities: Microfinance and Rural Credit Access for the Poor in India'. *Economic and Political Weekly* (2005): 1747–56.

Taylor, Marcus. '"Freedom from Poverty Is Not for Free": Rural Development and the Microfinance Crisis in Andhra Pradesh, India'. *Journal of Agrarian Change* 11, no. 4 (2011): 484–504.

MIDDLE CLASS

Pavan K. Varma

The Indian middle class consists of an entire swathe of people who are above the poor and below the very rich. In the Indian context, anybody who has a home to live in and can afford three meals a day for the family, with access to basic healthcare, public transport and schooling, and some disposable income to buy such basics as a fan or watch or cycle, has already climbed on to the lowest level of the middle-class bandwagon. By these parameters, the middle class could well be more than half of our total population of nearly 1.3 billion, below the 2 per cent of the very rich and above those below the poverty line or those not destitute but still very poor.

Even by an economic criterion, the size of the growing middle class is very large today. If we define a middle-class person as anyone who belongs to a household whose monthly income is between 20,000 and 100,000 rupees a month, the middle class would be, as per estimates, anywhere in the vicinity of over 300 million people. According to a recent study done by the McKinsey Global Institute, by 2025, the middle class would have expanded to 583 million, with incomes increasing by eleven times over what they are today.

This middle class will play an increasingly important role in the further evolution of India. There are several reasons for this. First, for the first time, the middle class has reached a numerical size which constitutes a significant critical mass in the electoral arithmetic of the nation. Second, this growth in numbers has reinforced the incipient homogeneity of this class to a point where, more than ever before in our history, it constitutes a *distinct* class with an identity that significantly transcends class loyalties. Third, this numerically sizeable class has for the first time acquired a footprint which is pan-Indian in scope, meaning that it is represented in all parts of India. Fourth, this middle class has never been younger, with the bulk of its members being around the age of 25. Fifth, the powers of this class have undergone a verifiable revolution with respect to information and communication, and consequently of influence, due to mobile telephony, social media and 24 × 7 news.

However, in spite of some occasions where it has come out of its behavioural insularity, the middle class is still far too self-obsessed, with little improvement in regard to its social insensitivity to the travails of the vast numbers of those who are below it, and lives in visible poverty and deprivation. The middle class still believes that its interests constitute the interests of the nation and has little time for the larger issues of poverty, illiteracy and malnutrition that plague our country. This is a weakness the middle class will need to overcome, in its own interest, because no class can secede to form its own Republic, and a nation has to grow holistically in order to benefit all its constituents. The challenge thus, before this powerful and emerging class, is to become 'modern' in the sense of values such as civic sensitivity, citizen responsibility and the imperatives of public welfare.

References

Beinhocker, Eric D., Diana Farrell and Adil S. Zainulbhai. 'Tracking the Growth of India's Middle Class'. *McKinsey Quarterly* 3 (2007): 50.
Saxena, Rachna, et al., 'The Middle Class in India', *Frankfurt* February, 2010.

NASBANDI (NASBANDĪ)

Poonam Muttreja

The Hindi term *nasbandi* refers to 'getting your tubes tied' – a surgical procedure for sterilization in which a woman's fallopian *tubes* are clamped and sealed. Nasbandi gained notoriety in the mid-1970s, when Prime Minister Indira Gandhi introduced forced sterilization of women and men as part of India's 'population control' programme. This happened during the state of 'national emergency' that was declared between 1975 and 1977, a dark era that saw the suspension of civil liberties. Forty years later, India's family planning programme is still to fully recover from the forced sterilization experience of the 1970s.

Many rational explanations are offered for why poor families in particular end up having more children than they desire. When child mortality is high, families tend to have more children than they would ideally like so that at least a few survive and there are more 'free' hands to work. Sadly, such explanations have compromised, if not ignored, the consequences of frequent and unwanted pregnancies on women's health.

Though *nasbandi* refers to both female and male sterilization, the onus of family planning has always been on Indian women. In 2015–16, female sterilization accounted for 75 per cent of contraceptive use in India – among the highest in the world. In stark contrast, male sterilization accounted for just over half a per cent of modern methods of contraceptive use. Most Indian men do not seem to care about the reproductive health of their wives, a sad reflection in women of the stranglehold of patriarchy, the resultant subjugation of women and women being denied their rights to fertility decisions.

As a transformative move, in 2017 the Government of India introduced two new free contraceptives, in its bid to promote temporary methods of contraception and widen the basket of choice to meet the population's family planning needs. Also, every once in a while, positive-deviant stories emerge from unexpected quarters. Chedi Mandal or 'Nasbandi Baba' as he is called, a respected, fearless and active educator of health issues, has motivated twenty men in his village in Bihar to opt for vasectomy. After watching *Main Kuch Bhi Kar Sakti Hoon [MKBKSH]: I, A Woman, Can Achieve Anything*, a behaviour-change-communication-oriented television soap opera, a group of men from Chhatarpur district in Madhya Pradesh, who were habitual wife beaters, have become empathetic partners and undergone vasectomy.

Inspired by Chedi Mandal and others like him, MKBKSH celebrates male vasectomy, while simultaneously shattering myths surrounding its impact on virility by referring to nasbandi as 'mastbandi'. In Hindi, the word *mast* means fun. When messaging in entertainment education programmes are modelled on markers like 'nasbandi–mastbandi', the audience observes and imbibes them. As we continue to stir up conversations around family planning and educate people on spacing methods, it is equally important to understand that we are fighting a mindset which cannot be changed until social norms change. The expansion of the digital media offers an opportunity. Entertainment education-oriented communication strategies can cause digital disruption. Mass-mediated storytelling can reach the unreached and inform the uninformed, to make a significant difference to people's lives.

References

International Institute for Population Sciences. *National Family Health Survey* (NFHS-4), 2015–16.
Wang, H. and A. Singhal, *Unfurling the Voicebook of Main Kuch Bhi Kar Sakti Hoon: Real-Time Audience Engagement, Rising Fandom, and Spurring of Prosocial Actions*. New Delhi: Population Foundation of India, 2017.

NREGA (NAREGĀ)

Reetika Khera

In the early days of the National Rural Employment Guarantee Act (NREGA), when we participated in awareness drives in rural India, we were greeted with bewilderment. That there could be a law guaranteeing one hundred days of employment to anyone who applies for it was beyond people's imagination and dreams. 'If the government fails to provide work, you are entitled to an unemployment allowance.' We thought that perhaps mentioning this provision would get them excited. It mostly made matters worse: being paid for sitting at home came across as a cruel joke.[1] Within five years of those days of awareness drives, *narega* in North India and *nooru naal vaele* (hundred days' work) in Tamil Nadu had become household words. Every year, about 50 million women and men are employed under NREGA, according to official data.

Beyond the promise of employment, NREGA has other noteworthy features: there is a mandatory minimum share (one-third) of employment for women; work is to be provided within five kilometres of one's residence; at least half of NREGA funds are to be spent by elected local councils; village assemblies select and prioritize NREGA projects; there are strict norms for transparency and accountability; workers are entitled to basic worksite facilities. Further, people are to be employed for the creation of productive assets, such as approach roads, water-harvesting structures, contour trenches and various works on private land (e.g. levelling or construction of wells). There have been some achievements thus far, but many hurdles still remain in realizing its full potential for rural transformation. Women participate in large numbers and, especially in North India, they appreciate the opportunity to earn the minimum wage in their own village. Though NREGA is primarily perceived as a social security programme, it can also play an important role in the creation of productive assets in rural areas.

However, NREGA has been a battle from the word go. To have such a law enacted was in itself a battle in the prevailing political and economic climate. While that battle was won, it opened up a bigger battle: the implementation. Even creating awareness of rights under the Act, the very first requirement of successful implementation of the law is a challenge – not just because the people concerned are often unable to read or write but also because they tend to have little faith in the state.

Another major challenge is to develop a sense of accountability, which is sorely lacking, among functionaries responsible for the implementation of NREGA. For over a decade now, we have found that those in charge of implementing the Act do not necessarily empathize with the labourers or share the vision of the Act. Often, they are part of the corrupt nexus that sees the programme primarily as an opportunity to milk the system. Breaking this nexus has been an important part of the employment guarantee battle.

It was expected that in its second term (2009–14), the United Progressive Alliance (UPA) government would build on the foundations laid earlier and address what had thus far been termed 'second-generation' issues. These included improving technical inputs for the programme, ensuring the provision of basic worksite facilities and streamlining wage-related issues, among others. Instead, one witnessed an unhealthy trend towards centralization of the NREGA. An ill-conceived 're-engineering' of the NREGA began at the behest of the Unique Identification Authority of India (UIDAI), which issues a unique identification number to every resident, with biometric authentication called the Aadhaar. Aadhaar began to be imposed in NREGA processes, such as distribution of job cards and payment of wages. The advantages of this are negligible; there is mounting evidence of considerable damage.

Further, the real wages of NREGA workers have declined or stagnated for a few years. Though the demand to index NREGA wages to the price level was agreed to in early 2011,

---

[1] In the second term of the United Progressive Alliance government, 'Mahatma Gandhi' prefixed to it NREGA (making it MGNREGA), an attempt by the Congress Party to earn political capital through superficial measures.

the revisions are often tokenistic. The scale of employment has also more or less stagnated since 2010–11 (even though there is still a large unmet demand for NREGA work). Delays in wage payments cause fatigue among rural labourers and push them towards lower-paid, more exploitative forms of employment in the private sector. These adverse developments indicate that even as hostility towards NREGA appears to have subsided, the Act's modest achievements are in danger of being reversed.

An encounter in Surguja District (Chhattisgarh) with seven men belonging to the Pahari Korwa community provided a glimpse of the promise of NREGA. Pahari Korwas (earlier classified as a 'primitive tribal group') are forest dwellers and live on the margins on society. A group of researchers and myself met with these men, who lived in the hills of one of the remotest village of Lakhanpur Block. Yet we found that they were all familiar with NREGA, proudly showed their job cards and bank passbooks, and had all worked on NREGA worksites. We asked them how they had spent their wages. Often, people elsewhere would report that their wages are spent on subsistence needs. Instead, in this case, one said that he had invested his earnings in a bicycle, another to buy a bullock, the third man said he had repaid a debt incurred when his brother was sick. Yet another had set them aside to buy textbooks for his child's education. And, finally, one used it to meet social obligations. Next, we asked what work had been undertaken in that area. It turned out that the main activity was levelling their fields. They were pleased about this too as they felt that it could double their crop yields. It is experiences such as these that make the battle for employment guarantee seem worth fighting.

References

Khera, Reetika, ed. *The Battle for Employment Guarantee*. New Delhi: Oxford University Press, 2011.
Sankaran, Kamala. 'NREGA Wages: Ensuring Decent Work'. *Economic and Political Weekly* (2011): 23–5.

OUTSOURCING

Souvik Mukherjee

In 2005, Thomas Friedman conceptualized the world as 'flat', a concept that emphasized the powers of outsourcing. Imagining himself embarking on a journey for India like Columbus, he nevertheless concluded that the world, as traversed via his Lufthansa flight to Bangalore, is flat. As proof of his conclusion, he has the following example: 'The Infosys C.E.O., was showing me his global video-conference room, pointing with pride to a wall-size flat-screen TV, which he said was the biggest in Asia. Infosys, he explained, could hold a virtual meeting of the key players from its entire global supply chain for any project at any time on that supersize screen. So, its American designers could be on the screen speaking with their Indian software writers and their Asian manufacturers all at once. That's what globalization is all about today […] Above the screen there were eight clocks that pretty well summed up the Infosys workday: 24/7/365.'

Keywords for India

In the grand vision of Globalization 3.0, Friedman sees the Indian entrepreneur and her or his American counterpart vying equally for business for 'when the world is flat, and anyone with smarts, access to Google and a cheap wireless laptop can join the innovation fray'. Friedman goes on to provide many other examples from India and indeed claims that the idea of the flattened world occurred to him from something the Infosys CEO had said about levelling the playing field. No wonder 'outsourcing' is now part of the common parlance in Indian languages and is even used as a 'verb' quite often. Together with it, the associated words 'offshore' and 'onshore' are often heard.

Put simply, 'outsourcing' is the way that work can be digitally transferred to people across different countries and continents, often at cheaper rates, thus significantly reducing production costs and maximizing profits. This is also informed by what Manuel Castells calls the 'network society' or 'a society whose social structure is made up of networks powered by micro-electronics-based information and communications technologies'. For example, the Paris-based videogame developer Ubisoft has sections of the same game being constructed separately in Montreal, Sofia and Pune. In fact, the concept itself affects language: for example, websites such as 'Outsourcing Translation' provide a specially constructed basic vocabulary of languages such as Hindi, Kannada and Telugu meant for communications by those in the BPO (business process outsourcing) system. The 'flatness', however, is easily challenged. Pradip Ninan Thomas, charting the digital growth of India, cautions, 'Even as it is right to celebrate the success of the IT industry in India [...] while one can certainly argue that the industry and the BPO sectors have resulted in spillover effects and [...] transcend barriers that have hitherto acted as a break on information access and use, the benefits of this revolution have accrued, on most occasions to the already privileged segments of the Indian population.'

Outsourcing, once the favourite buzzword in US industry, is now much less popular as it is viewed as a threat to local employment. In India too, the word has begun to metamorphose into intriguing synonyms. Rajesh Rao, of the videogame company Dhruva, calls it 'co-development', as reported in a CasualConnect video, signalling the changing perceptions of the word in the Indian context as well. In a 2017 report in the *Hindustan Times*, it is stated that NASSCOM (National Association of Software and Services Companies) estimates that more than one million people work in the Indian BPO industry and more than five hundred companies offer outsourcing services in India. The word itself and its cultural connotations have a far wider reach, despite its recent vicissitudes. 'Outsourcing' vies for a top position with other loan words from English into Indian languages.

References

Castells, Manuel, ed. *The Network Society: A Cross-Cultural Perspective*. Cheltenham: Edward Elgar Publishing, 2005.

Friedman, Thomas L. 'It's a Flat World, After All'. *The New York Times*, 3 April 2005. Available at: https://www.nytimes.com/2005/04/03/magazine/its-a-flat-world-after-all.html (accessed December 2018).

POLICY PARALYSIS

Vipul Mudgal

The term 'policy paralysis' has been around for a while but it found a new ascendency and context sometime around 2011–12. The immediate context was that economic reforms had slowed down around the second half of the United Progressive Alliance II (UPA II) government, led by Prime Minister Manmohan Singh of the Congress Party. By the middle of the year, there was huge rise in the usage of this phrase, along with its occasional variants 'policy inaction' or 'policy gridlock'. In Hindi-language papers, the term appeared in variants of *nitigat jadta* (roughly, 'policy deadlock'), and over time a number of parallel terms were coined by India's vibrant regional press in more than twenty-two languages, spread over the length and breadth of India.

It is difficult to pin down the origin of this phrase, but it can be safely said that it has a strong Indo-US connection. One of the earliest stories in this period, published by the *Economic Times* on 13 May 2012, talked about the influential US–India Business Council (USIBC), the apex body of American corporates doing business in India, which had written a 'secret' letter to US president Barack Obama and told the White House that there was a 'vacuum' at the central government in India. The USIBC story and the quote, which made a mockery of the letter's claimed secrecy, was carried by dozens of papers and channels, not to mention hundreds of websites and videos in the same week.

Policy paralysis was used in the context of the government's failure to implement pro-industry labour laws and lower the cost of capital, besides accelerating key economic reforms such as allowing foreign direct investment (FDI) in sectors like the insurance, airlines and the retail business. News stories blamed policy paralysis for slowing down the gross domestic product (GDP) growth rate and a downgrade of the country's ranking by global rating agencies. Never mind if the economic growth was slowing down in 2012 not just in India but all over the world. Also, jobless growth, as witnessed simultaneously, then was, it seems, a non-issue for the media.

Most reports in which the phrase policy paralysis was used as a keyword quoted important people advising or warning the government to immediately address the 'reforms'. An *Economic Times* report quoted steel tycoon L. N. Mittal as saying that policy paralysis is condemning millions to remain poor, with a useful hint that Mittal's whopping US$ 30 billion projects were awaiting clearance. This serves as an example of a highly selective use of a term loaded with political and ideological meanings, clearly aimed at policy modification in favour of corporate India. It is equally important, therefore, to point out what the phrase does not mean.

It is interesting that except in stories about slowdown of economic growth or delay in reforms, the term policy paralysis was hardly ever applied to India's perennial policy-related problems, such as hunger, agrarian crises or farmers' suicides. Around the same period when its usage was growing exponentially, a meticulous search failed to find a single story in the mainstream press that put the blame for the country's chronic hunger on policy paralysis. For instance, policy paralysis was never used to describe India's broad failure in meeting the Millennium Development Goals (MDGs) such as targeting poverty, providing safe drinking water and toilets to the poor or reducing gender discrimination.

Keywords for India

In the middle of a media blitzkrieg of 'policy paralysis' attacks, Prime Minister Manmohan Singh released a report on chronic hunger called *The HUNGaMA Survey Report 2011*, brought out by the NGO Nandi Foundation. Singh called hunger and malnutrition India's national shame. Dozens of news stories and comments in the mainstream papers chastised successive governments for their failures, but it never occurred to any reporter or commentator to apply the term 'policy paralysis' to chronic hunger which, as the report brought out, was a result of faulty or misplaced policies followed by the successive governments.

The usage 'policy paralysis' was rampant in India just before the 2014 elections. From January to March 2011, the mention of policy paralysis in mainstream Indian media was around ten a month, which jumped tenfold to between 100 and 150 from June to October that year, according to a Reuters Report. In November and December, it crossed 400 and 450, respectively, and rose almost steadily to touch 600 in June 2012. The Reuters report and graphic 'Indian Rupee and Policy Paralysis', based on media monitoring by Factiva, reveals that the usage surged across all (English) media with the fall of the Indian Rupee. The report noted that 'the references have surged just as the rupee tumbled to a record low of 57.32 against the dollar on June 22'.[1] By the middle of 2012, the term policy paralysis had entered thousands of economic/financial websites, blogs and YouTube videos and the government was clearly on the defensive. It was probably among the two most important ideas and expressions (the other being Lokpal or anti-corruption ombudsman) which may have had a role in bringing down the UPA government.

A meticulous tracking of the term or its variants in the entire Indian media would require enormous time and resources, but it is safe to assume that the usage continued to grow until the next elections in 2014 in which the Congress-led UPA was trounced by the right-wing Bharatiya Janata Party (BJP). The phrase continues to be used in India but its currency has declined significantly after Congress Party lost to BJP, led by Prime Minister Narendra Modi, who is seen as market-friendly and pro economic reforms. The usage of policy paralysis is particularly conspicuous in its absence in TV debates after 2014, but it will be interesting to track its journey in the future. Its future connotations will be most eagerly watched because sooner or later all governments face populist compulsions and are forced to ignore free-market prescriptions.

References

The Economic Times. 'Policy Paralysis: India "Condemning" Millions to Remain Poor, Says L N Mittal', 21 June 2012.

Nandi Foundation. *HUNGaMA: Fighting Hunger & Malnutrition, The HUNGaMA Survey Report – 2011*. Hyderabad: Nandi Foundation, 2012. Available at: http://www.naandi.org/wp-content/uploads/2013/12/HUNGaMA-Survey-2011-The-Report.pdf (accessed 31 March 2018).

---

[1] See graphic in http://archive.indianexpress.com/news/policy-paralysis-indias-new-catchphrase/967796/ Retrieved on 6 December 2019

POLLUTION

Shahzad Gani and Pallavi Pant

The word 'pollution' is derived from the Latin verb *polluere*. Synonyms include contamination, adulteration and impurity. However, for a long time, the word was used in reference to human beliefs and was commonly used to describe instances with moral judgements. By mid-1800s, there was some use of the word with respect to the environment, but it wasn't until the 1950s that the word began to be used extensively with the natural environment.

In the *Oxford English Dictionary*, and in contemporary discourse, the word pollution is described as 'the presence in or introduction into the environment of a substance which has harmful or poisonous effects'. In India, it is also used when discussing social norms, with reference to 'purity' of caste. But, it is more commonly used in the environmental context and can refer to soil, water, air and noise pollution. In common parlance, it is common to hear phrases such as *gaadi ka pollution check* ('Get your car's emissions checked'), *sarkār pollution ka kuch karti kyun nahin* ('Why doesn't the government do something about pollution!') and *kitna pollution ho gaya hai* ('It has become so polluted'). The use of the word pollution is most often associated with 'air pollution' in the media.

Pollution is one of the biggest health risks in India and is becoming an increasingly mainstream topic of discussion, both in the media and among the masses. Sridhar and Kumar observe that nearly 75 per cent of all surface water is contaminated with biological or chemical contaminants including chemicals, disease agents and other waste. In terms of air pollution, most districts in the country have levels higher than the guidelines stipulated by the World Health Organization (WHO).

Exposure to pollution, either through ingestion of contaminated food/water or through inhalation of polluted air, is linked to a variety of health effects. Common ailments associated with unsafe water include cholera, dysentery, hepatitis A, jaundice and so on. On the other hand, air pollution is related to several respiratory illnesses, such as shortness of breath, asthma, bronchitis as well as cardiovascular diseases. A report by Indian Council of Medical Research (ICMR), Public Health Foundation of India (PHFI) and Institute for Health Metrics and Evaluation (IHME) states that unsafe water and sanitation, closely linked to water pollution, contributes to 5 per cent of the country's disease burden, while air pollution is responsible for 10 per cent of the country's disease burden.

In terms of governance, India has a wide range of environmental laws and regulations that restrict discharge of pollutants into the environment, including the Water (Prevention and Control of Pollution) Act of 1974, the Water (Prevention and Control of Pollution) Cess Act of 1977 and the Air (Prevention and Control of Pollution) Act of 1981. Central and state pollution control boards are responsible for monitoring and controlling pollution. One of the biggest legal cases on air pollution has been fought in the city of Agra in Uttar Pradesh where the impact of air pollution on the Tājamahala has led to long-term action on air pollution, albeit with limited results. Several dedicated projects focused on polluted rivers have resulted in limited improvements, and despite the sacred status of many Indian rivers, pollution continues unabated.

In the last few decades, 'pollution' has also come to be used in the environment versus development debate. In many cases, pollution is considered a necessary evil for the country to grow and expand. However, in recent years, there has been a growing demand for clean air and water from the general public, and the issue has gained media attention as well. In fact, Article 21 of the Indian constitution has been interpreted by the courts of the land to include the right to clean environment for Indian citizens.

References

Indian Council of Medical Research (ICMR), Public Health Foundation of India (PHFI) and Institute for Health Metrics and Evaluation (IHME). *India: Health of the Nation's States: The India State-Level Disease Burden Initiative*, New Delhi: ICMR, PHFI, and IHME, 2017. Available at: http://www.healthdata.org/sites/default/files/files/2017_India_State-Level_Disease_Burden_Initiative_-_Executive_Summary%5B1%5D.pdf (accessed December 2018).

Sridhar, Kala S. and Surender Kumar. 'India's Urban Environment: Air and Water Pollution and Pollution Abatement', MPRA Paper No. 43810 (December 2012). Available at: https://mpra.ub.uni-muenchen.de/43810/1/MPRA_paper_43810.pdf (accessed December 2018).

PUBLIC PRIVATE PARTNERSHIP

Bibek Debroy

Public private partnership (PPP) is an expression widely used, often for disparate projects. Therefore, it is best to have an official definition. There is a PPP Cell (set up in 2006) in the Infrastructure Division of the Department of Economic Affairs (DEA), and this keeps tabs on all PPPs of the union government. India is a union of states, and the state governments are also vital partners in PPPs. The DEA's general and formal definition states, 'PPP means an arrangement between a government or statutory entity or government owned entity on one side and a private sector entity on the other, for the provision of public assets and/or related services for public benefit, through investments being made by and/or management undertaken by the private sector entity for a specified time period, where there is a substantial risk sharing with the private sector and the private sector receives performance linked payments that conform (or are benchmarked) to specified, pre-determined and measurable performance standards.'

This definition makes three points clear. First, PPP isn't only about greenfield development, as is sometimes assumed. There can be management or maintenance contracts as well. Second, it isn't only about physical infrastructure (transport is the most obvious). There can be, and are, PPP projects in skills, education, healthcare and water supply too. Third, many states have PPP projects. In the broad area of infrastructure, at the moment, there are 1,529 projects in various stages of implementation.

Why PPP? The broad reasons are superior management compared to the public sector, better technology and incremental resources. There are detailed guidelines and there is the Public Partnership Appraisal Committee (PPPAC) of the union government. The level at which approval is granted is a function of the project cost. The current thresholds are below 100 crore rupees, 100–250 crore rupees and above 250 crore rupees. If the PPP project is for infrastructure, one should mention the Viability Gap Funding Scheme (this proves a capital subsidy) and India Infrastructure Finance Company Limited (for long-term debt).

There were indeed some problems with PPPs and, in 2015, a committee under the chairmanship of Vijay Kelkar was set up to examine these problems for the infrastructure sector. The Kelkar Committee stated, 'The sectoral spread of PPPs has been fairly diverse in hard infrastructure sectors such as transport (roads, airports and ports), which has seen the largest share in terms of numbers and success. The new airports at Delhi, Mumbai, Bengaluru and Hyderabad and the large dimension of highway projects are part of the programmatic success of PPPs in the country.' It has also convincingly addressed some myths that are widely prevalent, such as the following: (a) profit motive of private sector is incompatible with the service motive of public sector; (b) PPPs increase user tariffs; (c) money for PPPs comes from private 'pockets'; (d) once a private sector partner is brought in, there is little or no role for the public sector; (e) PPPs do not provide value for eventual cost to the public sector; and (f) private operators are not committed to protecting the environment.

There must have been some problems. Otherwise, there would have been no reason to set up this committee. Those problems concern global issues, judicial/statutory authority orders, legal and regulatory frameworks, financing issues, multiplicity of institutions and overlap, problems internal to the private sector and contractual frameworks. For the PPP performance to be better, these problems will have to be addressed.

References

Planning Commission. 'Chapter 3: Financing the Plan'. In *Twelfth Five Year Plan 2012-2017: Faster, More Inclusive and Sustainable Growth*. New Delhi: Government of India, 2013.

Vijay Kelkar Committee. *Report of the Committee on Revisiting and Revitalizing Public Private Partnership Model on Infrastructure*, submitted to the Department of Economic Affairs, Ministry of Finance in November 2015.

PUBLIC HEALTH

Poonam Muttreja

The term 'public health', although self-explanatory, often leaves lingering questions on what it really means even among those working in this field. Regardless of whether one is a community activist, a number-crunching analyst, a serious scientist and researcher or a policy adviser, the goal of public health is fairly obvious. Public health has people and their well-being as its only focus. Seventy years ago, in 1948, the World Health Organization (WHO) defined the health of an individual as 'the state of complete physical mental and social well-being' and not merely the absence of disease. The promotive intent is to stay fit, and the preventive intent is to avoid getting sick or hospitalized.

The significance of public health has declined over the centuries with the remarkable ascendance of allopathic medicine that has found treatments and cures for deadly diseases. Nevertheless, it is important to underscore that the largest gains in child survival in the United Kingdom and other countries in Europe during the nineteenth century came from promoting personal hygiene and public sanitation and not by building hospitals or producing gynaecologists and paediatricians. Over the years, the field of public health has evolved to embrace different disciplines to assure holistic well-being: by promoting critical medical interventions, such as the immunization of children to personal hygiene, and addressing the social determinants of health – which refers to addressing issues of caste, class and gender – that deny people equal opportunities when it comes to accessing health services, basic education and even livelihood opportunities.

In 1977, the 30th World Health Assembly coined the slogan 'Health for All by the Year 2000 A.D.' This meant that primary healthcare would be made universally accessible. In 1978, the famous Alma-Ata World Conference acknowledged primary healthcare as the mainstay of 'Health for all by 2000 A.D', In May 1979, the World Health Assembly endorsed the Declaration of Alma-Ata and, in order to achieve its goals, invited member states to formulate a National Health Policy (NHP), as Singh and Singh have detailed. Strong political will, community participation and intersectoral coordination were required to lay the foundation of primary healthcare and 'Health for All' – if at all the public was to be brought into public health and every individual was mobilized. The responsibility of the state to provide comprehensive primary healthcare as per the declaration led to the formulation of India's first NHP in 1983, revised again in 2002 and 2017. Despite India's commitment to the Alma-Ata Declaration, preventive community-based primary healthcare wasn't given priority.

Over these decades, India has witnessed a significant shift in the role of the public within public health from being a passive recipient of public health services to becoming an active participant. The introduction of communization processes under the National Health Mission, such as Community Action for Health (CAH), has placed people at the centre of its processes to ensure that the health needs and rights of the community are being met. The inclusion of CAH exemplifies a paradigm shift and is an acknowledgement of the fact that equitable and universal healthcare cannot be achieved in isolation. However, it is still a work in progress and we have a long way to go.

Speaking of equality, Michelle Obama said, 'Communities and countries and ultimately the world are only as strong as the health of their women.' Sadly, we are far from imbibing the true essence of these words in our society. Women are still discriminated against and violence against women, recognized globally as a fundamental human rights violation, still finds wide prevalence in India. A 2013 World Bank report by Duvvury et al. estimates that one in three women across the globe has experienced physical and/or sexual assault at some point in their lifetime. The report also demonstrates the significant health and economic impacts and states that every form of violence, including physical and sexual violence, against women is undoubtedly as much a public health concern as any other disease.

Within the realm of global commitments such as the Sustainable Development Goals (SDGs), it is the need of the hour for public health systems to realign and redefine their priorities. It is imperative to understand that public health is and will remain a cross-sectoral concern – it is a concern with domestic violence as much as with environmental pollution, food contamination, non-communicable diseases, like cancer or diabetes, or, for that matter, a concern with the failure of the state to regulate the private sector and protect its people from market failures that adversely affect their health. It is time to bring back the public into public health and look for long-term sustainable health solutions. In the words of Thomas Carlyle, 'For he who has health has hope; and he who has hope, has everything.'

References

Duvvury, Nata, Aoife Callan, Patrick Carney and Srinivas Raghavendra. *Intimate Partner Violence: Economic Costs and Implications for Growth and Development*. Women's voice, agency, and participation research series no. 3, Washington DC: World Bank, 2013. Available at: https://openknowledge.worldbank.org/handle/10986/16697 (accessed December 2018).
Singh, A. R. and S. A. Singh. 'The Goal: Health for All; The Commitment: All for Health'. *Mens Sana Monographs* 2, no. 1 (2004): 97–110.

REFUGEE

Paula Banerjee

There is a common misunderstanding that all forced migrants are refugees. A refugee is a forced migrant but so are many others such as the internally displaced, trafficked and the stateless who are forced out of their homes and habitat. A refugee is a legal and official entity as opposed to the forced migrant, and the definition of a refugee, as given by the UN Convention Relating to the Status of Refugees of 1951, says that a refugee is a person who: 'As a result of events occurring before 1 January 1951 and owing to well-founded fear of being persecuted for reasons of race, religion, nationality, membership of a particular social group or political opinion, is outside the country of his nationality and is unable or, owing to such fear, is unwilling to avail himself of the protection of that country; or who, not having a nationality and being outside the country of his former habitual residence as a result of such events, is unable or, owing to such fear, is unwilling to return to it.'

The UN mandated that the status of refugee could only be offered by the United Nations High Commissioner for Refugees (UNHCR) or by a sovereign state. UNHR notes three traditional durable solutions to the refugee problem. These are the following: (a) resettlement in third countries, (b) local integration and (c) voluntary repatriation. The 1951 Convention was seriously criticized by many, as B. S. Chimni notes, because it was thought to be too soft on countries from the global North and who, even after being signatories, did not follow the letter and spirit of the convention. It did not take into account either the major causes of conflict-related displacements in Asia and Africa or the exigencies of the borders of countries in these regions, as observed by Myron Weiner.

The Organization of African Unity (OAU) Convention of 1969 expanded the definition of refugees. Apart from the reasons given in the 1951 Convention, it added that refugee status should be given to 'every person who, owing to external aggression, occupation, foreign domination or events seriously disturbing public order in either part or the whole of his country of origin or nationality, is compelled to leave his place of habitual residence in order to seek refuge in another place outside his country of origin or nationality'. Thus, for the first time, colonial persecution began to be counted as a ground for seeking asylum. But, sadly, the 1969 OAU Convention was focused on members of the African Union only. People from other regions, such as Asia and Latin America, were deprived from its benefits.

In 1984, representatives of South America put forth the Cartagena Declaration, which further expanded the definition of refugees by adding that 'persons who have fled their country because their lives, safety or freedom have been threatened by generalized violence, foreign aggression, internal conflicts, massive violation of human rights or other circumstances which have seriously disturbed public order' should be eligible for asylum. In the post-1989 period, the situation of poor and vulnerable populations has become even more precarious. Massive groups of people began to be displaced as a result of local conflicts, development projects, climate-related reasons, genocide, statelessness and many other reasons.

In the new millennium, concern arose over the protection of extra-Convention refugees, who were called in such terms as 'de facto refugees', 'OAU and Cartagena-type refugees' and 'humanitarian refugees'. They were actually seeking 'complementary protection' but were totally absent from international treaties. An EXCOM conclusion adopted in October 2005 specifically referred to 'complementary protection' but did not define it, Jane McAdam has observed. But after 2005 they became part of the discourse. The other groups that appeared in discussions on refugees were 'climate refugees'. They were also outside the 1951 Convention. By 2016, the number of displaced population worldwide rose to over 65 million, of whom 22.5 million were refugees. In the second decade of the new millennium, a majority of the refugee population is made up of children and less than 1 per cent of these are beneficiaries of third-country resettlement. It is a myth that refugees flood the countries of the global North as most often they are accommodated in the same region where they were displaced. Most people are resettled through kith-kin networks and only a minority get to stay in camps.

References

B. S. 'Status of Refugees in India: Strategic Ambiguities'. In *The Refugees and the State*, 444–5, edited by Ranabir Samaddar, 2nd edn. New Delhi: Sage Publications, 2008.
Organisation of African Unity (OAU). 'OAU Convention Governing the Specific Aspects of Refugee Problems in Africa', adopted on 10 September 1969 by the Assembly of Heads of State and Government, entered into force on June 1974. Available at: http://www.achpr.org/files/instruments/refugee-convention/achpr_instr_conv_refug_eng.pdf (accessed 22 March 2018).

RESERVE BANK OF INDIA

Raghavendra Lal Das

Reserve Bank of India (RBI) is the central bank of the Republic of India (not to be confused with the Central Bank of India, a state-owned commercial bank). A central bank is tasked with the onerous responsibility of regulating the money supply as per the needs of the economy, not a penny more and not a penny less. It has monopoly over currency and it usually oversees the markets and commercial banking of the country.

The RBI started functioning from 1 April 1935 by terms of the Reserve Bank of India Act of 1934. The preamble to the Act enjoins the RBI 'to regulate the issue of Bank notes and keeping of reserves with a view to securing monetary stability in India and generally to operate the currency and credit system of the country to its advantage; to have a modern monetary policy framework to meet the challenge of an increasingly complex economy, to price stability while keeping in mind the objective of growth'. RBI is one of the few full-service central banks in the world. Its activities range from currency management, formulation of monetary policies, acting as banker to the government and banks, supervision of the banking system, overseeing the different segments of the financial market and management of forex and development activities including rural credit and development.

Like any other central bank, the RBI has its own lexicon. The daily pink broadsheets and economic journals use those words like jargon without explaining what they mean. This entry will therefore make an attempt to explain some of such oft-quoted words in the context of the RBI.

- *Mint street*: An alternative name given to the RBI by the paparazzi. The location of RBI's headquarters is on a street in Mumbai which was known as Mint Street decades ago.
- *Legal tender*: Banknotes (currency notes) and coins which have to be accepted by all as mode of exchange.
    - *Demonetization*: Bank notes or coins of any denomination which ceases to be legal tender as per the decision of the RBI. Such notes and coins are withdrawn from circulation.
    - *Essential features of a currency note*: These make a piece of paper to be a currency note. These are number series, issuing authority, promissory clause, signature of the RBI governor and the guarantee by the Government of India.
- *Currency chest*: Storehouse for currency notes and coins owned by the RBI but operated by the agency (commercial banks).
- *Lender of the last resort* (LOLR): Provider of the cash support to the eligible financial entities when they are faced with liquidity crunch or financial insolvency.
- *Monetary policy*: Deciding the cost of very short-term funds from the RBI with the objective of price stability.
- *Policy rate*: The rate at which RBI lends to the eligible borrower on the strength of collateral.
- *Repo rate*: The rate at which RBI lends to eligible borrowers on the strength of the security. The date of liquidation of the loan is prefixed.
- *Reverse repo rate*: The rate at which RBI borrows from eligible entities while parting with government securities. This rate is always less than the repo rate.
- *Cash reserve ratio* (CRR): A portion of specified deposits of the bank to be parked in their current account maintained with the RBI.

Keywords for India

- *Statutory liquidity ratio* (SLR): The portion of specified deposits of the bank to be kept in the form of cash, gold and unencumbered approved government securities.
- *Open market operations* (OMO): A mechanism to contract or expand the volume of cash or liquidity in the system by sale/purchase of government securities.
- *Public debt*: Borrowing by the government from the public and the institutions. This does not include liabilities arising out of small savings.
- *Risk*: Exposure to loss.
- *Credit risk*: Risk arising out of the inability of the counter party to honour the commitment.
- *Market risk*: Risk emanating from the movement in market prices or rates away from the contracted price or rate.
- *Operational risk*: Risk of loss on account of disruption in the business.
- *Risk-weighted asset*: Every asset is assigned a risk weight as per the risk perception.
- *Capital to risk-weighted assets ratio* (CRAR): It is calculated by dividing the capital of the bank with the aggregated risk-weighted assets. It is an indicator of the level of capitalization of the bank.
- *Non-performing asset* (NPA): Any asset not generating income for the bank is dubbed as non-performing. Non-performing assets are categorized in three brackets, depending on the nature and the length of irregularity in repayment. These are substandard, doubtful and loss.
- *Exchange rate*: Rate at which foreign currency is converted into local currency and vice versa.
- *Spot*: Sale and purchase of currency, commodity and security on the current price and immediate delivery.
- *Forward contract*: Sale and purchase of currency, commodity and security at contracted price and delivery at a future date.

References

Kisch, Cecil, 'The Monetary Policy of the Reserve Bank of India'. *The Economic Journal* 59, no. 235 (1 September 1949): 436–8.

Warrier, M. *India's Decade of Reforms: Reserve Bank of India at Central Stage*, Notion Press, Incorporated, 2018.

SENSEX

Hoshang Netarwala

'Sensex' is a term familiar to every person in Mumbai, India's financial capital. Its daily gyrations can cause considerable angst and exuberance all in the space of a few hours. New kids on the block dabble in the market daily to make a quick buck, but more often than not end up burning up the stash they started with. The Bombay Sensitive Index, or its popular short form, the 'Sensex', is a conglomeration of thirty of the most actively traded shares listed on the Bombay Stock Exchange (BSE), the oldest exchange in Asia with over 5,400 companies listed on it. The Exchange was established in 1875 by Premchand Roychand. Word has it that the initial broker meetings were held outside the city's town hall. As the number of brokers increased, they shifted from place to place, before finally moving to Dalal Street, where the exchange now has its headquarters, at Jeejeebhoy Towers, named after one of the longest serving members of the exchange. Earlier, trades were done through an outcry system on the floor of the exchange where brokers indulged in high energy physical trading involving a combination of gesticulation and lung power creating an ambience not unlike that of a fish market. The exchange transitioned to screen-based trading in 1995. Today, the online trading platform of BSE, known as BOLT, lays claim to be the fastest in the world.

In the mid-1980s, the BSE decided to set up a mechanism to monitor the performance of the major stocks traded on the exchange, to give investors an insight into the markets and the Indian economy as reflected by the performance of these actively traded stocks. With this idea, the Sensex was born. The thirty stocks comprised in the Sensex account for 50 per cent of the exchange's market capitalization. Different weightages were assigned to the thirty stocks that comprised the index, based on their market capitalization, with the total weightage of the index at 100. In the early days of the index, unscrupulous elements would manipulate the Sensex stocks and mislead people on how the scrips and the economy were performing. Fortunes were made and lost by punters hitching their wagons to the brokerage calls farmed out by market manipulators. The most famous of these scams was probably the Harshad Mehta scam of 1992, where the stock broker manipulated the markets using worthless bank receipts and swindled close to 5,000 crores rupees. The scam exposed loopholes both in the Indian banking system and the stock exchange. However, with the introduction of stringent controls by the Securities Exchange Board of India (SEBI) and the staggering growth of the stock market, manipulations of such a large magnitude by an individual are a rarity, though the odd scamster still gets away. The Sensex first pipped the 1000 points benchmark in July 1990. In May 2009, in reaction to the United Progressive Alliances win, the Sensex vaulted over 17 per cent, the single largest day gain in its history and trading had to be halted for an hour. Today, the Sensex stands at 38,000 – a towering reflection of how the Indian economy has grown over the last couple of decades. Succinctly stated, an investment of 100 rupees in the Sensex stocks when the index was introduced would now be worth 38,000 rupees – a good hedge against inflation.

The Sensex itself has metamorphosed over time. Its composition is periodically changed to reflect current market conditions. Laggards are dropped and new companies with large market capitalizations are introduced to keep it relevant. The index is calculated on a free-float capitalization method. While initially the Sensex was dominated by manufacturing companies, a number of these companies have now been discarded and replaced by new-age market icons. A majority of the stocks in the original Sensex don't exist in its new avatar today having either been discarded or wound up. Today, the stock with the largest weight in the Sensex is the petroleum behemoth Reliance Industries, closely followed by infotech giants Tata Consultancy Services (TCS) and HDFC Bank. Over time with the growth of the stock market, the Sensex has spawned a number of new indices, most notably the Nifty 50 index. With that the Sensex has lost some of its sheen and competes for the numero uno benchmark with other pretenders to the throne. Market mavens who wish to invest in specific sectors have a host of indices to fall back on. With globalization of the world economy, the Sensex is no longer insulated from international crises which can impact its performance. But despite the introduction of multiple indices to track various segments of the market, the Sensex is no slouch – it still remains the gold standard for old hands of the trade who want a snapshot of how the markets are shaping up.

References

Ignatius, Roger. 'The Bombay Stock Exchange: Seasonalities and Investment Opportunities'. *Indian Economic Review* (1992): 223–7.
Yalawar, Yalaguresh B. 'Bombay Stock Exchange: Rates of Return and Efficiency'. *Indian Economic Journal* 35, no. 4 (1988): 68.

SOCIAL MEDIA

P. Vigneswara Ilavarasan

Social media is an electronic platform where two or more people communicate with each other either directly or indirectly. The use of social media is dependent on the internet and electronic devices whose access or ownership cost is fast declining. The communication can be through any form – text, images, audio, video or just emoticons – and can be both synchronous and asynchronous. Piskorski notes that the platforms are successful as they cater to the unmet social needs of the people by reducing social and economic costs. For instance, if I am looking for a casual physical relationship, 'single' status in Facebook or having a profile on Tinder will help me avoid spending in local bars and possible social rejection while asking multiple people if they are also seeking partners. Given this, unmet social needs are multiple and diverse for India, due to its plurality. The extant research on social media platforms in India is mostly in information systems and related management disciplines, and insights from cultural studies and other social sciences are limited.

There are more non-users of social media in India, since only 33 per cent of its 1.3 billion population have access to the internet as of 2018. There are more urban users than rural ones with differential preferences for content and language. However, there is the saying, 'Whatever you say is true in India, the opposite is also true.' This applies to the internet, especially social media, as well. Narayan and Narayanan note that Shubhpuja and OnlinePrasad are e-commerce firms that offer religious services, such as priests, live broadcast of rituals and astrology consultation. Most of the popular temples in India also live broadcast important festivals. On the other hand, India repeatedly figures in the top ten consumers of porn. When Google offered free Wi-Fi at the railway stations, pornography topped the list of domains accessed.

There are home-grown social media platforms, some of them imitate their counterparts. For instance, Zomato is a restaurant-review platform which is similar to Yelp in the West. Sharechat is similar to WhatsApp. When these platforms evolve in India, there are customizations to meet the Indian demands. Zomato has added more restaurants than Yelp, with detailed menu and timings. Sharechat claims to be a 'no-English-network' and focuses on local languages. There are some India-centric platforms which thrive on Indian cultural traits. Pagalguy.com has all possible content related to business school admissions in India. Shadow education or dependency on coaching centres is common in India. Pagalguy is an extension of the same. Indian consumers expect high quality at a lower price and like to argue and complain. Mouthshut.com populates its platform with complaints and reviews about consumer products and reviews uploaded by the users. There are platforms where Indians dominate usage and participation. India was the greatest source of traffic on Quora, a question-and-answer community platform, in February 2018. The number of Indian users on that platform is only next to the United States, and India is the only developing country among its top ten users.

More males use Facebook than females in India. Hence, Facebook is a masculine space in India, with more likes for electronic products, female celebrities, politics and sports. In the mid-2010s, it was noticed that Indian men tended to use fake names and profile pictures to defraud people from foreign locations. This is not much different from the mid-2000s when a person was called as 'Orkutiya' when he relentlessly solicits romantic relationships through 'Orkut', a popular social media platform back then. Sometimes Indian men go to extremes, as in a case from South India, where a young man stabbed a woman who he befriended on Facebook to death because she rejected his proposal for love. Also, Facebook and WhatsApp messages have been used as evidence in an increasing number of divorce cases in Bangalore from the mid-2010s onwards.

Citizen activism for social changes, in the lines of neo-social movements, is on the rise. Either coming together against corruption (Indiaagainstcorruption), gender violence (Nibhaya), upholding ethnocentric practices (Jallikaṭṭū) and others, social media users have been busy in the last decade. Most of them are reactions to the non-responsiveness of the government. The common people also compensate the inability of the government to execute its responsibilities. For instance, in 2015, during the Chennai floods, disaster management efforts were led by the public mostly through social media. People were uploading and authenticating information related to water levels, missing people, food demand, medicine supply and relocation efforts.

The 2014 general elections were hailed as social media elections by the media due to the heavy use of social media platforms by the political parties and their leaders. Prime Minister Narendra Modi was also recognized as one of the top thirty influential persons on the internet in 2016 by *Time*. Presently, the Indian government is making efforts to bring more people online either through its capacity-building activities under Digital India and is attempting to deliver public services online. The election commission is engaging Facebook to bring more voters to the roll list and voting. Though there are mixed results, a future wherein most of the citizens are online and be part of policy contemplations cannot be ruled out.

There are other consequences of social media platforms as well. YouTube is slowly becoming a part of learning resources in Indian classrooms. Premier educational engineering institutions are using YouTube to even out the quality differences in learning experiences by uploading class lectures for entire courses. New careers in the domain of content creation are emerging. Freelancing YouTube stars and travel bloggers can garner a significant number of followers and generate revenues. Microentrepreneurs and self-employed artists can expand their market opportunities by low-cost social media marketing. Social media is a major part of leisure practices and will pave the way for learning for the urban poor.

At the same time, it has also to be noted that social media has been occasionally banned by the state, ostensibly for reasons of internal security. In some parts of rural India, local elders ban mobile phone usage by younger women as access to social media is perceived as spoiling them. There is also the concern that the young population is spending too much time on social media platforms and is likely to spend less time with real friends and runs the risk of developing an addiction.

References

Ilavarasan, P. V. 'Social Media Research in and of India: A Snapshot'. In *Emerging Markets from a Multidisciplinary Perspective*, edited by Y. K. Dwivedi, N. P. Rana, E. L. Slade, M. A. Shareef, M. Clement, A. Simintiras and B. Lal. New York: Springer International Publishing, 2018.
Piskorski, M. J. 'Social Strategies that Work'. *Harvard Business Review* 89, no. 11 (2011): 116–22.

START-UP

Souvik Mukherjee

The Indian government now has a dedicated website (startupindia.gov.in) for start-ups and with that a detailed definition that covers the Indian context:
  'Start-up means an entity, incorporated or registered in India:

- Upto a period of seven years from the date of incorporation/registration or upto ten years in case of Start-ups in Biotechnology sector
- As a private limited company or registered as a partnership firm or a limited liability partnership
- With an annual turnover not exceeding Rs. 25 crore for any of the financial years since incorporation/registration
- Working towards innovation, development or improvement of products or processes or services, or if it is a scalable business model with a high potential of employment generation or wealth creation.'

The attention paid to start-ups by the government shows that they are viewed as an important part of the country's economic and political systems. In the networked world, start-ups are easier to float and they can often address niche requirements that other less flexible corporate structures cannot. A couple of other terms are associated with start-ups, such as 'incubator' and 'indie'. Incubators are collaborative programmes aimed to help start-ups succeed. They provide workspace, seed funding, mentorship and training. One such incubator is NASSCOM (National Association of Software and Services Companies), which started its '10,000 Startups' initiative in 2013. The other word often connected to start-ups is 'indie'. Indie or 'independent' probably originates from the independent rock music scene, where the music produced would not be connected to big labels or brands. In the context of the start-up ecosystem, indie would mean any business or designer not associated with a large corporate and can also define the consumer who chooses to support small business, independent record labels and handmade items rather than shopping at big chain stores. Start-ups need not necessarily be connected to indie but this can often be the case.

Often, in the digitally connected world, start-ups make use of crowdfunding initiatives whereby many people the world over can contribute varying amounts ranging from a token US$ 1 contribution to large denominations using online payment portals and credit cards. One of the most famous crowdfunding portals used by start-ups is kickstarter.com. Start-ups are also often associated with open-source software and with code-sharing, such as on portals like GitHub. The concept of the start-up is still quite niche and urban, although some of these like the eco-friendly clay-based Mitticool refrigerator attempt to address the needs of the rural and underprivileged populace. Start-ups are becoming significantly popular in the IT-driven global ecosystem. This is also a term (and a concept) that is here to stay as more entrepreneurs start following the start-ups model.

References

'NASSCOM 10,000 Startups Serves up Inspiration and Innovation with the Startup Product Series', *YourStory*, 6 February 2018. Available at: https://yourstory.com/2018/02/nasscom-startup-product-series/ (accessed December 2018).

'Startupindia, Department of Ministry of Commerce and Industry, Government of India', Available at: https://www.startupindia.gov.in/ (accessed 20 April 2018).

TAX

Saba Sharma

According to the *Online Etymology Dictionary*, the word 'tax' evolved from the Latin *taxare*, meaning 'to estimate or assess', and its early fourteenth-century Anglo-French use as *tax*. Given its wider contemporary usage in India as a contribution levied by a sovereign power, such as a government, it is interesting to see that in much of Northeast India, particularly areas that have known insurgency and/or separatist movements within or against the Indian state, the word 'tax' is commonly used to mean an amount of money levied by militant groups and/or students' unions.

These taxes are levied on businesses, government officials, villages or communities and individuals, as well as toll tax on the highways, and on state-funded development projects. Different insurgent groups levy different 'rates' of tax, sometimes depending on the economic status of the person or business being taxed, and rates can also be negotiated. Alternative words like 'donation' and 'extortion' are also used, often highlighting the degree of acceptance of the practice from the point of view of the speaker. Government officials or the police, for instance, would use the word 'extortion' instead (as Sarita Santoshini notes in a report), as might some academics (for instance, Rakhee Bhattacharya) and locals (as Patricia Mukhim observes). Interestingly, the official (government) tax base in Northeast India is not very wide, as they do not have much industry, and scheduled tribes (STs) in the region (who constitute most of its population) are exempt from income tax.

Usage of the word tax to denote what is essentially considered an illegal practice by the formal state apparatus brings up questions of what constitutes legitimate governance in Northeast India. One strand of argument, seen in Rakhee Bhattacharya's work, is that insurgency is entirely driven by economic incentives, with insurgent groups collecting money through tax/extortion, which is then spent on lavish lifestyles and accumulation of personal wealth for leaders. Subir Bhaumik's analysis of the budget of one such group, ULFA (United Liberation Front of Assam), shows, however, that much of the money is used in cadre salaries, arms deals and operational costs as well as investments in stocks and companies to secure the future of the organization. Another strand of thought, suggested by Sanjib Baruah, is that ethnic militias such as the ones that levy taxes in fact fill a vacuum that the state leaves in these neglected areas, where state institutions are not able to guarantee security, and thus it is in these groups that people's loyalties are vested.

People's experiences of this taxation system are also complex. In Nagaland, for instance, a citizen's group called Against Corruption and Unabated Taxation (ACAUT) has challenged rampant taxation by several militant groups, including the largest and most powerful National Socialist Council of Nagalim (Isak-Muivah) (NSCN [I-M]). The NSCN(I-M) responded to this demand by reiterating the importance of tax collection to further the cause of Naga nationalism and positioning itself as the sole legitimate authority to collect taxes in Nagaland. The same group (ACAUT), however, does not uniformly condemn tax collection but engages and lobbies with them as civil society do with governments elsewhere. So, for instance, when the 'one-nation-one-tax' regime (GST, as it is popularly now known) was rolled out across India, ACAUT appealed to Naga insurgent groups to do the same. Here, the legitimacy of their political authority is not just gained through their official status but also by these performances of governance, as also reflected in many insurgent groups handing out receipts after collecting tax.

Differing usages of the word 'tax' in Northeast India, as opposed to the rest of India, highlight already prevalent difference between these regions of India and the disparity in experiences of state and governance. Tax collection by rebels is but one illustration of this wider phenomenon.

References

Baruah, Sanjib, *Durable Disorder: Understanding the Politics of Northeast India*, New Delhi: Oxford University Press, 2005.
Bhaumik, Subir, *Troubled Periphery: Crisis of India's North East*, New Delhi: Sage Publications, 2009.
Santoshini, Sarita, 'In India's Nagaland, a Tale of Taxes and Corruption', *Al Jazeera*, 14 April 2016. Available at: http://www.aljazeera.com/indepth/features/2016/04/india-nagaland-drowning-taxes-corruption-160411062725238.html (accessed 15 September 2017).

CHAPTER 4
INTIMACIES: CULTURE AND MATERIAL CULTURE

AZAN (AZĀN)

Hilal Ahmed

Azan (*adhan* in Arabic) is an Islamic call delivered by a *muezzin* (person who recites the azan) from the mosque five times a day. The purpose of azan is to invite Muslims for the obligatory (*farz*) prayers, the *salat* (or what is also called *namaz* in North India).

There is no universally acceptable form of the recitation of azan. In fact, there is a debate between Sunnis and Shias on the very origin of the idea of azan itself. The Sunni sects argue that the azan – using human voice to call worshippers for prayer – marks the distinctiveness of Islam.

Shia scholars, however, do not subscribe to the Sunni argument. They suggest that the azan had a divine origin. They believe that Allah commanded the Prophet to tell his companions the words, sequence and mode of delivery of the azan. Shia schools also challenge the authenticity of the Sunni azan. It is claimed that a few words, such as 'Prayer is better than sleep' (recited only for the *fajr* prayer), were added by the second caliph, Umar. Therefore, these words are not divine.

Such Sunni–Shia differences aren't the only unsettled issues with regard to the azan. There are a variety of azans among the Sunnis as well. For instance, the azan is recited very differently in North Indian Barelavi mosques. It begins with the *durud* (an Arabic *dua* [invocation] dedicated to the Prophet), followed by usual phrases of the Sunni azan and culminates with a *na't* (a poem usually composed in Urdu to praise the Prophet), especially on the occasion of the weekly Friday prayer. However, this is not an acceptable practice in the Deobandi or the Ahl-i Hadis mosques.

The use of loudspeaker in mosques for azan is another contentious issue. Fatwas issued for and against the use of machines for Islamic prayers have had a long and interesting history in colonial and postcolonial India. It is believed that the loudspeakers were first introduced to mosques in the 1920s. These machines were used for two purposes – recitation of the five-time azan and the diffusion of the voice of the imam (lead worshipper) for a large congregation so that the worshippers might follow him directly, especially on the occasion of the Friday prayers and the annual Eid prayers. Azan, in this sense, was not a serious issue since using an efficient mode to call on the worshippers is religiously justifiable. However, the use of a machine for disseminating instructions during namaz was not so straightforward.

Maulana Ashraf Ali Thanwi, one of the leading Deobandi ulema, offered a way out. In his opinion, the loudspeaker actually helps in spreading the voice of the imam (in the case of namaz) and muezzin (in the case of azan) to the public and therefore does not distract the congregation at all. This fatwa paved the way for similar arguments in favour of the public address system of mosques. Despite this religious sanction, though, the debate on loudspeakers for azan has not died down. In fact, it has led to a new set of questions. What does one do when the azan is delivered from two or more mosques at the same time? What are the religiously permissible etiquettes, protocols and manners to recite the azan on the loudspeaker? How does one respond to a situation when the loud sound of the azan is opposed by non-Muslims? Different Islamic sects have responded to these questions in a variety of ways in postcolonial India. Despite this multiplicity, there is consensus that the recitation of azan – with or without a loudspeaker – should always create a soothing effect.

References

Khan, Naveeda. 'The Acoustics of Muslim Striving: Loudspeaker Use in Ritual Practice in Pakistan'. *Comparative Studies in Society and History* 53, no. 3 (2011): 571–94.
Metcalf, Barbara Daly. *Bihisti Zewar: Perfecting Women* (Maulana Ashraf Ali Thanawi's Bihishti Zewar: A Partial Translation with Commentary). Berkeley: University of California Press, 1990.

BADH (BAḌH)

Punam Tripathi

The Hindi word *badh* is akin to the English 'flood'. It is a noun derived from verb *badhna* which is a modified form of the 0 word *vardhan*, meaning 'increasing, growing and thriving'. The dictionary meaning of the term badh is 'to overflow'. When a water body is unable to contain its water within its basin, it overflows and inundates the surrounding land area. This results in a flood, that is, an overflow of a large amount of water beyond its normal limits, especially over what is normally dry land. The synonyms for badh are *jal pralay* and *sailab*. In Sanskrit, the term *plavan* is used to refer to a flood. It is a feminine noun. Therefore, to denote an approaching flood, the phrases *badh aa rahi hai* and *badh aa gayi* are used.

References to badh can be found in many spiritual texts of Indian origin. The earliest records are found in Sanskrit texts. According to legend, Lord Vishnu's first avatar was the *matsya* (fish), which rescued the first man, Manu, from a great flood. Across the varied belief systems of India, floods are the most common means employed by gods to destroy civilization as an act of divine retribution or out of jealousy. The oft-quoted legend of the sinking of Mahabalipuram (where the shore temple of Tamil Nadu is located today) is that the city was so magnificent that jealous gods unleashed a flood that swallowed the city up in a single day. It is also believed that the ancient city of Hastinapur was destroyed by a flood. In the *Arthashastra*, Kautilya has identified eight kinds of 'providential visitations' and includes the flood as one of those.

Today, floods are viewed as a destructive phenomenon that claims lives and livelihoods, damages crops, livestock and infrastructure. But, floods are not an 'un-natural' phenomenon in the northern plains of India. In fact, floods have contributed in the genesis and the fertility of the 'Great Plains', that is, the Indo-Gangetic plains. The Great Plain is a badh *ka maidan* (or floodplain) of the Indus and the Ganges–Brahmaputra river systems and encompasses an area of about 700,000 square kilometres. Floods are an annual phenomenon in these plains. The summer heat leads to melting of the glaciers and increases the volume of water in the river channels. The summer heat is also responsible for drawing monsoon winds, which are moisture-laden winds that move from the surrounding oceans towards the Indian landmass. Three-fourths of the annual rainfall in India occurs during the four monsoon months, that is, from June to September. Because of this concentrated rainfall and the melting snow, the rivers overflow their banks resulting in floods. The damage resulting from the encroachment of the floodplains for economic activities and various interrelated factors, such as deforestation in the watershed, sedimentation, change in land use, diversion of river courses and construction of dams, reservoirs and barrages.

Badh is a common phenomenon that occurs in all physiographic regions of India. Indeed, every Indian language has a distinct word for it. In Punjab, the land of five mighty rivers, where floods are very common, they are called *hara*. Another region characterized by annual floods is the lower Gangetic–Brahmaputra plains of Assam and West Bengal. In this part, floods are known as *banna*, while in neighbouring Odisha they are referred to as *banya*. If we come to the western part of the country, they are known as *pur* in Gujarati and Marathi. In the four Dravidian languages, namely Telugu, Kannada, Malayalam and Tamil, floods are known as *pravaahamu*, *huccuhole*, *veliyerram* and *vellam*, respectively. Other related Hindi terms/phrases are *badhgrast hona* (under flood water), *badh prabhavit* (flood-affected areas), *badh peedit* (affected by floods), *badh rahat* (flood relief) and *badh rahat kosh* (flood relief fund).

References

Kapur, Anu. *Vulnerable India: A Geographical Study of Disasters*. New Delhi: SAGE Publications, 2010.
Williams, Monier. *Sanskrit-English Dictionary* (revised, 2008). Available at: http://www.sanskrit-lexic on.uni-koeln.de/monier/ (accessed 12 August 2017).

BALTI AND LOTA (BĀLṬĪ AND LOTA)

Shivani Chopra

Balti is a Hindi/Urdu word for 'bucket', and 'lota' is Hindi/Urdu term that could refer to a 'mug or a small tumbler', also referred to as *mugga* in some dialects. The lota is made of brass, steel, iron, aluminium or hindalium. Now a days, balti and lota are mostly manufactured in plastic because it is easier to maintain and cheaper to buy. The balti and lota are an essential part of bathroom use in Indian households across castes, classes and regions. Water would be stored in the balti and it would be poured out with the help of a lota. They are primarily used for bathing and washing clothes. Since bath tubs or showers are rarely found in middle-class homes, a large majority of the Indian population enjoys bathing with the balti and lota. Even today, many small-town hotels do not have a shower head in their bathrooms. They only provide a tap and a balti and lota for their guests to bathe. One is meant to fill the large balti with water and carefully use the lota to pour water over oneself. One may have to squat down or one can sit on a small raised platform or seat while bathing so that the water covers more surface area in one pour. This mode of bathing is also eco-friendly as one is constantly measuring out water, unlike in the shower, where one does not know how much water is spent. So, in regions where there is water scarcity, such as in India, bathing with the balti and lota is prudent.

The balti also represents a time gone by. The balti has replaced big clay or metal pots (*matka*) that were used for water storage in households. Even up till a few decades ago, tap water was still rare in many villages, and the main sources of water were rivers and wells or handpumps. In those cases, the balti arrived as a convenient alternative to the clunky and breakable matka, to effectively pull water out from the well or out of larger drums and tankers or at the base of a handpump. This is the reason why, for a very long time, brass or steel balti and lota were an essential part of the dowry that was given to the groom's family, along with utensils and other utility items.

In Southern India, many restaurants use small baltis to store and serve rice, gravies and curries. In Northern India, *sevak*s (volunteer workers) in temples and gurudwaras serve food in a balti to every devotee or whosoever has come to the shrine. This is how food used to be, and still is, served for large gatherings, such as in weddings. This has changed, albeit slightly, with the advent of privatization and multinational companies. While serving food in the new set of Westernized restaurants, which is a popular choice among youngsters, is not with the balti and lota, we still see traces of the ubiquity of the bucket in the 'bucket of fried chicken' of KFC, and in South India where the current rage is the 'bucket biryani', where you can takeaway biryani for a small group of say eight people in a plastic bucket – and you can keep the bucket after polishing off the delicacy!

Reference

Balaram, Singanapalli. 'Design Pedagogy in India: A Perspective.' *Design Issues* 21, no. 4 (2005): 11–22.

BEHENJI (BAHANJĪ)

Ajoy Bose

The Hindi word *behenji*, which literally means 'respected sister', has three different connotations in the Hindi-majority states of North India.

The first and most common usage is to describe young ladies belonging to the middle and upper classes in a manner which is at once familial and yet respectful in tone. For instance, a shopkeeper addressing a woman client as 'behenji' expresses both regard and friendliness by adding the honourific *ji* to the familial *behen* (sister). This is the direct female equivalent to the term *bhaisaheb* (the honourific *saheb* added to the Hindi word for brother, *bhai*). Interestingly, in Bengali, the terms used to express the same are *didi* and *dada*, meaning elder sister and elder brother. In Hindi, since behen is usually qualified by *badi* (elder) and *choti* (younger), it became imperative to create the new word behenji as a key word in the Hindi lexicon that allowed men to address with a degree of familiarity, if not affection, and without any sexual connotation, women neither much younger than themselves to be called *betis* (daughters) nor much older to be addressed as *mausiji* (auntie) or *dadiji* (granny).

The term behenji was further amplified when it entered the Indian political lexicon after it became the title of the firebrand Dalit leader Mayawati from the early 1990s onwards. This appellation was popularized by her mentor Kanshi Ram, founder of the party she now heads, the Bahujan Samaj Party (BSP). Interestingly, Behenji for Mayawati has run parallel to similar terms combining endearment and respect for two other powerful women leaders in other parts of India in recent years. Didi is the popular title of Mamata Banerjee, chief minister of West Bengal and chief of the Trinamool Congress, and Amma (meaning 'mother') is the title for the late J. Jayalalithaa, former chief minister of Tamil Nadu and All India Anna Dravida Munnetra Kazhagam (AIADMK) supremo.

The third connotation of behenji denotes exactly the opposite of love and respect. It is a derisive term that the English-speaking upper-middle-class youngsters use for women who are considered sexually unattractive and not smart enough. The 'behenji stereotype' would be a girl who has her hair in oily pigtails, who only dresses in salwar kameez, is unable to speak fluent English and is timid in her interactions with the opposite sex. The term usually implies someone from a lower social – if not economic – status, from a conservative family background and possibly rural or small-town upbringing. While Behenji was a very common put down by the smart young set in the 1960s and 1970s for those who did not fit in with their social benchmarks, it has seen a decline in the past several years. This may well be because young girls, even from the lower social and economic strata, with small-town backgrounds, have started dressing quite sharply in Western clothing, if not in the original brands, and are also quite bold in their interactions and relationships with boys. Most importantly, the ability to speak fluent English in the correct accent, which was a clear distinction between the urban chic and the behenjis, is no longer considered a very important mark of social prestige.

References

Bose, Ajan. *Behenji: The Rise and Fall of Mayawati*. New Delhi: Penguin Random House, 2012.
Sandhu, Priti. *Professional Identity Constructions of Indian Women*. Amsterdam: John Benjamins Publishing Company, 2016.

BHADRALOK (BHADRALŌK)

Supriya Chaudhuri

The Bengali term *bhadralok* (from Sanskrit *bhadra*, 'auspicious, blessed, good', and *loka*, 'the world' but also 'inhabitants of the earth, people'), as used from around the beginning of the nineteenth century and documented in early periodicals such as the *Samāchār Darpan* and the *Samāchār Chandrikā*, describes a respectable gentleman, usually belonging to one of the three upper castes of Hindu society, Brahmans, Vaidyas and Kayasthas. Over the course of the century, this meaning expanded to include the ideas of middle-class refinement or civility, education and a measure of prosperity. As a singular noun, bhadralok is initially restricted to a Bengali Hindu male with these caste and class attributes, the female of the same species being described, somewhat later in the nineteenth century, as *bhadra-mahila* (from Sanskrit *mahila*, 'woman'). In Bengali, moreover, several other terms with a wider range of application are commonly used along with bhadralok, such as *bhadra-samaj* (polite or respectable society, the upper-caste Hindu educated class), *bhadralok-gosthi* (the social group formed by bhadralok families) or *bhadra-sampraday* (gentlefolk, the educated middle class). John Broomfield, therefore, describes the bhadralok at the end of the century, as 'distinguished by many aspects of their behaviour – their deportment, their speech, their dress, their style of housing, their eating habits, their occupations, and their associations – and quite as fundamentally by their cultural values and their sense of social propriety'.

Thus, the bhadralok is a self-constituting, even aspirational category. Despite its initial, and persisting, religious and caste connotations, allows for some exceptions. Even low caste was not an absolute barrier to the acquisition of bhadralok status through education and economic empowerment, and right through the nineteenth and early twentieth centuries, members of other religious denominations in Bengal – Muslims and Christians in particular – formed bhadralok communities that intersect with those of the Hindus. While the term defines a social status – and most members belong to the professional middle class, espousing bourgeois ideals despite a largely non-bourgeois social base – bhadralok is not constituted as a class, and the label is more a marker of social pretension or 'distinction' in the Bourdieusian sense. Nevertheless, there are points of intersection with class, caste, interest group and status formation.

It remains to ask whether these intersect with the domain of gender. For some historians, such as Parimal Ghosh, the answer appears to be no. Yet, by the beginning of the twentieth century, the emergence of women in the public domain of professional and intellectual labour complicates the definition of bhadralok as a male category.

The decline of the bhadralok – a self-constituted elite seeking to instrumentalize education, professional skills and cultural investment to secure its social position – was inevitable, given the political and economic storms that shook twentieth-century Bengal. Ravaged by famine, Partition, migration, displacement, economic recession, Marxist class struggles and their populist counterparts, Bengali society entered a period of flux in the later twentieth century. The bhadralok, barely managing to survive the onslaught of workers' movements and class wars, was finally undone by economic liberalization. Forced to surrender both the cultural field and the moral high ground, the figure of the bhadralok may appear today as no more than a phantom, a historical delusion.

References

Bhattacharya, Sabyasachi. 'Notes on the Role of the Intelligentsia in Colonial Society: India from Mid-Nineteenth Century'. *Studies in History* 1, no. 1 (January–June 1979): 89–104.
Broomfield, John H. *Elite Conflict in a Plural Society: Twentieth Century Bengal*. Berkeley: University of California Press, 1968.
Ghosh, Parimal. *What Happened to the Bhadralok*, 12–42. Delhi: Primus, 2016.

BHAILO/BHAIYA/GHANTI/PAKLO

Rochelle Pinto

Bhailo is a Konkani term that literally translates as 'outsider'. The term is used in recent times to 'other' those who are not part of the mainland Goan identity. In a literal sense, the term is comprehensive as it does not denote any particular race or ethnicity or class. An entry in Fr Angelus Francis Xavier Maffei's *An English-Konkani Dictionary* of 1883 translates the words 'outer', 'exterior', 'exotic' and 'foreigner' as bhailo. As ethnocentric anxiety shifts its focus, however, bhailo may be assumed to carry its most pejorative charge when referring to working-class migrants to Goa.

The three terms *bhaiya*, *ghanti* and *paklo* reference historical changes in the articulation of difference in colloquial Konkani as spoken in Goa. Of these, paklo may be the oldest, deriving from the time of Portuguese colonial rule between 1510 and 1961. Unlike the term *aṅgrēja*, which has quite a specific reference to the English, paklo originally referred to a generic 'foreigner', denoting whiteness rather than a specific nationality. It could be considered an emic usage along with *mestis*, a Konkani rendition of *mestiço* (mixed-race Goans), and *cafre*, denoting the black race. Both mestis and cafre are derivatives from other languages, but paklo is not.

Bhaiya connotes the labouring or small trading class that has migrated from the north of the country, without specifying a particular state or ethnicity, with the assumption that the migrant is Hindi-speaking. Ghanti refers to communities from the hill ranges, the Western Ghats that divide Goa from the Deccan. In the early twentieth century, lineage and family links persisted between the plains and the ghats, evident when families claimed their share in cultivable land in the village councils which were called *gaunkaria* in Marathi and Konkani.

The surge in land prices and neoliberal policies from the 1990s created an environment conducive to the unrestricted conversion and sale of land and a sharp increase in the number of migrants into Goa as property owners and labourers. The word bhailo in current use carries a pejorative connotation and the perception of threat to ethnicity, cultural continuity and the immediate physical neighbourhood. Likewise, with increased urbanity, the associations between urban life and civilization have intensified to the point where to call someone a ghanti is not only an insult denoting a lack of social grace but also an insult that approximates to caste insult, because the assumption is that ghantis are outside of settled society.

Given the preoccupation with caste-based purity, one might think that mestis and paklo, both denoting race, would also acquire pejorative overtones. In fact, some interpretations of these terms suggest that they express indigenous and/or casteist contempt for the other or humorous innuendo hinting at racial miscegenation. However, race, religion and caste simultaneously defined hierarchy and identity in Goa, and the interpenetration of their usages suggests that the term paklo after political independence is often used with no negative connotation, as it denotes fairness akin to that of a foreigner today, an attribute that hierarchises identity in former colonies. The term mestis may denote an actual racial group, but paklo, when not specifically used to indicate a foreigner, indicates lightness of skin colour.

The region was considered as marginal to the political formation of India and has been positioned within the national economy as a space for either stigmatized hedonistic excess or extraction of natural resources, providing a context within which such terms increasingly denote a polarized and xenophobic identity in Goa. Neoliberalism has facilitated a culturally and homogenizing populist discourse that favours singular aspirational identities and has increased hostility towards the *bhailo*, the *bhaiya* and the *ghanti*.

References

Goswami, Rahul. 'An Accidental Bhailo'. In *Behind the News: Voices from Goa's Press*, edited by Frederick Noronha, 148–56. Saligao, Goa: Goa, 1556, 2008.
Wardhaugh, Julia. 'Beyond the Workhouse: Regulating Vagrancy in Goa, India'. *Asian Journal of Criminology* 7, no. 3 (1 September 2012): 205–23.

BHUKAMP (BHŪKAMP)

Punam Tripathi

The Hindi word *bhukamp* translates to 'earthquake' in English. Bhukamp is a *tatsam* word, that is, it has come into Hindi without any modification from Sanskrit. It is a blend of the words *bhu* and *kampa*. Bhu is a Sanskrit root word that has different meanings depending on how it is used. As a verb, bhu is used to indicate an action, a state or an occurrence. It also means 'to exist', 'to dwell' or 'to be'. It also refers to 'the place of being, space or world' and is therefore a synonym for earth (*bhumi*). As a prefix, bhu in bhukamp refers to the 'earth' while the word kampa has been derived from the Sanskrit *kampana*, which means to 'tremble'. Thus, the word bhukamp, means 'the tremble of the earth', as can be experienced during an earthquake. Synonyms of the word in Hindi are *prithvikampa*, *bhuchal* and *bhudol*: *prithvi* is a synonym of bhumi; the noun *chal* is derived from the verb *chalna*, which means 'to walk or move'; the verb *dol* means 'to sway'. In common parlance, however, bhukamp is also known as *jaljala*.

The word for earthquake is similar in all Indo-Āryan languages, differing only in its pronunciation, as these have all been derived from the same Sanskrit roots. In Marathi, for instance, it remains the same, that is, bhukamp, bhuchal, bhudol and sometimes it is also referred to as *dharanikampa* which is similar to Gujarati's *dharatikampya*. Another word popular for earthquakes in Gujarati is *bhumikampya*. In Bengali, the word used is *bhumikampa*. In Assamese, it is *bhuinkampa*, while in Nepalese it is *bhuinchalo*. In Punjabi, the word is bhuchal. Out of the four Dravidian languages, in three the word for earthquake seems to have been borrowed from Sanskrit: in Kannada, it remains as *bhukampa*; in Telugu, it becomes *bhukampamu*; in Malayalam, it is *bhuchalam*. In Tamil, the word used is *nilatukkam*. Thus, bhukamp is the most common word used for earthquake across India.

The earliest reference to bhukamps can be in found in Varaha Mihira's *Brihat Samhita* dated to the fifth or sixth century CE. The *Brihat Samhita* has postulated several causes for the bhukamp. One of the causes is that once upon a time the Himalayas could fly and they fell frequently on the earth causing earthquakes. At the request of the earth, Lord Indra (the lord of thunder) clipped the wings of the mountains so that the earth became stable but also added that the four elements, namely, wind, fire, *varuna* (water) and *indra* (thunder), would shake the earth from time to time from four directions in order to reveal the good and bad effects of actions to the world. Another explanation is that the earth was saved from sinking by Varaha, the boar avatar of Vishnu, and rests on its tusks. The earth quakes when Varaha is restless and needs to relieve his fatigue. Since powerful earthquakes result in damage and destruction, they have also been linked to the demonic forces.

References

Kapur, Anu. *On Disasters in India*. New Delhi: Foundation Books and Cambridge University Press, 2008.

Williams, Monier. *Sanskrit-English Dictionary* (revised, 2008). Available at: http://www.sanskrit-lexicon.uni-koeln.de/monier/ (accessed 12 August 2017).

CHAPPAL (CAPPAL)

Gopika Nath

The Hindi word *cappal*, meaning 'footwear or slipper', has been in use in India since the third century CE. Related terms in Hindi and other Indian languages include *panhi* in Hindi, *chappalan* in Punjabi, *chappien* in Kashmiri, *choutti* in Bengali, *saandala* or *chappala* in Marathi, *champalu* in Sindhi, *champal* or *pagarkha* or *panai* in Gujarati, *pagarki* in Rajasthani, *chaippulu* and *seruppu* in Tamil, *cheruppu* in Malayalam and *syaandal* in Kannada. Most of these words have been derived from the Sanskrit roots *pa* or *pada* (foot), *charan* (foot/to walk) and *upanat* or *upanah* (to tie/bind). Combinations such as *charan-panhi* or *charana-upanah* to *chapanhi* or *chapana* may have led to the term now in use 'cappal'. In fact, the word *padaka* is used in the Rig Veda to denote 'a small foot'. In later texts, such as the Mahābhārata, this term becomes *paduka* to denote 'a sandal or shoe or slipper'. The paduka, also called *khadava* or *khadaun*, was possibly the oldest footwear, whose earliest surviving example, excavated from East Bengal, is dated circa 200 CE. The attitude of reverence for the foot and the footprint followed with the footwear, where Rama's paduka served as an object of veneration for his subjects until he returned from exile in the Rāmāyaṇa.

The religious and cultural significance of feet in Indian traditions is unique – both sacred and humble, it is paradoxically the most polluting part of the body. From within these concepts is the worship of feet and footprints, whether on the ground or on a fabric, and the romantic sentiment of cherishing the touch of the beloved's foot, with particular attention given to the adornment of this icon of sensual desire. The wayward seek forgiveness by prostrating at the feet of the wronged, as a mark of the surrender of their ego. Showing the sole of the shoe or hitting someone with it is an ancient insult, and placing your shoe on your head signified ultimate humility and submission. In *Rajatarangani* (dated to the twelfth century CE), when cutting his finger didn't appease his sovereigns' wrath, Sanjapala tied a turban around his neck, placed a shoe on his head and ate humble pie. During the national freedom struggle, Gandhi had also urged Indians to make their own chappals, alongside promoting khadi, as a symbol of self-reliance.

Sculptures of Buddha from the Gandhara region depict footwear of the simplest kind with a sole at the base, a strap passing across the instep and another connecting this strap to the tip of the sole, at the gap between the big and second toe. From these depictions, the precursor to the modern cappal may have originated. Today, there are many different kinds of chappals in India. They range from the kohlapuris of Maharashtra to the blue- and white-rubber flip-flops or hawai chappals of Bata and Shantiniketan cappal of West Bengal. The cloth or grass pula cappal of the Paharis and the Osho cappal of Pune in Maharashtra. Right up to the fancy cappal, replete with heels and studded stones, worn by fashionistas, matching the mood of their dress or the occasion.

If one wonders why it is so important to discuss chappals, we need only turn to Anjali Joseph's novel *The Living*, which paints a poignant picture of the kohlapuri through the eyes of a cappal maker, whose family has made chappals for generations but whose son is not interested in the trade anymore. Musing while varnishing and checking the chappals his family makes, the cappal maker's son questions why he cares for something a man will put 'between his feet and the ground'. He soon recognizes that the cappal is a constant companion, more so than a spouse. He also laments that 'when they're gone, it will be as though they had never been there' but advises us that these old chappals that we have lived-in have to stay, for new ones inevitably harass the skin.

References

Jain-Neubauer, Jutta. *Feet and Footwear in Indian Culture*. Ahmedabad: The Bata Shoe Museum Foundation and Mapin Publishing, 2000.
'Sole Stories: The History of Footwear in India', *Cox & Kings*, blog post. Available at: https://blog.co xandkings.com/sole-stories-the-history-of-footwear-in-india/ (accessed December 2018).

CHOOLAH (CŪL'HĀ)

Shahzad Gani and Pallavi Pant

The Hindi word *choolah* (stove) refers to an apparatus that is used for cooking or heating. The word 'choolah' is similar to the Sanskrit word *chuli* and probably has a Dravidian origin. It generally refers to the traditional Indian cooking stove, which is heated by burning solid fuels such as wood (including twigs, sticks and logs), charcoal, animal dung briquettes or agricultural/crop waste. While its usage is more prominent in rural parts of India, it is also widely used in cities, typically in low-income households. Even modern stoves, which use cooking gas/electricity, are sometimes referred to as choolah in North India.

Prevalent societal norms across India, with a few exceptions, dictate that women take responsibility for managing the household, including cooking and procuring fuel (biomass) for the chulhas. This is best exemplified by the common Hindi phrase that is often used in daily life and can also be heard on TV shows and in movies: *choolah chowka sambhalna aurat ka kaam hai* ('It is a woman's responsibility to take care of the house'). Women often leave the safety of their communities in search of fuel and are also at high risk from exposure to a variety of harmful air pollutants while cooking with the conventional choolah. By virtue of spending most of their time with their mothers and other female relatives, infants and young children are also exposed to this risk from an early age. Clean alternatives to solid fuel-burning chulhas can drastically reduce fuel consumption and exposure to harmful emissions.

References

Cooking Clean Alliance. Website. Available at: http://cleancookstoves.org (accessed December 2018).
Subramanian, Meera. 'Global Health: Deadly Dinners'. *Nature*, 28 May 2014. Available at: https://www.nature.com/news/global-health-deadly-dinners-1.15286 (accessed December 2018).

COOLIE

Harish Trivedi

Coolie is a word of uncertain origin and may have derived from a Tamil word through the Portuguese. The word signifies an indigent person employed to perform strenuous physical labour for low wages. The term came into wide use in English after 1833 when slavery was abolished. To replace liberated black workers on sugar plantations, etc., poor peasants mainly from India and China were recruited by British imperial authorities and shipped halfway across the world, mainly to the Caribbean, various parts of Africa, Mauritius and Fiji. Coerced into signing (or often thumb-printing) an agreement for indenture, usually for a period of five years, such labourers came to be called coolies by their white employers. They called themselves *girmitiya*, in a Bhojpuri adaptation of the 'agreement' they were bound by. This pan-imperial colonial practice, which Hugh Tinker has aptly labelled 'a new system of slavery', was strongly opposed by Indian nationalist leaders led by M. K. Gandhi, who saw it practised all around him during the early years of his career in South Africa. Most descendants of the original girmitiyas have stayed on and now form a substantial proportion of the population in many of the former British colonies named above, contributing vitally to the hybrid culture there and, after Independence, vying with native or black-immigrant populations to fill high positions, including those of the offices of the president or prime minister.

In India, the term is used for plantation workers and other labourers in the hills and, more ubiquitously, for porters on railways platforms. In Mulk Raj Anand's novel *Coolie* (1937), the term is somewhat arbitrarily stretched as the 14-year-old Munoo is forced to work successively as a domestic servant, a market porter of old ladies' shopping bags, as a millworker in Bombay where Communist union leaders seek to politicize him and finally as a rickshaw puller for a British memsahib in Shimla who even takes a passing erotic fancy to him before he dies of consumption at the age of 15. A more iconic Indian portrayal of the term is to be found in the Hindi film *Coolie* (1983), in which Amitabh Bachchan plays a railway porter. The theme song of the film, *Sari duniya ka bojh ham uthatehain* ('We carry the burden of the whole world'), features him with a group of coolies in red kurtas who declare in the song that they earn their bread the hard way, have only one holiday in the year on the day of Eid (as all the coolies here happen to be Muslims, oddly enough), that they are exploited and may not have much to eat but try and cope with the help of a drink of water and *paan-beedi* and that while passengers come and go they remain forever on the platform which is their home.

Before wheels were reinvented, so to say, and attached to travellers' bags a couple of decades ago, it was considered not only impractical but also *infra dig* for a self-respecting passenger to carry her or his own bags. Older Hindi films abound in scenes where the hero at the end of a rail journey stands in the doorway of his carriage and even before alighting shouts 'Coolie! Coolie!' Notions of class and (in)dignity are inseparably attached to the term 'coolie', which often carried a racist slur as well. The use of the word has recently been banned in several former colonies, including South Africa and parts of the Caribbean, where the practice was dominant; the preferred term now is 'indenture'. In an ironic evocation of this complex history, call-centre workers in India who work at a fraction of the wages payable to white American workers whom they replace were called 'cyber-coolies', as a reminder that similar forms of neocolonial exploitation continue to exist.

References

Kumar, Ashutosh. *Coolies of the Empire: Indentured Indians in the Sugar Colonies, 1830–1920*. Cambridge: Cambridge University Press, 2017.
Trivedi, Harish. 'Cyber-Coolies, Hindi and English', Letters. *TLS: The Times Literary Supplement*, 23 June 2003: 17.

CRICKET

Boria Majumdar

'Cricket is an Indian game accidentally discovered in England.' These poetic words were penned by Ashis Nandy in his seminal *Tao of Cricket* (1989). Given the financial muscle of Indian cricket in 2017, Nandy, it must be said, had prophetic foresight. It was in the early nineteenth century that the sport in its modern form was appropriated by the ruling English gentry and turned into a tool to bind the contours of the British empire together. It was brought to India around the mid-nineteenth century by men of the empire, and the first natives who played the game were the sepoys residing in cantonment towns across Northern and Central India.

It is an interesting question as to why the sepoys and then some Indian princes and middle-class patrons readily appropriated the British sport of cricket. From a pragmatic point of view, it may be surmised that they saw in them a worthwhile cultural tool to reassert their hurt self-esteem and injured masculinity. On the other, cricket had the potential to be assimilated as means of crossing swords with the British imperialist. At a time when the ills of an unequal political and economic structure threw up contradictions, which quite naturally had a deep impact on the social psyche of Indians, sport might have provided a level-playing field. Failing to attain power and prestige within the army or in the society, the sepoy and later the middle-class Indian nationalist searched for apolitical ways to counter British humiliation.

Indian cricket came of age when the erstwhile British colony played its first recognized test match at Lord's on 25 June 1932 under the captaincy of C. K. Nayudu. And though it took India twenty years to win its first test match against England (at Chennai in 1952), the game was already well grounded in the country at the time of Independence in 1947.

Cricket as an industry, however, owes its origins to India's World Cup triumph in England in 1983. Things changed overnight. A sport turned into a national obsession and corporate India was forced to take notice. Soon enough, the rights to host the World Cup moved to the subcontinent in 1987 and with liberalization and the opening up of the Indian economy in 1991, the Board of Control for Cricket in India (BCCI) managed to sell telecast rights of Indian cricket for a whopping 650,000 dollars.

. India's position as the new nerve centre of world cricket has been strengthened in recent times, thanks to the impact of the IPL on world cricket, modelled on Major League Baseball and the National Football League.

The BCCI, which is entrusted with the task of governing cricket in India, is made up of multiple state associations. It governs and works on assignments for the Indian national cricket teams for both men and women and also for age group teams at the U-19 level. It also runs the IPL. Finally, it is entrusted with the task of setting up coaching clinics across the country and has established the National Cricket Academy in Bangalore and zonal cricket academies in Kolkata, Mumbai, Delhi and Chennai. The adoption of a conscious talent-nurturing policy by the BCCI ensured that economically underprivileged youngsters no longer had to worry about training facilities. A look at the Indian national team and the impact is evident. More than half the team is from small towns, making Indian cricket a meritocracy of sorts.

References

Nair, Nisha. 'Cricket Obsession in India: Through the Lens of Identity Theory'. *Sport in Society* 14, no. 5 (2011): 569–80.

Nandy, Ashis. *The Tao of Cricket: On Games of Destiny and the Destiny of Games*. Oxford University Press, 2000.

CYCLE-WALA (SĀ'IKILWĀLĀ)

Jean Drèze

The term Cycle-wala (or Cycle-wali, as the case may be) is being used here in the twin sense of 'a person who cycles' and of the 'cycle mechanic'. Both seem to me to be endangered species in India, or at least in urban India, so let me try to contribute to their posterity.

I came to India forty years ago, and I swear not a single screw or other part of the ordinary Indian bicycle (say, your good old Hero Jet) is different today from what it was in 1979. The odd 'mountain bike' has appeared in the meantime, but the less said about it the better – it does not even have gears, in most cases. The ordinary bicycle, of course, has no gears either. Nor does it have lights, a striking fact if you think how dangerous it is to cycle at night without lights and if you compare the cost of a bicycle light with that of a road accident.

You might think that the Indian bicycle is the same as before because it has achieved perfection. This idea, however, is hard to square with the absence of gears or lights. And it is not just that. Over the same period, bicycles in other countries (from Europe to China), which already had lights and gears of course, have seen a series of technological innovations – electric bicycles, foldable bicycles, *trottinettes* and, yes, real mountain bikes. If this is possible elsewhere, why not in India?

The same observations apply to the Cycle-wala, as a mechanic. His dilapidated toolbox, like the bicycle itself, is exactly the same as forty years ago. It consists mainly of a few spanners, a bunch of ball bearings, some basic spare parts and of course a heavy all-purpose hammer. Oh, and I forget the museum piece, the heavy-metal bicycle pump with bits of tyre strung around it at the bottom. I doubt that there are many places left in the world where it often takes two persons to inflate a bicycle tyre, one to hold the nuzzle (because it has no screw) and one to pump.

The Cycle-wala is just one example of a class of occupations that might be called 'stagnant jobs'. There are many other examples, from the *chaiwala* (tea-stall manager) to the street cobbler. Like the Cycle-wala, they are doing the same thing with the same tools or utensils as forty years ago, at least in the cities I am familiar with, mainly in North India.

I am trying to draw attention to the striking stagnation of the technology of everyday life in India or rather the everyday life of the poor. Not only do cycles still lack gears, but kitchens still have no chimneys, bathrooms no pegs, mosquito nets no stands and wall switches no colour scheme to distinguish fans from lights. And the failure rate of simple items like taps, latches, switches, zips, plugs, not to speak of toilets, is depressing. All this contrasts with the amazing speed of improvement, year after year, of the gadgets and gizmos used by the privileged classes – motorbikes, smartphones, drones, air conditioners and, of course, the world-class crazy-expensive trophy bicycle with more gears than you can count but which nobody actually rides.

I may be wrong, but I suspect that it has something to do with the caste system and its obsession with hierarchy and the division of labour. One principle of the caste system, for instance, is that the thinkers and doers are different people. The cycle mechanic is not expected to be a kind of barefoot engineer who also designs better tools. As for the accredited engineer, it is below her or his dignity to work on the design of a better bicycle pump – a rocket or laptop is far more suitable.

None of this, of course, is immutable. What I have said of bicycles would have applied just a few years ago to cycle rickshaws. But some people did apply their mind to the design of better rickshaws, and the new ones are far more driver-friendly than the old ones. Even the improved cycle rickshaw, however, does not have gears. And I was amazed, one day, when I asked a *rickshawwala* how he felt about gears and discovered that he had no idea what bicycle gears were. So, there is still much to do all around.

Mind you, the Hero Jet is really cool – I wouldn't want a different bicycle.

Reference

Sainath, P. 'Where There is a Wheel'. In *Everyone Loves a Good Drought*. New Delhi: Penguin India, 2000.

DANDA/LATHI/LATHI CHARGE (ḌAṆḌĀ/LĀṬHĪ/LĀṬHĪ CHARGE)

Manindra Thakur

Though the Hindi word *ḍaṇḍa* has multiple meanings in Indian intellectual traditions and in the wider social milieu, essentially it stands for the coercive power of the state. For instance, concepts like *daṇḍa samhita* (penal code) or *daṇḍa vidhan* (rules for punishment) mean the collection of rules or laws of the state for taking punitive action. *Dandadhikari* is the one who has the authority to punish. Daṇḍa is also one of four classic strategies of confronting one's enemy and settling disputes. The other three are *sama* (conciliation by praising, mutual benefit, using personal or social relations), *dana* (placating with gift) and *bhed* (using secrets, creating mutual suspicion). In this sense of the term, daṇḍa stands for punishing by plundering or destroying the enemy's property, harassing or killing the enemy.

In this tradition, the science of law enforcement is called *dandaniti*, and it is one of the four areas of knowledge. The other three are *anwikshki* (logic or philosophy), *trayee* (Vedas) and *varta* (Arthashastra). Dandaniti discusses the principles of just punishment. It is believed that unjust punishment would destroy the legitimacy of the punishing authority and that of the state or the king; therefore, it should be based on sound principles and should be adequate. Dandaniti constitutes a significant part of texts like the *Manusmriti*, the Mahābhārata and Kautilya's *Arthashastra*.

In its material form 'daṇḍa' stands for a stick, representing the state authority or hierarchy of the social authority. Officers of the state responsible for adjudication and announcing punishment used to carry such a daṇḍa, symbolizing their state-sanctioned authority. In the social hierarchy in ancient India, the Brahmin, the intellectual class, was supposed to carry a daṇḍa as tall as the person's height; the Kshatriya, the warrior class, of the height of their forehead; and the Vaishyas, the trading class, was supposed to have it equivalent to the height of their nose. Also, the suggestion was made that the Brahmins should keep a daṇḍa made of Palas wood or Bael wood, whereas the other two castes should use a Daṇḍa made of Peepal or Pilu wood. It is interesting to note that all three plants are known for their medicinal values in Indian culture.

The more colloquial equivalent of daṇḍa is *lathi*, a stick made out of bamboo, that the Indian police carries. In the hands of the policeman, lathi symbolizes state power in a cruder sense, as it is used to demonstrate the force of the state. During the early colonial period, the British government provided lathi to policemen to control the crowd and with this began the practice of 'lathicharge'. The lathi also symbolizes power in a more general sense in the Indian villages, where most members of the agrarian classes carry it with themselves to public meetings or otherwise. Though it has multiple uses, such as to ensure protection from animals or reptiles and to carry something heavy by using the shoulder as a fulcrum, the central use of a lathi is to demonstrate force. During the zamindari system, people trained in using the lathi as a weapon were quite valued and they were appointed as security guards by the zamindars (feudal lords). During this period, demonstration of the skill of using lathi for defence and attack also became a kind of sport in Indian villages. There are several proverbs using the word lathi. For instance, *jiski lathi, uski bhains* ('The one who has more power in his lathi gets the buffalo', meaning, the powerful control the resources). Similarly, when someone says that he is oiling the lathi, it means that he is preparing for a fight.

References

Bhaduri, N. 'Dandaniti: Prachin Bharatiya Rajshasira'. *Sahitya Sangsad, Kolkata* (1998).
Shah, K. J. 'Of Artha and the Arthaśāstra'. *Contributions to Indian Sociology* 15, no. 1–2 (1981): 55–73.

FEMALE FOETICIDE

Ravinder Kaur

Foeticide is the deliberate act of causing the death of a foetus. The destruction of the foetus – or aborting the foetus – has a long history, both legal and illegal. The commonly used word in Hindi for foeticide is *bhrunhatya*. *Stree* or *kanya bhrunhatya* refers to the murder of a female foetus, the word stree referring to 'woman' and kanya referring to a 'young female child'. It is interesting that although the sex ratio at birth is much worse in China than in India, the term female foeticide has clung much more to descriptions of the phenomenon of sex-selective abortion of females in India.

The term 'female foeticide' gained currency in India in the mid- to late 1980s. It was used to refer to the wanton destruction of female foetuses that was made possible by new procedures and technologies, such as amniocentesis and ultrasonography. With the arrival of ultrasound machines in this decade, non-invasive procedures of sex determination (*jaanch karvana*) became easy. If the foetus was detected to be female, it would be aborted (*girva dena*; literally, to let drop the child). This practice intensified both latent and overt son preference, especially in the north-west parts of the country, leading to a steep decline in the child sex ratio (the number of girls relative to a thousand boys). This was because female foeticide was seen to be more acceptable as it was facilitated by the use of technology and was therefore a modern way of shaping the sex composition of the family. It did not carry the shame or guilt associated with female infanticide; rather, it was seen as a scientific and rational way of planning the family.

Amartya Sen made the cause of 'missing women' popular through his 1990 *New York Review of Books* article, but it was somewhat later that the focus shifted to 'missing daughters', the phenomenon popularly captured by the Indian use of the term 'female foeticide'. Writers in the media have evoked images of the holocaust by terming the sex-selective abortion of female foetuses as a 'gendercide'. The *Economist* used the term in its cover story on 4 March 2010, calling the large-scale abortion of female foetuses in India and China 'the war on baby girls'. With a yet to live down reputation of satī, dowry and female infanticide, this became the new scourge India became known for. Images of female foetuses being dumped in dustbins and discarded carelessly began to shock the world.

Feminists, however, were upset with the use of phrases such as female foeticide and gendercide as these terms collapsed the distinction between legal and illegal abortion, arguing that the use of the word foeticide brought to mind images of murder, making people fall into the trap of thinking of abortion as child murder. They therefore, popularized the use of the longer phrase 'sex-selective abortion' or 'female sex-selective abortion' to clarify their stand that while they supported women's right to abort, they did not support selective abortion of female foetuses. The courts faced a thorny issue – if a woman could exercise the right to abort a foetus, why could she not, by the same logic, choose to abort a female foetus? Contextualizing the large-scale abortion of female foetuses that has led to a sharp skew in the child sex ratio, the courts pronounced that selective abortion of female children could not be allowed. Campaigns by women's rights activists eventually led to the passing of a law in 1996 prohibiting sex determination.

While the feminist stand on the use of the term 'female foeticide' and its implications led them to coin a different vocabulary, the term continues to resonate with ordinary people and with activists. This is partly because it helps people distinguish it from 'female infanticide' and connect it to the use of modern sex-determination technologies that make possible the prevention of the birth of a female. Past histories of discrimination against girls and women provide resonance to the term female foeticide, and it is unlikely that the common use of the term will be abandoned in the near future in favour of more politically correct language.

References

Croll, Elisabeth. *Endangered Daughters: Discrimination and Development in Asia*. London and New York: Routledge, 2001.

John, Mary E. 'Sex Ratios and Sex Selection in India'. In *Routledge Handbook of Gender in South Asia: History and the Present*, edited by Leela Fernandes. Abingdon: Routledge, 2014.

FOOD

Jasmine Anand

Chai pani

This term is believed to have originated in India with the practice of tea breaks that factory owners and mill owners arranged to keep their workers happy during the First World War. This habit of drinking tea and its symbolic welcoming nature soon entered Indian homes. Today, the term is used for an arrangement of a cup of tea, coffee or soft drink and snacks for guests at home or for social obligation over work. Chai pani, or *chai nashta/nashto*, also refers to high tea or the welcome drinks that are served when a groom visits the natal home of the bride for the first time or arrangements made for a retirement party. Chai (tea) was a borrowed welcoming custom that the Indians took from British. Back then, for a majority of Indians, drinking tea was far too expensive. So, offering chai was a special endeavour. However, all over India today chai has become commonplace. There are many variants, such as 'cutting chai', which is served around middle part of India made with more water and less milk and served in a half-full small glass; *gavati chai* made with lemon grass served in Maharashtra; *nathdwara/srinathji* chai of Rajasthan, tea made with a tinge of mint; *kulhad chai* of Kolkata, which is served in earthen pots/*kasauras*; masala chai, which is a tea brewed along with spices like fennel, cinnamon, cardamom and ginger; *kahwa* served in Kashmir, which is a kind of black tea brewed with spices like nutmeg, fennel, cinnamon, cardamom and saffron and sprinkled with crushed nuts; and *Sulemani chai*, which is a black tea served with a slice of lemon in the Irani style. The chilled *pani* could refer to the roadside *shikanji* or *nimbu pani*, which is a mixture of lemon, cold water, sugar and salt; the sweet rose water or *roohafza* or *jigarthanda*, made of *gond katira* (the gum known as tragacanth) mixed with *roohafza* which is made with rose and watermelon juice; *banta* soda, which is a local aerated drink; and *jaljeera*, which is made of tamarind pulp, rock salt, mint leaves, roasted cumin powder and sugar mixed in cold water. The snacks offered along with tea and drinks are known as *nashta* or *farsan*. Biscuits, rusk, cake, *brun maska*, *khaari*, *murukku*, *pakoda*, *bhajji*, *samosa*, *tikki*, *patty*, *idli*, *vada pav* and *dal kachori* are a few snacks that are served as accompaniments to chai pani. India now has many *thelas* (tea huts/shops and cafes) that serve lavish chai pani. These chai pani *thelas* form the only spaces of *aḍḍā* (public sphere where discussions can be held). In offices, arrangement for chai pani is generally made through roadside *thelas* or *khobchas* (hole-in-the-wall establishments).

The phrase 'chai pani' can also allude to a small bribe to appease someone, specifically a bureaucrat. The usage is not negative but admissible everywhere; in fact, if the offering is not enough, the recipient may insist that the 'chai' was given but not the 'pani'. An instance of Hindi usage of the phrase in a sentence is as follows: *inke chai pani ka bandobast/intzaam kar do* or *kuch chai pani milega?*. At times, chai pani may also be used to mean alcohol. Hence, the phrase 'chai pani' is ambiguously used materially, monetarily and metaphorically.

Dhaba

The term is believed to have originated after Partition in 1947. Dhabas were initially started by Punjabi refugees and catered to those who were uprooted by Partition by serving basic tandoori and Punjabi food. Generally speaking, the dhaba is an open-air informal resting and eating place on the highways, especially near petrol pumps. The word 'dhaba' probably also stems from the rustic Punjabi tradition of women preparing their dough at home and taking it to communal, open-air village *tandoors* to bake into *rotis* (breads). The *tandoor* is a traditional clay oven heated with hot charcoals placed inside it. Dhabas chiefly have an open kitchen with not much of a choice of Punjabi meals. *Parathas* with dollops of fresh white butter, curd, *lassi* and jaggery are staple in any dhaba. Cots with a wooden plank to serve as a table along with mud-plastered kitchen with *chulhas* (stoves), a *tandoor* and brass/steel utensils are characteristic features of a dhaba. Gradually, dhabas began to be mostly visited by men in transit or truck drivers. It gave them a feel of simple home-made food while on the road for days. Dhabas also became the centre of alcohol, gambling and sex work with the overwhelming footfall of primarily men. However, these days dhabas are visited by one and all. The place is typically inexpensive in comparison to restaurants. Currently, some dhabas are covered and fully air-conditioned and are also present within cities. Such posh dhabas serve an elaborate spread of Punjabi food such as *daal makhni, kadhi pakoda, sarson ka saag, paneer bhurji, sabji, chole, rajma, kukad, meat, chawal, roti, parantha, makhan, dahi, lassi, gur, saunf and chaa*. However, what remains the same with all dhabas is the major aromatic effect of charcoal that infuses every dish with a smoky flavour. Also, in dhabas, food is usually slowly cooked with whole spices that not only adds to the taste but also to the shelf life. The dhabas that serve only vegetarian food are known as 'vaishno dhabas'. Today, dhabas have also begun to serve an eclectic mix of food not only from within the different parts of India but also from all over the world. Sometimes, entire meals, except the tandoori roti, are prepared on cooking gas rather than on charcoal. At a few places, a complimentary glass of *chaas* or *lassi* is given to every customer. Another important feature of the dhaba is that it provides a snippet view of Punjabi culture and life with the help of decoration and layout within the premises – such as statues, replicas, miniature setting of Punjabi village life and sometimes even small shops selling Punjabi clothing and accessories for women.

Dhabas nowadays are all about good food, fun and are quirky, lively places. For instance, Rangla Punjab, a dhaba on Jalandhar Highway, has created a huge impact on youngsters and families due to innovations in space. Another example is Garam Dharam, a dhaba which projects an upscale exoticized Punjabi appearance along with cut outs, graffiti, dialogue and posters from the film actor Dharmendra's Bollywood films especially *Sholay*.

Khichdi/khichda/dal chawal

The word *khichdi* originates from Sanskrit word *khichha* which means 'a combination of rice and lentils'. Rice and *dal* (lentils) is a staple all over India. Generally, this one-pot meal khichdi is made using *mung* (green gram) or *moongi–masari* (red-and-yellow split dal). The pulses are cooked along with rice in equal proportions with water. Khichdi can be accompanied by pickle, curd, *papad* and *kadhi*. Nowadays, however, khichdi is cooked with all kinds of lentils, legumes, vegetables and caramelized onions and garlic. It is believed that the English *kedgeree* was influenced by the Indian khichdi. Ibn Batuta, the famous Moroccan traveller, refers to the dish in his travelogue as *kishri*. Abu Fazl's *Ain-i-Akbari* mentions several versions of khichdi preparations including those that used saffron, spices and dry fruits. Another travelogue by the Russian traveller Athanasius Niktin refers to Jahangir's fondness for spicy khichdi that he had named *lazeezan* meaning 'the delicious'. Aurangzeb is said to have liked *alamgiri khichdi*, which was cooked with a dash of fish and boiled eggs. Khichdi is both a low-key and high-end affair, depending on the addition of ingredients like ghee, spices, vegetables and nuts, or its usage for festivity or otherwise. Khichdi is both eaten for fasting as well as feasting. The festival of *Makar Sankranti* is marked by cooking khichdi. The khichdi is especially prepared to welcome a new bride and groom at their married home after marriage in northern India. This easy, comfort food is also a baby's first solid food in many parts of India. Without the addition of ghee, khichdi is consumed by people who are sick. Ritualistically, in some homes, khichdi is consumed as a simple mourning food as well. A variant of this dish from the state of Karnataka is known as *baath* or *bhath*, the additions to the base dish being tamarind, jaggary and curry leaves. Another variant from Tamil Nadu is called as *kanji*. A Himachali variant involves cooking rice and dal in curd. The Hyderabadi *khichda* is cooked with an inclusion of minced meat. In north India meals begin with the khichdi, whereas in western India meals end with the khichdi. The term has also come to mean any work which takes a lot of time or is progressing at the pace of a snail with the commonly used phrase '*Birbal ki khichdi*'. According to legend, this kind of khichdi took a long time to cook as the cooking pot was kept 5 feet above the fire.

In literary tradition, the term khichdi has also come to refer to 'polyphonic dialogues' or 'a heterogeneous mix of people sharing community life' in India. To express someone's unending love for a friend or loved one, ghee and khichdi are exemplified together as a reference point and the phrase used is *ghee khichdi hona*. Contrarily, the usage *apni khichdi alag pakana* refers to dissent and turning away from another. Recently, the Indian media unofficially designated the khichdi as the national dish and it is being globally promoted by the Government of India as the 'queen of all foods'. The Union Minister of Food Processing Industries Harsimrat Kaur Badal is quoted by various news agencies as having said, 'Khichdi is considered nutritious, healthiest food in India, and it is eaten by poor and rich alike, irrespective of their class. It symbolizes India's great culture of unity in diversity.'

Tiffin/dabba

The word 'tiffin', which could also refer to the lunchbox or *dabba*, is believed to have come to India through the British. The English borrowing comes from the slang word *tiff*, which means 'to eat and sip'. The word 'tiffin' is used to refer to a light midday meal after a light breakfast and before a heavy dinner. This meal is generally eaten between one and three in the afternoon. The city of Chennai has 'tiffin rooms' for people in transit. Maharashtra has *dabbawallas* who deliver home-cooked food as lunch to offices in dabbas or tiffins. Tiffins and lunchboxes are usually prepared in the morning for school-going children and used to be round or square containers made of brass, aluminium or stainless steel. With the coming of microwave ovens, tiffin boxes are today made of plastic, acrylic and glass. The equipment generally consists of vertical set of containers or a single container is divided into many parts. Usually, there are three separate containers: one for rice, one for meat or a vegetable dish and the other for chutneys or the bread. The three containers are then clasped together and loaded into an outer case that keeps the food warm and prevents spillage. While tiffin seems to refer to the equipment or a simple home-made food, in actual it has come to refer to a lot more in the form of the aesthetics of taste, nostalgia, love, caring and sharing. An internationally acclaimed film named 'Lunchbox' was recently made on the incident of an Indian wife preparing tiffin/dabba for her husband daily and the work of dabbawallas of Mumbai.

References

Achaya, K. T. *The Story of Our Food*. Hyderabad: Universities Press, 2002.
Sen, Colleen Taylor, *Feasts and Fasts: A History of Food in India*. London: Reaktion Books, 2015.
Sen, Colleen Taylor, *Food Culture in India*. Westport: Greenwood, 2004.

GODMEN

Akshaya Mukul

The concept of godmen is as old as the gods themselves. Among Hindus, holy men are variously referred to as *sant*s, *mahatma*s, *yogi*s, *rishi*s, *swami*s, *sanysasi*s or *guru*s and by several other names based on the differences in their approach, rituals and practices. The Vedas and the Upanishads talk of rishis and sages. There are hundreds of *sampradayas* (sects) manned by its own gurus.

Who is considered a sant or a yogi or a guru? Monier-Williams defines them thus: 'One who lays down or deposits; one who abandons or resigns; an ascetic, devotee; especially one who retires from worldly concerns, and is no longer bound to read *mantras* and perform sacrifice, but only to read the Aranyaskas or Upanishads.' There are other interpretations as well. According to Oriya Baba, sants have been categorized into *acharyakoti* (teacher-like) and *avadhutakoti* (one who has discarded the world). Avadhuakoti sants are not generally genial in behaviour, and their manners and teachings are not suited to everyone. Only a genius can fathom their talent. But even without the outward appearance, they are still considered sants. Acharyakoti sants are the ones who are the conventional gurus, endowed as they are with the qualities of peace, geniality, equanimity and complete lack of arrogance.

One of the very well-known orders of sants is the one established by Shankara to take on Buddhism in eighth century CE. Following this, highly orthodox orders were established at Puri in Odisha, Badrinath in Uttaranchal, Dwarka in Gujarat and Sringeri in Karnataka. The heads of each of these orders are referred to as Shankaracharya and exert immense influence in contemporary society. The vast network of educational and health institutions they run adds to their influence.

Then there are various other sects like Brahma sampradaya (founded by Madhava), Nimavats (founded by Nimbarka), Rudra (founded by Vallabha), Sri sampradaya (founded by Ramananda), sects of various denominations run by Nagas and the Swaminarayan sect of Gujarat. The followers of Chaitanya Mahaprabhu have carved out a distinctive place for themselves within the Madhava sect.

Among yogis, the best-known sect is the *nathapanthi* followers of Gorakhnath. The current chief minister of the state of Uttar Pradesh, Yogi Adityanath, is the leader of this sect.

In post-Independence India, there has been a concerted attempt to control and use the influence of sadhus and sects over their followers for political ends. Be it the formation of Akhil Bharatiya Sadhu Samaj or nominating sadhus as contestants in polls, politics has entered the world of the godmen in a big way. The reputations of sadhus or gurus have also seen a decline in society. Since politics and power play were no longer anathema to them, there is no premium on renunciation, which was earlier a key ingredient to become a sadhu or a guru.

Today, a big cast of godmen has emerged in Indian politics, starting with Swami Karpatri Maharaj, the founder of the Ram Rajya Parishad; Mahant Digvijaynath of Nathpanth, who also became the head of the right-wing organization Vishwa Hindu Parishad (VHP); and Swami Rameshwarananda, who became a member of parliament and was a key actor in the 1965 attack on the parliament in the name of cow protection. Every five years, the BJP gives tickets to certain *sadhus* (or sant) or *sadhvis* (female sants) who enter parliament and have even become ministers. Former chief minister of Madhya Pradesh, Sadhvi Uma Bharati, is just one of them.

As noted in *Controversial New Religions*, the 1950s saw the beginning of New Religious Movements (NRMs) across the world. Controversy is second name to some of these NRMs that emanated from India. And, founders of these movements often had another career before turning spiritual and giving it a twist. The International Society for Krishna Consciousness (ISKCON) was one such movement that was established by Swami Prabhupada, owner of a pharmaceutical business, in the United States in 1966. Taking advantage of the lifting of the Oriental Exclusion Act in 1965 that resulted in a big wave of migrants to the United States, Prabhupada set up his first temple in Manhattan's lower East Side. Young Americans, primarily 'hippies who had dropped out or disaffected hippies who had burned out', were among Prabhupada's early recruits. ISKCON soon spread all over the world. They even established a temple in Vrindavan, considered the birthplace of the god Krishna.

Mahesh Prasad Verma was also an engineer who left his material life after an encounter with his guru Brahmananda, one of the Shankaracharyas. His first ashram was in Rishikesh and in 1959, he set up his first US-based ashram in Los Angeles. But it was not until the visit of the Beatles to learn his Transcendental Meditation (TM) that he came to international limelight as Mahesh Yogi. This was because TM promised 'bliss and prosperity not only to the mediators but also to the entire world'. But there was a precipitous decline in Mahesh Yogi's stature as a new-age godman when he faced multiple challenges in the 1980s. First, there were a series of lawsuits in the United States, and in India his 'right-hand man' Ravi Shankar broke away from him and named his movement 'Art of Living'. Ironically, the name of his movement was based on Mahesh Yogi's book *The Science of Being and the Art of Living*. Ravi Shankar's Art of Living has now spread all over the world and his vast network presents him as a spiritual man who has solutions for everything, from the crisis in Pakistan and Kashmir to the Ram Temple in Ayōdhyā.

The most irreverent of the NRMs was the one started by Bhagwan Rajneesh. His open advocacy of permissive sexual behaviour mixed with tenets of modern psychology had the world worshipping at his feet. From his ashram in Pune to the massive operation he started in Oregon, United States, in 1981, Rajneesh's cult, popularly known as the Osho movement, faced massive legal problems in the United States. His lavish lifestyle – ninety-three Rolls-Royces and gun-toting bodyguards – created an outrage in Oregon and eventually he had to return to Pune. His death in 1990, followed by a period of intense succession battle, was a setback to the movement. But now Osho has been posthumously revived through his books, videos, tapes and films. *Controversial New Religions* notes that Lady Gaga endorsed Osho in 2011, and in India the Pune ashram attracts people from all over the world.

No account of Hindu gurus can be complete without the story of Sai Baba of Shirdi and Sathya Sai Baba of Puttaparthi. The later claimed to be the incarnation of the former. Sai Baba of Shirdi was unlike all the godmen we have discussed thus far. He had disciples from across religions, lived a frugal life and performed both Hindu and Muslim religious prayers. He is believed to have had supernatural powers, and his fame grew steadily. Shirdi, where he stayed, is today a holy town. Sathya Sai Baba, a Telugu by birth, claimed at the age of 13 to be an incarnation of Sai Baba of Shirdi. This made him famous, but what drew people to him was his supposed magic powers that could heal. Politicians, bureaucrats and commoners became his disciples. In fact, a large Sai Baba network exists in government, especially among bureaucrats. A vast network of hospitals, schools and colleges are still run by his close aides after his death.

The past few years have, however, been particularly bad for godmen in India. Two of them, both prominent – Asaram Bapu and Guru Ram Rahim – have been put behind bars on charges of rape of their female disciples. The smartest of the modern gurus, however, has been Baba Ramdev, who is considered close to the ruling dispensation. Through his yōga and naturopathy, Ramdev now runs one of country's biggest FMCG companies. Spiritual life to corporate ascendance is only the latest in the long history of innovations Indian godmen have made at home and abroad.

References

Baba, Oriya. *Sant Ka Swarup* (Types of Sants) Gorakhpur: Gita Press, 1937.
Lewis, James R. and Jesper Aagaard Petersen, ed. *Controversial New Religions*. New York: Oxford University Press, 2014.
Mukul, Akshaya, *Gita Press and the Making of Hindu India*. New Delhi: Harper Collins, 2015

GODREJ ALMIRAH (GODREJ ĀLMIRAH)

Dipti Kulkarni

The Godrej almirah is quite an important element of the India story. Born in 1923, this steel cupboard, manufactured entirely in India by Godrej, was to become a part of people's lives.

In those days of scarcity and limited resources, owning anything from a phone to a cupboard or a television was a matter of immense pride. For middle-class India, the Godrej Storwel (the brand name) had an aspirational value. People who could not afford it, rented it. The almirah was a sturdy steel cupboard which because of its weight was almost a fixture in the house. This cupboard was where the family kept all its prized possessions – from certificates to special clothes and sarees to gold and cash. The almirah was also an important part of the wedding trousseau. If the newly-weds lived in a joint family, who had the keys to the almirah's locker was an important aspect of family dynamics. In those times when people lived in *wadas* or *chawls*, neighbours were like extended family and the family who owned a Godrej almirah often had to oblige neighbours by safeguarding their important goods. That the almirah was an important cultural artefact can be seen from its presence in literary texts, such as Satyajit Ray's *Adventures of Feluda* in which a character named Dhiru Kaka offers to keep the doctor's ring in his Godrej almirah and this offer completely relieves the doctor of his anxiety!

All of this has undergone a change in the decades gone by. The company altered the original and came up with newer offerings that were lighter in view of a more mobile customer. Today, there is more choice in terms of colour and size. From the point of view of the customer, the story of the Godrej almirah has gone from 'pride' to 'hide'. Now that large wooden wardrobes are in style, people struggle to make space for this beast from the past. Some 'hide' their almirah by covering it with wallpaper or paint. Some make a wooden exterior and keep the steel almirah inside it. The altered sentiments towards the almirah are a reflection of the preoccupations of young Indians, who have very little to do with the India of the previous century. Global trends influence what they aspire in their lives as in the objects they wish to possess.

References

Alladi, Harini, 'Cultural Branding in India: The Case of Godrej "Storwel" Cupboards (1944-1991)'. *Journal of Historical Research in Marketing* 10, no. 3 (2018): 224–41.

Ray, Satyajit. *Complete Adventures of Feluda*, vol. 1. Penguin Books India, 2004.

HARAM/HALAL (HARĀM/HALĀL)

Amir Ali

The paired Islamic concepts of *haram* and *halal* are binary opposites. The dividing line appears to be extremely clearly demarcated, establishing what is permissible (halal) and what is absolutely forbidden (haram). It is important to stress that haram has a certain pre-eminence over halal as it forms one of the five values classifying the goodness or badness of human conduct, the *ahkam-al-khamsah*. The five ahkam-al-khamsah are acts that can be (a) obligatory, whose performance is rewarded and omission is punished (*wajib*); (b) recommended, where performance is rewarded but non-performance does not bring punishment (*mustahab*);

(c) permitted, where there is an indifference to the performance or non-performance (*mabuh*); (d) acts met with disapproval but which are acceptable with reluctance (*makruh*); and (e) acts that are completely prohibited (haram).

For most people in India, the most familiar form of halal is meat from an animal slaughtered in the ritually prescribed Islamic manner. However, the category haram/halal is also applied to decide the legitimacy of money and wealth that is earned or inherited. Income from sources where there is commensurate effort on the part of the individual would be halal, whereas income from interest payments or usury, for instance, would be haram. Further, money from gambling or other such games of chance are haram. Any attempt to usurp the wealth of the vulnerable, such as orphans, is absolutely haram. Sexual morality would be another realm in which there are fairly elaborate and clear guidelines about what is permissible and hence halal. Homosexuality, for instance, is considered haram.

The haram/halal distinction applies most prolifically in the ethical realm. One however notices an uncoupling of the haram/halal binary in one realm – the theological. In the realm of Islam's almost uncompromising monotheism, it is absolutely forbidden and hence haram for a believing Muslim to associate any god or deity with Allah. This would constitute *shirk* and can be considered as the most severe application of the category haram for the Muslim. One notices here an application of the concept of haram without the companion concept of *halal* playing any role whatsoever. This reinforces the point about the pre-eminence of haram mentioned earlier.

Quite often, it has been surmised that the implications of the categories of haram/halal are a clear demarcation of boundaries on the part of *ulema* (religious scholars) through the instrumentality of issuing *fatwas* (opinions). The influence of the ulema is then understood as a form of social control over the community. Thus, it is not unknown for practices that may have a syncretistic element in them to be declared haram and thereby forbidden, perhaps on the basis of not being Islamic enough. There have been instances when fatwas have disapproved the wearing of a sārī or short skirt on the basis of their being non-Muslim attire. The application of vermilion by Muslim women has been frowned upon. In this context, it may be kept in mind that the fatwa is a legal opinion and not a religious diktat, as is quite often projected through popular media representations. Once a person has received the fatwa, she or he is free to seek another religious opinion, much in the manner that an individual seeks a second opinion from a doctor. Also, it is common for fatwas to end with an admission of their own limitation by suggesting that it is only Allah who knows best. However, the more flexible and, dare it be said, creative role of the fatwa has undergone a change with the transformations wrought in Islamic jurisprudence by modern legal systems. As a result of such transformations, the haram/halal category perhaps lends itself to becoming more flexible as a form of social control.

References

Faruki, Kemal. 'Al-Ahkam Al-Khamsah: The Five Values'. *Islamic Studies* 5, no. 1 (March 1966): 43–98.
Kugle, Scott Alan. 'Framed, Blamed and Renamed: The Recasting of Islamic Jurisprudence in Colonial South Asia'. *Modern Asian Studies* 35, no. 2 (2001): 257–313.

IZZAT/SHARAM/HONOUR KILLING (IZZAT/ŚARAM)

Shivangini Tandon

The word *izzat* refers to 'honour, reputation or prestige'. It is an Urdu word derived from the Persian *ezzat* and the Arabic *izza*. In his work on the concepts of honour and grace in anthropology, Pitt-Rivers points out that honour is 'the value of a person in his own eyes, but also in the eyes of the society'. The word *śaram* originates from the Urdu language and is translated as 'shame' in English. Michela Canepari argues that its English translation is restrictive in comparison to the original term. For instance, shame only denotes embarrassment, humiliation, disgrace, dishonour and being infamous. Śaram, on the other hand, means much more than that. It could mean modesty, decency, a moral act, being courteous and respectable. It is often used interchangeably with words like *lajja* and *laaj*, its synonyms in languages like Hindi and Bengali. Frank Henderson Steward, who has written extensively on the concept of honour, has emphasized that honour involves two aspects: inner and outer honour. He uses internal honour as a term for 'a personal quality' (honourableness) and external honour as a term for 'reputation'. Following Steward's theory, honour can be described as a concept which regulates the relationship between an individual and a group which they belong to or identify with. Honour groups could be large and extensive (e.g. nations, clan and family) or small and limited, but in either case they are defined and regulated by distinctive honour codes. It is actually this latter aspect of honour translating into reputation that has increasingly led to the crimes of killing in the name of safeguarding the izzat or śaram of the family or community or incidents of honour killing, in many parts of the world.

The term 'honour killing' refers to the structured practice of killing a woman (and, in some cases, her male partner as well) if her family believes that her behaviour has threatened the izzat of the family. In such a scenario, killing her is seen as the only solution to protect the honour and śaram of the family. The practice of honour killing has been known since ancient Roman times, when the seniormost member of the household had the right to kill an unmarried but sexually active daughter or an adulterous wife. Honour-based crimes were also known in medieval Europe, where early Jewish law mandated death by stoning for an adulterous wife and her partner. Today, this practice is common in regions of North Africa and Middle East. However, the aim here is to talk about the practice of honour killing as it exists in many parts of India, particularly in the states of Haryana and Punjab. In a largely male-dominated or patriarchal society, a family's reputation is perceived to rest on a woman's obedience and chastity. In case the woman marries without her father's permission, marries outside her caste, seeks divorce or has an adulterous affair, she is considered to have violated the family honour and this becomes a justification for the endorsement of honour killing. The punishment given as a part of this practice can take multiple forms – shooting, beheading, dismemberment, flogging, burning by acid or fire, strangling, drowning and forced suicide. Prem Chowdhury, who works on popular perceptions of masculinity in rural North India through oral traditions, throws light on one such popular belief or cultural pattern that objectifies women and treat them as mere objects devoid of any subjectivity and agency. He writes, *Zamin joi zor ki / Zor ghati hor ki* ('Land and wife can only be held by force / When force fails, they pass into other hands').

Honour killing targets a woman's autonomy and seeks to control her sexuality and choices. In India, women in interfaith and inter-caste relationships are subjected to immense torture and coercion at the hands of their families, communities and also fascist political parties. Since a woman is considered to be a man's property, honour killings find an easy justification in society. In order to combat this practice in India, strict and specific laws against 'honour crimes' and a general change in mindset are sorely required.

References

Chowdhry, Prem. 'Popular Perceptions of Masculinity in Rural North Indian Oral Traditions'. *Asian Ethnology* 74, no. 1 (2015): 5–36.
Lesnie, Vanessa. 'Dying for the Family Honor'. *Human Rights* 27, no. 3 (2000): 12–14.

JAGANNATH/JUGGERNAUT (JAGANNĀTH/JUGGERNAUT)

Jatindra Kumar Nayak

It is rather strange that a deity supposed by many to be of tribal origin and with half-formed limbs should even be remotely associated with a word that means an unstoppable destructive force for over seven centuries in the Western imagination. The history of this imagination invokes among others, *The Travels of Sir John Mandeville* (1357–71), 'The Curse of Kehama' (1810) by Robert Southey, Balzac's *Le Pere Goriot* (1835) and the bête noire in the popular American comics series *X-Men*, created by Stan Lee.

Situated in the coastal town of Puri, Jaganath (literally, 'Lord of the Universe') became the centre of the Vaishnavism, in what is today the state of Odisha, with the arrival of Ramanuja, a Bhakti saint from the south, in the twelfth century CE and the Bengali Bhakti saint Chaitanya in the sixteenth century. Jaganath embodies and stands at the centre of an assimilatory and fascinatingly syncretic culture that has its roots among the Sabara tribe of Odisha and was included in the Hindu pantheon much later. An exception on numerous accounts, Jaganath resides with his elder brother Balabhadra and sister Subhadra (as opposed to living with his consort Lakshmi) in Jaganath temple which was built by King Ananatavarman Chodaganga Deva of the Ganga dynasty in the twelfth century. While some scholars contend that the temple was initially a Jain temple, there are others who are convinced of the presence of Buddhist relics in the temple. In fact, Buddha is considered an incarnation of Jaganath. The iconography of Jagannāth is in itself a unique field of enquiry, for, unlike other Hindu deities, Jaganath and his siblings are neither anthropomorphic nor zoomorphic. He is identified by his large round eyes, his black face and the absence of fully formed limbs, which have contributed to a great many popular lore. The wooden body, again a notable exception from other deities who are carved out of stone, also points to the tribal origins of the deity.

But what remains perhaps the most popular aspect of the Jaganath cult is the annual chariot festival, the *rath yatra*. The English term 'juggernaut' is not so much derived from any of the features of the god himself but from the gigantic chariot whose wheels are supposed to have crushed many who offer their lives in order to attain salvation. While the deaths might have occurred mostly due to accidents, colonial imagination and inadequate documentation might have steamrolled various facets of the overwhelmingly grand occasion into one horrifying image. For the people of Odisha, however, no other religious occasion matches the grandeur of the chariot festival.

References

Dube, Ishita B., *Divine Affairs: Religion, Pilgrimage, and the State in Colonial and Postcolonial India*. Shimla: Indian Institute of Advanced Studies, 2001.
Eschmann, Anncharlott, Herman Kulke and Gaya Charan Tripathi, *The Cult of Jagannath and the Regional Tradition of Orissa*. New Delhi: Manohar, 1978.

JAGRAN/KIRTAN/BHAJAN (JĀGARAṆ/KĪRTAN/BHAJAN)

Jaskiran K. Mathur

Though very closely related, these three terms are not identical. *Jagraṇ, jagraata, jaag* or *ratjagga* quite literally mean 'vigil or an all-nighter'. It usually refers to an event where the rendering of devotional songs (the *bhajan* or *kīrtan*), that narrate the glory of god or specific deities, is carried out as a community exercise. Jagraṇ could as easily refer to any other celebratory group activity requiring the participants to stay awake all night – be it a political event, a sport or a night of bacchanalian revels.

In the most popular usage of the term, jagraṇ more often than not includes bhajans and kirtans sung in praise of a revered deity on an auspicious day (*parv*) or festival (*tyohaar*) designated by the Hindu lunar calendar. A jagraṇ may also be organized to mark a familial celebratory thanksgiving. The collective nature of the activity is fundamental to this phenomenon, wherein the group subsumes the individual, bestowing instead a shared impetus, fervour and gratification. In this community-bolstering exercise, someone often takes the leadership role owing to either their sacramental status, their musical ability or their organizational aptitude. Such a gathering provides room for both anonymity and spontaneity. While the sense of community and belonging assures inclusiveness, the comforting potential of ritual observance serves to fuel and reaffirm faith. A similar purpose and objective could well be attributed to any jagraṇ that may be categorized as secular.

The words bhajan and kīrtan are often used interchangeably, share subject matter, form of expression and context as both belong to the genre of devotional performance art. While bhajan is less formal, kīrtan is more structured. But both involve the presence and participation of a congregation as well as spiritual or religious renditions. Bhajan quite literally means 'to share'. As the aim is to bring home the message, popular film song tunes too have been used in bhajans to draw and hold the attention of the gathering. Kīrtan may be translated as a musical form of narration or shared recitation. *Shabd kīrtan* (recitation of the word of the guru; *gurbani*) has evolved as the very form of communal worship in Sikhism, for instance. Kīrtan has its roots in the Vedic tradition and is practised with regional and denominational variations across the subcontinent. Often, ragas are prescribed and various musical instruments employed – oration, drama, dance, moral narration, allegory, humour, poetic prowess are all very much a part of this practice as is audience participation (*sankirtan*).

The bhajan is intrinsically associated with the *bhakti* movement, which was a medieval devotional phenomenon and had significant syncretic potential and grass-roots representation. Inspired by a multitude of saint-poets, the emergence of bhakti can be traced to eighth-century Tamil Nadu and Kerala. By the fifteenth century, it had embraced the eastern and northern regions of the subcontinent as well. While it may be debatable if the movement was truly a rebellion against orthodoxy, there is no doubt that the status quo was being questioned and an inevitable recontextualizing emerged within the parameters of the Hindu tradition. It is thus no surprise that this successful motivational format played a significant role in community organization in nineteenth- and twentieth-century colonial society when protesters and freedom activists used early morning processions (*prabhat pheri*) to voice inspiring political messages combined with bhajans. In fact, this influence is also visible in the expressions of protest adopted by Indian indentured workers in lands as far away as Guyana, Trinidad and Fiji.

References

Hawley, John Stratton. *A Storm of Songs: India and the Idea of the Bhakti Movement*. Cambridge: Harvard University Press, 2015.

Kaivalya, Alanna. *Sacred Sound: Discovering the Myth and Meaning of Mantra and Kirtan*. Verlag: New World, 2014.

JHAROO/TEEL JHAROO/EERKALI CHOOL (JHĀḌŪ//TEEL JHĀḌŪ/EERKALI CHOOL)

Susan Visvanathan

Most children in India grow up with the sound of the *eerkali chool* (Malayalam) or *teel jharoo* (Hindi), which their mothers use to sweep the yard or clean watery spaces, where dried-grass brooms will not work. Separate brooms are used for each workspace. As the teel jharoo is made from the spine of the coconut leaf, if left in water, or not maintained, they tend to decompose, and there is nothing more horrible than holding a wet teel jharoo to clean. It is made of a hundred or so thin strands, each of which once supported each laminae or segmental leaf, and the work of separating it from the leaf to make the jhadoo takes time.

Since coconut trees are an important source of revenue across households in Kerala, it would be instructive to look at how this process is done in that state. All over Kerala, workers employed in a house will set to de-spining the coconut leaves, which involves tearing the rib-like reed from its surrounding leaf. The quantum of such fibres used for personal use is thrice what is available in the market, as the utilitarian aspect of these brooms is valued in every home. Since the work is tedious, the actual space of involvement is that of the domestic servant sitting down after lunch and working to produce a broom as a leisure-time activity. Children surround her, and she works systematically through the afternoon, till it is time to make those coconut delicacies which the children love, such as *korikatta* (steamed rice balls, with a filling of jaggery and coconut inside).

The making of coconut brooms is often associated with Ezhava families, who are well versed in the collection of toddy (palm wine) as well as the enumeration of the coconut harvested from trees. Leisure thus is associated with gainful work, and the presentation of perfection is something which is defined as 'acceptable' by the master/mistress of the household or the merchant. Teel jharoos and eerkali chools are assessed by their weight and the strength of their fibres.

The eerkali chool or teel jharoo, in some way, with its simplicity and austerity, and its sense of compounded unity as a bundle of sticks, integrated together, used to clean effectively the dirty spaces of the house is a welcome symbol in contemporary politics (the Aam Aadmi Party has in fact adopted the jhadoo as its symbol). Not surprisingly, children were disciplined by using a single 'stick' of the eerkali chool. The sting of the fibre was not hard enough for the parent to feel that she or he was being cruel, and like the disciplinary pinch (*picchu*) was a customary way of reprimanding children.

Every morning in Kerala, the sound of the chool can be heard. A swept yard or staircase, the clean bathroom and the clean kitchen are essential to a sense of mental equilibrium. The symbolic association with blue skies, fresh air, the smell of coffee, the wisp of smoke from the wood fire on which rice is already boiling, the call of the fisher as she/he makes the rounds and the brushing sound of the eerkali chool, all these are the associated imagery which arise in the mind of a Malayali far from *naad* (country), as she or he sets about doing the daily chores, before rushing to catch the bus or train to work in an office.

References

Tripathy, Jyotirmaya. 'The Broom, the Muffler and the Wagon R: Aam Aadmi Party and the Politics of De-Elitisation'. *International Quarterly for Asian Studies* 48 (2017).
Wyatt, Andrew. 'Arvind Kejriwal's Leadership of the Aam Aadmi Party'. *Contemporary South Asia* 23, no. 2 (2015): 167–80.

JOOTHA (JŪṬHĀ)

Rama Kant Agnihotri

The Hindi adjective *jootha*, in the sense of 'defiled' or 'polluted' food, is used in rather specific contexts, such as in *vahkisiikaa jootha (khaanaa) nahiin khaataa* ('He does not eat the food leftover/touched by anybody else', i.e. 'already polluted/defiled by being eaten by somebody else'). It could have come from the Sanskrit *jushth* or the Pali word *jutth*. In this sense, it is integral to the Indian binary of the pure/polluted that comprehensively cuts across social, religious and cultural life even though a simple binary where the 'polluted' is forbidden and the 'pure' alone is recommended may not do justice to the complexities it encompasses.

The related feminine noun *juuthan* literally means 'leftover'. These leftovers were meant for animals, by definition outside the human sphere, but they were often served to the Dalits, people outside the hierarchical caste system and at the lowest level of society, the 'untouchables'. The horrifying implication here is clear. The abject poverty and social degradation that the Dalits have suffered in India is encapsulated in the autobiographical narrative *Joothan* by Omprakash Valmiki (1997).

There may be some feudal contexts of yore in which expressions such as *juuthan giraanaa* may have been used. For example, *aajaa phamaareyahaan juuthan giraaneaaiye* ('Please visit us for a meal'), suggesting that the leftovers will come handy for the cooks (who may have been women) and the lowly, the expression being honourific for the invited (maximizing the praise for the other) and displaying humility on the part of the person inviting and his family (minimizing self-praise). This usage is certainly dated. On the contrary, some members of a family or friends may take pride in saying *ham sab ekhiiplet men khaatehain* ('We enjoy eating together in the same plate'; i.e. 'We don't mind eating each other's jootha').

Though the pure/polluted binary is possibly universal, it seems to take very specific forms across different cultures (as Mary Douglas has noted on the Jewish notion of *kosher* food, for example). In India, the concept jootha derives from and is inextricably linked to the overarching and hierarchical caste system. However, its linguistic expression varies across the country. The Telugu equivalent of the word is *engali*, while Malayalam uses the word *echil*; thus, there is a strong possibility that this word entered languages like Bengali, where it is known as *entho*, via Dravidian than Indo-Āryan routes. This is a power word that is used in many Indian languages as an adjective as well as a noun. Its strength as cultural practice remains strong and continues to be uniquely – while not admirably – part of Indian social structure in the twenty-first century.

References

Valmiki, Omprakash. *Joothan*. New Delhi: Radhakrishan Prakashan, 1997. Translated into English by Arun Prabha Mukherjee as *Joothan: An Untouchable's Life*. New York: Columbia University Press, 2008.
Verma, Ramachandra. *Shabd-sadhna*. Benaras: Sahityaratnamala Karyalaya, 1990.

KABBADI, GILI DANDA, JALLIKATTA (KABAḌḌĪ, GILLĪ ḌAṆḌĀ, JALLĪKAṬṬŪ)

Souvik Naha

Kabbadi

The term 'kabbadi' probably comes from the Tamil root words *kāʾi* (hand) and *pidi* (catch). The sport is played between two teams of seven players each. The players take turns raiding the other team's refuge and the team with the maximum successful raids over two twenty-minute halves wins. The raider tries to touch as many opponents as possible, holding one's breath, before trying to return to one's zone safely, while the opponents try to pin her or him down to diffuse the challenge. The sport is highly popular in South Asia, especially in rural areas, as no equipment is involved. Its rules were formalized after the All India Kabbadi Foundation was established in 1950. The senior national championship started in 1952. A new organization, the Amateur Kabbadi Federation of India, set up in 1972 is now governing the sport in the country. The first Asian Kabbadi Championship was held in 1980. International visibility of Kabbadi increased with its inclusion in the First South Asian Games (SAF) in 1984 and in the Asian Games in 1990 and the beginning of the Kabbadi World Cup in 2004. India usually triumphs in every tournament it participates in, making kabbadi the most decorated sport in the country. Kabbadi has been featured in many films and numerous works of fiction as a plot point.

The inception of Pro Kabbadi League in 2014 has revolutionized the sport today. Apart from organizing the game indoors, in an attractively built environment, the organizers modified the standard rules to encourage more aggressive play. Every season has proven to be highly popular, with increase in television audience across India, revealing that with proper overhaul, an indigenous sport such as kabbadi can favourably compete with the likes of cricket and football for viewership.

Gilli danda

The name of this sport comes from the practice of participants hitting a short stick (*gillī*) with a long stick (*daṇḍa*), both made of wood. This game is referred to as Tipcat in English and is known by many other names across India and the world, most notably as Danguli in Bengal, Kuttiyumkolum in Kerala, Kittipul in Tamil Nadu, Billamgodu in Andra Pradesh, Dandibiyo in Nepal, Pathellele in Indonesia, Konko in Cambodia and Lappaduggi in Afghanistan. It is played between individuals or two teams with an equal number of players and no upper limit. The players first dig a small hole on the ground on which they place the gillī. A player inserts the daṇḍa underneath the gillī to first lift the latter up in the air, and then strike it, before it touches the ground as far as possible. She or he gets three attempts to hit the gillī, failing which she or he is declared out. Opponents can get her or him out by either catching the gillī while it is airborne after the strike or, if it had already fallen to the turf, by collecting it and directly hitting the daṇḍa, which should be placed above the hole after the hit. There is no universal scoring system, even though gillī daṇḍā is not entirely an amateur or recreational sport any more. The Indian Gilli Danda Federation, established in 2016, is currently working towards standardizing the rules of the game.

Jallīkaṭṭū

A collection of Tamil Sangam poetry called *Kalithogai*, written between 400 BCE and 300 CE, mentions a sport called 'eruthazhuval' ('embracing the bull'), in which a group of men try to tame a bull. This sport is believed to have evolved into what is today known as jallikatta. Usually conducted on the second and third days of the Pongal festival, this sport involves men holding on to a bull for a certain period of time while the animal tries to break free. Persons able to maintain their grip on the bull for the longest time are declared winners. In a way successful bull-taming has been a marker of one's masculinity, power and self-sufficiency. The bulls which prove most difficult to tame are identified as the strongest and used for breeding strong calves, while the weaker ones are used for agriculture and transport. Tamil culture usually envisages the sport as a symbol of human–animal connection, in which the animal becomes part of the family and is treated with care.

The change in the way this ancient sport is conducted has sparked protests from various animal rights organizations, particularly since the 2000s. They have been campaigning against the cruel manipulation of bulls used in the sport. If Eruthazhuvuthal was a one-to-one combat between the bull and the man, jallikatta is a spectacle in which many people try to grab a single raging bull, which is often made to drink alcohol or provoked with injuries to be more aggressive. Other than unethical treatment of the animal, the ritual of masculinity, casteism and gambling around the sport has also been called into question. The Supreme Court of India accepted this opposition and banned jallikatta in 2014, which led to massive protests against supposedly exaggerated accounts of violence and perceived affront to Tamil culture in the state of Tamil Nadu. The agitation forced the Government of India to reverse the ban in 2016.

References

Alter, Joseph S. 'Kabaddi, A National Sport of India: The Internationalism of Nationalism and the Foreignness of Indianness'. In *Games, Sports and Cultures*, edited by Noel Dyck, 81–116. Oxford: Berg, 2000.

Singh, Java. 'Jallikattu: Post-Humanistic Coefficients and Coloniality in South Asia's Ergic Sport'. *South Asian Review* 38, no. 1 (2017): 29–48.

KAI (KĀI)

Vanamala Viswanatha

With a four-page entry in F. Kittel's comprehensive *Kannada–English Dictionary*, kai is a Kannada word which refers to the human hand. Every Kannada child masters this word first when s/he learns at home about the parts of the body and also later in school when the teacher, ready with a cane, thunders, *kai chaachu*! ('Stretch your hand!'). This word is also commonly used in other South Indian languages such as Tamil and Malyalam.

The word *kai* is as versatile as the organ itself. In conjunction with a verb, it changes its meaning and, before you know, it can mean the opposite. *Kai kodu* literally means 'to give hand', but it can also mean 'to deceive, to let down'. But *kodu kai*, used as one word *kodugai*, refers to 'a generous person'. *Kai bidu* literally means 'to leave the hand', meaning 'to give up, to drop'. *Kai maadu* literally means 'to make hand', meaning 'to attack'. *Kai haaku* means 'to venture into', *kai hidi* means 'to marry', while *kai chellu* means 'to drop helplessly'. *Kai kaayuvudu* means 'to depend', and *kai nadeyuvudu* refers to a time 'when the going is good'. *Kai suttukolluvudu* literally means 'to burn one's hand', refers to suffering. *Kai beesu* refers to 'walking without a burden'. *Kai torisu* means 'to consult an astrologer'. While *kaigetegeduko* means 'to undertake'; *kaigebaru* means 'to reap', that is, as a grown-up son who is useful; *kaigoodu* means 'to accomplish'; and *kaivasha* means 'to conquer, to hold control'. *Kai mara* refers to the manual signal on a track. *Kai magga* refers to handloom and *kaikola* refers to the handcuffs. *kaigada* means 'a temporary loan'; *kaigatti* is a 'small knife'; *kaithuththu* is a 'morsel' and *kaichalaka* is 'exemplary skill'. While *kaifiyaththu* is 'signature', *kaibaraha* refers to handwriting, and *kaiyyaare* means 'with his/her own hands'. *Angai* and *mungai* refer to the palm and back of the palm, respectively. *Kaikoosu* refers to an 'infant', *Kaijodisu* literally means 'to surrender', and *kaitege* means 'to withdraw'. While *kaimeeri* can mean 'to get out of one's power', *kaisere* means to 'arrest, to be in captivity'. *Kaikelage* is used to refer to 'under an authority' and *kaikodali* is a small axe.

Ever since 'the hand' became a symbol of the Congress Party, *kai* has been used in a telling manner to indicate the candidate's status – *kaihididaru* is to 'join the party'; *kaibittaru* is 'to get ousted from the party' and *kaikottaru* is to 'defect from the party'.

Reference

Kittel, Ferdinand. *A Kannada-English Dictionary*, vol. 1. Basel mission book and tract depository, 1894.

KAYAKA (KAYAKA)

N. Manu Chakravarthy

The concept of *kayaka* is central for the Lingayat movement that flourished in Karnataka, about the twelfth century CE. This was one of the most crucial phases of the sociocultural and intellectual life of Karnataka and Kannada language. There are innumerable narratives on the period, coloured by diverse ideological positions. However, a concept that is integral to the ethos of that period and which continues to influence and shape Kannada consciousness, is 'kayaka'. More specifically, 'kayaka' refers to 'work', to 'physical labour', but the concept profound philosophical and political implications and is, therefore, quite central to contemporary cultural politics.

At the philosophical level, kayaka suggests the strong shift from the privileged positions of metaphysical speculation, intellectual reflection and epistemological practice to the great meaning and significance of 'labour', signifying the value and importance of all working classes in a social context. The privileging of knowledge, which marginalized the enormous contributions of the laboring communities, was severely interrogated by the Vachana poets of the Lingayat movement leading many thinkers to regard it as a period that foregrounded notions of equality and justice. Hence, the concept kayaka occupies a crucial position in contemporary discussions of democratic principles of an egalitarian society.

In addition, the concept has led to the contemporary expression *kayakave kailasa*, negating the idea of gaining redemption/salvation and thereby rejecting the very belief in the reality of a heaven that lies beyond this temporal world. The phrase 'kayakave kailasa', suggests that labour/work itself is *kailasa* (Lord Shiva's abode), clearly underlining the belief that dedicated work itself is true spiritual transcendence. Thus, ideas of rebirth and salvation beyond the spatial–temporal, and notions of spiritual transcendence, are erased in favour of the essential value of earthly labour. For these reasons, kayaka is part of the vocabulary of contemporary thinkers and activists who emphatically resist various philosophical and political hierarchies.

References

Īshwaran, Karigoudar. *Religion & Society among the Lingayats of South India*, vol. 19, Vikas Pub, 1983.
Waghmare, Nalini. 'Basaveshwara's Concept of Kayaka and Dasoha Relevance to Modern Times', Faculty Publication, Tilak Maharashtra Vidyapeeth, Pune, 2013.

KHADI (KHĀDĪ)

Tridip Suhrud

Khādī refers to any cloth made from two processes of spinning and weaving done by hand. Khādī was not an invention by Gandhi. Spinning and weaving are as old as human civilization. But, in the modern Indian imagination, khādī has come to be etched as an idea, a process and a possibility deeply and inviolably connected with Gandhi. It does signal to his capacity to understand and grasp universal human impulse and innovation and bring it into the realms of contemporary political economy and political action.

The production of khādī involves two processes, the preparation of yarn by spinning and the act of weaving on a handloom. Traditionally, in large parts of India there is gender-based division of these two activities. Women spin and men weave. Gandhi chose the activity associated with women's labour and made it his own. So deep was his identification with the object, the process, the product and its symbolism that the spinning wheel became his lifelong companion, often its repetitive movements obliterating his need for *namasmaran* (taking the name of God).

For Gandhi, the charkha and the loom and the cloth that it produced came to signify the possibilities of a civilization where machines were not the measure of men, where human worth was not located outside the human person. Gandhi was captivated and moved not only by the civilizational possibilities of khādī but also its redemptive potential – its potential to free India from poverty, hunger, debt, lack of productive work, nakedness, bondage and the need and necessity to deny others the dignity of freedom. In that sense, khādī was the true 'livery of freedom', as Pandit Jawaharlal Nehru spoke of it.

If the poet Rabindranath Tagore saw the charkha with its repetitive movement and the coarse yarn it produced as unaesthetic and hence an anaesthetic that would hold masses of India in perpetual bondage, Gandhi saw it as the only true *dharma* (duty) available to him. The creativity of the charkha was enough for him.

The grotesque charkhas that now abound the urban landscape of contemporary India are a perfect symbol of the fate of khādī and Gandhi in the India of today. Once a symbol of deep urge for freedom, it has now come to symbolize poverty – poverty of the spinner and the weaver, poverty of our imagination and the cessation of the Indian state from the lives of its poor.

And yet, like all potentially liberating acts and artefacts, khādī survives. It survives because of its universality, its deep civilizational roots in human subjectivity, in our capacity to imbue the simplest of artefacts and processes with our capacity to imagine and strive for freedom. And, in that sense, khādī remains a 'livery of our freedom'.

References

Jain, Jyotindra and Jasleen Dhamija, eds. *Handwoven Fabrics of India*, Mapin Publishing Pvt. Ltd, 1989.

Tarlo, Emma, 'The Problem of What to Wear: The Politics of Khadi in Late Colonial India'. *South Asia Research* 11, no. 2 (1991): 134–57.

LAKSHMAN REKHA (LAKṢMAṆ RĒKHĀ)

Rukmini Bhaya Nair

The English phrase 'to draw a line' has echoes in many cultures. For much of human history, lines have been drawn to demarcate boundaries on maps, in battle and in law. They have also been implicated in large philosophical enquiries of the sort: can a clear line, a boundary, ever be drawn between fact and fiction, between subjective experience and objective reality, between self and other?

On the Indian subcontinent, the metaphor that perhaps most graphically captures these challenging features of boundaries is the 'Lakshman Rekha', now an intrinsic part of our everyday moral vocabulary. The Lakshman Rekha is a line drawn by the prince Lakshman to protect his sister-in-law, Sita. Sita's husband, Rama, has gone in search of a golden deer that she has spotted in the forest and that she longs for. However, Sita is worried because Rama has been away for long hunting for this deer. She therefore sends Lakshman off in search of her husband. Once she is left alone, however, the enemy king Ravana comes to her in the guise of a wandering mendicant. When she unsuspecting crosses the line (rēkhā) in order to give Ravana his alms, she is carried off and this become a key incident that provokes the great war between Rama and Ravana in the epic Rāmāyaṇa.

In this myth, characters seem to be summoned up from the mists of antiquity with all their failings intact. Sita is shown yielding to temptation, enchanted by a possibly illusory golden deer. Further, she deliberately crosses the line drawn by Lakshmana, again putting herself in harm's way by an act of volition. Unlike Helen of the Odyssey, abducted for her beauty, Sita is very much a self-possessed agent here. When she steps across the boundary line, she does so out of empathy for a poor man seeking alms. Acts of kindness, of desire and of delusion thus combine to present us with a series of conundrums about human nature and human motivations in the Lakṣmaṇ Rēkhā story. Sita's actions in this tale seem to call up a moral conflict between two sorts of codes – one based on being obedient and staying within the line drawn by Lakshmana, the other based on the altruistic premise of giving alms to a poor stranger. She may have been duped in this myth but she has nevertheless succeeded in redrawing a moral boundary at the close of the story. In this sense, every Lakshman Rekha is arguably a 'Sita Rēkhā' as well, making Sita the sort of 'boundary-crosser' that anthropologists such as Mary Douglas (1966) suggest signify trouble in many cultures. Deep fears of loss of 'purity' are aroused when a cultural 'rēkhā' is crossed.

More generally, the point the story makes is that concepts of the good life and good society (e.g. moderation, modesty, duty and purity) are stereotypically exemplified by a person's ability – often a woman's ability – to remain within socially specified limits, not without considerable cost to oneself. However, resistance to these constricting stereotypes appears also to be built into the Lakshman Rekha myth. Such myths often enable a subtle but ceaseless critique of those several boundary lines of caste, creed, gender, economic status, language and education that a hierarchical and highly stratified culture such as the Indian is given to drawing.

In India, where there is a high tolerance on the ground of rules being changed and lines being redrawn at a moment's notice, ambiguous stories like that of the Lakshman Rekha constitute a cognitive recourse wherein we can return to the Rāmāyaṇa to ask counterfactual questions such as the following: had Sita not stepped beyond the boundary line that day, would no great war have taken place? But if so, how would good be shown to performatively triumph over evil? A reconsideration of the concept of the Lakshman Rekha could in this sense allow an examination of the psychological and social consequences of 'border disputes' across a number of cultures.

Umberto Eco (1992) has argued, for example, that the boundary line was a foundational concept in Western culture. Lines served to separate the city of Rome from nomadic barbarian invasions. Bridges were drawn up so that moats into the city could not be crossed. Linearity represented not just 'civitas' but logical, rational thought. Once a line was drawn, time and space were considered irreversible. Even God could not change the linear laws that he had set in motion.

Does the rēkhā or line have similar implications for us in India? Prima facie, it appears that there is little obsession in India with the linearity that Eco suggests is a defining feature of Western thought. An alternative approach to 'rational thought' seems to consist in the knowledge that once a line is drawn there's always the logical possibility not only that it will be *crossed* but also that it will be *redrawn*. In the narrative space of India, ambiguity and nuance often replace the strict divide that allegedly separates 'fact' from 'fiction' in the Western paradigm. In such a culture, the counterfactual possibility is not banished. Time *can* be turned back; bridges (between Lanka and Bharat, for example). Bridges (*setu*) are *not* 'sacrilegious' as Eco avers that they were in the Roman world but are 'sacred' even – or especially! – when built by a monkey brigade. The 'solution' to the divisive paradox of the line is to recross it, thus both proving its existence and yet denying its supreme authority.

The Indian narrative of the Lakshman Rekha reminds us that cultural materials, unlike physical matter, are typically untidy. Space-time is perhaps mathematically describable as a harmonious, curving grid exquisitely fashioned by an Eco-logical God. Cultural vitality, however, might be understood more aptly as a set of overlapping boundaries. Multiple Lakshman Rekhas comprise our social existence, but they are typically both affective and negotiable. It may take years, even centuries, to retrieve the damage caused by the crossing of a 'red' line – in Kashmir or in the United States, for example – but the 'Lakshman Rekha' legend seems to imply, unlike the story of the founding of imperial Rome, that such redemption is not impossible.

References

Douglas, Mary. *Purity and Danger: An Analysis of Concepts of Pollution and Taboo*. New York: Praeger, 1966.
Eco, Umberto and Steffan Collini. *Interpretation and Overinterpretation*, Cambridge: Cambridge University Press, 1992.
Nair, Rukmini Bhaya. 'Epithymetics: The Psychology of Desire'. In *Psychology Volume II, Cognitive and Affective Processes. ICSSR Research Surveys and Explorations*, edited by Girishwar Misra, 204–270. Delhi: Oxford University Press, 2019.

MADA, NALL (MĀD, NĀL)

Alito Siqueira and Asawari Nayak

In Konkani, the word used for the coconut tree is *mada* and the coconut fruit is called *nall*, which is derived from the Dravidian root *neera* (literally, water; and thereby meaning 'fruit containing water'). The coconut tree is the state tree of Goa. Although it is also an important crop in other states of South India such as Kerala, Tamil Nadu, Karnataka and Andhra Pradesh, in Goa (as perhaps in other regions too) it has a strong sociocultural significance.

Culturally, mada is regarded as one of the members of the Goan family and is often thought of as being one of the children (perhaps a son, since mada is masculine). When a coconut tree that is planted around one's house grows to be lush and healthy, it is believed that the family too will blossom, in terms of lineage and economic status. Because of the cultural importance of this tree, a Goan would hesitate to even think of chopping a coconut tree down and would only settle to do so if there is no other alternative.

The mada and the nall are also very much present in the religious events of the locals. Traditionally, a new Goan mother is expected to start the naming ceremony of her child by watering a coconut tree on the twelfth day after the birth of the child and take blessings from it. Here, the coconut tree may be thought of as the ancestor of the family and a fertility symbol. Similarly, in Goan Catholic rituals, during *ros* (a pre-wedding ceremony), coconut milk is applied to the bride and the groom by the family members while singing songs that bless the couple.

The nall is also a culturally significant object. Its appearance is likened to a human head because of its shape, fibrous 'hairy' exterior (coir) and the three 'eyes'. In Goan folklore, the coconut is supposed to represent God (some believe it looks like Lord Shiva since he also has three eyes) and also an ancestor of the family. Traditionally, a coconut was also used as a juristic symbol, that is, one was made to swear an oath on a coconut.

References

Kosambi, D. D. *An Introduction to the Study of Indian History*, second edition. New Delhi: SAGE Publications, 2016.

Noronha, F. 'Why Has Goa Decided the Coconut Palm Is no Longer a Tree?' *BBC News*, 28 January 2016. Available at: http://www.bbc.com/news/world-asia-india-35417168 (accessed December 2018).

MELA (MĒLĀ)

Chandan Gowda

A *mela* usually refers to a large religious fair. It is a place for commerce too: various kinds of goods are bought and sold here. And it is a spectacle to behold and rejoice in. A random coming together of people, though, does not bring about a *mela*. Indeed, a *mela* happens in a designated place at a specified time. And the latter details are known to the participants not through formal announcements as much as in the nature of ingrained details of a community calendar.

The 1899 edition of the Monier-Williams Sanskrit–English dictionary defines a *mela* as 'association, assembly, company, society'. A crucial feature of a *mela* is that the participation in it is open to all. The invocation of a collectivity of people in a *mela* does not admit of social distinctions. In other words, social hierarchies and the hard facts of power do not find explicit space in the imagination of a *mela*.

Furthermore, interactions in a *mela* are not tightly bound by rules. Things fall in place, as it were, on their own. There is a freeness to how people interact without the gathering risking slipping into chaos or anarchy. Also crucial: people can come in and leave as they wish.

In the meeting held at the Sevagram Ashram a few years after Gandhi's assassination in 1948, Vinobha Bhave held up the model of a *mela* to characterize the organization most suited for advancing the work of Gandhi in independent India. For him, a formal organizational structure was ill-suited to the task. The ensuing discussions at the meeting illuminate several other dimensions of the concept of *mela*. Arguing that financial reserves were unimportant for carrying on the work of Gandhi, Vinobha pointed out, 'The *melas* and gatherings of the religious people of this country have never needed funding.' In supporting Vinobha's proposal, Maulana Azad, singled out the special freedoms that lay in the experience of a *mela*: 'A mela is an open fair, a carnival. No one attending it needs to know the others. No one has responsibility of any kind. An open fair is a throw about of people and purposes."

The 1894 Kannada–English Dictionary compiled by Reverend Ferdinand Kittel extends the range of meaning inhering in *mela*: 'meeting', 'union', 'a large concourse of people collected at stated periods for religious or commercial purposes', 'a fair', 'a band of musicians', 'a set of dancing girls, musicians and singers and their performances', and 'mirth, merriment, jest, sport, joking fun'.

A sense of fun, gaiety, blitheness and festivity are integral to the imagination and experience of a *mela*. This is probably a reason that *mela* is also used in relation to performers, musicians and entertainers. While *mela* as a fair or a large gathering brings up the idea of an assembly of people in the abstract, it can admit of gender distinctions when used to refer to a chorus of musicians.

A *mela* can also refer to the union or the conjoining of two objects or people. For instance, 'this literary work invokes *shringara rasa* to portray the *mela* of *prakriti* (nature) and *prema* (love)'. Indeed, *melaisu* (to create a *mela*-like relation) means a bringing together of different elements in a harmonious way and, at times, a sexual union.

As a space of general social mixing melas extend opportunities for promiscuous encounters too. The anonymous nature of the mixing is perhaps reflected in the Kannada word, *meladava*, which literally means a man of the *mela* or a man who has emerged from the *mela*. In the Kannada dictionary compiled by the famous writer, Shivaram Karanth, *meladava* is defined as 'a prostitute's son' and 'an intimate associate of a prostitute'.

Additionally, *mela* can surface as a term of derision and sarcasm to scoff at a gathering that is crowded or has turned into a comical affair or a state of confusion. A lineage to the sense of a comic occasion is illustrated by the old Kannada words, *meladaata* (a male buffoon) and *meladaake* (a female buffoon).

Over the decades, the word *mela* has become hitched to modest, limited-purpose occasions. Consider the following phrases: mango *mela*, loan *mela*, saree *mela*, *udyog mela*. In all of these instances, no one is under any illusion about the depth of the *mela* experience. *The Great Indian Mela* sale announced by an online retailer recently promised the *mela* experience in digital space, among a virtual community of consumers.

References

Boralingaiah, H. C., ed. *Karnatakada Janapada Kalegala Kosha (A Dictionary of the Folk Arts of Karnataka)*. Hampi: Kannada University Press, 1996.

Knighton, W. 'Religious Fairs in India'. *The Nineteenth Century: A Monthly Review* 9 (1881): 838–48.

MISSED CALL

Satish Padmanabhan

Indians are addicts of the 'missed call'. A highly popular and often intricate form of communication despite its non-verbal nature, a missed call in India is used to market services and even to attract people to activist and political causes and to mount recruitment drives. A missed call bypasses language barriers and costs nothing if it is not picked up. Here is an example of the complex communication that a missed call can accomplish in India. Anil Singh in Khopa village near Malla Ramgarh in the hills of Kumaon goes down to the village road and gives Santosh Dharmwal a missed call whose house lies on the hill-step below him. On cue, Santosh comes out on to his terrace. Anil asks him if the gas cylinder truck has come to Malla. Santosh calls Mahesh Da, the gas dealer. He then 'cuts' his call, which means the truck hasn't come. Mahesh Da in turn gives Hemu a missed call at the Indane Gas godown in Bhowali. After three rings his call is disconnected and he gets a call back immediately. This is the SOP to say the gas truck has left Bhowali. Santosh tells Anil to go to Malla in half hour to get his cylinder.

A 'missed call' is a new kind of Morse code, a mime act, a nod-tilt of the hat-lowering of the 'eye' set piece in a gangster film, where nothing is said but everything is understood. Opinion pollsters tell you to give a missed call to, say, 9898012345, if you agree with their question or to 9898012346 if don't. Insurance companies ask you to give a missed to call to a certain number to know more about their schemes. You can give Tata Sky a missed call and they will call you back with new offerings. Girlfriends give boyfriends a missed call to ask them to come out of their hostels. Missed calls can be loaded messages in estranged relationships.

References

Donner, Jonathan. 'The Rules of Beeping: Exchanging Messages Via Intentional "Missed Calls" on Mobile Phones'. *Journal of Computer-mediated Communication* 13, no. 1 (2007): 1–22.

Sivapragasam, Nirmali. 'Hit Me with a Missed Call: The Use of Missed Calls at the Bottom of the Pyramid', *3rd Communication Policy Research South Conference (CPRsouth3) Beijing, China*, 2008.

PRAKRITI/SANSKRITI (PRAKṚTI/SANSKṚTI)

Ranjeeta Dutta

Prakriti means original or primary, that which can develop into *sanskriti* (culture). It also means 'nature', 'matter' and 'temperament'. Like sanskriti, the word prakriti also appears in the names of several institutions and retreats because of its association with nature. In Ayurveda, it also means the constitution of the body, which is made up of three components: *vatta* (air), *pitta* (fire) and *kapha* (body resistance). There are several food programmes and articles that state 'Know your prakriti' and then enlighten the audience or reader about the *vatta, pitta* and *kapha*.

According to Monier-Williams, in Hindu philosophy, prakriti is a significant concept, meaning 'making or placing before or at first, the original or natural form or condition of anything, original or primary substance'. It is the primordial source for the birth of the universe and represents the phenomenal universe. Samkhya philosophy has it that the universe consists of two distinct realities, *purusha* (soul) and prakriti (matter). Neither of them need god as an original cause – nor can they be identified with god. According to the yōga school, prakriti was an effect of the will of god. Samkhya metaphysics endows prakriti with three *gunas* (qualities): *rajas* (creation), *sattva* (preservation) and *tattva* (destruction). The equilibrium between these three gunas is the basis of material reality. Prakriti also refers to the feminine aspects of the universe and is symbolically represented as a woman. In the Jain tradition, prakriti is related to the theory of *karma*.

Sanskriti is derived from the word *sanskrit/samksruta*. The etymological derivation of this word is *sam+krita/kriti*, where '*sam*' is the prefix meaning 'very good' or 'perfect', *kru* is the root verb, meaning 'to do', *kruta* is the past participle form meaning 'done' and *kriti* is the noun meaning 'activity' or 'creation'. Thus, *sanskriti* means a very well/perfectly done creation/action. '*Kru*' is also the root for words, *prakriti* and *vikriti*, which means 'degeneration', 'perversion' and 'distortion'. When *prakrit/prakriti* or something that is raw is developed and well formed, then it becomes *sanskriti*; when distorted or degenerated, it becomes vikriti. Worth nothing too is the fact that *sanskrit/samskruta*, meaning a perfectly made, completely refined, very well-polished language.

The word *sanskriti*, in English usage, is usually translated as 'culture', implying development and sophistication. Like the words 'culture' and 'cultured' in English, the word '*sanskriti*' is identified with refinement, honour and aesthetic good taste. Thus, *sanskriti* also includes activities/engagements with the arts, architecture, dance, music crafts, literature, cuisines, languages, philosophy and ideas, all considered to be important for the development of a society, its outlook and the expansion of people's minds.

The present state of *sanskriti* in any society is a result of its long-standing historical evolution, development and legacy. Often, *sanskriti* is used in conjunction with the word *sabhyata*, as *sanskriti aur sabhyata*, approximately translated as 'culture and civilization'. Sanskriti and *sabhayata* are not, however, synonyms. The spirit of enquiry, intellectual curiosity, inventions and discoveries for the welfare of mankind and posterity is considered as *sanskriti*, while lifestyle, food habits, behaviour and so on are a part of *sabhyata*. While *sanskriti* generates knowledge and an intellectual capacity that creates inquisitiveness and enables mankind to question, *sabhyata* is related to the material conditions and improvement in those conditions. Therefore, eating good food, wearing good clothes and possessing wealth and property is *sabhyata*, and engaging with the natural environment around us, seeking knowledge and making innovations in the arts, science and philosophy that create intellectual development, and are not material, is *sanskriti*. *Sabhyata* informs various aspects of *sanskriti*, and *sanskriti* forms the bedrock of knowledge, on the basis of which society can think and act and improve its conditions, leading to progress. Knowledge and the research generated, as a consequence, and their use for the welfare of people are at the core of *sanskriti*, and making proper/ beneficial use of that knowledge system is understood as *sabhyata*. Knowledge and inventions that harm humankind and generate negativity are described as *asanskriti*, and misuse of the arts, science, philosophy and ideas are considered as *asabhyata*. The social environment and physical conditions influence *sanskriti* and its further growth. The dissemination and diffusion of *sanskriti* is understood to occur through communities, group of people and the society. Therefore, it is not the individual but the collective that plays an important role in carrying forth the ideas from one generation to another. Although capacious, *sanskriti* is not a homogeneous omnibus category, not is it static with elements being added to it from time to time. Thus, arts, philosophy, language, architecture, music and dance, all change and acquire different shapes with time and comprise different components representing diverse ideas and attitudes.

The histories of India, the changes from one stage of social and economic interaction to another are all identified with Indian *sanskriti*. The intellectual outputs of Bodhayana, Bhaskaracharya and Aryabhatta, in mathematics and astronomy, with the pioneering invention of zero, the contributions of Kanad and Varahmira in physics, Nagarjuna in chemistry, Sushruta and Charaka in medicine, Patanjali in yōga and several others are part of a shared *sanskriti*. Literature, folklore, crafts, visual and performing arts, festivals, manuscripts, antiquities, museums – the entire heritage of the subcontinent counts as Indian *sanskriti*. In addition, the concept of the *Bharatiya sanskriti* is used in political and cultural discourses and ideals to emphasize the various ideas of a nation.

'*Bharatiya sanskriti*' translates as 'Indian culture'. The Ministry of Culture today is, for example, known as *Sanskriti Mantralaya*. This ministry regularly organizes the *Rashtriya Sanskriti Mahaotsava* (National Cultural Festival) and has a mobile app called *Sanskriti* that provides information about events in India related to dance, music, arts, films, theatre and exhibition. The website of the ministry also has a *Sanskriti* channel (indiaculture.nic.in).

References

Dube, S. C. *Manav aur Sanskriti*. New Delhi: Rajkamal Prakashan, 2016.
Monier-Williams, Monier. *Monier William's Sanskrit-English Dictionary*, second edition, 654. London: Oxford University Press, 1899.

RAMZAN (RAMZĀN)

Hilal Ahmed

Ramzan (Ramadan in Arabic) is the ninth month of the Islamic calendar (*Hijri*). This month is considered to be the most sacred month of the year by Muslims all over the world for two primary reasons. First, it is the month of fasting. It is obligatory (*farz*) for adult Muslims to observe fast during the month of Ramzan (except those who are suffering from an illness, those who are travelling, those cannot fast due to old age and women who are pregnant, breastfeeding or menstruating). The *saum* (or what is called *roza* in the subcontinent) is one of the five pillars of Islamic religiosity. The other four pillars of Islam are the following: *shahada*, the faith that there is no God but Allah and Mohammad is his Prophet; the five-time *salat*, also known as *namaz* in the Indian subcontinent; *hajj*, the annual pilgrimage for those who can afford it; and, *zakat*, the obligation on affluent Muslims to donate one-fortieth of their wealth for the poor and the needy. Observing roza from dawn to sunset is not entirely about refraining from food, drink, smoking and sexual intercourse. The *rozedar* (the person who observes the fast) is expected to not get involved in any sinful behaviour and observe her or his roza as an instrument to purify her or his spiritual engagement with Allah. In this sense, the physical act of fasting is a means to achieve moral–spiritual ends. Second, Ramzan is also marked as a sacred month because of its intrinsic relationship with the Quran. It is believed that the verses of the Quran were first revealed to Prophet Mohammad in the month of Ramzan. The Quran itself underlines the significance of Ramzan in the following verse in Sura Al Baqra: 2: 185: 'The month of Ramadhan [is that] in which was revealed the Qur'an, a guidance for the people and clear proofs of guidance and criterion. So, whoever sights [the new moon of] the month, let him fast it; and whoever is ill or on a journey – then an equal number of other days. Allah intends for you ease and does not intend for you hardship and [wants] for you to complete the period and to glorify Allah for that [to] which He has guided you; and perhaps you will be grateful.'

An additional congregational prayer called *taraweeh* is also performed in mosques during Ramzan to recite the Quran collectively. These taraweeh prayers are led by *hafiz* (those who memorize the Quran). Although there is a disagreement between Shia and Sunni Muslims on the religious importance of taraweeh, there is a consensus among all sects of Islam that the Quran must be read and recited extensively in the month of Ramzan. Ramzan involves a lot of cultural festivity. Special food and drinks are prepared for *sehri* (pre-fast meal) and *iftar* (collective breaking of the fast). Ramzan ends with sighting of new moon and the very next day is celebrated as Eid-ul-Fitr.

References

O'Brien, Peter. 'Secularism'. In *The Muslim Question in Europe: Political Controversies and Public Philosophies*, 144–98. Philadelphia, Rome and Tokyo: Temple University Press, 2016.
Robinson, Neal. *Islam: A Concise Introduction*. Washington: Georgetown University Press, 1999.

SHAMSHAN (ŚAMŚĀNA)

Ipshita Chanda

In Sanskrit, *shma* means 'corpse' and *shyan* means 'bed'. The *shamshan* (colloquially, mashan) refers to the 'cremation grounds', where according to Hindu practice, corpses are confined to flames. The cremation grounds are presided over by the Dom community, a Dalit community from Bengal, who are traditionally assigned the task of cremation. According to the *Bhagwat Purana* (Skandha 4, Adhyay 4), Siva presides over the cremation grounds and it is occupied by his followers who are adept in the tantric art. The cremation ground is generally located on the banks of a river, as flowing water is needed to immerse the ashes to symbolically aid the soul with crossing the mythical Baitarani River on its way to the other world. The corpse is placed on the pyre with the feet facing south. After the principal mourner lights the pyre by placing the brand in the mouth of the corpse, the body becomes an offering to the gods. This is the place of *kayanta*, where the body ends.

One among the numerous cremation grounds of legend is the Manikarnika ghat on the banks of the Ganges in Varanasi, the only city that Siva is supposed to have not destroyed in his grief following the death of his wife Satī. According to legend, Satī is invited to a celebration in her natal home, where she is disturbed by the arrogance and insults her father Daksha heaps upon her cremation ground-dwelling husband. In protest, she immolates herself. Siva takes the blazing body to the Himalayas, where he lives; Vishnu sends his weapon, the *sudrashan chakra*, to cut Satī's body into pieces and scatter the pieces across the country. Legend holds that places were a part of her body fell have now become places of worship of the female energy and are known as Shakti Peeth. At Manikarnika ghat, Satī's ear jewel is believed to have fallen. The smashaan at Manikarnika ghat is ruled by Mahakaal, also known as Yama, the god of death. It is believed that those cremated here achieve *mōkṣa* (salvation) most easily. This is why Varanasi is also known as kasha or mokshadayini (she who offers salvation to the soul).

Besides, as the liminal world between the living and dead, the shamshan also hosts several Shiva-worshipping cults which use the death rituals and corpses as part of their devotional and disciplinary practice. At the cremation grounds in Varanasi, the cults include the Aghori tantric worshippers of Siva as Mahakaal. These worshippers believe in infringing on the taboos within Hinduism such that their path to salvation is hastened. Other cremation ground-dwelling devotees of Siva include the *vetala* (spirit messengers of Siva), whom worshippers have to appease in order to become *vidyadhar* (masters of the secret arts). The shamshan is also known as the *pitr-bhasmakanan* (the garden of ashes of the ancestors) and ruled by Shiva-worshipping *kapalik* (skull men), who use human skulls for their rituals.

In Islam, the graveyard is where the dead are buried. Here, the death rituals comprise the ritual bath (*ghusl*) performed by the relatives of the deceased, who belong to the same gender. Then the body is covered in a white shroud (*kafan*) and brought in a final procession (*janaaza*), after the reading of the *salaat* (prayer) for the occasion. While the funeral prayers are being performed, loud recitation and loud mourning or sitting are frowned upon; hence, the solemnity of the ceremony is maintained. The graveyard, therefore, is a place of prayer and contemplation. Graves are tended to and offerings are made by some sects and frowned upon by others.

References

Ballard, Roger. 'The Logic of Cremation in Indic Contexts: An Anthropological Analysis', 2008. Retrieved from: http://crossasia-repository.ub.uni-heidelberg.de/466/1/1_Logic_of_Cremation.pdf (accessed 6 December 2019).

Gupta, Ravi and Kenneth Valpey, eds. *The Bhagavata Purana: Sacred Text and Living Tradition*. Columbia University Press, 2013.

SOGADU (SOGĀRŪ)

N. Manu Chakravarthy

The Kannada word *sogadu* means the quintessential quality, flavour, temper of whatever is linked with it. *Sogadu* is used to foreground the inherent nature of a land, a language (to mean the richness of its idiom) and even extends to include agricultural produce (food grains, fruits and vegetables). It draws attention to the uniqueness and vitality of communities and individuals.

Sogadu could also be used to strongly indicate the heterogeneous nature of all elements – animate and inanimate – and, because of the resonances of diversity and uniqueness it carries, the word helps imply resistance to easy classifications and categorizations that come from homogenizing attitudes. However, even as it points to the uniqueness of all temporal elements, *sogadu* works horizontally to avoid any kind of privileging of any single entity. It is inclusive and is not exclusionary in any sense.

Contemporary cultural discourses in Kannada deploy the word *sogadu* to open up larger questions that resist notions of 'purity' of caste, religion, linguistic expressions, food habits, music, dance and other forms of artistic expression. 'Sogadu' could be regarded as a concept that confronts dominant stereotypes as regards the sociocultural contexts of divergent communities.

SUSEGAD (SUSSEGĀD)

Alito Siqueira and Asawari Nayak

The *Rajhauns New Generation Konkani-English Illustrated Dictionary* defines the Konkani adjective *susegad* as a word used to describe a person (a situation or place) that is calm, content or 'at peace'. The word is from the Portuguese *sossego*. Other derivatives include the noun *susheg*, which means 'rest', 'calm' and 'peace'; the verb *susheg ghevap*, meaning 'to take rest'.

Susegad is often used as an epithet for Goa and Goans within the Indian context. The tourism industry also promotes this representation and presents it as one of Goa's chief selling qualities. In doing so, it appeals to visitors/tourists who want to escape the clamour of their busy lives. As a state of being, Susegado is often used as the antonym of a noisy, industrial, urban, harried life. Susegad is also used as a sobriquet for the Goan way of life within the global (predominantly Western) discourse of tourism. In his article 'You can do anything in Goa, India', Bandyopadhayay elaborates on this by quoting an excerpt from the Marika McAdam's work on Goa called *Lonely Planet*: 'Spend any time trying to figure Goa out, and you will get no closer to a tangible answer. Instead, surrender to the spirit of susegad – of relaxing and enjoying life while you can – by accepting that Goa is not so much a state of Indian but a state of mind … a state of simply "being"'. Bandyopadhyay further argues by saying that, often, such touristic representations are largely orientalist, reflecting a colonial fantasy of India (or Goa) being a 'timeless' 'west's pleasure periphery' and are ways in which outsiders can 'take control' over spaces wherein the natives continue to perform their roles to meet the pleasure needs of the tourists.

While susegad can be seen as a word used to describe the high aesthetic sense of Goans, it can also sometimes be seen as a 'weakness' that others (perhaps implying at non-Goans) may abuse or take advantage of. In the negative sense, the word may also be used to refer to the stereotype of 'lazy Goans'. One can find this stereotype evoked also by Goans themselves, when the government or the media wants to take attention away from actual structural issues (such as unemployment or the caste system), by claiming that these problems are manifestations of Goan 'sussegadness'.

This word has now entered other sister languages such as Marathi and Hindi. Although it may not find its place in the standard lexicons of these languages, it is used in popular media such as films and print media.

References

Bandyopadhyay, R. 'You Can Do Anything in Goa, India: A Visual Ethnography of Tourism as Neo-colonialism', *Tourism and Visual Culture* 2 (2010): 200–7.

'Vidharbaat Matadaan Sussegaad', *Maharashtra Times*, 10 April 2014. Available at: http://m.maharashtratimes.com/maharashtra/nagpur-vidarbha-news/voting-in-vidarbha/articleshow/33544927.cms (accessed December 2018).

STAMP PAPER

Ramanjit Kaur Johal

Stamp paper gets its name and value from bearing the 'stamp'. *Black's Law Dictionary* defines 'stamp' as 'an impression made by public authority, in pursuance of law, upon paper or parchment, upon which certain legal proceedings, conveyances, or contracts are required to be written, and for which a tax or duty is exacted. A small label or strip of paper, bearing a particular device, printed and sold by the government, and required to be attached to mail-matter, and to some other articles subject to duty or excise.' The origin of stamp duties lies in the Stamp Act of 1694 signed in England during the reign of King William and Queen Mary.

As Britain extended its empire to India, the coverage of stamp duty also increased. The purpose of this instrument was to raise revenue for the East India Company. The British first introduced stamp duty in India in 1797. Initially, it was limited to Bengal, Bihar, Banaras and Orissa (now Odisha), replacing a tax that was collected from Indian merchants and traders for maintaining the police. The government was run mainly from land revenue as there was no income tax, excise or custom duty. Court fee and revenue stamps were designed by the British to collect taxes from residents of some of the princely states as early as 1797. The designs included the name of the state as well as the type and amount of tax imposed. Early examples of stamp paper from British India and the princely states were colourless, much like a notary's seal, but were subsequently replaced by typeset or engraved stamps. Later, colour was added, and printings for some of the more affluent states were imported from the West. These collectors' items are found in museums, personal collections and in the market for their artifact value.

Stamp duty was first formalized by Act XXXV of 1860, soon after the administration of India was transferred from the East India Company to the British Crown. After several amendments, the present law, called the Indian Stamp Act, emerged in 1899. The Indian Stamp Rules were framed in 1925. The Act covers stamp duty in various forms, including on transfer of land, insurance policies, promissory notes and power of attorney. It also covers revenue stamps on receipts. The Act has been amended fifty-one times since 1899 (most recently in 2004), repealing and imposing stamp duties and granting exemptions. The Act has also been amended by various states and the rates of duty differ from state to state.

Under the Bombay Stamp Act of 1958, sixty-two categories of documents need to be legitimized by stamping them. For instance, stamp paper of 10 rupees is used for an affidavit/declaration/undertaking; stamp paper of 20 rupees for Special Power of Attorney; stamp paper of 50 rupees for General Power of Attorney/Agreement; stamp paper of 100 rupees for Indemnity Bond and Guarantee Bond.

There are of two kinds of stamp papers: judicial stamp paper, used for legal and court (*kacheri*) work for payment of court fees, and non-judicial stamp paper, used for registration/execution of documents, insurance policies and so on. Stamp duty paid for non-judicial stamp paper is paid under the Indian Stamp Act of 1899. The different denominations of non-judicial stamp papers include those of Indian Rupees 10, 20, 50, 100, 500, 1000, 5000, 10,000, 15,000, 20,000, 25,000. Stamp papers and stamps are distributed to nodal districts and reach the public through sub-treasuries and stamp vendors.

In India, some types of contracts need to be stamped to make them legally valid. For example, if an individual sells property as per a written contract which is not on stamp paper, or for which stamp duty is not paid, then such a document would not be legally binding. Sales deeds have to be executed on stamp paper and any deficiency invites penalty, which may be of the value of the insufficient stamp and fine or up to a certain multiple of the insufficient stamp duty. In India, the collector has the power to punish, impose fine and rule for forfeiture of the property. The payment of duty towards stamp enables the government to keep records of the documents for which stamp duty or stamp revenue was paid. Hence, ultimately, genuine documents would be preserved by government functionaries.

Revenue stamps and stamp paper are treated with awe and respect in India. Stamp paper has found its place in the vernacular as an embodiment of the gravity and promise of the documents that it is used for, thus when convincing another of the seriousness of their intent the poser often is, 'Would you have this committed on stamp paper?' It is interesting that stamp paper is perceived to establish the authenticity of a document. However, it does not in itself certify the genuineness or falsity of a document; it is the concerned authority that authenticates a document executed on a paper of a certain stamp value. The need to make this obligatory payment or else pay the penalty, in the case of inadequate postal stamp value, actually ensures the delivery of such 'bearing' (*barang*) letters where the penalty is collected from the recipient. This convoluted effect of surety of delivery has been captured eloquently in folk songs, such as in the Punjabi folk song which goes *Jaan taan sajjanaap millin, nahi chitthive barang pavin*, which loosely translates to 'my beloved, meet me in person or then mail me a "bearing" letter'. In 2002, India was rocked by the infamous Telgi Scam, which was a counterfeit stamp paper scam that was spread across seventy-two towns and eighteen states over a period of ten years. This scam dealt the Indian economy a shattering blow of a loss of about 32,000 crore rupees.

With the slogans of smart and citizen-centric governance, stamp paper usage is increasingly being done away with. Apart from withdrawing affidavit requirements for many non-judicial procedures, stamp papers are being replaced with more secure ways of paying stamp duty, such as e-challans and e-Secured Bank-cum-Treasury Receipts (eSBTR). E-stamping has made the procedure of stamping easier. The Stock Holding Corporation of India Limited (SHCIL) is the central record-keeping agency that has facilitated e-stamping in a number of states and union territories. It is a computer-based application and a secure way of paying non-judicial stamp duty to the government. It is the speediest and most convenient mode of stamping and also helps check counterfeiting. In fact, in states like Delhi all stamp duties are being compulsorily paid through e-stamping since 2016.

References

Aggarwal, S. 'Modes of Stamping in India', blog post on *lawfarm*, 29 July 2016. Available at: https://www.lawfarm.in/blogs/modes-of-stamping-in-india- (accessed 7 February 2018).
Misra, B. B. *The Administrative History of India 1834–1947: General Administration*. New Delhi: Oxford University Press, 1970.
Sims, B. J., J. B. Hodgson and A. K. Tavare, eds. *Sergeant on Stamp Duties*. London: Butterworth & Co. (Publishers) Ltd., 1963, 4th edition.

STREET CHILDREN

Harsh Mander (with Satya Pillai and Deepti Shrivastava)

According to the Inter-NGO Programme cited in *Strategies to Combat Homelessness* by the United Nations Centre for Human Settlements (Habitat), a street child is 'any girl or boy … for whom the street (in the widest sense of the word, including unoccupied dwellings, parks, parking lots, spaces under bridges, shop corridors, wastelands, etc.) has become his or her habitual abode and/or source of livelihood; and who is inadequately protected, supervised, or directed by responsible adults'. In general, street children suffer from many denials and vulnerabilities. These include deprivation of responsible adult protection; coercion to work to eat each day; work in unhealthy occupations on streets like rag-picking, begging and sex work; abysmally poor sanitary conditions; inadequate nutrition from begging, foraging and food stalls; a range of psychosocial stresses; physical abuse and sexual exploitation; and exposure to hard drug abuse. From our years of engagement with street children, we identify them as children who have abandoned their families, children whose families have abandoned them and children who have ties with their families.

Keywords for India

Although India, the second most populous and fastest-growing economy, is home to the world's largest population of street children, we still do not have any agreed definitive and accurate official figure of the number of children for whom city streets are home. They escape official attention and are not counted in censuses and surveys, as these are designed and conducted around counting housed people.

Children on Indian streets are brave but profoundly vulnerable survivors. They have run away from incest, violent and substance-abusing guardians, starvation, cruel step-parents and even horrendous massacres. They have been forced to live by their wits on the street, find food, work or beg to get money, fight for whatever they need, fend off older bullies and all the time carry a well of emptiness in themselves because the significant adults in their lives have failed them. These street children are free spirits. They do not take kindly to being locked inside a gate, being supervised closely and being corrected constantly. They therefore need comprehensive long-term residential care for the entire duration of their childhood and youth but in ways that are voluntary and non-custodial. Children from the street have proven to be able to learn and accept discipline when guidance is not accompanied by condemnation or rejection. They seem to have created a space around themselves, which served the purpose of self-protection when they were living on the street. They do not easily allow others to come into this shell. These children often carry the scars of earlier negative experiences of which they do not speak until they trust the people around them. They sometimes show a strange combination of the maturity of adults coupled with the joy, vulnerability and innocence of a child.

References

Mander, Harsh. *Living Rough, Surviving the City Streets: A Study of Homeless Populations in Delhi, Chennai, Patna and Madurai*. New Delhi: Planning Commission of India, 2009.

Shukla, P. C. *Street Children and the Asphalt Life: Street Children and the Future Direction*. Delhi: Isha Books, 2005.

STREET VENDORS

Ritajyoti Bandyopadhyay

Street vendors occupying public spaces such as pavements, parks and thoroughfares, and thereby appearing to deny access to their 'rightful' users has been, over the years, a highly contentious issue in major cities across the globe. In India, the question of the street vendors has received enthusiastic public attention with the passage of the Street Vendors (Protection of Livelihood and Regulation of Street Vending) Act 2014 (hereafter, SVA). In 2004, the first draft of the Act in the form of a national policy was made public for wider consultation. The SVA arrived at an eclectic definition of street vendor for the entire country: "'street vendor" means a person engaged in vending of articles, goods, wares, food items or merchandise of everyday use or offering services to the general public, in a street, lane, sidewalk, footpath, pavement, public park or any other public place or private area, from a temporary built up structure or by moving from place to place and includes hawker, peddler, squatter and all other synonymous terms which may be local or region specific; and the words "street vending" with their grammatical variations and cognate expressions, shall be construed accordingly.' Clearly, this definition attempts to bring together a vast array of trade practices and their regional dimensions within a coherent and recognizable structure of street vending. We may call this the moment of *nationalization* of the street vendor.

The term street vendor was not common in popular parlance in India until the 1970s. In the colonial archives of Calcutta, for instance, the term 'hawker' appears along with other similar terms, such as pavement seller, footpath seller and *pheriwala* (peddler) at least since the late nineteenth century. Whereas in everyday language of conversation, hawker emerged only after Partition, when the Government of West Bengal initiated economic rehabilitation projects for refugees by building a number of 'refugee hawker corners' in the city. The changing political circumstances after Independence also enabled various commodity sellers on the sidewalks to come together under trade unions. The trade unions also needed a generic name that could somehow manage to describe their subjects. This is the context for the emergence of the hawker as a population category. The term street vendor/street vending started becoming familiar to the street traders as the trade unions began to embrace the lexicon of informal economy to articulate their objectives and orientations.

Street vendors are the key players in rural–urban commodity circulation. They constitute one of the largest service sectors that keeps cities affordable to a large cross-section of the population. In early 1990s, All India Institute of Hygiene and Public Health conducted a survey on the street food sector of Calcutta led by I. Chakravarty and C. Canet. The survey was carried out on 911 consumers from various important commercial areas and transit points, of whom a staggering 80 per cent were men and the rest women. The survey revealed that in some of the prominent business districts of Central Calcutta, about 75 per cent officegoers obtained at least part of their midday meal from street vendors. The survey also considered the nutritional value of some of the most consumed food items and found that the street food 'may be the least expensive means of obtaining a nutritionally balanced meal outside home, provided the consumer is informed and able to choose the proper combination of food'.

In Indian cities, street vendors represent one of the largest, more organized and more militant sectors in the informal economy. Often, they negotiate eviction operations by virtue of complex patronage networks involving local state functionaries belonging to the ruling and opposition political parties. These relationships can hardly be reduced to electoral calculations, as street vendors do not form a clustered urban vote bank like slum dwellers and squatter groups. Rather, through everyday negotiations with pedestrians, shopkeepers, property owners, the state and themselves, the street vendors create, reconfigure and 're-function' materialities of infrastructures. In doing so, Mitchell notes, they periodically sidestep the bourgeois law of property, appropriate infrastructures and make infrastructures the focus of a collective existence. Often, they demand concessions from the government as a matter of right to livelihood in the city. They place such claims not as a matter of rule but as acceptable exceptions to the rule of property. At the time of competitive electoral mobilization in cities, according to Partha Chatterjee, such claims define the terms on which these groups are considered parties to the governmental negotiations.

References

Bandyopadhyay, R. 'Institutionalising Informality: The Hawkers' Question in Post-Colonial Calcutta'. *Modern Asian Studies* 50, no. 2 (2016): 675–717.
Mitchell, T. 'Introduction: Life of Infrastructure'. *Comparative Studies in South Asia, Africa and the Middle East* 34, no. 3 (2014): 437–9.

TEMPLE ENTRY

Dipti Kulkarni

Certain places of worship in India have followed discriminatory practices and have prohibited women and people belonging to the 'lower castes' from entering its premises to worship. Such practices of social exclusion have a long history and continue to this date, despite being unconstitutional. The basis of such segregation and exclusion runs deep. Persons belonging to the 'lower castes' and women are prohibited entry because they are considered impure. Notions of purity and impurity may be difficult to fathom for an outsider but are an intrinsic part of the practice of Hinduism.

Persons born outside the four broad *varnas* (Brahmin, Kshatriya, Vaishya and Shudra) may not only be prohibited from entering temples but are also denied access to public wells, roads and so on.

Efforts by the oppressed to gain access, in modern India, can be dated to the Vaikom Satyagraha in the 1920s. Temple entry agitations such as these were marked by the usage of Gandhian means of *satyagraha* (civil disobedience). Dr B. R. Ambedkar, a legal luminary, visionary and scholar, led many such protests for access to public utilities in the state of Maharashtra.

The question that often gets asked then is why do these women and Dalit groups feel the need to seek entry and worship these Gods anyway. To paraphrase the thoughts of Ambedkar on the matter: Entry into temples is not an end in itself. The oppressed must focus their energies on things like education and getting jobs, but it is still only one step towards gaining equal status in society. The final objective being the abolishment of gender prejudices and caste altogether.

References

Jeffrey, R. 'Temple-Entry Movement in Travancore, 1860–1940'. *Social Scientist* 4, no. 8 (1976): 3–27.
Kulkarni, Dipti. 'No Social Change Sans Dialogue: Case of Shani Shingnapur'. *Economic and Political Weekly* 51, no. 34 (2016): 34–5.

TRIBAL CUSTOMARY LAW

Melvil Pereira

Tribal customary law is defined as the body of traditional practices observed and procedures followed in an indigenous or tribal community. However, it is a contested term in the academia. Some scholars refuse to recognize it as law, treating it merely as one of the sources of law, because it lacks clarity, certainty, legitimacy and sanctions. Other scholars assert that it is indeed a system of laws consisting of all the customs and practices found in a particular community. These scholars hold that customary law, like statutory law, enjoys social sanction and promotes law and order in society.

Given these divergent views, it is useful to begin by distinguishing between 'custom' and 'customary law'. A custom is a usage or traditional way of doing things passed down the generations. A custom attains the status of law when it is recognized as useful or even necessary for maintaining harmony in society and its violation leads to penal action. Thus, customary law is part of social heritage and differs from statutory law, which is enacted by a sovereign or legislature. Tribal communities all over the world are falling back on their customary law in order to preserve their culture and identity.

There is no doubt that nowhere else are tribals more protected than in India. There is also no doubt that tribals have nowhere a greater say in managing their own affairs than in Northeast India. This is because of the special provisions in favour of tribal communities by virtue of Article 371 and the Sixth Schedule enshrined in the Constitution of India. For instance, Article 371A and 371G protect Naga and Mizo Customary Law, respectively, as they state that no Act of Parliament in respect of Naga or Mizo Customary Law and Procedure shall apply to the states of Nagaland and Mizoram unless their respective legislative assemblies so decide through a resolution.

Many of those who favour the continuation of customary law also recognize its limitations. Customary law is essentially patriarchal, resulting in the denial of rights to women in inheritance of property, maintenance and governance. It also systematically excludes women from decision-making forums.

References

Pereira, M., B. Dutta and B. Kakati, eds. *Legal Pluralism and Indian Democracy: Tribal Conflict Resolution Systems in Northeast India*. New Delhi: Routledge, 2018.

Singh, K. S. *Tribal Ethnography, Customary Law and Change*. New Delhi: Concept Publishing Company, 1993.

ZANANA (ZANĀNĀ)

Nazima Parveen

Zanana is a Persian word that is used by both Urdu and Hindi speakers in India. It originated from the Persian root *zan*, which means 'woman'. In its literal sense, zanana means 'of the women' or 'pertaining to women', that is, referring to a space in a house belonging specifically to women or a 'gathering of women'. The word *zanankhana* is an extended expression which specifically describes the space where female members of the family can take rest, chat, play, dance and entertain friends in private. Zanana is the antonym of *mardana*, which refers to a masculine space, that is, the outer apartments used for welcoming male guests and men.

In another sense, the word zanana is also used to describe the feminine tendencies of eunuchs, that is, men who have been castrated and *hijras* (who are identified at birth as male but who self-identify later as female or as neither male nor female).

Zanana space was intrinsically linked to the practice of *purdah*, as women were not supposed to enter the outside domain of men. This imposed restriction, nevertheless, has its own sociological implications. As feminine zones, zanana spaces produced a whole variety of womanly rituals, games, music and rich linguistic traditions, which are completely alien to menfolk. Begmati Zubaan, the language of the women of the aristocratic class of shahjahanabad, a coded language for secret conversation was a specially intersting development that is said to have taken place during the Mughal period.

The Hindi–Urdu controversy, after the Independence, gradually replaced zanana by the Sanskritized Hindi term *mahila* and the English word 'ladies'. However, as an expression, zanana still remains a tongue-twisting favourite of Urdu lovers.

References

Lal, Ruby. *Domesticity and Power in the Early Mughal World South Asian*. Cambridge: Cambridge University Press, 2009.

Minault, Gail. 'Begamati Zuban: Women's Language and Culture in Nineteenth-Century Delhi', *India International Centre Quarterly* 11, no. 2 (June 1984): 155–70. Available at: http://www.columbia.edu/itc/mealac/pritchett/00urdu/umraojan/txt_minault_begamatizaban.pdf (accessed December 2018).

CHAPTER 5
EMANCIPATORY IMAGINARIES

ADIVASI (ĀDIVĀSĪ)

Virginius Xaxa

Several terms are used to denote groups and communities that have been described as 'tribes' in India. The most common among them are *adimjati, vanyajati, janjati, anusuchit janjati, vanvasi* and *adivasi*. In Hindi, adimjati meaning 'primitive community' is applied to tribes. This word encapsulates notions of savageness and primitiveness conventionally associated with tribes. Voluntary associations Gandhian social workers formed to uplift tribal people from their economic and social conditions were often prefixed with the word adimjati. Thakkar Bappa, a well-known Gandhian, started an organization with branches in different parts of India named Adim Jati Sevak Sangh nearly nine months after Gandhi's assassination. Another term in use, vanyajati, had a limited circulation. The tribes have also been described as janjati. Ray has equated *jana* with an egalitarian form of social organization as against *jati* (caste) with a hierarchical system of social organization. Other scholars, such as Beteille, have contested this view, pointing out that any attempt to identify jana with the present-day tribals today is not without difficulty. In fact, 'anusuchit janjati' meaning scheduled tribes is routine administrative parlance in dealing with tribes.

For a little over two decades, the new term 'vanvasi', meaning 'inhabitants of the forest', has been in wide circulation to refer to people described as tribes. This term originated in the deliberations, discourses and writings of the ideologues of the Rashtriya Swayamsevak Sangh (RSS). All its affiliates, such as Vishwa Hindu Parishad, Bajrang Dal, Sewa Bharti, Ekal Vidyalaya and Vivekananda Kendra refer to tribes as vanvasis. In fact, the key organizations run by the RSS among tribal communities – Vanvasi Kalyan Ashram – goes by this name.

The terms above are, ironically, outside the lexicon of tribal communities. Some of them do use janjati and anusuchit janjati as part of administrative practice, even though these words remain outside their consciousness as tribal people. What does exist as a part of conceptual vocabulary is the category of Adivasi.

'Adivasi' (*adi* meaning 'original' and *vasi* meaning 'inhabitant') is an equivalent of the term 'indigenous people' used worldwide and has been current among tribal people in India, especially in Eastern, Central, Western and Southern India. However, such usage is markedly absent in Northern and even in Northeast India where nearly 12 per cent of India's tribal population live. In Northeast India, the term adivasi is applied to communities that were brought in as indentured labour by colonial British tea companies to work in tea estates they opened in Assam from the middle of the nineteenth century. The Adivasi tag was acquired by these groups in the places of their origin. Adivasi is used in the region as a convenient label, shorn of the notion of indigeneity evoked by the term. This is not to say that tribal communities in Northeast India do not identify themselves as indigenous. They do and many organizations representing them have been participating in international events concerned with indigenous peoples.

The idea underlying Adivasi or indigenous peoples did not have its origin in tribals/Adivasis themselves. It originated with British administrator-scholars, ethnographers and, more importantly, Christian missionaries, Sengupta notes. Other terms in vogue among British administrator-scholars and missionaries were autochthonous, aborigines, etc., which literally meant original inhabitants. With this, the idea of these peoples belonging to a different racial, linguistic and cultural stock emerged. While the administrator-scholars and ethnographers described them as such, Christian missionaries made them aware of it. This divide sharpened with increasing interaction between tribals and non-tribals, which was far from symbiotic and harmonious. Marked by exploitation and domination, this situation was instrumental in shaping the new consciousness of indigenous peoples.

Since then this idea has become an important marker of self-identity. Even non-tribals today identify and address them as Adivasis. In fact, the idea of Adivasi has edged out the idea of primitiveness attached to the other categories. Such awareness and identity did not take shape in Northeast India as tribes there were isolated from Indian civilizational centres and therefore escaped its grip even as tribes in mainland India had begun to experience colonization before the advent of British rule. The British hastened and intensified the process that was already at work.

On the eve of Independence, the tribes were marked by economic and social backwardness on the one hand and on the other with rampant alienation of land from tribes to non-tribes coupled with the denial of rights over forest and other resources that they had enjoyed for centuries. The former entailed the idea of primitive and the latter of the original inhabitants, the Adivasis. The nationalist leadership, however, viewed Adivasis primarily from the lens of adimjati and hence considered their problems of social and economic backwardness as one arising from isolation. The exploitation was acknowledged, but this remained dormant. The integration of tribes with the so-called mainstream became the buzzword and the making of state agenda in post-Independence India. The special provisions enshrined in the Constitution for tribes must be seen in this light.

The Constitution provides for three distinct kinds of provisions for the Adivasis. These may be referred to as reservation, development and protection. Reservation is provided for under Part III (fundamental rights), development under Part IV (directive principles) and protection under Part X (scheduled and tribal areas) of the Indian Constitution. To reinforce the provisions made in the Constitutions, legislations have been enacted from time to time both by the central and state governments. The acts were concerned broadly with such issues as restriction on alienation and restoration of tribal land, money lending, governance, forest rights, atrocities and so on. Administrative steps were also taken for the implementation of reservation as were the policies and programmes for their economic and social development.

Despite these measures, Adivasis remain the most marginalized community of India today. The number of Adivasis living in poverty is high, the level of literacy is low and health indicators are poor. There has been a phenomenal increase in the number of landless and people with diminishing land areas. The alienation of land from tribes to non-tribes on the one hand and on the other by the displacement of tribes by state-driven projects, such as industries, mining, dams, power, roads, railways and wildlife sanctuaries, were the causes. It is estimated that as many as 21.3 million people were displaced by various development projects in India between 1951 and 1990. Of the total displaced, 8.54 million have been enumerated as tribals. Tribals constitute more than 40 per cent of the internally displaced population, though they are only about 8 per cent of the total population. However, benefits of these development projects did not accrue to the tribal people. All these suggest that the protection that the Constitution and law provides for the Adivasi has been sacrificed for the larger cause of national development and development for population groups other than the tribes.

References

Beteille, A. 'The Concept of Tribe with Special Reference to India'. *European Journal of Sociology* 27, no. 2 (1986): 297–318.

Planning Commission. *Report of the Steering Committee on Empowering the Scheduled Tribes for the Tenth Five Year Plan (2002-07)*. New Delhi: Government of India, 2001.

AMBEDKARITE

V. Geetha

Fundamentally, an Ambedkarite is one whose understanding of society is shaped by Dr B. R. Ambedkar's views and arguments on the Indian social order, polity and economy. An Ambedkarite is also one who espouses 'Ambedkarism', a world view that brings into a unified perspective Dr Ambedkar's ideas on a range of subjects – justice, the state, revolution and ethics – as these unfolded in the course of his life's work and writings.

Keywords associated with Ambedkarism and which an Ambedkarite would hold important include equality, fraternity, democracy, justice, rule of law, oppressed minority, adequate representation, communal electorates, Dalits and political power, constitutional morality, republic, graded inequality, untouchability, annihilation of caste, non-violent social revolution, cause of labour, socialism, conversion out of Hinduism, Buddha, dhamma and maitri.

These terms could be assembled together in diverse ways, and an Ambedkarite's distinctive politics would then depend on the relative importance afforded to this or that term and to the relationship that is established between all these terms. What might unite plural positions is an avowed commitment to the annihilation of caste. In this sense, one might legitimately speak of an 'Ambedkarite' inhabiting a variety of political spaces and being part of different political movements. It is thus possible to be an Ambedkarite and yet be part of a communist party, as the career of the late R. P. More of Maharashtra illustrates; it is equally possible that an Ambedkarite is supportive of regional and ethnic politics, especially when it comes to negotiating Indian federalism, and examples of such Ambedkarites are not wanting in a state like Tamil Nadu. On the other hand, an Ambedkarite might choose to identify with parties that are explicitly committed to Ambedkarism, such as the Republican Party of India and the groups that emerged from it.

Beyond indicating a political identity, being an Ambedkarite marks a certain social disposition: standing in for ways of being and acting that nurture and foster equality and justice in practical ways. Thus, an Ambedkarite might be one who undertakes educational work in specific neighbourhoods, helping children and young people from Dalit communities gain access to schools and colleges; or she or he could be one who mediates state welfare, by providing information and advice on how Dalits might make use of this or that state provision, earmarked for their economic and social progress. Ambedkarites are also at the forefront of struggles that protest day-to-day violations of Dalit dignity and the right to equality; they are likely to be and have been part of campaigns to end inhuman cultural practices imposed on Dalits by dominant castes. In parts of the country, an Ambedkarite could also be a neo-Buddhist, who might not be politically active but is engaged in organizing dhamma meetings or Buddhist cultural events in and through a local *vihara* (educational centre). In the most expansive sense of the term, an Ambedkarite is one who invites people to be part of a new fraternal universe, where mutual human interaction is welcome and necessary for the greater common good.

In political debates, the term 'Ambedkarite' has proved contentious. For instance, in both popular and critical left understanding of Dr Ambedkar's life and work, and Dalit movements, an Ambedkarite is viewed as a 'liberal', looking to state measures to achieve a modicum of social and economic justice; a 'legalist' who does not wish to go beyond what is allowed by the terms of law and the Constitution; and as one who prefers to engage with social rather than economic contradictions and who, therefore, does not view class contradictions as primary. From the Ambedkarite point of view, the philosophy she or he adheres to is committed to ending one of the oldest forms of social injustice, which, in essence, also contains economic injustice and which requires one to vigorously criticize, oppose and opt out of the Hindu faith and on that account work towards the annihilation of the caste order. This position is deemed no less revolutionary than the one that seeks to wage revolution against Capital and a society based on class divisions and economic exploitation.

Ambedkarism sits fruitfully with other distinctive philosophies of social justice and equality. Thus, in Maharashtra, one might often encounter individuals and groups committed to Phule-Ambedkarite thought or to what might be called Phule-Ambedkarite-Marxism. There is also BAMCEF (Backward and Minority Communities Employees Federation) which is active across the country and has consistently put forth a social and cultural philosophy which combines various anti-caste traditions and world views, including those that have to with countercultural figures who have challenged what they define as Brahminical ideals and practices. BAMCEF endorses Ambedkarism as salient to its concerns and has drawn on Ambedkar's arguments to do with Dalits accessing political power to explain and justify the politics of the party that it supports – the Bahujan Samaj Party. In Southern India, Ambedkarism is often aligned to E. V. Ramasamy Periyar's movement and his views on social change, and this relationship has been both fraught and productive.

Ambedkarite feminists or feminist Ambedkarites are a vocal group of people whose complex politics addresses gender realities as these shape the caste order and as they unfold within intimate and familial spaces. The new feminism that pervades the writings of Ambedkarite women places caste oppression, as Dalit and lower-caste women experience it, in the course of their labouring and social lives at the centre of its understanding of patriarchy.

In the twenty-first century, especially in the course of its second decade, Ambedkar Students Associations have emerged in different parts of the country, with a new generation of Ambedkarites redefining and reinterpreting meanings of ideals inherited from the past and from a variety of anti-caste sources. Such associations have attracted not only Dalit students but also young people from diverse social communities.

Since Dr Ambedkar's death in 1956, Ambedkarites have grown in number and a rich, layered and complex literature continues to be produced by those who debate his legacy. The growth of social media and the internet facilitates communication across languages and borders, enabling interesting and significant conversations between those committed to ending the injustice that is caste and those working on issues to do with race or ethnic exploitation. Thus, Ambedkarism has well and truly taken its place alongside other universal philosophies of emancipation – and Ambedkarites, like revolutionaries, belong to a large global community of actors against race, caste and other forms of xenophobia.

References

Omvedt, Gail. *Dalits and the Democratic Revolution*. New Delhi: SAGE Publications, 1997.
Pai, Sudha. *Dalit Assertion and the Unfinished Democratic Revolution: The Bahujan Samaj Party in Uttar Pradesh*. New Delhi: SAGE Publications, 2002.

AMIR GHARIB (AMĪR/GHARĪB)

S. Imtiaz Hasnain and Masood Ali Beg

In casual conversation, the literal meaning associated with both *amir* and *gharib* can be understood in most generalized sense as either 'having something' or 'not having something'. Their denotative capacity further allows them to be used in a wide range of contexts, linguistically, communicatively and situationally. Interestingly, in the South Asian context both amir and gharib dichotomy always allude to antagonistic classes purely in terms of rich–poor. This dichotomy represents an inversely designated cultural and intellectual heritage, which euphemistically identifies cultural poverty with the rich and invests opulence of culture with the poor. For example, expressions like *gharib brahman* or *gharib munshi* (the literate elite) or *gharib maulawi* are reflective of such nuances which are completely glossed over when viewed from the perspective of straight-jacketed, Euro-centric economic parameters alone. *Mera tariq amiri nahi, taqiri hai; khudi na bech gharibi mein naam paida kar*, is a relevant verse by Iqbal in this instance, which means: 'the way of the hermit, not fortune, is mine; sell not your soul! In a beggar's rags, shine.' As separate and distinct words, 'amir' and 'gharib' have other meanings.

Amir is from the Arabic *amara*, which means 'to command'. In this sense, amir along with *sardar* refers to leader, military commander, ruler, prince, a nobleman, chief or a head. It brings richness in literature by providing a range of synonyms such as *rais* or *syed*, all bringing the sense of honour and respect to a referent to which they get attached, for instance, *raisul waqt* (the richest, at a given point), *saiyadul shohda* (the noblest of martyrs) and *saiyadul bashar* (the noblest of humans).

When used to form a compound of the type noun + noun, it undergoes a morphological process of clipping to form *mir* (head, the chief). For instance, *mir-e-mahfil*, *mir-e-karwan* (leader of the caravan mission). Here both *mir-e-karwan* and *amir-e-karwan* are in free variation. This process of compound formation is fairly productive and the likely explanation for amir to change to mir comes from poetics. It is the requirement of metre that generates a couplet like *khuda khud mir-i-majlis bud andar-ul makan Khusro* ('Khusro! God itself leads an assembly in [inside] a celestial place').

As mentioned at the outset, as an adjective, amir in the sense of 'rich' or 'wealthy' or 'affluent' is frequently used in the Hindi and Urdu speech context, such as in *amir admi* and *amir log*. But these seemingly innocuous constructions are laced with sarcasm in the discourse of economically deprived sections of society. For instance, it is quite common to hear expressions like *amir log hamari fikr kyon kare?* ('Why should the rich care for us?') or '*voh ab amir admi ho gaya hai*' ('He has now become a rich man'), said more with a tinge of sarcasm coupled with abhorrence. Its use in opposition to gharib is also fairly common: *karti hai jo gharib ko ham pahlue amir* ('What brings a poor together with the rich'). The following couplet by Iqbal also shows, in a restricted sense, the use of amir (represented as *shaikh*) in the sense of an exploitative capitalist and a merciless feudal lord: *aye Shaikh, amiron ko masjid se nikalwa de* ('O Lord! Please get the rich thrown out of the mosque [as they have not paid money to the poor]').

Today, the term amir does not evoke honour or respect. While in the Arab context, it is perceived in the sense of a chief or head (head of the state or a vice chancellor of university is called Amir), in the South Asian context, amir was rarely in use in the sense of leader. On the contrary, in this sense the term *qaid* was more in use, for example, *qaid-e-azam* (with reference to M. A. Jinnah) or more recently with reference to the late prime minister Atal Bihari Vajpayee ('*mere qaid Atalji nahi rahe*', 'My leader Atalji is no more').

Gharib, in Perso-Arabic tradition, literally means 'strange, uncommon, outlandish, foreign, extraordinary, poor, needy, humble, gentle and docile'. It is very commonly used as part of Arab names, particularly in the context of foreigners. In terms of philology, both gharib and its plural g*haraib* mean 'rare', 'unfamiliar' and consequently 'obscure' (*nadir/munfarid*). With this meaning, its use as the title of several books is very common.

The Arabic word *gharb* means 'west'. The term 'west' semantically can be extended to mean something which is not the 'east' and, therefore, 'foreign'. Hence, in the non-technical, laudatory sense of 'unfamiliar' (sometimes even 'original'), gharib also occurs in works on literary theory, where it is appropriated to evoke the notion of nativity (and, thereby, purity) in language use. The attitude of condemnation towards the use of gharib or unfamiliar was further extended to include in its ambit both prose and oratory.

There is yet another connotation of the term gharib, *namely* poverty. Its use in the sense of 'poor' or 'needy' is not inherent in Arabic usage. However, in Hindi and Urdu speech context this notion is very common, for example, *gharib log, gharib admi*. This meaning may be connected to Sufism, which is etymologically derived from the Arabic word *suf* (wool). The woollen garments of early ascetics were often identified with 'the importance of manifesting spiritual poverty through material poverty' through the use of poor rough clothing. It is in this sense of poverty that relates the Sūfī to the Arabic term *faqir* (mendicant) or its Persian equivalent *darvish* (wanderer), who is regarded as poor on account of hardship borne during his travels.

In the sense of 'journey' or 'traveller', *ghurbat* (derived from gharib) is commonly used. In Urdu poetry, there are many instances showing the use of ghurbat in the sense of 'journey' or 'traveller'.

To conclude, the sense of affluence (amir) and poverty (gharib) is quite pervasive in the political discourse in India and is invariably a strong constituent of election slogans. It has thus been completely incorporated as an integral part of political oratory. The passive acquiescence of and demonstrable resilience to the sudden, knee-jerk proclamation caused by demonetization by a strong section of society could, in fact, come about because of the delusion that it is amir, the Other, who is now the immediate victim. Amir, as an exploiter responsible for making of the 'Self', gharib emboldens the perceived sense of assurance that the grief has finally struck the 'Other'.

References

Bonebakker, S. A. 'Gharīb'. In *The Encyclopaedia of Islam,* edited by B. Lewis, C. H. Pellat and J. Schacht, Assisted by J. Burton-Page, C. Dumont and V. L. Menageas, vol. II. Leiden: E.J. Brill, 1991.

Renard, John. *The A to Z of Sufism.* The A to Z Guide Series, No. 44. Lanham, Toronto, Plymouth: The Scarecrow Press, Inc., 2009.

ANGANWADI (ĀṄGANAVĀḌĪ)

Sarojini Ganju Thakur

The word *āṁganavāḍī* is intrinsically linked to a universal programme of the Government of India, the Integrated Child Development Services (ICDS), a mother and preschool education and child care programme launched in 1975. This programme was meant to penetrate across the length and breadth of the country, including both rural and certain urban areas, through the establishment of āṁganavāḍī centres of the ministry or departments of women and child welfare working in close coordination with the ministry/department of health. These centres provide 'integrated' health, nutrition and preschool education services to children in the 0–6 years group and pregnant and lactating mothers. In recent years, their mandate has also been extended to adolescent girls. Anganwadis are based on the premise that the overall impact of individual services will be greater if they are provided in a convergent manner.

Etymologically, the word *angan* can be translated as 'courtyard', a confined space usually within a house. Then āṁganavāḍī would literally translate to 'courtyard shelter', and in the programme the public space for the programme notionally defines the accessibility, protection and familiarity of the more private space. Interestingly, while 'angan' is a Hindi/Urdu word, through its link with the programme the concept of āṁganavāḍī has come to be accepted, used and understood throughout India.

The ICDS has approximately 7,000 projects and 14,000,000 āṁganavāḍī centres spread over the twenty-nine states and seven Union Territories of India. The funding pattern of ICDS between the central and state governments varies from state to state. For special-category states like Himachal Pradesh, it is 90:10 but for other states it is 60:40. According to the scheme, all children up to 6 and pregnant and lactating mothers of the country are covered by this scheme. Anganwadis visibly embody the penetration of governance to every corner of the country and, in contrast to the overall top-down nature of governance, it also represents the localization of governance. Given the huge impact and coverage of this scheme in some states, development partners such as UNICEF, WFP, WB and DFID have also been involved with the implementation of certain aspects of the scheme.

The scheme is primarily welfarist, offering a package of six services, namely, supplementary nutrition (SN), preschool non-formal education, nutrition and health education, immunization, health check-up and referral services.

SN is a very important aspect of the scheme and in fact has often overshadowed other services. SN is intended to meet the gap between the average daily intake of children and the recommended dietary allowance. It takes the form of snacks and hot meals for children belonging to the 3–6 year age group who come to the āṁganavāḍī and take-home rations for children under the age of 3 and pregnant and lactating mothers and includes provision of folic acid for adolescent girls and pregnant and lactating mothers to deal with iron deficiency. The actual nutrition provided varies from state to state.

The ICDS team comprises the Aṁganavāḍī workers (AWWs), āṁganavāḍī helpers, supervisors, child development project officers (CDPOs) and district programme officers (DPOs). The AWW is usually a woman who belongs to the local community where the āṁganavāḍī is located and is considered an honourary worker. She gets an honourarium, contributed to by both the central and state governments. AWWs have often raised questions about the quantum and nature of the honourarium, given the time and responsibility attached to working in the āṁganavāḍī. Āṁganavāḍī helpers assist the AWW, generally, but are often involved in meal preparation, assistance in looking after the children and in general cleanliness of the āṁganavāḍī. In addition to these workers, medical officers and accredited social health activists (ASHAs) are also actively involved with the AWWs to ensure immunization and vaccination of the children, thus achieving convergence of different services.

Evaluation of the impact of the programme also varies from state to state. However, in general terms, the āṁganavāḍī has been responsible for spreading awareness of and ensuring immunization, monitoring the growth and weight of children, knowledge of antenatal and postnatal care, preschool education and supplementary nutrition. In recent years, there has been an effort to strengthen and restructure the ICDS through a series of programmatic and management reforms. These reforms have been aimed at certain qualitative aspects, such strengthening the early childhood care and education (ECCE) aspect and focus more significantly not only on children under 3 years of age, identification of severe and moderate malnutrition and improved monitoring of the programme but also on the provision of improved infrastructure, including construction of buildings for āṁganavāḍī centres in a phase-wise manner.

In fact, anganwadis embody the presence of government, and their influence and ambit extend to the implementation of most initiatives at grass-roots level. This includes the organization of self-help groups for women or the schemes for adolescent girls but are equally critical for the successful implementation of the National Rural Health Mission. In the recent past, āṁganavāḍī workers have been involved with the registration of children under the Ādhāra scheme and in the electoral process as well! The āṁganavāḍī program in India is the world's largest for early childhood development and is a very visible aspect of the presence of Government of India even in its remotest corners.

References

Gupta, Akhil. 'Governing Population: The Integrated Child Development Services Program in India'. *States of Imagination: Ethnographic Explorations of the Postcolonial State* (2001): 65–96.

Palriwala, Rajni and N. Neetha. 'Care Arrangements and Bargains: Anganwadi and Paid Domestic Workers in India'. *International Labour Review* 149, no. 4 (2010): 511–27.

AYUSH (ĀYŪṢ)

Madhulika Banerjee

AYUSH, acronym for Ayurveda, yōga (and naturopathy), Unani, siddha (and sowa rigpa) and homeopathy, is the official name given to living traditions of medical knowledge, practised widely across the Indian subcontinent and now also across some parts of the globe. Yet, of them Ayurveda, yōga and siddha most clearly originated in India, while the other four were founded elsewhere and then took root here. Unani, as the name suggests, has its origin in Greece, in the tradition of Socrates, Hippocrates and Galen. It evolved in West Asia through an interesting combination of healing traditions, including those from the Indian subcontinent, at the court of the Persian rulers. When it came to the Indian subcontinent with the wandering Sufis and later rulers, it expanded its pharmacopoeia by learning from, as well as lending its knowledge to, the medical knowledge systems that were already in use here. Homeopathy was an eighteenth-century German medical knowledge system that came to India by the nineteenth and then flourished in many parts of the subcontinent. While it continues to flourish here even today, it exists on the margins in Germany and other parts of Europe. Naturopathy developed in Europe, as part of the struggle to retain the vestiges of the knowledge of the herbal medical system that was rendered obsolete by biomedicine. Sowa rigpa is a Tibetan medical tradition that is based on Buddhist literature and has its origins in the Himalayan ranges. These living traditions of medical practice existed separately, yet in close relation to each other for a very long period of time. They contain within themselves great diversity and the umbrella term under which they come together, AYUSH, is a curiously modern identity created by the contemporary postcolonial nation-state of India.

The beginnings of the AYUSH traditions, with the exception of homeopathy and naturopathy, date to about 3000 BCE to the early years of this millennium. They each have clearly worked out epistemologies in written texts, though operationalized with reference to the specific contexts in which they are rooted. At the same time, they have also continuously innovated on the basis of learning and lending with each other. This process of enrichment of these systems encountered a different path in their encounter with biomedicine, the medical knowledge that evolved in post-Enlightenment Europe. While the early encounters continued the trajectories of mutual exchange, the paradigmatic difference with biomedicine marked the predominant development of the AYUSH systems from the nineteenth century onwards.

The commonality in the epistemology of these systems is derived from their understanding of the body: in external terms, in its agro-ecological context, and in internal terms, a mélange of humours and organs in symbiotic relationships with each other. Thus, there are distinctive methods of diagnosis, prognosis and treatment regimens, the latter including procedures as well as materials. The first foundational commonality lies in their understanding of the relationship of human beings with nature. That they both belong to the same elements yields significant insights – that the harmony within the body is guided by the harmony without; so, they can never be separated from each other. This aspect has implications for their relevance in contemporary times, which will be discussed later on.

One of the most important aspects of the contemporary AYUSH is its legacy from the experience of colonialism through the gradual domination of biomedicine. Biomedicine did not come as a finished, complete medical knowledge system with the onset of colonialism but actually evolved throughout the colonial period. But its perspectives of mind–body duality, the identification of microbial causes for disease, its systems of diagnosis, prognosis and externalizing of treatment drew it as one apart and away from all the AYUSH systems. Its remarkable achievements complemented those in firepower, commerce and bureaucracy, altogether constituting a network of power that undermined the knowledge structure of not just AYUSH but also those ranging from shipbuilding to weaving to agricultural practices and irrigation systems.

A great many scholars have characterized it as an encounter in which the AYUSH systems were challenged, belittled and undermined as credible medical systems, positioned clearly as the Other of biomedicine. Many scholars have pointed to the vigorous response offered by these systems. These were through processes of mass manufacture and the advertisement-led marketing of their medicines, the creation of modern teaching and research institutions for these systems, printing of their textbooks in English and other Indian languages and adoption of the modern title of 'Doctor' – markers of modernization and homogenization, leading mostly to creating a Double of biomedicine. However, each tradition undertook this process in its own way, leading to a great variety of doubles available. In this too, it must be pointed out that there was a real struggle by each of the systems to retain some of the 'glory' and their specificity as markers.

In this process, these systems have shown remarkable resilience, developing capacities to adapt and to learn. Practitioners of these systems are able to read and analyse diagnostic tests continuously developed in the biomedical world, keep track of new research and findings published in the best journals and also know the specific properties of new molecules and formulations that continuously hit the market. No doubt this is a response in defence, in order to keep up their practice, a great majority of them having lost confidence in the systems they were trained in, opting to prescribe in the allopathic mould. There is a proportion of them, however, that do this in order to actually proffer a translation of categories across epistemological divides and a furthering of medical knowledge that only such a detailed and nuanced exchange can bring. This is an aspect of the AYUSH community that is not known to even the common allopathic medical practitioner community, which harbour biases and reservations about their counterparts much like the common public does. This is unfortunate because of a lost potential of dialogue between medical knowledge systems that could actually break through frontiers of medicine and which are instead mired in received structures of power. Much of the responsibility for this rests with the politics of the postcolonial state and its policies towards these systems.

During the anti-colonial struggle, visionary practitioners of Ayurveda and Unani had created and vigorously lobbied with nationalist forces to recognize them and give them credibility. The dominant segment of nationalists was keen on modernization in general and not interested in traditional knowledge systems. So, for AYUSH, in addition to the struggle against the colonial state, it was a struggle against the dominant nationalists as well, an aspect that was carried over to the postcolonial period. Numerous committees and reports recommended institutional and regulatory frameworks for traditional medical knowledge systems, but the bottom line remained that the bulk of the outlay of government expenditure was always on biomedicine and a very small portion on all seven of the AYUSH streams put together. Following long years of struggle by AYUSH practitioners, a Central Council for Indian Medicine and seven Central Councils for Research, one for each of the streams, were established. This caused a transformation of the locus of institutional interest in them, leading to the creation of a separate wing of the Ministry for Health and Family Welfare in 2000 (initially called 'Indian Systems of Medicine and Homeopathy' [ISM&H]). The NDA government that took over in 2014 created a separate ministry for AYUSH. It is important to note, however, that the financial outlay proportions between allopathy and AYUSH remain the same.

As stated earlier, one of the strong counters to the colonial regime and its espousal of biomedicine was the creation of modern, mass manufacturing units of ayurvedic and Unani medicines. Between 1885 and 1910, a whole array of companies was set up – Dabur, Hindustani Dawakhana, Baidyanath, Zandu, Kalpataru Medical Company, Sharifi Dawakhana, Arya Vaidya Sala Kottakkal, Arya Vaidya Pharmacy Coimbatore and Hamdard. Each of these is easily recognizable even today – indicating a story of ingenious adaptation and innovation undertaken by these companies to keep the AYUSH systems a force to contend with commercially. The earliest expectation from creating these companies was that consumers, who were familiar with these products culturally, would be more inclined to use them when able to access them off the shelf readily at the market, just like the pills and syrups of allopathy. Familiarity and trust were expected to be the twin foundations of the prosperity of these firms. From this point, they standardized the mass production of the 'classical medicines' (those spelt out in the source texts), adapting modern machinery created for other purposes to undertake the arduous processes of grinding, filtering, straining, condensation, experimenting with fuels for boiling and slow cooking and using the tableting machines of modern pharma companies to create the complex measures of pills that had been made by hand before. They adapted the capacity of traditional practitioners to create unique formulations based on those given in the classical texts, into the modern category of patent and proprietary medicines, supported by the law by an amendment to the Drugs and Cosmetics Act in 1974. For both categories, they adapted, too, their traditionally prescribed systems of quality control both to the machinery and the new perspectives, continuously having to defend their practices to modern regulatory and market imperatives. For this, they conducted simple validation experiments to complex clinical trials, having to continuously adapt the parameters they were forced to use, as received from the modern disciplines of biochemistry and the pharmaceutical industry. Further, they had to accept and respond to the market's innovations on packaging, to keep their feet firmly in the contemporary.

By far the most important innovation that these companies have made was to position a great part of their products as fast-moving consumer goods (FMCGs). The AYUSH systems are founded on the belief that food is medicine/medicine is food, and that a range of natural products within easy reach can take care of daily health requirements. This foundational idea is transformed into the FMCG sector – the category that commercial enterprises understand

and consumers can relate to. The outcome is a range of everyday cosmetics and nutritional and health supplements, supported by ingenious marketing that points to the judicious mix of tradition and modernity in these products, with an appeal to the nationalist pride of the beleaguered middle class. It is important to point out, however, that not everyone necessarily followed the trajectory of classical medicines to proprietary medicines to FMCG – a company like Hamdard, for instance, began its presence in the market with RoohAfza, a sherbet that is popular to this day, before it was known for its other formulations.

It is this segment of the pharmaceutical market that realized its potential in the global wave of 'the herbal' in the 1990s. The search for new molecules by companies in the United States and Europe and for preventive and less harsh medicines by consumers had generated a demand for herbal medicines that they had relegated to their obsolescent past not so long ago. This had already created a niche market there and given the leadership they provided for markets worldwide, it was clear that this trend would catch on in the Global South as well. AYUSH manufacturers could see this coming and, for the first time, they were able to mount a collective and somewhat united pressure on the central government to demonstrate its commitment to creating policies that would help them both at home and in the world. The creation of the ISM&H department, the first separate policy on traditional medicine in the country, predating the one from the World Health Organization (WHO), formulating Good Manufacturing, Laboratory, Agricultural (for raw materials) and Trade practices were all initiatives aimed at preparing this sector for legitimacy and credibility in the international market. The process was not easy – they faced quick reprisals internationally by way of official committees in the UK and Europe slotting them in hierarchies that would clearly disadvantage them. In the United States, ill-informed and poorly argued academic debates in established scientific journals around the content of heavy metals in Ayurvedic medicines served to create an abiding doubt about their veracity. Those battles continue and AYUSH products still cannot be sold or dispensed as medicines – they can only be prescribed and sold as food supplements. But the practitioner-entrepreneurs, from India at least, are not about to give up. They are engaged in continuous lobbying for a change in policy, while the practitioner-researchers are engaged in working on the efficacy of these medicines in collaboration with mainstream research institutions like the National Institutes of Health in the United States.

If there is a possible exception to this trajectory from within the AYUSH, it would be that of yōga. Principally, because it was not material product-oriented body of knowledge, it was not involved in the processes of commercialization such as was Ayurveda, Unani, siddha, sowa rigpa or indeed even naturopathy. While it is known to have been around for a very long period of time, the presence and spread of yōga in precolonial and colonial India have not been systematically studied. It was known to be the niche practice of those who devoted their life to religious study, but if it ever belonged to the everyday routine of ordinary people is not exactly understood. Like all other systems, the widespread and diverse nature of yōga is evident in the existence of the many schools, the principles and practice of which may have been known to a close circuit of yogis. Its movement across nations, along with the religious ideas of Hinduism in the nineteenth century, is well known and documented.

If this account of contemporary AYUSH were to indicate that it is the state, the market and institutional debates where it is housed, nothing could be more insubstantial. In India, where so much of significance lies outside the realm of the state, the market and other institutions, AYUSH does so likewise. Community health initiatives, non-governmental organizations as well as discrete individual interventions characterize the presence of these systems all over the country. As elsewhere, contestations, negotiations, debates and innovations characterize this space and it is as lively and active as the other two. A range of initiatives are being carried out across the country, such as creating systems of legitimizing non-institutionally trained, but widely accepted as legitimate, healers, forging programmes of accountability for public health programmes, drives for setting up home herbal gardens in both rural and urban settings, creating small units for making herbal medicines under the guidance of local practitioners for local consumption at nominal rates and encouraging farmers to take up the cultivation of medicinal and aromatic plants that would fetch good prices and supplement their incomes. Of these, the setting up of home herbal gardens to make people more comfortable with using plants to heal themselves, as also the attention to local production of medicine for local use, challenges the modern health concepts of dependence on chemical-based medicines and the centralized, unsustainable form of manufacture considered necessary to make affordable medicines accessible to all. These are, in many ways, more interesting, because this is where the possibilities of collective action around health are best played out, as also the explorations of the future sustainability of AYUSH – commercially and climatically. From the WHO's call for 'Health for All' in the Alma-Ata declaration of 1978, expected to be reiterated forty years hence in 2018, this is the space that has the potential to transpose the slogan to 'health by all'.

References

Alavi, S. *Islam and Healing: Loss and Recovery of an Indo-Muslim Medical Tradition 1600–1900*. Ranikhet: Permanent Black, 2007.
Arnold, D. *Science, Technology and Medicine in India*. New Delhi: Cambridge University Press, 2000.

BHAICHARA (BHĀ'ĪCĀRĀ)

Satish Aikant

Bhaichara (literally meaning 'brotherhood', from *bhai*, Hindi for 'brother') has characterized Indian society since the earliest periods of history as a significant organizing principle of social life. All tribal groups in the past had shared strong bonds of solidarity, reflected in successive social formations. Myths and rituals have played an important part in promoting solidarity among various groups. Fairs and festivals in India bring about cultural integration and play a crucial role in bringing about bhaichara among communities. Usually celebrated in the carnivalesque, open-space festivals like Holi, Deepavali and Eid constantly challenge the categories of 'public' and 'private'. Interstitial outside of public spaces, such as bazaars and street corner shops, acts as the meeting point of several communities.

The antecedents of the concept of bhaichara can be found in the composite culture which came into existence with the influx into India of travellers, invaders and migrants, including first the Aryans and later the Mughals and then the British. Indeed, India is an amalgam of several religious communities. It is the spirit of bhaichara which characterizes this syncreticism. Ashoka (304–232 BCE) embraced the concept wholeheartedly after the Kalinga War. The reign of Akbar (1542–1605 CE), especially, was marked by the spirit of Hindu–Muslim synthesis and harmony, as displayed in the new religion that he founded, Din-i-Ilahi (Religion of God). However, it is the medieval bhakti poets who laid the strong tradition of bhaichara among the people by breaking down barriers of caste and religion. Kabir (1398–1448) was a great votary, as were Ravidas (1398–1540), Guru Nanak (1469–1539) and Jyotirao Phule (1827–1890). Amir Khusrau (1253–1325), a great Sūfī poet, made seminal contribution to the composite culture of North India. The teachings of these saints and poets found their fruition in what has come to be known as the *Ganga-Jamuni tehzib*, that is, the culture of the land between the two rivers of Ganga and Yamuna, though composite culture is not essentially restricted to North India.

The Progressive Writers' Movement in 1930s and 1940s North India further underscored the discourse of social harmony. Premchand's well-known stories like 'Mandir aur Masjid' and 'Himsa Paramo Dharmo' are not only literary masterpieces but also show deep impact on his mind of India's composite culture.

In modern India, Mahatma Gandhi showed unequalled passion and commitment to communal harmony. His crusade was directed not only against the British colonial power but also at fighting social injustice and untouchability which he considered to be the foremost evil. Gandhi spread the message of Hindu–Muslim unity and worked for it. Nehru's idealistic and secular approach to politics laid the foundation for the ethos that has prevailed in India since Independence. He carried the principle of brotherhood to the international arena. It is he who in his idealistic exuberance coined the slogan *Hindi Chini Bhai Bhai* ('Indians and Chinese are brothers'), even though the relations between India and China had not always followed this normative framework.

Bhaichara has found much favour in popular culture in India, especially in Bombay cinema. The Nehruvian era was characterized by idealism and the moral vision of films such as *Paigham* (1959) and *Dosti* (1964). The 1977 blockbuster Hindi film *Amar Akbar Anthony* which celebrates 'unity in diversity', bridging religious divisions between Hindu, Christian and Muslim, can be read as a parable of secular India.

A disturbing feature of clannish solidarity which runs counter to the spirit of bhaichara is the social institution of khap panchayats in Northern India, which represent themselves as 'custodians of honour', claiming to be autonomous from the state to avoid legal sanctions. They are medieval remnants of regressive tribal societies that have persisted in the modern liberal age. Barring such aberrations, bhaichara as a felicitous concept continues to be the bedrock of social/communal harmony in India.

References

Chakrabarty, Dipesh. *Habitations of Modernity: Essays in the Wake of Subaltern Studies*. Ranikhet: Permanent Black, 2002.

Dwyer, Rachel and Christopher Pinney, eds. *Pleasure and the Nation: The History, Politics and Consumption of Public Culture in India*. New Delhi: Oxford University Press, 2001.

CHANDRAYAAN (CANDRAYĀṆ)

Gopal N. Raj

The name 'Chandrayaan' has become inextricably linked with Indian Space Research Organisation's (ISRO) programme for robotic lunar exploration. ISRO had initially suggested calling the spacecraft it proposed to send to the Moon 'Somayaan'. But, when Prime Minister Atal Bihari Vajpayee announced India's first voyage of cosmic exploration in his 2003 Independence Day address, he christened it 'Chandrayaan-1'.

A Moon shot was a radical departure from ISRO's well-defined trajectory, which produced satellites for remote sensing, communications, broadcasting and weather monitoring and place them in orbit around Earth; these activities were not glamorous but served practical needs. The eye-catching lunar mission, on the other hand, created tremendous excitement and pride within the space agency as well as among the wider Indian public. It was also noticed internationally, adding to the sense of India making its mark as a rising global power.

Although many spacecrafts had already gone to the Moon and humans had walked on it, important scientific questions about Earth's natural satellite still remained. The Chandrayaan-1 was designed to orbit the Moon while its instruments took images and gathered data. The probe carried instruments made by ISRO's own units as well as from abroad. A small 'Moon Impact Probe' that detached from the spacecraft and fell to the lunar surface – to plant the Indian flag, as it were – was included at the suggestion of former president, late A. P. J. Abdul Kalam.

Chandrayaan-1 drew on ISRO's years of experience in building, launching and operating satellites. It was launched on 22 October 2008 and entered lunar orbit on 8 November that year. But, malfunctions that began less than three weeks after the launch (although not made public at the time) led to the mission's premature termination after only about ten months in space.

Even so, the mission accomplished a great deal before it ended, including giving ISRO the experience to undertake more challenging efforts at space exploration. India's subsequent, and much lauded, Mars probe launched in 2013, which the popular press named 'Mangalyaan' (ISRO called it simply 'Mars Orbiter Mission'), was a direct offshoot.

More recently, in 2019, ISRO launched its second lunar mission, Chandrayaan-2. A robotic lander, carrying a small rover, crashed in the final moments of its descent to the lunar surface. However, an orbiter, equipped with eight scientific instruments, is circling the moon.

More planetary exploration is planned. Another spacecraft that will go to Mars is on the anvil and a mission to Venus is being prepared. Others will doubtless follow. Chandrayaan-1 marked the start of this chapter in ISRO's history.

References

Current Science, Special Section: Chandrayaan-1, 96, no. 4 (2009): 486–546.

Kasturirangan, Krishnaswamy. 'Space Science in India: Two Recent Initiatives', Sir Jagdish Chandra Bose Memorial Lecture, delivered at The Royal Society, London, 2004.

DALIT (DALIT)

Gopal Guru

Dalit is a modern word whose origins have been traced by Romila Thapar to Pali, the language of ancient Buddhist literature. However, the term acquired political salience in the early twentieth century in the writings and speeches of Babasaheb Ambedkar. In the post-Ambedkar period, this word finds spectacular presence in the 1972 manifesto of the Dalit Panthers. Today, the word has acquired wide political currency in India, In the field of formal academic scholarship, scholars have used the word quite freely. This free use of the word does not have any bearing on the original meaning that this word was infused with in the manifesto of the Dalit Panthers. The manifesto sought to see this word as founded on the singular meaning of caste exploitation. It strongly connoted victimhood: Dalits were victims, physically and mentally ground down by caste exploitation. This is a passive definition set against the expansive meaning adopted by the Dalit Panthers. However, reading Dalit exclusively in terms of caste has acquired currency today in politics and the mass media.

The concept Dalit is no doubt sociologically constituted and historically arrived at. But it refuses to be defined in terms of victimhood and political passivity. Non-Dalits also use this word as if it is a concrete object, a pathological object. In fact, the word Dalit is politically constituted only in opposition to other contending words such as Harijans, SCs and Buddhists. In fact, the word Dalit militates against the word Harijan, which is removed from social contradiction. Harijan is a word that places itself in a position in which people are no longer responsive to understand the concrete world, which is organized around the cognitive world of differentiation, polarization and classification. Harijan takes itself out of a position of contestation and locates itself in the realm of the theological and the spiritual, both of which are fundamentally non-cognitive. Unlike such a word, Dalit participates in the political project and makes it intensely contestable.

Similarly, the word Dalit is different from 'scheduled caste' or 'SC'. SC is found in the language of legal rights and acquires relevance within the logic of a policy regime. SC is part of the pacifying structure controlled by the state. The word Dalit, on the other hand, exists outside this patronizing location. It is a word of struggle; it is a word which acquires its essence through the assertion of one's moral right to dignity. In fact, this word has come up in the context of the limits of the language of individual rights, which may guarantee a Dalit the advantage of self-esteem but not of self-respect. Self-esteem based on positional good can be developed by using the support of state institutions, but self-respect can be acquired only outside patronizing state institutions. Dalit carries a political charge and is confrontationist in orientation. In its political expression, it carries the intense power of resistance.

The word Dalit is not available to quotidian polemics. It is not a polemical word in the sense that it is suffused with unified and rigorously controllable meaning. In polemics, on the other hand, the looseness of the internal content of a word allows the polemicist to play with its different meanings. Thus, for the postmodernist polemicist, words are used only for meaning-making. Meaning with effective degree of coherence acquires its essence not from other words but from the reality which stands outside the word but ultimately becomes integral to it. The word Dalit, however, establishes it rigour through its oppositional relationship with other words. The identity of this word is not secured by definition but by a process involving a display of its power vis-à-vis the pacificatory power of Harijan, SC and even non-Ambedkarite Buddhists. The word Dalit becomes transparent through its power display. It does not hide its power. Because of its determinative force and internal coherence, it refuses to be reduced to either 'untouchable' or its extension 'Mahadalit'. In other words, it is neither extendable in terms of its instrumental use by interested parties nor is it expandable in terms of its transformative meaning which is still at its core.

The ground of the meaning assigned by the upper castes to the word Dalit is constitutive of the incarcerated and stigmatized lives of millions of Dalits in India. The innocent use of the word Dalit tends to stabilize itself in the limits of its very meaning. When used with such intention, the word Dalit is pushed into a state of frozenness and is forced to encounter its semantic death. Dalit then gets reduced to an empty shell, an empty signifier. Thanks to the cast of mind that celebrates this death of a live word. Is not Dalit then a keyword to access the complexities of the casts of mind?

References

Omvedt, Gail. *Dalits and the Democratic Revolution: Dr Ambedkar and the Dalit Movement in Colonial India*. SAGE Publications India, 1994.
Webster, John C. B. 'Who Is a Dalit'. *Untouchable, Dalits in Modern India* (1999): 11–19.

DEMOCRACY

Peter Ronald deSouza

In an opinion survey conducted in 2006, as part of a larger study on the state of democracy in South Asia, 5,205 respondents were asked an open-ended question: 'Why is democracy understood differently by different people. According to you what is democracy?' The question was translated in all the Indian languages. They were entitled to give two responses each. Ninety-nine different responses were received which were then grouped into the following seven clusters: (i) people's rule, (ii) parties and elections, (iii) law and institutions, (iv) rights and freedom, (v) social justice and equality, (vi) development and welfare and (vii) peace and security. A few had a negative attitude to democracy. From the varied responses, we see that not only does democracy in India carry the whole normative burden of development, justice, rights, equality, peace and government formation, it also has, since Independence, acquired the status of a common sense in Indian politics. Democracy in India is the magic potion that will solve all ills and meet the myriad expectations of ordinary people. In the village gram sabha, local disputes are settled by a show of hands. While *gantantr* or *prajatantr* are Hindi translations of the word democracy, it is fair to say that the word democracy itself has become a keyword in all the Indian *Bhasas*.

The credit for this must go to the Indian Constitution. With the stroke of the pen, and not because of a long struggle, the people of India were given the gift of universal franchise. All adult Indians irrespective of gender, education, caste, community, property or status acquired the right, as Schumpeter described it, to choose who was to govern them for a fixed period. In spite of a freedom movement, and of the colonial constitutions of 1919 and 1935 where there was limited democracy, it was the adoption of the Constitution of 1950, by 'we the people', which installed the architecture of democracy and inaugurated the era of popular control over decision makers and of political equality. It was the inspired leadership at Independence and, it must be acknowledged, a postcolonial romance about a new nation that set India on this irreversible democratic path.

Indian democracy has all the elements of a vibrant democracy: regular elections which are free and fair; peaceful succession; a competitive party system; a fairly independent press; an articulate but fragmented elite; an autonomous judiciary; separation of powers into legislature, executive and judiciary; elected representatives at all tiers of government: national, state and local; oversight institutions such as the SCI, CAG, ECI, CVC and CBI; diverse social movements; and many non-party political formations. India also has a long culture of philosophical and political dissent from Buddhism onwards to Naxalism today. It is a plural cultural space that finds manifestation in the process of intense political contestation.

Seventy years of a working democracy have qualitatively transformed, and is transforming, the social landscape of an old society and an older civilization. Although Indian democracy has all the problems and challenges that democracies elsewhere experience, such as elite capture of institutions, arrogance of political leaders, a criminalization of politics, ethno-religious mobilization, excessive influence of money power, invisibilization of the protests of those excluded, a structure of law often inhibiting the delivery of justice and the domination of the public discourse by an elite, Indian democracy has still succeeded in converting the social landscape from a hierarchical to an aspiring egalitarian one. Democracy in India is work in progress. Any inconvenience is regretted.

When analysing Indian democracy, two questions need to be asked together: What is democracy doing to India? – the transformation question detailed earlier – and the converse, what is India doing to democracy? This latter question implies that Indian democracy offers conceptual challenges to the global discourse on democracy beginning with the normative overload which the concept carries, to the fashioning of relevant terms to describe it, such as non-party political formations instead of civil society, or *dharanā, rasta roko* and *ghērāva*, as forms of protest, or *satyagraha* as civil disobedience. Responding to both questions gives one a sense of the unique historical transformation that is currently underway in India, because of democracy.

References

deSouza, Peter Ronald. 'The Indian Commonsense of Democracy', no. 576, Seminar-India, 2007, New Delhi.

Sheth, D. L. *At Home with Democracy*, edited and an introduction by Peter Ronald deSouza. New Delhi: Palgrave Macmillan, 2017.

DISABILITY

Annie Koshi

Historically, disability has been understood as the 'inability' to function according to certain standards set by society. How did we come to understand a difference as an inability? To answer this question, an examination of the connotations and meanings of a few words in some of our languages, in the light of recent advances in disability studies, is germane.

In the Hindi-speaking belt, the terms *seedha* and *seedhi* are often used to address individuals who are not capable of divergent, abstract thinking, alongside terms such as *bholi*, *bawla* and *bhola* for individuals who are generally slow in cognition. The term *budwak* is used in Bihar, *bhondu* in western Uttar Pradesh and *mandabuddhi* in Kerala for individuals with mental retardation. In casual talk, these words also often lend themselves as derogatory terms for the non-disabled as well. The same is the case with other terms used for physical impairment: be it *zuk-zii-skyon-ba* in Bhoti or Ladhaki or *loola* and *langda* in Hindi for people having issue with mobility. In a slightly different case, the name of the blind Bhakti poet, Surdas, has come to be used to mockingly refer to persons with visual impairment. In all, it can be safely said that most words that have been used to denote disability in one form or the other have crossed over from being used to just describe people with specific disabilities and entered generic conversation for casting aspersions on others.

The dichotomies in our parlance are 'normal' versus 'abnormal', 'abled' versus 'disabled' and 'typical' versus 'atypical'. All of these situate the challenged within a socio-medical framework. They have far-reaching implications on perceptions, attitudes and consequent interventions. A case in point is the word *divyang* (divine limbed) that has recently seen a surge. This word for disability was popularized by Prime Minister Narendra Modi in his monthly programme on the state radio and TV channel, *Mann ki Baat*. Besides using the word divyang, he had also specifically referred to persons with visual impairment as *pragyachakshu* (wise-eyed). It meant to be in opposition to *viklang*, which strikes a direct reference to lack of ability. Despite the negative connotation that viklang carries, its usage was official. The word figured on the names of institutions and organizations that worked for the visually challenged. Following the prime minister's directive, the Ministry of Social Justice and Empowerment ordered an official change in terminology. The state had effectively stepped into a renaming that was actually a perspective-building.

A study of the usage and promotion of the term 'divyang' suggests that the term sets us back a few years in terms of disability rights. Conferring a benign status to people with disability obscures the real problems they face and is flagrantly patronizing. However, phrases such as these in truth centre perceive disability only as a 'weakness' to be viewed by the non-disabled as worthy only of charity. Such perspectives do not to fully entitle the disabled to equitable employment, medical care or education and therefore inclusion.

This brings us to the question: what then is disability? Is it an individual's problem or a social construct tinged with attitudes and perceptions that construct the narrative around the word which calls for weeding out nonconformity or the atypical? Disability is a state that is imposed and recognized by society and governmentality. The pseudo-valorization of the disabled as objects of charity or medical cases distances us from a rights-based approach, where society is required to modify infrastructure and environment to accommodate the individual, rather than requiring the individual to change and adapt. In other words, when disability is seen as an abnormality and ascribed divinity, there is less emphasis on how the environment needs to be structured, rather society delineates and marginalizes the group because they are unable to adapt to existing structures.

Transcending conventional ideas of intellectual and physical impairment to include social and financial challenges, disability studies contribute to inclusion/exclusion studies as well. Such studies will help celebrate rather than rue diversity.

References

Bhattacharya, T. 'The Language of Disability: A Linguistic Analysis'. University of Delhi, 2009.
Prime Minister's Office. 'Text of PM's speech at SamajikAdhikaritaShivir for distribution of aids and assistive devices in Varanasi'. Delivered on 22 January 2016. Available at: http://www.pmindia.gov.in/en/news_updates/text-of-pms-speech-at-samajik-adhikarita-shivir-for-distribution-of-aids-and-assistive-devices-in-varanasi-22-01-2016/?comment=disable (December 2018).

DOWRY (DAHĒJ)

N. Jayaram

Dowry (*dahej*, in Hindi) is an institutionalized practice of giving gifts in cash or kind or both to a bridegroom or his (extended) family on behalf of the bride's family at the time of the wedding or very soon after. It is a common marital tradition in the Indian subcontinent, dating back centuries. It ostensibly emphasizes marriage as a relationship not just between two individuals but also between two families.

Dowry is different from 'brideprice' or 'bridewealth', which is a transfer of resources from the bridegroom's family to the bride's family in acknowledgement of the transfer of rights over the bride's productive and reproductive capabilities. It is a form of compensation to the bride's family for the loss of her labour. Whereas dowry is seen as a sort of compensation to the bridegroom's parents for taking on a 'non-productive' family member, as a sort of 'pre-mortem inheritance', in societies where daughter's inheritance rights in parental property are assumed to be commuted into dowry given at the time of her wedding.

There is no consensus on the origins of dowry in India. Generally, there is a correlation between the bridegroom's educational qualification and occupational standing, on the one hand, and the amount of money and the monetary value of gifts given, on the other.

Giving or receiving of dowry, especially what and how much is given or received, reflects the prestige of the families involved; it may mean upward mobility for the bride and thereby her natal family. Over the last century, many lower and middle caste groups which formerly gave brideprice or bride wealth now insist on receiving dowry. Dowry has also gained ground among non-Hindus – Christians, Muslims and tribal communities – whose religious ethos gives it no explicit approval.

Parents start saving for their daughter's dowry from her birth, placing a heavy financial burden on families of lower socio-economic background. At the same time, the practice of dowry results in the circulation of wealth within the endogamous sub-castes, contributing to sub-caste solidarity. Given the predominantly patriarchal family system in India, dowry is also assumed to be a form of 'bribe' to ensure fair treatment of the bride at her in-laws' household and insurance to cover any eventuality the bridegroom may face regarding his health or economic position.

Demanding dowry as a precondition for marriage is now regarded as extortionate and a punishable offence. The Dowry Prohibition Act, 1961 (amended in 1983) and Sections 304B and 498A[9] of the Indian Penal Code prohibit the request or demand and payment or acceptance of dowry 'as consideration for marriage'.

Law, however, has had limited effect. The highest number of crimes committed against married women is by husbands and their family due to dowry. An average of 302 such cases, including 20 dowry deaths, are reported every day, but the conviction rate is a dismal 35 per cent. Another deleterious fallout of the practice of dowry is the psychological ill treatment meted out to brides who cannot meet the bridegroom's or his family's dowry demands, such as abetting her suicide. The preference for the male child and female infanticide/foeticide, resulting in a skewed sex ratio unfavourable to girls, is also attributed to the practice of dowry. The pathology of dowry, therefore, exposes the contradiction between a regressive social practice and an ineffective social legislation.

References

Basu, Srimati. *Dowry and Inheritance*. New Delhi: Women Unlimited, 2005.
Kohli, Hari Dev and Suman Nalwa. *Law Relating to Dowry, Dowry Death, Cruelty to Women and Domestic Violence*. New Delhi: Universal Law Publishing Company, 2011.

GANDHIAN

Sudarsan Padmanabhan

The term 'Gandhian' has been inspired by the historical Gandhi. Interestingly, it is attached less to the persona of Mohandas Karamchand Gandhi and more to the larger than life figure of Mahatma Gandhi, known variously as the Great Soul or the apostle of peace. The term 'Gandhian' has been iconized in the form of Gandhi and vice versa. While the term also kept evolving with the twists and turns of Gandhi's life, it exemplifies only some of the attributes of Gandhi's mystique. It is also pre- and post-Gandhi, as some of the qualities that were valued were ascribed to Gandhi and some of Gandhi's qualities began to be encapsulated in the term Gandhian. The term Gandhian has also continued to expand in scope to include phenomena according to the spatio-temporal contexts, for example, Occupy Wall Street protests in the United States against the influence of multinational corporations on politics. Thus, the term Gandhian is not reducible to Gandhi alone. In that sense, the term Gandhian represents a dynamic and continually evolving idea. As we parse what the term signifies or connotes, the legend of the term continues to grow with what could be considered an increasingly un-Gandhian epoch. The Gandhian becomes what is not un-Gandhian. Ironically, thus, the idea of a Gandhian is also enriched by its opposite. What does the term Gandhian signify?

In the contemporary epoch, the term Gandhian could be analysed from the moral-ethical, economic, political, social and environmental aspects. In the case of moral-ethical framework, the emphasis on *satya* (truth) and *ahinsā* (non-violence) is the constant refrain of a Gandhian understanding in the public imaginary. In the case of economic policy, self-sustainable, local and village-based economic development models are identified with the Gandhian economic thought. Gandhi's disciple, J. C. Kumarappa's *The Economy of Permanence* details a life in synchronization with the rhythms of nature that is organic, environmentally sustainable and harnessing the local natural and human resources judiciously so that they can regenerate, without exhausting them, satisfying the needs of the community and not the greed of the individuals to amass wealth and involving the local populace in various economic activities and financial decision-making process. E. F. Schumacher's 'Small Is Beautiful' is an example of the Gandhian model of economic philosophy. When it comes to the social aspect of Gandhian thought, social evils like untouchability, gender discrimination and inter-religious strife should be forsworn. In the political realm, Gandhi espoused an ethic of duty and responsibility towards fellow human beings over a rights-based approach. He saw the rights-based approach as individual-centric and not based on a sense of love for the other. For Gandhi, rights emanated from duties and politics cannot be divorced from ethics.

While Gandhian philosophy is hailed as a precursor to deep ecology, in his voluminous and prolific writings, he did not speak much about ecology or the environment. The Chipko (tree-hugging) movement in the 1970s was led by rural women village heads of the Himalayan region to protect forests from being ravaged by unregulated lumber mafia. This movement was later made famous by the Gandhian Sunderlal Bahuguna's 5,000-kilometre walk along the Himalayas. The concept of *sarvodaya* (universal upliftment), an integral part of the Gandhian oeuvre, was an inspiration to the Save the Forest movement in the Garhwal region of the Himalayas. Though there were no explicit environmental policy formulations in Gandhi's writings, the way of life that was practised in his ashram was simple, clean, austere, hygienic and contented. Gandhi also emphasized the connection between physical labour and spiritual satisfaction. Hence, mass production and wholesale consumption were considered to be injurious to the living environment and human well-being.

The Gandhian social construction programme was designed to address five major issues plaguing India before Independence. Hence it was aimed at socio-economic measures to alleviate poverty, social reforms including Hindu–Muslim unity, women's equality, abolition of untouchability, political empowerment of villages, building a rural economy through cooperatives, land distribution to the poor, strengthening civil administration and reducing the size of the army, environmental protection and providing quality education with emphasis on the vernacular as the medium of instruction with Hindi and English to provide a national and international dimension to the education.

References

Gandhi, M. K. *Collected Works of Mahatma Gandhi*. New Delhi: Publications Division, Ministry of Information and Broadcasting, Government of India, 1956–94.
Weber, Thomas. *Gandhi, Gandhism and the Gandhians*. New Delhi: Lotus, 2006.

GAON (GĀNV)

Jitender Parsad

The term *gaon*, which stands for the English word 'village', is derived from the Sanskrit word *grama*. According to M. M. Williams, grama refers to an inhabited place, village and hamlet. In the *Rig Veda*, the term refers to the collective inhabitants of a place, community, race and any number of men associated together, such as in a multitude or troop (especially of soldiers). Opposed to the term grama is the Hindi word *shaher*, which derives from the Sanskrit word *nagar* used to refer to a town/city.

Basham notes, 'The basic unit of Aryan society was family.' He further observed, 'A group of related families formed a sept or grama, a term which later regularly meant "village", but which in the Rig Veda, usually refers to a group of kinsfolk, rather than to a settlement and the family was staunchly patrilineal and patriarchal.' Any discussion of grama or gaon will necessarily involve studying the family and kinship structures.

The term gaon refers to a cluster of huts, small and large, often grouped round a well or some river basin that served people in organizing cultural activities. Historians have also observed that such gaons were walled or stockaded for protection from ferocious animals and invaders. The sociocultural life inside a gaon was characterized by cohesion, solidarity and strong bonds of kinship. The term gaon, therefore, invokes the feeling of communal solidarity. And, the people residing in a gaon formed a self-conscious community and often had an energetic community life. Culturally speaking, the term gaon gets associated with community, that is, a 'primary group' where people had face-to-face contact, physical proximity, identity of interest and strong normative orders bound by the feeling of fraternal solidarity. The so-called nuanced expression of gaon also centres on native terms like *gama, desh, khera, mazra, dehat, khap, gohand, peend* and *dhani*. These are some alternatives for gaon in certain linguistic regions. Each of these expressions carry its own meaning but they all go to suggest strong bonds of kinship that characterize their relationships.

In the writings of sociologists and social anthropologists, the term gaon is rarely used. The English term, 'village' is used synonymously to refer to rural society, agricultural community, peasant community and tribe. While in the mid-twentieth century, a number of sociologists emphasized the importance of the village as representing the basic structure of Indian society, there were some sociologists who pointed out the continued existence of urban society. Thus, the term, shaher as opposed to gaon, came to be used to characterize the dichotomous structure of Indian society. M. S. A. Rao, while editing a classic work on urban sociology in India, discussed rural as against urban in dichotomous terms. The first urbanization in the Indus Valley civilization is dated to *c.* 2500 BCE.

Before sociologists of Indian origin began discussing the Indian village as basic to understanding the sociocultural framework of Indian society, British colonial administrators considered gaon to be a revenue unit. This colonial perspective was born out of their own perception of studying Indian society with a financial motive. They also perceived the village as a monolithic and unchanging entity. The leading and founding administrator of British colonial rule in India was Charles Metcalfe, whose popular passage suggests that village communities of India might be termed as 'Little Republics' that enjoyed independent and autonomous character. Whatever may be the perception of Charles Metcalfe, the fact that remains undisputed is that their construction of the gaon as an idyllic and utopian political community and characterized as an autonomous enduring group was a romanticized depiction of the village. Their construct was born out of the orientalist perspective, which viewed from the point of view of a group having customs and traditions of the indigenous population. As against the oriental perspective, there existed the Anglicist's view which treated native customs and traditions with a certain degree of contempt. Thus, treating the traditionally settled inhabitants, the village, as a revenue unit was their main concern. From the point of view of administration, at times they showed concern with the customs and traditions of the rural society, but whenever they needed to have administrative control over the village, they used law and court as legitimate institutional instrument. However, the colonial construct of treating the village as a revenue unit was criticized by the Marxist scholars like Irfan Habib, who saw the village as a 'cohesive exploited whole'.

The colonial construct of the village also had an element of ethnocentric bias with a political agenda that treated village as a core category. However, for nationalist leaders like M. K. Gandhi, B. R. Ambedkar, Jawaharlal Nehru, Rabindranath Tagore, Rajendra Prasad and Vallabhbhai Patel, the Indian village epitomized the core civilizational ethos. Gandhi considered the village as harbouring the soul of the people and therefore insisted that if India has to develop, the village must be centre stage.

The term gaon is also viewed from the perspective of representing communities and traditions. Robert Redfield provides a useful list of four major characteristics of the 'little community' of a village: smallness, distinctiveness, homogeneity and self-sufficiency. For him, the little community, that is, the village, is a 'cradle-to-grave arrangement'.

Village life was also characterized by barter transactions, and such transactions have long been integral elements of its agrarian economy. *Jajmani* relations (patron–client relations), that is, the landed and the dominant caste extended patronage to their clients normally in exchange of services rendered by them, were popular for a long time in the rural areas. The serving castes of low status had a *jajman* (patron) from high caste and the serving castes were termed as *kamin* (client). The nexus of relations existing between them was characterized by both patronage as well as exploitation.

The term gaon finds a place in the writings of Indologists. Iravati Karve has discussed the gestalt of three types of villages in Maharashtra. First, the nucleated village with a habitation clearly defined from the surrounding cultivated fields. The second type of villages are generally strung along length-wise on two sides of the road, without any sharp distinction between the habitation area and the cultivated area. In such villages, the land is exploited for both horticulture and agriculture. The third type of village is found in Satpura mountains, where the houses are situated in their own fields in clusters of two or three huts all belonging to a single closed kinship groups. In the last type of village, we understand that the expression gaon can also suggest corporate or a cohesive group reinforced by kindred relationships, caste groupings and family status.

However, it must be noted that a village may consist of more than one caste group. In North India, the villages are clan-based settlement. Thus, multi-clan villages may also exist. There is a tendency on the part of dominant clans to form clusters of villages known by as *athgaon* (group of eight), *chaubisi* (group of twenty-four), *chaurasi* (group of eighty-four), etc., where the rules of *gotra* (clan) govern social relationships such as marriage. Any contravention may be considered a violation of customary rules. Thus, in some cultural regions, the rules of gotra exogamy and village exogamy suggest the cultural survival of customary practices. The cultural formations of groups of such villages are called *khaps*. In Haryana, the clusters of neighbouring villages constitute numerous khaps and the elderly within the khap act as the custodian of the norms and traditions of the khap panchayat. These khaps may play a predominant role in social and civil matters.

References

Basham, A. L. *The Wonder That Was India*. Delhi: Rupa, 1982.
Chauhan, B. R. *The Rural Studies: A Trend Report in a Survey of Research in Sociology and Social Anthropology*, vol. 1, edited by M. N. Srinivas. Bombay: Popular Prakashan, 1974.

HIJRA (HIJDĀ)/LGBT

Ashley Tellis

Hijra, an Urdu word (Arabic root *hjr*), used mainly in North India, is one of several terms (e.g., *aravani* or *tirunangai* in Tamil Nadu, *jogappa* in Karnataka) used for a member of an indigenous community found across India and the subcontinent comprising people who identify as women and dress up as women and desire men. This category includes castrated men, hermaphrodites/eunuchs, intersexed people and biological men who are part of a very structured *guru–chela* (master–student) and kinship system. Syncretic in terms of religious beliefs, many in the Hijra community borrow from regional variations of mythological stories (e.g., Bahuchara Mata in North India, Goddess Yellamma in Karnataka, Lord Aravan in Tamil Nadu). Historically, they were part of the royal court and guarded the harem. Their status declined in the nineteenth century when the British deemed them a criminal tribe. They earn their living through performing certain rituals, begging and sex work.

Hijras must be distinguished from transgender, a term of US origin meant to signify several things that hijras are not. These include a desire to transition from one sex to another, a sense of fluid, non-binary identities and a range of expressions of these as variant from their assigned sex in a characteristically US and naive belief that principle of sexual difference might be simply circumvented by an act of will and a sleight of hand. Hijras are firmly located in the principle of sexual difference.

The conflation of these two categories has led to much confusion over the Transgender Persons (Protection of Rights) Bill 2018, which has been hijacked by a fledgling but influential upper-caste and upper-class movement of trans people, influenced by, indeed formed in the crucible of US trans politics and demanding absurd legal definitions of gender as entirely self-nominated and endlessly proliferating, while hijras without basic rights lose the possibility of gaining these through the law.

LGB (lesbian, gay and bi) in India are also, like the T mentioned above, urban, upper class and upper-caste identities adopted by urban Indians from the Euro-US contexts of these movements that in the West fought for rights since the 1960s. Of these, only gay politics has been prominent largely via the legal demand to read down (and not repeal) Section 377 of the Indian Penal Code which, while it does not mention homosexuality, penalizes buggery and 'acts against the order of nature'. This legal campaign asked for the decriminalization of private sexual acts between consenting same-sex adults when these were never outlawed in the first place.

While the Delhi High Court upheld the reading down of Section 377 as unconstitutional in 2009, the Supreme Court first reinstated it as perfectly constitutional and in no need of reform in 2013 and then read it down in 2018. Both sides of the argument, however, miss any real political movement for LGBT rights in India. The reason for this and for the anomalous nature of LGBT politics in India is that it came with the opening of the Indian market through the process of globalization or neoliberal economics. It came as a ready-made language and politics without any social struggles on the ground. One indication of this is the adoption by Indian LGBT politics of contemporary Western LGBT campaigns, like the one for gay marriage, given the eventual assimilation of the Western movements into the neoliberal economy without any sense of the prehistory of those movements in the West. It also came through the politics of aid and funding for HIV/AIDS, through NGOs, and NGOization must not be mistaken for a social and political movement on the ground.

While there is some sort of LGBT movement that predates contemporary LGBT politics (which in its current form is certainly not a movement) in India, this has been sporadic, intermittent, evanescent and not yet mapped as a historical narrative at all. Whether it was the AIDS Bhedbhav Virodhi Andolan in Delhi, which fought for the repeal of Section 377 and worked around HIV/AIDS awareness in the late 1980s and early 1990s, the work of figures like Shyamala Nataraj and organizations like the South Indian AIDS Awareness Programme (SIAAP) since the 1980s around AIDS, sex workers and sexual minorities in Tamil Nadu, the lives and careers of individuals like Hoshang Merchant in Hyderabad and some gay men who lived courageous lives as self-identified gay men and, even in the neoliberal moment, an organization like the short-lived Campaign for Lesbian Rights (CALERI), an independent formation that came out of the Hindu Right's attack on Deepa Mehta's *Fire* in the late 1990s.

An LGBT movement in India is yet to be born and will need to craft its conception away from this neoliberal efflorescence that passes as a movement in India and the hegemonies of class, caste and global empires like the United States with their worldwide propaganda of a certain language and politics. This is a difficult proposition but a good place to start.

References

Dube, Siddharth. *No One Else: A Personal Story of Outlawed Love and Sex*. Delhi: Harper Collins, 2015.
Merchant, Hoshang. *The Man Who Would Be Queen: Autobiographical Fictions*. New Delhi: Penguin, 2011.

JANTA (JANTĀ)/PUBLIC

Rama Kant Agnihotri

Janta literally means 'public'. It derives from the root *jan*, which means 'person, fellow, people'. Janta may not be formally related to jan, but it does give the sense of 'collection/ gathering of people'. Several other words in the Hindi–Urdu lexicon are used in the same sense, including *logbaag, samaaj, samudaay* and *aavaam*. Janta is generally used to refer to a community, collective or a group and could refer to all the people of a country. Association with a specific geographical region such as a state, a larger territory subsuming several adjoining states or the whole country/nation is a necessary feature of the concept of janta. One can perhaps *not* talk of the janta of the whole world, because the expression is central to the concept of a nation-state.

The word gained currency in the political discourse with the formation of the Janata Party at a moment when the democratic ethos of India was at stake. When in 1975, the Government of India declared Emergency in the name of national security, several political parties got together to constitute the Janata Party, which defeated the ruling party in the post-Emergency 1977 elections. It is therefore not surprising that many political parties have the words janta or *janataa* or jan in their name, for example, Bhartiya Janata Party (BJP; the party in power at the Centre now), Janata Dal, Janata Party, Rashtriya Janata Dal, Lok Janshakti, Bahujan Samaj, etc.

In several contexts, the word janta can also be treated as 'plebeian', 'masses' or 'ordinary', as opposed to 'elite'. One could, for example, hear, 'This film will do well with the *aam janta*', that is, this movie will be a great success among the masses but may not appeal to the elite.

Before we conclude, a word about the alternation in the pronunciation of janta and janataa. According to the standard Hindi phonological rule, word final 'a' is not pronounced. For example, the inherent 'a' of 'l' of the name 'Kamal' is not pronounced. An extension of this rule says, if a word ends in a long syllable, the inherent 'a' of the preceding consonant is not pronounced. Hence, jantā. However, Sanskritized pronunciation favours maintaining the inherent 'a'. Hence 'kamala' and 'janataa'.

References

Malik, Yogendra K. and V. B. Singh. 'Bharatiya Janata Party: An Alternative to the Congress (I)?' *Asian Survey* 32, no. 4 (1992): 318–36.
Swain, Pratap Chandra. *Bharatiya Janata Party: Profile and Performance*. New Delhi: APH Publishing, 2001.

LOVE MARRIAGE

Rajni Palriwala

Asha told me that her son and daughter-in-law had chosen each other themselves – they had met at the company they work in. She was a Jain, whereas they were Baniyas. I exclaimed that was nice; theirs was a love marriage. Asha was quick to deny this, saying that it had been a proper arranged marriage, with all the ceremonies and events, done as grandly as they could. This brief conversation encapsulates much of the meaning, discourse and signification around the idea of love marriage in contemporary India, an idea and a possible practice for which the English words are used rather than the various languages in which it may be spoken of in the Indian context (such as *prem vivah*).

It is difficult to trace the etymology of what is at times a hyphenated word, as Perveez Mody notes, at times a phrase and at times a noun with an adjectival qualifier. It is the last that perhaps has the earliest resonances, with orientalists of colonial and native origin, anthropologists and traditionalists who feared the deluge of Western mores. All, in different ways, sought to distinguish cultural practices of Europe and the subcontinent. Marriage in this region, they held, was arranged by family elders on the basis of social compatibility and was not a consequence of shared romantic love between future spouses. Thus, this twinned word, 'love marriage', referred to an emotion and to an institutionalized relationship, both taken as being universal with equal emphasis on both parts. It was in their conjunction that a specificity and a distinction that were signs of modern conjugality as manifested in the European ideal were being claimed.

'Love marriage', as an idea, has since been studied by a range of scholars across the humanities and social sciences, where two themes have been to point to a long history of romantic love and the variety of marital practices and marital emotions across time and social groups in the subcontinent, as Francesca Orsini observes. Yet, as has also been emphasized, connotations, meanings and practices of love marriage suggest a phenomenon different from earlier constructions of romantic love or conjugal love or conjugal-erotic love or conjugality. What continues in social narratives is the idea of romantic love as possibly transgressive, tragic and doomed, especially when it precedes marriage and the careful social and community orchestration of choice. The shadow of the socially illicit hangs over much of love marriage, even as political ideologies validated the idea and modern law enabled the legalization of the socially illicit, though not absolutely and without question in practice (Mody 2008). Across diverse streams within the movement for national Independence, including some social reformers, Gandhian socialists, the left and modernists, love marriage was rightfully transgressive, as it would enable inter-caste marriage, dowryless marriage and a simple wedding, which formed a route to break caste divisions, 'wasteful' practices and democratize marital and familial relations. These have been themes in modernist literature and a central motif in popular cinema. At the same time, inter-caste marriages and simple weddings were not synonymous with the idea of marriages following romantic love and passion, as such marriages were also initiated and arranged by friends or parents of such ideological and political inclination.

It is striking that in much of the articulations, love marriage was and is seen in terms of its defined opposite – the arranged marriage. Starting from very different vantage points – those who wish to uphold 'Indian' tradition and those who question the division between the free individuals of the modern West and the absence of individual agency and emotion in the tradition-bound Orient – this dichotomy has been questioned. For the first, the argument is that in arranged marriage, both sexual and companionate love comes after the wedding and will persist and make for happier and lasting marriages as the social and cultural compatibility of spouses and a wider network of relationships have been ensured. The second stream of critique highlights the social determinations of 'free choice' and cultural and class isogamy in the shaping of love and marriage selection in the West (Khandelwal, 2009) and questions the distinction between emotion and rationality in personal choices. This also suggests a third and empirical blurring of the dichotomy in contemporary times through uncovering the continuum between the two opposites: from marriage arranged by family elders using old and new modes to find a match and with greater or lesser right to refuse the match on the part of the young (clearly only possible as age of marriage has risen), matches initiated by friends and comrades and even family elders in which individual emotional compatibility and desire is given more space and perhaps time to develop before the decision to marry and certainly before the wedding itself, self-arranged marriages in which elements other than the emotion of individual romantic or sex love is primary, to love marriage which is consequent on romantic and erotic love and a desire for a shared life together, whatever the difficulties it may entail. Common across the continuum is the idea of compulsory heteronormative marriage.

In contemporary India, the conjoining of love and marriage carries different meanings and social implications for people of different classes, ages, cultural milieus and life trajectories. There has been an upsurge of studies of 'love marriage' couples and their families, in different generations, while media and popular cultural forms carry a constant conversation on love marriage, in which an influential, but not singular, diaspora is also a participant (Uberoi 2006). For the cosmopolitan, urban, middle-class youth, it is a sign of their distinction, their individual autonomy, modernity and necessary to the life they desire; for their parents, it may also be a claim to modernity or inescapable if their 'modern' children so choose as long as the choice meets community (caste/religion) and class criteria or a way out in a context of difficulties in arranging a 'proper' match, given rising dowry and increasing intra-community differentiations; the last may also be the case for poor working-class parents whose daughters find a spouse at work or elsewhere; for others – both urban and rural – it is a threat to the family, as it signals that their children no longer accept their authority, that their daughters-in-law are way too forward and will not 'adjust' and that conjugal love will displace the filial love on which a cared-for old age depends. For them, love marriage is an invitation to social chaos and loss, as for many young men, who are struggling to find their place in the economy and in their communities and for whom love marriage reduces the pool of possible matches from which their parents can select. For many young women, love marriage also reduces the possibilities of post-marital natal support, as it may result in rupture of kin and community ties and the impossibility of speaking of problems in a self-chosen marriage, unlike in arranged marriages where parents have continuing expectations of and responsibilities for their married children.

In fear of love marriage and of the stigma of love that may not lead to marriage, the parental control of the movements of young women, even to the extent of stopping their education, is practised and justified. Part of and consequent to the socially illicit colour of love marriage is the exclusion of the couple and possibly their natal families from the community with consequences for social support and the marriages of other children. Those love marriages that are likely to get parental approval in the subcontinent are those as in the conversation above – between people of compatible class and community, which can be celebrated in the manner appropriate to their communities and enable a post-wedding extended familial life, even if not extended household living. In other words, those that can be given the colour of an arranged match. Other love marriages may not be possible except through elopement, the loss of the natal family and, even then, constantly under danger of separation. One tactic adopted by parents and kin opposed to a love marriage of their daughter is to file a case that their daughter is below the legal age of marriage and consent and has been abducted. It is well-nigh impossible to estimate the spread of the practice of love marriage, the visibility of the opposition to it perhaps leading to its overestimation. The threat of love marriage to community, to control by tradition and the continuation of traditional authorities has been deeply politicized and responded to with violence. The latter is evident in the phenomenon of 'honour killing' and the call to fight *love jehad*. The first has been witnessed primarily among dominant castes across North India but also in southern parts of the subcontinent and among all castes and communities. The second – an oxymoron meaning religious war through pretensions of romantic love – is a campaign by the Hindu Right to fight intercommunity love marriages posited as a concerted attempt by Muslims to outnumber Hindus by seducing young Hindu women, taking advantage of their naivety, innocence and incapability of making decisions for their own life. In all the different articulations of love marriage, by its proponents and its opponents, there are glimmerings of ideas of whether young people, especially women, can and should make their own life choices and implications for equality and authority within marriage and the family. At the same time, many young people look for love and romance before their marriage, without any plans that it should lead to marriage. For them, especially young women, the material and emotional support of their natal kin is more reliable than the love of a man on whom they will have to depend, since so little else has changed in their economic and social possibilities.

References

Chowdhry, P. 'Private Lives, State Intervention: Cases of Runaway Marriage in Rural North India'. *Modern Asian Studies* 38, no. 1 (2004): 55–84.
Khandelwal, M. 'Arranging Love: Interrogating the Vantage Point in Cross-Border Feminism'. *Signs: Journal of Women in Culture and Society* 34, no. 3 (2009): 583–609.
Mody, P. *The Intimate State: Love-Marriage and the Law in Delhi*. Delhi: Routledge, 2008.
Orsini, F., ed. *Love in South Asia: A Cultural History*. Delhi: Cambridge University Press, 2007.

MAA (MĀṀ)

Geetanjali Shree

Maa (mother) is a pivotal word in the Indian cultural lexicon. It is derived from the Sanskrit word *matri*, which is inherited from the Proto-Indo-Iranian *maataa*. It has many variants across the Indian cultural-linguistic spectrum, such as *mai, maiya, maai, aai, maat, maatu, maatrikaa, maateshwari, amma, mahtaari, matahari, maadar, ammi*, mummy, mom and mamma.

The inclusion of 'mummy', 'mom' and 'mamma' among the variants of maa is dictated by a linguistic-cultural trend which over the years has been getting increasingly irresistible. Whereas these were words that were till some time ago used only by a more anglicized upper-class section of the population, it is now part of the common person's mode of addressing her or his mother.

Maa is a magical word. It evokes, spontaneously, some of the finest human feelings, such as love, reverence, gratitude and the readiness to sacrifice. Its temporal spread and psychocultural depth are indicated by the fact that it belongs equally to two clusters of terms selected for this lexicon – classical heritages and intimacies.

Maa, the term and the relationship, is not tied to the umbilical cord. It applies, equally, to a foster mother. Indeed, there are venerable discussions on who the 'real' maa is, the one who gave birth or the one who brought up the person like her own child. The mythological characters of Krishna and Karna in the Mahābhārata constitute two classic examples of this situation. Forsaken by their biological mothers immediately upon their birth for very different reasons, both treat their foster mothers as their maa. The unmatched veracity of mythological testimony apart, we have in the extraordinary bonding between Anandomoyee and Gora in Tagore's eponymous masterpiece *Gora* a memorable portrayal in our own day of this phenomenon.

Not just confined within the family, maa is imbued with larger symbolic/figurative connotations embracing geography and culture. Embodying the quintessential nurturer, the term is attached to the land of one's birth, *matribhoomi* (mother land; or, more specifically, *Bharat Mata*, Mother India), and to the language imbibed through one's mother's milk, *matribhasha* (mother tongue). The earth – the supreme nurturer – is *prithvi mata*. Similar deferential recognition of the sustenance, they provide, produces variants like *Ganga maiya* and *Jamuna maiya*.

Maa is also redolent with divinity. Depending upon who uses it, and the state of mind in which it is used, maa for one's earthly mother or Bharat Mata can be suffused with divinity. Besides, there is an endless and still-growing pantheon of goddesses (*devimatas*), such as Parvati, Sarasvati, Kali, Durga, Vaishno Devi and so on.

Maa carries a benign aura around it. Be it an individual mother or the earth, indeed even maatribhoomi, there is no hint of evil about her. In real life, though, an individual or a group may act egregiously and still feel – even be – absolved on the pretext of the deed having been done for maa. She/it, thus, helps sustain a comforting individual and collective self-image.

This idealized image of maa rests on the excision of all but the savoury aspects of the otherwise complex phenomenon that the term denotes. It, in turn, transmits its aura to the no less complex allied phenomena denoted by derivatives like matribhoomi and, certainly in our day, matribhasha and *gaumata* (mother cow). This is achieved by turning a blind eye to real-life experience as also to the insights of our ancient seers and folk imagination. These insights recognize the complexity of life and relations within it, as is reflected in, for instance, the venerable pantheon of both benign and terrifying *devi*s – matas – like Durga and Kali. In fact, mother goddesses as a genre represent not only a mother figure (fertility) often surrounded by children but also *shakti* (feminine energy) that not only destroys demons but – symbolizing the endless cycle of birth and death – also devours her own children. There is, besides, more specific filicide, too, like in the portrayal of Ganga who kills her seven sons as soon as they are born. (I read this story without the gloss that her filicides were meant to ease the curse of seven Vasus that they would have to be born as humans.)

The idealized patriarchal image of maa, and the intricate nexus of institutions, beliefs, values and behaviour patterns that it serves to valorize, is now coming under radical scrutiny, especially from women writers. To cite such an exceptionally powerful voice, Krishna Sobti has shown maa in her fullness. A normal person with normal needs, desires, dreams and vulnerabilities, she is a nurturer too but not the venerable self-effacing self-sacrificing nurturer. The mother – as in Sobti's *Ai Ladki* – may seem self-obsessed and domineering and searing in her criticism of her daughter, without ceasing to care for her. Remember also the layers of mother uncovered in Mahashweta Devi's intense stories, such as 'Standayini' and 'Hajar Chaurasir Ma'.

I may also mention my own first novel, more so as it bears the title *Mai*. (The same title, significantly, has been maintained in its English, German, French, Serbian and Urdu translations.) The mother in *Mai* is seen by the new-age children as weak and subordinate to everyone's wishes but in fact is silently creative and manipulative, certainly not subservient to the views or directives of the males.

And, of course, there is always the mix of the sublime with the ridiculous, the inane with the epic, the stereotype with the specific, all nonetheless resonating with the music and values around the term maa. Thus, even as this radical questioning gains edge and ground, every moviegoer in North India – perhaps elsewhere too – quotes with a smile from the movie *Deewaar* where Amitabh Bachchan, playing a mafia don, is silenced by Shashi Kapoor, an honest police cop and his brother in the film. Pointing to the enormous wealth he has amassed, the former asks in a taunt what the latter has. *Mere pas maa hai*, retorts the honest cop.

Or the joke about Jesus being a Bengali. The proof: Every Bengali mother believes her son to be God, and every Bengali son believes his mother to be pure and a virgin.

On balance, the future seems to belong, ideationally and empirically, to a new maa. With women from the middle and upper classes fast ceasing to be mere housewives and claiming perfect and substantive equality with men, the concept of maa is poised to be radically transformed. So also hopefully, as a sequel, will derivative concepts like matribhoomi.

References

Devi, Mahasweta. *Breast Stories*, translated by Gayatri Chakravorty Spivak. Calcutta: Seagull Books, 1997.
Devi, Mahasweta. *Mother of 1084*, translated with an introductory essay by Samik Bandyopadhyay. Calcutta: Seagull Books, 1997.

MADRASA (MADRASĀ)

Mohd. Sanjeer Alam

The term *madrasa* is derived from the Arabic word *darasa* which literally means 'to tell something' or 'to teach something'. Thus, the word madrasa broadly refers to a place of teaching and learning.

Historically, the institution of madrasa has been at the heart of the evolution and progress of Islamic civilization. In the initial phase of Islamic civilization, mosques served as the locus of activities of the believers. Apart from being a place of worship, they also served as centres of teaching and learning. The teaching was confined to reading and recitation of the Quran. With passage of time and spread of Islam far and wide, a formal system of education was needed. It thus marked the separation of institutions of learning from mosques, although the latter continued to be a space for elementary learning. In course of time, a hierarchized network of institutions came into being to mark the Islamic system of education.

Structurally, Islamic educational institutions can be distinguished as *maktab*, *madrasa* and *jamia*. A maktab, often attached to mosque and mausoleum and mostly subsisting on local charity, is like an elementary school, where a child begins to learn the art of writing and to read elementary (Islamic) texts. After finishing maktab successfully, a child graduates to the madrasa for higher learning, where subjects other than the Quran, such as the Hadith (sayings of the Prophet) and *fiqh* (Islamic jurisprudence), are also taught. For further higher learning there are institutions called jamia, equivalent to the general university, although in many instances a madrasa functions and labels itself as jamia. While many rational subjects, such as mathematics, sciences, philosophy and so on, began to be taught in madrasas early on, excessive focus remained on religious education, for the primary aim of madrasas has been to equip individuals with the knowledge of Islam and to produce scholars (*ulema*) who would be torchbearers of Islam.

In the Indian subcontinent, madrasas began to be built with the establishment of Muslim rule. But the first madrasa that finds mention in historical accounts was Madrasa Firozi built in Multan (now in Pakistan) by Nasiruddeen Qubacha. Renowned thirteenth-century Persian chronicler and historian Minhaj-al-Shiraj informs us that he was in charge of this madrasa in 1226 CE. Nevertheless, establishment of madrasas with liberal grants from rulers and nobles became common throughout the medieval period. In many cases, madrasas were also built by individual scholars and by the collective effort of people in a locality. These madrasas imparted education free of cost and to wards of both patricians and plebeians alike. Those graduated from these institutions not only became ulema, who would take Islam into the future, but many of them were also to be part of the state apparatus. Seen thus, not only did madrasas play an important role in spreading education among Muslims, they also had a multilayered functional relationship with medieval society.

However, the expansion of madrasas experienced a jolt after the 1857 uprising against the British. In the colonial administrative circles, it was widely held that madrasas were part of the conspiracy against the colonial regime. Consequently, the colonial regime blocked the resources to madrasas, which forced many of them to shut down. The new system of education introduced by the colonial regime also undermined the significance of madrasas as centres of education. For one, not only did the colonial system provide a robust alternative system of education, it was also the site of educational credentials crucial to join the colonial bureaucracy. Although there were efforts at reviving the madrasa system in the nineteenth century (such as the establishment of Darul Uloom Deoband and Madrasa Mazahirul Uloom) to counter the growing popularity and influence of the colonial education system, madrasas failed to regain the glory they once had.

Estimates abound on the number of madrasas running at present. Different sources put out widely varying figures. The source of error lies in the tendency of conflating the madrasa with the maktab. Whatever may be the exact number, there are thousands of madrasas spread across the length and breadth of India. While madrasas are inclusive in their intake in terms of social class location of students, they have been known for gender-based segregation. Even in the twenty-first century, gender continues to separate madrasas as one for boys and other for girls. There are, of course, separate madrasas for girls, but their number is far less compared to boys.

Indian madrasas differ from each other in terms of the financial resources with which to operate. Most of them are run by community resources such as *zakat* (religious obligation to give alms or tax) and donations from affluent Muslims. By virtue of this, they stand as autonomous institutions. Yet, there are many that receive some grants from the state as well. Nor are madrasas homogeneous in terms of syllabi. The syllabus called *dars-e-nizami* (named after its founder, Mullah Nizamuddin) framed in the seventeenth century stressed on the teaching of rational subjects, such as mathematics, logic, philosophy and jurisprudence. The Quran and the Hadiths were marginally studied. However, it has undergone modification time and again. Another popular syllabus followed by many madrasas is *dars-e-aliya*, initiated in in the late eighteenth century. Under this system, a student takes fifteen years to complete education. Much akin to SSC (Senior Secondary Certificate) pattern, students are required to appear for and have to pass examinations at various levels. Apart from religious books, the syllabus includes subjects such as mathematics, sciences, social sciences and literature.

In recent decades, madrasas have come under public scrutiny for allegedly producing *jihadis* (encouraging militant Islam). There is tremendous pressure on these institutions for curricular reform and to bring education imparted in them into the mainstream of universal trends. Given that the primary aim of the madrasa is not to impart modern education or to produce workers for the modern labour market, the idea of modernization of madrasa would defeat its very *raison d'etre*.

References

Ahmad, Aziz. *Studies in Islamic Culture in Indian Environment*. New Delhi: Oxford University Press, 1999.

Qasmi, Muhammadullah Khalili. *Madrasa Education: Its Strength and Weakness*. New Delhi: Manak, 2005.

MODERNITY

Kavita Panjabi

Modernity, in most major Indian languages, indicates not just a sense of the current and the new but also the transient and changing. Thus *adhunika*, the commonest term for 'modern', signifies *nutan* (new) as well as *na take tevu* (that which will not last, ephemeral) in Gujarati; *aajkal ka* (of current times), *vartaman ka* (of the present) and *naye zamane ka* (of the new times) in Hindi; and *bartaman* (present), *sampratik* (recent) or *nabin* (new) in Bengali. As *navina* in Tamil, it indicates that which is modern or up to date.

Modernity in Europe may be dated as far back as the transformations of the Renaissance and Enlightenment; or, more specifically, to the processes of secularization and rationalization attendant on the transition from feudalism to capitalism and industrialization; or, even more recently, to the beginnings of modern warfare with the World Wars. In the Indian context, it is usually represented with reference to the beginnings of British colonialism. In the founding of India as a modern nation, the anti-colonial thrust propelled India's critiques of Western modernity. These critiques inflected India's self-definition about its own governance, socio-economics and scientific and technological investments. Central to Indian modernity, across the differences in vision of most of its makers, was the value of human worth, selfhood and dignity intertwined with critiques of modern forms of violence and social inequity – not surprising for a populace impacted by devastating inequities and multiple histories of subjugation.

Nehru upheld the project of modernity but was critical of Western modernity for failing 'to have solved the basic problems of life'. His aim was to humanize science; he advocated a 'blend of science and humanism', Gyan Prakash observes. The destructive potential of science and technology that had already wreaked havoc during the First World War underlined Tagore's *Talks in China*, as he reached out to China in the hope that an alternative vision of modern civilization could emerge from the East. The question of non-violence was of course at the core of Gandhi's philosophy of *satyagraha* (civil disobedience) and his advocacy of 'soul force' over the 'brute force' taking over the modern world. Based on his critique of the violence of technology, Gandhi also elaborated an alternative vision of modernity as self-governance in *Hind Svarāj*. He launched a trenchant critique of 'the craze for machinery, not machinery as such', of the system of competitive and destructive social, cultural and political relations attendant on the accumulation of capital and the unthinking propagation of technology. Tagore declared nationalism, in the modern capitalist world, to be 'an epidemic of evil' because of similar reasons; he privileged ethical human values over the political in his assertion that 'a country is not greater than the ideals of humanity'. In fact, the very first line of his *Nationalism* draws attention to the sectarian and hierarchical nature of society: 'Our real problem in India is not political. It is social.'

The post-Independence Dalit critique of Indian modernity has been incisive. It issued a powerful challenge to the common sense of the secular modern in its protest against the casteist Brahmanical character of the politics of the public sphere. Ambedkar, the principal architect of the Constitution of India, argued for the criticality of the social rooting of constitutional values, emphasizing that 'Indians today are governed by two different ideologies. Their political ideal set in the preamble of the Constitution affirms a life of liberty, equality and fraternity. Their social ideal embodied in their religion denies them.' And Periyar, the leader and philosopher of the Self-respect Movement in Tamil Nadu, brought the focus sharply on to the everyday experience of humiliation in the lives of non-Brahmins, on to the question of 'their very selfhood – deemed low, dishonourable and untouchable by their religion, and which had to be redeemed, re-possessed in the name of a common and universal humanity', as V. Geetha notes.

The notion of transience, read together with the sense of the new and the present in most Indian terms for modernity, also offers a critical key to understanding the uniqueness of Indian modernity as a process of constant recasting of older or 'traditional' significations. Suhrud observes that Gandhi had viewed modern civilization as transient and ephemeral, implying that it was destructive and certain to be destroyed. Yet modernity in India is also marked by an ironic resilience, not as a break or departure from the past but in an underlying continuity in transformation. Reconfigurations of the substance of religion, spirituality, sociopolitical relations and material processes both undergird and serve as camouflage for political and socio-economic power struggles. On the one hand, the inequities of 'tradition', such as of caste and religion, continue to persist within modern political systems, transforming themselves to endure firmly. In fact, Periyar rejected Indian nationalism precisely on the grounds that 'it sought to compromise the new with the substances of an older tyrannical religious ideology'. On the other hand, departures from 'tradition' draw upon the very weight of 'tradition' to establish themselves. So, the re-emergence of the phenomenon of 'satī' in Rajasthan in the 1980s had little to do with the religious myth of Parvati and Siva that it evoked; it was a new artefact of modernity, a patriarchal response to modern laws of inheritance and a culture of widow immolation propagated through a pervasive socio-economic network to secure the marital family's control over the widow's inheritance, as Sangari and Vaid convincingly argue.

Such reconstitutions of 'tradition' work both ways – they serve to reinforce older modes of patriarchal and sociopolitical power in altered contemporary contexts and they also facilitate liberal transformations, as in literary and artistic innovation. Faiz Ahmed Faiz, one of the pioneering poets of the Progressive Writers Association, drew upon the Indo-Islamic poetic tradition and the egalitarian spiritual power of Sufism to spearhead new modes of political engagement and secularization. Ritwik Ghatak broke through the limitations of atheistic approaches and drew upon transformations of religious archetypes in his films to plumb the ruptures of subjectivity resulting from Partition. Girish Karnad enacted his critique of religious beliefs and practices and ushered in a 'modern' sensibility through theatre, precisely by deploying history and myth to give him the distance to comment on contemporary realities.

As multiple modernities were forged, fresh assessments of the 'modern' self-reflexive, egalitarian and progressive gendered elements of certain past 'traditions' also began to challenge the notion of the colonial beginnings of modernity. Were the secular and the sacred at all viewed as distinct realms by Amir Khusrau and Chaitanya or by Kabir, Mira and Bulle Shah? It is significant that they too drew upon the language of the sacred as a resource for egalitarian and secular negotiations from as early as the thirteenth century onwards. Our focus on the colonial legacy has sidestepped much else that was happening within the Indian subcontinent. The elements of modernity that underline the Sūfī, Bhakti and Sant traditions, for example, press for the need to rethink the very basis of periodizing modernity that we have settled for across South Asia.

Finally, one of the most telling features of modernity is the silence which shrouds the internally conflicted subjectivity resulting from Partition. Over 14 million people were displaced across both borders between India and Pakistan and over one million were killed; as the World Wars and the Holocaust underlined twentieth-century modernity in Europe, so did the experience of Partition in this subcontinent. Political subjectivity was reoriented along nationalist, even jingoistic lines. Yet the loss of a homeland continued to haunt processes of interiority in critical ways – both immediately and later in nationalist and communal or fundamentalist appropriations. Literature and art became sites 'for the elaboration of a selfhood at odds with the geometry of selves put into place by partition', as Aamir Mufti observes. The struggle against a divided sense of self and the devastating impact of violence made for groundbreaking lyric poetry and a powerful body of hard-hitting prose, such as that of Faiz and Manto. Yet, in the literary periodization of the *Adhunik* (modern) period there is no classificatory acknowledgement of the radically modern transformations catalyzed by Partition. The repressed subjectivity of the experience of Partition haunts the nether realms of modernity while its sectarian appropriations ravage the Indian subcontinent even today.

References

Geetha, V. 'Who Is the Third That Walks Behind You? Dalit Critique of Modernity'. *Economic and Political Weekly* 36, no. 2 (2001): 163–4.

Sangari, Kumkum and Sudesh Vaid. 'Institutions, Beliefs, Ideologies – Widow Immolation in Contemporary Rajasthan'. *EPW* 26, no. 17 (27 April 1991).

Suhrud, Tridip. *Reading Gandhi in Two Tongues*. Shimla: Indian Institute of Advanced Studies, 2012.

MOHALLA (MŌHALLĀ)

Nazima Parveen

According to the *Oxford English Dictionary*, the word *mohalla* means 'an area of a town or village' or a residential 'community'. Although the word originated from the Arabic word *mohaalla*, it is used in many languages, such as in English, Spanish, French, Hebrew, Turkish, Portages, Italian and German with the same meaning. In Urdu, it means a locality or a ward. Related words such as *mohalladar* (neighbours) and *mohalladari* (neighbourly feeling) to describe spatial associations are no longer used in everyday conversation in North India. But, the term mohalla still survives as a powerful marker to express belongingness.

The word became very popular in the subcontinent as the Mughal dynasty began establishing capital cities as centres of their empire between 1400 and 1750 as centres of their empire. A system of mohallas and *katras* (a unit of mohalla, comprising a large compound with a number of families living in different houses or residential lanes) was developed to suit the caste-craft- and class-based homogenous community structure. However, the pattern of homogeneity was contextual representing different groups residing in *galies* (streets) and katras of a mohalla. Although the meaning of mohalla has remained the same, its trajectory in relation to the community identified with it reveals an interesting transformation of community-space relation and its political manifestation in colonial and postcolonial North India.

Delhi is a good example to underline this transformation. Broadly speaking, the story of Delhi's mohalla can be divided into three phases: (a) mohalla as a self-sufficient unit during the Mughal rule; (b) the evolution of mohalla as a political constituency at the time of British colonialism; and finally (c) mohalla as an antithesis to urban planning in postcolonial period.

In Shahjahanabad (the original name of what is now known as Old Delhi), different residential mohallas were interwoven with the Mughal *thana* (police station) system. Each mohalla came under the jurisdiction of a thana situated near to its location. The *thanedar* (head of a thana) policed the neighbourhood, collected duties, regulated trade and industries and kept a record of the local population and immigrants. The mohalla, in this sense, was not merely an area but also an administrative unit. These mohallas also practised *kuchabandi* (the practice of barricading a mohalla with high walls and a gate) and had a *chowkidar* (guard) for the purpose of security. These mohallas were in fact named either after the *amirs* (aristocrat) and nobles who lived there or a feature of the main professional activities performed by its inhabitants and/or the commodities sold in these areas. They were headed by chiefs (*chowdhuries*) of caste councils (*panchayats*). They were called *meer-mohalla*. The meer-mohalla settled inter-mohalla and intra-mohalla quarrels, judged disputes over land and property and decided questions on ritual status and other matters of common concern.

The events that took place after the 1857 revolt changed the way these mohallas were organized and identified in Shahjahanabad. British officials found the traditional mohalla system, especially the narrow lanes, and the practice of kuchabandi was viewed as a problem of security and surveillance. The area from Red Fort to Kashmiri Gate was cleared to establish British cantonment in the city immediately after its takeover in September 1857. As for the residential mohallas, the officials conducted a selective clearance and rehabilitation drive on the lines of the religious identity of the residents. Those mohallas that were populated mainly by people belonging to the Mughal family and the amirs, Muslims of the city in general, who were believed to be the main culprits of the uprising, were cleared as punishment. The Muslim population was resettled in and around the *shehar faseel* (city wall) within two years. This selective treatment of a residential population not only disturbed the traditional caste- and craft-based living pattern but also set the terms of discourse of the identification of Delhi mohallas and their political manifestations in later years.

The new form of policing the city established under the Police Act of 1861 abolished the administrative organization of the mohalla. The practice of kuchabandi was also eliminated. Mohallas came to be defined as administrative 'wards' in official vocabulary. Each of these wards was controlled by a non-official member of the government appointed as a member of the municipality. The introduction of local self-government in Delhi in 1883 and the debates on separate electorates established these residential wards as electoral constituencies. Eventually, these mohallas were identified as 'Hindu-dominated', 'Muslim-dominated' and 'mixed' political constituencies. The use of terms like 'majority' and 'minority' paved the way for the articulation of collective claims over space, further complicating the meanings of belongingness. These developments completely transformed the way communities associated themselves with their residential space in the later years of colonial politics. A mohalla, which strongly represented the socially ingrained caste identity of residents, was identified through politically constructed Hindu and Muslim categories, which multiplied social conflicts, thereby converting the mohalla into a field of multiple contestations.

The debates on urban planning in postcolonial Delhi produced the mohalla as a contested category in all senses of the term. As an administrative unit, mohallas and overcrowded katras posed a challenge to the modern urban planner. The deteriorating condition of these mohallas led them to declared 'unsuitable for human habitation'. Second, traditional living patterns showed an amalgamation of commercial and residential activities. The existence of small-scale industries (*karkhanas*) and other trades running in different mohallas also came in conflict with the parameters of city planning along modern lines. Thus, the separation of commercial and residential space became an important aspect of the redevelopment of Shahjahanabad under the first Master Plan of Delhi, 1961.

Although the word mohalla is still used in the same sense to represent a residential community, the symbols of their identification with politically constructed identities – Hindu, Muslims and now Dalit – have transformed them into the antithesis of a progressive, modern and inclusive idea of the city.

References

Gupta, Narayani. *Delhi between Two Empires, 1803–1931: Society, Government and Urban Growth*. Delhi: Oxford University Press, 1981.

Parveen, Nazima. 'The Making of Muslim Ilaqe'. *Seminar*, November 2014. Available at: http://www.india-seminar.com/2014/663/663_nazima_parveen.htm (December 2018).

NEHRUVIAN

Madhavan Palat

The term 'Nehruvian' is employed both in a positive sense and with a negative connotation. In the positive sense of the term, it could denote parliamentary democracy, secularism or religious pluralism, unity without uniformity, in formulaic terms, 'unity in diversity'; Indian, rather than Hindu, nationalism; cosmopolitanism transcending nationalism; state-led industrialization through planning and the rhetoric of socialism; and carving out an independent position for the Indian state in the world, expressed as 'non-alignment'. The pejorative connotations are democracy that did not go deep enough, secularism as pandering to minorities (especially Muslims), respecting difference to the extent of national fragmentation, as with special provisions for Kashmir or Muslim personal law; refusing to promote India as the land of Hindus or at least of Hindu civilization; cosmopolitanism as diluting Indian tradition; socialism and planning throttling economic enterprise; and non-alignment leading to insecurity and overdependence on the Soviet Union.

Parliamentary democracy was the constitutional structure chosen by the Constituent Assembly in 1949, but it is peculiarly associated with India's first prime minister, Jawaharlal Nehru, because of his unflinching adherence to its principles and the respect for its institutions. By democracy, he understood the parliamentary and multiparty variety and not democratic dictatorship through electoral legitimation. But he also understood it as a mass democracy, that is, an electoral system with adult suffrage. He multiplied democratic institutions, hence the *panchayati raj* (democracy at the local level of the district and the village). In the event, it was three-tiered, the Parliament at the apex, the state assemblies in the provinces and the panchayats below them. His firm commitment to these institutions and their practices has contributed decisively to the Indian understanding of political life; few can imagine an Indian democracy that would be plebiscitary, however charismatic the leaders who offer themselves from time to time; and still less can they imagine a military dictatorship in India.

Secularism is quintessentially Nehruvian. This implies allowing all religions and communities the freedom to function provided they did not hinder the rights of other communities. It does not entail rejection of any religion and still less any form of persecution of one. On the contrary, it calls for respecting the minority communities, whichever they were, and making special provision for the protection of their culture and practices. But this runs counter to the pure logic of majoritarian democracy, which therefore denounces such secularism as favouring minorities. Nehruvianism is a liberalism that imperatively embeds a minority discourse within the democratic one.

Nehruvian nationalism is what is known in nationalist theory as civic and, in India, as secular. It is inclusive and composite, with every Indian citizen finding a place equal to that of any other; this is Indian nationalism, set off against all other nationalisms that are exclusive or ethnic, in particular Hindu nationalism. Other nationalisms, whether Muslim or Sikh, or of tribes and regions, are minorities within India and cannot pretend to be Indian nationalism. However, Hindu nationalism can and does claim to be Indian nationalism on the ground that Hindus are in majority. The Nehruvian rebuts this claim.

It also goes beyond the nation to global citizenship. It is only a stepping-stone to the ultimate goal of arriving at a single, if diversified, civilization of humanity. Hence, nationalism is not a final end and acts as a constraint to the cosmopolitan ideal. His support to the demand for the continued use of English in India is deplored as an aspect of such cosmopolitanism.

'Unity in diversity' is pendant on nationalism. It sustains both the unity of the Republic and of local cultures. This is regarded as both high statesmanship and as pursuing contradictory goals. It allows space for those who wish to integrate India through a single culture; but it also permits multiple local ones to flourish under this umbrella, constitutionally in each of the states. For this reason, the Nehruvian vision has been accused of both imposing homogeneity and tolerating fragmentation.

Planning and socialism, upheld and derided as Nehruvian, derive from the state-led strategy of development and never were independent values in themselves. As the state cannot function like a private capitalist, it structures economic development through a national plan. Socialism was the rhetoric employed; but India was never a socialist economy and Nehru did not intend it to become one, although he periodically declared his preference for it while deploring Soviet and other forms of communism. The developmental state was the Nehruvian ideal; but its instruments, both planning and socialist rhetoric, are now understood as Nehruvian.

Nehruvian also denotes non-alignment. This is a foreign policy goal which aimed to preserve Indian independence of choice in a global polarization and division into armed camps during the Cold War. It was neither neutrality nor an attempt at forming another bloc, as Nehru repeatedly explained. While independence in foreign policy retains its primacy today, its specific form as non-alignment has atrophied since the end of the Cold War.

References

Arnold, David. 'Nehruvian Science and Postcolonial India'. *Isis* 104, no. 2 (2013): 360–70.
Sangari, Kumkum. 'A Narrative of Restoration: Gandhi's Last Years and Nehruvian Secularism'. *Social Scientist* 30, no. 3/4 (2002): 3–33.

PARIVAR/SAMAJ/BIRADRI (PARIVĀR/SAMĀJ/BIRĀDARĪ)

Nilanjan Mukhopadhyay

Going by the dictionary meaning, *parivar* denotes the smallest unit and comprises a group of people who are members of a family, related to one another by birth and/or marriage. *Samāj* is numerically and socially larger and can normally consists of either several *parivars* or individuals and designates a community connected by commonality of faith, pursuit, shared objective or social identity. Associations formed on basis of caste, community and creed are often established to impart an identity that is distinctive from the rest in society. These are set up chiefly with the intention of preserving cultural traditions, securing rights, pursuing projects, holding festivals to further heritage and identity and to promote social interaction within the *samāj*.

Biradri too is almost similar, although in certain regions and among specific communities, it is moderately more expansive and historically, its members were interlinked by patronage as well as kinship. Because of its origin in Persian and subsequent integration into linguistically inclusive Hindustani, *biradari* is often used as a counterbalancing and inclusive idea as against the relatively *shuddh* or puritanical Hindi words, *parivar* and *samāj* which in recent decades in India have also been used as a lapel of exclusion by the Indian right wing. However, there are still large swathes in South Asia where language is not religion-specific and *samāj* and *biradri* are not exclusionary.

Biradri is also used as suffix for socially inclusive initiatives that are not specific to a single caste or community, while *parivar* and *samāj* when utilized consciously do not reach out beyond rigid social identities. *Biradri* is treated as a concept to bond too inwardly, especially at times of strife, hardship and conflict when there is need to rally like-minded – or similarly-threatened – people to restore peace and harmony.

Previously, from early nineteenth century, the word *samāj* was used to delineate social groupings and name reform movements. These initiatives were carved out of society as mark of protest against social orthodoxy, practise and customs. The Brahmo Samaj was among the first such societies and Ram Mohun Roy's initiative at social reform catalyzed other social endeavours, most prominently the Arya Samaj. More often than not, *samāj* has been used in the name of either a social reform movement or a political outfit committed to reversal of existing social norms.

Of the three words, *parivar* has been used most regularly in recent years, especially after the Bharatiya Janata Party and other organizations affiliated to the Rashtriya Swayamsevak Sangh began its political ascent. In the social sphere, the word *parivar* is used for relatives who like to display unitary identity but in the political arena, it has come to be used almost exclusively for the sangh parivar. The word is also used to disparage political families, and *parivarwad* or dynasticism is presented as a major aberration in Indian politics, especially in the Congress Party.

The RSS has popularized the idea of the sangh parivar, and this nomenclature is now among the most easily comprehended in India. It denotes an interwoven phalanx of an estimated a forty-odd organizations committed to the idea of Hindutva. A political fraternity, it is spread across almost every sector ranging from peasantry, working class, students, women, tribals, Dalits, middle-class professionals and lobbyists and are united by common goals and objectives. It is only in rare instances that members of the sangh parivar work at cross-purposes.

Significantly, the RSS was established without a formal name but just referred as *sangh* or collective. Several months after the RSS was established the name was chosen from a shortlist of four, two of which ended with the word *mandal* or association and the other two had *sangh* as the last word. It was eventually decided upon for because it was considered more intimate. Significantly, in its early years, RSS grew principally due to the personal loyalty *pracharaks* or preachers were able to secure among *swayamsevaks* or self-servers/volunteers who were inducted into the *parivar*.

In contemporary India, when political contestation has progressively become more strident, the three words no longer evoke what they did generically. Instead, they have emerged as flags which are either flaunted or displayed to attract other like-minded individuals.

References

Ahmed, Mughees. 'Local-Bodies or Local Biradari System: An Analysis of the Role of Biradaries in the Local Bodies System of the Punjab'. *Pakistan Journal of History and Culture* 30, no. 1 (2009): 81–92.

Chaudhry, Abid Ghafoor, et al. 'Perception of Local Community and Biradari on Panchayat: An Exploratory Anthropological Study of Biradari in Village Saroki, District Gujranwala, Pakistan'. *Advances in Anthropology* 4, no. 2 (2014): 53–8.

PATRIARCHY

Uma Chakravarti

Patriarchy, the term by which the contours of a set of related institutions is now understood, has been described by Sylvia Walby as a 'system of social structures and practices, in which men dominate, exploit and oppress women'. It is important to stress the characterization of patriarchy as a *system*, because this helps us to reject biological determinism as the basis of difference in the power and status of men and women as well as to understand that men's power over women is not an individual phenomenon but is part of a structure. According to Gerda Lerner, patriarchy 'is the manifestation and institutionalisation of male dominance over women and children in the family and the extension of male dominance over women in society in general. It implies that men hold power in all the important institutions in society and that women are deprived of access to such power'. She also points out that this does not mean that women are 'either totally powerless or totally deprived of rights, influences and resources'. It also does not mean that every individual man is always in a dominant position and every individual woman is in a subordinate position. What is important, however, is that under the system we have called 'patriarchy', there is an ideology that men are superior to women and that women are, and should be, controlled by men, with women regarded as the property of men.

A significant aspect of such an approach in defining patriarchies is that we can see its linkages with other institutions such as class, caste, state and ideologies (whether religious or secular); we can also grasp the fact that since the formation of patriarchy has a relationship to history and is not static but has changed, its dominance can also be ended through the struggles of women, and men, committed to a more egalitarian society.

Certain questions are central to an understanding of patriarchy: when we talk about women's subordination to men in the patriarchal system, what exactly do we mean? In what ways do men dominate women and what do they control? In what way does their control over women link up with their control over resources and why do they need to control women at all? With the development of intensive agriculture, the exploitation of human labour and the sexual control of women became closely linked; women's sexuality was thus sought to be controlled, and such control intensified with the development of private property and class-based exploitation. Patriarchy is related fundamentally to both class and the state and even the earliest states in history were organized in the form of patriarchy and had an interest in the maintenance of the patriarchal family.

Apart from the control over women's sexuality under patriarchy, women's subordination to men also enables the latter to control women's productive or labour power. Women's productivity within the household, and outside, is controlled by men who also determine whether women will work outside the household or not. The control of women's labour means that men derive economic gains from the subordination of women. To maintain this double control – over women's sexuality and their labour – women's mobility is often stringently controlled through practices such as confining women within the house or within certain defined spaces. The entire structure of controls is facilitated by depriving women of independent access to productive resources and making them dependent on men.

Other kindred concepts are the terms 'paternalism' and 'paternalistic dominance'. In their historical origins, the concepts come from family relations as they developed under patriarchy (paternalism is a subset of patriarchy) in which the father held absolute power over all the members of his household. In exchange, he owed them the obligation of economic support and protection. Further, for the maintenance of paternalism, it is essential to convince the subordinated that their protector is the only authority capable of fulfilling their needs. The most significant aspect of paternalism is that while it softens the harshest features of the system of male dominance, it also weakens the ability of the subordinated to see their subordination in political terms. At the same time, the ideology enables the dominant to convince themselves that they are extending paternalistic benevolence (rather than dominance) to people inferior and weaker to themselves.

Paternalism has been extremely successful in India, as elsewhere, and was reinforced by pre-Independence and post-Independence thinkers and policymakers, and has easily adapted itself to moderate reforms in the status of women without changing the power relations in any way between men and women in the family or in the wider society.

Two features of the system of patriarchy in terms of its ideology is that it produces consent: women 'cooperate' in the working of patriarchy as they provide consent to it by internalizing the ideologies of male dominance. Thus, they become complicit in the system. Cooperation or consent was in a sense extracted, rather than freely given, because of the material structure in which women were excluded as independent actors; it must be understood, therefore, that patriarchy is not merely a system, it also has a material basis.

Although the subordination of women is a common feature of almost all stages of documented history and is prevalent in large parts of the world, the extent and form of that subordination has been conditioned by the social and cultural environment in which women have been placed. Even within South Asia, there is great regional diversity in the patriarchal formations. Apart from many communities in Kerala, Lakshadweep and Northeast India, which are matrilineal (where succession passes from mother to daughter) within a larger structure of patriarchy, there are many types of family and kinship arrangements. The dominant form of patriarchy in many parts of the subcontinent has been termed Brahmanical patriarchy in recent feminist scholarship. Brahmanical patriarchy is a set of rules and institutions in which caste and gender are linked, each shaping the other, and where women are crucial in maintaining the boundaries between castes. Patriarchal codes in this structure ensure that the caste system can be reproduced without violating the hierarchical order of closed endogamous circles, each distinct from and lower or higher from the others. Brahmanical patriarchal codes for women differ according to the status of the caste group to which they belong in the hierarchy, with the most stringent control over female sexuality for the highest castes. The norms of Brahmanical patriarchy are often drawn from the prescriptive texts and shape the ideologies of the upper castes in particular, but the norms are also sometimes emulated by the lower castes, especially when seeking upward mobility.

Just as graded inequalities mark the caste system, graded patriarchies mark the nature of women's subordination in South Asia. The mechanism of control through which both caste hierarchy and gender hierarchy were reproduced in this region is threefold: the first device is ideology, internalized by women as *pativrata* (wifely fidelity), whereby women aspire to chastity and wifely fidelity; second, law and custom as prescribed by texts or regional practices; and the third, the state itself, both in early history and in more recent times. In the cultural models of Brahmanical patriarchy, through its mythologies, women were socialized into believing in their own empowerment through chastity and fidelity; through the ideology of sacrifice and of passive acceptance, features of the pativrata woman, women saw themselves as achieving both sublimation and a special strength. Women then believed that they had a different and distinctive power, a higher and more spiritual power that could even bring about miracles. Working together paternalism and cultural models of womanhood virtually erased subordination; it was thus much easier for women to be complicit in the patriarchal structure that governed their lives.

Both the structure of Brahmanical patriarchy, customary and regional variations of patriarchy and paternalistic ideologies are being opposed today by democratic and egalitarian ideologies and norms enshrined in the Constitution. Movements and struggles addressing the issue of women's subordination, their exploitation at home and outside it and the range of oppressions they experience 'inside the family' have been occurring in many parts of India. Along with other democratic struggles against caste and other oppressive institutions, the women's movement has been a dynamic force in the political process; it has also spearheaded the very significant women's studies movement, which has provided us with a set of terms by which we can understand women's subordination.

References

Chakravarti, Uma. *Gendering Caste: Through a Feminist Lens*. Kolkata: Stree, 2003.
Lerner, Gerda. *The Creation of Patriarchy*. New York: Oxford University Press, 1986.

POLICE REFORMS

Prakash Singh

The police organization in India is based essentially on a legislation enacted in 1861. Its historical background needs to be understood. There was a revolt in the country against British Rule in 1857. This uprising was crushed, but it had shaken the foundations of British rule in India. The colonial masters felt that they must have a police force that would be at their beck and call and carry out their diktat, right or wrong. And so, the Police Act of 1861 was passed to raise a 'politically more useful' police.

After Independence, several states appointed police commissions and submitted their recommendations to the state executive, but their core recommendations were never implemented. In 1977, the Government of India appointed a National Police Commission (NPC) as it felt that 'a fresh examination is necessary of the role and performance of the Police'. Between 1979 and 1981, the NPC submitted eight detailed reports that listed comprehensive recommendations covering the entire gamut of the working of the police. Unfortunately, these set of recommendations too received no more than cosmetic treatment at the hands of the central executive.

In a landmark judgement on 22 September 2006, the Supreme Court of India issued comprehensive directions for police reforms. These were as follows:

a) To constitute a State Security Commission in every state to insulate the police from external pressures.

b) Director General of Police (DGP) of the state to be selected from among the three seniormost officers of the department, empanelled for promotion to that rank by the Union Public Services Commission (UPSC) and, once selected, she or he shall have a minimum tenure of at least two years, irrespective of her or his date of superannuation.

c) All police officers on operational duties, such as inspector general of police (IGP) in charge of a zone, deputy inspector general of police (DIGP) in charge of a range, superintendent of police (SP) in charge of a district and station house officers (SHO), should also have a prescribed minimum tenure of two years.

d) The investigating police shall be separated from the law and order police in, to start with, towns/urban areas which have a population of ten lakh or more and gradually extended to smaller towns/urban areas.

e) Constitution of a Police Establishment Board, comprising DGP and four other senior officers of the department to decide all transfers, postings, promotions and other service-related matters of officers of and below the rank of deputy superintendent of police (DSP). This board shall make appropriate recommendations to the state government regarding the postings and transfers of officers of and above the rank of SP.

f) The setting up of a Police Complaints Authority at the state level to look into complaints against officers of the rank of SP and above and, at the district level, to look into complaints against junior officers up to the rank of DSP. These will be headed by retired judges.

g) The Centre shall set up a National Security Commission to prepare a panel for selection and placement of chiefs of central police organizations and also to review measures to upgrade the effectiveness of these forces.

The aforesaid directions were to be complied with by the Centre, state governments and the Union Territories by 31 March 2007.

The states have dilly-dallied in the implementation of the court's directions. Seventeen states have passed laws and the rest have passed executive orders. However, these Acts and executive orders go against the letter and spirit of Supreme Court's directions. The Centre has also not enacted the Model Police Act, even though a draft of the same was submitted by the Sorabjee Committee in 2006. Justice Thomas Committee (2008–2010), which was appointed by the Supreme Court to monitor the implementation of its directions in various states, expressed 'dismay over the total indifference to the issue of reforms in the functioning of Police being exhibited by the States'.

Apart from the core areas identified by the Supreme Court, reforms are urgently required in some other policing related fields as well:

a) Manpower shortage needs to be addressed,

b) Infrastructure (transport, communications, forensics, housing) needs upgradation.

c) Modernization of police forces needs to be given impetus.

d) Registration of cases calls for drastic improvement.
e) Working hours of police personnel need to be limited; at present, they are considered on duty round the clock.
f) Greater promotional opportunities need to be made available for subordinate ranks.
g) Crime and Criminal Tracking Network and Systems (CCTNS) project, which seeks to network all police stations across the country, needs to be implemented with vigour.

Police reforms, it must be emphasized, are not for the glory of the police. They are to give better security and protection to the people of the country, uphold their human rights and improve governance. It has been rightly said that police reforms are 'too important to neglect and too urgent to delay'.

References

Alexander, Koshy. *Police Reforms in India: An Analytical Study*. New Delhi: Discovery Publishing House, 2006.

Khadem, Mohammad Bashir Mia. 'The Emergence of Modern Policing System in the Indian Subcontinent: A Review of Major Reform Initiatives'. *Social Science Review* 32, no. 1 (2015): 71–86.

RTI

The MKSS collective

RTI is a contemporary Indian abbreviation for 'Right to Information' and is used as a noun, verb, adjective or even adverb. The RTI, defined by people's movements in India, is not only a legislation but also a political construct. Rajasthani villagers often say that the easier word is Hindi and the more difficult English. By that definition, RTI is now a 'Hindi' word and has come to stay.

The RTI grass-roots movement has its origins in the struggles of the rural poor in mid-1990s central Rajasthan. The Mazdoor Kisan Shakti Sangathan (MKSS) held its first rural *jan sunwai* (public hearing) in Kot Kirana, Pali district, on 2 December 1994 and demanded the right to access all government documents and the right to public audit. Through these hearings, numerous scams were exposed and the basis of the culture of secrecy perpetuated by the colonial Official Secrets Act (OSA) of 1925 was implicitly questioned. The jan sunwais galvanized both victims and perpetrators. They expanded the notion of right to information beyond the 'freedom of expression' (guaranteed by Article 19 of the Indian Constitution), by intrinsically connecting it to the right to life (Article 21) and to equality (Article 14), thus changing the global discourse of access to information movements.

Two years after the first jan sunwai, in April–May 1996, MKSS organized a forty-day *dharanā* (sit in) at Beawar in Rajasthan. The success of this protest led to the formation of a National Campaign for the People's Right to Information (NCPRI) later that year, transforming a local struggle into a national demand for state and central legislation. Consequently, some states passed

RTI legislations, and the state laws themselves and debates around them began to contribute to a pan-India build-up of the movement. The decade-long campaign by NCPRI continued with its dialectic between street protest and lawmaking. RTI became a part of the lexicon for the demand for a law in the form of ideas and slogans used widely – 'our money, our accounts', 'right to know, the right to live'. 'Social audits' and the experience of the jan sunwais demonstrated how people could use information to actually participate in democratic governance.

The Right to Information Act was eventually enacted on 15 June 2005 and came into effect on 12 October 2005. The RTI and its use ingeniously derives from the wisdom of ordinary citizens. It requires an application on a piece of paper with a fee of 10 rupees, and the public authority is bound to respond to the application within a specified time frame. Its impact has been electric on a malfunctioning system. As one user from Punjab said, 'The RTI has, for the first time, inversed accountability, and put the system on the mat!' Today, a network of about sixty to eighty lakh users routinely challenge corruption and the arbitrary use of power. They call power to account right be it in a village or in the Parliament. Questions are asked every day, and parliamentary and legislative sessions alone do not anymore define 'question time'. As a democratic tool, RTI has empowered people to participate in governance on a continuous basis. People own and support the Act. Armed with proof from official records, they have been able to establish both legitimacy and agency.

The ignominious killing of more than seventy RTI users since 2005, and the continued threat to current RTI users, has not served as a deterrent. It is perhaps the only legitimate weapon for millions of Indians who live on the margins, economically, socially and politically. It allows them to exercise their sovereignty – to change the culture of secrecy and establish one of openness. The RTI is participatory democracy in action.

A senior administrator and teacher at the national administrative training institute remarked a few years ago, 'Administration in independent India, can be divided into "pre-RTI" and "post-RTI" eras. For the citizen, RTI has completely changed their relationship with government. "Let's file an RTI! (RTI *lagadenge*!)" is a statement of resolve; a challenge to abusers of power, especially governments. The governments dread what follows an application: dismantling of power and secrecy, and drawing people into public debate. Disclosure creates an avalanche of challenges.' As this essay is being written, the threatened power elite attempts for a third time around to amend and weaken the law – this time by reducing the independence and authority of the Information Commission, which is empowered to enforce the legislation. In response, millions who use the RTI raise their voices against this attempt to dilute the law, and the amendments are once again deferred. The RTI is destined to be a contested space; and, at the same time, it is destined to be the source of many more stories that celebrate the creative relationship of people and language.

References

Roy, Aruna and the MKSS Collective. *The RTI Story: Power to the People*. New Delhi: Roli Books, 2018.
RTI Assessment and Analysis Group, and the National Campaign for Peoples' Right to Information. 'Safeguarding the Right to Information: Report of the Peoples' RTI Assessment', 2009. Available at: http://freedominfo.org/documents/india-safeguarding-executivesummary.pdf (accessed December 2018).

SHAKTI (ŚAKTI)

Vrinda Dalmiya

Shakti (from the root *shak*, 'to be able') is power or force. It makes things happen. This aligns it to notions of ability and potentiality. The former captures the agential dimension of making something happen, while the latter its temporal or modal aspect – the state of possibility before and from which something emerges as real. When the 'something' is the world in general, shakti references that which brings it about as well as the unmanifest potentiality prior to its actualization. What is distinctive, however, is that such power is gendered: it is conceptualized – and visualized – as being feminine or female. Thus, we find here a conception of femininity that is explicitly *not* aligned with passivity.

In the Shakta traditions, shakti becomes the Ultimate Reality that manifests itself in different forms. It signifies the metaphysical root of the world that is of the nature of pure consciousness (*jnaaana, cit*), has a desire to multiply (*ichhaa*) and, most importantly, the capacity to change or act (*kriyaa*). Since emergents share in the nature of their cause, dynamic consciousness is the 'true' nature of all objects. In some schools of tantra, the generative moment or shakti is the free play of delight wherein consciousness imaginatively projects a 'you-ness' and then self-reflexively sees itself through the eyes of the latter. Thus, in the structure of awareness, the wide gap between the first person or 'I' and its inert object or the third-personal 'it/that' is mediated through the act of *addressing* it as a 'you'. This address calls into being the second person which is both other to and the same as the self (*paraapara* or identity in difference). This intermediary space is the enabling ground of proliferation and is shakti.

When such abstract ontology is theologized and gendered, Shakti comes to signify the goddess. Female divinities as personifications of Ultimate Reality are worshipped in multiple forms – from the powerfully martial Durga, and the beneficent Lakshmi, to the terrifying Kali. Male deities now are the metaphysical ground (consciousness) that always needs activation by the goddess. This is dramatically represented in art and iconography through the figure of the *ardhanarishvara* – a body that is half male and half female, Shiva–Shakti. Sometimes goddesses become 'consorts' – separate figures attached to male divinities personifying their energy and animating force. This image resurfaces in vernacular wordplay. Men jokingly refer to their wives as their 'shakti' and in misogynist political humour, female leaders (like Indira Gandhi) can be referred to as 'Shakti' indicating unbridled (political) power like the more destructive images of the goddess.

In classical Indian philosophy of language, shakti as power appears as the capacity of a word to mean something or refer to an object. This semantic articulation of the concept has led to vibrant technical debates over linguistic signification being eternal or conventional and over the nature of this relation which is presupposed in testimonial knowledge.

References

Dupuche, John R. 'Person to Person: *Vivaraṇa* of Abhinavagupta on *Parātriṃśikā* Verses 3-4'. *Indo-Aryan Journal* 44 (2001): 1–16.

Ganeri, Jonardon. *Semantic Powers: Meaning and the Means of Knowing in Classical Indian Philosophy*. Oxford: Oxford University Press, 1999.

SCIENTIFIC TEMPER

Ranjit Nair

The phrase 'scientific temper' first appeared in the nineteenth century in a garden-variety sense to describe the behaviour of a scientist who loses his temper. It was the philosopher Bertrand Russell who deployed the term in the manner we do today, to connote rational inquiry untrammelled by dogma. Four decades later, in his tome *Discovery of India*, Jawaharlal Nehru used it as a key marker to differentiate between medieval and modern attitudes to understanding the world and ourselves as part of it. One may plausibly argue that Nehru, who was an avid reader, acquired the phrase from Russell.

Among the leadership of the postcolonial world, Nehru stood out for his understanding of the key role that science and technology played in the modern world. 'It is science alone that can solve the problems of hunger and poverty, of insanitation and illiteracy, of superstition and deadening custom and tradition, of vast resources running to waste, or a rich country inhabited by starving people. ... Who indeed could afford to ignore science today? At every turn, we have to seek its aid. ... The future belongs to science and those who make friends with science.' Max Perutz, a Nobel Prize winner in Chemistry, in his collection of essays entitled *Is Science Necessary?* highlights this statement by Nehru and gives as an example of the Green Revolution which M. S. Swaminathan was able to bring about, ensuring that food grain production kept pace with India's rising population.

For Nehru, the scientific temper carried larger social implications. According to him, 'The scientific approach, the adventurous and yet critical temper of science, the search for truth and new knowledge, the refusal to accept anything without testing and trial, the capacity to change previous conclusions in the face of new evidence, the reliance on observed fact and not on pre-conceived theory, the hard discipline of the mind – all this is necessary, not merely for the application of science but for life itself and the solution of its many problems.'

At the helm of affairs as prime minister of free India, Nehru acted on his belief that scientific temper was key to national development by establishing institutions of higher education and research at a furious pace, as if to make up for opportunities lost during the long night of colonial subjection that had reduced the country to abject penury. Nehru valued the company of scientists and was instrumental in creating a chain of national laboratories, several Indian Institutes of Technology (IITs), the nuclear and space programmes, setting India on track to become a major world power in the twenty-first century. In 1946, in fact, Nehru had jumped the gun, averring that 'India today is one of the four great powers of the world' – yet this was by no means an unreasonable statement, considering the carnage inflicted by the Second World War in the European and Asian theatres of war to which he was witness.

In 1926–7, Nehru visited several European countries and was impressed by the Soviet approach to planned development, which he viewed as an application of the scientific approach to social affairs. On his return, he wrote to Mahatma Gandhi, expressing disagreement with the *Ram rajya* ideal that the latter extolled. Yet, when Aldous Huxley charged Gandhi (and Tolstoy) with advocating mass slaughter by rejecting modern science, Nehru wrote to Huxley that he had committed a 'grave wrong' and that Gandhi's attitude to science was 'very far from being hostile' and that he welcomed its benefits. It was because the colonial power's industrialization had destroyed traditional Indian industries that Gandhi was critical of modern industrialization and taken to reviving cottage industries which could mitigate, to some extent, widespread immiserization across rural India. He argued that free India, rid of colonial parasitism, would undertake rapid industrialization.

Scientific temper was written into the Constitution of India in 1976, vide the Forty-Second Amendment, in Part IV-A Article 51-A, on the 'Fundamental Duties' of citizens, of which Article 51-A (h) enjoins citizens 'to develop scientific temper, humanism and the spirit of inquiry and reform'. With Prime Minister Indira Gandhi having declared a national emergency, these amendments did little for the cause. In 1981, a group of scientists and academics associated with the Nehru Centre in Bombay issued a 'Statement on Scientific Temper' that castigated the rise of obscurantism and superstitious beliefs. A 'Counter-Statement' was then issued by the social psychologist Ashis Nandy who charged the signatories of elite disdain towards 'vulgar common folk' and advocating instead a 'humanistic temper', which was welcomed by traditionalists.

Scientific rationalism is often seen as subversive of religious dogma and rightly so. Belief in miracles and hatred towards rationalists who debunk them has angered traditionalists within the religions of India. Some rationalists have been murdered and others have become voluntary exiles fearing for their lives. Scientific temper, however, remains alive and well for the most part, despite being dangerous to the health of its advocates.

References

Singh, Baldev, ed. *Jawaharlal Nehru on Science and Society: A Collection of His Writings and Speeches*.
    New Delhi: Nehru Memorial Museum and Library, 1988.
Nair, Ranjit, Review of Baldev Singh (ed.) in Seminar 363, November 1989.

SELF-RESPECT

V. Geetha

Self-respect might appear a word that needs no gloss. For most people, it signifies a human disposition that is taken for granted. Historically, the term has a distinctive valence, particularly in the Indian context. It is associated with an anti-caste movement that emerged in colonial South India, in the province of Madras in the 1920s. Identified with its founder E. V. Ramasamy (or Periyar, as he was known) and his iconoclastic, rational and atheistic world view, the movement set itself against a social order founded on the basis of caste divisions and given to the practice of untouchability and women's subordination.

The self-respect movement emerged as a response to the Indian nationalist movement under the leadership of M. K. Gandhi. It took issue with nationalists on the question of social justice or the importance of recognizing caste-based discrimination and inequality and working to remedy it – through envisioning and putting into practice a system of communal representation that would ensure that Dalits and non-Brahmins access higher education, government posts and places in the legislature in proportion to their numbers in the population. Unconvinced of the Indian National Congress' intent in this regard, Periyar, originally an ardent follower of Gandhi, broke faith with the party and subsequently with Gandhi. Periyar was dismayed by Gandhi's continued endorsement of *varnashrama dharma*, the Hindu religious logic that sanctified caste divisions.

Periyar counterposed to the nationalist espousal of *svarāj* (self-rule) the ideal of self-respect. He argued that svarāj cannot be considered one's 'birthright' as nationalists were wont to, since one's birth was determined on the bases of caste. Rights assigned on the basis of caste were discriminatory, argued Periyar, and therefore one ought to work against the logic of birth-based social status before one could claim self-rule as one's birthright. What was desirable in this context therefore was not self-rule but self-respect. For, in caste society, one was told to respect one's so-called superiors and look down on one's so-called inferiors. This did not and could not make for a healthy sense of the self, and it was important for caste selves to be transformed – and such remaking was to be achieved through the practice of self-respect.

To respect oneself meant myriad things in Periyar's semantic universe and the meanings of the term were actualized in plural ways by those who came to be part of the self-respect movement. The movement came to protest the following: the hegemony of Brahmins in modern political and social spheres; the hold of religion, particularly obscurantist beliefs and practices, presided over by a pliant and corrupt priesthood, composed of Brahmins; the authority of the rich; and finally, the power and privileges that men had and withheld from women. Positively, self-respect became the badge of a creed that espoused social and political comradeship in place of caste-based social relationships; social equality, including gender equality; women's freedom, especially when it came to matters to do with marriage, motherhood and divorce; a rationalist world view; atheism or, at the very least, a critical attitude towards faith and scripture pertaining to all religions; and in a broad sense, socialism.

When aligned to political ideas, the notion of self-respect referenced a distinctive politics. Periyar argued that for a self-respecter socialism would have to be more than a question of economic justice and embrace what he termed *samadharma*, as opposed to *manudharma* (the creed of the *Manudharmashastra*, which justified social inequality). Samadharma pertained to the realm of common and inalienable rights that accrue to all of us as human beings and it had to be brought about through the repudiation of the caste order. In this sense, self-respect-samadharma represented an ethics that would help refashion the self, freeing it as it were from the stranglehold of caste, even as socialism freed all from an exploitative economic system.

The self-respect movement was unique in that it sought to create alternative cultural and social practices, including, of self-respect marriages – which were now deemed contractual rather than sacramental and not requiring the presence of a Brahmin priest to solemnize the conjugal tie. The self-respect marriage was rendered legal only in the 1960s though such marriages were in vogue right from the 1920s! Other cultural practices included putting in place a repertoire of songs and music on self-respect themes, building self-respect theatre forums, reading and propaganda groups and evolving an alternative journalism. Self-respecters were committed to a rationalist world view and many were avowed atheists who thundered against all faiths, yet their greatest ire was reserved for Hindu practices and beliefs.

The self-respect movement was committed to social revolution and looked to the state to enact appropriate legislation to enforce radical and modern ideas of equality. Politically, it endorsed socialism, but its followers were not all socialists. Some were nationalists, others socialists and yet others came to endorse Tamil nationalism. In 1944, a substantial number of self-respecters became part of a new organization, the Dravidar Kazhagam (DK), formed to safeguard Tamil or Dravidian political and social rights and interests on the eve of Independence. The DK protested the idea of India and argued for a more federal polity, including the right of provincial ethnic, linguistic and other groups to secede and form nation-states of their own. While the political agenda of the DK remained a piece of political propaganda, its social and cultural campaigns which targeted 'northern' 'Āryan' faith was, in essence, a repudiation of upper-caste, especially Brahmin, dominance and authority in matters of culture, religion and politics.

References

Geetha, V. and S. V. Rajadurai. *Towards a Non-Brahmin Millennium: From Iyothee Thass to Periyar*. Kolkata: Samya, 1998, reprint, 2008.
Pandian, M. S. S. 'Towards National-Popular: Notes on Self-Respecters' Tamil'. *Economic and Political Weekly* 31, no. 51 (1996): 3323–9.

SEVA (SĒVĀ)

Tridip Suhrud

The garden is magical, the distant hilly sky crimson, the two faces aglow with light, almost beatific light, the younger man clad in translucent dhoti sits pressing the legs of an older man in a diaphanous lower garment which is undone. In the distance an undecipherable image, like God who shall not be captured by human eye and three figures, one of them unmistakably of a woman, in meditative silence or a conversation so deeply intuitive that words are superfluous. This is Bhupen Khakkar's 1986 oil on canvas 'Seva', one of the most evocative paintings of modern India.

The painting captures the entire gamut of meanings – said and unsaid, uttered and inarticulate – of the act called *seva*, translated all too often as 'service'. Seva is derived from *saha* and *eva* meaning 'together with'. It is suggestive of a mode of being in the world, with nature and with fellow beings as also with the divine who refuses to reveal her true nature. Understood thus, seva is the epitome of fellowship, of a state of communion with the self, other beings and the divine.

By its very root meaning, seva is an act performed with others and also for others. Seva cannot be self-serving, self-aggrandizing, self-seeking. Even the search of the self in seva is through this act of communion. It is an act of being with others, being that is non-acquisitive, being that seeks only to serve that pain is alleviated, suffering made bearable, joy experienced and the divine made immanent. This makes seva the preferred mode to be free from sin, and if one cannot be free from sin, for atonement. Seva creates a fellowship based on shared pain and care of those in pain. To care is to perform seva.

Such a mode of being in the world has been described in the *Bhagavad Gita* as a state of *yajna*, as sacrifice not of the others but of the self, through unattached service. Thus, seva and yajna are used interchangeably, or the term *sevayajna* is coined. Herein lies the attraction of the life of seva. Seva is also both a vocation of freedom and a paean to it. It is a mode of freedom where freedom is sought and experienced not as an assertion but by a process where the self is surrendered to others in and through service. The greater the surrender, the deeper the freedom. And yet, or perhaps for that very reason, seva is an act of self-volition. In this sense, seva is the complete opposite of servitude and slavery, where both self and self-volition are denied.

For these reasons, seva has captured our imagination. It allows for a search of the divine by being in the world as an act of service. This very ideal moves the philosophy and practice of relatively recent religious formations like the Sikhs. The practice of *kar seva*, bodily service rendered to others and through them to truth, captures (despite its horrific and destructive usage as we have rendered) the spirit. In the last century and a half, seva acquired an organizational structure, for example in the formation of the Ramakrishna Mission, wherein the age-old institution of *sanyasa* (of renunciation) is sought to be imagined as a life of unceasing service unto others. Seva found a different embodiment in the life of Charles Freer Andrews, who sought to combine a Christian dedication to the poor and the disposed with an impulse of seva such that he became a *deen bandhu* (brethren of the poor, literally but more beautifully 'a poor brother' as well). For many dying, emaciated, neglected and forgotten Saint/Mother Teresa embodied seva, which has few parallels in our lives and times.

It was M. K. Gandhi who brought seva from a personal, religious, ethical universe into the realm of the political. If his personal god was *Satyanarayana* (Truth as God), it was equally true of *Daridranarayana* (Poor as God). If Satyanarayana takes one to satyagraha and svarāj, Daridranarayana takes one to *asteya* (non-stealing) and *aparigraha* (non-possession or poverty). An ethical person, for Gandhi, is one who recognizes the pain of others. And together, they create a mode of freedom where the ethical is ever present not only as a philosophically negotiated ground but also as the last person, the most dispossessed, the 'meekest' her that we have been 'together with', been sevak of.

Violence is the perfect opposite of seva. Seva as service, as care, as non-acquisitive selflessness is a necessary condition for *ahinsā* (non-violence or, more aptly, love). Violence unto the others occurs when they are pushed outside the realm of care and of seva. Seva denies the legitimacy of violence as an act of freedom, as more we take to violence, the more we recede from ourselves. Violence is denial of the self, seva is affirmation of the self, living together with others.

References

Ciotti, Manuela. 'Resurrecting Seva (Social Service): Dalit and Low-Caste Women Party Activists as Producers and Consumers of Political Culture and Practice in Urban North India'. *The Journal of Asian Studies* 71, no. 1 (2012): 149–70.

Handy, Femida, et al. *From Seva to Cyberspace: The Many Faces of Volunteering in India*. Delhi: SAGE Publications India, 2011.

SARVA SHIKSHA ABHIYAN (SARVA ŚIKṢĀ ABHIYĀN)

Vimala Ramachandran

SSA is the abbreviation for Sarva Shiksha Abhiyan, a campaign by Government of India to ensure education of all children. Following the World Education Conference held in Jomtien, Thailand, in 1990, a global campaign for universal primary education, popularly known as 'Education for All' or EFA, was launched. It took time to set root in India. It was only in 2000–1 that the Ministry of Human Resource Development (MHRD) of the Government of India announced an ambitious programme of universal elementary education. This meant ensuring education for all children in the 6–14 year age group by ensuring them access from grade one to grade eight. This programme was called Sarva Shiksha Abhiyan (literally, 'Education for All' campaign). According to the MHRD website, 'SSA (sought) to provide for a variety of interventions for universal access and retention, bridging of gender and social category gaps in elementary education and improving the quality of learning. SSA interventions include inter alia, opening of new schools and alternate schooling facilities, construction of schools and additional classrooms, toilets and drinking water, provisioning for teachers, regular teacher in service training and academic resource support, free textbooks and uniforms and support for improving learning achievement levels/outcome.'

Since 2003, when SSA covered the entire nation, the term has become synonymous with universal elementary education. Today, the term SSA is used to denote school education in newspapers, reports and common everyday conversation on education. Interestingly, when we use SSA we essentially refer to government efforts and government schools and not private schools and private efforts in the same direction. Equally significant is the common perception that SSA means free education. Since the mid-2000s some non-governmental organizations, such as Pratham India and Educational Initiatives, have started assessing what and how much children are learning as a result of this intervention. Their work indicates that SSA is essentially about brick-and-mortar inputs to augment school infrastructure and hiring more teachers. Their argument was based on the finding year after year that over 50 per cent of children in grade five cannot read grade two text or do simple arithmetic problems. As a result, at least in the public perception, SSA is perceived as an opportunity for rent-seeking and corruption – with the accent on utilization of infrastructure budget, ticking off completion of activities like the mandatory twenty-day teacher training, providing ramps for differently abled children and so on. In 2006, the Comptroller and Auditor General of India's report on SSA highlighted the siphoning off of several crores of rupees meant for training and purchase of teaching and learning material. This assessment was reiterated in 2017.

SSA is essentially a Hindi phrase that has now been accepted across the different linguistic regions of India. While it started as a specific programme, over the last seventeen to eighteen years (since 2001) it has come to mean something specific – the government schooling system. The abbreviation is used as a word by the media and sometimes even in scholarly articles. It denotes the Indian way of centralized top-down planning and implementation of school education programmes. I say 'the Indian way' because if one reads the rhetoric of SSA, it speaks of bottom-up district planning to ascertain needs and provide solutions. However, in reality the programme provides a tight template that districts and state administration are required to use to plan. The template is linked to strict financial norms – and regardless of whether a district is based in a remote mountainous region or a flood-prone coastal area – the financial norms for building, for pupil–teacher ratios, for academic and administrative supervision are the same.

References

Ministry of Human Resource Development (MHRD). 'Sarva Siksha Abhiyan'. Available at: http://mhrd.gov.in/sarva-shiksha-abhiyan (accessed 29 September 2017).

Ramachandran, Vimala and Prerna Goel Chatterjee. 'Evaluation of Gender and Equity Issues under Sarva Shiksha Abhiyan'. *Indian Journal of Gender Studies* 21, no. 2 (2014): 157–78.

SUDHAR (SUDHĀR)

Tridip Suhrud

Before *svarāj*, both in the sense of self-rule or home rule and rule over the self, captured the imagination and aspirations of people of the Indian subcontinent, it was *sudhar* or its cognate *sudharo* which had moved the people of the subcontinent in the second half of the nineteenth century. Sudhar is *su-dhar*, the good path and also the one that holds, contains. It is in the former sense that the term was used and the practice attendant to it was created. The idea was represented in English most prevalently by the term 'reform'.

At the most immediate level, what had to be reformed, reshaped, created anew was the self, the person and, at a larger, more basic level, the civilization. The second half of the nineteenth century was marked by this anxiety, this endeavour. It was also marked by equally deeply felt need to resist this move to cast order of things anew. In theory and practice, sudhar involved thinking anew the practices related to worship, food, dress, conjugality, relationship with others – both individually and societally – and advent of new modes of doing things and thinking about these newer modes. Sudhar, though externalized, was in a fundamental sense about the self, the person as an autonomous, individuated being. And yet, not surprisingly, the battleground was the subjectivity, the minds and the bodies of women. Women had to bear the burden of being the primary bearers of continuity, tradition and also change. The desire to reform and to conserve forced men to engage with the 'women's question' in a manner never evident before.

The practice of self-examination gave rise to two forms of cultural self-expression: the autobiography and the novel. The former was predicated upon the autonomous individual self and the latter on the desire to capture what Govardhanram Tripathi called 'the drama of transition'. The self-practices of the reformers came to be identified with the modern. And still, the chasm between thought, aspiration and practice gave rise to deep ambivalence both among those who sought to reform and those who wished to conserve. The present for both became oppressive and they sought release from it in either an imagined future or in a fantastic past which would make the future more bearable.

The desire to recast the self and society gave rise to a quintessentially modern and 'secular' institution called 'society' (*samāj*) or as the Gujarati term goes *mandali*. As an organizational structure, samāj is the harbinger of the modern artefact called the political party. The demand for political reform followed after the need for reform of the self and society. During much of the second half of the nineteenth century, sudhar, reform and hence the modern was a positive value, an aspiration worth cultivating and emulating. This conception of sudhar was questioned and, for some time, altered by M. K. Gandhi, who in his philosophical dialogue, *Hind Svarāj*, spoke of sudhar in multiple semantic frames. For Gandhi, sudhar was civilization, modern civilization, ephemeral civilization, change, progress, reform and that which will destruct itself. For Gandhi, modern civilization had enslaved India. This formulation of Sudhar as the oppressive and enslaving impulse sought to change both the conception of sudhar and the practices attendant to it. Gandhi argued that India's salvation lay in svarāj, as rule over the self, where the performance of duty and recognition of morality was the ground from which civilization, true sudhar emerged and was sustained. In performance of duty and in moral action lay Gandhi's mode of being in the world, which was *seva* (service to others). Sudhar was that mode of conduct which allowed one to perform seva and through that claim for oneself the capacity for self-rule.

This conception of sudhar as that which de-civilizes and of 'true' sudhar as one that enables freedom remains unique to Gandhi. This usage was not something that Indians of his times or the times after him were and are ready to accept and adopt. The liminal space that Gandhi's *Hind Svarāj* occupied in his times and the contests that we have with it today emanate largely from Gandhi's insistence that sudhar is not a civilizing idea but its opposite, one that grounds under its heels human autonomy and self-volition. By casting aside this conception, contemporary India has restored a largely positive value to the term sudhar and our search for self-volition continues to be in the realm of the modern.

Reference

Gandhi, Mohandas Karamchand. *Hind Swaraj or Indian Home Rule*. Madras: GA Natesan and Company, 1921.

SUKH-DUKH (SUKH-DUKH)

Aditi Mukherjee

The expression *sukh-dukh* has two constituents: *sukh* and *dukh*. Independently, they seem to be in a binary relationship, representing two poles of experience. Literally, 'sukh' would approximate to 'happiness, well-being, joy' and 'dukh' would mean the opposite, that is, 'unhappiness, misery, distress'. However, these two words are often paired together, with mutually exclusive meanings, in Indian philosophy and literature. The following line from *Bhagavad Gita* (Chapter 2, verse 38) can be cited as an example: *Sukha dukhe same kritwa laabhaalaabhau jayaajayou* ('happiness distress treat alike, gain and loss, victory and defeat'). That is, in the battlefield at Kurukshetra, Lord Krishna urges Arjuna to treat happiness and distress, loss and gain, victory and defeat with equanimity. A similar pairing is found in the

Hitapodesha to indicate that happiness and unhappiness in life rotates like a wheel: *chakravat parivartante dukhani cha sukhani cha* ('like a wheel it undergoes cyclic change from sorrow also and from happiness also'). The Sūfī saint-poet Kabir says, *Dukh mein sumiran sab kare, sukh mein kare na koye/Jo sukh mein sumiran kare, to dukh kahe ko hoye* ('Everyone prays to Him when they are unhappy, none remembers Him in happy times/if one prayed at happy times, why should unhappiness come').

In all the three examples above, sukh and dukh are juxtaposed as semantic opposites. However, when sukh and dukh are joined to form the compound 'sukh-dukh', the semantics is no longer binary or additive as sukh plus/and dukh. The meanings of the constituent words do not add up to give the meaning of the whole compound. Like the Yin and Yang, an element of complementarity is introduced. The semantics is now non-compositional and covers an entire spectrum with a wide range of experiences between the two seemingly opposite poles of happiness and unhappiness. Such non-compositional compounding is quite common in Indian languages. The spectrum could be: (a) spatial: as in *upar-neeche* (above-below), *aage-peeche* (front-back), *idhar-udhar* (here-there), *yahaan-vahaan* (here-there); (b) temporal: as in *subah-shaam* (morning-evening), *raat-din* (night-day); (c) transactional: as in *lena-dena* (to take-to give), *naap-tol* (measure-weight); or (d) experiential: as in sukh-dukh (happiness-unhappiness). Following are some contexts where sukh-dukh is used to cover a range of emotions and experiences which need not necessarily consist of either sukh or dukh. The first two are from Hindi, the third is a Bengali sentence and the fourth is a Telugu sentence: *Sukh-dukh mein padosi kaam aate hain* ('Neighbours come in useful in all situations'); *Aao thodi der baithkar sukh-dukh ki batein kar lein* ('Come, let us sit down and share our life experiences'); *Dui bondhute mile onek sukh-dukher kotha holo* ('The two friends met and chatted shared their life experiences'); and *Waaru sukha-dukhaalu pacchkunTaaru* ('They shared their life experiences').

References

Easwaran, Eknath. *The Bhagavad Gita:(Classics of Indian Spirituality)*, vol. 1. California: Nilgiri Press, 2007.

Grover, Shalini. *Poor Women's Experiences of Marriage and Love in the City of New Delhi: Everyday Stories of Sukh aur Dukh*. Diss. University of Sussex, 2005.

SWARAJ (SVARĀJ)

Dunu Roy

The teeming cauldron of mass dissent against English rule in India exploded into what the imperialist English called the Mutiny of 1857 but later nationalist Indian historiographers termed as the First War of Independence. Thus, 'dissent' may be seen differently by those who face it and those who create it. Much the same may be said for the word *swaraj* (literally, 'self-rule') when, two decades after the 'mutiny', Dayananda Saraswati, founder of the Arya Samaj, first used it to project a vision of 'India for Indians'. But he was not just posing it as liberation from English rule; he was equally, if not more, concerned about the cultural degradation of Hindus and the many forms of idol worship and rituals that took away from 'Vedic purity'. In the manner of many ascetics, he wandered for almost twenty-five years in spiritual pursuit of the 'truth' before writing *Satyarth Prakash* to throw light on the meaning of truth as revealed in Vedic writings.

At the same time, he was a vocal advocate of equal rights for women, education for all, a staunch critic of caste discrimination and child marriage and a votary of scepticism and rationality. His eclectic preaching and the public debates he had with other Sanskrit scholars had a galvanizing effect on the nationalists of the times, influencing spiritualists like Madame Cama and Swami Shraddhanand, Hindu conservatives like Vinayak Damodar Savarkar and Lala Lajpat Rai as well as revolutionaries such as Ram Prasad Bismil and Ashfaq Ullah Khan – each charmed by swaraj in their own way but all coming together in the tumult of the struggle for freedom.

It should, therefore, not be surprising that two decades later, in 1898, Bal Gangadhar Tilak, another scholar of Sanskrit who wrote a commentary on the *Bhagvad Gita*, gave the clarion call: 'Swaraj is my birth right and I shall have it.' Through his two newspapers, Tilak exposed the cruelties and excesses of British rule and raged against the suffering of the mass of Indians at the hands of their colonial masters. He denounced the famines and epidemics as a result of misrule and was an outspoken critic of the moderate policies of the Indian National Congress. His swaraj, therefore, did not denote religious reform but a radical departure into *sampoorna swaraj* (full freedom).

Another decade later, M. K. Gandhi picked up from both Saraswati and Tilak and wrote *Hind Swaraj*. Acknowledging that, 'No one realised the evil of the existing system of government as Tilak did', Gandhi went beyond Tilak to postulate his swaraj, which transcended merely getting rid of the Englishman and posed a moral challenge to the evil of the Englishman's system of government, its institutions, its foundational beliefs and its unjust, exploitative and alienating structures as seen through the lens of a colonized people. Thus, Gandhi visualized a completely different set of structures, with self-respect, self-realization and self-responsibility integrated into self-rule.

Thus, prior to the English leaving the subcontinent to its own devices (although there was much that the subcontinent internalized from English rule, such as its body of law, its governance and administration, the armed forces and concepts of 'development'), the meaning of swaraj may be seen to emerge in the three dimensions of religious reform, political freedom and moral reconstruction – as represented by the three stalwarts Saraswati, Tilak and Gandhi. A major difference between the three was that while Saraswati and Tilak tried to reform or revolutionize Hindus on the basis of past glories, Gandhi tried to draw all faiths into his call for a secular future.

The idea of freedom embodied in swaraj also resonated in the call for *swadeshi* ('of our country') given by Surendranath Banerjea (who was dismissed from the Indian Civil Service) to protest the partition of Bengal in 1905. In 1906, Dadabhai Naoroji (a cotton trader who was the first Indian to be elected to the House of Commons) was inspired by Saraswati to declare swaraj as a political objective when delivering the Presidential Address at the Indian National Congress. In 1923, Motilal Nehru and Chitta Ranjan Das constituted the Swaraj Party to contest elections to the Central Legislative Assembly (winning almost half the seats), before the Congress gave the call for *poorna swaraj* ('complete freedom') in 1929.

In 1938, four years before the Congress launched the Quit India movement that eventually led to freedom, there was an opportunity to realize Gandhi's vision of swaraj, when the Raja of Aundh, Bhavanrao, was persuaded by Maurice Frydman (a Polish engineer who became Swami Bharatananda) to hand over the reins of state to his people. Gandhi helped draft the Swaraj Constitution and the administration was reorganized with village *panchayat*s (local self-government) being elected by all adult voters to administer all services and welfare, with each panchayat choosing a president to represent them at the taluka council. For the next six years, this island of swaraj took remarkable strides, until India arrived at her tryst with destiny in 1947.

After Gandhi's assassination in 1948, his spiritual successor Vinoba Bhave constituted the Sarva Seva Sangh to continue experimenting with swaraj, also launching the *bhoodan* ('land grant') movement in 1951. By 1955 about 2.5 lakh acres had been granted in the villages of Koraput, Orissa, for Bhave to initiate another experiment with swaraj Annasaheb Sahasrabuddhe, who had been part of the Aundh experiment, was placed in charge. Two achievements were reported initially: a large number of illiterate people were quickly trained for technical and managerial tasks, and the Government readily granted the funds. Yet, the experiment failed because bureaucratic procedures did not match with Gandhian precepts.

Other efforts interpreted swaraj differently. In 1956, Khasa Subba Rao began a weekly magazine called *Swarajya* as a 'first coherent intellectual response to Nehruvian socialism', championing 'individual liberty, private enterprise, minimal state, and cultural rootedness'. In 1973, students in Ahmedabad went on strike to protest against a hike in hostel food fees, and the unrest spread to successfully demand the government's resignation. Students in Bihar also embarked on a similar agitation and veteran Gandhian Jayaprakash Narayan declared that *sampoorna kranti* ('total revolution') was unfolding against all oppression and injustice. This tide of protest eventually led to the State of Emergency in 1975.

Some other notable examples were in 1984 when the Bhopal gas tragedy occurred and Banwarilal Sharma and Rajiv Dixit laid the foundation of the Lok Swaraj Abhiyan to summon Union Carbide to account. Later, in 1992, they also launched the Aazadi Bachao Andolan as a 'national movement in India to counter the onslaught of foreign multinationals and western culture'. Then the Seventy-Third Amendment (which devolved power to the panchayats) was extended to Scheduled Areas in 1996, and Brahma Dev Sharma, who made significant contributions to make this possible, became the inspiration for the Hamara Gaon Hamara Raj movement in tribal areas. This later manifested as the Pathalgadi movement in Jharkhand in 2017.

The most recent development was in 2012 when Arvind Kejriwal, leader of the Aam Aadmi Party that emerged out of the India Against Corruption movement led by veteran Gandhian Anna Hazare, wrote his own version of *Swaraj*, arguing that political power must be decentralized to the units of direct democracy, the *gram sabha*s and *mohalla sabha*s. In 2015, a faction led by Yogendra Yadav and Prashant Bhushan formed the Swaraj Abhiyan, claiming the higher moral ground of swaraj by launching the Jai Kisan Andolan to mobilize farmers for debt relief and remunerative prices and to pursue litigation in the Supreme Court to ensure the proper functioning of the Public Distribution System.

Thus, the idea of swaraj has been resurrected time and again with different interpretations, depending on the era and context. At the core lies the notion of 'freedom', of charting one's own unfettered course, but much depends upon who is seeking freedom from what and for whom.

References

Anand, Y. P., comp. 'Hind Swaraj or The Indian Home-Rule (1909): The Gandhian Concept of Self-Rule'. Available at: http://www.mkgandhi-sarvodaya.org/hindswaraj.htm (accessed 27 May 2018).

Anjaneyulu, B. S. R. 'Gandhi's "Hind Swaraj": Swaraj, The Swadeshi Way'. *Indian Journal of Political Science* 64, no. 1/2 (January–June 2003): 33–44.

VIRANGANA (VĪRĀṄGAṆĀ)

Usha Mudiganti

Virangana is a unique expression of Indian womanhood combining power and virtue. The Sanskrit word *virya* signifies the 'heroic' and is used for brave men, whereas the word virangana is meant to describe a woman who embodies heroism. Although a virangana seemingly blurs gender lines, there is not only an acceptance but also a celebration of such an expression of womanhood in India. It is an alternative to the image of the meek, docile and domestic Indian woman.

Despite large-scale admiration for this expression of womanhood, it is rare to come across a contemporary woman who would be given this title. For a woman to be described as a virangana, she has to take up tasks culturally deemed to be those performed by men while retaining traditionally cherished feminine traits. While there would be countless modern working women who have a successful career and are also excellent homemakers, they would not be considered viranganas. A virangana is a woman who takes up the responsibilities of a man on the untimely death of her husband and successfully performs all the duties left incomplete by the man. She is a woman who unexpectedly, but efficiently, steps into the shoes of a male predecessor and in his absence continues his struggle for a worthy cause.

India has a long tradition of queens who have been described as viranganas. There are descriptions of warrior queens in the Mahābhārata who can be called the foremothers of modern-day viranganas. Scholastic studies of the Indian Revolt of 1857 have thrown up names of many warrior queens who led their people against the takeover of their kingdoms by the British East India Company owing to Lord Dalhousie's Doctrine of Lapse. The long list includes queens as well as common women who fought along with their queens. Some of the famous warrior queens are Rani Lakshmibai of Jhansi, Rani Avantibai of Ramgarh and Begum Hazrat Mahal of Awadh. Some common women who fought alongside their queens in this revolt are Jhalkaribai of Jhansi, Uda Devi of Awadh and Azizun Bai of Kanpur. These queens and common women have become ideals for many contemporary women's rights activists. Feminist scholarship has traced an entire historical and legendary tradition of viranganas fighting for just causes and for the betterment of their people. The one thing all these warrior queens have in common is that they were trained in their childhood in the skills required for warfare and/or governance by their father or an older male relative but were married to a prince at a very young age and settled into lives within royal households till the death of their husband necessitated their stepping in as regents, at which point they showed their efficiency in governance or warfare, as was required of their particular situation. Their visual depictions usually are of a woman astride a horse and geared for war with arms and armoury but also wearing feminine jewellery.

However, some queens who never took up arms, and depicted as traditionally garbed widows, are also celebrated as viranganas. These are women who have nurtured and inspired their sons into bravery and rebellion against oppressive kings. The most famous among such viranganas is Jijabai, mother of the Maratha king Shivaji. Another such Maratha queen from the mid-eighteenth century, Ahilyabai Holkar, is known as a virangana not only for the immense amount of social work led by her in her kingdom but also for organizing a regiment of women. A couple of centuries later, another all-women regiment was formed for India's freedom struggle. It was the Rani of Jhansi Regiment raised under Subhas Chandra Bose's Indian National Army. It was headed by Captain Lakshmi Swaminathan and was named for the most famous virangana of the Revolt of 1857, Rani Lakshmibai of Jhansi. Lakshmibai's story circulated through folk legends, songs and poems to such an extent that the Hindi phrase *jhansi ki rani* has become a metaphor for bravery and is frequently used by the people and the media in India to describe a courageous young woman. The phrase has also been used as a metaphor for some modern Indian women politicians just as it is used for common Indian women who lead local struggles. Quite often, the phrase is used with a tinge of admiration to warn men against making unwelcome overtures towards a brave young woman.

References

Hansen, Kathryn. 'The Virangana in North Indian History: Myth and Popular Culture'. *Economic and Political Weekly* 23, no. 18 (1988): WS28–33.

Singh, Harleen. *The Rani of Jhansi: Gender, History and Fable in India*. New Delhi: Cambridge University Press, 2014.

VISVA-BHARATI (VIŚVA-BHĀRATĪ)

Partha Ghose

The Sanskrit word *visva* refers to the 'world' or the 'earth'. The Sanskrit word *bharati* stands for the Hindu goddess of knowledge and music, also known as Saraswati. As a name, Bharati is primarily a feminine name but was also part of the name of the great Tamil nationalist poet Subramania Bharati, who was male; or titles for members of a religious sect like Shri Krishna Chaitanya Bharati; or the name of an organization connected with teaching and research, such as India's first research facility in the Antarctic, called Bharati. The word visva has found usage in organizations such as Vishwa Hindu Parishad, names of various firms and encyclopaedias such as the *Vishwa Katha Kosha*.

Visva-Bharati is the name given by Rabindranath Tagore, Nobel laureate Indian poet, to the centre of creative learning he established in 1921 at Santiniketan in West Bengal. Its motto is *yatra visvam bhavati ekaneedam*, a verse from the *Rig Veda*, which means 'a single nest for the world'.

It was Maharshi Debendranath Tagore, Rabindranath's father, who first visited the area in 1863, developed a special liking for it and acquired some land to build a large country house and plant tall trees. He named the house Santiniketan, the abode of peace, because he envisioned it as a sanctuary for seekers after the formless Brahman, the transcendent and immanent ultimate reality. Far from the madding crowd, it was a quiet and serene place with time for meditation and study. Debendranath put the property in the care of a trust which would operate it as an *ashram* (a hermitage). The trust deed also had a provision to establish a Brahmo school (along the lines of the monotheistic reformist religious movement called Brahmo Samaj). A tinted glass prayer hall was built in 1891. The asram was open to everyone, regardless of caste, creed or religion, but image worship or sectarian religious practices were prohibited. The entire area surrounding the ashram soon came to be known as Santiniketan.

Rabindranath visited the place from time to time and, in line with his father's general approach, established a school there called Asram Vidyalaya on 25 December 1901. Studies were combined with plays and songs. Students and faculty lived simply, subsisting on simple meals and doing many menial chores themselves. The school was later renamed Patha Bhavana.

His subsequent travels and interactions with eminent people across the world led to a broader and more complex vision: the creation of Visva-Bharati. This vision, born out of Rabindranath's personal disenchantment with rote learning prevalent in his time and his vision of the essential unity of life, was to establish a creative education centre that would stand apart from the typical educational institutions established following Lord Macaulay's 'Minute on Indian Education of February 1835' whose single purpose was the mass production of 'a class of persons, Indian in blood and colour, but English in taste, in opinions, in morals and in intellect'. On the contrary, the aim of Visva-Bharati was to understand the West from the standpoint of the East and to seek out the essential unity and humanity of the various religions and cultures of the world. Visva-Bharati combined education of children in a free and nature-loving environment, the use of music and arts as instruments for emotional development, social work to help neighbouring villages, the promotion of rural development and higher research in philosophy, cultures and so on. The key elements in the structure were the school Patha Bhavana, the centre for fine arts Kala Bhavana and the centre for music Sangeet Bhavana. Besides these, he also established a department of Chinese language and culture called Cheena Bhavana in April 1937.

In 1951, the Government of India declared Visva-Bharati a centre of national importance and passed the Visva-Bharati Act of 1951, thereby declaring it as a central university. As warned by several eminent parliamentarians who took part in the debate that followed the introduction of the Bill in Parliament, this governmental move has changed the original character of the institution because the question of equivalence of degrees across India came up, and the Academic Council of the new university decided to conform to the standards prevailing in the country. The very character of the institution that Rabindranath compared to 'a vessel that carries the best cargo of my life' was eventually sacrificed.

Leonard Elmhirst, who went to Santiniketan together with his wife Dorothy to help Rabindranath in his rural reconstruction work at Sriniketan, later established the Dartington Hall project in South Devon, England. Inspired by the ideals of Visva-Bharti, Dartington Hall works towards providing progressive education and rural reconstruction. This is one among many other centres across the world that have been directly or indirectly inspired by the ideals of Visva-Bharati.

Thus, the word Visva-Bharati has come to acquire the connotation of a centre of alternative education to promote peace, conservation of nature and propagating universal humanism based on ancient Eastern wisdom informed by Western values, with music, dance and seasonal festivals playing a central role.

References

Tagore, Rabindranath. *My School*. Montana: Kessinger Publishing, reprint, 2010.
Tagore, Rabindranath. *Creative Unity*. London: Macmillan & Co., 1922.

VOTE BANK

Manisha Madhava

With the adoption of the Constitution in 1950, a liberal democratic political system with modern political institutions was established in India. However, these democratic political institutions were actually superimposed on a traditional particularistic society based on caste. The interplay between these two gave rise to what is popularly referred to as the politics of 'vote bank'. Vote bank refers to a block of voters, who on the basis of certain considerations such as caste, religion, language and identity, loyally support a particular candidate or a party in an election. The term was first introduced by the noted sociologist M. N. Srinivas in his classic *The Social Structure of a Mysore Village*. In Srinivas' formulation, 'vote banking' involves three actors – individual voters, political parties and village-level middlemen – bound together by a vertical hierarchy of caste and 'influenced by patron–client relationship'. The relations of patronage between voters and middlemen are mediated by caste and class, with the middleman often belonging to the higher caste and class and the masses belonging to the lower castes, obliged by social, economic and ritual ties. These 'bonds' between the two are mediated by relations of social trust. At election time, these social ties are activated in order to deliver votes to a preferred party or candidate. Elucidating on the Congress Party-dominated political system of India, Rajni Kothari points out that the party's power hinged on 'intermediate networks which take on the form of autonomous sub-systems'. Similarly, Kohli describes how the 'Congress system' operated through a 'chain of important individuals stretching from village to state, and eventually to the national capital, welded by bonds of patronage'.

After Independence, support for the newly established institutions came from a coalition of interests of both caste and class. However, political institutions were largely controlled by a dominant upper-caste elite. Marginalized communities, such as the Dalits, constituted the vote banks of mainstream parties dependent on vertical relations of patronage – clients. This served the interest of the dominant caste elites in maintaining their positions within the framework of the modern democratic system. Vote-bank politics was however subject to much criticism as it militated against the notion of the individual as an autonomous, independent voter exercising her or his free political will.

The nature of vote-bank politics in India has undergone significant change over time. From 1950 till 1967, the political landscape of the country was dominated by the Congress Party, which held power both at the national and the state levels, drawing support from a broad spectrum of upper castes, middle classes, scheduled castes, scheduled tribes and Muslims. The steady decline of the Congress Party in the 1970s, due to the growing size and politicization of the Indian electorate, excessive centralization and the resultant failure to accommodate the interests of all sections as well as the rise of regional political parties altered patterns of political patronage, as Jaffrelot notes. It was, however, the implementation of the recommendations of Mandal commission in 1989 by the V. P. Singh-led National Front Government at the Centre that gave a new salience to caste and vote-bank politics. The Mandal Commission recommended reserving 27 per cent of seats in educational institutions and jobs for the Other Backward Classes (OBCs). While caste identity had always been politically important, after 1989, 'vote bank' was no longer what a single patron commanded. Rather, it denoted a collective political preference defined principally by primordial identity, of caste or religion or language, of a particular interest group. As Ranajit Guha points out, 'vote banks' are constituted by shared material or moral interests.

Dalits today constitute the core support base of regional parties such as Bahujan Samaj Party (BSP), Samajwadi Party (SP) and Rashtriya Janata Dal (RJD). Their support is not on the basis of patronage but on the basis of identity. As Chatterjee notes, 'Community groupings are offering votes in exchange for material benefits' and this needs to be understood as part of a broader 'strategic politics' through which the urban poor are making claims on the state. Another point of view, forwarded by Schaffer, is that vote-bank politics, where votes are exchanged for material benefits, lends it the character of market purchase and is more harmful to democracy than patronage and has negative implications for democratic accountability. The debate now is whether the emergence of new forms of vote banks wherein material goods and particularistic benefits are directed towards caste- and community-based social groupings in exchange for a block vote represent exploitative politics in which the poor are excluded from true democratic participation or if vote banks possess the possibility of redistribution of justice and mass emancipation.

References

Kothari, Rajni. 'The Congress System in India'. *Asian Survey* 4, no. 12 (2016): 1161–73.
Srinivas, Mysore Narasimhachar. *The Social Structure of a Mysore Village*. Indiana: Bobbs-Merrill, 1960.

YOJANA (YŌJANĀ)/PLANNING

Nalini Nayak and Pulin B. Nayak

The idea of 'yojana', or planning, has been an essential part of Indian economic thinking and its regular usage may be traced to the pre-Independence period. Pandit Jawaharlal Nehru, in particular, was a strong votary of planning as an instrument to bring about a rapid social and economic transformation of India's poor and underdeveloped economy. In 1938, the Congress Party, under the presidentship of Netaji Subhash Chandra Bose, set up the National Planning Committee (NPC) of which Pandit Nehru was made the chairman. With the onset of the Second World War, India's independence seemed imminent and the purpose of the NPC was to formulate policies and strategies to bring about rapid economic development in India.

In Nehru's words, the NPC was 'a strange assortment of different types' but it soon set about the task of addressing the critical issues concerning agriculture, industry, education and health, among others, and the urgent task of poverty eradication and achieving self-sufficiency. It is possible to hold the view that under the NPC the state was expected to play a lead role in the development process. Soon after, there was a separate effort by several prominent businessmen, who came up with the 'Bombay Plan' of 1944, which acknowledged the influence of the NPC. However, the formulators of the Bombay Plan were keen to emphasize the role that the private sector and the market were to play in the national planning exercise.

On assuming the prime ministership after India gained Independence, Pandit Nehru was keen to introduce planning as a vital component of the development exercise. The Planning Commission was established on 15 March 1950 with the prime minister as its chairman. The country soon embarked on the First Five-Year Plan (1951–6) which focused on a balanced growth of agriculture and industry. A very important question centred on the issue of providing for consumption versus capital goods. A higher allocation for capital goods entailed lower consumption today but a higher growth rate for the economy that would benefit the future generations. The Second Five-Year Plan (1956–61) was formulated with the help of the statistician-physicist P. C. Mahalanobis, which placed emphasis on the capital goods sector. This was critiqued by many observers who felt that there was a neglect of the wage goods sector, which was detrimental to the development process.

During the early years of planning, the public sector was to play a crucial part in the development process. Nehru was of the view that the 'commanding heights' of the economy should be in the hands of the state and accordingly a significant role was earmarked for the public sector in, for example, steel, coal, heavy industries and electricity generation. The government also allocated substantial funds for education, health, science and technology, and it was during the 1950s that the state-funded teaching and research institutions, such as the IITs, IIMs, AIIMS, CSIR, etc., were given a strong push.

During the first three decades of planning, the average growth rate of the Indian economy however remained in the 3.5 to 4 per cent range. The critics of the planning process argued that the bureaucratic licence-permit system gave rise to rent-seeking and served as a fetter on economic efficiency. In 1991, under the prime ministership of Shri P. V. Narasimha Rao, with Dr Manmohan Singh as the finance minister, significant economic reforms were introduced. The market mechanism was now accorded a much greater role in the development process, though the Planning Commission still remained functional and continued to address the issue of channelizing investment into socially desirable areas. The growth rate of the Indian economy picked up substantially, and during 2005–8, the average annual growth rate of GDP exceeded 9 percentage points.

In 2014, a new government led by the Bhartiya Janata Party came into power with Shri Narendra Modi as prime minister. In a significant break from the past, the Modi government disbanded the Planning Commission. In its place, the NITI (National Institution for Transforming India) Aayog has been constituted. The age-old problems of poverty, unemployment, regional imbalance and accentuation of inequality, among others, continue to be major problems confronting the Indian economy, and it is too early to assess the performance of the new body. It is however worth remembering that if India is one of the fastest-growing major economies of the world today, the basis for this must have had something to do with the planning process that the country had adopted, howsoever imperfectly, for sixty-four years of its existence as an independent nation.

References

Chakravarthy, Sukhamoy. *Development Planning: The Indian Experience*. New Delhi: Oxford University Press, 1987.
Nehru, Jawaharlal. *The Discovery of India*. Calcutta: The Signet Press, 1946.

CHAPTER 6
LANGUAGE AND SELF-REFLECTION

ADDA (AḌḌĀ)

Manas Ray

Old Bengali dictionaries give the meaning of *adda* as the meeting place of the mischievous – wasting time in idle frolic and meaningless chats. As a cultural phenomenon, adda has, however, grown in prestige and popularity from the early twentieth century, attributing a distinct texture to Bengali modernity. Venerable cultural critics like Buddhadev Bose and Gopal Haldar maintain that, notwithstanding some ambiguity about the origin of the word, as a cultural practice, adda blossomed in Bengal. As a matter of fact, there seems to be unanimity among commentators that nothing expresses the 'soul' of modern Bengali culture better than adda. The way the history of adda links with the emergence of Bengali literary modernity, the cultivation of a distinct cultural and political self and the formation of a reading public with its attendant spaces of the coffee house, bookshops, movies, plays and magazines is not to be found in otherwise similar patterns of socialization in the rest of India.

Like any other evolving cultural practice, adda defies neat definition. Broadly speaking, addas are spontaneous, free-flowing talk-shops of a group of mostly men (never less than three and rarely more than ten) where all topics under the sun, no matter how serious or trivial, global or local, public or private, are welcome. No digression causes any disruption in such discussions, which are often spiced with good-humoured banter and leg-pulling. Narration of events (invented or true) are quite often exaggerated. Backbiting and a tinge of mischievous – even malicious – criticism of those not present give adda its special flavour. Its gradual democratization, as part of the rise of the urban middle class and an emerging nationalist modernity towards the beginning of the last century, has endowed the environment of adda with a sense of assumed equality. This was also the time when the venue of addas started shifting from the drawing rooms of the rich to tea shops, cafes and, what in Bengali is called, *rawk* – an outdoor verandah or raised slab of a house, mostly adjacent to the road. Showing off or name dropping kills adda, and habitual do-gooders are better kept outside the ambit of adda.

While discussions must never touch vulgarity, adda is not responsible for guiding the world or achieving any practical purpose. Here lies its essential difference from the Habermasian public sphere which, as a matter of fact, is neither private not public – it is not private because members are not supposed to talk about their personal problems and it is not actually public, for only a select few have access to it. Ideally, these are spaces of normative freedom for making principled arguments based on rational, critical discourse. In contrast, there is no obligation for addas to be politically correct or didactic or to offer practical solutions. Though issues (especially political but at times even aesthetic) may invite fervent discussion, addas are far less about knowledge transacted and much more about presentation and performance. They are a mode of living in the world, giving meaning to it and thus making it habitable. What matters is a sense of intimacy and informality. This is in sharp contrast to Western club gatherings, which are formal affairs with specific codes of dress and conduct and which require a monthly or annual subscription. Each adda has its own sense of relevance and propriety as well as its own repertoire of private jokes and references – in short, its own poetics. While topics can quickly change and the tone varies from very serious to utterly frivolous, all must gel during these chats. Hence, addas are a form of life – an accepted and recurrent cultural practice with their own style of language, specific patterns of behaviour and an embedded history.

From early in the last century, poets and writers have had their own addas, as have journalists, all of which has had a ricocheting effect on the addas of student hostels in the city. From the 1930s onwards, addas in drinking places have become a regular feature. More well known of these is the heady, dimly lit joint at Khalashitola in the port area of the city. Such places (including inner-city pubs and the coffee houses) with all the fervent literary and political discussions give Calcutta its reputation as a city of caffeine, alcohol, brawls and floating tar.

If adda has genealogical links with *chandimandap* – the age-old homosocial culture of gossip at the courtyard of the temple of goddess Chandi by the upper-caste village elderly – it also carries elements of *majlish* – gatherings in the drawing room of the affluent in nineteenth-century Calcutta. Between these two ends, that is, rustic vulgarity and show of pomp and erudition, adda as a cultural practice paved its way into the twentieth century as part of the trajectory of Bengali cultural modernity. In the course of this contingent journey, it has also become hegemonized by the Bengali middle class. The highbrow literary adda of the first half of the last century was replaced in the post-partition era by a group of angry young writers, whose 'addresslessness' was their much-vaunted identity. This was also a booming time for government jobs and there was a consequent rise of the salaried class as well as the coming into being of a kind of cinema, music, literature and the phenomenal growth of little magazine culture that catered to the middle class' tastes. All of these served the right *dispositif* for the popularization of adda, which became the principle vehicle for world-making in a vastly transformed urban scenario. With the spread of university education, women's participation remained less remote.

Recent decades have witnessed a decline in the culture of adda, as erstwhile residential houses have given way to multi-storeyed apartment blocks, street corner teashops are being taken over by chains of cafeterias, the educated youth has begun to out-migrate and evenings are monopolized by different televisual fares and social media playing the role of what might be called electronic chandimandap. Thanks, mainly to the television channels, adda is now an important item in the ongoing retro celebration of Bengali culture, much of which looks out of place, even fossilized. Here, the anchor takes the role of an adda jockey as prominent personalities 'engage' in an adda that is solely meant for consumption.

References

Bose, Pradip. 'Adda, Parocharcha, Gultani'. In *Bangali Jiboner Tattatalash*. Delhi: Parampara Publication, 2016.

Chakrabarty, Dipesh. 'Adda, Calcutta: Dwelling in Modernity'. In *Provincializing Europe: Postcolonial Thought and Historical Difference*. Princeton, NJ: Princeton University Press, 2000.

ADJUST

Santosh Desai

The idea that life is a ceaseless state of negotiation between one's desires and one's circumstances and that some room can be contrived through inventive forms of compromise is what animates the idea of 'adjust'. Encountered, most graphically, when travelling by public transport, being asked to adjust is, in effect, a way of squeezing in twice the number of people in any defined space. The entreaty to adjust a little is met with a look of resigned acceptance and some shuffling takes place – the new entrant gets a small perch which is, over the course of journey, gradually expanded till all the passengers have an equal if constricted amount of space.

The underlying logic of the idea of adjust is that if everyone settled for a less-than-ideal solution, then perhaps the desires of an incremental few could be accommodated. Desire for a little more is not considered illegitimate, nor is its complete fulfilment considered essential. Located firmly in the group of people that call themselves the 'middle class', making adjustment is seen as a way to contrive aggregate satisfaction at the cost of the individual. It highlights the belief that compromise is inevitable and, in fact, desirable for life to proceed at a permanently imperfect level. Adjustment allows things to move forward with relative ease – something that the quest for perfect solutions does not allow.

Implicit in the idea of adjust is the idea of a commons that precedes the claim the individual has over any product or service, particularly one which is present in a public space. In this sense, the notion of ownership eludes definitiveness; in practical terms, it becomes the right to first use, rather than an absolute entitlement. Newspapers carried in a bus or a train can be picked up by one's neighbour without a need felt to seek permission, and the notion of 'reserving' a berth is seen more as a convention than a rule. The ability to extract value out of suboptimal and partial answers is visible in many ways. Matric-fail is deemed a qualification, as is *chauthi*-pass (one who has passed the fourth grade). Reservations in trains carry an intermediate classification – that of RAC (Reservation Against Cancellation) which assures one of a seat and keeps hopes of getting one's berth alive. The 'missed call' made from overseas communicates the safe passage of a loved one without incurring any cost.

Over the years, 'kindly adjust' has become an established Indianism and finds mention in popular culture particularly in television parody shows and advertising. As a mark of Indianness, it represents both scarcity and a reluctant form of generosity that allows the collective to accommodate the needs of the (n + 1)th person and contrive a degree of satisfaction out of constraints. It has its critics too – people who argue that this trait of suboptimal accommodation becomes a disincentive in the pursuit of perfection. The idea of order, which rests on the ability to separate categories and drawing lines between things, gets compromised when one is open to 'adjusting' one's needs.

References

Kundani, Lalit. 'Kindly Adjust: The Spaces Of India'. *Huffington Post*, 13 December 2014. Available at: www.huffingtonpost.in/lalit-kundani/kindly-adjust-the-spaces-_b_6273698.html.

Singh, Amita Tyagi and Patricia Uberoi. 'Learning to "adjust": Conjugal Relations in Indian Popular Fiction'. *Bulletin (Centre for Women's Development Studies)* 1, no. 1 (1994): 93–120.

AKSHARA (AKṢARA)

Aditi Mukherjee

The Sanskrit word *Akshara* literally means 'imperishable', 'indestructible' or 'fixed'. It is derived from the root *kshara*, meaning 'perish' or 'melt away', and the prefix *a-* which indicates 'not'. Sanskrit phrase, *na ksharati iti akshara* would translate as 'something/someone that does not perish'. The word is used to refer to the Supreme Being. It is also one of the thousand names of Lord Vishnu – one whose greatness never diminishes over time. In the Sanskrit/Indian writing system, Akshara refers to a character that represents a syllable, a minimal unit of sound, that cannot be further atomized. Also, it could perhaps be related in some way to the literal meaning of the word – imperishable – in the sense that the written symbol, which is the visual representation of speech, is relatively more permanent than an oral utterance.

In the Devanagari script and its derivatives in different Indian languages, vowels (long or short) and consonants, are represented by distinct characters. The vowels, by definition, form the nucleus of a syllable and, therefore, represent the syllable. Each vowel has two forms – one, when it occurs independently and, the other, known as *matra*, when it is attached to a consonant. On the other hand, each character for a consonant includes a default short vowel to form a syllable. In Hindi and many other Indian languages, this vowel is *schwa*. In Bengali (*Bangla*), Assamese and Odia, it is 'o' pronounced as in the English word – call. In some Dravidian languages, like Telugu and Kannada, the presence of the default vowel is indicated by a mark on the top of the character. The word for this mark, in Telugu, is called *talakattu* – literally meaning 'a mark on the head'. To indicate the absence of the inherent vowel in Sanskrit, a mark known as *halant* is added to the bottom of the consonant character; the halant is still in use when writing Sanskrit. However, due to certain historical processes of sound change, many Indo-Āryan languages have lost the final vowel syllable. For example, the Sanskrit words *veda* 'Veda' and *samataa* 'equality' are pronounced as 'ved' and 'samtaa' in Hindi. The default vowel after 'd' and 'm', in the two words, respectively, is absent and, in the written form, the *halant*, which should have been used is, likewise, absent. The use of the halant sign is becoming increasingly rare in most languages of Indo-Āryan origin. However, the Dravidian scripts like Telugu and Kannada behave differently; they not only indicate the presence of a vowel including the default vowel but also maintain the tradition of signalling its absence with a sign (equivalent to the halant) that replaces the 'presence' sign on top of the character.

When two consonants come together, without a vowel between them, they form a consonant cluster. For example, 'pr' in the English word 'pride' is a cluster. Indian scripts have different ways of representing consonant clusters. These are known as *yukta* akshara (yukta 'combined/joined' + akshara). Some of them have merged into distinct characters. Thus, there are specific *yukta aksharas* for clusters such as 'tra', 'kta', 'ksha', etc. The yukta aksharas usually have complex shapes and new learners find them difficult to acquire.

There are two interesting derivatives of the word akshara – *saakshara* 'literate' and *nirakshara* 'illiterate'. These two terms have acquired a social value now. They are used in connection with 'education'. A *saakshara* person is deemed to be educated and thus socially empowered as opposed to the *nirakshara* person who is perceived as ignorant and, thus, backward.

BAAT-CHEET (BĀTCĪT)

Rama Kant Agnihotri

The origins of *baat-cheet* (feminine noun) may be from the Sanskrit words *vaartaa* meaning 'speech, story, dialogue' – leading to *baat* – and *chintan* 'to think/reflection' leading to *chiit*, but etymological enquiry is hardly ever foolproof. For us, in contemporary India, the Sanskrit vaartaa and chintan are two distinct words, while the Hindi baat-cheet is just a single word. Even if the words are related, it remains difficult to trace the exact trajectory of the journey. Even though baat does exist on its own, there is no word like 'chiit' in Hindi. In fact, there must be very few words in the Hindi language that would match the frequency with which baat-cheet is used in North India; there may also be only a handful that cover a comparable semantic range.

Kumar and Kumar mention several, including *kaanaaphuusi*, *phusphusaahat* (focus of the talk 'secrecy') and *vaartaalaap*. Other words like *samvaad* (serious conversation/dialogue), *khickhic* (annoying talk), *charchaa, paricharchaa* (discussion), *bhentvaartaa* (interview) and *paraamarsh, vichaarvimarsh* (focus on advice) may have the meanings associated with baat-cheet; none of these words, however, quite have the semantic scope of baat-cheet. This polysemous word could mean anything from an ordinary conversation between two or more friends to the most serious international negotiations of nuclear weapons (a summit MoU) between two countries.

Consider some everyday uses of the word in Hindi – '*aaj hamein apne bete ki shaadi ki* baat-cheet *karne jaanaa hai*' ('today we will go to talk about our son's wedding'), '*un donon deshon ki* baat-cheet *kaa vishay duniyaa kii aarthiik stithi hai*' ('the subject of discussion between those two countries is the economic condition of the world'). The conversational use of baat-cheet could include, say, matrimonial negotiations and also religious discourse; hence, the high frequency of its use is no surprise and its functional relevance is enormous. As noted above, the word also subsumes the meanings of words like dialogue, discussion, discourse, consultation, interview, conference, conversation, etc. There exists something of a parallel in Bangla, in the East, with the word *kothaa batraa* and in Malayalam, in the South, with *vaartaamaanam*; as a result, the pan-Indian flourish to the word baat-cheet is indubitable.

References

Kumar, Arvind and Kusum Kumar. *Brihat Samanta rKosh*. New Delhi: National Book Trust, 2013.
Verma, Ramchandra, ed. *Manakhindikosh*. Allahabad: Hindi SahityaSammelan, Prayag 1990.

BHASHA (BHĀṢĀ)

Karthika Sathyanathan and Rajesh Kumar

The word *bhasha*, in Hindi, means 'language'. As per the *People's Linguistic Survey of India*, our country is a land of over 780 languages and 66 different scripts. They are all spread over five different language families. According to the Government of India Census of 2011, there are about 122 languages (spoken by more than ten thousand people) and numerous minority languages; of the 122 major languages, 22 are scheduled languages (included in the 'Eighth Schedule' of the Constitution of India). The linguistic diversity of the country is well depicted in the aphorism *kos-kos par badle paani, chaar kos par baani* ('The language spoken in India changes every few kilometres, just like the taste of the water'). The etymology of the word bhasha is in the Sanskrit word bhasha, which also translates to 'language' and, thus, cognates with multiple Indian languages such as Marathi, Nepali, Nevari, Bhojpuri, Gujarati, Malayalam, Tamil and Telugu.

Synonyms of bhasha in Hindi are *jabaan*, *baat* and *boli*. On hearing the word bhasha, the first thing that comes to the mind of a Hindi speaker is standard language(s). Jabaan literally means tongue and boli could mean spoken languages, dialects and slangs. The word boli derives from the verb *bolna* (meaning, to speak), as is evident from the example, '*kya tum* Bhojpuri *bolti ho?*' ('Do you speak Bhojpuri?'). Bhasha and boli are sometimes interchangeably used in spoken Hindi; one may ask 'kya *tumhari* boli Bhojpuri *hai?*' ('Is your dialect Bhojpuri?'). However, in the written language, the terms are marked by clear distinctions. Bhasha stands as a symbol of formality and purity, while boli is used to imply colloquialism. Hence, it is seen appropriate to write '*uski* boli Bhojpuri hai' ('His/her dialect is Bhojpuri') as opposed to '*unki* bhasha Bhojpuri hai' ('His/her language is Bhojpuri'). It also becomes evident with word collocations such as *maatri*-bhasha 'mother tongue' and *rashtra*-bhasha 'national language', wherein the term boli cannot replace bhasha. When the term bhasha becomes a part of the words rashtra and maatri, the compound word stands as a marker of identity and nationality. Quite often, Hindi speakers distinguish bhasha from boli in its association to a written script, antiquity and number of speakers. Bengali (*Bangla*) has a script and is, hence, considered a language, while Maithili, in lacking a script of its own and possessing lesser number of speakers, is seen as a spoken language/dialect of Hindi. Many people believe that Sanskrit, being one of the oldest languages of the country, is the mother of all Indian languages. Such distinctions are people's perceptions built around languages; these constructed notions are proved wrong by linguists. Language and dialects, therefore, are attached to dichotomies such as the standard and the local, the pure and the impure, the formal and the informal.

Jabaan, on the other hand, is an Urdu word with the literal meaning 'tongue'. The usage of tongue to imply language is prevalent in English language as well – an example is the compound word 'mother tongue'. Slip of the tongue, for example, translates to jabaan *fisalna*. A few more examples are as follows – '*apni* jabaan *par kaaboo rakho*' ('hold your tongue') and 'jabaan *sambhaal ke*' ('mind your language'). The use of jabaan is predominant in areas dominated by Urdu-speaking communities. Another synonym of bhasha is baat, as used in the sentences '*mujhe* tumhari baat *samajh me nahi aayi*' ('I didn't understand what you said') and '*mujhse* baat *mat karo*' ('don't talk to me'). In this context, baat refers to talk, speech or saying.

The term bhasha exposes quite a few sociolinguistic realities. The very fact that the term has travelled from Sanskrit to multiple Indian languages is indicative of the porousness and flexibility of languages. Languages do not have rigid boundaries. They borrow and mix with one another very easily, thereby proving that notions about purity of languages are constructed and do not exist in actuality. This leads one to the fact that there exist numerous misconceptions and myths surrounding language. It is quite ironical that the word bhasha, the supposedly standard and pure form of usage (to imply language or speech), brings to light the myths constructed around purity and standards of language.

References

Agnihotri, R. K. 'Multilinguality, Education and Harmony'. *International Journal of Multilingualism* 11, no. 3 (2014): 364–79.

Singh, Shiv Sahay. 'Language Survey Reveals Diversity'. *The Hindu*, 22 July 2013. Available at: https://www.thehindu.com/news/national/language-survey-reveals-diversity/article4938865.ece (accessed 18 June 2018).

EIGHTH SCHEDULE

Om Prakash

Following Macaulay's famous *Minute on Education* in 1835 and Charles Wood's Education Dispatch in 1854, it was the Constituent Assembly of India, which discussed the issues of languages and policy in India extensively. The Constituent Assembly Debates continued over a period of almost three years from 1946 to 1949 and culminated with the enactment of the Constitution of India on 26 January 1950. Given the multilingual and pluricultural context of India, the Constituent Assembly Debates and consequent language policy framing drew a far-fetched impact on administration, education and functioning of constitutional bodies in Independent India.

The Constitution of India had a dedicated section in Part XVII on 'Official Language', consisting of Articles 343–351, dedicated to the matters of official languages of India and the states. The section is devised in four chapters: Chapter One addresses the issues of the official language of the Union and the Commission and Committee of Parliament on official language in Articles 343–344; Chapter Two addresses regional languages, covering the issue of official language or languages of the state, official language for communication between one state and another or between a state and the Union and special provision relating to language spoken by a section of the population of a state in Articles 345–347; Chapter Three addresses the issue of the language to be used in the Supreme Court and in the High Courts and for Acts, Bills, etc., and the special procedure for enactment of certain laws relating to language in Articles 348–349; and Chapter Four is concerned with the language to be used in representations for redress of grievances, facilities for instruction in mother tongue at the primary level, special officer for linguistic minorities and the directive for development of Hindi language in Articles 350–351.

The Constitution has twelve Schedules for detailing and specifying matters contained in the corresponding Articles. The Eighth Schedule mentions all the languages that have been recognized by the Constitution of India as official languages of the Union and the special provision relating to languages spoken by a section of the population of a state. In accordance with the Articles 344(1) and 351, twenty-two languages are included and listed as official languages of the Union in the Eighth Schedule. These languages include Assamese, Bengali, Bodo, Dogri, Gujarati, Hindi, Kannada, Kashmiri, Konkani, Maithili, Malayalam, Manipuri, Marathi, Nepali, Odia, Punjabi, Sanskrit, Santhali, Sindhi, Tamil, Telugu and Urdu. These languages have appeared in alphabetical order, with various amendments and renumbering, and do not represent any hierarchy. Originally, the list contained fourteen languages, besides Hindi. In subsequent amendments – Seventh Amendment in 1956, Twenty-First Amendment in 1967, Seventy-First amendment in 1992 and Ninety-Second amendment in 2003 – eight more languages were added to the list: Sindhi in 1967; Konkani, Manipuri and Nepali in 1992; and Bodo, Dogri, Maithili and Santhali in 2003.

It was conceived that all the languages included in the list would qualify for representation on the Official Language Commission, and they would be the enriching sources for strengthening Hindi: 'The President shall, at the expiration of five years from the commencement of this Constitution and thereafter at the expiration of ten years from such commencement, by order constitute a Commission which shall consist of a Chairman and such other members representing the different languages specified in the Eighth Schedule as the President may appoint, and the order shall define the procedure to be followed by the Commission' (Article 344 (1), pp. 212–13).

The inclusion of languages in the Eighth Schedule mandates the Government of India to promote Hindi along with other languages included in the list as Official Languages. The Official Language Resolution 1968 states, 'WHEREAS under article 343 of the Constitution, Hindi shall be the official language of the Union, and under article 351 thereof it is the duty of the Union to promote the spread of the Hindi Language and to develop it so that it may serve as a medium of expression for all the elements of the composite culture of India.' Thus, it is imperative for the Government of India to work towards promotion and development of the languages listed in the Eighth Schedule, as resolved in the Official Language Resolution of 1968: 'WHEREAS the Eighth Schedule of the Constitution specifies 14 major languages of India besides Hindi, and it is necessary in the interest of the educational and cultural advancement of the country that concerted measures should be taken for the full development of these languages; ... The House resolves that a programme shall be prepared and implemented by the Government of India, in collaboration with the State Governments for the coordinated development of all these languages, alongside Hindi so that they grow rapidly in richness and become effective means of communicating modern knowledge.'

The importance of the Eighth Schedule also gets underlined as it offers equal opportunity to the speakers of other languages listed in the Schedule as the 1968 Resolution mandates the same: 'AND WHEREAS it is necessary to ensure that the just claims and interest of people belonging to different parts of the country in regard to the public services of the Union are fully safeguarded:

This House resolves –

   a. that compulsory knowledge of either Hindi or English shall be required at the stage of selection of candidates for recruitment to the Union services or posts except in respect of any special services or posts for which a high standard of knowledge of English alone or Hindi alone, or both, as the case may be, is considered essential for the satisfactory performance of the duties of any such service or post; and

b. that all the languages included in the Eighth Schedule to the Constitution and English shall be permitted as alternative media for the All India and higher Central Services examinations after ascertaining the views of the Union Public Service Commission on the future scheme of the examinations, the procedural aspects and the timing.'

This is the reason that has fuelled demands for inclusion of more languages to the Eighth Schedule and 'at present, there are demands for inclusion of thirty-eight more languages in the "Eighth Schedule" to the Constitution'. These languages include Angika, Banjara, Bazika, Bhojpuri, Bhoti, Bhotia, Bundelkhandi, Chhattisgarhi, Dhatki, English, Garhwali (Pahari), Gondi, Gujjar/Gujjari, Ho, Kachachhi, Kamtapuri, Karbi, Khasi, Kodava (Coorg), Kok Barak, Kumaoni (Pahari), Kurak, Kurmali, Lepcha, Limbu, Mizo (Lushai), Magahi, Mundari, Nagpuri, Nicobarese, Pahari (Himachali), Pali, Rajasthani, Sambalpuri/Kosali, Shaurseni (Prakrit), Siraiki, Tenyidi and Tulu.

The Eighth Schedule of the Constitution of India reflects the statutory acknowledgement of Indian linguistic diversity and plurality. The growing demand for inclusion of more and more languages in the Schedule represents the aspirations of other languages that require institutional support and constitutional protection. This tendency is encouraging and required, to keep the multilingual fabric of India intact.

References

Department of Official Language, Government of India. 'THE OFFICIAL LANGUAGE RESOLUTION, 1968'. Available at: http://rajbhasha.nic.in/en/official-language-resolution-1968 (accessed 28 June 2018).
The Constitution of India. Available at: https://www.india.gov.in/my-government/constitution-india/constitution-india-full-text (accessed 28 June 2018).

ENDANGERED LANGUAGES

Jatindra Kumar Nayak

About twenty years ago, Ken Hale of Massachusetts Institute of Technology (MIT), linguist and language activist, while expressing concern about language death, observed that when a language is lost, a culture is lost because the latter is encoded in the former. A knowledge repertoire is lost too. When Boa Sr – an Indian Great Andamanese elder, the last person fluent in the Aka-Bo language – died in 2010, the language Bo died with her as did the knowledge that came with the language; she could correctly anticipate a tsunami and knew precisely where she would be safe. The British linguist and language activist, David Crystal, has remarked that of about the six thousand languages in the world today, about a half of them will be extinct by the end of this century and just around six hundred languages would be ruling the world of language.

As part of some affirmative action in this regard, UNESCO has categorized languages in terms of their endangerment status: safe, at risk (shrinking domains of use), disappearing (speakers noticeably shifting to another language), moribund (not transmitted to children), nearly extinct (very few elderly speakers alive) and extinct (one or no speakers alive). In the UNESCO list of the endangered languages, there are 197 languages of India. There is disagreement about a few of the entries on this list, but that does not reduce the gravitas of the matter.

Responding to this situation, in 2014, the Government of India instituted the Scheme for Protection and Preservation of Endangered Languages (SPPEL) of India. Central Institute of Indian Languages (CIIL), Mysore, which monitors it, has collaborated with some of our universities for this project. Documentation of the languages or tongues spoken by less than ten thousand people is the main aim of this effort, since threat perception is more crucial for these languages. Documentation of these languages cannot simply be restricted to the preparation of their grammars and sample lexicons. The tales, songs, proverbs, wise sayings, naming systems and beliefs, among others, of the concerned speech communities, their knowledge of their environment and the way they negotiate with it must also be carefully documented by properly trained and sensitive persons.

In multilingual environments, because of various pressures and, sometimes, governmental policies, people shift to other languages and a stage comes when the language comes under the threat of extinction. Let not a language die when its last speaker dies; with proper documentation, the language can have, at the very least, an archival life.

References

Pandharipande, Rajeshwari. 'Minority Matters: Issues in Minority Languages in India'. *International Journal on Multicultural Societies* 4, no. 2 (2002): 213–34.
Sengupta, Papia. 'Endangered Languages: Some Concerns'. *Economic and Political Weekly* 44, no. 32 (2009): 17–19.

ENGLISH

K. Narayana Chandran

The first learners of English were the two hundred-odd Indian employees of the East India Company (EIC), on the eve of the Battle of Plassey (1756). They probably spoke a 'pidgin', which was effectively the lingua franca of the local traders and suppliers of victuals for the Company officials. The Indian record keepers of the Company were *dubashi*s who widened its trade network in India. They were fluent in multiple *bhasha*s (languages) and in English as well. By 1660, the Company's trade posts and factories, besides the Christian mission schools, made for the wider use of English among the Indians. In 1792, Charles Grant proposed to the Court of Directors of the EIC that the Indians will benefit from English education. The language, he hoped, would instil noble Christian values among the superstitious, though intelligent, Hindus who might even begin to appreciate the munificence of their trading partners. It is not surprising that Ram Mohan Roy's letter to Lord Amherst, demanding modern English education and the institution of a General Committee of Public Instruction, coincided in 1823. The Indians were demanding English and the British were all too willing to oblige them.

It was, however, T. B. Macaulay's 'Minute on Education' (1835) that proposed and institutionally heralded English education in India. While Macaulay had the whole-hearted support of Anglicist British administrators and scholars, he was opposed by the Orientalists and the Vernacularists who pleaded for the promotion of an education in Indian classical and local languages, respectively. The first Indian universities were located in the three presidencies – Madras, Calcutta and Bombay – in 1857. English has, since then, remained the sole medium of modern education throughout India. The passing of the *Official Languages Act of 1967* by the parliament settled, once and for all, the case for English and its inevitable presence in India as the first language of civil administration and higher education. English continues to be the 'associate official language' besides Hindi, the official language of the Indian Union.

As English became more entrenched in India, it began to establish a small but influential tradition for itself. Its growth among and coexistence with at least two other bhashas in nearly all linguistic regions, besides Hindi, in most Indian cities, have contributed meaningfully to a triadic multilingualism among the professional middle classes. Despite its non-Indian provenance, English graduated into a 'second language' for many Indians who completed their university education and joined the ranks of civil and military administration. In the 1960s and 1970s, the spread of English was phenomenal, despite some political opposition to its manifest power and the values it was alleged to espouse. If it was not quite the mother tongue for the upper and upper-middle classes, it was allegedly the 'other tongue'. In the absence of the native tongue, English was perhaps, for the elite young of India, their 'auntie tongue'. Even today, we occasionally hear the rumblings of this old debate when political leaders and intellectuals see English as both enslaving and dominating our minds on the one hand and their opponents seeing the great opportunities India has had among the new globalizing economies on account of its demographic dividend strongly fostered by its command of English. The influential public and electronic media call the political bluff of *angrezi hatao* ('English out!') campaigns of the bhasha fanatics, who, ironically, send their wards to the elite English-medium schools in the country.

Even the Indian nativists concede the easy adaptability of English, one that they find both charming and irresistible, while mixing or switching codes in their respective languages. Salman Rushdie's *chutnification* comes closest in characterizing this linguistic mix and adaptation of English by creative users in India. The word, of course, captures the ease, instantaneity and pep that the regionally varied chutneys have for those Indians who cannot do without them.

In an awkwardly curious way, English has become increasingly aspirational and covetable for the youth of economic-liberalized India while it continues to retain its colonialist aura of privileged distance and exclusivity. In other words, English shares the basic characteristic of the club (pride in the privileges it bestows on its highly selective membership) which the colonial administration brought to India. It is, still, not quite readily accessible to larger sections of the economically and socially disadvantaged Indians. Put differently, English has some strange way of distancing Indians from themselves and making way for unfair discrimination and stigmatization, for engineering and sustaining democratically untenable schisms between and among workers, institutions and communities. More perniciously, all these divisions and differences are hard to trace directly to a language or a culture – a source called English – an authority that seems to emanate from some unknown centre outside India; a supervening power to which none of the privileged classes in India are able to meaningfully respond, let alone offer self-determined resistance. In absenting itself from the immediate scene of political action, English has succeeded, nonetheless, in promising to the new India a modernity other societies are unlikely to acquire without it or in offering multiple projects and prospects under its aegis that are bound to remain unfinished. The crucial question English raises, now, is whether the Indian elite wants the modernity that still remains unfinished even in their own understanding of it. Certainly, this grim vindication of the Gandhian scenario of 'English rule without the English' calls for debate every time someone calls English one of *our* bhashas.

References

Kachru, Braj B. *The Alchemy of English: The Spread, Functions, and Models of Non-Native Englishes*. Urbana-Champaign: University of Illinois Press, 1990.
Ramanathan, Vaidehi. *The English-Vernacular Divide: Postcolonial Language, Politics and Practice*. Hyderabad: Orient BlackSwan, 2005.

FILE

Shiv Visvanathan

In a Gutenburg Galaxy, a file is a cosmos that determines your existence. When you begin life, a file is opened on you, that means you demand and require attention. A file exists because citizenship is an act of the continuous processing of information. Your life ends when your file is closed. You disappear when your file disappears. Your embodied existence does not matter, your presence lies in the file so that in Decartian sense, you are when your file exists. When your file goes missing, you enter a world of Kafka and Alice rolled in one. The lethal power of the file to make or unmake a people as an act of governance needs to be understood. Right to Information (RTI) activists have shown that government departments have declared many villages as dead. As a result of being non-persons, they lack claim to retirement benefits, the right to apply to a loan. Resurrecting a file is an act more miraculous than reincarnation. A file is cartography of identity and entitlements. It defines the very ontology of being, stating when you were born, when you died and both need the gravitas of a certificate. A file archives the rites of passage in a modern world. A certificate is a statement of the veracity of existence, a verification of a claim to entitlements. The survivors of the Bhopal Gas Tragedy were often denied entitlements because they lacked existence in a file. An unrecorded suffering is meaningless as an untold story. A file legitimates you as in being. Without a file, modernity as non-being begins.

A file captures the universe of power of a bureaucratic thought. A file conveys a sense of the sacred. Filing and defiling citizenship are real acts of governance. When a file is opened, it is the inauguration of a creation; when a file is closed, it is a closure of a textual kind. A file as archive captures memory. I remember an anecdote related to me with a grin by one of India's finest scientists. He had met P. N. Dhar, director of the Institute of Economic Growth. Dhar had told him that the two doyens of social science – V. K. R. V. Rao and M. N. Srinivas – were squabbling over a petty decision. Dhar had patiently listened to Rao complain about Srinivas and quickly forgot it. One day Rao came and demanded an old letter of complaint. Dhar was in a panic as he had forgotten all about Rao's complaint, and he appealed to his assistant, who assured him that that was not a problem at all. He brought out a file labelled 'Fight: M. N. Srinivas *vs* V. K. R. V. Rao'.

A file captures the ethnography of decision making in bureaucracy. When you enquire anxiously about your application, the clerk assures you indifferently, *File abhi tak pass nai hua.* ('Your file has not been passed as yet.') It implies you belong to the liminal world of in between, where waiting as time can extend from a day to a lifetime. It captures the sheer helpless of citizenship and invents a new space for corruption. A bribe is an incentive to open, close or speed up a file. A bribe provides the alchemy of the file, turning it from an indifferent space to a miracle of concern. Rules define the mechanical universe of a file. Bribes define the alchemical world of a file. A file and the permutations of a file define the infinite possibilities of corruption. A file is inert, till a bribe declares it alive. The elasticity of a file to move from delay to miraculous speed is one of the great events of modern governance. Corruption is a rule game that increases the infinite possibilities of a file. A cynical observer with an acute sense of power said, 'It is a pity that Marx talked of the dictatorship of the proletariat. He had no sense of the clerk as a Leviathan of the archive, of the dictatorship of the Filariat; for that you needed Weber and Kafka.' Modern sociology or management theory has still not captured the world of a file. A file is geography of an imagination, it encodes the everyday and provides a chronography of time and is the ultimate act of violence. All genocide or displacement demands is that a clerk closes the file on you.

References

Patel, Sheela and Carrie Baptist. 'Documenting by the Undocumented'. *Sage Journals* 24, no. 1 (2012): 3–12.
Subbaraman, Ramnath, et al. 'Off the Map: The Health and Social Implications of Being a Non-Notified Slum in India'. *Environment and Urbanization* 24, no. 2 (2012): 643–63.

FIRANGI/ANGREZ (PHIRAṄGĪ/AṄGRĒZ)

Gilian Wright

These two words are used as an adjective, meaning 'Western' or 'British', or as a noun, meaning 'Westerner' or any 'white person', sometimes disparagingly or with hostility. The word *firangi*, often spelt *firinghee*, is derived from the word 'Frank', referring to Germanic peoples who established their rule in Europe after the collapse of the Roman Empire and from whom France takes its name. In Arabic, the Franks were known as *al-faranj* or *firanji* and the Persian term was *firingi*/firangi or *firing*/*firang*. Persian was, in earlier days, a widely used Indian language and it may be from Persian the term became common across India. In Hindi/Urdu, as well as many other Indian languages, firangi now means a Westerner or Western and particularly those of the colonial period. In Tamil, the term *parangi* was originally used specifically for Portuguese. The scholar Jonathan Gil Harris has demonstrated that before the British *raj*, firangi was also used for Christian migrants from non-European countries – Christian slaves from Africa, as well as for Jewish migrants, aside from Muslims who had once served Christian masters. The word *angrez* is derived from the Portuguese *ingles* meaning English, and *angrezi* is therefore the English language. Like firangi, angrez can be used for Westerners generally. In the context of India's experience of colonialism, it too can be used negatively.

Both terms imply foreignness. For example, a Hindu ascetic objected to the American-born Baba Rampuri from becoming a *naga sadhu* by saying, 'Many of our lineages have been filled up with non-Brahmin castes, but there are no … angrez! They will say … that you are a bad omen.' The Bengali author, Sunil Gangopadhyay, in his historical novel *Those Days*, plumps for firinghee over angrez to describe the British, for example, 'The firinghee is our common enemy and must be driven out.' Modern writers also use the term to describe the European soldiers in Indian armies, for example, those employed by Shah Jahan or Maharaja Ranjit Singh of the Punjab, and the term is also used for Europeans who came to India, adopted Indian customs and settled here. The historic European presence is remembered in place names like Chittagong's Firinghee Bazaar, Kolkata's Firinghee Kali Bari (temple) and Firangi Mahal, the Lucknow centre of Islamic learning, at first housed in a building formerly owned by a European. It has also been argued that paintings of the 'Company School', commissioned by Frenchmen in India with no links to the East India Company, should be called 'firinghee Paintings'.

In modern times, author and conservationist, Mark Shand, describing his experience of riding across India mounted on the elephant Tara, recalled people straining to get a glimpse of 'the firinghee mahout'. The naturalist M. Krishnan noted in his article 'The Genus Feringhee' that the Tamil version of the word, parangi, also means a pumpkin and a disease that Westerners brought with them to India. However, it is not used for an Indian who apes the West – for which the Tamil term is *dorai* – but rather Europeans of the past, for example, the one depicted being devoured by Tipu Sultan's famous clockwork tiger. For Krishnan, the firangi, as a rule, completely missed the culture of the country and led insular lives; but this was not true of all. 'But for the Feringhee', he writes, 'there would have been no rich lore of natural history in India'. He concludes, 'I am quite willing to confess that my life has been profoundly influenced by Feringhee values – you may, probably, deny this influence in your own, though I am writing this in the language of the feringhee and you are reading it!'

References

Crooke, William, ed. *Hobson-Jobson: A Glossary of Colloquial Anglo-Indian Words and Phrases, and of Kindred Terms, Etymological, Historical, Geographical and Discursive*. Delhi: Munshiram Manoharlal Publishers, 1979.

Harris, Jonathan Gil. 'India, The Firangi Mahal'. *Outlook*, 2 February 2015. Available at: https://www.outlookindia.com/magazine/story/india-the-firangi-mahal/293191 (accessed 26 May 2018).

GAALI (GĀLĪ)

Praveen Singh

The Hindi word *gaalii* – may be translated as 'profanity', 'swear word', 'cuss word' or 'slang', among others. It is the kind of language used to offend or revile someone when you want to hurt them because you are angry or want to be disrespectful. However, it would be wrong to suggest that only the strong words/phrases used in this manner are understood by the term gaalii. It may be that two people use expressions that would otherwise be offensive to an outsider but form a way of bonding the two and serve as a mark of informality between them. Gaaliis may also be used to draw someone's attention to a point being mentioned or to convey one's disapproval of someone or something. In other words, they perform many more functions in speech other than merely serving to offend others.

Gaaliis can be measured for their impact on people, if one wished to do so – people of a given community, speaking a particular dialect, will be expected to agree on the extremity of the 'swear word' used which would involve finding out what and how something was said. A word such as *chuutiyaa*, in Hindi, has come to mean 'stupid/dumb' (even though it literally means 'having been born of a vagina') and is considered less offensive than the extremely vulgar *bhos(a)Ri-ke* (meaning 'born of a loose vagina'). Even a phrase like *ullu ke paTThe* (meaning 'son of an owl') evokes less extreme emotions amongst people. Some other more common abuses are *haraamii* ('of illegitimate birth'), *namak-haraam* ('treacherous'), *bak-chod* ('stupid blabberer'), *behen-chod* (literally 'sister fucker'), *beTii-chod* (literally 'daughter fucker'), *bhaRwaa* ('pimp'), *maadar-chod* (literally 'mother fucker'), *suar kii aulaad* ('son of a pig') and so on.

There is no doubt that there exists a general tendency among people to avoid being rude or impolite, so much so that we tend to use euphemisms such as *swarg sidhaarnaa* (literally 'go to heaven') or *parlok siddhaarnaa* (literally 'go to the other world') instead of the more common expression *mar gaye* ('to die'); but, there can be contexts in which a person may choose to use a taboo word to express a fact if only to emphasize the point. So, in a context where a widow (*vidhvaa*) or a widower (*vidur*) is getting married for the second time and if someone wishes to reveal their disapproval, the person may use taboo words such as *raanD* and *ranDu(v)aa* to emphasize the inadmissible social status of the widow and widower, respectively.

Nevertheless, gaaliis are so much a part of our everyday existence that it is really difficult for one to get away without hearing it in the streets and, in fact, very few can claim to have never used them. Psychologist Timothy Jay found that 'on average 0.7 per cent of the words people use in a day are taboo ones', notes Melissa Mohr (2013). They also impact us differently psychologically and physiologically. For instance, Mohr mentions that research has shown that it is easier to remember swear words compared to other new words that are learnt and also that they help increase one's ability to 'deal with physical pain'. They may be used to humour oneself or others too. Songs and verses based on taboo words can be heard on occasions of marriages and other events where they are intended to offer richness to the whole event. Of course, sometimes they are also sung to register protest of some kind but only in a symbolic manner. For instance, the songs sung by the bride's side on the event of her send-off from her parents' house after the wedding ceremony is over.

Gaaliis in languages can be based on any number of things. People may use the region, religion, class, caste, race/ethnicity, sex, birth, occupation, physical appearance, resemblance to another animal, kinship, colour of skin, behavioural traits, skill levels, efficiency, etc. of a person to revile him/her. Just to give a few examples: *nauaa* ('barbar'), *chamaar* ('member of an Indian caste whose caste-occupation is leatherworking'), *kaafir* ('infidel'), *moTaa* ('fat'), *sikRaa* ('very thin'), *kaaliye/kaale-kaluuTe* ('of black colour') and so on. Almost anything can form the basis for a gaalii. Even an individual's or a group's ideological and/or religious leanings can be used as a word to abuse them or their whole group.

Several extremely offensive gaaliis are based around the female/male sexual organs or around notions of incest. Even among those, it is common for people to use taboo words that mostly involve females and incest, such as *maadar-chod, behen-chod, beTii-chod* and so on. One can learn about the history and cultural practices of a community through these swear words for they, like any other word of the community's language, carry a thread of history in them and it is possible for etymologists to find out more about societies/communities and their practices (Hughes, 2006). Different societies have, at different times, adopted some or the other approaches to cope with what they believed about swear words – some have curtailed the use of swear words through regulations while others have been just casual about them. No matter what we think about them, gaaliis in Hindi have a texture which is hard to translate or describe, and perhaps the same may be said of the swear words of all the different languages of the world.

References

Hughes, Geoffrey I. *An Encyclopedia of Swearing: The Social History of Oaths, Profanity, Foul Language, and Ethnic Slurs in the English-Speaking World.* London: M. E. Sharpe, 2006.
Mohr, Melissa. *Holy Shit: A Brief History of Swearing.* New York: Oxford University Press, 2013.

HELLO-JI (HĒLŌ JĪ)

Maidul Islam

Hello-ji is a form of greeting in North India. Generally, it is used in a casual manner for an informal greeting instead of the anglicized 'hello'. However, on some occasions, it is used as an expression of surprise in order to attract someone's attention. The cultural equivalents of hello-ji in India are many; while *namaste* or *namaskar* is a more traditional and formal greeting in Hindi, *adaab* serves the same purpose in Urdu. Similarly, in Assamese, *nomoskar* is used. In Bengali, *nomoshkar* is the cultural equivalent of a formal greeting, while *pronam* is often used as an informal greeting. In Odia, namaste or namaskar is also regarded as a general greeting. In Telugu, namaste is also known as *dandamuor namaskaram* for singular use and *dandaalu* or *namaskaralu* for the plural form. Unlike the Bengali pronam which is used primarily as an informal greeting, *pranamamu* is also used in formal Telugu. In Kannada, *namaskara* is used for the singular and *namaskaragalu* for the plural. In Malayalam, namaskaram is used. In Tamil, namaste is known as *vanakkam* which is derived from the root word *vanangu* meaning to bow or to greet. Namaste, in the Hindu custom, means, 'I bow to the divine in you.'

Hello-ji is devoid of any religious cultural connotations unlike namaskar or its various regional forms in India. Similarly, it is also devoid of several religious cultural connotations other than the Hindu custom, like *sat sri akaal* (true is the name of God) used as a greeting by the Sikhs or *Salaam* meaning peace (the short form of Assalaamu'alaykum – may peace be upon you – or of the further extended form, Assalaamu 'alaykum warahmatullahi wabarakatuh – may the peace and mercy of Allah be with you) used by the Muslims or 'grace and peace to you from God, the Father and the Lord, Jesus Christ!' used by the Christians. In various parts of North India, the word 'ji' is used at the end of someone's name to convey respect. In this regard, hello-ji is relatively more non-traditional than a simple hello, it is often used as a respectful greeting, although it sounds strangely synthetic.

The mildly autobiographical novel of author, commentator and corporate manager Gurcharan Das, *A Fine Family* (1990), has a reference to hello-ji as a form of greeting. In the novel, a character jokingly responds to 'hello-ji' by laughingly saying 'what an odd thing to say. Either you say "hello" or you say "namaste ji". You don't mix them up.' It is also referred to as a form of greeting by those *desis* (native Indians) who want to be anglicized. Hello-ji has, thus, been used in several Indian novels in English and has become a part of the postcolonial vocabulary of popular Indian fiction in English. Hello-ji is often expressed with the following three words: *ki haalchaal* or *ki haal hai* (meaning 'how are you?'). A song named 'Beautiful' by, the popular Punjabi music composer and singer, Honey Singh, starts with 'Hello-ji, ki haalchaal'.

References

Anand, Mulk Raj. 'Pigeon Indian: Some Notes on Indian-English Writing'. *World Literature Written in English* 21, no. 2 (1982): 325–36.
Das, Gurcharan. *A Fine Family*. Delhi: Penguin Books India, 1990.

INDIAN WRITING IN ENGLISH (IWE)

G. J. V. Prasad

IWE (Indian Writing in English) is now the most accepted term/acronym for the work produced by Indians in the English language. It has taken a while to arrive at this nomenclature. This literature has been called by many names – Anglo-Indian literature, Indo-Anglian (even, for an awful, though short, time, Indo-Anglican) literature, Indo-English literature, Indian English literature (or, less frequently, Indian Literature in English) and Anglophone Indian literature. Anglo-Indian literature, now, denotes writings by the British who lived in India during the *Raj*.

The term Indo-Anglian literature was popularized by K. Srinivasa Iyengar and stood its ground for a long time; indeed, it is not uncommon to see it being used even now. However, this seemed to indicate a relationship between two nations, something Iyengar seemed to endorse when he said that the writer can be called an Indo-Anglian but not an Indo-Englishman, which would be unthinkable. Thus, Indo-Anglian writing would have its feet in both nations. Indo-English literature fell out of favour, to denote original IWE, soon after it was proposed; many, including Sujit Mukherjee and V. K. Gokak, preferred the term as a signifier of Indian literatures in English translation. It must be noted that Iyengar moved on to call this literature

Keywords for India

IWE (the name of his iconic book published in 1962). Indian English literature has had the strongest run so far, with the Indian Academy of Letters – Sahitya Academy's – acceptance of the term and its use, in M. K. Naik's ever popular *History of Indian English Literature* which was first published in 1982 and is still in print.

However, the emphasis, in this term, is on the language – Indian English – and thus, its fate is twinned with that of the existence and validation of such a language (this, perhaps, is the reason some prefer to call this Indian Literature in English). Indian English seems to be a language, often artistically created by writers themselves, with constructions and words from Indian languages, appearing to mimic Indian languages by seeming to be translations while actually being original constructions! Thus, Indian English literature seems to be one that plays with and constructs a language, and it should not surprise us that the best-known writers in Indian English live or lived outside India, starting from G. V. Desani.

Anglophone Indian literature bestows a global context and makes this literature a part of various literatures in English that have emerged from different parts of world, expectedly, due to colonialism or other contacts. However, this term is more inclusive than simply 'postcolonial' literature (since it also looks at contemporary forms of imperialism, the impact of globalization, etc.) as well as more exclusive (not including any indigenous language or, indeed, any other language of colonization). Thus, it seems to be an avatar of new literatures in English or commonwealth literature. IWE does not have any special advantage over Indian literature in English – both can be erroneously assumed to include works in translation and both have the same problem of definitions of boundaries in that they must decide who is an Indian writer, one of Indian origin writing anywhere or of Indian origin, writing from within the nation-state. It seems that IWE seems to lay emphasis on Indian writers writing from within the boundaries of India, but perhaps IWE scores as an acronym over IEL (Indian English Literature) or ILE (Indian Literature in English), in popular academic imagination, and is thus used more often.

References

Iyengar, K. R. Srinivasa. *Indian Writing in English*. Mumbai: Asia Publishing House, 1962.
Naik, M. K. *A History of Indian English Literature*. New Delhi: Sahitya Akademi, 1982.

JUGAAD (JUGĀḌ)

Lallan Baghel

Etymologically, the word *jugaad* has its origins in the Sanskrit word *yukti* and means making an effort to produce something new by bringing together something existing (*samayojan* in Hindi). In colloquial Hindi, the word jugaad has emerged from the word *jugat* which goes back to its Sanskrit origin yukti. Hence, in day-to-day language, it denotes jugat *lagana* or coming up with makeshift changes/solutions, pertaining to material as well as non-material processes.

There are two ways in which the term jugaad is used. The first, is when it is used for local technological innovations and the second usage is to denote the gain of personal favours through the bypassing of formal institutional norms and procedures in the public domain. In the first sense, jugaad came into popular usage to describe indigenous technological innovations to meet local needs at nominal costs, by creative individuals with not much formal training in the realms of science and technology. Jugaad is not as much about a new innovation as it is about the assembling of already existing technology, in order to make it more suitable to local needs while also being cost-effective. One example includes an indigenous vehicle developed, in the hinterlands of North as well as South India, by farmers by attaching a mechanical irrigation pump to a cart, to transport the produce to the market or to fetch fodder from the farm to their home. This jugaad item has multiple uses as it is used as a tractor also. Another example is the use of electrical mixer-grinder without using electricity – put on the backseat of a bicycle and connected by a pully, the jar of this Jugaad mixer-grinder churns perfect lassi and milk shakes for the workers of a local NGO in cities like Chandigarh. It is in the mechanical domain that most of the jugaad happens in small towns and villages of India. However, in cities like Bangalore, it is put to creative technological use by entrepreneurs who want to save money on research and development in order to reduce cost value of their product and to maximize their profits. Jugaad, here, applies to any kind of creative and out-of-the-box thinking or life knacks that maximize the resources for a company and its stakeholders. It is not that jugaad has not been recognized by the formal scientific community in India; some of the noted scientists, including Professor Yash Pal – a leading science communicator – have endorsed and recognized the value of jugaad for economically poor societies like India's.

In its second sense, it is difficult to find an exact translation of the word jugaada. A very close translation could be 'to fix matters through hook or crook'. In this sense, it is used to denote the bypassing of formally laid down institutional norms and procedures, by a person, in order to gain special favours from the system. It is important to note that in everyday life, it is an accepted norm in the political and bureaucratic culture of India. 'Promotion/posting/ *naukri ke liye jugaad lagana*' ('to use jugaad to get a promotion, a posting or a job') is an acceptable norm which, on one hand, points towards the malleability of the system and, on the other, hints at the vulnerability of the masses who have to find a 'connection' in order to get things done. In a way, jugaad is an apt example of the working of Indian democracy where, despite formal equality, there lies a wide chasm when it comes to sharing the pie that the state has to offer. For a slum dweller, it might mean finding the right connections and some money to get an electricity connection. For a local businessman, it might mean being able to tweak the system to run a private university.

The word jugaad is also used to denote the formation of governments by political parties, in a way where they bypass the constitutional norms. Jugaad *ki sarakāra* (Government of Jugaad) has been much in use during the past few decades, in Hindi media, to denote the moral corruption of political parties when it comes to the formation of the government. Jugaad, here, means not having the required mandate and yet the formation of a government, by influencing the political office of a state governor or the president or indulging in horse trading or other such manoeuvring tactics to gain power.

Jugaad, as a word, ironically expresses the strength as well as weakness of Indian society and democracy. In its more positive sense, it points to the creative enterprise of Indian masses who innovate and use technology for their own empowerment, without ever bothering to claim the jugaad as their own. Jugaad, here, is innovation sans patents. In its negative connotation, jugaad points to the vulnerability of masses and craftiness of the society and system at the same time. In a deeper sense, jugaad points to where the Indian democracy falls short.

References

Jauregui, Beatrice. 'Provisional Agency in India: Jugaad and Legitimation of Corruption'. *American Ethnologist* 41, no. 1 (2014): 76–91.
Prabhu, Jaideep and Sanjay Jain. 'Innovation and Entrepreneurship in India: Understanding Jugaad'. *Asia Pacific Journal of Management* 32, no. 4 (2015): 843–68.

KARPU

Antony Arul Valan

This Tamil term is often translated to mean 'chastity' or 'conjugal fidelity'. While the ancient texts *Tirukkural*[1] and *Tolkappiyam* (*karpiyalcutrams*) discuss *karpu*, the concept finds a strong advocate in the epic *Silappadikaram* by Ilanko Atigal, dating back to the time of the three Tamil kingdoms, a little after the Sangam Age. The second, of the three stated aims of the epic, is, in fact, to show how 'great men everywhere commend [the] wife of renowned fame'.

Since 'Indianness' transcends today's geopolitical boundaries, it would be pertinent to draw upon perspectives from another country in the subcontinent – Sri Lanka. Pertinent because the protagonist of *Silappadikaram*, Kannagi, is the guardian deity of the island and is worshipped, as Pattini, even today by Sinhala Buddhists and ethnic Tamils, as documented by Gananath Obeyesekere. Mala Kadar, of Ilankai Tamil Sangam, describes the evolution of the concept of karpu with the progression of Kannagi's character arc in the epic: 'urged on by a patriarchal, hegemonic principle, the concept of chastity (karpu) for Tamil women evolved as a form of learned self-denial of sexuality, tolerance, submissiveness and bashfulness that combined to form a benevolent power (sakthi).' She reports the two etymological observations of the word karpu – the first is from Tolkapiyar (who composed the *Tolkappiyam*), who defines karpu as 'the act of giving away the bride to the bridegroom'. This view finds support in Abraham Mariaselvam, who notes that according to the *Tolkappiyam*, karpu is 'the life of wedlock'. However, as Kadar notes, 'By the Sangam age, karpu exclusively referred to marital fidelity.' The *Tolkappiyam* is the earliest extant work of Tamil literature, predating works of the Sangam Age. Moreover, this also corroborates with the second etymological observation that Kadar makes, offered to her by Dr Selvy Thiruchandran: 'the word "karpu" has its origins in the word "kal" which means to learn.' V. S. Rajam notes that karpu meant 'acquiring profundity' in the time of the Sangam Age and, in course of time, male learning (man's karpu) was 'separated from

---

[1] Kural 54, G. V. Pope's translation reads 'what is more excellent than a wife, if she possesses the stability of [Karpu]?' Pope translates 'karpu' as 'chastity'.

the overall semantic realm of learning (karpu)' and 'equated with acquiring traditional skills or education (*kalvi*), whereas "female profundity/learning" (woman's karpu) was restricted to mean "chastity"'. So, while the word karpu is not gendered, the act of learning chastity seems to have become confined to women.

What does karpu mean to Tamils today? According to Jacob Pandian, the word 'evokes a number of associations that include supernatural power, sacrifice, suffering, penance, virtue, morality, justice, ethics, austerity and asceticism'. George Hart argues that the contemporary pan-Indian chastity/spirituality complex had its origin in Tamil civilization. According to Periyar, Rajadurai, Geetha and Rawat note, chastity and prostitution were dialectically linked to each other – that is, 'one cannot exist without the other'. The concept is also a frequent plot device in popular culture, more specifically movies and serials on the television – women kill themselves once they are raped, women are threatened with rape, women are blamed for what they wear, how they speak and walk if they are raped. Today, Karpu exists all around us as part of the popular imagination and is invoked to mark the 'fallen' woman. There are at least two ways in which news articles about rape refer to the act – they call it *karpazhippu* (literally, the destruction of chastity) or *vanpunarvu* (literally, forced coitus). While in progressive media and Tamil LGBT/queer circles, the latter is used to refer to rape, the former is widely used among the general public. It is to this expression of the concept, karpazhippu, that I refer when I say karpu is all around us.

Kadar poignantly notes that after her death, Kannagi is worshipped 'in temples as a paragon of wifely loyalty [and] chastity' today and, I would add, she is studied in schools today as a symbol of Tamil virtue, but 'the idea of Kannaki as a vociferous, eloquent woman who argued for justice, who put forth evidence, was not to be entertained'.[2] Much, perhaps, like women in our country today, whose chastity is perceived to underpin the honour of their family – even when it is a small girl of 8 from a nomadic community in faraway Kashmir who had to be punished because the presence of her family and community was not desirable for some.

References

Kadar, Mala. 'The Myth of Kannaki: The Concept of Chastity and Power'. *Sangam.org*, 13 October 2003. Available at: http://www.sangam.org/articles/view/?id=27 (last accessed 31 May 2018).
Rajadurai, S. V., V. Geetha and Vidya Bhushan Rawat. 'Periyar and His Ideas'. *CounterCurrents.org*, 28 September 2016. Available at: https://countercurrents.org/2016/09/28/periyar-and-his-ideas/ (last accessed 31 May 2018).

---

[2] A popular 1964 film production on the epic (*Poompuhar*, directed by P. Neelakantan) nuances Kannagi's argument in the Madurai Royal Court after her husband's execution. According to the film script, penned by Karunanidhi, her argument is threefold – the unjustified haste in executing the accused, lack of trial or even permitting the accused a hearing and a convincing physical demonstration that the anklet is hers. It is important to mention this here because Karunanidhi's literary output, among that of others, was important to the cementing of Dravidian politics in Tamil Nadu. As Perianayagam Jesudoss observes, 'The DMK's unchallenged grip over the audience is thanks to its rhetoric on "Tamilness", which was constructed in part by notions of *maanam* (honor) and valor.' And, therefore, bringing Kannagi's story of karpu and valour on-screen was a powerful political project.

KATHA, KAHANI, QISSA, DASTAAN (KATHĀ, KAHĀNĪ, KIS'SĀ, DĀSTĀN)

Mahmood Farooqui

The Sanskrit word *katha*, the Arabic *qissa* and the Persian *dastaan* are all subsumed under the common Hindustani word *kahani*. All describe a story, a tale, a speech, discourse, a fable, recital narrative or even a recitation. South Asia is a land of stories where all stories flow and from where stories flow out. An Arabic qissa, like the *One Thousand and One Nights*, becomes a filmy kahani in the 1980 film *Alibaba aur Chalees Chor*. The dastaan, a long oral epic meant to be performed, takes on a different valence to become a part of the famous Hindi song, '*ajeeb dastan hai ye, kahan shuroo kahan khatam*'.

In one word, all of them mean a tale or a story, but in practice, their usages differ greatly. Katha, the oldest of them, is in simple words, a story. A katha is also a mythological tale, like a tale from the Puranas. So then, katha becomes more open-ended, more timeless and also acquires an element of sacrality. In this last sense, the *Jataka* about Buddha's life is also a katha. To recite a katha is to provide its *varnan* (description); it is to present a scene, a *vrittant*. In Sanskrit theoretical and poetic usage, a katha is a distinct literary form and has its own offshoots such as katha *prabandh* (a composed story), katha *prasang* (a literary composition) and katha *rup* (the context). Katha *sanyukt* refers to the literary composition; katha *vartta* to speech, discourse, controversy, news, report and rumour; and, finally, *kathopkathan* referring to conversation, dialogue and narration.

The dastaan is the other end of the spectrum. It is derived from the Arabic and Persian long narrative tradition and refers to an exalted performance form, *dastangoi*. Dastans emerge from telling, often improvised, possibly never-ending narratives where adventures, love, war and romance are the dominant themes. In India, the dastaan took on a very distinctly Indic life when trickery or *aiyyari* and sorcery or *tilism* became more and more important and, with that, the dastans began to grow longer and longer until, when finally published at the end of the nineteenth century, the Indian *Dastan-e Amir Hamza* came up to a whopping forty-six volumes. That is over forty-six thousand pages of a single narrative cycle, consisting of high-quality Urdu poetry and prose, almost all of which was generated during oral performances and much of which was extemporaneously composed. The mastery of literary language thus required and the calibre of drama that it could create on the spot – suspense, mystery, action and most of all humour – make this the greatest achievement of Indian oral storytelling.

Qissa and kahani, often compounded together as in *qissa-kahani*, is the most demotic and democratically used of all these words. The great eighteenth-century poet Mushafi used the phrase as '*na vo raatein a vo baatein na vo qissa kahani hai*' ('neither those nights, nor that talk, nor that qissa-kahani remain'). A qissa is a short tale, sometimes related, but also meant to be recited. Whereas the katha often contained a moral lesson, the qissa was a mere fable, possibly an invention. To create a qissa was also to create friction or discord hence leading to the innumerable Urdu-Hindi compounds such as qissa *khatam karna* (to end a chapter or to finish the matter), qissa *barhana* (to aggravate matters), qissa *faseel* hona (all meaning to resolve matters), qissa *khara* karna (to create a discord) and qissa *mukhtasar* karna (to cut a long story short).

Kahani is, in a nutshell, a story. Kahani *sunana* is, of course, the most popular pastime in South Asia. But kahani *banana* is to embellish, to falsify or to tell a fictitious tale. In that sense, a kahani is not real and hence, the couplet: '*Khuda mile to mile ashna nahi milta/Koi kisi ka nahi dost sab kahani hai*' ('it may be possible to find God but not a comrade/nobody is anybody's friend, it is all mere fiction').

In modern Hindi writing, the word kahani has also come to stand for a self-conscious modern short story. It could also refer to a modernistic story as in the *Nai Kahani* movement of the 1960s. The modern Urdu short story, on the other hand, calls itself an *afsana*, derived, in turn, from *fasana* which, colloquially, means an invented or an exaggerated tale. In the early 1950s, after he published his short story *Kata Hua Dibba* or 'The Severed Coach', the Urdu writer Intizar Husain was told by the poet Nasir Kazmi ,'yaar Intizar, this kahani of yours has become a katha'; what he probably meant was that the story contained such different variations of time and space that it had the hallmark of a katha and thus, in its open-endedness and its infiniteness, it had become bigger than a story. When all is done though, all that we are left with is a story, a kahani. '*Teri kya* kahani hai *bhai*' ('Brother, what is your story?'); nobody writes qissas anymore.

References

Cowell, Edward Byles, ed. *The Jātaka: Or, Stories of the Buddha's Former Births*, vol. 5. Delhi: Motilal Banarsidass Publ., 1990.
Pritchett, Frances W., ed. *The Romance Tradition in Urdu: Adventures from the Dastan of Amir Hamzah*. New York: Columbia University Press, 1991.

KHARI BOLI (KHAḌĪ BŌLĪ)

Abhay Kumar Dubey

The linguistic entity called Khari Boli was the main vehicle of conversation for the speech community that lived in and around the Meerut–Delhi geographical area, also known as Kuru desh. However, unlike several other dialects of Indian subcontinent, it refused to remain confined in its original cultural zone and the conspiracy of history pushed it to travel across regions and religions. Perhaps this tendency of proliferation, along with other unique qualities, made it attractive to the nationalizing elite who were looking for the possibilities of a pan-Indian link language. This might be considered one of the main reasons why the onset of Indian modernity, especially in the post-1857 period, saw a complex process involving the tools of Khari Boli that ultimately got metamorphosed into the principal harbinger of modern Hindi, today's superordinate link language. Khari Boli not only provided the basic vocabulary, grammatical structure and tone that gave Hindi its initial register but it also went on to stamp its name on a long-running unique linguistic experiment through which Hindi evolved in various stages as the lingua franca and literary apparatus of North India. Not only this, the basic structure of spoken Khari Boli paved the way for various Hindi(s), such as Dakhani, Kalkatia and Bambaia, which gave it the aura of a link language for non-Hindi provinces.

The prose and poetry, that Hindi users of today take for granted, took roots and later developed through a highly contested cultural politic. Annals of linguistic history remind us the number of battles fought by Khari Boli, initially for its *gadya* and later for its *padya*. Looking at the positive side, it is precisely due to this cultural politics that we have, today, a developed language which can be used for various discourses across distinct cultural zones. Contemporary proponents of Hindi do not even acknowledge its historic role as the precursor of the language of the Indian Union. Khari Boli was the marker of difference that gave Hindi its distinctiveness in the era where Braj Bhasha ruled the courtly and other domains of culture.

It is difficult to find a consensus about the origins of such a historically significant linguistic entity. Scholars are still debating whether it sprung from Kauravi or Shaurseni or if it emerged from Apabhransha or Prakrit. Dr Bhola Nath Tiwari tells us that this Boli is structured into a sophisticated mixture of the elements of Eastern Punjabi, Bangdu, Braj and other dialects of Punjab, Delhi and Western Uttar Pradesh. However, this does not spell out the full import of the creative impact that Khari Boli has on our day-to-day expressions. Dharmavir, a great scholar of Khari Boli, ventured to link this impact with Sadhukkari Bhasha and regaled us with a series of words that sound the same but have different meanings, such as *sadhukkad, akkhad, dhumakkad, bhujhakkad, bhukkhad, piyakkad, nukkad, fakkad, bakkad, jhakkad, dhaakkad, kakkad, lakkad, bhulakkad, rokkad, makkad, thukkad* and *tukkad*.

Even the simple meaning of the word 'khādī' eludes scholarly unanimity. For some, it means a language which always stands and fights, but for others, khādī means *khari* that is more or less, pure or unadulterated. While the former characteristic denotes the constant struggle of this boli against the well-entrenched *janpadeeya* bhashas of the early nineteenth century, the latter one can be corroborated by at least one historical fact. John Gilchrist of Fort William College instructed his portage, Lalluji Lal, to look for a linguistic register which can claim equal distance from Arabic and Persian, on the one hand, and from the Sanskrit, on the other. Accordingly, Lalluji Lal decided to compose his *Prem Sagar* in Khari Boli, due to its relative independence from these classical languages. In fact, Khari Boli was culturally embedded with two major sociological tendencies: it had a constant aversion to the dominance of Brahmins and Sanskrit and never found itself at the right side of Arabic and Persian influences. This is not to suggest that Khari Boli and Urdu do not converge; in fact, the original habitat of Khari Boli also proved to be a fertile ground for Urdu. Dharamvir recommended the inclusion of Urdu poetry in Hindi courses for the obvious affinity between the two, in contrast to Braj or Awadhi, for instance. When the members of a twenty-first-century literati conduct political-cultural discourse across the vast area of more than 350 million people (Uttar Pradesh, Bihar, Rajasthan, Madhya Pradesh, Punjab, Haryana, Delhi, Uttarakhand, Rajasthan, Chhattisgarh), it hardly occurred to them that it was the inherent power of Khari Boli that gave them the ease and precision to communicate with the masses as well as classes.

References

Dr Dharamveer. *Hindi ki Atma*. New Delhi: Samta Prakashan, 1998.
Dwivedi, Mahavir Prasad. *Hindi Bhasha ki Utpatti*. New Delhi: Anang Prakashan, 1907/2001.

KOLAVERI (KŌLĀVERĪ)

Fahima Ayub Khan

There are words, across languages, which distinctly represent the zeitgeist of a certain period in history. Sometimes, cultural contact and other intractable interactions might lead to the borrowing of words from one language to another by speakers of that language. It happens rarely that a word from a language represents the spirit of people across the world. The word *kolaveri* from Tamil became an epochal referent that appealed to people, especially the Tamil diaspora. It is a compound word formed by the free morphemes *kolai* and *veri* in the noun form. The first morpheme translates as 'murder' and the second refers to a mad fury. When translated, it literally means 'murderous rage', referring to the immense irrationality that affects one's decisions. The implementation of the word in everyday conversations is not given a conscious thought. It functions as a rhetorical device and, in most cases, it is used to express sarcasm.

For a word that is colloquially used in conversations among Tamil speakers, it became a phenomenon by late 2011. It came to light with the song 'Why this kolaveri di?', written for a Tamil movie 3 that was released in 2011, as Singhal notes. The song captures the use of Tanglish, among the young Tamil speakers in South India. Tanglish is a mixed code of Tamil and English, a product of widespread code-mixing which is considered to be 'a spontaneous behaviour of bilinguals', observes Kanthimathi. Despite the lack of syntactic coherence in the lyrics, the song gained unusual popularity, particularly, among the younger generation since 'code-mixed songs tend to be more attractive for the younger generation, who find them relatively easy to connect with', Kazim argues. The word kolaveri, transcending linguistic borders, can be perceived as a result of the song's unprecedented acclaim. This word was infrequently used by the Tamil speakers before it featured in the song and eventually emerged as a pop culture phenomenon. In the time that followed the release of the song, kolaveri, as a word, lost its literal meaning in contemporary usage. The repeated mention of the word in the Tanglish song has reduced the scathing intensity of rage expressed by the word and in turn rendered its connotative meaning redundant. The song quickly gained prominence among youngsters across India, generating the catchphrase, 'Why this kolaveri di?' Now the word exists only in rhetoric and appears as a hyperbole in common discourse.

References

Kanthimathi, K. 'Tamil-English Mixed Language Used in Tamil Nadu'. *The International Journal of Language Society and Culture* 27 (2009): 47–53.

Kazim, Rafia. 'Subverting the Rules of Grammar: Is Kolaveri Di the Subalterns' English? Does the Tamil-English Code Mixing in a Popular Song Herald a New Variety of English?' *English Today* 29, no. 2 (2013): 27–32.

Singhal, Divya. 'Why this Kolaveri Di: Maddening Phenomenon of Earworm'. http://dx.doi.org/10.2139/ssrn.1969781.(2011).

LANGUAGES AND LINGUISTIC STATES

Rama Kant Agnihotri

Indian grammarians and philosophers of language have always been concerned about the ontological and epistemological issues concerning language. The tension between language as a rule-governed, homogeneous system and language conceptualized as fluid and heterogenous has always been there. Bhartihari was, indeed, a class apart and argued that the only path to cognition is through language. However, we all know that Vedic Sanskrit and Sanskrit, like Greek and Latin, soon ceased to be living languages and gave way to Prakrits and Apbhranshas and, finally, to the contemporary Indo-Āryan languages of North India including Hindi, Punjabi, Awadhi, Gujarati, Marathi, Bengali, Assamese and Odia, among many others, each defined not so much by its homogeneity as by its heterogeneity. All these languages celebrate their glory in the multiplicity of their linguistic and literary articulations rather than in just one codified *shuddh* (pure) norm.

Given this background, it is unfortunate that elite cultures have forced social groups to see themselves as predominantly monolingual rather than multilingual. What has been central to human existence is variability in linguistic behaviour which, as Pandit tells us, has been a facilitator in human communication than an obstruction. It is not just in India, but across the world, that languages tend to flow into each other rather than remain contained in social groups and geographical boundaries. Sounds, words, syntactic structures and patterns of discourse do not require passports and visas to walk across to other languages in spite of social, political, geographical and linguistic boundaries. It is not the elite culture, cultured in terms of select refinement of exclusive texts, arts and monuments, that encompasses multilinguality; it is the cultures and languages (*bolis*, as they are called) of the common people that celebrate multilinguality through *katha*, *kahani*, *satsang*, *vrat* and *pravachan* in the North and *burra katha* and *villu paatu* in Andhra Pradesh and Tamil Nadu, respectively. Every part of the world has similar celebrations of multilinguality.

In this multilinguality, the division of human articulation of the aesthetic experience into oral, musical, visual, performative and written breaks down. In a 2008 work, I discussed the case of the *barahmasa* (twelve months) in Bengal, also found, in variable forms, in other parts of the country including Rajasthan, Bihar and Gujarat. It could be associated with the agricultural calendar or songs of separation; there is no reason to believe that similar folk traditions will not be available in other cultures as these are always fluid and open to other varieties. As Madan points out, 'These songs are a well-known and well-developed component of folk culture all over north India, from Bengal in the east, to Gujarat in the west.' It is rooted in the folklore associated with agriculture and complex relationships between man and woman and nature. This folklore is not normative in character and is marked by patterns of behaviour that are in a state of flux.

These spaces of multilinguality, in fact, constitute spaces for protest and subversion, I had noted in 2002. Satchidanandan discusses forms such as *vacanas*, *warkari*, *chandayan* and *lallesvari* and makes a distinction between the *sramana* and the *brahmana* traditions, the former being associated with protest and innovative heresy and the latter with the Vedic hegemony and power even though there were always points of intersection. The Vachankaraka and Warkari traditions used symbols and structures that would make sense to the common people across the country. All of these traditions revolted against the elite cultural and linguistic norms.

Even the myth of 'one nation-one people-one religion-one language' which had gained considerable supremacy during the colonial and post-war period was seriously questioned and it became obvious that the countries, hitherto regarded as the ultimate examples of monolinguality like the United States, the UK and various European countries, were essentially multilingual. Even when 'a language' was associated with 'a community', it was obvious that the range of variability in terms of region, age, sex, socio-economic status was so substantial as to merit different linguistic labels. This multilinguality is, of course, built on a shared 'universal grammar' that informs all linguistic behaviour at some abstract level. We need this multilinguality not only to negotiate our day-to-day encounters that multiply exponentially in complexity as persons, places and topics of conversation change but also to construct, transmit and continuously enrich our culture.

The paradigm example of documented multilingualism is India. Despite Grierson's *Linguistic Survey of India* and several Census surveys, it has not been possible to precisely determine the number of languages spoken in India. According to the 1961 Census, India had 1,652 languages belonging to five different language families: Indo-Āryan, Dravidian, Tibeto-Burman, Austro-Asiatic and Andamanese. The 1991 Census showed that there were 10,400 mother tongues used by the people of India. Through a 'thorough linguistic scrutiny, editing and rationalization', the number of these mother tongues was reduced to 216 and 85 were subsumed under the 18 (now twenty-two) languages listed in the 'Eighth Schedule' of the Constitution. Languages such as Awadhi, Bhojpuri, Bundeli, Chattisgarhi, Mewari, etc., most of which had a long literary heritage, were subsumed under the rubric of Hindi. Today, these parents of Hindi are called its dialects. G. N. Devy's *People's Linguistic Survey of India* showed that there were 780 languages in India and of these 480 were spoken by tribes and nomads. What it showed, once again, was that India spoke in a multiplicity of languages and scripts. It also showed, clearly, how cultures of the elite ignored the cultural heritage of those it had pushed to the margins.

The linguistic and cultural ethos of India forbade its division on the basis of language and in spite of the promises made by the Congress Party, great visionaries like Gandhi and Nehru were against it. The JVP (Jawaharlal Nehru, Vallabh Bhai Patel and Pattabhi Sitaramayya) Committee dismissed the idea of reorganization on a linguistic basis in April 1949. Yet, within a span of three years, the Government of India was forced to create the state of Andhra Pradesh. There was turmoil in the Telugu (once a contender for being the national language)-speaking state and the leader of the movement, Poti Sriramulu, died after a fifty-six-day hunger strike on 15 December 1952. Since then, there has been no respite in demanding separate states in India. The country that started as a Union consisting of nine provinces, some princely states and five Union Territories today has twenty-nine states and seven Union Territories. Even though in the creation of all new states, language was a main factor, all states ended up being multilingual. Ambedkar put forth three basic considerations for setting up the linguistic states: first, viability of the state should be ensured; second, the communal balance should be taken care of; and third, all people speaking one language need not be put in one state. India has always maintained the spirit of having multiplicity of languages and people in the same place. All this has helped to sustain and nourish the multilinguality that has been constitutive of the Indian genius.

References

Agnihotri, Rama Kant. 'Identity and Multilinguality: The Case of India'. In *Language Policy, Culture, and Identity in Asian Contexts*, edited by A. B. M. Tsui and J. W. Tollefson. Mahwah: Lawrence Erlbaum, 2007.

King, Robert D. *Nehru and the Language Politics of India*. Delhi: Oxford University Press, 1997.

MATLABI (MATLABĪ)

Shiv Visvanathan

Indians discovered their own response to power and their adaptability to power and success centuries ago. It is embodied and epitomized in the word *matlabi*. Matlabi combines shades of nuance. One is calculating, pragmatic, amoral, devious, deceptive, adaptable, even rational, as one enacts the world of the matlabi. The word goes beyond the pragmatic and the instrumental and commands a polysemic calculus of its own. A matlabi maximizes the intentions of his world while ignoring or manipulating the interest of the other. It is an art of survival which is indifferent to ethics. As a matlabi survives and grows in power, he develops his own vocabulary.

Think of words which exude a hybridity of meaning like 'contact' or 'oblige' or 'service'. These are English words which have a Hindi or Punjabi meaning. Indians use English to say what the English could not say. Let us consider the word 'contact'. Contact is an open sesame of a word going beyond what Ali Baba can dream. A friend of mine was teaching Kafka's *The Castle* to a bunch of students from the north, explaining the pathos and poignancy of the hero's entry into the castle. His students looked puzzled. One of his students asked, '*Kuch contact nahin tha?*', meaning 'Didn't he have any contacts?' Contact conveys the magical, matlabi sense of entry. Entry and access are the first rituals of matlabi strategy. To know the right place and to sense the right man ushers the matlabi into the world of power. A matlabi needs to understand middlemen, brokers, because it is they who oblige you. The way the tout says *Kuch oblige kar sakte hai* (literally, 'Can you please oblige?') opens out the world of reciprocity, of service, of mutuality. A dog should not eat dog when it can accommodate the other.

Matlabi is a keyword in the folklore of corruption. Corruption secularizes power, the matlabi instrumentalizes entry and a utilitarian world of service and reciprocity is born where a matlabi maximizes survival and mobility. The word matlabi conveys the sense of tactics and strategy in world of everydayness. A matlabi has no permanent friends without permanent interests. He becomes a cameo contrast with the innocent idealist bumbling in a world where values are stumbling blocks and interests grease the way to power. A matlabi is the power politician of the ordinary. If goodness can be used to maximize gain, a matlabi would be angelic. A matlabi created the folklore of Machiavelli long before Machiavelli was born. Mobile, fluid, protean, a matlabi demonstrates the art of survival in an unforgiving world. Yet, he is creature of the folk imagination, envied, immortalized in many Bollywood film. The following fragment from *Roy* captures it: *Matlabi ho ja Zara Matlabi/Duniya ki sunta hai kyu/Khud ki bhi sun le kabhi* ('Become self-interested, dear Matlabi. Why listen to the world? Sometimes, just be interested in yourself').

References

Kingston, Christopher. 'Social Capital and Corruption: Theory, and Evidence from India'. *Amherst College*, 2005. https://pdfs.semanticscholar.org/918a/673257256f78779801f8ec9afb717a31b935.pdf (accessed 30 August 2019).

Ruud, Arild Engelsen. 'Corruption as Everyday Practice: The Public—Private Divide in Local Indian Society'. *Forum for Development Studies* 27, no. 2. Taylor & Francis Group, 2000.

NARA (NĀRĀ)

Navprit Kaur

Etymological roots of the word *nara* could be traced back to the Arabic word *naar*. In English, the word nara can be translated into slogan. Naras are short phrases or words, generally coined or weaved together by a leader (ranging from the leader of a local sweeper's union to the prime minister), a group of people, social, religious, cultural and political movements, a political party or a government. Naras are the most common mode of raising demands, political mobilization, protest and collective expression in the public domain in India. Naras express disapproval or support for public authorities and governments (slogans against the local junior engineer for lack of electric supply or for demands of *azadi* [freedom] in Kashmir), events and happenings (such as a dowry death or the American president's visit to India), ideas and movements (from a Bollywood film to the Naxalite movement) and policies. Expressed through a variety of mediums, naras are an integral part of the spatial composition of a public place in India. Naras could be found in the form of posters hanging from electric poles, pasted on public chowks or scribbled on walls. One example is the naras by Indian Railway's workers on walls all along the railway tracks throughout India. During protests, public meetings and political rallies, naras are raised in a high-pitch voice and are accompanied by the raising of a fist. Prefixing with a word, which could be the name of a person, a public authority, a government, a political party or a nation, and following it with either *zindabaad* ('Hail!') or *murdabaad* ('Down with!') are two most commonly used naras to express support and resentment, respectively.

In fact, one can trace the journey of India, and gauge the political mood of its people at a particular time in history, or simply get to know the issues faced by masses at various junctures by looking at the most popular naras. In the context of the Hindi-speaking regions in contemporary India, naras could be divided into two: those belonging to the colonial period and those belonging to the postcolonial period. The naras of the colonial period represented the various streams of thought within the Indian freedom movement. If *angrezo bharat chhodo* ('Britishers quit India!') represented Gandhian aspirations of peaceful mobilization of the Indian masses, then *jai hind* and *tum mujhe khoon do, main tumhen azaadi doonga* ('Give me your blood, I will give you freedom!') by Subhash Chandra Bose represented the radical stream of gaining political independence. Slogans like *vande mataram* ('I praise you, motherland!') by Bankim Chandra, *satya mev jayate* ('Truth alone triumphs!') by Madan Mohan Malviya and *swaraj mera janam sidh adhikaar hai* ('Self-government is my birth-right!') by Bal Gangadhar Tilak represented the Hindu nationalist thought within the Indian freedom movement.

Inquilaab zindabaad ('Hail the revolution!') by Maulana Hasrat Mohani, and popularized by Bhagat Singh, reflected the radical stream of thought but is now used in a more popular sense by the left during protests.

In the postcolonial period, there were naras related to the new vision of independent India. Naaras like *roti kapda aur makaan* ('Food, clothing and shelter') represented the socialist vision of Indian state during the Nehruvian era. Similarly, Lal Bahadur Shastri talked of *jai jawan, jai kisan* ('Hail the soldier, hail the farmer!') in the backdrop of the Indo–Pak war and the food crisis of the 1960s. Indira Gandhi produced the slogan *garibi hatao* ('Alleviate poverty') to build a self-sufficient India. In the post-Emergency period, the Jayaprakash Narayan-led movement popularized the slogan of *Indira hatao, desh bachao* ('Remove Indira, save the country!'). Apart from the governments, various political and social movements have also coined their own slogans. Some of the most famous slogans of the women's movement are *naari shakti zindabaad, pitrasatta murdabaad* ('Hail women's power, down with patriarchy!') and *halla bol halla bol, pitrasatta pe halla bol* ('Attack patriarchy!').

Apart from this, the most common slogans used across the political spectrum are *jo humse takrayega choor ho jaayega* ('Those who challenge us, will bite the dust'), *awaaz do hum ek hain* ('Hail our solidarity') and *taanashahi nahi chalegi, nahi chalegi, nahi chalegi* ('Down with dictatorship!').

References

Ahmed, Ishtiaq. 'The 1947 Partition of India: A Paradigm for Pathological Politics in India and Pakistan'. *Asian Ethnicity* 3, no. 1 (2002): 9–28.
Nayar, Kuldip. *The Martyr: Bhagat Singh Experiments in Revolution*. New Delhi: Har-Anand Publications, 2000.

NETA (NĒTĀ)

Manish Thakur

Neta, in singular and masculine meaning leader/political leader, has its etymological roots in Sanskrit and is a ubiquitous term in many Indian languages such as Hindi, Marathi and Bengali; *netri* is the singular and feminine term for the same. In Urdu, a leader is called *quaid* – the term is famously used to refer to Mohammad Ali Jinnah (*Quaid-e-Azam*/Great Leader); a political leader/politician is also called *siyasatdaan*, particularly by the Urdu speakers of Pakistan.

While many terms exist for the leader in India, it is neta (masculine, singular) which is the most common. Generally speaking, it exhibits a range of connotations from respect to parody. When suffixed with the honourific *ji* as in *netaji*, it refers to some of the tallest mass leaders marked for the reach and scale of their support base. For example, in the Hindi-speaking belt, Netaji has come to stand for Mulayam Singh Yadav, the founder of the Samajwadi Party and former chief minister of Uttar Pradesh. However, not all political leaders, some perhaps more eminent than Mulayam Singh Yadav, are addressed as Netaji. Atal Bihari Vajpayee and Lal Krishna Advani, for example, are called Atalji and Advaniji, respectively; they are neither netaji nor Netaji.

At a pan-Indian level, Netaji is recognized to be used for Subhash Chandra Bose, the famous freedom fighter and nationalist leader. His name is either prefixed by Netaji or simply used as a proper noun. A large number of public roads, buildings and localities in post-Independence India carry his name in either of the two forms; history (text) books do the same too. In this usage, evidently, the term Netaji is used as a marker of some of the stellar attributes of leadership like courage, conviction, valour and other cognate abilities to lead the people. Bose's founding of the Azad Hind Fauz/Indian National Army and his victory as the president of the Indian National Congress (despite Gandhi's opposition to his candidature) and his bold and radical attempt during the Second World War to ally with the Axis powers for the sake of India's independence, might have cumulatively given him that sobriquet. Here, again, no other leader of the nationalist pantheon has this moniker. There are others like Sardar, Maulana, Mahatma, Pandit, Lokmanya, Deshbandhu, but there is only one Netaji with a capital N.

The term neta, in itself, though, does not necessarily mean a political heavyweight or a leader who has a pan-Indian (visibility and) recognition. It denotes leaders of all sorts – from those stationed in New Delhi with access to a *lāla battī* (red beacon) Ambassador cars, down to a village leader. At times, it is locally used in a pejorative sense to make fun of unemployed youth who idle away their time gossiping and are always ready to offer opinion on any issue. Such people are seen as indulging in *netagiri* (the act of being a neta) rather than providing *netritya* (positive, sincere, ideal) leadership. There are also combinations of multiple types where a person is a trader and a neta, a *paan* shop owner and a neta, a teacher and a neta, a lawyer and a neta and the likes. Such netas, in popular parlance, are an inalienable presence in the Indian landscape, both urban and rural. It is no hyperbole to suggest that every neighbourhood, village and town has their own netas. They are a common sight in the teeming *bazaars* (markets) and *mohallas* (streets) and they become more visible and approachable during elections. Local people know them by their sartorial distinctions, food habits and/or penchant for good life and other related traits that matter locally.

Generally, anyone who takes to politics in a recognizable way or is concerned with public/community affairs is a neta in the eyes of the locals even when (s)he might be just an ordinary member of the local branch of a state- or national-level political party. Moreover, unlike their more established, bilingual and sophisticated metropolitan colleagues, the political universe of the local netajis goes beyond the requirements of electoral arithmetic and attendant mobilization. They are not merely confined to party offices and do not always follow the *diktats* (dictates) of the party high command.

The adjective neta has given rise to an interesting verb netagiri *karna*, which is the act of being a neta. It is quite common to hear the expression in the Ganga-Yamuna plains: tum netagiri *kar rahe ho* or netagiri *karne ki zaroorat nahi hai*. Here, netagiri is seen as an act of creating unnecessary public nuisance. Effectively then, neta means someone who can mobilize others on an issue or a set of issues. This mobilizational power of the neta can very well act as a threat to those who maintain the status quo in manifold ways. They are scorned because they seem to unsettle the status-quoist common sense of the day, where public affairs are, more often than not, merged with the hitherto existing power hierarchies.

In many cases, political parties do not have permanent offices worth their name. Yet, many makeshift offices crop up during election times. The lack of a permanent address is hardly a deterrent, both for the neta and the hoi polloi. A visitor to a small town will, in all likelihood, encounter the neta either in the party office (if there happens to be one) or, say, in prominent and not-so-prominent public places.

(S)he, in the second case, may come to know that a particular small teashop is the parking place for Sharmaji's vehicle (usually a two-wheeler), Sharmaji being the local neta who religiously visits it at a preordained time and delivers all-absorbing lectures on themes ranging from Bush to Saddam, Ghulam Nabi Azad to Lalu Prasad Yadav, cricket diplomacy to Pakistani threat and so on. Similarly, one may run into a Vermaji in a sweetmeat shop, relishing his usual staple of *Aaj* and *Dainik Bhaskar* and talking animatedly on the sociopolitical problems facing India and the world in contemporary times.

The predominantly male, local universe populated by netas like Sharmajis and Vermajis, as is obvious, hardly finds any mention in standard textbooks on theories of democracy and the state. It connotes a political world where old values sit comfortably with the new-found radicalism emanating from the ideas of rights and equality. It is a world where democratic values and articulations collapse into the conventional hierarchies of status and wealth. However, it is not that nothing is changing. It is a world which reminds us that there can be something more to our lives than the traditional obligations of caste, kinship and village. With all their limitations, our mofussil netajis are the creators of the public sphere in a country in which one's understanding of the world is always circumscribed by one's location in a particular social station. Our omnipresent netas, despite the occasional pun and general disdain, reveal the most significant and contemporary facet of our Indianness, which is that democracy has struck deep cultural roots in India.

References

Krishna, Anirudh. 'Gaining Access to Public Services and the Democratic State in India: Institutions in the Middle'. *Studies in Comparative International Development* 46, no. 1 (2011): 98–117.
Manor, James. 'Small-Time Political Fixers in India's States: "Towel over Armpit"'. *Asian Survey* 40, no. 5 (2000): 816–35.

PRAVACHAN (PRAVACAN)

Rama Kant Agnihotri

The words *pravacan* and *bhaashan* can, in many contexts, be used interchangeably; in fact, all pravachans could legitimately be called bhaashans (speeches). However, the vice versa is certainly not true. Pravacan, by definition, carries religious, spiritual and moral connotations. In principle, a pravacan can be delivered anywhere but it is generally marked for person, place, topic and audience. The place may be a temple, a mosque, a church or a gurudwara or places specifically designated for religious discourses, such as the Ramakrishna Mission or the Radhaswami Satsang (*satsang* literally means a gathering of religious people). The person, *pravachankaarak* – a saint or a monk – delivering the pravacan, is generally a theology scholar/philosopher; the topic invariably concerns the way we should live our lives, with frequent references to moral consequences and life hereafter.

This word owes its origins to Sanskrit; it is a masculine noun, referring to the recitation and exposition of religious texts, consisting of philosophical, spiritual and ethical ideas, shared with a sense of gravity for the welfare of the listeners. *Rig Veda* verses 10.35.8 and 4.36.1 use the word in the sense of recitation of Vedic texts. It is the Vedic *pravaachan* which becomes the post-Vedic Sanskrit pravacan. A satsang, or a religious congregation, is the place most commonly associated with pravacan and in India, there are hundreds of such sects. One of the leading spiritual forums is the Ramakrishna Mission started by Ramakrishna Paramhamsa and his disciple Swami Vivekananada. Another, the Radha Soami Satsang Beas (RSSB) has millions of followers. In recent years, we have unfortunately seen some such 'spiritual' satsangs which, under the garb of religious activities, indulge in crime, money laundering, rape and murder.

The word bhaashan could also subsume some religious discourses, but is often used for a public lecture; it covers a wide semantic range. It could, in Hindi, refer to a public lecture given by a philosopher, historian, sociologist, linguist or a scientist. Lectures given by politicians may often be called a bhaashan; they would never, however, be called a pravacan. The lecture given at a university convocation is referred to, in Hindi, as *dikshaant* bhaashan – a lecture given by the chief guest at the moment when students have completed their education (*dikshaa* means 'knowledge' and *ant* mean 'end', in Sanskrit). The art of delivering bhaashans does involve a certain oratorical skill – the use of rhetorical devices that help capture the attention of the audience. 'Dr. Ambedkar Ke Bhaashan', 'Bhaarat Ke Mahaan Bhaashan', 'Bhaashan Kalaa', etc., are all possible titles of books that one may come across. The way one speaks has remained a central concern in all cultures; for example, when in the Bhagavad Gita (2.54), Arjuna wants to know the defining features of a person with a stable mind (his own mind being so unstable), he asks Lord Krishna – *sthita-prajnyasya kaa bhaashaa samaadhi-sthasya keśhava | sthita-dhiḥ kiṁ prabhaasheta kim aasita vrajeta kim* ('Oh Lord, how do you define a person with a stable mind? How does he speak, how does he sit and how does he walk?'). The widely used term bhaashan often carries a note of sarcasm in almost all the Indo-Āryan languages. When you get irritated by someone constantly getting on your nerves by suggesting 'do this, do that, this is not what you should be doing', etc., your reaction might be 'stop your bhaashan *baajii*'.

References

Apte, Vaman Shivram. *Sanskrit-hindi kosh*. Delhi: Motilal Banarsidass, 1986.
Beckerlegge, Gwilym. *The Ramakrishna Mission: The Making of a Modern Hindu Movement*. New Delhi: Oxford University Press, 2000.

SETTLED

Shiv Visvanathan

The word settled should rank high in any *Hobson-Jobson* of the modern world. It captures the common-sense art of problem-solving, the result of looking at the world not as a given but as something to be constructed out of negotiation. A problem is settled but never settles down. The ritual of settle demands skills of diplomacy, adjustment, adaptation of a mutual give and take which makes society possible as a coexistence of difference. *Hum settle kar dege* (literally, 'We will settle [it]') is a promise of delivery. *Settle ho gaya* ('I/they have settled') gives a sense of comfort, closure and ease, a promise that worry does not crease your eyes. Settle evokes both open-endedness and promise of closure. It needs brokerage, the tout and that great invention of modern power, the personal assistant (PA), who can settle any bureaucratic problem even if his bosses cannot, if given the right incentive. Settling is an art, a craft, a repertoire of skills which power demands. Nothing is unsolvable in a world of touts, brokers and PAs.

Settling also gives the sense of a different kind of social. Here the social bridges two worlds, inner and outer, indigenous and alien, and the word 'settle' derives from the hybridity of a mind that is at home with differences and yet seeks an ease of translation where a solution does not have to be ideal or utopian, merely something which allows for adjustment and adaptability on both sides. A bribe also provides the poetic grease, the incentive to adjust between two cultures or contending groups.

The idea of settling is always easy with difference and asymmetry. The negotiator seeks adjustments, bringing his skills of negotiation and reworking the word to recreate the world as it exists. Settling is thus a perspective about the world, a way of resolving differences and the skills that it demands. Most 'settlers' are middlemen and as a villain in a movie toasted them, 'Thanks for middleman, for those who settle things, they make the world possible.'

Settled also is a signal for not touching or tinkering unnecessarily with an issue, of not reopening it too often. *Settled ho gai hai* is a way of saying cease worrying about it when the world is at peace with itself. A tout put it succinctly, *Shadi ho ya supari, settle to karna hi padega* (It may be a wedding or a killing: either way, the matter has to be settled).

SHRUTI AND SMRITI (ŚRUTI AND SMṚTI)

Praveen Singh

Shruti (also spelled *Śruti*) has its roots in Sanskrit which means 'that which has been heard'. In the context of Hinduism and Indian Philosophy, it refers to that strand of knowledge which is said to have been 'revealed' to the ancient *Rishis* also referred to as *drishtaa* (seers) who were able to 'hear' the divine word through their meditation and discipline. They were, in some sense, the *drishta* or the 'seers', who were not only able to understand the vibrations of the cosmos but also able to pass it on to the progeny (see Lochtefeld 2006). This knowledge was initially in the form of oral knowledge that was handed down and which later got codified in the form of the *Vedas*, the most authoritative of all texts considered to be sacred and having no known origin in any human being. These have, thus, been called *apaurusheya* (without any origin in humans). This divine origin thus adds to their authority and status of being the revealer of incontrovertible truth and any doubt cast on their authenticity is deemed unacceptable.

The term Veda comes from the Sanskrit root 'vid' which means 'to know' and implies divine knowledge, Dalal argues. The Vedas are said to be four in number, namely the *Rig Veda*,

Sama Veda, *Yajur Veda* and *Atharva Veda* and each of these have their special functions. The Vedas comprise four kinds of texts, namely, *samhitas* or 'the hymns to the gods', *brahmanas* or 'the ritual manuals', the *aranyakas* or the forest books containing some speculative thought and the Upanishads, which may be said to be the earliest texts carrying the germs of serious philosophical enquiry (ibid). Scholars, such as Sharma (1960) have observed that the Vedantins consider even the Upanishads as shruti and treat them at par with the Vedas. The shruti texts are said to enjoy the highest authority in all matters and in the case of any dispute between the texts that have been referred to as the smritis and the shrutis, it is the latter that is to be considered as the final having a privileged status. However, we are told that Sankara, a great exponent of *Advaita Vedanta*, was of the opinion that even the shruti should not be believed blindly and that reason should be used to determine if what it says is correct.

While the shrutis are said to have no human authors, there is another body of texts in Hinduism, generally referred to as the *Smriti* texts which are said to be compositions by humans. The word 'Smriti', too, comes from Sanskrit which means 'that which is remembered'. In other words, smritis are the result of some kind of reminiscence or recollection of something that one may have heard or thought about. Since it is remembered and has human authorship, there is a likelihood that the smritis may be wrong. That possibility is accepted and in case of any doubt, the shrutis are expected to form the basis of the final knowledge or understanding. Smritis comprise a greater body of work which includes 'dharma literature, the sectarian compilations known as *Puranas*, the two great epics (Mahābhārata and Rāmāyaṇa), the *Bhagavad Gita* and the *Tantras*, which are manuals detailing the secret, ritually based religious practice of tantra followers', according to Lochtefeld. Some of the famous smritis are the *Kalpa Sutras* that are books that carry 'aphorisms on sacred law' and are comprised of three parts, namely 'prescriptions for Vedic rituals (*Shrauta Sutras*), prescriptions for domestic rites (*Grhya Sutras*), and prescriptions for appropriate human behaviour (*Dharma Sutras*)', Lochtefeld notes.

The Puranas are another genre of popular smriti texts that are full of sacred Indian mythologies. There are said to be eighteen major puranas, of which some of the major ones are *Markandeyapurana, Shiva Purana, Bhagavata Purana, Agni Purana* and *Vishnu Purana*. Among the popular *Dharmashastra* texts, which are another genre of Smriti texts, are the *Manu Smṛiti* (a book on the laws of a good social order and life) and *Yajnavlakya Smṛiti*. As has been mentioned earlier, the Smriti texts are less authoritative than the Shrutis but they are more in number and have been known to undergo changes with time and different commentators have offered different interpretations of the original smriti. They are, in that sense, a little flexible and undergo change, whereas shrutis are not expected to change with time.

References

Grimes, John, Sushil Mittal and Gene Thursby. 'Hindu Dharma'. In *Religion of South Asia: An Introduction*, edited by Sushil Mittal and Gene Thursby. London and New York: Routledge, 2006.

Lochtefeld, James G. *The Illustrated Encyclopedia of Hinduism*. New York: The Rosen Publishing Group, 2006.

THALAIVAR (TALAIVAR)

Sudarsan Padmanabhan

The Tamil term *thalaivar* is equivalent to the term 'captain' in English, derived from its Greek and Latin origins. Thalaivar is a reference to a leader in masculine gender. In the ancient Sangam literature, the term *talaivan*, in singular-masculine, is always accompanied by *talaivi*, its feminine. In latter genres of Tamil poetic and prose literature, the talaivan–talaivi template has continued as *nayaka–nayaki bhava*, in Vaishnavite Puranas, incandescently beautiful verses of medieval Vaishnative and Saivite poet-saints, Alwars and Nayanmars, respectively, and, more contemporaneously, in theatre, films and creative art forms as hero–heroine duo.

Thalaivar, in classical Tamil literature and ancient and medieval social milieu, also indicates a leader of stature in military, royal court, local village bodies, religious institutions and artisanal or business classes. Interestingly, there are also exceptions in the Sangam literature to this talaivan–talaivi categorization by way of the Buddhist and Jain literature. Texts such as *Manimegalai* and *Neelakesi* are against the traditional Vedic *asrama* system that believes in the four sequential stages of life leading towards final release and follow a *sramana* philosophy, which emphasizes renunciation as the direct path to liberation. The main characters in most of these epics are renouncers or aspiring ones. The term thalaivar, in the contemporary context, is twofold, one is salutary and the other mirthful. As in the Classical literature, the term thalaivar carries the mantle of leadership, especially in politics.

In movies, the talaivan–talaivi trope reaches its apogee due to the confluence of poetry, prose, drama, music, dance and comedy. During India's freedom struggle, many powerful leaders emerged over the course of two centuries with the tallest of them all being Mahatma Gandhi, who also matched the categorical characteristics of thalaivar. Two of the most famous contemporary actors in Tamil are, first, Rajnikanth known as Thalaivar, affectionately by his film aficionados but less seriously and in jest by those who are not inimical to his on-screen persona.

The other popular actor, who is laconically called *tala*, which literally means the head, is Ajith Kumar or simply Ajith. While Rajnikanth's thalaivar is expansive and theatrical, Ajith's tala is measured and understated. The original Thalaivar, in whom the on-screen persona and real-life personality seamlessly coalesced to create Tamil Nadu's most charismatic and talismanic political icon, was, however, the late M. G. Ramachandran or known as just MGR. M. G. Ramachandran understood the power of the mass media and used the talaivan–talaivi archetype in his films, tellingly to capture the imagination of the people of Tamil Nadu and India in general. Even when MGR was not given any official political position in his parent Dravida Munnetra Kazhagam (DMK), the leadership recognized his immense popularity and harvested it for many an election victory; he was an undisputed mass leader. As his popularity soared, the DMK expelled MGR from the party on a flimsy pretext, which only culminated in astounding political success during the most testing period in Indian politics, the Emergency. His protégé, the late J. Jayalalithaa, who was his on-screen romantic interest, also used the talaiva–talaivi *topos* to achieve great political success.

Another thalaivar figure who was also associated with Tamil films, theatre, poetry and literature, who successfully transitioned into a powerful political leader rivalling both MGR and Jayalalithaa, was Muthuvel Karunanidhi who is known for his bewitching oratorical skills, prolific writing and unabashed espousal of Tamil causes. The term thalaivar, therefore, reveals a dynamically evolving broad appeal yet at once a rootedness in the social context of the epoch.

References

Herbert, Vaidehi, trans. 'Sangam Poems'. Available at: https://sangamtranslationsbyvaidehi.com/ (accessed December 2018).

Ramanujan, A. K. *The Interior Landscape: Classical Tamil Love Poems*. New York: New York Review of Books, 2014.

TENSION

Anushka Rajesh Patel and Merdijana Kovacevic

A word is rarely *just* a word. The subtext undergirding a single word – navigating context, tone, speaker and listener – can render it a dynamically coded message. 'Tension', is one such word that has been absorbed into the Indian ethos with a ubiquity that is equally intriguing and confusing.

The *Oxford English Dictionary* defines tension as 'the act of stretching'. Technical, as this definition is, it aligns perfectly with how we understand tension in inanimate objects. Tension is a term used in physics to animate properties of inanimate objects and create quotidian appliances. For instance, a tension rod strains itself to perform the arduous work of holding up our curtains! However, the meaning of tension does not stop at defining a physical property. In fact, it is contextually rich and alludes to complex and lively states. The same dictionary, thus, proffers another definition that aligns more closely with how tension is socially constructed and reified among Indians: tension connotes 'a strained condition of feeling or mutual relations which is, for the time, outwardly calm, but is likely to result in a sudden collapse, in an outburst of anger or violent action of some kind'. Indeed, when tension is understood this way, it exemplifies our inner emotional experiences and the impact it has on complex social relationships.

Scholars from medicine, anthropology and psychology have been intrigued by the use of tension in India. It has been culturally appropriated – verbatim in the English form – into several linguistic groups including Kannada, Hindi and Marathi. Similar to its physical meaning of being stretched, the use of tension in relational contexts conveys a sense of feeling stress from being pulled in many directions. Tension is crucial for understanding mental health, because it acts as a loaded message, coded in sensitive cultural information. In other words, tension is an idiom of distress. An idiom is a way of communicating one's distress to optimize the chance that it will be recognized in a cultural setting and addressed by people who can decode the meanings laden within the idiom. As such, this concept helps convey a complex set of psychological states with mere mention of 'taking tension', 'having too much tension' or stating a desire to 'get rid of tension'. Every culture has its idioms of distress. Unlocking the wealth of culturally coded information embedded, in tension, can improve communication around it. In turn, clearer communication impacts healthcare dialogue (by recognizing, diagnosing and treating tension) and everyday discourse (by destigmatizing the experience) in powerful ways.

Careful anthropological study has revealed how people experience their tension, what they believe causes it and how they seek help for the same. For instance, tension is commonly thought of as an idiom conveying depressive and anxious symptoms, particularly among women. However, tension encompasses various components beyond this symptomology. Individuals using tension largely describe bodily distress, including episodic somatic problems (such as increased blood pressure, headaches, malaise, fatigue, insomnia, lack of appetite, aches and pains) and chronic ailments (such as gynaecological problems and stress-related diabetes). Tension may also encompass cognitive complaints (e.g. rumination, increased worries, suicidality), behavioural symptoms (e.g. crying, hitting others) and negative emotionality (e.g. persistent irritability, anxiety).

Interestingly, the types of problems most emphasized during tension depend on the group in question and the research foci. While women in psychological research have emphasized the depressive and anxious pathology when 'having tension', women examined for physical health conditions (e.g. sexually transmitted diseases or diabetes) highlighted their medical health concerns as related to/caused by tension. Despite diversity in symptoms of tension, some common ideas prevail regarding how tension relates to health. A prevailing notion across most groups is that 'taking too much tension' can impair one's health. Additionally, physical discomfort – be it through episodic somatic problems or chronic physical conditions – is a commonly reported feature of tension. As such, tension has been identified, most often, in primary care settings.

Given the complex states conveyed by tension, what could possibly cause it? The causes of tension are as wide-ranging as its symptoms. Simply put, tension has been linked with anything from daily irritants and chores causing low-grade cumulative stress to more severe and chronic forms of structural violence that are cyclical and entrap people in vicious cycles of tension. Interpersonal stress has emerged as a common theme across research, particularly among women. For example, concern for loved ones, inability to meet others' expectations, and marital/domestic discord or violence cause tension.

So far, tension has emerged as an idiom conveying complex psychological states of distress, with somatic symptoms being more commonly reported. This finding has intriguing implications: if the experience of tension includes both somatic *and* psychological symptoms, why are somatic problems being highlighted more often? We conjecture two reasons for this premised on Dr Lawrence Kirmayer's work on the significance of somatic idioms of distress. First, tension is an idiom operating in a healthcare context with limited psychological avenues for seeking recourse. As such, it may be more functional to highlight the somatic experience involved in tension as these symptoms can be 'fixed' through the healthcare infrastructure of doctors and holy healers already in place. Indeed, when doctors query people about tension, people readily discuss the symptoms and causes of their tension; in turn, doctors take tension to mean depression. Second, Dr Leslie Jo Weaver, a medical anthropologist who has studied tension among diabetic women in India, posits that tension conveys distress effectively precisely because its ambiguity is its strength. Put differently, reporting tension allows a woman to articulate distress vaguely enough that she cannot be faulted for 'complaining' about her mental health or relational problems in a highly relational cultural context. In turn, this idiom can garner psychosocial support without being alienated.

Recalling how relationally linked the causes of tension are, this ambiguity is necessary and adaptive for expressing distress without rupturing relationships. Thus, the richness of using tension to convey one's distress is situated precisely here. Tension is a cultural chameleon. It allows one to hint a wealth of charged information without giving much away at the surface. Tension can unlock a great deal – including symptoms, causes and coping – without saying much more than the three little words: 'I have tension.'

References

Cork, Cliodhna, Bonnie N. Kaiser and Ross G. White. 'The Integration of Idioms of Distress into Mental Health Assessments and Interventions: A Systematic Review'. *Global Mental Health* 6 (2019).

Pereira, B., G. Andrew, S. Pednekar, R. Pai, P. Pelto and V. Patel. 'The Explanatory Models of Depression in Low Income Countries: Listening to Women in India'. *The Journal of Affective Disorders* 102, 1–3 (2007): 209–18.

Weaver, Lesley Jo. 'Tension among Women in North India: An Idiom of Distress and a Cultural Syndrome'. *Culture, Medicine, and Psychiatry* 41, no. 1 (2017): 35–55.

THREE LANGUAGE FORMULA

Jatindra Kumar Nayak

In 1968, after consultation with the states, the union government formulated a policy of language education at the school level (classes one to ten), known as the 'three language formula' and expected the state governments to implement it in their respective states. According to this formula, the student has to learn three languages but learn them in a graded manner. First, from classes one to four, (s)he must learn only one language, namely the mother language or the regional language. Then, in addition to this, a second language was introduced between classes five and seven, which could be Hindi – the official language of India – or English – the other official language of the country – or a modern European language. Finally, a third language is added to the aforementioned two for classes eight to ten; this language, for the Hindi-speaking states, would be a modern Indian language (preferably one of the southern languages) and for the non-Hindi-speaking states, Hindi, if not already learnt as the second language. The objective was to develop emotional integration among the people and to enable them to study science and technology, the main language of which is English.

This well-intentioned formula has, however, not worked. Tamil Nadu was very uncomfortable with it, viewing it as strategy to impose Hindi on the non-Hindi states. The people of the Hindi-speaking states were reluctant to study a southern language; for them, it was an unnecessary burden – if everyone in the country was studying Hindi and English anyway, the third language would have no real function for them. So, many states found ways of avoiding learning either Hindi or a southern language, as the case may be for them. Besides, this policy privileged those whose mother tongue was the regional language of the state and those who did not benefit from mother tongue education were among the marginalized sections of the society – tribal language speakers, temporary migrants and even speakers of the non-standard varieties of the regional language. Despite all its limitations, this formula, even in its defective implementation, provided bilingual education, making people bilingual in the process.

References

Annamalai, E. 'Nation-Building in a Globalised World: Language Choice and Education in India'. In *Decolonisation, Globalisation: Language-in-Education Policy and Practice*, edited by Angel M. Y. Lin and Peter W. Martin, 21–38. Clevedon: Multilingual Matters Ltd., 2005.
Mohanty, Ajit. 'Multilingual Education in India'. In *Encyclopedia of Language and Education*, vol. 5: Bilingual Education, edited by Jim Cummins and Nancy Hornberger, 1617–26. New York: Springer, 2008.

TIME-PASS

Vanamala Viswanatha

Craig Jeffrey's book *Timepass* (2010) refers to the politics of a new India in which its youth, especially young men, while away hours of their waiting for something to come about – a job, an exciting or exacting event or even a romance. These 'in between' passages of time are spent in banter, in movies, theatres or simply doing nothing. Yet, such is the cultural variation in India that the very same compound word, in a different cultural space, namely the state of Karnataka in South India, has a slightly extended connotation. Pronounced *tamepas*, this supposedly English phrase (to pass the time) refers to peanuts in Kannada. Typically, you hear this expression from vendors shouting, 'tamepas, tamepas, tamepaaaas', in as many unusual, insistent intonations (a simple fall, an uncomplicated rise, a fall-rise, etc.) as they can manage, to grab your attention to the roasted, unshelled peanuts they sell in the bus and train stations, between Bengaluru and Mysuru. Another scenario is, there is a mound of roasted but unpeeled nuts with their brown/dark brown shell intact; people sit around this mound as the sun goes down, feeling the warm peanut shell in their hands as they break the shell expertly between their left forefinger and right thumb and throw the nut into their mouths, while chatting interminably about things.

There is a brilliant scene of tamepas in a classic short story by the Kannada *Dalit* writer, Devanuru Mahadeva, titled, 'Odalaala'. Pushed to the brink, a deprived *Dalit* family is forced to steal a sack of peanuts from their landlord. The hungry family sits around the fire and polishes off the entire sack of nuts, throwing the shells into the fire. When the police arrive, there is no sign of either peanuts or the shells, anywhere! Tamepas had swallowed up both evidence and time.

References

Fuller, Chris. 'Timepass and Boredom in Modern India'. *Anthropology of this Century*, no. 1 (2011).
Jeffrey, Craig. *Timepass: Youth, Class, and the Politics of Waiting in India*. California: Stanford University Press, 2010.

TRANSLATION

Rita Kothari

On an extremely congested road, ironically called Relief Road, in the city of Ahmedabad, is a city civil court. As you navigate that traffic to reach the court, you come across some people who have their chairs and desks laid out outside the court. They translate documents from English and other languages into Gujarati. In the world of Europe, this form of legal translation would require formal training and a licence. In this case, it is done out of experience, intuition and, more importantly, as one of the means of livelihood. Incidentally, the current cost of translating a document from English to Gujarati is 80 rupees, approximately one US dollar. This purely functional and pragmatic need is in no conversation with the medical, literary or corporate translation.

A classic question about India, and it's over a thousand recorded languages, is how does India manage communication amidst such linguistic diversity? Surely translation must be the only way. And yet, as mentioned above, a large number of untrained translators go through ad hoc assignments for a very meagre pay. While a small number does derive intellectual joy from it, translation as a practice is mostly perceived as a means towards an end. If the movement from one language into another happens all the time at home, at work, on trains and buses, how is translation special? It is ubiquitous and pervasive, not requiring a name, leave alone training. The 'excess' of a multilingual reality has made translation not distant enough for cerebral theorization or economic compensation and social or intellectual recognition. That being said, a gamut of forms and approaches of cultural and linguistic transfer obtain under different names in different languages of India.

If one were to look at the various ways in which translation evolved and was termed in various Indian languages, a host of varied names crop up – sometimes one language has several words for the process of 'rendering' or retelling, sometimes several languages having common words albeit with different shades of meaning. Some of the terms for translation include *anuvad* (to speak after or to tell in turn), *bhashantar* (a change of language), *roopantar* (a change of form), *mozhipeyarttu* (*mozhi* meaning language and *peyarttu* meaning 'to dislodge, to carry across or to migrate' in Tamil), *parivartan* (a transformation), *tarjuma* (used in Islamic literature to refer to the biography of a Sūī, saint or scholar but later came to be used for translation), *deshantar* (a change of locale), *veshantar* (a change of dress or attire), *kaalantar* (a change of historical period), *bhavanuvad* (a rendering of emotion), *gagdyanuvad* (a rendering of prose) and so on.

Anuvad, or speaking in turn, is often elicited as a distinguishing temporal aspect of the Indian notion of translation when compared to translation in the West, which, etymologically, has the spatial aspect to 'carry across'. Several words for translation in India involve the suffix *antar* which generally denotes change. For instance, deshantar would be a rendering in which the original locale or setting is adapted to the target locale and country. The notion of change or 'antar', as already inherent in the activity of translation, means that a translated text is, already and always, distant from the 'original'. However, this difference is not seen as a dilution or a corruption of the 'other'. Antar, which is both a spatial and a temporal metaphor, denotes simultaneously 'interval' and 'distance'. Furthermore, antar also refers to 'the inner' or 'of the self', which implies an organic link between 'text' and 'translation'.

Keywords for India

The activity of translation, thus, is not a movement away from the text but a change within itself. This notion of internal change and interaction seems vital to an understanding of an Indian sense of translation. The philosophical underpinnings of the terms demonstrate how the idea of the 'original' and the treachery attached to the history of translation in the West, as also its attendant anxieties of fidelity, have not been central to the Indian subcontinent. In fact, the word 'translation' falls less easily on the tongue, signalling a degree of formalization and self-consciousness. Unsurprisingly, the term *bahubhashiyata* for multilingualism also has a touch of new coinage to it. Both terms point to an imaginary formation through a process of translation.

The puzzling absence of translation theory in India's long-standing linguistic and civilizational life has been seen by scholars like Harish Trivedi as constituting 'the history of non-translation'. Trivedi's much-cited article 'In Our Own Time, on Our Own Terms: Translation in India' is an extremely important intervention and argues that 'the traffic in translation was never thick throughout the premodern period in India, that is, right up to the impact of the West in the eighteenth century, and whatever little translation there was, was all in one direction, from the Indian languages out' (Trivedi 2006). But what is translation in the Indian context? Does it have to be linguistic in nature? Does it need to refer to written texts only? Does 'it' need to be called translation, or is it an unstable and hybrid category that has increasingly begun to get stable in a more self-conscious and academic understanding of translation? Does criss-crossing of languages, often captured in misleadingly transactional terms such as 'borrowing' and 'loan words', not constitute translation? Do vocabularies from diverse regions not constitute what comes to be claimed as 'purely' indigenous languages, hinting at yet other processes of translation at work? To ask such questions is to remind ourselves not to assume what is perhaps best not assumed – the absence of a presence, called translation.

References

Bassnett, Susan and Harish Trivedi. *Postcolonial Translation: Theory and Practice*. London: Routledge, 2012.
Trivedi, Harish. 'In Our Own Time, on Our Own Terms'. In *Translating Others*, vol. 1, edited by Theo Hermans, 102–111. Manchester : St Jerome, 2006.

VIP

Shiv Visvanathan

Modern democracy needs a language of conspicuous consumption not for commodities but for power, to demonstrate an ethology of display, a ritual dance of power. No word captures it better than VIP. A VIP is a 'very important person' who has to be seen as a very important person. In a world of scarcity, he is surrounded by excess. He can demand entry, space, the right seat and the best chair. When everyone is sitting on the ground in a community of equals, the VIP needs a sofa. In a community of equals, he is more equal than others. His power always needs a noisy display, a semiotics of access ranging from sirens, to security, to a chorus of sycophants fluttering over his presence. A VIP who is not noticeable is a non-person.

A VIP is singular but never single. He needs an entourage around him, a combination of kin, sidekick juniors who thicken his presence. These are roles to be taken seriously. Without it, power cannot be an act of conspicuous consumption. Someone must fan him, repeatedly offer him that fresh glass of water, flatter him with attention and excessive concern, because without excess, that abundance of attention which must evolve into a ritual of display a VIP diminishes in power. Excess as display is the only economy he can understand. A potlatch of sycophancy must accompany him. If a VIP visits an area, it must be cleaned, whitewashed, even if it is abandoned for a year later. A VIP's visit to any area must be an event, at least for a day, even if cows sit lazily munching posters, he has left behind, a day later. A VIP's presence in an area is a historical marker which divides history into before and after. If a VIP visit does not cause unnecessary traffic jams, delay traffic, create obstructions so that people feel his presence, he does not feel like a VIP. A VIP is a man who has the right access or can provide the right access to power, to exclusive spaces. He is pampered as patron of an entourage whose well-being he caters to.

The ritual of time and space becomes critical to a VIP. If an event is packed with people, seats will be reserved for him. He does not have to join the Darwinian world of the ordinary. He is above subsistence. His absence, like his presence, must exude power. A VIP who is punctual is an oxymoron. Being late is a sign of power; keeping people waiting shows how busy you are. Punctuality is one art that eludes the VIP. In fact, in a world obsessed with ranking, there could be a delay index of power. Politicians and film stars would head the list, with bureaucrats playing lesser mortals. Conspicuous delay is a VIP art form. There is also a temporariness to VIPs. Government secretaries in Delhi who walk like lions around India International Centre (IIC) shrink bodily when they retire. The absence of power literally deflates them. An ex-MP, an ex-bureaucrat is emasculated when he loses the hyperbolic power which officialdom confers on him. It is this sense of closure that makes VIPs as theatre hyperbole. They lack the authenticity of power. As actors they lack an epic quality, convey the sense of a skit, the spoof, an absurd drama of power without the sense of brutality or ruthlessness. They always remain part of the scaffolding of power, people who are important because they are seen as important. Their image defines their reality.

References

Thakur, Ramesh. 'India's VIP Culture: Forget Lincoln's Definition of Democracy. India's Government Is of VIPs, by VIPs and for VIPs'. *Times of India*, 4 September 2018. Available at: timesofindia.indiatimes.com/blogs/toi-edit-page/indias-vip-culture-forget-lincolns-definition-of-democracy-indias-government-is-of-vips-by-vips-and-for-vips/.

Thakur, Ramesh. 'VIP Culture Is a Blight on India's Democracy'. *Policy Forum*, 1 May 2018. Available at: www.policyforum.net/vip-culture-is-a-blight-on-indias-democracy/.

CHAPTER 7
POLITICS AND THE POLITICAL

AFSPA AND OTHER DRACONIAN LAWS

Ujjwal Kumar Singh

On 9 August 2016, a curious drama played out in the precincts of a court in Imphal, the capital of Manipur. Irom Sharmila, popularly called the 'Iron Lady of Manipur', was present in court. Since November 2000, following the killing of ten civilians by army personnel of the Assam Rifles, Sharmila, a human rights activist working for peace in the region, took to fasting as a form of public protest. For sixteen years, she was on a continuous fast against the draconian Armed Forces Special Powers Act (AFSPA). Charged under section 309 of the IPC for attempting to take her own life, Sharmila was incarcerated in a hospital-prison, where she was force-fed through a nasal tube. This incarceration involved the playing out of an annual ritual, with the government bringing her before the court each year, where she declared her intention to continue her fast; she was then taken back to her prison-hospital and the life-saving paraphernalia of force-feeding re-installed. Her appearance in court on 9 August 2016 was, however, different. She had come to court this day to declare that she was giving up her fast but would persist with her resistance through other means, including electoral politics.

In a rented hall within the same precincts, another group of women was preparing to take the struggle against the AFSPA forward by fighting for its repeal in court. The women called themselves members of EEVFAM (Extrajudicial Execution Victims Families), set up in 2009 from the proceeds of an international award given to Irom Sharmila. The EEVFAM had petitioned the Supreme Court in 2012 to repeal AFSPA because of widespread human rights violations, asking in particular if 'the next of kin of the victims of AFSPA, have any rights at all, other than receipt of monetary compensation?' They asked the court to set up a Special Investigation Team (SIT) of police officers from outside the state of Manipur to investigate instances of alleged extrajudicial executions and prosecute the offenders in accordance with law. In its judgement delivered on 8 July 2016, the Supreme Court concluded that irrespective of any enquiry the Manipur government would undertake, 'in situations of the kind that we are dealing with, there can be no substitute for a judicial enquiry'. The court also argued that the use of 'excessive force or retaliatory force' was not permissible, and all such deaths must be thoroughly enquired into.

The security state architecture in India is made up of three kinds of legal regimes: preventive detention laws, anti-terror laws and laws for 'disturbed areas'. The preventive detention system is based on minimal due process and gives pre-eminence to executive decision making and its 'satisfaction' in the initiation and affirmation of extraordinary proceedings.

Anti-terror laws like the Terrorists and Disruptive Activities Prevention Act (TADA) of 1985 and 1987, Prevention of Terrorism Act (POTA) of 2002 and the Unlawful Activities Prevention Act of 1967 (amended in 2004, 2008, 2012 and 2019) constitute the second set of laws. While both the preventive detention laws and anti-terror laws enhance the powers of the executive, the security regime of anti-terror laws puts in place the jurisprudence of necessity appropriate for extraordinary conditions. While TADA and POTA are no longer on the statute books, the Unlawful Activities (Prevention) Act (UAPA) is a permanent law, which, along with special state laws, is used to tackle terrorism.

AFSPA is an example of a different regime of laws, which applies to 'disturbed areas', giving special powers to the armed forces to come to the 'aid' of civil administration and perform the function of 'internal-security'. In the context of Partition, armed forces were deployed in large numbers in the border regions of Bengal and Punjab for long periods under the Disturbed Areas (Special Power of the Armed Forces) Ordinances for Bengal and East Punjab in 1947. The Armed Forces (Special Powers) Ordinance 1942, promulgated by the colonial state to curb the Quit India movement, is largely seen as the precursor of the 1947 Ordinances. The idea of 'special powers' and the legal and institutional arrangements that went with it were found useful, and in 1958, when the Nagaland National Council rose in insurgency, the AFSPA was enacted with the claim that it was merely shifting, under logistical compulsion, powers of ordinary policing to the army in Assam and Manipur. Once the governor of a state declares that an area is 'disturbed', 'special powers' under AFSPA become available to officers of the armed forces. These powers include the use of force by opening fire, even to the extent of causing death in areas where prohibitory orders have been issued, power to destroy hideouts or training camps and search premises without warrant and arrest persons on suspicion. Armed personnel enjoy legal immunity under the Act and connot be prosecuted for 'anything done or purported to be done in exercise of powers conferred by the Act', except with the previous sanction of the Centre. AFSPA was extended to the entire North-East (except Sikkim) in 1972 and to Jammu and Kashmir in 1990.

Between 1980 and 1982, the Naga People's Movement for Human Rights (NPMHR) along with other democratic rights organizations filed a petition before the Supreme Court questioning the constitutional validity of AFSPA. In 1997, the Supreme Court delivered its judgement and upheld the constitutionality of AFSPA.

Opposition to AFSPA mounted among those who saw it as an instrument of territorial control and gained momentum with Irom Sharmila's fast. It was, however, only in the summer of 2004, when a young Manipuri woman Thangjam Manorama was picked up by the army on the suspicion of assisting insurgents and her body, bearing marks of sexual assault, was discovered that there was a surge of protests. Most notable was the naked protest by the social movement called Meira Paibis (the torchbearers), in front of the headquarters of the Assam Rifles in Imphal, challenging the jawans to 'take their flesh'. The Apunba Lup, a body of thirty-two women's organizations of Manipur, made the repeal of AFSPA its primary concern. The state government of Tripura revoked AFSPA in May 2015, stating that insurgency was on the wane in the state. The state had been under AFSPA since February 1997. The continuation of laws like AFSPA manifest the contradictions and duality of state processes in a democracy.

References

EEVFAM vs Union of India, W.P. (Crl) No.129/2012, judgement delivered on 8 July 2016. Available at: http://kanglaonline.com/wp-content/uploads/2017/07/judgement-for-wpcril-case-reportable.pdf (accessed December 2018).

ATROCITY

Chandraiah Gopani

The word 'atrocity' as a noun means 'wicked or cruel'. In its adjective form, 'atrocious' means the quality or state of atrocity. The idea of atrocity is associated with acts of inhuman assaults and violence against an individual or group. The word atrocity describes both the act of cruelty as well as the nature of cruelty. The word comes from Middle French *atrocite* or from the Latin *atrox*, both of which mean 'terrible or cruel'. The term is used depending on the nature of the offences in parlance with humiliation, genocide, caste violence, gendered violence, rape, ethnic cleansing, mass murder, slavery, torture and social boycott. In Indian languages, 'atrocity' is used in different ways, for example, as *kroorata* and *atyaachaara* in Hindi, *attuliyam* in Tamil and *duragatam* in Telugu. All these words encompass the act of cruelty and violence.

In India, 'atrocity' has come to mean a legal intervention as well. Scheduled castes (SCs), or the Dalits (ex-untouchables), are historically marginalized, subjugated and stigmatized in the Hindu social order. The scheduled tribes (STs), generally known as tribal or Adivasis, are aboriginals who are geographically isolated and carry distinctive sociocultural features that have been historically delegitimized by the social order in India. Dalits and Adivasis are victims of the caste system in India. Ghanshyam Shah notes that caste is a structural violence on Dalits and that it is constitutive, relational, historical and deep-rooted in Hindu religious and ideological structures. The system is pervasive both in formal and informal institutions. To map the terrain of caste violence and discrimination, the category 'atrocity' is drawn into law from social experience in India. In the context of the growing rampant violence in the mid-1980s against the Dalits and Adivasis, the Scheduled Castes and Scheduled Tribes (Prevention of Atrocities) Act of 1989 (SC-ST PoA Act 1989) came into existence and was enacted in 1995. In common legal parlance, it is also known simply as the 'Atrocities Act'.

In a judgement involving the state of Madhya Pradesh, under the SC-ST PoA Act 1989, it was argued that 'the offences of atrocities are committed to humiliate and subjugate the Scheduled Castes and Scheduled Tribes with a view to keep them in a state of servitude. Hence, they constitute a separate class of offences and cannot be compared with offences under the Indian Penal Code.' While the Act does not define 'atrocity', the Act lists eighteen types of atrocities: force-feeding of obnoxious substances; dumping waste matter on land; intimidation during voting; compulsion to vote for a particular candidate; mischievous litigation; false information; public humiliation; denudation; wrongful land dispossession; bonded labour; outrage of modesty; sexual exploitation; fouling of water resources;

obstruction of entry to a public place; eviction of habitation; mischief with explosive; destruction of building; and suppression of evidence. Through a Constitutional Amendment in 2017, the Centre added a few new offences such as imposing social and economic boycott, tonsuring of head and/or moustache or similar acts derogatory to the dignity of SCs and STs and garlanding footwear. The Act also rationalized rehabilitation funds to victims and provides special courts at various levels for speedy and transparent justice. In the absence of a clear definition of the term 'atrocity', various interpretations, meanings and understandings are drawn depending on the context and nature of the offences. The case aforementioned suggests that 'in order to constitute atrocity, there must be an element of cruelty, brutality or wickedness in the commission of a particular offence or it should have the background of having been committed with a view to teach a lesson to the Harijans (Dalits)'. Due to difficulties in establishing some of these elements, there are contested views on the implementation and usage of the Act.

In the discourse around atrocity cases, it is apparent that dominant caste perpetrators abuse the law and the very officials entrusted to uphold it abandon their responsibilities. Our understanding of atrocity has to acknowledge the politics of resisting caste violence. And the various aspects of atrocities against Dalits listed above have to be enshrined in the state's use of the term. The rich body of Dalit writing will help us in this regard as it captures these varied forms of atrocities.

References

Kumar, P. Kesava. 'Politics of Atrocity: Towards Understanding of Caste Violence'. Uploaded on 25 November 2012. Available at: http://untouchablespring.blogspot.in/search?q=atrocity (accessed December 2018).
Shah, Ghanshyam, Harsh Mander, Sukhadeo Thorat, Satish Deshpande and Amita Baviskar. *Untouchability in Rural India*. New Delhi: SAGE Publications, 2006.

AYODHYA (AYŌDHYĀ)

A. K. Verma

Ayodhya is a small town in Faizabad district of Uttar Pradesh (UP), India. Situated on the banks of the river Sarayu, Ayodhya is famed as the birthplace of Lord Ram. The word 'Ayodhya' means 'invincible, not to be fought against'. The city represents religious and cultural confluence in India. It is not only, according to legend, the birthplace of Lord Ram but also a meeting place of the Buddhist, Jain and Islamic faiths. The Jains believe that about five *thirthankar*s (spiritual teachers) were born in Ayodhya. During the Mughal period, Babar constructed a few mosques in this town, of which the eponymous Babri Masjid is famous.

Ayodhya is a city of antiquity. We find its earliest reference in the Atharva Veda: 'That which has eight chakras and nine entrances, such a city of Ayodhya is full of divine powers. The divinity of this place makes it like heavens' (Part I: 10/2/31-2699). Valmiki's *Ramayana* (fifth century BCE to first century BCE) comprehensively talks about Ayodhya, Lord Ram and his entire lifecycle. It is believed that by the first century BCE, Ayodhya was completely deserted. Then, King Chandra Gupta Vikramaditya (379–413 CE) located several places connected with activities of Lord Ram in Ayodhya and is said to have constructed 360 temples there. But the first detailed account of Ayodhya as a geographical location is found in the sixteenth-century work *Ain-I Akbari* (vols II–III, pp. 182–3) written by Abul Fazl, prime minister in the court of the Mughal king Akbar: 'Awadh (Ajodhya) is one of the largest cities of India … It is esteemed as one of the holiest places of antiquity. … It was the residence of Ramachandra who in the *Treta* age combined in his own person both the spiritual supremacy and the kingly office.'

Babar's minister Mir Baki is believed to have constructed the Babri Masjid by demolishing the Ram Temple at Ayodhya in 1528. In 1855, following riots in Ayodhya and the Muslim claim to take over the temple Hanuman Garhi, the disputed area was roughly divided equally between Hindus and Muslims. On 29 January 1885, Mahant Raghubar Das of Ayodhya filed a suit in the District Court of Faizabad against the secretary of state of India for the construction of a temple at the 'Ram Chabootra', on which the *charanpaduka* (footprint) of Lord Rama was inscribed. A counter-suit was filed by Mohammed Asgar, *mutallavi* (guardian) of the Babri Masjid. The Faizabad Trial Court disallowed Mahant's suit on grounds of possibility of further riots. This status quo was maintained from 1885 to 1949. On 23 December 1949, some Hindus forced entry into the disputed area and placed an idol of Lord Ram within the Babri Masjid. The police on duty lodged an FIR. Ever since, Muslims have not been able to offer prayers and Hindus have had to take *darshan* (to see the deity) from a distance. However, the court restrained rival parties from removing idols and obstructing puja. This position continued till 25 January 1986, when Advocate Umesh Chand Pandey petitioned to the district judge of Faizabad to open the locks at Ayodhya so that pilgrims could have darshan from inside. On 1 February 1986, district judge of Faizabad K. N. Pandey directed the district magistrate and superintendent of police of Faizabad to open the locks. The opening of the lock catapulted the dispute to the national level and triggered a chain reaction leading to the demolition of the disputed Babri Masjid structure on 6 December 1992 by a large crowd of *kar sevak*s (volunteers for a religious cause).

In October 1991, the Kalyan Singh government in UP had acquired the premises in dispute along with some adjoining area for 'development of tourism and providing amenities to pilgrims in Ayodhya'. This move was then challenged in *Mohd. Hashim vs. State of UP* and other cases. The Supreme Court struck down Section 4(3) of the Acquisition Act which had directed abatement of all pending suits, as unconstitutional and invalid, resulting in the revival of all earlier suits pertaining to the Ayodhya land dispute in the High Court of Allahabad. The High Court, by a majority of 2–1, decided on 30 September 2010 to divide the title to disputed land among Muslims (Sunni Wakf Board), Hindus (Ram Lala Virajmaan) and the Nirmohi Akhara – three parties to the dispute. Now the matter is pending before the Supreme Court.

Today, Ayodhya has come to be a recurrent communal flashpoint. Hindus, represented by activist groups, want to retrieve lost glory by building a grand temple at Ayodhya, and Muslims, represented by activist groups, insist on retaining the Babri Mosque. Efforts are still on to resolve the Ayodhya dispute.

References

Carnegy, P. *Historical Sketch of Tahsil Fyzabad, Zillah Fyzabad*. Lucknow: Publisher unknown, 1870.

Griffith, Ralph T. H. trans. *The Ramayan of Valmiki*. London: Trübner & Co. and Benares: E. J. Lazarus and Co., 1870–74. Available at: https://www.gutenberg.org/files/24869/24869-pdf.pdf (accessed December 2018).

BABU/SARKAR/REVENUE OFFICER (BĀBŪ/SARKĀR/REVENUE OFFICER)

Tabish Khair

It is best to begin by taking up a different word: *munshi*. Like *babu* and *sarkar*, munshi is a precolonial term: I use 'colonial' in the specific sense of being ruled from outside the geopolitical territory, and hence, in India, it applies only to European colonization and not to the various conquests and incursions before it. Babu and Munshi were equivalent honourifics in the precolonial and/or early colonial period, both usually applied to literate gentlemen, often employed for various bureaucratic purposes by Indian regimes. Their etymology is different: babu deriving from the Sanskrit for 'father' and munshi from the Arabic root *insha* meaning 'to educate or to compose'. The babus ('baboo') and munshis ('moonshee') one encounters in the early colonial period were basically scribes and bureaucrats from reasonably affluent and literate Indian families. In this sense, the words still meant what they meant in the precolonial period.

However, the shades of meaning attached to them were to change. Babu, a designation used largely in Greater Bengal (the first region to be extensively colonized by the British East India Company), moved both upwards and downwards, while munshi moved steadily downwards. Upwardly mobile babus came to be associated with the bureaucracy of the colonial government, while downwardly mobile munshi came to be associated – as the *Hobson-Jobson Anglo-Indian Dictionary* notes in passing – with pedagogy and literacy in 'languages like Arabic, Persian and Urdu'. It is not incidental that in the late colonial period, the great writer Premchand, who started off writing in Urdu and switched to writing in Hindi, was known as Munshi Premchand. By then, the babus were obviously English-speaking and English-writing Indians, though munshi still had some status in *bhasha* (Indian languages) circles.

This reveals the other route taken by the word 'babu': even as it came to be associated with colonial power, it also came to be associated with being Anglophone, and that inevitably led to dismissive noises by the English. The munshi, as hybrid as the babu, remained where he was and hence was not seen as hybrid *in* English. But the babu – *now* that was another matter. He had become the threat to the identity that Homi K. Bhabha associates with hybridity. This led – and still leads – to a confusion of terms, best exemplified by the difference between 'Babu English' (a pejorative description) and the 'babu', when used as a honourific by ordinary Indians in many languages.

One could argue that 'Babu English' is a different matter from babus and English, and it raised the hackles of educated Indians way back in the nineteenth century. Usages like

'Babu English' were and remain a different matter from many other usages of 'babu'. For instance, a rickshaw puller in Bihar is not making a sarcastic reference to your English when he addresses you as a babu even today. What he means is an affluent and educated man, often, but not necessarily, in Western clothes.

In short, 'babu' as a pre-British term continues to be a term of social class and respect in discourses that have not been confined to those of postcolonial English-language babuness. A one-sided objection to the usage of 'babu' as an emblematic term, while necessary within a certain colonialist discursive context, is also at the same time an indication of the objector's inability to step beyond the colonial context. In that sense, it indicates the tendency of 'postcolonialism' to circle round and round, inevitably, in the discursive space of 'colonialism' while ignoring the 'pre', 'para' and entirely 'post'-colonial.

The babu had become not just what he was intended to be when Macaulay and his ilk pushed for European education in India in the early nineteenth century, a buffer between the natives and the Europeans. He had also become a dilemma. This comes across most powerfully in Rudyard Kipling's writings; despite his clear preference for 'martial Indians' from the edges of the empire, such as Afghans and Gurkhas, Kipling has his hero exclaim 'What a beast of wonder is the Babu!' in the novel *Kim*. He is referring to Hurree Babu, the quintessential colonial babu, a man with what we would call 'nerdy' and anglophile interests, obese, inscrutable, not physically brave, always faintly ludicrous, but who nevertheless saves the entire British Empire by a sustained act of physical and intellectual bravery.

The word 'babu' and the word 'sarkar' are closely associated. Sarkar derives from the Persian and Urdu, where it was a compound word made of *sar* (chief/head) and *kar* (agent/doer). Sarkar came to be used to refer to and address any person in a position of direct authority and to authority/government itself. The babus, in that sense, helped run the sarkar and could be addressed as 'sarkar', especially if they had risen to a high administrative status, while by the twentieth century the 'munshi' had become a much smaller cog in the governmental machinery.

What was this governmental colonial machinery? It was pretty diverse in the early twentieth century. But it had largely started off under the East India Company and later, after 1857–8, under the British crown, as a revenue-collecting machinery. Collecting revenue was seen as the main function of the colonial head (mostly British) of Indian districts, under whom many babus worked. So much so that even in the 1970s, when the British 'district collector' had long been replaced by Indian 'district commissioners' and 'district magistrates', in taluk towns like Gaya, where I grew up, the district magistrate/commissioner was still referred to as the 'collector'.

It is an interesting indication of how far we have moved from the colonial period and how close we still are to it in our 'postcolonial' period, seventy years after Independence, that the words 'babu' and 'sarkar' and the designation 'revenue officer' (also in its neo-Hindi version of *raajasavadhikaaree*) still suggest empowerment and authority, except to Anglophone academics who cannot manage to get beyond their English, while the word 'munshi' has diminished to a non-status. The rickshaw puller or auto driver *is* being slightly offensive if he calls you 'munshi' anywhere in North India but not if he calls you 'babu' or 'sarkar'. The trajectories of *wordly* prestige – as the difference between 'master' and 'mistress' indicates – are excellent markers of power flows.

References

Khair, Tabish. *Babu Fictions: Alienation in Contemporary Indian English Fiction*. New Delhi: Oxford University Press, 2001.
Nair, Rukmini Bhaya. *Lying on the Postcolonial Couch: The Idea of Indifference*. Duluth: University of Minnesota Press, 2002.

BORDER

Yogesh Snehi

India shares international territorial mainland borders (*sarhad* in Hindi) with Pakistan, China, Nepal, Bhutan, Bangladesh, Myanmar and Sri Lanka. Unlike maritime borders, which remain fragile, mainland borders are potentially definable and therefore defensible. The Indo–Pak border that stretches from Sindh–Kutch–Gujarat, Bahawalpur–Rajasthan, Punjab and Jammu and Kashmir has, especially after the wars of 1947, 1965, 1971 and 1999 with Pakistan, and the 1962 war with China, been heavily militarized and permanently fenced. Violent political conflict in Punjab and J&K have made these regions one of the most volatile zones in contemporary times.

The Partition of Punjab in 1947 weakened the economy and social fabric of most border village and towns. Among the road and rail links that once connected overland and maritime trade and cultural exchanges between Punjab, Bahawalpur, Sindh, Multan and Afghanistan, only a few remain extant today. Partition demographically transformed the region into a Muslim-dominated West Punjab (in Pakistan), and Sikh-/Hindu-dominated East Punjab (in India). Identitarian movements and ethnic conflicts have been a hallmark of these territorialized zones. In 1966, East Punjab was further reorganized and a new state of Haryana, and subsequently Himachal Pradesh, was carved out of the region identified with colonial Punjab. Sikhs, for the first time, emerged as a dominant majority in reorganized Punjab, defining the social and political contours of the state thereafter. Today, Muslim, Hindu and Sikh Jats control the socially conjoined spaces of West Punjab, East Punjab and Haryana. However, the geography of sacred shrines rupture this project of nation-state and region formation in South Asia.

Meanwhile, historic agreements between Indian and Pakistan led to the beginning of Samjhauta train service in 1976 and bus service in 1999 called *sada-e-sarhad* (call from across the border) along Lahore–Amritsar–Delhi that passes through Atari–Wagah border check posts.

Borders, it is clear, shape the lives of people who live along them. Access to agricultural land inside 'no man's land' (the land between the actual border and the fence) that a farmer may rightfully own, and the right to cultivate it, is dependent on permissions granted by the Border Security Force (BSF). War often looms in the memories of border towns, which were emptied on several occasions, and so do tales of rationing of grain and offering services to the standing army. Nationalist distress narrows the possibility of social and economic wellness of people who inhabit border zones. It is not a surprise, then, that borders are also zones that are severely affected by drug abuse. Some civil society groups like the Hind-Pak Dosti Manch have tried to build bridges and connect people across borders through peace marches, candle light vigils on Wagah and *mushairas* (social gathering where Urdu poetry is read) to create an alternate discourse on borders.

Maintenance of borders is thus an important nationalist imperative. At the Wagah retreat ceremony, which began in 1959, we see both India and Pakistan creating, rehearsing and performing rituals that define their 'modern' nation-state identities. Borders sustain the otherwise complex narrative of the nation-state that has been continually contested by assertion of ethnic and linguistic identities in both India and Pakistan. The Wagah border post has large gateways on both sides, like entry points to sacred shrines, defining those inside and outside the realm of faith, devotion and bodily performance.

Every day, at least an hour before the actual retreat ceremony begins, a soldier on both the sides arouses nationalist emotions through loud 'patriotic' music. Later, when 'Indian' Border Security Force soldiers and 'Pakistani' rangers perform at the daily retreat ceremony – involving lowering of their respective national flags – they stage synchronized drill and similar rituals of opening and closing of entry gates. As tension escalates between India and Pakistan, the mood of the drill becomes vigorously masculine and is performed with loud thuds.

Yet another contemporary phenomena concerning borders are their depictions in several Bollywood films. Most border films have been plotted around the 1971 Indo–Pak war (from *Haqeeqat* [1964] to *Lakshya* [2004]). Then there is the war/dispute in the J&K (*LOC Kargil* [2003] or Wagah (*Kya Dilli Kya Lahore* [2014]). Other, more nuanced films have problematized borders (from *Henna* [1991] to *Begum Jaan* [2017]) and engage directors/actors from both India and Pakistan. These films predominantly feature heroism, hate and love in the midst of war along borders.

However, it has to be noted that rivers, winds, birds, insects and music do not recognize borders. Insects, particularly *tiddi dal* (swarms of locusts) that devour standing crops, have metaphorically remained alive in the historical memory of people along Indo–Pak borders. The Indus Water Treaty between India and Pakistan has tried to resolve distribution of waters. But these very rivers often erode the border fence. Winds systems, similarly, do not follow the logic of borders. In recent times, India has blamed pollution from Pakistan for the smog in North India. There has also been a long tradition of musicians (for instance, Nusrat Fateh Ali Khan) whose compositions do not accept the tyranny of the Indo–Pak border.

References

Athique, Adrian M. 'A Line in the Sand: The India–Pakistan Border in the Films of J.P. Dutta'. *South Asia: Journal of South Asian Studies* 31, no. 3 (2008): 472–99.
Nayar, Kuldip. *Wall at Wagah: India–Pakistan Relations*. New Delhi: Gyan Publishing House, 2003.

BUREAUCRACY

Aakar Patel

Modern Indian bureaucracy turned 160 in 2018. Of course, nobody really planned on celebrating it because the bureaucracy, especially the lower one that citizens actually interface with, is and has always been terrifying.

One hundred and sixty years ago, a year after the Mutiny, the Government of India Act of 1858 transferred rule from a private corporation's board of directors to Queen Victoria's government and its civil servants, the Indian Civil Services (ICS) (later renamed Indian Administrative Services [IAS]). But much before that, the Mughal bureaucracy had been equally threatening. European travellers have described it in detail. The emperor sat on a platform behind a series of barricades. Entry into the spaces between the barricades was restricted by rank and only the highest were allowed before the final barrier. Petitioners and justice seekers were held by the hand by one of the nobles (to communicate closeness and trust) and taken before the emperor – or as close as they could get. There they had to first perform the *kurnish*, the Persian three-step bowing salute that Alexander the Great was enamoured enough to adopt, upsetting the Macedonians. And then they had to hope the emperor actually took notice. Gifts usually helped, as we know even in our time.

Transfer to the ICS made things less arbitrary for the Indian citizen. But things were not necessarily more efficient. Lord Curzon, who came fifty years after the Mutiny, likened the Indian bureaucracy to an elephant: 'very stately, very dignified, but very slow in its movement'. To make it move faster, he said he was 'prodding the animal with the most vigorous and unexpected digs, and it gambols plaintively under the novel spur'. He said nothing was done in less than six months. 'When I suggest six weeks, the attitude is one of pained surprise; if six days, one of pathetic protest; if six hours, one of stupefied resignation.'

It is easy to see why the civil servant inspires feelings of such dread. The word 'cracy' denotes a particular form of government: democracy, autocracy, plutocracy and so on. A bureaucracy is rule by 'desks' (the meaning of the French word *bureau*). By definition, it announces its interference in the everyday life of the citizen. And who can deny that in India this interference is true? The bureaucrat is a potentate with the power to deny without reason, your right to travel, eat, drink or even be free. This may seem an exaggeration to the outsider, till she notices how important an influence the bureaucrat is, in the issuance of passports and Aadhaar cards, licences and ration cards and the other paraphernalia which keeps the bureaucrat busy.

Gandhi thought the Indian bureaucracy was 'top heavy and ruinously expensive'. He felt it was useless and 'even law and order and good government would be too dearly purchased if the price to be paid for it is the grinding poverty of the masses'. S. R. Maheshwari tells us in *Indian Administration* that Indira Gandhi thought the bureaucracy was a 'stumbling block' on the road to economic and social progress. In 1969, the Congress complained, 'The present bureaucracy, under the orthodox and conservative leadership of the Indian Civil Service, with its upper class prejudices, can hardly be expected to meet the requirements of social and economic change along socialist lines. The creation of an administrative cadre committed to national objectives and responsive to our social needs is an urgent necessity.' Both Gandhi and Indira knew a thing or two about statecraft, but those who have been in positions of governance in the subcontinent have developed a healthy respect for the 'steel frame' that is the IAS.

Stephen Cohen, a scholar of India's armies, notes two differences between bureaucrats in India and those in the United States. For the Indian, rank was important. He would refuse to meet anyone lower than his direct counterpart even though the official assigned was empowered to decide on the issue. And second, the Indian immediately regurgitated the history of the issue, going back decades, while the American was concerned only with the contours so far as they affected the current position. The bureaucrat sees himself as the guardian of the administration and also its conscience. He knows he is indispensable and not easy to replace systemically. The bureaucrat is in not a few ways more important to the citizen than the politician.

Historian Sir Jadunath Sarkar has an interesting theory on the decline of the Mughal Empire. The incompetent Jahangir lost Kandahar to the Safavids in 1649. This stopped the Mughals from using the land route west to Mecca (empowering the Europeans because of their naval dominance). And it stopped the highly sophisticated Persian Shia from travelling east for bureaucratic work in India. According to Sarkar, the Persian Shia could not be replaced by local Indian talent and the empire began to be mismanaged and declined quickly. For 160 years, the ICS/IAS has tried to show that Sarkar's observation about the Indian administrator's quality was not true in perpetuity. Whether they have successfully or not is I think still up for debate.

References

Maheshwari, Shriram. *Indian Administration*. Hyderabad: Orient Longman, 1990.
Sarkar, Jadunath. *Fall of the Mughal Empire-Vol. I*, 4th edn., vol. 1. New Delhi: Orient Blackswan, 1991.

CHUNAV (CUNĀV)/ELECTION

Mona Mehta

The birth and journey of many a word is directly tied to the advent of political processes and institutions that have become emblematic of modern India. The Hindi word *chunav*, which means 'election', is one such word that started gaining currency in the early twentieth century, a word that is deeply entwined with the story of Indian democracy. The etymology of chunav can be traced to Sanskrit, specifically to the root word *chi*, which means 'to select'. The word election in Sanskrit is *nirvaachan*. A medieval cognate *chunana*, which also means 'to choose', was in use as early as 1354, long before chunav's relatively recent popularity. Today, chunav has come to denote an instrument, a process, an event. It is a verb and an adjective. And, it is impossible to imagine contemporary India without it.

As a political phenomenon, chunav emerged in British India. In order to elect representatives to the provincial and central legislatures, the colonial rulers began to subject the population to the process of electoral exercise. It was around this time that the innocuous-sounding word chunana began to acquire the specific meaning we associate with chunav. However, chunav remained a tame and insipid word during these early decades of the twentieth century when elections were a colourless event. This is because elections were being organized on a limited elitist suffrage, open only to those who owned property, paid direct taxes or had educational qualification. The masses had little interest in a system that was designed to exclude them. Chunav began to enter mass consciousness only when the Indian National Congress, which was at the vanguard of the nationalist freedom movement, decided to participate in the provincial assembly elections of 1937. This was a decisive moment in the history of the term chunav; it marked a shift in its connotation from a non-participatory political process to a public event, resulting in a corresponding change in popular perception. The masses that made up the Congress-led freedom movement began to perceive chunav not merely as an arena of political contestation but also as an extension of the freedom struggle (*azadi ki ladai*). Every Congress candidate who contested a chunav was seen as a soldier of the freedom struggle. Chunav was finally on its way to be a currency of mass circulation.

However, this euphoria was short-lived. In 1939, Indian National Congress resigned from all provincial governments to protest against the British decision to drag India into the Second World War, against its will. The patriotic fervour expressed through chunav of the late 1930s transformed into a defiant anger of the Quit India Movement of 1942. In the ensuing years, it appeared as if chunav had lost its way amidst the bloody turbulence of the partition of the Indian subcontinent and the ambiguous uncertainties of a newly independent nation in 1947.

Few perhaps could have anticipated chunav's spectacular re-emergence in its new avatar as *aamchunaav* (general election) that was held in 1951. This election heralded the birth of India as the world's largest and most complex electoral democracy. But this post-Independence version of chunav that indexed the transformation from colonial subjects to citizens was no ordinary avatar. It was loaded with the incredible transformative power of universal adult franchise supplied by a new Constitution of India inaugurated on 26 January 1950. It was to set in motion an unprecedented churning within the age-old society of India with a promise of sociopolitical empowerment and fulfilling economic aspirations.

Chunav began to be perceived by millions of Indians as the operating system of Indian democracy where the *mut* (vote) was their password to progress. It is difficult to find many examples of a word depicting a government-sponsored and government-regulated event like chunav being used as extensively by ordinary people in their daily life as a noun, verb or adjective. For instance, a regulating body like Chunav Ayog (Election Commission, enjoys a rather unique place in people's perception). The Chunav Ayog is responsible for overseeing the entire *chunav vyavastha* (electoral machinery) and it regularly carries out *chunav ghoshna* (election announcement). It is interesting that words such as *prakriya* (process), *aacharsanhita* (moral code of conduct) or *adhikari* (official) when coupled with an adjective like *chunav* suddenly acquire a popular understanding which goes beyond their narrow official definitions.

While *chunav prakriya* (electoral process) may mean the nitty-gritty of the laid-down procedure, *chunav gati-vidhi* (activity) tells us a different story. Then, there is *chunav yachika* (election petition) which can be filed either before the Chunav Ayog or a court of law. The physical boundaries of the *chunav kshetra* (electoral constituency) drawn up by the Chunav Ayog either for the Lōk Sabhā (lower house), Vidhan Sabhā (upper house) or *nagara palika chunav* (local municipal body elections) are a multivalent entity that holds tremendous significance for different groups. For the *umeedvar* (contestant) her or his constituency (*kshetra*) is always a battleground for *chunaavi jung* (election battle) that must be fought through *chunavi ran-niti*. From the perspective of the resident-voters of a constituency, chunav offers them the power to make or break the political fortunes of leaders. Political history is replete with fabled stories about the rise and fall of politicians associated with specific constituencies. In this way, the demarcation of an electoral constituency acquires personal and historic dimensions.

A chunav ghoshna (poll announcement) might deal with mere dates and time of the contest, but a chunav ghoshna *patra* (election manifesto) may deal with anything under the sun. Indeed, the manifesto contains an amazing thing called *chunaavi vaada* (election promises) – the real stuff of which a *chunav abhiyan* (election campaign) is made of. However, *chunav abhiyan* might involve a host of logistical and organizational activities, like putting up banners, sticking posters or distributing pamphlets, but it is *chunav prachaar* (election propaganda) which ignites the real spirit of the contest. It conjures up the vision of a mass mobilization involving road shows, and mass rallies, generating the real heat, dust and noise of a hot contest, the *chunaavi muqaabla*.

But even this may not be sufficient if not followed by a *chunaavi daura* (mass contact at the hustings) by the *umeedvar* where the *umeedvarneta* (leader candidate) comes knocking at the doorstep or appears at the local street corner. At the end of the day, a *daura* involves *jan sampark* (mass contact). Of all the institutions designed to order human society in India, chunav is perhaps that ultimate equalizer bestowed with the potential to challenge and erase sociopolitical hierarchies and inequalities.

Cynics might dismiss this high-pitched frenzy as a *chunaavi jumlā* (an electoral subterfuge which may degenerate into a carnival of corruption). But there are others who call this *lokaparva*: a celebration of democracy. They look at election as a mass catharsis without which political contestation might degenerate into violent conflict. No matter how you look at it, it is difficult to imagine an Indian landscape without chunav.

References

Banerjee, Mukulika. *Why India Votes*. New Delhi and Oxford: Routledge, 2014.
Shani, Ornit. *How India became Democratic: Citizenship and Making of the Universal Franchise*. New Delhi: Viking/Penguin, 2017.

COALITION DHARMA

E. Sridharan

'Coalition dharma' is a peculiarly Indian English term used to denote the ethics and modalities of behaviour in a coalition, building on the Sanskrit term *dharma* in its sense of ethics or what is right behaviour. As we know, in a parliamentary system such as India's, a coalition in politics is never the ideal situation from a political party's point of view. Political parties want, ideally, to win power and rule on their own without having to share power. But when this is realistically not possible, they have perforce to form either a pre-electoral coalition to contest elections, followed by, if the coalition wins, a post-electoral coalition to form government; or if they contest alone and are unable to win, a post-electoral coalition – if one can be put together – to acquire majority support and form a government.

Coalitions of both the pre-electoral and post-electoral kind involve compromises with one's coalition partners. In pre-electoral coalitions, this means giving up some seats for one's partners to contest and persuading one's base to vote for the partner party's candidates, with the partner parties expected to reciprocate. It also means making compromises on one's electoral, ideological and policy platform with one's partner parties to evolve a common platform. In post-electoral coalitions, it means making compromises not only on the ideological and policy platform of the government to be formed but also on the all-important question of the sharing of power, that is, of ministerial portfolios. Such compromises are never ideal, never easy and run the risk of alienating one's own support base. This is where the question of behaviour towards one's coalition partners comes in, that is, the ethics or dharma of coalition behaviour.

Forming and steering a coalition through an electoral cycle or the duration of a government requires both ethics and skill in managing relationships, including reading, reacting to and sending out signals, tolerating brinkmanship by one's partners up to a point and the like. While there is no codified dharma in coalition management in India, unlike, say, the codified dharma (not law, but inter-party consensus) of the Model Code of Conduct for electioneering, there have evolved two coalition management mechanisms over the twenty-five-year coalition era of 1989 to 2014 (the coalition era still continues since the Bharatiya Janata Party [BJP]-led National Democratic Alliance in power from 2014 is still a coalition despite the BJP having a majority on its own). These are: (a) the evolution of the mechanism of a common minimum programme between coalescing parties, which can apply to pre-electoral coalitions or to coalition governments; and (b) the evolution of the mechanism of a steering or coordination committee of the coalescing parties to manage differences that might arise and coordinate policy. While these are useful mechanisms and have helped the management of coalitions in India (as they have in other national contexts), coalition dharma is ultimately not just about mechanisms and skills but also about that intangible, political judgement and ethics.

References

Ruparelia, Sanjay. *Divided We Govern: Coalition Politics in Modern India*. New Delhi: Oxford University Press, 2015.
Sridharan, E., ed. *Coalition Politics in India: Selected Issues at the Centre and the States*. New Delhi: Academic Foundation, 2014.

COMMUNAL VIOLENCE

Harsh Mander

In South Asia, episodes of violence where persons are attacked because they belong to particular religious identities are commonly described as communal riots. The word 'communal' in other parts of the world has quite different and often positive connotations, viewed as a source of integration and social solidarity, and its breakdown, a major source of violence and strife. In a comprehensive review of the chronology of communal violence, B. Rajeshwari suggests that 'whenever conflicting groups from two different religions, which are self-conscious communities, clash, it results in a communal riot'. An event is identified as a communal riot if (a) there is violence and (b) two or more communally identified groups confront each other or members of the other group at some point during the violence. It is commonplace to use the word 'riot' to describe communal violence, both in reportage and scholarship, but the difficulty with the term is that it suggests implicitly that people of two communities battle each other, usually spontaneously. But this may not be the case if the violence is one-sided or engineered by dedicated groups, as is very often the case. For instance, it is a travesty to describe the violence against the Sikhs in Delhi in 1984 as anti-Sikh riots, because it was exclusively the Sikhs who were victims of violence in almost all these attacks. The same is the case with many, if not most, other episodes of communal violence. The use in reportage as well as survivors' own testimonies of the terms, such as storm, are now more popular – the Gujarat survivors widely describe the anti-Muslim violence in 2002 as *toofan* (storm) – but this alternate terminology is more evocative than analytical. Scholars sometimes deploy the term carnage, slaughter or bloodbath, which is a more accurate description of the character of such violence.

The more pertinent terminology could be 'hate communal violence' or 'targeted communal violence'. In South Asia, the word 'communal' has a specific meaning of social and political mobilization of persons based on their religious identity, usually in opposition (sometimes violently) to persons of other religious identities. The prefix 'communal' carries negative connotations of hate propaganda, mobilization and sometimes violence against a religious (or as the Sachar report put it, 'socio-religious') community. This is because of the peculiar history of the subcontinent's bloody partition on grounds of religion and the continued fractures created across South Asia by religious identity. Today, when we speak of communal violence, we are concerned conventionally with a specific kind of hate violence which targets people *for* their religious identity.

The word 'communal' is also closely tied up with the idea of communalism or the social and political mobilization of people on the basis of their religious identities. Bipin Chandra describes three stages of communalism: beginning with the belief that people of one religion have common interests; going on to the belief that the common interests of people of one religion are different from those of another; and the most aggressive stage of communalism founded in the belief that the common interests of people of one religion are in implacable opposition to those of another. Chandra views communalism as an ideology comprising these three basic elements or stages; each element functions as an assumption upon which the next is based. The three also form a continuum, feeding into each other. The intensity of acrimony towards other religious groups increases as people move from one stage to the next.

A few more points are in order in the language of scholars and lay observers regarding communal violence. One relates to the prefixing of the word 'mass' to communal violence. When does a communal, targeted, hate attack become a mass attack? Is it merely a question of numbers? Is communal killing of one person not mass violence, whereas if three are killed it is mass violence? This demarcation is, in the end, subjective. Also, it can invisibilize seemingly discrete, small acts of communal violence, including the recent rise of mob lynching, each not 'mass' in character when seen individually but which actually are part of a larger orchestrated plan.

It is also important to recognize that hate and targeted violence can be directed at people not only because of their religious identity but also because of their caste (as in anti-Dalit atrocities), ethnicity (such as attacks of persons of the north-east in Delhi's cities), gender (such as in violence against women), region (such as the historical attacks in Mumbai on persons from South India and now from Uttar Pradesh and Bihar), language, sexuality (such as attacks against homosexual men and transgendered persons) and occasionally stigmatized ailments (such as attacks on people living with leprosy or HIV/AIDS). The particularly gendered nature of sexual hate violence, which regards the woman as the property of the men of that community, and sexual violence, the ultimate humiliation of the community and its men has to be underscored.

There is also the question of what constitutes violence as distinct from discrimination or segregation. Religious minorities are subjected to a great deal of discrimination. These include a number of disabilities in accessing housing, jobs, credit, entry into educational institutions and access to basic services in their habitations, such as drinking water. These can also be seen as forms of passive violence. Even more pertinently, there can be communally charged taunts and insults in classrooms, workplaces and places of community gathering. There can be active hate propaganda. And then there is active physical, targeted and hate violence, involving attacks on the body and property of persons of the designated 'other' religion, involving culpable heinous offences such as murder, rape, injury, arson and looting.

Finally, hate propaganda. Usually, scholars separate questions of discrimination from active physical hate violence, and hate propaganda stands in a somewhat twilight zone in between. Many recognize that hate propaganda incites violence and therefore regard it to be criminally culpable; even if it is not active violence in itself, it still instigates such violence.

References

Chandra, Bipan. *Communalism in Modern India*. Delhi: Vikas Publishing House, 1984.
Rajeshwari, B. 'Communal Riots in India: A Chronology (1947–2003)'. Institute of Peace and Conflict Studies Report, March 2004.

CORRUPTION

C. Rammanohar Reddy

'Corruption' is a word that is everywhere in India, perhaps as much as, if not more than, 'poverty', 'jobs' and 'communalism'. It dominates politics; it is always in the media and seems to crop up frequently in private conversations. There is a broad agreement that corruption is an identification mark of Indian society and that the phenomenon is crying out for urgent action. The corruption that is most common in public discourse is the abuse of office for private gain by those elected and appointed to the government. This abuse takes the form of demanding payment for services rendered which may even be legitimately due to the citizen or may even be illegal services.

Corruption in high places involves payment of huge bribes, often made outside the country, for allocation of natural resources, large public works contracts and change in policy to benefit particular entrepreneurs. In the middle layer of government, entrepreneurs need to pay bribes for permissions to run their business and also to evade the application of certain laws. At lower layers of government, honest citizens find themselves oppressed when they are expected to make payments for housing permits which should be provided out of duty. There is also petty corruption by low-level officials in charge of basic services. The weak pay their own bribes to police, such as in payment of *hafta* (protection or permission money). Every aspect of daily life of the citizen is touched by bribery.

Historians point out that texts from ancient India do not have any definite Sanskrit word for 'corruption'. They, however, also argue that this does not mean that there was no corruption at the time, only that transgressions which one would today equate with corruption are referred to as violations of one's duty. Centuries later, under colonialism, early colonialists like Robert Clive, who benefitted from personal plunder and bribery, sought to explain away their riches as an unavoidable enrichment in a society where monetary corruption was considered the norm. The nationalists of the early twentieth century, in turn, sought to explain corruption in India as something that was exacerbated if not actually introduced by colonial powers. Soon after Independence, it was the Santhanam Committee of 1962 that made the first systematic attempt at studying corruption in India. Whatever the historical evidence on the prevalence of corruption in pre- and post-Independence India, the perception in India is that in its spread and magnitude, the malaise of monetary corruption, is only growing over time.

In fact, there have been major cases of corruption in India from the very first decade after Independence. All of these to a greater or smaller degree became election campaign issues in national and state elections. However, none of these compare to the issue made out of the major allegations of corruption made in the late 2000s and early 2010s against the then ruling United Progressive Alliance (UPA) government, which led to new political agendas and had important political outcomes. While there were some doubts about the quality of estimates of 'notional losses', there was no question of the impact these 'scams' had on public consciousness.

The word 'scam' became a part of newspaper headlines. The scams of the 2000s at the national level led to the 'India Against Corruption' movement of Anna Hazare in 2011, which later resulted in the formation of the Aam Admi Party, the first major political party which, initially at least, put corruption at the heart of its political platform. This impact, however, was outstripped by the centrality of corruption in the campaign for the parliamentary elections of 2014, when the Bharatiya Janata Party was able to make political capital out of people's disgust with the scams of the UPA government and ride to power.

There is no evidence to suggest that corruption in the private sector is any less than that in government. It just does not get the same attention. However, as the extent of such corruption in the form of fraud and embezzlement has increased in recent years, this too has entered public discourse.

Another kind of corruption that has made its presence felt more and more is what is considered the unhealthy transformation of a uniquely Indian way of life. The destruction of the Indian way of life by external influences is an old meme, but with globalization, the core of Indian culture is seen to be increasingly 'corrupted' by certain 'Western' influences which are causing a decay of the social fabric. This could be described as a framing of corruption in moralistic terms.

The most unusual aspect of corruption, at least in high places, has been the very few cases of conviction of people in positions of power. In the handful of cases where elected representatives have been convicted, the legal proceedings have stretched over more than a decade. The causes of such delays and a low rate of conviction are both political and legal. The end effect is despair among the citizenry. In the routine, there is no moral opprobrium associated with the corrupt whether they are serving or elected officials. Anger surfaces only when corruption leads to, for example, poor quality work which causes death and injury. The acceptance of corruption as a part of everyday life has, however, raised questions about the distrust it breeds in the rule of law.

This discussion inevitably leads to asking if India is one of the most corrupt societies in the world. Global attempts to rank countries are subjective and of little value. These show India occupying only the middle ranks in the global league of countries. However, with the rule of law so routinely violated and punishment so rare, public perception is that India is indeed one of the most corrupt countries in the world. Society's deep concern about corruption has led some to believe that a constant focus on the phenomenon has made it out to be a bigger problem than it actually is and has bred a cynical mood among the citizenry. The validity of such an argument cannot be established, but what has been established, even if only with numerous pieces of anecdotal evidence, is that corruption touches everybody at different points of their lives and in different aspects.

References

Myrdal, Gunnar. *Asian Drama*, Single edn. London: Pelican, 1971.
Viswanathan, Shiv and Harsh Sethi, ed. *Foul Play: Chronicles of Corruption 1947–97*. New Delhi: Banyan books, 1998.

DESIVAD (DĒSĪVĀD)

Bhalchandra Nemade

Desivad, from *desi*, which means 'of the land' and *vaad* (the suffix '-ism'), has been a most widely debated theory in Marathi and other Indian languages since 1980s. This has been, partly, a response to the postcolonial situation, anxiously reclaiming the dormant hoary traditions, and partly as an attitude towards the dilemma of homogenizing internationalism and indigenous pluralism encountered in Indian literary culture of enormous varieties-ethnic, religious and linguistic. Being desi is asserting a particular code of the land, self-evident in the inherited lifestyles of immense diversity found in every different region and sometimes in the same place.

Desivad has thus both benign and aggressive dimensions: it sensitively recognizes individuality of each of the numerous tribes, subaltern groups, castes and faiths or religions strikingly expressed in their literature; on the other hand, it confronts any uniform, national, transnational, universalist or cosmopolitan standards, which are bound to be ideologically charged and induce rootlessness in societies. Desivad rejects theories of evaluation that judge the product of one culture by the standards of another, refusing to count native systems as subsets of some abstract national or international systems, because such haphazard praxizes culminate in the breakdown of interrelationships between biodiversity, cultural diversity and linguistic diversity.

Rooted in physical and cultural environments of existing mores of society, rather than in the historical archival repositories, desivad asserts plurality of distinct native styles of living.

Different population groups have acquired characteristics designated by their geographical and genetic isolation for millions of years, ensuing psychological adaptations and, in turn, cultural differences between peoples are attributed to geographical and environmental causes as well as reproductive isolation. Thus, every human group has evolved its own culture and there is nothing like a universal human culture. Similarities do exist; however, differences are more fecund, especially in human creative faculties.

Basic environment and choice are active in structuralizing an inherited tradition which makes itself distinct from another. Hence the unique value of legacy or heritage in every human group. Despite the characteristic geopiety it manifests, desi-ness may lead to self-centredness, inbreeding and insularity. A vital and ongoing process in all cultures necessitates *desikaran* (nativization). It entails interdependence between cultures under various historical processes of culture contact, leading to borrowing, often forms, and rarely even features, from 'other' cultures, both intra- and international, into the receiving culture.

The borders between desi consciousness and other xenophobic tendencies, such as fundamentalism, chauvinism and revivalism, naturally grow in the interstices of democratically nurtured multicultural society like the Indian subcontinent. The borderline between such degenerate tendencies and desivad appears to be thin; nevertheless, it does exist, is distinctly visible and perspicuous. However, there is a prevailing political strategy to deliberately blur the barriers in order to exploit desi emotions. Every great author, whether Shakespeare or Goethe, wrote for her or his time and place and for her or his own language community. Similarly, every work of art inevitably bears the birthmark of the soil in which it is born. From the desi viewpoint, international recognition, however high in relief, is purely accidental, determined by circumstances, ideologically conditioned and subject to the sociology of reception.

References

Katzenstein, Mary F. 'Origins of Nativism: The Emergence of Shiv Sena in Bombay'. *Asian Survey* 134 (1973): 386–99.
Paranjape, Makarand R. *Nativism: Essays in Criticism*. New Delhi: Sahitya Akademi, 1997.

DHARNA/RAIL ROKO/BANDH/HARTAL/GHERAO (DHARNĀ/RĒL RŌKŌ/BANDH/HARTĀL/GHĒRĀV)

Samir Kumar Das

These five words refer to various forms of political protest, with an Indian idiom. The Hindi word *dharna* means 'sitting in restraint, placing', originally meaning, lying flat on one's face in worship in front of a temple till one's vow is accomplished. In modern times, the word has undergone significant secularization of meaning and now describes holding of peaceful demonstration in front of an office/workplace. The word originates from the Sanskrit verb *dhar* ('to hold, to place'). Interestingly, the same verb also lies at the root of *dharma* (ethic) and is often mistranslated as (organized) religion. Because of its ethical connotation, the act of staging dharna is marked by a certain kind of intransigence insofar as the protesters refuse to leave till their demands are met or at least some promise towards their fulfilment is made. Dharna emerged as a political practice in the villages of Kathiawar in Gujarat against the British authorities in the early nineteenth century and was popularized in modern times by Gandhi. It is often accompanied by fast unto death, self-flagellation or other forms of self-torture, even self-immolation.

The second term *rail roko* has two components: the English term 'rail' and the Hindi term *roko*. This simply means squatting on the railway tracks while obstructing or halting the movement of trains, usually to publicize local issues. The word rōkō is derived from the Hindi word *rukna* that implies 'to stop, to hinder, to obstruct'.

While rail roko is organized by the general public, railway workers' strike is one in which the workers refuse to report to work in order to pursue their demands and railway traffic comes to a standstill. That brings us to the third word *band*, which comes from the Sanskrit word 'bandh' meaning 'to bind, pledge'. The word subsequently underwent a transformation of meaning to now connote any striking of work.

The fourth word, *hartal*, is derived from the Gujarati word *hannatala*, meaning 'closing of shops in the market'. The word is formed from two Sanskrit words: *hanna* which means 'market' and *tala* which means 'padlock'. Hartal is often accompanied by *bhukh hartal* (hunger strike), whether relay or indefinite. By all accounts, the word hartal was first used during the freedom movement in India. It refers to a form of mass protest involving total shutdown of shop floors, workplaces, offices, markets, courts of law, educational institutions, industries and so forth, as part of civil disobedience organized to bring home the unacceptability of a government decision.

While hartal and band often appear as synonyms, there are significant differences between the two. First, while hartal is usually called on a much wider scale on issues that are of general character (such as imposition of Goods and Services Tax or withdrawal of subsidies from agricultural inputs), a band is organized on a smaller scale and usually involves local issues. Second, a band may be sudden, spontaneous and unorganized. A hartal, on the other hand, is unlikely to be so, because organizing it on a wide scale requires some level of planning and leadership. Third, in 1997, the High Court of Kerala distinguished hartal from band by holding that while calling of a band per se is illegal and unconstitutional, calling of a hartal is not. The court noted that it is the enforcement of a hartal by force, intimidation and coercion that makes it illegal and unconstitutional insofar as it violates the rights of others who refuse to observe it.

The next term in the sequence, *gherao*, is of Bengali and Hindi origin, but its first documented usage was in West Bengal. Gherao originally meant 'to encircle, to surround', and in the political scenario, it refers to a kind of protest where protesters do not allow the authority or employers to leave the office or workplace until their demands are met. This form of protest was introduced by Subodh Banarjee when he was the West Bengal state minister of labour welfare in 1967 and Public Works Department (PWD) in 1969. The National Commission of Labour in India, however, refuses to accept gherao as a legitimate form of labour protest on the grounds that it threatens to cause physical distress to the persons gheraoed and jeopardizes industrial harmony and law and order.

In Western parlance, each of these words may have its English equivalent with the effect that each may have travelled across continents and lost its distinctively Indian character. But, the

Indian words are nevertheless important in ways that are likely to set them apart from their Western equivalents for the following reasons: First, each of these forms is marked by a sense of ethicality and intransigence that distinguishes it from the commonplace forms of collective bargaining and trade union consciousness that expresses itself through such demands as increase in wages and improvement of work conditions etc. Each of them thus speaks of a deep sense of justice that catalyzes it. Justice Krishna Iyer maintained that a strike, even if illegal, could be very well justified. Second, unlike in the West, these practices of protest are also reflective of some form of affect. Often family, caste, kinship and neighbourhood ties play a role in reinforcing or undermining the otherwise political solidarities that form through these practices of protest. Third, the ethical element underlining many of these forms of protest has a tendency of overshadowing the democracy understood conventionally as the regime of numbers. Fourth, these forms of protest face the risk of losing their edge insofar as they get routinized because of their overuse. Sometimes bandhs and hartals are organized more as a show of strength than to fulfil demands.

References

Denning, Lord. 'Gherao: A Pernicious Technique of Agitational Politics in India.' *Pressure Groups and Politics of Influence* 8 (1997): 330.

Spodek, Howard. 'On the Origins of Gandhi's Political Methodology: The Heritage of Kathiawad and Gujarat'. *The Journal of Asian Studies* 30, no. 2 (1971): 361–72.

DM/BDO

Ashok Thakur

The DM (district magistrate) is the executive head of a district in India. The office is a legacy of the Raj, having been introduced by Lord Warren Hastings in 1772, to head and to represent the government at the district level. Interestingly, the model was more akin to the Prefecture system in France, offering unity of command and centralized administration, which the British needed for faster consolidation of acquired territories.

At present, there are 707 districts in India's 29 states and 7 Union Territories. The officers heading these posts belong to the Indian Administrative Services (IAS), the successor to the Indian Civil Services (ICS). The selection into the IAS is done by an arm's length agency of the Centre, that is, the Union Public Service Commission (UPSC), which selects around 150 candidates each year out of 400,000 who appear for the exam, making it one of the toughest in the world. After an initial two years of training and another three as sub-divisional magistrate (SDM) and additional district magistrate (ADM) she or he is posted as a DM. Apart from the term DM, the office is also known as collector in states where, historically, collection of land revenue was important. In some states, the appellation of DC (deputy commissioner) is also popular.

Generally speaking, there are three broad roles as head of the district. The first one is that of maintaining law and order, which makes the DM technically the head of the police and executive magistracy. The superintendent of police (SP) of the district is supposed to report to her or him on all important matters relating to the subject. Supervision of jails is also one of the duties. The office had judicial powers too, which ended with the separation of judiciary from the executive in 1973. At present, their judicial powers are limited to hearing cases under preventive sections of the Criminal Procedure Code (CPC). Conducting elections fairly and peacefully in the district is another important role, as it is the bedrock of the country's democracy.

The second role is as that of head of land administration, wherein one is responsible for collection of taxes (now no longer important), proper maintenance of land records, protection of government lands from encroachment and arbitration in land acquisition cases. As collector, she or he is assisted by district revenue officer and several sub-collectors and tehsildars. In times of natural disasters like drought, flood, fire and earthquake, this office takes the lead role.

The last hat that she or he wears is that of the head of 'development administration', which implies improving the living standards of the rural families, especially those living below the poverty line, by implementing a host of livelihood and income-generation schemes. Creating tangible rural assets/infrastructure is also an important objective. These schemes are funded by the Ministry of Rural Development and Poverty Alleviation of the Government of India with the state government chipping in. Besides this, most of the major development programmes of line departments of the state government are chaired by DM for effective coordination. Thus, the buck stops with the DM for matters related to the district. The reporting officer of DM is the commissioner who has several districts under her or his control. In turn, she or he reports to the state government for overall coordination and control.

The BDO (block development officer), on the other hand, is a subordinate of deputy commissioner in the area of 'developmental administration'. Typically, there are about five to ten developmental blocks in a district, each headed by a BDO. The institution of BDO came into existence in 1952 with the launch of the Community Development Programme in the country, with the objective of bringing about social and economic transformation in rural India. The strategy was to increase the income of farmers through increased agriculture production, improving their livelihood opportunities, bettering rural connectivity and augmenting primary education enrolment. The office of the BDO was to be the focal point for all the block-level functionaries of the line departments, namely agriculture, horticulture, industries, fisheries, cooperatives and rural development department and work in coordination under the leadership of BDO, who in turn is answerable to the DM. With the introduction of Zila Parishad under Panchayati Raj (local self-government), the position of the BDO has become complex as she or he now reports not only to the deputy commissioner but also the Block Samiti chairperson.

The institution of DM as well as the BDO are undergoing major changes today due to the increasing role of the elected representatives. The political leadership controls the bureaucracy (DMs and BDOs are no exception) through the instrument of transfer, promotions and posting. The average tenure of a DM in some states is less than a year, which leads to the post becoming less effective. In many states, the line departments headed by ministers now no longer report through the BDO/DM. The Police Department is a case in point where they tend to function independently on most occasions. The 'steel frame', as the IAS was referred to in the past, is fast losing its relevance due to the pressures of the changing times.

References

Mukhopadhyay, Asok. 'Changing Role of the District Magistrate'. *Indian Journal of Public Administration* 43, no. 3 (1997): 696–702.
Sinha, Chandan. *Public Sector Reforms in India: New Role of the District Officer*. New Delhi: SAGE Publications India, 2007.

DOMINANT CASTE

Ghanshyam Shah

In the mid-1950s, social anthropologist M. N. Srinivas coined the concept of dominant caste to explain rural sociopolitical dynamics. It was based on a village study in south India. A dominant caste that is, *jati* (a local social group in which members have an interpersonal relationship of exchange of food and matrimonial network) is not necessarily high in the ritual hierarchy, but it is also not too low in the social order. It numerically preponderates over other castes and also wields significant economic and political power. In the context of rural India, economic power is embodied with landholding and political power – control over caste and village councils. Later, Srinivas added two more attributes to the notion of dominant caste: (Western) education and (non-farm white-collar) occupation.

The dominant caste is not necessarily the same in all villages of a district or block. It may vary from village to village. All dominant castes do not necessarily have all or even most of the attributes of dominance. It is possible that a caste with numerical strength without economic power may enjoy dominance in some spheres but not in all. And, a caste numerically insignificant but economically powerful might enjoy political influence and dominance.

According to Srinivas, when a caste enjoys one form of dominance, it is frequently able to acquire the other forms as well in course of time. Thus, a caste which is numerically strong and wealthy will be able to move up the ritual hierarchy if it Sanskritizes its ritual and way of life and also loudly and persistently proclaims itself to be what it wants to be. The more forms of dominance which a caste enjoys, the easier it is for it to acquire the rest. However, traditionally, untouchable castes do not enjoy an opportunity for upward mobility.

A caste with all the above attributes enjoys *decisive* dominance. Though there is reciprocity among the castes in socio-economic relationships, dominant caste, more so when it enjoys decisive dominance, enjoys coercive power over other castes. In this scenario, members of the non-dominant castes 'may be abused, beaten, grossly underpaid, or their women required to gratify the sexual desires of the powerful men in the dominant caste'.

Srinivas showed that at the village level a dominant caste resolves inter-caste as well as intra-caste disputes. Ritually high-caste Brahmins and even Muslims sought the help of patrons of the dominant caste to settle their disputes. However, untouchables did not refer their disputes to the dominant caste. But his observations were confined to a study of one village in South India in the 1950s. Since then, with increased urbanization, coupled with industrialization and the Green Revolution, rural India in different parts of the country may have changed considerably. The scenario of inter-caste relationship observed in the 1950s seems to have undergone shifts in many parts of the country where non-dominant castes resist, protest and confront the dominant caste. At the same time, it seems probable that caste dominance does not easily dissipate. Some sociologists have shown that land ownership in Indian villages moves towards the dominant caste. Correspondingly, landless labourers from a dominant caste have a greater chance of becoming landowners than members of other castes. This is also true for education and white-collar employment.

In their studies on elections and state/region politics, political sociologists thus continue to use the concept of a dominant caste. At a regional level, for example, a jati-cluster that successfully mobilizes other jatis perceived as belonging to a similar denomination will have the numerical strength to constitute a dominant caste. Rajni Kothari observed that 'politics serve as a medium of integration' of these jatis 'though adaptation and change'. These caste clusters may be called dominant political castes. Such dominant castes vary from region to region. They compete with each other in electoral politics and distribution of resources. All of them are not necessarily economically powerful. Though political sociologists use the concept of dominant caste, so far very little effort has been made to conceptualize the idea of a dominant political caste in contemporary times.

References

Kothari, Rajni. *Caste in Indian Politics*. Hyderabad: Orient Longman, 1970.
Srinivas, M. N. 'The Social System of a Mysore Village'. In *Village India*, edited by McKim Marriott, 21–35. Chicago: University of Chicago Press, 1955.

EMERGENCY

Suhas Palshikar

The word 'emergency' would ordinarily mean merely a situation of some unforeseen urgency. But, in the context of Indian politics, it refers to certain constitutional provisions, a brief period of effective suspension of democracy and an evocative political polemic implying an authoritarian tendency. The Constitution envisages three types of emergencies: national emergency, state emergency and financial emergency. The third has remained a dead provision as it has never been used in independent India's political history thus far. The second, more popularly known as 'president's rule' in the states of India, has been controversial right from the beginning but seldom referred to as emergency. That leaves us with the 'national emergency' that is declared under Article 352 of the Constitution of India.

When such an emergency is declared, the union government assumes extraordinary powers to suspend fundamental rights and to take away the powers of India's states – thus, converting the country temporarily into a non-federal and even non-democratic state. This was not always the case. Emergencies were indeed declared when India faced wars with its neighbours, but the severe effects of those emergencies were never felt. It was only the Emergency of 1975 that has created history: it was not declared on grounds of threat of external aggression but rather on grounds of threat of internal disturbance. The argument of the government was that a spate of agitations across the country tended to weaken the Indian state, the alleged appeal by Jayprakash Narayan to the armed forces and the police not to obey illegal orders of the government amounted to a threat of rebellion and that there was an international conspiracy to destabilize India. While the period immediately preceding the Emergency was indeed a period of severe anti-government political activity, critics of the Emergency of 1975 point out that there was hardly an anarchic situation and certainly no organized political violence.

During that Emergency, large-scale arrests of political opponents took place and these arrests were in the form of preventive detentions, that is, there were no specific charges, no trials, no convictions. In a case known for its non-democratic tenor, the Supreme Court refused to entertain the right of the detainees to use the writ of habeas corpus, thus effectively admitting that during Emergency, the fundamental rights to life and liberty did not exist anymore. While India has a system of collective responsibility of the Union Cabinet, the declaration of Emergency in 1975 was not approved by the Cabinet before it went to the president for his assent. He did not inquire about Cabinet approval and accorded his assent. In the absence of most members of the opposition, a major amendment to the Constitution was made (Forty-Second Amendment). Elections were due in 1976 but using the Emergency provision, elections were postponed and then the duration of Lok Sabha was extended by one year – from five to six so that elections would be necessary only in 1978. However, the government actually called for elections in early 1977 and the sitting government was defeated by a combined opposition. This was the first time in independent India that the sitting national government was ever defeated in elections. In the political folklore of India, the defeat was attributed to 'excesses' during the Emergency and the outcome was hailed as a second freedom.

Thus, Emergency has become a political code word. It is not merely about the specific political developments of 1975–7 but a reference point. It refers to the possibilities of ushering in authoritarian government through constitutional means. It refers to complete decimation of political opponents using state power. It refers to the failure of the judiciary to protect the Constitution and uphold democracy. It refers to the unprecedented atmosphere of fear and suspicion that practically suspended open competitive politics. It refers to the contingent possibility that people themselves may remove a sitting government if it engages in political excesses. Above all, in the political lexicon of India, the term Emergency refers to two things. One, it refers to unleashing a reign of terror to tame the opposition. Two, it refers to a proclivity to personalized authoritarian rule propped up by use of the bureaucratic apparatus.

In the aftermath of the Emergency and the elections of 1977, some mechanisms of damage control were adopted. For instance, by an amendment to the Constitution, the reasons for declaring Emergency were more strictly defined as war, external aggression or armed rebellion. It is also now mandatory that the advice to the president to declare a state of Emergency must come in a written form by the Union Cabinet. Declaration of Emergency must be approved by the Lok Sabha within one month and after that, it can remain operative only for six months. Extending it beyond six months requires approval of the Lok Sabha for each period of six months.

Since 1975–7, Emergency powers have never been invoked. But the word Emergency continues to have resonance in political rhetoric. Besides the use of Article 352, Emergency refers to a possible curtailing of rights, including the freedom of expression, and a general political environment of fear, suspicion and intolerance. The Congress Party often receives criticism for its infamous use of Emergency powers in 1975–7 (because it has never formally distanced itself from what its leadership did in the 1970s nor has it accepted that it made a mistake). On the other hand, critics of Prime Minister Narendra Modi have pointed out to his alleged authoritarian style of functioning, his emphasis on personal popularity and power and the instances of unofficial harassment and/or violence against those with opposing views. The criticism of the prime minister is that without invoking the constitutional provision of Emergency, he is causing an 'Emergency-like' political atmosphere that suspends dialogue and brands opponents as threat to the nation.

Thus, beyond its constitutional ramifications and subtleties, the term 'Emergency' has assumed a political connotation that draws attention to authoritarian tendencies that are active inside the democratic sphere of competitive politics in India.

References

Nayar, Kuldip. *The Judgement: Inside Story of the Emergency in India*. New Delhi: Vikas Publishing House, 1977.
Park, Richard L. 'Political Crisis in India, 1975'. *Asian Survey* 15, no. 11 (1975): 996–1013.

FATWA (FATVĀ)

Irfanullah Farooqi

A *fatwa* is a legal opinion given by a *mufti* (scholar trained in Islamic law) in response to a question raised by an individual. As an opinion, it responds to a matter/issue that has a bearing on religious conduct. While fatwas have become part of popular discourse quite recently, its history, as a practice of seeking opinion on matters of religious conduct, is very old. It is held that the companions of Prophet Muhammad used to seek his opinion on a range of issues and matters. What is important to note is that on many occasions, Muhammad would refrain from giving his own opinion and wait for revelation on the matter.

Contrary to the prevalent understanding of fatwa, a result of series of simplistic-yet-politically motivated formulations, it is non-binding. In case the inquirer is not convinced with the response, she or he can always approach another mufti. While in most cases a fatwa is sought or requested so as to know the dictate of the *shariah* (Islamic legal code) about a specific issue, there are instances when a mufti, on his own, announces his jurisprudential opinion on a matter that, according to him, merits an intervention in the light of shariah.

If we look at the sudden prominence of the word fatwa across the globe since the late 1980s, it becomes quite clear that it created an overwhelming corpus of knowledge around the institution of fatwa giving that reduced it to the binary of orthodox/conservative versus liberal/progressive. Rather than understanding it predominantly as a response to an individual's genuine curiosity around a new social practice and the possibility of its reconciliation with the Islamic legal codes, fatwa has been understood as a declaration that is invariably in line with violence and bloodshed or against freedom and human agency. Starting with the fatwa in support of suicide bombers to the highly infamous fatwa against Salman Rushdie, it comes across as violently antithetical to the peaceful functioning of the human world. Interestingly, this massive coverage of political fatwas of a certain bent conveniently overlooks fatwas that were equally political yet signalled the liberal and rational aspect of Islam as a religion. For instance, little or no attention was given to fatwas that openly condemned violence and declared that suicide bombing was against the teachings of Islam and those that made a case for coexistence and accommodation, spoke in favour of gender equality, publicly denounced bigotry in the name of religion and so on.

Given how rapid changes in any society merit the critical intervention of fatwa, it is not difficult to make sense of the massive increase in fatwas in the recent past. Massive movements of labour forces to developed countries, increased mobility and access, technological development, new trends in governance, religious revivalism and so on have all jointly led to a very genuine concern around the assimilation of a series of new social practices within the larger frame of shariah. As against the commonly held perception, interventions through fatwa, in many cases, revealed flexibility within Islamic discourse by stretching the limits of Islamic law. The huge number of fatwas on insurance, investment in share markets, use of technology, political participation and several other important issues categorically hint at, alongside a means of providing religious legitimacy, Islam's accommodative spirit towards reforms.

One of the most fundamental reasons behind the prevalent sinister understanding of fatwa as a deterrent is to do with the focus of fatwa discourses being restricted to the mufti and absolute neglect of the *mustafti* (the person who seeks the fatwa) and *istifta* (the request for fatwa). A mustafti ideally should be driven by a deep and earnest urge to know shariah's say in the matter concerned. She or he must find a qualified mufti and must be willing to travel to find one in case there is none in her or his area. In fatwa as a process, both mustafti and mufti are to fulfil a set of desirable qualities. Personal preferences should not come in the way and *taqwa* (God consciousness) should remain at the core of their engagement with the issue.

Looking at India in particular, even a cursory look at the range of fatwas during the colonial period urges one to discard the 'fear' of a fatwa. Ever since the beginning of the nineteenth century, fatwas were issued one after another against colonial rule. By the beginning of the twentieth century, serving the British army was declared *haraam* (forbidden). There were fatwas that openly asked Muslims to express solidarity with the Indian National Congress and, in their opposition to colonial rule, cooperate with the Hindus. The fatwa in support of Gandhi's call for non-cooperation signed by five hundred muftis followed by an endorsement of a similar scale during the Khilafat Movement remains well-documented.

A holistic understanding of fatwa politics in India must take us beyond the convenient reference to supremacy of Muslim orthodoxy or their contentious role in regulating the lives of ordinary Muslims. Invoking fatwa's anti-progress and anti-reform aspect, a certain political ideology is quite keen on projecting it as something that is against the national interest. Repeated references to fatwas against co-education, music, fashion, modelling, watching TV and films, contraceptives, life insurance, uploading of photos, birthday celebrations and so on have created a world that holds the community responsible for its poor showing. Alongside this huge pile that is moved to articulate fatwa's role as an impediment in nation-building, what also slips between the cracks are the fatwas against doing the yogic *surya namaskar* and chanting the

Hindu *saraswati vandana* and the nationalist slogans *vande mataram* and *bharat mata ki jai*. As a result, there arises a peculiar mixture of secular, communal and national concerns around the institution of fatwa. These concerns then underline the rigidity of Islamic law and push for doing away with Muslim Personal Law. Needless to say, this fatwa politics that eventually enters the realm of culture feeds sawdust into the already burning fire of communal hatred in India. There is an urgent need to check the sinister meaning that fatwa has acquired. Such false equivalences will prove extremely damaging to the plural ethos of a country like India. Muftis must seek recourse to the much-cherished reticence in calling every other practice un-Islamic and we as a society should be willing to give religious knowledge its due, on occasions that require an uncommonly deep engagement with issues related to rights and representation.

References

Agrama, Hussein Ali. 'Ethics, Tradition, Authority: Toward an Anthropology of the Fatwa'. *American Ethnologist* 37, no. 1 (2010): 2–18.
Masud, Muhammad Khalid. 'The Significance of Istiftā in the Fatwā Discourse'. *Islamic Studies* 48, no. 3 (Autumn 2009): 341–66.

GHAR WAPSI (GHAR VĀPSĪ)

Rudolf C. Heredia

Any consideration of conversion or reconversion must first come to terms with Babasahib B. R. Ambedkar's defining decision when he announced at Yeola on 13 October 1935: 'It was not my fault that I was born an untouchable. But I am determined that I will not die a Hindu.' Ambedkar's neo-Buddhist, navayana movement is an enlightening example of such a protest. The only response Hindutvawadis have had to this is to affirm that Buddhism is Hinduism, precisely the opposite of what Ambedkar was emphatic about. Neo-Buddhist Dalits today would consider this to be an act of Manuvādī obfuscation. Buddhists in other countries in Asia would certainly reject this as well. Here conversion is understood as a change of religion, *dharmantar*, not only a change of heart but also an *atmaparivartan* within the same religious tradition. Such religious conversions have been recently on the boil because of the Hindu reconversion imbroglio, euphemistically called *ghar wapsi* (which literally means 'homecoming'). Our tense and polarized situation demands an honest introspection so that converts and would-be converts are heard in their own right, not in the voices of those who ventriloquize for them.

Conversion from one religious community to another understandably makes the original community of the convert insecure, even hostile. Something held precious is being negated, and something else affirmed. The real concern ought to be, how valid is this negation, how meaningful the affirmation? To respond with reconversions, or ghar wapsi, is but a defensive playback in reverse. To put a cunning spin on the term and pretend that it is not a religious change but a homecoming, ghar wapsi, is disingenuous and cannot hide the patent political agenda under the garb of religion or culture. The issue here is whether the overlay of psychological and social, political and economic motivations which may well obtain, invalidate and even negate religious ones. If they do, then it would not be religious conversion but still a legitimate and ethical exercise of personal freedom.

Converts and reconverts in India and elsewhere often become pawns in the numbers game of converters and reconverters for their own purposes. Both converters and opponents need to carefully discern whether they foreground the best interests and freedom of the 'proselytes' or these are being instrumentalized and co-opted to alien causes. Surely, the need is to work towards better inter-religious understanding and dialogue. Those opposed to religious conversions also need to interrogate themselves as to why is it that the wretchedness of would-be converts merits so little attention, except in the event of their changing religious allegiance. They are not accepted in their own religious community, nor allowed to leave, and are virtual prisoners of a 'no entry, no exit' policy.

When religious conversions develop into a people's movement, then the political and economic interests they touch can arouse considerable protest. The movement itself is often both a protest against an oppressive political and economic situation and a hope for a better life. Here the concern ought to be whether such protest and hope is legitimate within the rights and liberties constitutionally guaranteed to our citizens. Religious conversion is an unavoidable stumbling block for any aspiration for religious harmony or any real hope of true religious understanding, both of which are so essential to contain the a faux idea of 'religious diversity' which can so easily divide rather than unite people. Extremism on either side leaves alarmingly little room for the middle ground of sanity and common sense free from prejudice and increasingly less space for an awareness of our inevitable prejudgements. Positioning ourselves on common ground, we must enlarge this to engage in a plurality of conversations with the willing. This common ground must be extended to include other areas of human values and concerns that may well be outside these religious traditions but can still serve to question and critique them. This common ground on which our exchanges are premised does not exclude the secular or the non-religious in so far as this helps to further a multifaceted dialogue. The alternative is the violence of 'might is right' which settles very little and destroys much.

When a culture entrenches its values and stakes as non-negotiable, a 'cultural disarmament' is the only 'way to peace', in the words of Raimon Panikkar, by bracketing our cultural differences for an engagement in open and equal dialogue. Today, we need similar commitment to a 'religious disarmament' to open a way to intra-/inter-religious harmony and intra-/inter-communal peace. However, tragically there is an inversion of roles today: the religious traditions that once emphasized propagation and proselytization are now converting to understanding and dialogue, and those that once stressed tolerance and inclusiveness are now becoming aggressive and exclusive. Ghar wapsi exemplifies this inversion.

References

Heredia, Rudolf C. *Changing Gods: Rethinking Conversion in India*. New Delhi: Penguin, 2007.
Panikkar, Raimon. *Cultural Disarmament: The Way to Peace*. Louisville: Westminster John Knox Press, 1995.

HINDU RASHTRA (HINDŪ RĀṢṬRA)

Pralay Kanungo

Hindu rashtra (Hindu Nation) constitutes the core ideology of the Rashtriya Swayamsevak Sangh (RSS), the fountainhead of right-wing ideology in contemporary India. In the milieu of intense identity politics, communal polarization and Hindu–Muslim riots, Dr K. B. Hedgewar, influenced by V. D. Savarkar's thesis on *Hindutva*, founded the RSS in 1925 at Nagpur, Maharashtra, to organize and mobilize Hindus.

Hindutva (lit. Hinduness), being coined by Hindu revivalists the late-nineteenth-century colonial Bengal, remained obscure till Savarkar made it a political ideology in his seminal work *Hindutva* (1923). He defined the Hindu as a person who regarded Hindustan as his *pitrubhumi* (fatherland) and *punyabhumi* (holy land); thus, while only Hindus constituted the Indian nationhood, Muslims and Christians fell outside its ambit as their holy land existed in the Middle East, beyond the sacred boundary of India. Interestingly, in contrast to the usual Indian use of *matrubhumi* (motherland), Savarkar's invocation of fatherland showed German influence. For Savarkar, Hindutva not Hinduism constituted the core of Hindustan; while the former is a history in full, the latter is only a derivative. Being an atheist, Savarkar had little to do with religion; he rather displaced Hinduism (religious) by *Hindutva* (political) as the foundational identity of a Hindu as well as of India.

Savarkar's nationalism became the guiding doctrine of RSS's ideology of Hindu rashtra/Hindu nationalism. Being more of a practitioner, Hedgewar innovatively put this ideology into action; he recruited young boys, set up *shakhas* (branches), imparted both *sharirik* (physical) and *boudhik* (intellectual) training regularly and despatched a dedicated and disciplined band of trained disciples as 'pracharaks' (propagandists) to open shakhas across India to inculcate in young boys the ideology of Hindu rāṣṭra.

M. S. Golwalkar, who succeeded Hedgewar as the second chief (*Sarsanghchalak*) of the RSS, further sharpened and amplified the ideology of Hindu rashtra in two ideological tracts *We or Our Nationhood Defined* (1938) and *Bunch of Thoughts* (1966). While *We* became controversial for its explicit and extreme anti-minorities pronouncements, and was later withdrawn, the 'moderate' *Bunch of Thoughts* (1966) was no less provocative as it identified three enemies of *Hindu Rashtra* – the Muslims, the Christians and the Communists. Golwalkar also propagated 'Hindi, Hindu Hindustan' (one language, one culture and one nation). Strategically, Golwalkar did not antagonize the British kept the RSS away from the freedom struggle, thereby enabling it to expand quietly and smoothly. When Hindu–Muslim riots broke out after India's partition in 1947, the RSS established its credentials as a 'defender' of Hindus.

In a highly charged communal atmosphere, in 1948, Mahatma Gandhi was assassinated by Nathuram Godse, who was a close disciple of Savarkar and a former RSS member. The RSS was banned as a result and its leaders, including Golwalkar, were arrested. The ban was lifted in March 1949, and the RSS pledged to adopt a written constitution and confine itself to the cultural domain. Adverse experiences during the ban led to the birth of its political progeny, the Bharatiya Jan Sangh (BJS) in 1951; this new political party, preserving the ethos of Hindu rashtra, would politically challenge the Nehruvian vision of a modern, secular and composite India. Golwalkar also systematically created affiliates like the Akhil Bharatiya Vidhyarthi Parishad (ABVP; the students' wing), Bharatiya Mazdoor Sangh (BMS; workers' wing) and Vishwa Hindu Parishad (VHP; religious wing) in order to penetrate and control various spheres of civil society. Thus, emerged a huge network of affiliates commonly known as the Sangh Parivar (RSS family).

Balasaheb Deoras succeeded Golwalkar in 1973. Known for his astute political sense, he soon anticipated a climate change in Indian politics and concluded that the time was right for the RSS to plunge into direct politics. Thus, he aligned with Jayaprakash Narayan against the authoritarian regime of Indira Gandhi, opposing the Emergency. A large number of RSS cadre went to jail, and the RSS was banned. The strategy paid off – New Delhi had the first non-Congress government in 1977, and the RSS became a key player. The BJS merged with the Janata Party; two of its prominent leaders – Atal Bihari Vajpayee and Lal Krishna Advani – became cabinet ministers. As the Janata Party experiment failed over time, the RSS launched the Bharatiya Janata Party (BJP) in 1980. While the new party got only 2 out of 543 seats in the Parliament in 1984, the RSS adopted a militant religio-political strategy to revive BJP's political fortune. Thus, the old Ram Temple–Babri Masjid issue was raked up and Vishwa Hindu Parishad (VHP), the religious affiliate, was given the lead role as it can passionately invoke Hindu religiosity and sentiment effectively. The Ramjanmabhoomi agitation was launched with the support of a large number of Sadhus. Advani's Rath Yatra (1990) ignited the flames of communal riots across India, and finally, the Babri Masjid was pulled down in 1992. The RSS was banned for the third time. But the Sangh Parivar had already demonstrated its political might through a mammoth mass mobilization unprecedented in independent India.

Ramjanmabhoomi agitation put Hindutva at the centre stage of Indian politics as BJP's number soared in Parliament and state legislatures. As a consequence, Vajpayee, an RSS member, became the prime minister, first for only thirteen days in 1996 and then for six years from 1998 to 2004. As Vajpayee was moderate and the BJP had to share power with disparate political forces, the core Hindutva agenda like the Ram Temple, Article 370 and Uniform Civil Code were put on the backburner. However, the government saffronized education, raised jingoistic nationalism during the Kargil War and, above all, empowered the RSS affiliates and cadre to expand and entrench. In 2002, unprecedented anti-Muslim riots broke out in Gujarat when BJP's Narendra Modi was chief minister. In the political wilderness, the BJP captured New Delhi again in 2014 under the leadership of Narendra Modi, an RSS pracharak. Though the ruling BJP had sworn by the secular Constitution and inclusive governance, yet discourses, rhetoric, icons and symbols, glorifying the ideals of Hindu rashtra, have today become familiar in the public domain.

Thus, the RSS, from its founder K. B. Hedgewar to the present chief Mohan Bhagwat, remains committed to the ideology of Hindu rashtra and works to achieve this objective with a calibrated strategy; political power had always given further momentum to their mission, perfectly manifested today in Bhagwat–Modi combine. Yet India's inherent pluralism and diversity continue to modify the tenets of an unreconstructed Hindu rashtra and PM Modi who has come to power with an impressive majority in the Indian General Elections of 2019 speaks today of an 'inclusive India', and 'sabka vishwas'.

References

Copland, Ian. 'Crucibles of Hindutva? VD Savarkar, the Hindu Mahasabha, and the Indian Princely States'. *South Asia: Journal of South Asian Studies* 25, no. 3 (2002): 211–34.
Raghavan, T. C. A. 'Origins and Development of Hindu Mahasabha Ideology: The Call of VD Savarkar and Bhai Parmanand'. *Economic and Political Weekly* (1983): 595–600.

HUMAN RIGHTS

Savita Bhakhry

Human rights are a set of generally taken-for-granted assumptions based on the premise that as all human beings are born equal, everybody has human rights. The contemporary dominant articulation of human rights worldwide draws from the United Nations system of promoting and protecting human rights, predominantly the 1948 Universal Declaration of Human Rights. It stipulates that all rights are universal, inalienable, interdependent, interrelated and indivisible as they belong to all of humanity because of their shared essence of dignified human existence. And, no one is to be discriminated against with regard to distinctions of any kind, either by the state or the community or the family. The Universal Declaration, though not legally binding, is also reflected in the Constitution of India. This has paved the way for a rights-based constitution in the governance of India after Independence.

The Constitution of India was adopted by the Constituent Assembly on 26 November 1949 and came into force on 26 January 1950. The Preamble, the provisions contained in Part III of the Constitution relating to Fundamental Rights and those in Part IV describing the Directive Principles of State Policy, directs the state to protect and promote human rights, more specifically, civil and political rights plus economic, social and cultural rights, including rights of women, children, vulnerable groups like persons with disabilities, scheduled castes and tribes, minorities and other weaker sections. Fundamental Rights, enshrined in Articles 12 to 35, are justiciable and substantially cover almost all the civil and political rights under six broad categories. These are rights that individuals and citizens have in relation to government and those in authority: the right to equality, right to freedom including the right to protection of life and personal liberty, protection in respect of conviction for offences and protection against arrest and detention in certain cases, right against exploitation and right to freedom of religion. These represent the basic values cherished by the people of India since Vedic times and protect not only the dignity of the individuals but also create conditions in which every human being can develop their personality to the fullest extent. Directive Principles of State Policy, Articles 36–51, focus on economic, social and cultural rights, essential in the governance of the country and it is the duty of the state to apply these while making laws. These have been held to supplement Fundamental Rights and are directed towards the ideals of building a true democratic welfare state by securing, protecting and promoting a just social order. These include right to livelihood, make effective provision for securing the right to work, education and public assistance in the event of unemployment, old age, sickness, disablement or other cases of undeserved want, equal pay for equal work, just and humane conditions of work, raising the level of nutrition and standard of living, improving public health and social and cultural opportunities.

It is important to remember that, conceptually, rights often come packaged with duties. Every right seems to have a corresponding duty, the two representing two sides of the same coin. If we have a right to life, a duty is also cast upon us to respect human life and not harm another person. This concept is reflected in Article 51-A (Part IV-A) of the Indian Constitution which enumerates the Fundamental Duties every citizen is required to follow.

The adoption of the Protection of Human Rights Act of 1993 in India is significant as it led to the establishment of the National Human Rights Commission (NHRC) and State

Human Rights Commissions (SHRC). An important function of the NHRC is to study treaties and other international instruments on human rights and make recommendations for their effective implementation. An equally vital function of the NHRC is to review the safeguards provided by the Constitution or any law in force for the protection of human rights and recommend measures for their effective performance. Submissions made by the NHRC to the government and UN Human Rights Council for India's universal periodic reviews confirm that implementation of the laws, the weakness of new Bills and delay in new laws are areas of concern.

Undoubtedly, India has a powerful and activist judiciary, a free media and watchful civil society, which guards human rights in an open society run by the rule of law. However, gross violations of human rights by the state apparatus continue, both loud and silent. 'Loud' violence is directed against children, women, scheduled castes and tribes, Muslims, Christians and critics of the government. Internal strife, custodial violence, illegal detention and torture are a few other grey areas of violation of human rights. Lack of accountability for abuse committed by security forces persists. The inhuman practice of manual scavenging, bonded labour and child labour continues. Blanket shutdown of internet services in troubled areas by the government is the latest form of curbing the right to freedom of speech and expression.

Some 'silent' violations of human rights are the pervasiveness of poverty, hunger, illiteracy, maternal deaths, considerably high infant and under-five mortality, sex-selective abortions resulting in sex ratio imbalance at birth, widespread malnutrition, prevalence of anaemia, poor quality of education and infrastructure in villages, child marriages, human trafficking and discrimination and abuse of LGBT individuals. There is often awareness of loud violations but not of such silent violations. With the recognition of the Human Development Index (HDI) as a new measure of development in the 1990s, silent violations were brought centre stage while integrating human rights with human development as a true measure of progress.

The biggest challenge that the state apparatus faces today is that there is no national action plan for human rights. The state needs to work on this if at all human development for everyone and the 2030 agenda of Sustainable Development Goals (SDGs) are to be achieved.

References

Lal, Chaman and Savita Bhakhry. 'National Human Rights Commission: A Retrospective'. *Journal of the National Human Rights Commission, India* 12 (2013): 149–90.
Verma, J. S. 'Human Rights Redefined: The New Universe of Human Rights'. *Journal of the National Human Rights Commission, India* 1 (2002): 1–17.

IAS, IFS

Yogendra Kumar

IAS (Indian Administrative Service) has become part of common parlance in all parts of the country, both urban and rural. It evokes an aura of state authority and a certain mystique rooted in the history of the British Raj when near absolute power and stratospheric elitism were the hallmarks of the predecessor service called the ICS (Indian Civil Service). Within the democratic and representative system of government in independent India, members of the IAS are still expected, by the wider public, to shed the image of 'unaccountable authority' and elitism even though the political leadership at all levels of hierarchy is far more powerful than the civil servants who are drawn from a much more diverse socio-economic background, especially from disadvantaged sections as a result of constitutionally sanctioned affirmative policy.

The power associated with a career in the IAS makes the recruitment process among the toughest anywhere in the world and invests its members with social renown and prestige incomparable with other careers which would, in any other society, be considered no less prestigious and professionally exclusive. Although much admired socially, at the individual level, a pejorative expression, 'babus', is also used in public discourse, especially in the clamorous, high-octane electronic media, to put public agitational pressure against government policy or its implementation and evoke the same negative attribute ascribed to them during the days of the British Raj. The word 'babu' itself gained currency in the early period of the Raj, as a respectful but also occasionally satirical British term for upper-class Indians educated in the British system and, often, employed in junior administrative positions.

Much like its earlier avatar, the ICS, the IAS is also a catch-all expression for a wide variety of non-technical higher services recruited and managed by the national government, irrespective of their deployment either in the national or provincial structures. These services range from the IAS itself to those relating to the police, taxation service, revenue service, accounts service, railways service, postal service, army cantonments and so on. These are clubbed together in this manner since they are all categorized as Class I services. Admired for offering considerable prospects for upward social mobility, members of these services receive much public approbation if they are seen as being 'humble' and as 'one among the people'. The historical context of such cultivated personality traits is not to be taken lightly as the Indian members of the ICS, maligned for being part of a colonial administrative system during the period of freedom struggle, feared losing their jobs at the time of India's Independence. Thanks to the non-violent and culturally eclectic nature of the Gandhian freedom movement, their services were, however, retained and many of them served in the government with great distinction. However, the nomenclature for the successor service was changed to IAS after Independence and the service association was renamed as the ICS/IAS Association, as was their official dress which nationalist leaders at time thought should be made of handloom fabric (khadi).

As in the case of the IAS, the IFS (Indian Foreign Service) also had a somewhat approximate predecessor service, called the 'Indian Political Service', an offshoot partially of the ICS. Members of the Indian Political Service were deployed in very high positions in various princely states that were in a relationship of subsidiary alliance with the British Crown. The nature of their work was politically delicate as well as administrative. Although influential in the Raj political system, they were not as well known as their ICS counterparts. The IFS was set up in 1946 to conduct independent India's foreign policy and was anchored in the idealism of the unique nature of India's freedom struggle. Although both the IAS and the IFS represent the same upper crust of the elite administrative services of the Government of India, the latter service gets subsumed by the former as a generic expression much like the other Class I services, causing, unsurprisingly, a certain heartburn among its members.

Although the wider public, notwithstanding the exponential increase in outgoing international tourism and the growing diaspora overseas, remains largely unfamiliar with Indian diplomatic missions, the mystique and elitism enveloping the persona of an Indian ambassador is even greater in the public eye. Being introduced as an ambassador, either in the government or the wider public circle, evokes a certain awe and smoothens many a passage in difficult situations, both official as well as personal. It is emblematic of the public perception of the pomp and circumstance of international diplomacy and the mesmerizing arcana of statecraft engaged in by the members of the IFS that the appointment of a foreign secretary is seen by the media as meriting a much more prominent coverage than the appointment of a cabinet secretary, the head of the civil services in the Indian administrative system. The nature of work of IFS officers is, however, little understood by the public, resulting in its diminishing popularity among the civil service aspirants largely hailing from non-metropolitan cities and socially disadvantaged backgrounds. In the same vein as the IAS, the effort of the higher Indian diplomatic echelons is focused on 'public diplomacy' at home to explain and to demystify the public purpose of Indian diplomacy.

The two expressions, 'IAS' and 'IFS', encapsulate the flow of Indian history and culture in the colonial and the postcolonial periods. Public admiration for these elite government functionaries is leavened by a certain distrust of the authority enjoyed by them in its name: the 'Indianness' of these characteristics makes for the mystique surrounding their status in society. In the vastly different circumstances of the twenty-first century, robustly democratic India, a conscious – governmental as well as personal – effort still continues to be needed to overcome the legacy of their historical origin in the high noon of the British Empire in India.

References

Krishna, Anirudh. 'Continuity and Change: The Indian Administrative Service 30 Years Ago and Today'. *Commonwealth & Comparative Politics* 48, no. 4 (2010): 433–44.
Maheshwari, S. R. 'Strengthening Administrative Capabilities in India'. *Public Administration and Development* 4, no. 1 (1984): 49–62.

INSURGENCY/TERRORIST/JIHĀDĪ/MILITANT

Sanjoy Hazarika

Labels are powerful weapons that transform public perception of a community. The Rohingya are a case in point. While newspapers were filled with reports of persecuted Rohingyas fleeing into Bangladesh from Myanmar, a Ministry of Home Affairs (MHA) advisory announced that forty thousand Rohingya in India were to be sent back, and that they pose 'grave security challenges'. They were seen as vulnerable and could be recruited to jihadist groups, seeking to cement the public perception from asylum seekers to terrorists. Such words impact audiences and are used as 'weapons' in and of communication against individuals and communities. It would be instructive to deconstruct the terms *aatankwadi*, *jihādī*, 'terrorist', 'militant' and 'insurgent' towards understanding the problems these labels pose. We will look at them in the specific context of Northeast India, which is a stage of multiple conflicts. Northeast India shares 96 per cent of its frontiers with other nations and is connected to 'mainland India' by a thin strip of land. The region is an exceptional case because of its extraordinary ethnic, cultural and linguistic diversity and the continued existence of rebel groups despite contemporary 'rationalist' agendas.

Insurgency, or 'asymmetric warfare fought within the boundaries of a state', usually aims at overthrowing the incumbent government. The word derives from the Latin *insurgere* which means to 'rise up' or 'rise against'. One who engages in such activity – an insurgent – uses certain non-conventional means to achieve this, including terrorism, propaganda and guerrilla warfare, as Robinson observes. Insurgency is often conflated with Naxalism, which former prime minister, Manmohan Singh, described as 'the single biggest internal security challenge'. However, numerous other areas such as the North-East, were seen as insurgency-hit and even labelled by the Centre-appointed Administrative Reforms Commission as 'stable anarchy'. The North-East is the cradle for South Asia's longest running insurgency – that of the Nagas. Local armed groups have fought for the idea of 'Nagalim' or a Naga homeland. Historically, most Nagas have considered themselves distinct from India. 'Nagaland' is a state but remains a political construct in the eyes of many Nagas. Such rebellions have also occurred in other states in the region, Mizoram, Manipur, Tripura and Assam. Even parts of Meghalaya and Arunachal Pradesh, considered to be more peaceful, have been impacted by some violence due to insurgency.

Terrorist movements in the North-East, while indigenous in nature, have often required foreign support and bases, particularly Myanmar, Bhutan and Bangladesh. While no single definition of terrorism exists, certain boxes need to be ticked: (a) violence as the means used; (b) the act needs to be politically motivated; and (c) the objective is the intimidation of the local population. The August 2015 attack near Kokrajhar in Assam demonstrated the deadly striking capacity of a small group of terrorists with sophisticated arms. The target was civilians. It was carried out by the breakaway Songbijit faction of the National Democratic Front of Boroland (NDFB). Like other factions, the Songbijit faction was birthed by those who felt 'betrayed' by leaders who forged agreements with New Delhi.

Insurgency and terrorism come together in the term 'ethnic terrorism'. This term foregrounds ethnic groups' use of violence and populist narratives of 'freedom' and liberation to grab attention, as Upadhyay notes in *India's Fragile Borderlands*. In Assam, for instance, the United Liberation Front of Asom (ULFA) announced its intent to free Assam from India's 'colonial' clutches. They have engaged in assassinations, ambushes, militancy, terrorist attacks and have created a parallel taxation economy. However, their influence has waned enormously over the years, as has their striking power.

Jihādī, from the Arabic *jehad* ('struggle'), refers to the struggle or fight for Islam. A jihādī is one who wages this war against the enemies of Islam. Muslim extremists are said to pose an incipient risk to the North-East region, particularly in Assam, in light of the state's large Muslim population (34 per cent) and that of neighbouring states and countries. Many of these militant groups allegedly operate from across the border, in countries such as Bangladesh. However, there is little independent verification of the influence or even the size of such groups which surface in occasional media reports or selective official briefings. Some security analysts see a possible threat from the Rohingyas, pouring out of Myanmar. Specialists contend that the Rohingya of Myanmar could connect to Bangladesh and, in the future, possibly draw in elements from Assam and the North-East. Facing such a growing wave of right-wing communalism, which governments are either unable or unwilling to tackle, is rendering the region more vulnerable.

The word 'militant' is derived from the Latin *militare* which means 'to serve as a soldier'. Much like insurgency, increased militancy in the North-East is drawn from anger growing at a range of unfulfilled demands for greater autonomy and changing demographics. For example, in Tripura, demographic change led to the rise of a number of tribal militant groups such as the Tribal National Volunteers (TNV), All Tripura Tiger Force (ATTF) and the National Liberation Force of Tripura (NFLT), with the aim of ousting Bengalis from the state. With the creation of states like Arunachal Pradesh, Meghalaya and Mizoram, numerous ethnic groups have increased the use of militant tactics to promote their causes.

Further, there are often connections between underground groups and state governments. For example, Bethany Lacina claims 'the resilience of armed groups in Northeast India is not because of the advantages traditionally associated with guerrilla groups. They thrive by taking advantage of the imperfections in the rule of law; they maintain ties with mainstream actors in politics and business, and engage in strategic violence.' Manipur, the state most affected by insurgency in the region, has suffered from successive blockades in 2017 organized by the United Naga Council (UNC) leading to a shortage of goods and services and violent unrest. The problem then resurfaces: how can such groups espouse themselves as representatives of the people? The latter are rarely, if ever, consulted in the matter.

Militancy is also often linked to criminality, where groups engage in illegal economic activities in order to increase their control over resources and administration. In doing so, a tapestry of crime and violence is created, fed by the identity politics of the region.

References

Lacina, Bethany. 'Does Counterinsurgency Theory Apply in Northeast India?' *India Review* 6, no. 3 (2007): 165–83.
Upadhyay, A. *India's Fragile Borderlands: The Dynamics of Terrorism in North East India*. New York: I.B. Tauris, 2009.

JUMLA (JUMLĀ)

Mona Mehta

The word *jumla* suddenly became popular in the Indian public discourse in 2015, taking on a life and meaning distinct from its conventional usage. Jumla is derived from the Arabic root *jumla* (pl. *jumal*) and refers to 'totality, sum, whole, sentence or clause' in Hindi, Urdu and Gujarati. Although the word itself is not new, its popularity in recent times was triggered when a prominent ruling party politician, speaking in Hindi, used jumla to refer to 'a mere statement made by his leader during an election campaign'. Defending his leader, he said, 'Such a jumla was not to be taken literally as an election promise.' Why has this seemingly innocuous word unexpectedly caught the public imagination at this moment in history?

The remarkable story of the word jumla's recent ascent from relative obscurity has to do, in large part, with the advent of post-truth politics in India and the world over. Specifically, jumla's popularity lies in its ability to capture the new realities of our contemporary political landscape, where doctored facts, fake news and false propaganda have rapidly come to occupy a central place in political campaigns and public discourse. Going beyond its standard meaning of a mere sentence or clause, jumla's current usages connote the ideas of 'empty promises', 'concocted statements' and patently 'deceptive claims'. For instance, commenting on the political leadership of India, one twitter user noted, 'The mice following the Pied Piper never realize their fate before it's too late. The Piper always has lots of jumlas to save himself.' Here the term jumla is used as a noun to mean 'tricks' to cover up the regime's faults or mistakes.

Jumla's tremendous plasticity as a word has meant that it can be deployed as a noun, adjective and verb, in various combinations with English and regional language words, and produce a fascinating repertoire of newly coined terms. Consider, for instance, these terms that reveal jumla's versatility: *jumlanomics* alludes to the manipulation of statistics to exaggerate economic performance; *jumlabaaz* refers to an individual who deploys tricks of deception to promote his personal interest; *jumlajayanti* is the birth anniversary of a person who is considered a *jumlabaaz*; or *chunaavijumla* is a false promise made during an election campaign.

Despite jumla's strong association with falsehoods, it should not be confused with the petty lies and assorted shenanigans of a street-smart politician typically on display in the daily life of any liberal democracy. Jumla is particularly applicable to a category of politicians who have recently emerged in liberal democracies the world over and who might be considered as 'elected autocrats'. Symbolizing the era of post-truth politics, these types of politicians come to power through popular democratic mandate and use their popularity to advance authoritarian agendas. Jumla may be understood as an authoritarian political strategy used by 'elected autocrats' who show scant regard for personal rights or individual dignity.

The execution of jumla uses various instrumentalities of the state, and as such it is possible to identify three types of jumlas, categorized on the basis of the objectives they are required to serve: 'projection jumla', 'demolition jumla' and 'diversion jumla'. 'Projection jumla' involves a carefully crafted media campaign to forge origin stories about the humble roots of a politician and her or his awe-inspiring rise to the pinnacle of political power through sheer grit and personal merit, beating all the odds of an unfair socio-economic system. Such projection jumla circulate, for instance, as comic strips on social media, published children's books or doctored photographs of a past humble life. While 'projection jumla' is used to craft a certain larger than life image of the elected autocrat, 'demolition jumla' is meant to destroy the credibility and career of a political opponent. Demolition jumla makes ruthless use of security agencies, tax authorities and even media to collect or even fraudulently dig up damaging information about the opponents' financial or personal life. In Russia, the term used for the deployment of such demolition jumla is *kompremat* (compromising material), which has already made its way into the *Oxford English Dictionary*. Perhaps the most audacious of all jumlas is the category of 'diversion jumla'. This may involve ruthless use of state power to wage war or undertake risky economic measures, which can destroy the lives of millions of innocent people. It is used as a diversion tactic to shift away attention from real problems through reckless events designed to create fear psychosis or hate frenzy. Jumlanomics may well work as a 'diversion jumla' when reckless economic adventurism is undertaken by launching dubious economic measures ostensibly to eradicate evils, such as corruption. Here jumlanomics becomes a diversionary tactic to convince segments of the society, such as the poor, that the policy was needed to improve their lot even as they were adversely affected by it.

Just as nobody could have guessed jumla's unexpected entry into contemporary Indian public discourse, it is difficult to foresee its future trajectory. Given that jumla's present currency is closely tied to the advent of post-truth politics, a lot will depend on the prospects of this form of politics and the ways in which the vulnerabilities of liberal democracies are addressed.

References

Kaul, Nitasha. 'Rise of the Political Right in India: Hindutva-Development Mix, Modi Myth, and Dualities'. *Journal of Labor and Society* 20, no. 4 (2017): 523–48.
Schöttli, Jivanta and Markus Pauli. 'Modi-Nomics and the Politics of Institutional Change in the Indian Economy'. *Journal of Asian Public Policy* 9, no. 2 (2016): 154–69.

LAL BATTI (LĀL BATTĪ)

Manish Thakur

Beacons in general are used intentionally to draw attention to places, people, objects and situations of importance. Beacons are of many types and are widely used for navigational, military (including law and order), traffic, security and various other purposes. They come in different colours, such as red, blue, yellow, orange and green. The colours and sounds beacons make indicate what they mean. Among all the coloured beacons, it is the red one that is generally most prominent. Across the world, red beacons can symbolize many things: the state, restricted or no access, danger, state of alert, failure, bankruptcy and so on.

In India, the red beacon or *lal batti*, in Hindi, was, until as recently as 2017, a symbol of all of these mentioned in the previous sentence but with a difference. Above everything else, the Indian public associated the lal batti with not just institutions of state/government but also with the latter's ability to wield legitimate power or, as Max Weber said, authority. It multiplied manifold in the event of the vehicle moving, either as part of a secured motorcade or independently, with the lal batti switched on, rotating in high speed and the (police) siren blaring. An unlit, static, silent lal batti then was a benign sign of state authority, while a lit, mobile and audible one stood for modern, sophisticated, legitimate political power.

Until recently, Indians saw a white Ambassador car fitted with a lal batti as the most palpable and publicly visible display of power. Those privileged to have a lal batti vehicle were the ones who had access to the state – the ultimate symbol of public legitimacy in the euphoric aftermath of India's Independence. Lal batti was not meant to be a brutal and archaic show of power. It was not one of those premodern insignias which often inhabited the dynasties and monarchies of the past. It was not even a deliberate genuflection to the much-derided VIP culture that ultimately led to the total ban on colour beacons (except for use in ambulances and police vehicles) in May 2017. The countrywide endorsement of the fact that 'Lal batti is Off', as one national daily put it, had more to do with the accumulated public dislike of the contemporary political class and their bureaucratic co-conspirators. In other words, it was the passing of the nētā–babu centric lal batti (VIP) culture and not the lal batti per se which received public approval. In effect, the power symbolized by the lal batti was never absolute. It was not necessarily a symbol of unalloyed state power intended to create islands of privileges in an otherwise poor country teeming with deprived millions. The character of the lal batti also meant that it fuelled aspirations for one and all. Amidst the general constraints of resources and myriad situations of powerlessness in the everyday lives of millions of compatriots, the lal batti, however, symbolized the concentration of real and effective power in the hands of a select few.

Even as the lal batti was a way of representing a person's privileged access to state power, it had the embryonic potential to signal a new and more 'enabling/empowering' type of social stratification. At the time, when old certitudes of caste, land, *khandaan* (clan) and *biradaari* (caste association) were fast disappearing or at least did not carry the same weight as they did in the past, lal batti turned out to be some kind of civic–secular way of displaying a person's 'achieved' status as against older forms of primordial identities/statuses. It connoted an individual's merit, hard work, sailing through stiff competition to come at the top, perseverance and other such virtues which were supposed to be the stuff that successful men and women were made of. But of course, at another level, the lal batti was, to reiterate, part of an assortment of other insignias – siren, security cover – that distinguished this class of people from other ordinary Indians. This lal batti-aided class, consequently, contributed towards the making of an oppressive, undemocratic political (lal batti) culture.

Throughout history, the state has required communicable signs and symbols to assert its authority over citizens or, more generally, the ruled. Mostly, they were symbolic of crystallized hierarchy. However, in a democracy, the idea of political equality birthed a discourse where overt display of power and its attendant hierarchy was frowned upon. Not surprisingly, the recent ban on lal batti evoked an all-round unadulterated appreciation and a huge sigh of relief. Indeed, there was and continues to be an inherent incompatibility between (lal batti-signified) VIP culture and the principles and practices of democracy. The opposition to lal batti and its subsequent and successful ban points towards the specific case of resistance by the *aam aadmi* (common man) towards state-constructed hierarchies of power and privilege. In a larger sense though, it also indicates the spread of egalitarian principles of democracy that have made lal batti one of the most illegitimate of contemporary symbols.

References

Gupta, Krishna. 'Political Marketing in India 2014: Case of New Political Product AAP', January 2015, SSRN Electronic Journal, DOI: 10.2139/ssrn.2917075.

Jauregui, Beatrice. 'Beatings, Beacons, and Big Men: Police Disempowerment and Delegitimation in India'. *Law & Social Inquiry* 38, no. 3 (2013): 643–69.

LOK ADALAT (LŌK ADĀLAT)

Siddharth Peter De Souza

The term 'Lok adalat', which means 'people's court', is used with reference to an alternative dispute resolution forum, aimed at introducing informality, conciliation and accessibility to the otherwise adversarial court system of the state in India. Upendra Baxi documented one of the earliest templates of a Lok adalat in Rangpur, Gujarat, which was organized by the prominent Gandhian Harivallabh Parikh and grew largely due to his personal goodwill.[1] This forum was designed to adjudicate both inter- and intra-village disputes as well as disputes with administrative units. Disputes ranged from those relating to violence against the bodily integrity of a person to disputes regarding payment of debts or ownership of land as well as disputes around domestic and marital issues. The sanctions of the Lok adalat in these disputes included fines, public censure and social ostracism.

Around the 1970s, Justices Krishna Iyer and Bhagwati, in reports about legal aid reform, spoke of the need for forums that reflected conciliatory and indigenous traditions to be included and utilized in the administration of justice, as they felt this would enable making justice more accessible. Gujarat was the first state to use the term 'Lok adalat' in 1982 for a state-backed legal aid initiative. In this instance, a group of retired and sitting judges, social workers and socially aware members of the bar worked out of a van, a 'legal aid ambulance', and visited several villages giving free legal advice and encouraging potential litigants to find ways to negotiate a settlement for their disputes.[2]

With Lok adalats gaining popularity, there was an increasing demand to institutionalize these forums. In 1987, the Legal Services Authorities Act was passed.[3] This Act gave the Lok adalats statutory recognition and mandated that they be organized by state and district authorities in a manner they saw fit. Today, the Lok adalat is made up of a bench of a judge, an advocate and a social worker. In September 2017, the first transgender judge in India was appointed to a Lok adalat in West Bengal, in fulfilment of the requirement for a social worker on the bench.[4] Lok adalats have the jurisdiction to determine or find a compromise or settlement for any case referred to it, whether the case is pending before a court of law or is at a pre-litigative stage, provided it is a compoundable offence.

The decision of the Lok adalat, according to the Act, is deemed as the decree of a civil court and binding on the parties with no appeal to any court. An amendment to the Act in 2002 introduced the idea of a 'Permanent Lok adalat', which deals with specific kinds of cases, particularly those related to 'public utility services' such as transport, postal services, power and sanitation issues. There are various kinds among the regular Lok adalats: (a) the 'Mega Lok adalat' is organized on a single day across all courts of a particular state (i.e. the high court and the district courts); (b) the 'Mobile Lok adalat' involves taking a van to different areas to resolve petty cases as well as to spread legal awareness; (c) the 'Daily Lok adalat' is organized on a

---

[1] Baxi (1976).
[2] Gujarat State Legal Aid and Advice Board, 'Gujarat Legal Aid Ambulance Project: Lok Adalat'.
[3] 'The Legal Services Authority Act 1987'. http://nalsa.gov.in/acts (accessed 3 November 2017).
[4] 'In Another First, Bengal Gets a Transgender Lok Adalat Judge | Kolkata | Hindustan Times'. http://www.hindustantimes.com/kolkata/west-bengal-gets-a-transgender-lok-adalat-judge/story-PoFwwMctcQtQ8UFJiT13MK.html (accessed 3 November 2017).

daily basis; (d) a 'Continuous Lok adalat' discusses issues for a number of days and encourages parties to reflect on the different terms of the settlement and (e) the 'National Lok adalat' is held throughout the country from the Supreme Court to the courts at the taluk level.

Lok adalats have been heralded over the past few years for also reducing pendency and backlog of cases. According to the National Legal Services Authority, as of 30 September 2015, 15.14 lakh Lok adalats have been organized across India and over 8.25 crore cases have been settled.[5] In 2016, National Lok adalats were organized for matters relating to family or marital disputes, bank loan recovery claims, motor accidents and insurance claims, public service disputes over electricity, water, telephones and for transport and municipal matters.[6] For these reasons, there has been a growing push by the government and the judiciary to increase awareness around Lok adalats. Doordarshan has recently tied up with the National Legal Services Authority to highlight how Lok adalts have helped settle lakhs of cases around India in a series titled, *Akele Nahin Hai Aap* ('You are not alone').[7]

Despite Lok adalats expediting justice delivery, relaxing procedures and reducing costs, they have also received much criticism. Justice Krishna Iyer, who was one of the major proponents of the forums, criticized the Act because he felt it produced 'clumsy imitations of courts, not social mobilization schemes'.[8] Marc Galanter and Jayanth Krishnan argue that the only clear benefit of Lok adalats has been that they reduced the 'transaction costs' associated with the formal court system. According to them, these forums were instead instances of 'debased informalism' because they were built on aspects of avoidance of trial in the formal court system, rather than the benefits of an alternative model of dispute resolution.[9]

The Lok adalat has been associated with multifarious adjectives – from being an 'innovative' Indian contribution to enhancing access to justice by providing a hybrid type of dispute settlement, to an informal and indigenous forum with relaxed procedures aimed at justice for the poor, to stinging criticism for being nothing more than a poor imitation of a formal court. The Lok adalat has divided stakeholders, from litigants, lawyers and judges to academics, but it remains central in the imagination of those prescribing justice reforms, especially in the fight against pendency and in terms of improving the affordability and accessibility of the legal system in India.

References

Baxi, Upendra. 'From Takrar to Karar: The Lok Adalat at Rangpur'. *Journal of Constitutional and Parliamentary Studies* 10 (1976): 52.
Galanter, Marc and Jayanth K. Krishnan. 'Bread for the Poor: Access to Justice and the Rights of the Needy in India'. *Hastings Law Journal* 55 (2004): 789.
Krishna Iyer, V. R. *Legal Services Authorities Act: A Critique*. Society for Community Organisation Trust, 1988.

---

[5]'Lok Adalat | National Legal Services Authority'. http://nalsa.gov.in/lok-adalat (accessed 3 November 2017).
[6]Ibid.
[7]'Doordarshan to Broadcast Series on Cases Settled in Lok Adalats | The Indian Express'. http://indianexpress.com/article/india/doordarshan-to-broadcast-series-on-cases-settled-in-lok-adalats/ (accessed 3 November 2017).
[8]Krishna Iyer (1988).
[9]Galanter and Krishnan (2004).

MINORITIES

Peter Ronald deSouza

The term 'minorities' has been a keyword in Indian political discourse particularly since the partition of India. The two-nation theory which argued that Hindus and Muslims constitute two nations who could not live together gained parallel political constituencies, as the Muslim League and the Congress, during the struggle for independence from colonial rule, campaigned respectively for and against the idea. Since then the Indian political project of state-building has tried to debunk the theory through a four-pronged strategy of laws, institutions, policies and political discourse. Although the term 'minority' entered the political lexicon of India as a result of the Census of India 1881, when groups got a sense of their numerical strength vis--vis other groups, it gained traction during the Constituent Assembly which gave protection to religious and linguistic minorities (Articles 25–30). In its political usage today, the term 'minorities' has been expanded to refer to sexual minorities, especially after the Supreme Court judgement of September 2018 that struck down Article 377 of the Indian Penal Code that had hitherto criminalized homosexuality and to refer to minorities within minorities, that is, to groups within religious minorities who struggle internally for reform and who face oppression by the orthodox elements of the religious community.

As a descriptor, 'minorities' is a relational term that only makes sense when seen in relation to another group that is a majority. By itself there is no minority. Unlike European and North American history when states have used different strategies to deal with minority claims, from genocide (Jews in Nazi Germany), to expulsion (Kurds in Turkey), to suppression (Palestinians in Israel), to assimilation (Arabs in France), to integration (Hispanics in the United States), India has adopted a policy of accommodation of minorities. Both the traumatic experience of partition, where the country faced communal violence and killing, and the inspired leadership at independence, especially that of Jawaharlal Nehru, gave newly Independent India a philosophy on how to deal with its minorities. It is this philosophy that has guided the actions of the Indian state till the recent (2014) coming to power of a majoritarian political party, the BJP.

One area where minorities have faced challenges both internally, from their own minorities, and externally from majority groups, is in the area of reform of their personal laws. While many minority groups have willingly reformed their personal laws, the orthodox elements among the Muslim community have resisted this reform. In such conflicts, the courts have intervened with cases such as the famous Shah Bano case of 1985 and subsequent cases where gender justice and individual rights have, in the last instance, overridden community resistance. There is also a robust debate in the public sphere on legitimacy of a Uniform Civil Code for all communities where the public positions taken by the various groups have ranged from gender justice to religious freedom to community rights arguments. The jury is still out on this proposed initiative by the Indian state.

The edifice of protections available to minorities, that is, laws, institutions, policies and discourse, each of which needs to be studied, has produced a politics in India where groups are seeking to be formally recognized as minorities. Three such attempts may be mentioned, the Lingayats of Karnataka, the Ramakrishnan Mission in West Bengal and the Jains across India. Only the last has succeeded.

References

deSouza, Peter Ronald, Hilal Ahmed and Sanjeer Alam. *Democratic Accommodation: The Minority Question in India*. New Delhi: Bloomsbury India, 2019.

deSouza, Peter Ronald. 'Minority Rights and Democracy in India', chapter 64, *The SAGE Handbook of Political Sociology*, 2 vols., edited by William Outhwaite and Stephen Turner. London: Sage, 2018.

NAGAR PALIKA (NAGAR PĀLIKĀ)

George Mathew

In India, a municipal council is called *nagar palika*. The word *nagar* comes from the Sanskrit word *nag* which means 'static', like a mountain or a tree, and, therefore, nagar is a locality that doesn't move. The word *palika* is from the Sanskrit verb *palan*, which means 'one who fosters or brings up'. In the Dravidian language Tamil, *nagaram* refers to 'town'.

In ancient India (*c.* 2350 BCE), Harappa, Mohenjodaro, Kalibangan, Lothal, etc., were cities. By 600 BCE, several cities emerged in the Indo-Gangetic plains, of which there is reference to about sixteen *janapadas* (city states), such as Varanasi, Vaishali, Champa, Saket and Kaushambi. The British colonial rulers, who concentrated their attention mainly on establishing coastal trading centres, established the first municipal corporation in Madras on 29 September 1687. It was modelled on the British town council. Madras municipality is the oldest in the Commonwealth outside of the United Kingdom. Viceroy Lord Ripon gave a big push to the idea of local government in his Resolution on 18 May 1882. His idea was to nurse the citizens to emerge as local, provincial and national leaders. It may be mentioned here that Jawaharlal Nehru, who became the first prime minister of India in 1947, was elected as the chairman of the Allahabad municipality during 1923–5. Likewise, Sardar Vallabbhai Patel, the first home minister of independent India, entered public life as a municipal commissioner of Ahmedabad municipality in 1917 and later became its chairman in 1924. Subhash Chandra Bose was the chief executive officer (CEO) of Calcutta municipality and became the mayor in 1930.

Municipalities were not an integral part of the Constitution of India, which came into effect on 26 January 1950. They were given constitutional authority only four decades later, on 23 December 1992, through the Constitution (Seventy-Fourth Amendment) Act. On 1 June 1993, it came into force as Part IX A of the Constitution.

At present, there are 2,796 municipalities at three levels in India: (a) 149 municipal corporations which have a population of over 300,000; (b) 927 municipalities which have a population of up to 300,000; and (c) 1,720 nagar panchayats/town panchayats, each of which have a population of 25,000 or above.

In the nagar palika, members are elected for a term of five years, who in turn elect their chairman (mayor in the council system). In some municipalities, mayors are directly elected. More than 33 per cent of the members and mayors are required to be women. State government officials are appointed to handle the administrative affairs of the nagar palikas. Eighteen subjects, including urban planning, water supply, public health and poverty alleviation, have been transferred to the nagar palikas, according to the Constitution.

References

Bhagat, Ram B. 'Rural-Urban Classification and Municipal Governance in India'. *Singapore Journal of Tropical Geography* 26, no. 1 (2005): 61–73.

Singh, U. B. *Revitalised Urban Administration in India: Strategies and Experiences*. New Delhi: Gyan Publishing House, 2002.

NATIONAL, ANTI-NATIONAL

Kaisser Rana

The word 'nation' originated from the Middle English *nacioun*, which was in turn borrowed from the old French word *nacion* and the Latin word *nationem*, both literally meaning 'birth'. Historically, the word nation constituted a stable community of the people, formed on the basis of a common language, territory, economic life and ethnicity.

Principally, nationalism is the outcome of the theory of nation that believes sharing a common language, history and culture should constitute an independent nation, free of foreign domination. In fact, the new system that emerged in the modern world is the consequence of the shattering of the old despotic rule of monarchs by the outbreak of revolution in some parts of Europe and later in other countries. Obviously, one can't deny the fact that the new system also brought in new types of despots who were scientifically more advanced, technically savvy and politically shrewd. So, we can conclude that though the mode of production changed with the arrival of a new system, the profit motive of the individual remained intact in the new system, that is, capitalism. Therefore, in the words of George Orwell, 'Nationalism is power hunger tempered by self-deception.'

Independence from tyrannical colonial rule gave rise to a new India that was in the early stages after being liberated. Historically, even before the arrival of Islam, Indian society has remained a diverse society – divided along lines of caste, language, religion and culture. The entire subcontinent was fragmented into small and big kingdoms. The invasion of the Mughals from West Asia did not transform Indian society and politics. Instead they fitted themselves within this framework by adopting the habits and manners of the society they encountered. These fragmentations continued to exist even during the British rule and in post-Independence India. That is the reason why the Indian Constitution never proclaimed the idea of one language, one religion and one identity. Though it declared India as a nation, it significantly stressed the idea of a country rather than a nation. This meant that India could not be called a nation objectively, as it could never be identified with the theory of nation in principle. However, ironically, there have been, in existence, groups that are against the policy of coexistence of diverse communities. They oppose the very idea of a secular India and advocate expulsion of minority communities from the country. In *Bunch of Thoughts*, M. S. Golwalkar, the second *sarsanghchalak* (chief) of the Rashtriya Swayamsevak Sangh (an organization that urges India to be a Hindu nation with one language and one identity), while hailing Hitler and Nazism, expresses, 'To keep up the purity of the race and its culture, Germany shocked the world by her purging the country of the Semitic races – the Jews. Race pride at its highest has been manifested here.' Further, writing on religion and politics, he targets Muslims, Christians and Communists while claiming that 'hostile elements within the country pose a far greater menace to national security than aggressors from outside'.

In recent times, both within the political establishment and in a section of society, the issue of nationalism or the nationalist is hugely debated. Most of these debates or discussions centres around either praising one as a nationalist or defaming a dissenting voice by labelling her or him as anti-nationalist and sometimes or occasionally a section as Pakistani or Maoist. The outcome of the 2014 parliamentary elections, especially, has given rise to a new trend in society; if you are against any of Prime Minister Narendra Modi's policies, or disagree with RSS's fanatical ideology, and if you voice it out publicly, then you are bound to be called anti-national one day or the other. The fallout of this sentiment is that Muslims are being publicly lynched, the atrocities on Dalits have risen to alarming heights and students who have traditionally held dissenting voices are not being spared.

Today, the words nation and nationalism need a deeper and wider debate, especially because of the emergence of a grave force of spectre which haunts minorities, progressive sections of society, women, students, the working classes and peasants. One also needs to exactly define with more accuracy the difference between nationalism and anti-nationalism. This is so that the crowd doesn't act as policeman, judge and executer.

References

Gorski, Philip S. 'The Mosaic Moment: An Early Modernist Critique of the Modernist Theory of Nationalism'. *American Journal of Sociology* 105, no. 5 (March 2000): 1428–68.
Greenfield, Liah. *Nationalism: Five Roads to Modernity*. Cambridge: Harvard University Press, 1992.

NAXALITE (NAKSLĀ'IṮ)

Bela Bhatia

The term 'Naxalite' entered the Indian political scene in 1967. An uprising of labourers and peasants against the oppressive *jotedar*s (landlords) in the villages of Naxalbari, West Bengal, was to open a new chapter in the history of the Communist movement in India. The uprising was carried out under the leadership of the more radical within the Communist Party of India (Marxist) (CPI[M]). Peasants forcibly occupied land and cancelled old debts by burning records. The uprising was brutally suppressed by the state government, ironically with the CPI (M) as its main constituent, leading to a split within the ranks of the party and the formation of the Communist Party of India (Marxist-Leninist) (CPI[ML]).

In its self-definition, the CPI (ML) was a revolutionary party and adhered to Marxism, Leninism and Mao Tse-tung as ideological guides. The uprising and the dramatic events that followed caught the interest of the media and in that flame of reportage was born the 'Naxalite' – the revolutionary who wanted not only practical change but also a change in the political order. The CPI (ML) was factious almost from the start. It had undergone one major split in 1971 even before the death of one of its main leaders, Charu Mazumdar. After his death in 1972, more splits and mergers occurred for ideological and other reasons.

Today, it is difficult to say exactly how many CPI (ML) parties there are. According to one estimate, there were dozens of CPI (ML) parties at one stage. These parties, along with those who remained outside it but also organized themselves into similar parties (e.g. the Maoist Communist Centre [MCC]), together form the Naxalite movement. Revolution is the common aim of all these parties, though differences on questions of strategy and tactics remain.

The CPI (Maoist), formed in 2004 after a merger of the CPI (ML), People's War and the MCC is considered as the largest party today. It is often overlooked that while Maoists are Naxalites, not all Naxalites are Maoists. For the people who are part of the mass base, however, they are *annas* (elder brothers, in Telugu), *sathis* (companions, in Hindi) or simply 'comrade'. *Lal salaam* is a familiar greeting in these parts.

State repression followed the initial spurt of the Naxalite movement in the late 1960s. Midnight knocks on doors by the police, torture in prison and thousands of stories of fake encounters shocked the nation. The declaration of Emergency led to the arrest of many leaders of the movement, while many others went underground. The second phase of the movement began after 1975. Those in prison were released, mergers followed and a phase of powerful mass movements began. Three features mark this phase. First, the Naxalites were effective in mobilizing those at the lowest rungs of society for their basic economic, social and political rights against the powerful feudal elements. Second, even though the Naxalites were armed during this phase, the nature and scale of violence was different. There were occasions when a struggle for minimum wage, payment of overdue wages, land rights or rape of labouring women took on the colour of war. Third, despite lethal conflicts between Naxalite parties in the Bihar of the mid-1990s, a parallel history of caste *senas* (armies) and numerous massacres perpetrated by them on the mostly Dalit landless labourers and farmers, and the fake encounters that had become routine, the Naxalite movement had become a force to reckon with. The third phase of the Naxalite movement can be said to have begun with the ushering in of the new economic policies in India in the early 1990s. Its practical ill effects on the ground could be discerned by the early 2000s in the tribal areas of Jharkhand, Orissa and Chhattisgarh, when memorandums of understanding (MoUs) with mining corporates surfaced. It is hard to think of the timing of the then prime minister's pronouncement of the CPI (Maoist) as 'the greatest internal security threat' as a mere coincidence. This war has included several operations from the side of the state, including the police, paramilitary and local vigilante groups. The most notorious of these vigilante operations is the *Salwa Judum* (purification hunt, in Gondi), which was a brutal exercise in 'strategic hamletting', initially projected as a spontaneous people's movement against the Maoists.

At the time of my research on the Naxalite movement in Central Bihar, in the mid-1990s, the term Naxalite was part of people's everyday vocabulary. The term, however, was understood in many different ways. Even those who were part of the movement gave very diverse answers when I asked them, 'Everybody calls you naxalites. What is your understanding of who a naxalite is, and what does the term mean?' People's responses revealed telling perceptions of the term and of the Naxalite movement itself.

Often, Naxalites were known mainly for their violent deeds, but there were many interesting variants as well, based for instance on thinking that 'naxa' means 'map' (*naksha*) or that 'lite' means 'light' (*prakash*) or the more upbeat view of 'naslite' as the 'next light'. The Naxalites were popularly called *garibon ki party* (The party of the poor) in Bihar.

'Naxalite', however, had also become a term of abuse in the hands of the upper castes, the administration and the police. Sometimes, the abuse was taken to ridiculous lengths. For example, pro-poor public administrators have also been labelled as Naxalites in Bihar.

The Naxalite movement is a class struggle and has had to face retaliatory anger from those who felt threatened by it. Without acknowledging the rights that the movement tried to uphold, rights that they were complicit in suppressing, these opposing forces focused only on the violence of the Naxalites and called them *ugravadi* (extremists) or *aatankvadi* (terrorists). This notion of the Naxalite also gained currency after the formation of the CPI (Maoist) and the large-scale military actions undertaken by the People's Liberation Guerrilla Army (PLGA). These actions, involving sophisticated weapons like improvised explosive devices (IEDs), have caused mass killings of security forces and politicians. Guerrilla warfare is resented also because it is seen as war by deception and, hence, cowardly.

Ever since right-wing governments have come to power at the state and national levels, talking of the movement as a terrorist movement has gained salience. Increasingly, the movement has been purged of its ideological content, and left and democratic forces have been branded as 'Maoist', *'naxali dalal'* (Naxalite agents) or 'Naxali sympathizer' (*Maoist samarthak*).

The future of the Naxalite movement is uncertain. On the one hand, the policies and circumstances that pushed people to join or support the movement continue. Counter-insurgency operations themselves, freely overstepping the rule of law, have contributed to the survival and spread of the movement. On the other, reliance on violence and fear can have corrupting influences and that applies to the Maoists as well. While the Indian state is primarily responsible for the creation of the Naxalite, perhaps the time has come for the Naxalite movement to reinvent itself.

References

Bhatia, Bela. 'The Naxalite Movement in Central Bihar', unpublished PhD dissertation submitted to the University of Cambridge in 2000.
Bhatia, Bela. 'The Naxalite Movement in Central Bihar'. *Economic and Political Weekly* 40, no. 15 (2005): 1536–49.

NORTHEAST INDIA

Pradip Phanjoubam

In the Indian context, the word 'northeast' is now a proper noun. Unlike what the name suggests, northeast no longer connotes just a region of India located in that direction but has come to have many layers of nuanced meanings. These include cultural, developmental, geographical, strategic and racial. Northeast points to a group of eight states in India's extreme east, connected to subcontinental India by a narrow corridor which, at its narrowest, is about twenty kilometres wide and is often referred to as the Siliguri corridor. What makes the region unique is that it shares only approximately 2 per cent of its boundary with the country it is part of, and the remaining 98 per cent with Bhutan, China, Myanmar, Bangladesh and Nepal. The immense cultural, linguistic and ethnic diversity of the region, therefore, is only to be expected.

The British formally annexed Assam in 1826 with the signing of the Treaty of Yandaboo with the then Ava (Burmese) kingdom which had invaded and occupied Assam. After its annexation, Assam was initially made a part of Bengal, and British administrative records began using the term North-East while referring to this new territory.

In 1873, the Bengal Eastern Frontier Regulation was introduced. This regulation created the contentious 'Inner Line' drawn along the foot of the hills which virtually surround Assam's two major river valleys, dividing the revenue districts in the plains and the non-revenue hills inhabited by 'wild tribes'.

Territories beyond the Inner Line were considered as backward tracts and largely excluded from modern revenue administration that the British introduced. In 1914, some hill tracts in North Assam were marked off as the North-East Frontier Tracts (NEFT). By the Government of India Act of 1919, the NEFT and all other territories beyond the Inner Line were classified as 'Excluded Areas' and left out of the newly introduced partly representative provincial government.

After Independence, NEFT was made a part of Assam state and in 1951 this region was renamed North-East Frontier Agency (NEFA). On 21 January 1972, NEFA became a Union Territory and was rechristened Arunachal Pradesh. On 20 February 1987, Arunachal Pradesh was given full statehood. While NEFA thus ceased to be the name, the phrase 'North-East' remained and began to be used to jointly refer to all the eight states of the region.

The British did not consider the North-East as emotionally, culturally and ethnically part of subcontinental India, and this outlook became pronounced as Indian Independence became imminent. Administrative notes by British civil servants are loud testimonies of this. Olaf Caroe, for instance, wrote a paper 'The Mongolian Fringe' (1940), which referenced the Himalayan region, including areas such as Nepal, Sikkim, Bhutan and Northern Assam, as racially different from 'India Proper', as it was inhabited predominantly by people with Mongolian ethnic affinities.

Indeed, this alienation continued after Indian Independence. No document is a more pronounced alibi than Sardar Vallabhbhai Patel's letter dated 7 November 1950 to Prime Minister Jawaharlal Nehru. In this letter, Patel is unambiguous about an irredentist suspicion of the 'non-mainstream' North-East: 'The undefined state of the frontier and the existence on our side of a population with its affinities to the Tibetans or Chinese have all the elements of potential trouble between China and ourselves.'

One of independent India's early efforts at coming to terms and undoing some of these psychological scars suffered was the formation of the North Eastern Council (NEC) in 1971. In 2001, the union government created a minor (state) ministry with independent charge, called Development of the North Eastern Region (DoNER) and the NEC came to be one of its charges. However, alongside these commendable efforts, the Northeast continues to be administered as a frontier inhabited by people with dubious emotional affiliations with the nation. The continued promulgation of the draconian Armed Forces Special Powers Act (AFSPA) 1958 in the region is evidence of the same. India has not heeded appeals, even by the United Nations Human Rights Commission, to repeal/modify AFSPA. Expectedly, charges of state atrocities on civilian populations in the Northeast and Kashmir are aplenty.

Besides AFSPA, there are two other laws peculiar to the Northeast: the Protected Area Permit (PAP) and the Restricted Area Permit (RAP). The PAP requires all foreigners who wish to travel to some Northeast states to first acquire a special permit. The RAP restricts foreigners from travelling to certain designated areas within these states even if they have the PAP. Since 1 January 2011, the PAP has been conditionally relaxed for extendable leashes of one year at a time. Foreigners, except nationals of Afghanistan, Pakistan and China, can now visit these states, though they are required to inform state authorities of their presence at their points of entry. The RAP areas have also been considerably reduced.

In recent times, economic stagnation and spiritual ennui have compelled many from the Northeast to migrate to the vibrant metropolises of India in search of better education and employment, Delhi and Bangalore being the choice destinations for now. In these cities, many of them are again exposed to the ugly reality of cultural clash. They discover in everyday civil life that 'the Mongolian Fringe' is generally seen as 'non-mainstream' in culture, food habits, dress and social mores. This is not always in hostile terms but also at times in wonderment, the way tourists would experience exotic cultures, people and landscapes – appreciative so long as the distance between the observer and observed is not allowed to collapse. Things however change when the exotic comes to be next door. The Northeast person then begins to suffer routine microaggressions, such as being condescendingly addressed as 'chinky', 'momo', 'pahari', etc. They also face widespread ignorance about their home states and are often asked if they are Indians. When they reply in the affirmative, their answers are met with disbelief. Earlier charms of the exotic also transform to images of primitivism, tribal affiliations, underdevelopment, , easy-going and laidback lifestyles and so on. It is amidst this milieu of hopelessness, stagnation and alienation, together with the historical disconnects that British administrators pointed out, that several violent ethnic insurrections, fighting for goals ranging from autonomy to complete sovereignty, came to be born.

In this sense, the Northeast is a challenge to its nation's capacity to reinvent the idea of India to accommodate the 'non-mainstream'. The effort has more often than not, descended to a paternalistic political correctness, marked by exaggerated overtures to avoid imagined hurts to the Northeast person, or else calling upon the latter to join the mainstream, implying inadvertently that the Northeast people as they are cannot be fully part of the idea of India.

The term Northeast carries all these meanings. It is, in short, the story of a postcolonial struggle of communities in the region on one plane, and India on another, to give a dignified place to an identity forged at its inception by colonial administrative needs.

References

Baruah, Sanjib. 'The Mongolian Fringe'. *Himal Southasian* 26, no. 1 (January 2013): 82–6. Available at: http://himalmag.com/the-mongolian-fringe/ (accessed 20 October 2017).
Scott, James C. *Art of Not Being Governed: An Anarchic History of Upland South East Asia*. Hyderabad: Orient BlackSwan, 2010.

PANCHAYATI RAJ (PAÑCĀYATĪ RĀJ)

George Mathew

The term *panchayati raj* refers to self-governing village communities characterized by agrarian economies that existed in ancient India. The word *panch* means five in Sanskrit. *Panchayat*s in the early days meant five people managing the affairs of their village. Panchayats could decide as to what those living in the village can or cannot do. Panchayats are mentioned in the *Rig Veda* which dates back to 1200 BCE. Panchayats were the line of contact with the higher authorities on all matters affecting the village. They had both police and judicial powers. Religion and custom elevated panchayats to the sacred position of authority leading to different castes in Indian society (mainly in the Indo-Gangetic plains) having caste panchayats to ensure that persons belonging to different castes adhered to its code of social conduct and ethics. In South India, village panchayats had village assembly with an executive body having members of various groups and castes. In both North and South India, panchayats were the pivot of administration and the centre of social life and solidarity. It remained unchanged right up to the medieval age.

During the Mughal period, judicial powers of the panchayats were curtailed, but local affairs remained unregulated from above. Village officers and servants were answerable primarily to the panchayat. Although Charles Metcalfe, a British provisional general of India, called these village communities 'little republics', they were caste-ridden and feudal and far from democratic and participatory. During the British colonial period, self-contained village communities and panchayats were replaced by formally constituted institutions of village administration. Lord Mayo's resolution of 1870 on local self-government revived the traditional village panchayat system in Bengal through the Bengal Chowkidari Act, which empowered district magistrates to set up panchayats of nominated members. The government resolution of 18 May 1982, providing for local boards with a large majority of elected non-official members, presided over by a non-official chairperson, is considered as the Magna Carta of local democracy in India.

In fact, village panchayats were central to the ideological framework of India's national movement. For Gandhi, his vision of village panchayats was a complete republic based on perfect democracy and individual freedom. The village panchayats were therefore included in the Directive Principles of State policy (Part IV, Article 40) of the Indian Constitution after Independence. In 1957, Balwant Rai Mehta committee recommended democratic decentralization and 'public participation in community works … through statutory representative bodies'. This report urged to accelerate the pace of constituting panchayats in all the states. The first Panchayat was inaugurated by Prime Minister Jawaharlal Nehru on 2 October 1959 in Nagaur, Rajasthan. The term Panchayati raj came into vogue conceptually as a process of governance only later, after the Parliament amended the Constitution on 23 December 1992, making panchayats the 'institutions of self-government'. Today, Panchayati raj refers to a system of organically linking people from *gram sabha* (village assemblies) to Lok Sabha, the lower house of Parliament. Elections are held to posts every five years at three levels: village, block and district. As of 2014, there are a total of 2,950,128 elected representatives in Panchayati raj institutions out of which almost 50 per cent are women.

References

Mathew, George. *Panchayati Raj from Legislation to Movement*. New Delhi: Concept Publishing Company, 1994.

Mathur, Mukut Vehari and Iqbal Narain. 'Panchayati Raj, Planning and Democracy'. In *Panchayati Raj, Planning and Democracy*. Bombay: Asia Publishing House, 1969.

PARTITION

Salil Misra

The twentieth century may be designated as a century of partitions. While a large number of partitions occurred throughout the century, the partition of the Indian subcontinent into two nation-states of India and Pakistan is in some ways the most unique. It is distinctive above all in its scale of violence and displacement. Close to 3 million people died in the violence that accompanied Partition and well over seventy thousand women were abducted, raped and displaced. The partition of India actually included two other partitions, the partitions of Punjab and Bengal. About 12 million people migrated from West Punjab to East Punjab and Delhi and from East Punjab to West Punjab and Sind. The migrations in Bengal occurred in a continuous, seamless manner. This is easily the largest migration in human history around a single event. What is more important, these migrations were driven not by a search for better opportunities but by the desire for survival. Often people left a life of comfort and settled for a life of penury and misery.

What was the partition and why did it happen? India was, and still is, a large and multireligious society. Before Partition, Muslims constituted nearly 25 per cent of the population in British India. They constituted a majority in four regions – Punjab, Bengal, Sind and the North-West Frontier Provinces (NFWP) – and were scattered in the rest of the country as religious minorities. On the whole, two-thirds of India's Muslims were organized as a regional majority and one-third as minority. With the beginning of modern politics in the twentieth century, different political claims for concessions and safeguards were made from time to time by political leaders and organizations claiming to represent Indian Muslims. These demands were sometimes made to the British colonial government and sometimes to the Indian National Congress, since it was the largest political organization that claimed to represent all Indians, irrespective of religion, region and language.

Around 1940, a novel claim was made by Mohammad Ali Jinnah, the president of the All India Muslim League. The claim was that Indian Muslims were not a religious minority needing safeguards but a separate nation and were therefore entitled to their own separate, representative and sovereign nation-state. The new demand was that Muslim majority provinces (Punjab, Bengal, Sind and NWFP) should be carved out from India and constituted into a single sovereign state. This demand came to be known as the Pakistan resolution and after prolonged and acrimonious negotiations involving the colonial state, the Congress and the Muslim League, it was conceded. In 1947, India became free and was partitioned. Punjab and Bengal, two provinces with significant non-Muslim minorities of nearly 44 per cent were also partitioned. Yet until as late as 14 August that year, most people in Punjab and Bengal did not know which districts would go to Pakistan and which to India.

Why did Partition happen? The question can be explained by explaining three major transformations that swept the subcontinent during the nineteenth and initial decades of the twentieth centuries: social, politico-ideological and programmatic. First, social transformation. An enormously large number of small, local, ritualistic and syncretic communities began to be transformed into pan-Indian, internally standardized, externally differentiated, religious communities. This was a fairly long process and resulted in the creation of the finished product of pan-Indian communities of Hindus and Muslims out of an extremely complex and diverse raw material of local communities. Second, politico-ideological transformation. This transformation was later designated as communalism; however, it began with looking upon religious communities as political constituencies and transform them as such. Communalism was initially confined only to the upper classes and only reached out to the middles classes in the 1920s. However, by the late 1930s, it had successfully reached the masses and had transformed into a mass force. Third, programmatic transformation. This was a transformation that occurred in the politics of the Muslim League. From an organization demanding safeguards and concession for Muslims as a minority, it transformed into a platform seeking nationhood for Indian Muslims as a national community.

The story of Partition is not simply that of an episode that occurred in 1947. It unleashed a huge chain of events which have cast their spell on the political and social life of South Asia. Partition was meant to solve the minority problem; but it actually ended up exacerbating the minority problem in both the new countries. This was also the beginning of the Kashmir problem, which remains unresolved even today. India and Pakistan have not really lived like happy neighbours, as was anticipated by some during Partition. The two countries have gone to war with each other four times (1947, 1965, 1971 and 1998). Pakistan was partitioned once again in 1971, with the creation of the new country of Bangladesh. Much of South Asia, therefore, still lives in the shadows of the Partition of 1947.

References

Kudaisya, Gyanesh and Tan Tai Yong. *The Aftermath of Partition in South Asia*. London: Routledge, 2000.
Singh, Anita Inder. *The Origins of the Partition of India*. New Delhi: Oxford University Press, 1987.

PATWARI (PAṬVĀRĪ)

Ramana Murthy V. Rupakula

Patwari is the traditional village administrative and revenue official at the grass-roots, with the assigned duties of keeping land records and statistical data for crop production. The term Patwari may vary from region to region; for example, near synonyms of the word include terms such as *Kulkarni, Karanam, Adhikari, Talati, Patel, Lumberdar,* and so on in different regions of India.

The historical roots of the office of the patwari date back to *Munsabdari* system, introduced by Sher Shah Suri in sixteenth century, improved by the Mughals and later modified by the British. Patwari traditionally came from the *Brahmin* and *Kayasth* castes and were subordinate to other villager officials called *Mali Patel* (the term varied) who would assess and remit irrigation cess to the treasury. These officials would in turn work under police as *patel* or *mansab* in charge of law and order. A patwari was trained in the measurement of land, cropped areas, agricultural production and the assessment of tax, and received a salary from the Mansabdar. Under this system, the post was acquired by inheritance and called *watandari*.

The role of the patwari changed with the introduction of *ryotwari settlements* by the British administration, under which individual property rights were introduced. In addition to the assessment of production and tax, the patwari was now assigned the duty of maintaining the

Record of Rights (Register of Land Titles); record of private lands and their mutation; and record of government lands, common lands, uncultivable wastes, roads, tanks, ponds, canals, tank bed and forest land.

After independence, when this agricultural taxation was abolished, the duties of the patwari concerned three things: (i) the maintenance of the records of rights and mutation, the record of public and common properties and the assessment of water cess; (ii) the maintenance of the statistical record of acreage under different crops and (iii) the maintenance of the statistical record of births and deaths, livestock, certification of caste, profession and income of village people. This is supposed to have involved maintaining sixty-four different registers.

Beyond the mundane functions of the patwari, his role in the political economy of rural affairs must be understood. As a revenue official he was an extractive agent in the Mughal period. In the colonial period, besides the traditional extractive role with discretionary power, he had acquired another important function: that of the custodian of the Registry of Rights. He thus wielded considerable social and political power in the village and possessed detailed confidential information. Property rights, always a bundle of rights, have to be associated with interpretation. Among a largely illiterate peasant society, the patwari thus enjoyed considerable socio-economic and bureaucratic power, with the predictable effect that his office could involve corruption.

There is an interesting continuation of bureaucratic power of the patwari even in the post-independent period, even as his functions underwent fundamental alterations. The postcolonial state, being a modern bourgeois welfare state, proposes several reforms and welfare measures. Now the functional role of patwari changed from being an extractive agent to that of a gatekeeper of *governmentality*. The collection of agricultural taxation gradually disappears during this period and water cess remains nominal, thus reducing an old source of power that the patwari previously had. However, new sources of power simultaneously open up. Land transfers remain a prominent area of rent-seeking and even fraud. Cases of land reform are even more notorious, where landlords manage to conceal swathes of surplus land with the active collusion of the patwari. Ironically, the office remains a subject and agent of the rural oligarchy, as governments often refused to pay salaries to the patwari in several states.

A similar situation obtains regarding welfare schemes for the poor. Several anti-poverty schemes are introduced by the state in rural areas over time, and these are resented by the rural elite since they fear losing control over labour processes. In many states, benefits are usurped by landlords again with the collusion of the lower bureaucracy. Issuance of ration cards, voter cards, caste and income certificates, employment guarantee schemes, pensions, scholarships, and so on, all involve the endorsement of the patwari, whose efficiency often reflects the prevailing configuration of class power in the countryside.

Having discussed the historical role of this office, it would be incorrect to say that it has not evolved. First, the inheritance or the *watandari* system and single caste dominance was abolished. Second, several state governments have recently made the office of the patwari a salaried and transferable post, so that their local influence is reduced. Of late, after land records have been computerized in several states, the role of the patwari in land transfers has been reduced, especially in the South Indian states. However, there is no denying that the patwari has played a significant role in shaping bureaucratic power in contemporary rural bourgeois society. At the present time, the patwari is capable of becoming a catalytic agent in urbanizing rural spaces, converting agricultural land into real estate. In the precolonial, colonial, as well as the postcolonial periods, the role of the patwari appears to have been pivotal in reflecting the political economy of society.

References

Baden-Powell, Henry. *The Indian Village Community: Examined with Reference to the Physical, Ethnographic, and Historical Condition of the Provinces; Chiefly on the Basis of the Revenue-Settlement Records and District Manuals*, 598, 735–6, 1896. Available at: https://archive.org/details/indianvillage.com/page/n8.
Dantwala, Mohanlal Lalloobhai and Shah, C. H. *Evaluation of Land Reforms: General Report*, 167, 179–80, Dept. of Economics, University of Bombay, 1971.
Mishra Prachee and Roopal Suhag, 2017, *Land Records and Titles in India*. Available at: http://www.prsindia.org/uploads/media/Analytical%20Report/Land%20Records%20and%20Titles%20in%20India.pdf-.

PEASANT MOVEMENTS

Muzaffar Assadi

Any explanation of peasant movements requires explanation of the social category called peasantry. The term 'peasant' originated from the fifteenth-century French word *paisant*, which means 'one from the countryside'. During this period, the equivalent terms of use in North India were *rayat*, *kisan* and *dehati*. Rayat is used in the common sense to mean farmers, while kisan is used for any cultivator who lives on agriculture for her or his sustenance. Another term used to refer to a peasant is dehati, which literally means 'rural bumpkin'. The terms used in South India to denote peasants include *raitha* and *raithulu* (in Telugu), *vivasaayikal* (in Tamil), *shetkari* (in Marathi) and *raithapi* and *krishikaru* (in Kannada). There are different categories within these broader peasant category: for instance, poor peasants are called *bada raitha*, middle peasants are called *madhyama raitha* and rich peasants are called *shrimanta raitha*. In academic discourse, two terms have come to be broadly used with the changing political economy: 'peasant' and 'farmer'. The peasant is often identified with the rural population, who depends on agriculture for her or his livelihood and uses simple tools and technology for their subsistence. The farmer is a new category of peasant who produces surplus. They are peasants who have transformed into a market-dependant social category as a result of the changing political economy and are, therefore, known as 'market-oriented autonomous farmers'.

Kulak is another term used as an academic category in India. The kulak is largely seen as rich peasant category with reactionary tendencies. The origin of the term lies in the European context and was extensively used by Karl Marx in the American context and Vladimir Lenin in the Russian context. Lenin used this category to analyse why kulaks became reactionary in the context of the Russian revolution. Indian Marxists have also used this term, but with caution, as Indian kulaks did not play the same role as their counterparts in Russia. On the contrary, Indian kulaks did play a significant role in defeating land reforms and cornering the benefits of the Green Revolution.

This brings us to the crux of this entry on peasant movements in India. Differentiations and multiple meanings of the term 'peasant' have distilled into understanding the peasant movements as well. In fact, peasant movements in the Indian context can broadly be divided into two neat categories: peasant movement and farmers' movement. The term 'peasant movement' is used to refer to those movements that surfaced much before the Green Revolution. Multiple terms have been used to describe such peasant movements: peasant resistance, peasant revolution, peasant revolt, including the fact that such movements were also treated as *satyagrahas* (non-violent civil resistance movements). Locally, they are referred to as *raithapi pratiroda, raithapi kranti, raitha chaluvali, raithara dhange, kisan prathirod, kisan sangarsh* and *kisan andolan*.

Many a times, such terms are coined by and during the movements themselves. Deccan peasant movements came to be known as the Deccan Revolt of 1875, the movement led by the Mapillas became the Mapilla rebellion or riots (1921), the Nagar movement of 1830–4 in modern-day Karnataka became known as Nagara Raithara Dange or peasant uprising. In such cases, the terms revolt, rebellion and uprising are used synonymously as they convey the meaning of a series of severe uprisings or resistances led by the peasants, spanning many years, against exploiters such as the zamindars, middlemen or even the state. Mostly, they are not free from violence.

Almost all the peasant movements that came under the influence, or were led by the nationalist movement or Gandhi, are categorized as peasant or kisan satyagrahas. For instance, Champaran, Bardoli and Kheda satyagrahas led by Gandhi and the Oudh peasant movement led by Kisan Sabhas are categorized as peasant movements. Two more terms are used for peasant movements: *kisan pratirodh* and *raitha chaluvali*. These are used to explain the peasants' opposition through different forms such as picketing, band, long marches and sitting in dharna. These protests occurred in post-Independence India and largely followed the Gandhian path of non-violent resistance. They protested against price rise, heavy taxation and deteriorating conditions of agriculture.

We now come to the second category of protests following the Green Revolution, that is, during the 1980s, known as 'farmers' movements'. In fact, the term farmer's movement has now been replaced in academic discourse with the phrase 'new farmers' movement'. Scholars such as T. J. Byrce, Tom Brass, Jairus Banaji, Zoya Hasan and Muzaffar Assadi have used this term to explain the arrival of a new set of farmers' movement in the states of Maharashtra, Karnataka, Uttar Pradesh, Tamil Nadu and Punjab. These movements conceptualized their rhetoric using the local idiom and used strategies such as *gav bhandi* (village closure), *chakka jam* (stopping production) and *chalo padayatra* (start of long march) in their struggle. Their demands included *kajra mukti* (freedom from debts), *sala manna* (loan waiver) and *lakshmi mukti* (freedom from dependency). And, the green cap (*hasiru topi*), green shawl and green flag they sported became symbols of their resistance.

An important question at this juncture is the following: can we refer to tribal struggles as peasant movements? While the terms Adivasi, *moola nivasi, budakattu* and *vanavasi* are used to identify populations whose practices are animistic or those who live in and depend on forest resources, they have been victims of land appropriation and physical violence by the state, market forces and global capital. Since tribals are subjected to land alienation and exploitation just like peasants, scholars such as A. R. Desai have treated their struggles as part of peasant struggle. This is why the academic discourse is filled with terms such as Adivasi *dhange* and Adivasi *horata*, despite being explained as either a 'struggle' or 'rebellion' or 'insurrection'. For instance, the following cases of tribal movements have been characterized variably as farmers' movements and Adivasi uprisings: the Halba rebellion (1774–9), the Koli uprising (1784–5), the Tamar tribal revolt (1794–5), the Kond tribal revolt (1850), the Santhal insurrection (1855–6), the Tana Bhagat struggle (1914), the Birsa Munda rebellion (1900), the Koya tribal revolt (1920) and the Gond revolt (1940). These inconsistencies show that such terms have no fixed meaning in academic discourse, rendering the demarcation of a movement from struggle or resistance rather difficult to identify. They have either become overlapping or ambiguous categories.

References

Banaji, Jairus. 'The Farmers' Movements: A Critique of Conservative Rural Coalitions'. *The Journal of Peasant Studies* 21, no. 3–4 (1994): 228–45.
Brass, Tom. *New Farmers' Movements in India*. London: Routledge, 2014.

POLITICAL PARTIES

Ashutosh Kumar

The word 'party' is derived from the Latin word *patir* which means 'to divide'. For close to two centuries, the term was usually applied in a negative sense to describe divisions along the lines of political ideas, support for a particular leader or personal interests which would threaten peaceful government and disturb national order. It was only by the early twentieth century, with the huge expansion of the electorate and an increase in the power of the legislative, that a number of competing political parties made their appearance. They began performing a range of tasks, including acting as a mediating link between citizens, candidates, lawmakers and government, and in the words of Schattschneider, modern democracy came to be considered as 'unthinkable save in terms of the parties'.

Among Asia, Africa and Latin America, India stands out as an electoral laboratory for the study of political party. A number of national as well as regional parties were formed in the country before it became independent. Some of those parties have survived into the present, such as the Congress (established in 1885), Muslim League (1906), Shiromani Akali Dal (1920), Communist Party of India (1925), National Conference (1939) and Dravida Kazagham (1944; rechristened as Dravida Munnetra Kazhagam in 1949). The last three decades, characterized as 'post-Congress polity', have been witness to a huge number of parties. While the number of national parties has remained relatively stable at seven as of 2018, there has been an unprecedented rise in the number of registered recognized parties (59) and registered unrecognized parties (2044), according to data from the Election Commission of India. Most of the newly emergent parties are regional-ethnic in character as they thrive on the assertion of identity politics, based on politicization of social cleavages and regional disparity. Decline of the Congress ('dominant or hegemonic or system-defining party') during the period along with other national parties with the sole exception of the Bharatiya Janata Party (BJP, formed in 1980; earlier as Bharatiya Jana Sangh in 1951) in terms of their electoral presence has created political space for the state parties, especially in the states where the BJP did not have electoral presence. The resultant fragmentation of party system has incentivized the powerful and ambitious state-level leaders, who have the support of a core social constituency that is created and cultivated through sectarian ethnic patronage and clientelism, to break away from their original parties and form state-level or substate-level parties of their 'own' to have greater political bargain in a coalition system.

While the rise of regional parties may be in line with the global trend, Indian 'exceptionalism' when compared with the 'older' democracies of the West is reflected in the fact that not only has the number of parties increased in India but the level of electorates' participation has also risen with every new election. Centre for the Study of Developing Societies –National Election Studies (CSDS–NES) data notes that poor and uneducated electorates tend to vote in larger percentage than the rich and educated. Also, the level of electoral participation in India goes up further in the elections held for lower bodies, attesting to the 'assertion from below' thesis. Indian 'exceptionalism' with reference to party and party system, what in Hindi is termed as *dal* and *daliya vyawastha*, Diwakar notes, also emerges from the 'complex interaction of various sociological, institutional, and contextual factors' that do not apply the application of the theories – such as Duverger's law – and classifications of parties developed in the context of the Western democracies.

References

Diwakar, Rekha. *Party System in India*. New Delhi: Oxford University Press, 2017.
Schattschneider, E. E. *Party Government*. New York: Farrar and Rinehart, Inc., 1942.

RAJYA SABHA, LOK SABHA (RĀJYA SABHĀ, LŌK SABHĀ)

Valerian Rodrigues

The upper and lower houses of the Indian Parliament are formally known as Rajya Sabha and Lok Sabha, meaning Council of States and Council of People, respectively. The party or coalition of parties that wield a majority in the Lok Sabha form the government.

The Rajya Sabha consists of 250 members, of whom 238 are elected by members of state assemblies and 12 are nominated for their contribution to science, literature, the arts and social service. While domicile in the concerned state was essential for contesting candidates earlier, it no longer is. Membership of the house widely varies from state to state, due to demographic difference, and few of them are represented by only a single member. No seats are reserved in the house on grounds of community or other preferential considerations. It is a permanent house, where a member has a term of six years. Every two years, one-third of the elected members make way for others.

The Lok Sabha consists of 543 member selected through universal adult franchise in a first-past-the-post system. The lower house also includes two nominated members from the Anglo-Indian community if it fails to have such representation among the elected members. Here too, membership of the house varies greatly across the states mainly due to demographic variation. Fifteen per cent of the seats in the Lok Sabha are reserved for the scheduled castes (SCs), the traditional defiling and marginal caste and communities, and 7.5 per cent for scheduled tribes (STs), the ethnic communities with strong indigenous moorings and distinct ways of life. These representatives are elected in joint constituencies where only candidates from the relevant category can contest. The term of the Lok Sabha is five years, unless it is dissolved earlier.

The two houses together pass legislation, decide public policy, air popular grievances and hold the government accountable. They also endorse emergency measures, including president's rule in the states. They are also the field where the complex system of constitutional amendments is brought to effect. While the Parliament cannot interfere with some provisions of the Constitution, it can amend most provisions. If there is a serious deadlock on a Bill between the houses, it can be resolved through the joint sitting of the two. While the Rajya Sabha has coeval powers with the Lok Sabha, there are a few cases when there is difference in power. In the case of money Bills, the powers of the Rajya Sabha are only recommendatory; money Bills are introduced in the Lok Sabha and passed by it. The Rajya Sabha can transfer a subject pertaining to state powers to the Union for a year, create All-India Services and approve a state of emergency under Article 352 of the Constitution when the Lok Sabha remains dissolved.

The vice president of India, who is elected by both houses of Parliament, is ex-officio chairman of the Rajya Sabha. The Lok Sabha elects its own presiding officer, the Speaker, whose term is coterminous with the house unless she or he resigns or is removed. The Parliament functions through a committee system of great complexity. While some of these committees do the housekeeping, others do the spadework for parliamentary chores, including estimates and accounts of public expenditure. Departmentally related standing committees, numbering twenty-four as of 2018, review and assess the functioning of departments under their charge and make recommendations to the Parliament.

The Parliament of India is an institution of unparalleled reach and hope, as the voice of the nearly 900 million electorate. While both the houses, particularly the Lok Sabha, have become more inclusive of India's proverbial diversity, the representation of women and Muslims remains woefully inadequate. Criticisms of the system are many. Through its command over enormous resources and control over ruling party/parties, the executive has tended to tower over the houses, manoeuvring consent and evading accountability. Grandstanding and obstruction to the functioning of the houses have replaced debate and discussion. There is shrinkage in the number of working hours of the houses due to boycott and obstruction. Members of the houses and political parties are more concerned with the electoral impact of their action rather than their responsibility as representatives. The zero hour, when members raise the great concerns of the day, has tended to overshadow long-term and wider concerns. And, private members' bills find little support in the houses. While the anti-defection law has reined in defection of elected representatives from one party to another, the law has made members too cautious to express their true opinions because they are apprehensive of offending the party leadership. The excessive focus on elections has led many criminals to become members of the houses, has stoked communal prejudices, curbed intra-party democracy and led to the enormous increase of corruption.

References

Pai, Sudha and Avinash Kumar, eds. *The Indian Parliament: A Critical Appraisal*. New Delhi: Orient BlackSwan, 2015.

Shankar, B. L. and Valerian Rodrigues. *The Indian Parliament: A Democracy at Work*. New Delhi: Oxford University Press, 2011.

RAPE

Mary E. John

Rape, as the universally known sexual violation of women without their consent, which became central to feminist campaigns worldwide since the 1960s, has been critical in contemporary India's history as well. So much so that the English word 'rape' finds equal mention in our contexts as do its equivalences in Indian languages, such as the Hindi *balatkaar*. The term rape officially entered the subcontinent through the Indian Penal Code (IPC) of 1860, devised by the British and formulated in the English language. Rape is a crime against the state and can be found in Section 376 of the IPC, where it was defined as peno-vaginal penetration by a man against the woman's consent. The term rape has withstood the test of time better (in spite of recent amendments suggesting the term 'sexual assault' instead) than have other sexual crimes in the IPC whose terminology confines them within Victorian frames of understanding. Consider for instance the phrase 'outraging the modesty of a woman' for sexual harassment (IPC 509) or the highly problematic notion of 'sex against the order of nature', which includes punishment for homosexual acts (IPC 377), which has now been reformed.

Everyone would remember the outrage caused by the gang rape of Jyoti Singh, the physiotherapy student who boarded a bus in Delhi with her friend on the night of 16 December 2012. The horrific and fatal nature of the gang rape undoubtedly played a large part in the national and international outcry that followed, including the state's response in setting up the Justice Verma Committee and the rapid enactment of the Criminal Amendment Act of 2013 and the Sexual Harassment at Workplace Act of 2013. It brought issues of sexual violence into public discourse in a way that decades of agitation had not been able to achieve. What is particularly noteworthy is that we gained many fresh insights into sexual violence through considerable effort, often by going against the kind of common-sense perceptions that the Delhi rape case was dangerously close to cementing – that the greatest danger to women lies in the stranger lurking in the streets after nightfall, and that the only way to curb such crimes is through the death penalty. During the protests, for instance, it was calls for women's freedom (*azadi*) that could be heard as much as demands for more stringent punishment. Moreover, new research (including scrutinizing rape data records of the police) revealed that by far the most prevalent form of rape in India is by perpetrators known to the victim (98 per cent of rape cases all over India are classified as acquaintance rape). In all likelihood, some rapes should not even be categorized as such; these include charges of kidnapping and abduction which are levelled against the boy in an eloping couple by the parents of the girl. On the other hand, however, the Delhi gang rape also crowded out media attention to the shocking avalanche of rapes of Dalit girls and women that were taking place during the same time in the neighbouring state of Haryana. These were often young girls too but whose vulnerable social position, in relation to the perpetrators, made justice much more elusive.

The women's movement in India has had quite a distinctive and extremely complex history of campaigning against rape. The first national campaign in 1978 took up the case of the custodial rape of a young Adivasi woman, Mathura, by two policemen in the precincts of a police station in Maharashtra. As commentators point out, it came as a shock to feminists that what seemed to determine whether a woman had been raped was not an assessment of evidence but her past sexual history. Equally shocking was the realization that the nation's rape laws had not been subjected to any review since when they were first prepared in 1860. Over the last few decades, the women's movement has foregrounded cases of rape which go beyond the kind of general characterization made famous by Susan Brownmiller's *Against Our Will*. Rape, as a form of extreme violence, is not incidental but systemic in ways such that women's relative vulnerability to men is further exacerbated by structures of power, whether they be those of caste hierarchy, class exploitation, communally charged contexts and especially state violence (such as by members of armed forces). Though campaigns against violence such as rape and legal reform have gone hand in hand, one might say that a sense of just redressal through the law has been few and far between, with conviction rates in India being very low. Only those perpetrators who are socially marginal (as was the case in the Delhi gang rape) seem to stand a greater chance of being brought to book, compared to so many high-profile cases whom the courts find some reason or another to acquit. Even so, neither the state nor judicial recourse to justice can be dispensed with.

References

Kannabiran, Kalpana and Ritu Menon. *From Mathura to Manorama: Resisting Violence against Women in India*. New Delhi: Women Unlimited, 2007.

Srinivas, Rukmini. 'The Many Shades of Rape Cases in Delhi'. *The Hindu*, 29 July 2014. Available at: http://www.thehindu.com/data/the-many-shades-of-rape-cases-in-delhi/article6261042.ece (accessed December 2018).

SAARC

Rahul Tripathi

The South Asian Association for Regional Cooperation (SAARC) was established in 1985 to promote economic, social and cultural cooperation among the member countries. Initially, it started with the membership of seven countries, namely, Bangladesh, Bhutan, India, Nepal, Pakistan, Maldives and Sri Lanka; Afghanistan became the eighth country to join the group in 2007. Headquartered in Kathmandu, SAARC has completed more than three decades of a rather lacklustre performance, which has often led to the criticism of the structure and functioning of the arrangement for a variety of reasons. Though a bit on the extreme, some commentators, such as Girish Mathur, have been quick to dismiss SAARC as a still-born baby!

The central issue that has hampered the spirit of the SAARC process is that of political dynamics. Even though SAARC was conceived as a forum that would keep political and bilateral issues out of deliberations, political friction between India and Pakistan and at times other smaller neighbours has vitiated regular interactions. The clause that mandates that decisions must be taken by consensus of all members often becomes the pretext for decision not been taken at all. Moreover, the bureaucratic-structural hierarchy that highlights the operational programme of SAARC gives greater onus to the structure of cooperation rather than its substance. SAARC works through a number of layered committees, including technical committees, council of ministers and summit meetings that often lead to signing of lofty declarations without appropriate provisions to translate them effectively on ground, leading to a number of initiatives remaining confined to just the declaratory phase. One such notable initiative is the SAARC Convention on Suppression of Terrorism, which has failed to become an instrument of effective cooperation countering terror in the region.

A major area where SAARC has been unable to utilize its potential pertains to its inability to tap the economic potentialities and complementarities that make the region a natural geographical and economic unit for cooperation in the area of trade, commerce, energy and infrastructure. Intra-regional trade within SAARC countries continues to be well below its potential compared to its global trade. The region has still not been able to make effective use of transboundary resources for energy and infrastructural cooperation and transport connectivity across borders. People-to-people contact within SAARC member countries remains limited. The Group of Eminent Persons report of 2001 has listed a number of studies and suggestions on how to take SAARC forward, but they are yet to make a deeper impact on policymaking within SAARC. The body needs to reinvent and revive itself to meet the emerging geopolitical and geoeconomic realities, which would otherwise make extra-regional cooperation more attractive for member countries. Being the only manifestation of regional spirit in South Asia, SAARC needs a greater focus on implementation and an abiding concern for improving the quality of life of 1.6 billion people who inhabit South Asia.

References

Mathur, Girish. 'SAARC: A Still-born Child'. *Link* 29, no. 15 (16 November 1986): 6–9.
Obino, Francesco. 'SAARC: The Political Challenge for South Asia and Beyond'. *Economic and Political Weekly* 44, no. 9 (28 February 2009).

SARKAR (SARKĀR)

Chandan Sinha and Neilabh Sinha

The word *sarkar* is derived from the Persian language in which it means 'chief agent' (literally 'head of affairs'), although the Persian form may have definite connotations depending on the context. During the reign of Sher Shah Suri, it referred to a large territorial administrative unit. In India, in its most common usage, sarkar refers to the government of the day. However, it does not connote local government bodies, such as a panchayat body, or a municipal corporation The usage of sarkar at all levels of the public sphere has been facilitated in particular by the media, which uses the word on a day-to-day basis while referring to the central, state or a foreign government and their representatives. From this usage of sarkar is also derived the adjective *sarkari*, meaning 'of the government'. Thus, the word sarkari may be prefixed to agencies, institutions, procedures and public policy pronouncements, among other things, to indicate their governmental provenance.

Another implication of the word sarkar has to do with its long-standing usage in popular social discourse. As such, sarkar has a feudal connotation and is used to refer to the ruler or landholder. It remains in currency at the level of local discourse and characterizes the relationship between rich and poor or landowner and peasant/sharecropper.

At the family level in early colonial Bengal, sarkar would often refer to the person in charge of running the household of a European. Entries in P. T. Nair's collection of correspondence and descriptions from eighteenth- and nineteenth-century Calcutta show that the sarkar (or 'sircar') sometimes acted as the personal creditor of the European employer, thereby making himself indispensable to the said employer. He was often also responsible for appointing or dismissing other servants. As an aside, such persons generally belonged to the Kayastha class, and the household title may have evolved into the eponymous last name commonly found in Bengal today.

Finally, sarkari also continues to refer to the central funds of a joint family household in North India, a connotation that resonates with an older Persian meaning of 'sarkar' as state or royal treasury. The joint family was the basic social unit in traditional rural India and has now given way to a large extent to the nuclear family of the industrial era. The joint family survives in some parts of the rural hinterlands even today. Joint families had a code of behaviour and functional arrangements that, although not necessarily written down, were followed punctiliously. The keystone of the arrangement was the family 'treasury' or fund. Revenue from commonly held property/land would flow into this fund. The everyday expenses of the joint family would come from this central sarkari fund. This connotation of the adjective is often used to refer to the common household funds from which presents for individuals in a family are purchased for festivals or other communal occasions.

References

Landau, Amy S. 'Reconfiguring the Northern European Print to Depict Sacred History at the Persian Court'. In *Mediating Netherlandish Art and Material Culture in Asia*, edited by Thomas DaCosta Kaufmann and Michael North, 67–8. Amsterdam: Amsterdam University Press, 2014 (and accompanying footnotes).

Nair, P. T. *A Tercentenary History of Calcutta, Volume 2: Calcutta in the 18th Century*, 168–9. Calcutta: Firma KLM, 1984.

SCHEDULE

Justice Suhrud Dave

The word 'schedule' has its roots in the fourteenth-century Latin term, *schedula*, which currently means appendix, part, appendage or list. The Constitution of India contains twelve schedules. Schedules are required in the Constitution for listing subjects that could not be conveniently included in the text of the Act but have been recognized in law as the part of the Act.

For example, the Eighth and Ninth Schedules are two important Schedules in the Constitution of India. A conjoint reading of the Eighth Schedule (official languages of the republic) and Article 351 (directive for the development of Hindi language) would reveal the duty cast upon the Union to promote the spread of Hindi language and to secure its assimilation with Hindustani and other languages specified in the Schedule. Because of this process of assimilation, it was believed that the forms, style and expression of the scheduled languages will gain promotion and development without any interference. Moreover, this Schedule lays the foundation for the preservation of the linguistic diversity of India. The First Amendment Act of 1951 along with Article 31-B added the Ninth Schedule to the Indian Constitution. This Schedule prevents any land reform laws enacted by the various state governments from being legally challenged so as to facilitate agrarian reforms. Therefore, it placed a set of laws outside the purview of judicial review. With the *Kesavananda Bharati v. State of Kerala* judgement, however, the Supreme Court held that despite such inclusion in the Schedule, any enactment of the Parliament could be challenged on the grounds of being violative of the basic features of the Constitution. So, the Ninth Schedule has played a crucial role in arguing for an essence of the Constitution, envisaged by the Constituent Assembly, that is inviolable by any Act of Parliament.

Regrettably, in our political and social discourse, the term 'schedule' has come to be pejoratively associated with certain castes and tribes. Articles 341 and 342 define as to who would be 'scheduled castes' (SCs) and 'scheduled tribes' (STs) with respect to any state or Union Territory within the Union, empower the president of India to draw up a list of such communities and specify enabling provisions which are provided in the Fifth and the Sixth Schedule of the Constitution. The inclusion of castes and communities as schedules is a prerogative of the legislature and is not pejorative at all. The Sixth Schedule, for instance, provides for the establishment of Tribal Advisory Councils to advise the governor on matters pertaining to the welfare and advancement of the STs and for the non-applicability of the provisions of the central and the state Acts. The inclusion of any caste or tribe or language in the concerned Schedule would come with many benefits and advantages, including the legally acknowledged concept of reservation in the fields of education, service and elections. The terms SC and ST have not been defined under the Constitution and any community would be regarded as so only on their inclusion in the Schedule as a consequence of social and legal battles. The Supreme Court was, until sometime back, vigorously engaged in deciding such battles. Moreover, the inclusion of certain castes or tribes, as SC or ST, has brought in a divide in popular opinion. However, this classification will have to persist for their betterment. The social and political forces, acting otherwise, shall have to be discouraged.

References

Bijoy, C. R. 'The Adivasis of India-A History of Discrimination, Conflict, and Resistance'. *PUCL Bulletin* (2003). PDF available on Academia. https://www.academia.edu/6171880/The_Adivasis_of_India_A_History_of_Discrimination_Conflict_and_Resistance.

Osborne, Evan. 'Culture, Development, and Government: Reservations in India'. *Economic Development and Cultural Change* 49, no. 3 (2001): 659–85.

SECULAR

Rajeev Bhargava

The term 'secular' comes from *saeculum*, meaning a century or age. Within Christianity, it began to be used for those clergymen who lived their lives in ordinary time, the time in this world as against those sections of the clergy who turned away from this world to spend their time in the monastic order, closer to eternal time. The contrast here was not between a comprehensive secularity wholly opposed to a comprehensive religiosity. Instead, one might say there are secular religious and religious religious people, those who are doubly, wholly and intensely religious. The Christian God has devised two sets of laws, one that applies directly and immediately in the church and the other indirectly mediated by a set of laws devised by political rulers. The separation of church and state was not a conflict within Christianity but an internal matter.

In the past three millennia, however, Christianity itself began to be undermined in the West. The idea of another world and eternal time was radically questioned and dismissed as implausible. Humans existing in this world in ordinary time have exclusive ontological validity. All that is real is secular; everything else exists only in human imagination, in their dreams and fantasies.

Political secularity or secularism comes in three principal variants in the Western world. In its most radical version, all matters pertaining to this world must be governed exclusively by laws devised by humans through the agency of the state. Since it is false and illusory, religion must be dispelled from political and public life. The second variant retains its original Christian character, suitably adapted to modern conditions. Here, all temporal matters come under the strict jurisdiction of the state, while all godly issues, those that pertain to eternity, fall under the jurisdiction of the church and its chief officials. There is nothing anti-religious about this form of political secularity; at best, secular here means non-religious. The third variant is predominantly non-religious but accommodates the values of the dominant church in society. Thus, in many aspects of political and social life, religion plays no role. But, at least in some matters, the traditional laws of the church continue to reign.

Even in Europe, then, the word 'secular' or 'secularism' has no single connotation. This is even truer as we move across cultures. As these terms travel outside the Christian West, they acquire new connotations by virtue of the historical and cultural trajectory of non-Christian societies. One such region is the Indian subcontinent. Indians inherited specific versions of secularism from the West, but they did not always preserve them in the form in which they were received. They added something of enduring value to them, drawing from their own cultural traditions and further developing the idea. One crucial point to grasp is that in India, the terms secular and secularism developed in the context of deep religious diversity. This makes the Indian version completely different from all Western variants, where it developed after the creation of predominantly single-religion societies.

In Europe, with the breakdown of Latin Christendom, wars erupted between Catholics and Protestants. Simultaneously, peacemakers began to explore ways of preventing violence. In the ensuing negotiations, a consensus to adhere to one principle emerged: 'one king, one law, one faith'. The idea behind this was to have each ruler within her or his territory declare or confess her or his allegiance either to Catholicism or to one or the other Protestant sects. It was agreed that the subject population within the ruler's territory would then be compelled to embrace the religion confessed by her or him. Those who did not comply were expelled or eliminated. This is how European societies were homogenized and England became Anglican, Scandinavia became Lutheran, Spain and Portugal became Catholic and so on. The wars of religion did not result in the birth of secular but of extremely religious, confessional states. Political secularism emerged only when the rulers and the subject populations, which they governed, began to view their church as socially oppressive and politically meddlesome and challenged them. Hence, the demand for state–church separation.

This historical context was largely absent in India, at least until the late nineteenth or early twentieth century. The first major religion-oriented war in the entire history of the subcontinent occurred at the time of India's Independence. Despite some exclusionary movements, religious diversity and pluralism have been the norm in India. Adherents of radically different religio-philosophical world views – the many different groups that fall under the umbrella term 'Hindu', Buddhists, Jains, Syrian Christians, Pārasī, Jews, Muslims, Latin Christians, Sikhs – have all lived together, despite friction from time to time. None saw the other as an existential threat. When the terms 'secular' and 'secularism' began to be used here, their connotation could never be anti-religious or simply non-religious but rather the principled management and accommodation of religious diversity. Those anxious to prevent the partition of the subcontinent along religious lines used these terms to refer to a principled distance of the state from all religions in order to promote a reasonable sociability among them. Secular as multireligious, or against communal self-aggrandizement, became its principal meaning. However, a distinction was also made between valuable religious practices and those that legitimated hostility to other communities or oppression of women and 'lower castes'. With this, it radically transformed the original Christian or Western meaning of the term, investing it with a significance that has enormous transcultural potential. Ironically, it was only during the period of the notorious Emergency in 1975–6 that the word 'secular' was formally incorporated, via the Forty-Second Amendments, into the Preamble to the Indian Constitution.

References

Bajpai, Rochana. 'The Conceptual Vocabularies of Secularism and Minority Rights in India'. *Journal of Political Ideologies* 7, no. 2 (2002): 179–98.
Nandy, Ashis. 'The Politics of Secularism and the Recovery of Religious Tolerance'. *Alternatives* 13, no. 2 (1988): 177–94.

SUBALTERN

Shail Mayaram

The concept of the subaltern as interpreted in the last quarter of the twentieth century has changed forever the idea of the political. Initially used to refer to a junior position in an army, the term was transformed by the intervention of a school of history called 'subaltern studies' to signal subalternity, a condition of deep marginality that arose from the intersection of knowledge and power. Phenomena such as peasant rebels and social banditry that had hitherto been seen as pre-political now began to be viewed as political. The focus on the subaltern was embedded in a conceptual framework, which was one of the few to have come out of the work of scholars working on India. Engaging with Gramsci's formulation of hegemony, Ranajit Guha, the founding editor of the editorial collective of subaltern studies, argued that British colonialism represented dominance rather than hegemony, the latter being based on the consent of the governed.

The collaborative research agenda of the group of scholars who gathered around Guha augured a new approach to history. It has been suggested that Ranajit Guha established the 'Guha dock'. The metaphor of the shipyard is significant as many ships continue to anchor and take off from here even though the official subaltern studies project has wound up after publishing twelve volumes. It has left in its wake, besides the essays of these volumes, a large number of monographs of individual authors of the subaltern studies editorial collective. The work of the collective reinterpreted colonial and postcolonial Indian history. Gyanendra Pandey highlighted the colonial sources of violence, challenging the communalism and secularism binary. Susie Tharu and Tejaswini Niranjana foregrounded the concern with caste and gender. The group also marked a fresh focus on Muslims and Dalits.

The early criticism of the collective had been of the romanticization of the subaltern rebel rather than seeing her agency as one that could collaborate with sovereignty or be co-opted by the dominant discourse. With the intersection of postcolonial theory, epistemic issues of representation and voice were raised. In her famous lecture of 1985 titled 'Can the subaltern speak?' Gayatri Spivak emphasized that subaltern speech is both silenced and gendered and that scholars cannot claim to 'give a voice' to subalterns, given the problems of translation. She remarked that what subaltern studies stood for is a theory of consciousness and culture rather than a theory of change vide modes of production.

There have been other lines of difference and internal debate as the category of the subaltern continued to evolve over time. Dipesh Chakrabarty challenged Ranajit Guha's use of terms such as false consciousness, pointing out that Kanu and Sidu, the Santhal leaders, represented different temporalities and cosmologies that assume imagined worlds in which gods and spirits, gurus and pirs figure. Nonetheless, subaltern studies have provided new ways of approaching the question of religion and secularity. Milind Wakankar's work seeks the 'prehistory of religion' before it became entwined with the nation, state and civilization as also the coexistence of the miracle and violence.

New questions regarding the deepening of subalternity and the understanding of the state continue to rise. Landlordism as usury has given way to corporate and finance capital as the dominant form of capital. Further, communities identified as subaltern, including significant sections of Adivasis and Dalits, have come to participate in genocidal terror. Simultaneously, there is a new edge to the subalternity of other sections of Adivasis trapped between state and revolution, as Maoists continue their onslaught on Adivasi culture while sovereignty assumes new forms with the state's use of paramilitaries and the war against terror that renders minorities particularly vulnerable.

References

Guha, Ranajit. *Domination without Hegemony: History and Power in Colonial India*. Cambridge: Harvard University Press, 1997.
Morris, Rosalind C. *Can the Subaltern Speak? Reflections on the History of an Idea*. New York: Columbia University Press, 2010.

THANA (THĀNĀ)

Santana Khanikar

A *thana* refers to a level in the police hierarchy in India with both geographical and institutional connotations. Spatially, a thana may refer to both the physical buildings and compound of a police station. Etymologically, the word is derived from the Sanskrit root *sthaanak* or Hindi *thaan*, meaning 'a station or a place'. Historically, however, the institutional structures or authorities performing police functions were not referred to by this term prior to the Mughal period. Griffiths and Singh note that historic texts such as Kautilya's *Arthashastra* and the edicts of the Ashokan empire tell us of systems of maintaining law and order in the cities, namely that of *nagarika*s or *kotwal*s and *rajuka*s, which were of a composite nature, embodying in them the functions of judiciary, investigator and executioner. Law and order was maintained in rural areas through a village-based system that survived until the British period, enforced by the village headman at times answerable to large *zamindar*s, assisted by one or more village watchmen or *chowkidar*s, Bayley observes. The word thana does not occur in these documents.

However, this system of policing, essentially based in towns managed by kotwals and in villages maintained by local landlords and village councils, continued during the Mughal period. Some changes in the administration of police, giving it a more military character, were made during this period, where responsibility of maintaining law and order at the provincial level was entrusted with a governor known as the *subedar*. Madan notes that the provinces were divided into large districts or *sarkar*s under a *fauzdar*, and the districts were further divided into *pargana*s, which were then further divided into thanas at the bottom, looked after by a *thanedar*, who was responsible for the maintenance of law and order.

The modern British colonial police system of the 1860s brought in a province–district model of administration. While the Police Act of 1861 provided the legal backbone to the system, composed of British officers at the top and a large rank and file of natives at the bottom, it failed to spell out the lower-level or subordinate formations at the thana level, resulting in a centralized management. Training programmes were devised for thana-level police officers, nonetheless, which detailed rules and procedures to be followed in a police station, such as maintenance of a station diary, weapons and people in custody, and also listed documents to be maintained, such as those recording individual and community crime histories, as Kumar and Verma point out.

In contemporary parlance, a thana, the point of direct contact between common people and the state coercive machinery, is a place that is seen as both a necessity and a problem. Popular Bollywood films have frequently represented images of thana and thanedars both as righteous heroes taking up social causes and as evil and corrupt men. Recent ethnographic studies of thanas and policing in Northern India, such as those by Jauregui, Wahl and Khanikar, narrate how thana-level policing is ridden with colonial vestiges of hierarchy, violence and inefficiency and are still routinely called to perform as the first line of sovereign power.

Police forces in contemporary India are organized at the state/provincial level and have slightly varying organizational structures. All police forces, however, have thanas at the bottom of the hierarchy, sometimes supported by police *chowki*s (outposts) further down. The Bureau of Police Research and Development under the Ministry of Home Affairs records 15,579 police stations or thanas in India as of 2017. These thanas are headed by an officer, usually of the rank of inspector or sub-inspector, drawn from the subordinate police, who are in charge of allocating work and supervising overall functioning.

Thanas are responsible for ensuring safety and security of people and property, and investigating crimes within the area under their jurisdiction, and operate round the clock by deploying personnel in shifts. In order to perform these functions, various mechanisms of record-keeping and surveillance, such as crime-record registers and patrolling, are used. Suspects are arrested and interrogated within the premises of thanas. There are holding cells for suspects, known as 'lock-ups', where, legally, the thana can hold a suspect for up to twenty-four hours prior to producing her or him in a court of law and up to fourteen days with permission from a judicial magistrate. In an attempt to make the space of the thanas friendlier for visitors from all sections of the society, some police forces in contemporary India have attempted to compulsorily employ women personnel at the level of the thana. The recruitment of subordinate police in such contexts thus sees reservations not only for constitutionally defined groups of scheduled castes, scheduled tribes and other backward classes but also for women.

References

Bayley, D. H. *The Police and Political Development in India*. Princeton: Princeton University Press, 1969.
Madan, J. C. *Indian Police: Its Development upto 1905, An Historical Analysis*. New Delhi: Uppal Publishing House, 1980.

UPSC

Maruthi Prasad Tangirala

Synonymous with 'civils' in the southern parts of the country and 'civilwa' in the northern, UPSC (Union Public Service Commission) is a convenient shortening of the rather unwieldy name of a venerable eighty-year-old institution and represents either a somewhat naive belief or a fairly passionate faith among a significant section of India's employment-age youth about the emancipatory potential of a civil service job. While it conducts many different recruitment examinations every year, UPSC is now predominantly associated with the annual recruitment examination to the Indian Administrative Service (IAS) and a number of other cognate government services. The examination extends the legacy of the colonial-era aspiration for Indians to be associated with governance activity into the more egalitarian present. There is some evidence in recent times of the diversification of the aspirant pool for the IAS examination, from a largely urban and English-medium educated elite into the vast Indian semi-urban hinterland. Successful UPSC cohorts now consist of a greater variety of Indians from different backgrounds.

In conversations across different languages, the term UPSC can signify a variety of disparate things. To many in the middle classes it represents an entrepot to a life of middle-class respectability, a yearning for a better life if not power and pelf. UPSC can also indicate the mad rush to join cramming shops and finishing schools, in view of the extreme difficulty of the examination that requires above all stamina and staying power. Consistent with this perceived toughness, the term is often used to denote the pinnacle of individual intellectual achievement, as in 'she's obviously very good because she's come through UPSC'. It signifies the fairness of the meritocratic process to some; for many others who may not succeed, it is a perfect example of a hopelessly intractable obstacle race.

In the lanes, hostels and libraries around Mukherjee Nagar or Karol Bagh in Delhi or in Ashok Nagar and Gandhi Nagar in Hyderabad, and many other cities and towns across the country, UPSC means many years of physical hardship and mental labour, personal expense and sacrifice and singular dedication to 'cracking' the exam. To prepare for UPSC is reason enough for parents to remit additional money to their children living away from them, and the admit cards for the exam have considerable evidentiary and exchange value in hostels and homes across the country. UPSC also represents bonds of friendship between aspirants often born even a decade apart, of hierarchies and relationships forged among fresh-faced first-timers and veterans who have made multiple attempts, bonds and alliances that persist in spite of intense competition and often last a lifetime.

Sometimes described as a favourite national pastime for the intellectually inclined, the repeated attempts made at the UPSC exams represent a perverse incentive and a colossal opportunity cost. For a number of senior employees of public sector companies and banks, UPSC represents what might have been if they had made it through the exam, and for those others who had not the foresight to opt for a fall-back job while taking the exam, UPSC denotes the many productive years laid to waste without hope of recovery.

UPSC can be described as a foundational institution, at least by virtue of the articles expended on it in the Constitution. Its incorporation represents a desire on the part of the founders of the republic to eschew the patronage principle in appointments to the permanent executive. In its recruitment role in appointments to the services of the Union, UPSC has maintained a quiet efficiency over the years and has managed to largely stay free from taint and notoriety, unlike its constitutional counterparts in some states that are beset with performance problems and allegations of corruption.

UPSC has, over its history, earned a place among the few successful institutions in independent India. The sense of pride – of being a UPSC recruit – is manifest among its alumni, and the public perception too largely treats them as deserving of praise and respect. Elements of the selection process, most notably the general studies papers and the IAS interview, have achieved cult status.

Problems persist, nonetheless. UPSC has been one arena where the tension between a neoliberal governance paradigm above and the newly assertive subaltern aspiration below has played out, and this has had its effects on both the organization itself and the public's perception of it. The annual list of selectees put out from Dholpur House (where UPSC has been housed since 1952) no longer remains unquestioned, and the disclosure of fine details of evaluation is aggressively sought as a matter of right. The stakes being what they are, every issue, every mark not given, every question not strictly within the published syllabus, every interview question asked or not asked, every statistical evaluation tool not disclosed is contested and litigated by unsuccessful candidates in an unending dance of hope and desperation. This mirrors the larger failures in the education system that has not been able to teach our youth the difference between failure and rejection. Then again, the intense contestation is also reflective of the narrow pathways for public service and the abysmally few opportunities available to the educated unemployed to engage meaningfully with the nitty-gritty of governance. In spite of its faults and follies, however, UPSC will continue to remain a powerful proxy for aspiration and hope for the foreseeable future.

References

Gopalakrishnan, M. 'Direct Recruitment to the Higher Civil Services of India – The Personality Test for the IAS Examination – Some Observations'. *Indian Journal of Public Administration* 22, no. 2 (1976): 174–96.
Shurmer-Smith, Pamela. 'Becoming a Memsahib: Working with the Indian Administrative Service'. *Environment and Planning A* 30, no. 12 (1998): 2163–79.

VIOLENCE

Neera Chandhoke

Of what is it that we speak when we speak of violence? The term possesses a great deal of rhetorical value, commands immediate attention and evokes strong reactions. But, we no longer seem to know the difference between torture in the police stations of Delhi and little babies dying of malnutrition in remote areas of India.

Consider these differences: the imposition of draconian acts such as the Armed Forces Special Powers Act (AFSPA), which grants immunity to army personnel during the course of their duty in the Kashmir Valley and in Northeast India, amounts to discrimination. When the owner of a textile unit makes his workers labour for long hours without adequate remuneration, that is exploitation. When millions of scheduled castes and scheduled tribes suffer from avoidable harm, continue to be subjected to rank indignities and die premature deaths, we call it social injustice. When security forces or militants fire upon unarmed people and cause death, we properly term this violence.

We can distinguish between four broad categories of violence. First, the quotidian incidents of violence we often see: road rage, domestic abuse, lynching, terror attacks, arson, destructive demonstration and humiliation of fellow citizens. The second kind of violence is that which is harnessed towards the attainment of specific ends. For instance, the aim of caste and communal violence is to redraw the normative map drafted by Indian democracy. In this case, violence tries to restore a pre-democratic social order based on hierarchy and exclusion and to reverse the new democratic order based on principles of non-discrimination and equality. The third category of violence is that which is employed to make demands upon the state and force changes in policy. Groups use violence to wrest collective benefits from the state, ranging from the extension of affirmative-action policies to this or that group to the demand for a separate state within the federal system. Fourth, a group can resort to violence because it wants to simply opt out and establish a state of its own. Notably, groups that want benefits from the state do not renege on political obligation but secessionists do. They renounce the sovereignty of the state and wish to establish a new one forged out of the territory and the people of the existing state. Keep your society unequal, corrupt, exploitative and rotten they seem to say, just give us a state of our own.

The issue is much more complex in this last case. While we do not agree with their use of violence, we recognize that revolutionaries, too, seek to transform the institutional context in which people live out their lives and make it more just. Unlike secessionist politics, revolutionary violence does not seek to break off a piece of the territory of the existing state and establish a new state. The group that wields revolutionary violence reneges on political obligation to the state but not on their moral obligation to fellow citizens, particularly the most deprived, oppressed and exploited and in general those who are victims of a history not of their making.

In India, democracy and violence occupy the same political space. When institutions of the democratic state foster injustice, when the interest of citizens are betrayed, this space should have been filled with democratic contestation, social movements, campaigns, marches, strikes and negotiations between the state and civil society. Instead, we have violence at our hands as an instrument of last resort. Certainly, the institutionalization of justice will not make violence go away. Violence is part of the human condition. The political trick is to make the beast stay on the margins and prevent it from occupying the space of democratic politics. The political negotiation of violence demands innovation, creativity and imagination, but it can be done. Otherwise, Indian society will continue to pay heavy costs for the waylaying of democratic justice.

References

Gupta, Akhil. *Red Tape: Bureaucracy, Structural Violence, and Poverty in India*. Durham: Duke University Press, 2012.

Urdal, Henrik. 'Population, Resources, and Political Violence: A Subnational Study of India, 1956–2002'. *Journal of Conflict Resolution* 52, no. 4 (2008): 590–617.

EPILOGUE

If the Introduction to this book was the elegant setting out of the philosophical reasoning that underlay our enterprise, this epilogue outlines the political reasoning behind it. If the former is persuasive and scholarly, this is polemical and blunt. We see our book as belonging firmly to the literature on the politics of knowledge as it seeks to partner the many attempts to flatten the knowledge asymmetries between the North and the South. It has subversive intent. It seeks to disturb the regular vocabulary of social sciences and humanities and to disrupt the flow of communication between the North and the South. It seeks to upset the complacency of scholars who think their language adequate to the task of representing their world of inquiry. It seeks to suggest that their language is deficient and that new words and concepts are required.

In our book, we hope to both enlighten and liberate – to enlighten scholars who want to know India and through such enlightenment discover that they need not be constrained by a settled academic language that is, in fact, limited and not up to the task. We hope to suggest to such scholars that there is a rich linguistic reservoir out there, the *baolis* of India, from which they can draw. This book is also an act of liberation because it will allow scholars from outside the metropolis to participate in discussions on India using vocabulary that they consider more authentic and to assure them not to feel constrained by their unfamiliarity with jargon fashioned in the academic corridors of the North. The language of representation has to be *asli* not *nakli*.

While we recognize that the word 'authentic' is a taboo word in fashionable circles, these days we are, by using it here, inviting a discussion on the need to align the thinking and feeling of the scholar in her attempt to construct and represent. Sometimes words from the high table seem inauthentic, such as landed gentry, when *zamindar* would do. To an organic scholar, a word must feel authentic for it belongs to the common sense of the world in which she lives and operates. This looming battle that we are hinting at, to represent the world with words and concepts from outside the metropolis, belongs to our struggle in the politics of knowledge. The epistemology of the South must share equal space in the seminar room with the epistemology of the North.

While many of the responses to this pervasive and persistent knowledge asymmetry between the North and the South – by which we mean a political location not a geographical one – have looked at the processes of production of the knowledge that is largely used by global knowledge communities, such as policymakers and consultants, universities and multilateral agencies; or to the structures of dissemination by which words and concepts arrive, such as at media corporations and publishing houses; or to the communication instruments by which they get nativized, such as YouTube and Facebook; or even to the processes of valorization of some words and the downgrading of others, such as *modus vivendi* and not *jugaad*, this book looks at the conceptual landscape within which we operate. It looks at language. It recognizes the plural language landscape in which we in India communicate and which, we are arguing here, must be the landscape from which we draw our concepts.

While mapping asymmetries in production, dissemination and valorization of knowledge needs to be done to expose the biases at the heart of a world dominated by the knowledge systems left behind by the colonizer, what K. C. Bhattacharya described as producing a 'shadow mind' in place of a 'real mind', this volume, by looking at language, opens a new front in this battle for the decolonization of the mind. It seeks to diminish the asymmetry between the colonizer's language and the *bhasas*, between the conceptual universe represented by the colonizer's language and that of the *bhasas*. It is a small beginning in the effort not just to seat Sanskrit besides Latin but also Bhojpuri alongside French at the festival of ideas on India. In this task it has a larger ambition. The book seeks to give the world a wider menu of concepts from which to draw as together we, attempt to understand the complexity and paradoxes of the human condition. The book will thereby make policy choices more informed. It is, hence, also a celebration.

We have been able to get here only because of the huge collaborative effort that was involved. With their eyes and with their words friends said to us 'aage badho, hum tumare saath hai', meaning 'go ahead we are with you'. With gratitude, we have in the Introduction acknowledged the contributions of our many collaborators. At the risk of being repetitive, let me add to what has already been said. With approximately 259 entries, ranging from 300 to 1,200 words, and with nearly 200 contributors from across the disciplinary and geographic landscape of India, we have produced a book that offers more than a peek into the cultural and intellectual topography of India. Over the several years of its making, the book grew in its promise as we hounded some contributors, badgered others at seminars, chased still others behind bookshelves at book shops where we met by chance, and managed to persuade and enthuse them about our project. Most joined us, some didn't because of other commitments, but in the process we have made what began as an intangible idea into a printed reality. We are truly grateful to those who have come on board.

The book that we offer is intended to be interesting and playful, provocative and intriguing. Readers will smile at some of the entries and occasionally wonder why obvious words are missing. We know that at the moment of its publication there will be a veritable storm of protest. Scholars will question the title of the book and argue that India should not be in it since a lot of India is missing. 'Why is so and so word excluded?' 'Why is this region under-represented and that over-represented?' 'How do you justify including such and such a word, as a keyword?' 'Surely you could have done better?' While the first three responses are understandable, even justifiable, we must take issue with the fourth since cajoling two hundred plus scholars to contribute an entry was difficult and since every conversation we had across the many meetings both of us attended, produced suggestions, possible entries and the search for willing authors. We were consumed with the project. We saw it evolve as some leads turned out to be duds and others proved to be very fertile. There were frustrations and disappointments. And there was also joy as the confirmations started coming in.

It was a challenging task to match the structure of the book with the received entry, to attempt a balance so that one section would not dominate another, to ensure that the collection would not be ponderous but playful and innovative in what it revealed of the dynamic cultural and linguistic landscape of India. We are pleased with the outcome. We think we've done very well thank you. This book is the first step in our hope that others will join us in plugging the gaps. Producing it was like filling a hole on the beach with water from the ocean. The tide is coming in. And there is still water in the hole.

Epilogue

That it would be a challenging task was to be expected. After Papua New Guinea, India is the most diverse language landscape in the world. Now only do we have many languages, some only oral and some both oral and written, we also have some languages with many scripts. To prepare a short list of words, and to find contributors for them, was near impossible since we did not know enough language speakers from all the languages who could contribute and who were willing. Yet we got 259 words. Early in the project we took a decision that our volume was not aiming to be comprehensive. It could not be. At the best of times, it would be a Hanumanian task and perhaps even Hanuman would not be able to complete it. So we abandoned the aspiration of being comprehensive and also gave up on the goal of being representative. Even if we restricted ourselves to only the twenty-two languages in the Eight Schedule of the Constitution, and excluded the many languages documented in Grierson's *Linguistic Survey of India* or Ganesh Devy's *People's Linguistic Survey of India*, and further, found words that opened the proverbial window to give us a view of the inside of India, the book would still be deficient. Comprehensiveness and representativeness were unattainable goals. All we have been able to do is to illustrate what is available and what is possible. We expect this book to seed a curiosity and whet an appetite.

In this epilogue, let us describe the strategies we adopted to make the book a contribution to the larger battle in the politics of knowledge. Four approaches were tried simultaneously in our effort to select and reject, include and exclude. These are to infiltrate, elevate, appropriate and populate. Let us now detail the thinking behind each of these strategies.

The first is to 'infiltrate' the conceptual vocabulary that scholars and students use when speaking about India. The desire to infiltrate comes from our feeling that internally scholars hesitate to use concepts from the *bhasas*, and from the high languages of India, because it is considered inappropriate and perhaps indicative of a deficient education. Aime Cesaire saw this as the colonial process of inferiorization, a feeling, produced by colonization, that the culture of the local is inferior to the culture of the colonizer. This includes language. In the humanities and social sciences community when we want to represent India, we must speak English not Vinglish. So it is freedom instead of swaraj (*svarāja*), or non-violence instead of ahimsa (*ahinsā*), or honour instead of *izzat*, or even tribal instead of *Adivasi*. This hesitation is because we still have to attain the 'swaraj in ideas' that K. C. Bhattacharya talked about. We still feel diffident to use a vocabulary that is not the vocabulary of the metropolis. Salman Rushdie in his *Midnight Children* did not suffer from such diffidence. But other children born after midnight do.

Social sciences' work in, and about, India is done in English. This must naturally be so since English is the language of academic communication across the world. Fair enough. And therefore the challenge before us is to colonize this English. We have to make it more Hinglish or Bonglish. Further, if internally there is a hesitation to use words from the *bhasas*, then externally, to compound the problem, we experience a disapproval of words that the international community of scholars does not understand. If we have to represent India, we have to do so in their language not ours. So we are all expected to speak of India's zeitgeist not *asmitā* or political protest not *dharnā*. This is just not level.

The way to expand the field of available concepts is, therefore, to infiltrate the vocabulary of the humanities and social sciences in India with words and concepts from the larger linguistic terrain of India. The objective is to bring into this vocabulary words and concepts that have already achieved philosophical depth within the Indian philosophical traditions and then to offer them to the world not just because they are more representative of the Indian social, political and cultural landscape but also because they carry with them meanings that help us understand better the Indian civilizational universe and thereby, in doing so, contribute to our understanding of the diversity of the human condition. Concepts such as *dharma* and *lila* or *harām* and *halāl* are rich in meaning, have been extensively debated within their respective *weltanschauung* where fine distinctions have been made and have, over the years, produced a vast literature on their multiple usages. Such words are available. When one goes through the list of words in our book, one will get a sense of the infiltration we have attempted of the existing vocabulary of social sciences and humanities in India. The goal was not only to disturb the complacency of the scholar but also to deepen the resource base of concepts on India.

The second strategy that was used was to 'elevate'. Many things needed elevation –words into concepts, colloquial expressions into respectable phrases, acronyms into words and terms into ideas. Take *foto* or *herō* or UPSC or *cyberbhakt* or *bhailo* for example. They constitute small windows into the contemporary cultural world of India. These are both descriptive terms and conceptual categories for they allow us to name an action or a practice and also to place it within a distinct semantic context. During this exercise of finding words that represent contemporary India, we found words that bring alive contemporary India. 'Herō', for example, when deconstructed tells us a great deal about Indian modernity. 'Cyberbhakt' is a good window on how politics in India relates to the digital world. 'UPSC' is an acronym, which has become a word, that describes aspiration, achievement and social power. 'Foto' when opened up tells us much about the new mass culture, about emancipation and about the democratization of technology. 'Bhailo' refers to relationships of competition and hostility as 'the other' is constituted by communities across India. The bhailo is the other of the self in Goa. To elevate, therefore, is to give respect to words and terms that have hitherto been ignored and that have, so to speak, not appeared on the conceptual radar of the social sciences and humanities. To elevate a word into a concept is an act of resistance to the hegemony of the metropolis, to Northern epistemology. While English or French may be the base language of the humanities and social sciences, these base languages must borrow more widely, and more readily, from the languages of the other societies that they strive to interpret.

To elevate is to equalize concepts from the periphery with those of the metropolis. It shifts the burden of diffidence from the periphery onto the legatees of the hegemon. Elevating a word, which is much used in communication in the public sphere in India, whatever the location of such a word might be, such as *thalaiva* or *aḍḍā* or just *matalabī*, into a concept equalizes it with other concepts from the North such as Sir or gossip or dissimulation. Such equalization is necessary to flatten the asymmetry. It is also fun. Our favourite is a word such as *baat-chiit*. It is a word that spans a range of meanings from conversation, to discussion, to negotiation, to dialogue, to achieving understanding between persons, families and even nations. Why have we in India kept it beyond the periphery? We do democratic dialogues, not democratic *baat-chiit*. We have family arbitration not family *baat-chiit*. Another term that must be elevated is the description of the welfare state in India as *mai-baap sarkar*. It refers to government that is both mother and father, in its literal translation, and thereby to government that will provide livelihood security, when seen from the left, and rob one of initiative, when seen from the right. It is a term that signifies not just the reach and care of the state but also the dependence of the vulnerable citizens on it. To talk about India's economic policies of welfare, without using the term *mai-baap sarkar*, is to limit the discussion to the Lodhi Estate community and to not extend it to the many policy discussions and academic sites that flood the Indian plains.

Epilogue

For their own good, the Bretton Woods institutions better learn this language of *mai-baap sarkar*. It will ease their communication with the wider Indian world. Elevation as strategy comes from the belief that India cannot remain a non-contributor of concepts to the global policy discourse. We must try and make words into concepts, that is, inhabit them with meanings that come from diverse usages, and sometimes try and make concepts into theories such as *bhoodan and sarvodaya*. But we are not there yet.

The third strategy that has been deployed simultaneously with the earlier two is to 'appropriate'. Here we reverse the direction of flow, not from the *bhasas* to English but from English to the *bhasas*. As an illustration, let us take two English words that can be found in most Indian languages, 'tension' and 'adjust'. If one were travelling in a crowded metro train or a city bus, one will soon see that the last passenger to board, looking for a place to rest her weary body, will move towards a crowded seat and ask its occupants to 'adjust'. In translation, this means make a little place for me please. In most cases, passengers willingly comply. There is a shuffling of bums, and from nowhere, like a P. C. Sorcar trick, a tiny space appears just enough to seat a little bum and a weary soul. No rules of only two per seat work here. Sharing of common resources is the norm. A concession is made by the others occupying the seat who, by a small adjustment in a finite space, create an opening in which the recipient of that concession soon sits as if by right. We may be over-reading the small event that happens across buses in India but this is mainly to explain how the word 'adjust' travels across linguistic space in an Indian bus. Interestingly, adjust is not a word used in the London Underground to accommodate the last person to board. It must. 'Tension' enjoys similar acceptance in many of the other Indian languages. Here an English word carries many of its meanings into the *bhasas* and lives on in a range of situations. Recently, I was in a hospital ward where many of the staff came from the different linguistic states of India and where a kind of English-Vinglish was on full display. 'Tension' was the common word used by the nurses when bantering about their work. 'Last night I had toooo much tension no, because the ward was full.' 'Sir don't worry about the drip running out of fluid, don't take tension.' And so on, an English word making perfect sense in many Indian languages. Ask a taxi driver in Delhi whether you will reach your meeting on time and he will probable reply, 'sir tension mathh lo' ('Don't be worried you will reach on time'). One appropriates not just words but also acronyms. VIP in India, while it does mean very important person, has spawned a whole semiotic universe of Indian political culture. Seats are reserved for VIPs. Airport lounges can only be used by VIPs. There is a separate queue at many temples for VIPs. Aspiring for the status of a VIP is important for those who want to announce their importance to the community and to the society in which they live. VIPs walk differently, eat separately, dress distinctly. And since the class of VIPs has grown in size because of democracy – an indicator of the ease of political mobility that is available to all citizens in Indian democracy, an indicator which is not unlike the ease of doing business recommended by the World Bank – a special category of persons has emerged called VVIPs. If VIPs have a section of seats reserved for them at the Republic day parade in Delhi, VVIPs get the first row in this section. To discuss Indian polity and society by ignoring this class of persons is to miss a great deal about Indian democracy. Our book has included words such as adjust, tension and VIP. As we have stated before, this is just a beginning. Our list of words can only be illustrative not exhaustive. It can only provoke others to add to the list. We welcome additions to the lexicon of words that have been appropriated from English by the many Indian languages and that have acquired considerable use in the public sphere. For example 'herō' or 'missed call' tells us a great deal about the dynamic linguistic landscape of India and about how it is influenced by both Bollywood and technology. We wanted to have '420' in our lexicon, the section in the Indian Penal code that deals with crooks, but were unable to get a contributor. This discussion of appropriation of English words is like a 'selfie' of contemporary India.

While infiltrate, elevate and appropriate are useful strategies that have been adopted in our struggle within the politics of knowledge, the fourth, 'populate', gives this struggle the numbers we need. If one goes through the list of 259 keywords in 7 categories, one sees many words that have been included and that had hitherto been excluded. The exercise of populating comes from our goal to flatten the asymmetries in the flow of concepts across the world and not to create an alternative vocabulary. We recognize, and accept, that English and French are the dominant languages of social science and humanities production so far and so our goal is more modest, to add to the vocabulary words from other Indian languages, words that are closer to the ground, that better represent the world being described. Often words that come from outside the cultural universe of India, such as 'kulak', describe less than what an Indian equivalent word such a 'zamindar' would do, or 'sarkār', in the colloquial instead of 'governor', 'fatwa' instead of 'edict' or 'rajdharma' instead of 'norms of governance'. While many in the list of 259 words and concepts are from the conventional vocabulary of the humanities and social sciences, especially words on the Indian economy, their elaboration has an Indian touch. For example the sport cricket is the same game in the ex-British colonial world but in India, as in the South Asian subcontinent, it has the additional status of a religion. To populate is to add to the set of words. Our 258 words have done just that.

When these words, and others, enter the lexicon of keywords for India, then we will have diminished the power of the epistemology of the North. Angry critics from the North will describe our exercise as an attempt to create an alternative vocabulary that is bound to fail. This is caricature. We seek to add diversity not to substitute, to offer conceptual options not to compel the social reality to fit a social science concept that has been fashioned elsewhere. As was stated in the beginning of this epilogue, the philosophical underpinnings of this project were outlined in the Introduction. Here we have merely attempted to make a political statement.

Peter Ronald deSouza

CONTRIBUTORS

A. G. Krishna Menon is an architect and urban planner and founding member of the Indian National Trust for Art and Cultural Heritage.

A. K. Shiva Kumar is a development economist who teaches economics and public policy at the Harvard Kennedy School and at Ashoka University, India.

A. K. Verma is former Chair, Christ Church College, Kanpur. Currently, he is Honourary Director of Centre for the Study of Society and Politics (CSSP), Kanpur, and Editor of *Shodharthy*, a social science journal in Hindi.

Aakar Patel is Managing Trustee of Amnesty International India and a syndicated columnist.

Abhay Kumar Dubey is Professor at the CSDS where he directs the Indian Languages Programme. He has recently published *Hindi Mein Hum: Aadhunikta Ke Aine Mein Bhasha aur Vichar* (2015).

Aditi Mukherjee is Visiting Faculty at Language Technologies Research Center (LTRC), IIIT Hyderabad. Her publications include *Language Maintenance and Language Shift among Panjabis and Bengalis in Delhi* (1996) and *Literacy in India: The Present Context* (2002).

Aditya Dasgupta is Assistant Professor of Political Science at the University of California, Merced.

Ajoy Bose is a journalist and author. He was Executive Editor of *The Pioneer* and India correspondent of *The Guardian*, London. His books include *For Reasons of State: Delhi under Emergency*, *Behenji: The Rise and Fall of Mayawati* and *Across the Universe: The Beatles in India*.

Akshaya Mukul is an independent researcher and a journalist. He is the author of *Gita Press and the Making of Hindu India*. He is working on the first English biography of Hindi writer Sachchidanand Hiranand Vatsyayan Agyeya.

Alito Siqueira is former Associate Professor of Sociology at Goa University. His research interests include culture and development with a focus on pedagogy and questions of inclusion.

Amir Ali is with the Centre for Political Studies, Jawaharlal Nehru University, New Delhi. Previously, he taught at the Department of Political Science, Jamia Millia Islamia, Delhi.

Annie Koshi received her doctoral degree from IIT Delhi and did her masters in educational management from Oxford Brookes (UK).

Contributors

Antony Arul Valan is a graduate student with the Department of English at Ashoka University, India, and formerly senior editor at Orient BlackSwan, an academic publishing house.

Anushka Rajesh Patel is a PhD candidate in clinical psychology, focusing on trauma-related sequelae, at the University of Tulsa, Oklahoma.

Arjun Ghosh teaches at the Department of Humanities and Social Sciences, IIT Delhi. His latest book is an edited translation of Bijon Bhattacharya's *Nabanna*.

Arun Kumar is Malcolm Adiseshiah Chair Professor at the Institute of Social Sciences, New Delhi. He was formerly Professor of Economics at Jawaharlal Nehru University, Delhi.

Arun M. Kumar is Chief Executive Officer at KPMG India and formerly Assistant Secretary of Commerce for Global Markets and Director General of the U.S. and Foreign Commercial Service (USFCS) in the administration of US president Barack Obama.

Asawari Nayak is Executive Editor of *Jaag Monthly*, a Goan literary magazine in Konkani. Her research interests include gender studies, pedagogy, diaspora and policy studies.

Ashley Tellis is a teacher of English and gender studies, editor and journalist.

Ashok Thakur, currently an honourary professor at Panjab University, Chandigarh, belongs to the 1977 batch of the Indian Administrative Service. He retired as Education Secretary, Government of India.

Ashutosh Kumar is Professor, Department of Political Science, Panjab University, Chandigarh. His edited collections include *Globalisation and Politics of Identity in India* (2008), *Rethinking State Politics in India: Regions within Regions* (2017) and *How India Votes: A State-by-State Look* (2019).

B. N. Goswamy is an art historian and professor emeritus of Art History at Panjab University, Chandigarh. Recipient of several honours, including the Padma Shri and the Padma Bhushan, his publications include *Nainsukh of Guler* (1997) and *The Spirit of Indian Painting* (2014).

B. N. Patnaik is former Professor of English and Linguistics at Indian Institute of Technology (IIT), Kanpur. Previous publications include *Retelling as Interpretation: An Essay on Sarala Mahabharata (2013)* and *Language Matters* (2018).

Bela Bhatia is an independent researcher based in Bastar, Chhattisgarh. Questions related to truth, justice, human rights and democracy have informed her work over the last three decades.

Bhalchandra Nemade is a Marathi writer, poet, critic and linguistic scholar from Maharashtra, India. His debut novel was *Kosala* (1963), and he is a recipient of the Sahitya Akademi and Jnanapith awards.

Contributors

Bibek Debroy is an economist and Chairman of the Economic Advisory Council to the Prime Minister. His recent publications include a ten-volume unabridged English translation of the Mahabharata (2014). He was awarded the Padma Shri in 2015.

Bijoy Boruah is Visiting Professor of Philosophy at the Indian Institute of Technology (IIT), Ropar. He has earlier taught at IIT Kanpur, and IIT Delhi. His area of research interest is in the metaphysics of the self.

Bina Agarwal is Professor of Development Economics and Environment at The University of Manchester, and former Director of the Institute of Economic Growth, Delhi. Her recent books are *Gender and Green Governance* (2010) and a compendium of her selected papers, *Gender Challenges* (2016). Her honours include a Padma Shri in 2008, and the International Balzan Prize 2017.

Boria Majumdar, senior research fellow in the School of Sport and Wellbeing at the University of Central Lancashire and visiting lecturer at the University of Chicago, is a sports journalist, academician and author. His latest book is *Eleven Gods and a Billion Indians: The On and Off the Field Story of Cricket in India and Beyond* (2018).

Brahma Prakash is assistant professor of Theatre and Performance Studies at the School of Arts & Aesthetics, Jawaharlal Nehru University, New Delhi. He is the author of *Cultural Labour: Conceptualizing the 'Folk Performance' in India* (New Delhi: Oxford University Press, 2019).

C. Ramachandraiah is Professor of Geography at the Centre for Economic and Social Studies (CESS), Hyderabad. Recent publications include articles in the *Economic and Political Weekly* (2016) and *IASSI Quarterly* (2016).

C. Rammanohar Reddy is Editor of *The India Forum*. He was earlier editor of the *Economic and Political Weekly*. Previous publications include *Demonetisation and Black Money* (2016).

Chandan Gowda teaches at Azim Premji University, Bengaluru. He has translated U. R. Ananthamurthy's story, *Bara* (2016) in English, and edited *The Way I See It: A Gauri Lankesh Reader* (2017) and *Theatres of Democracy: Selected Essays of Shiv Visvanathan* (2016).

Chandan Sinha is an IAS officer of the 1989 batch and a writer. His publications include *Public Sector Reforms in India: New Role of the District Officer* (2007) and *Kindling of an Insurrection: Notes from Junglemahals* (2013); *Kabir - Selected Sakhis: The Vision of Wisdom*, his forthcoming work, is due for publication in 2020.

Chandraiah Gopani is an Assistant Professor at the G. B. Pant Social Science Institute, Allahabad. He does extensive fieldwork in South India and writes for magazines and journals in English and Telugu.

Contributors

Darryl D'Monte served as Resident Editor at *The Indian Express* and *The Times of India* in Mumbai. Chairperson of the Forum of Environmental Journalists of India, his publications include *Temples or Tombs: Industry versus Environment* (1985) and *Ripping the Fabric* (2002).

Debraj Ray is Julius Silver Professor in the Faculty of Arts and Science and Professor of Economics at New York University. Fellow of the American Academy of Arts and Sciences, he is co-editor of the *American Economic Review* and author of *Development Economics* (1998).

Dipak Dasgupta is Distinguished Fellow at The Energy and Resources Institute, New Delhi. He was earlier principal economic adviser to the Ministry of Finance, India, and board member at the international Green Climate Fund. His recent publications include the (co-authored) book *Moving the Trillions* (2015).

Dipti Kulkarni is Assistant Professor of English at NMIMS University, Mumbai. Her recent publications include *No Social Change Sans Dialogue: Case of Shani Shingnapur* (2016) and *Self-Repair in Instant Messaging Interactions* (2016).

Dunu Roy is a chemical engineer by training, social scientist by compulsion and political ecologist by choice. He is currently with the Hazards Centre, New Delhi, and is a contributor to the edited volume *Alternative Futures: India Unshackled* (2017).

E. Sridharan is the Academic Director and Chief Executive of the University of Pennsylvania Institute for the Advanced Study of India (UPIASI) in New Delhi. He has recently published *Coalition Politics and Democratic Consolidation in Asia* (2012) and *Coalition Politics in India: Selected Issues at the Centre and the States* (2014).

Fahima Ayub Khan is a postgraduate student of Developmental Linguistics at the University of Edinburgh. Her research interests include child multilingualism and the interface between developmental disorders and language acquisition.

G. J. V. Prasad is Professor of English at JNU. His recent publications include three edited volumes – *Violets in a Crucible: Translating the Orient* (co-edited with Madhu Benoit and Susan Blattes); *India in Translation, Translation in India*; and *Disability in Translation: The Indian Experience*.

Gangeya Mukherji teaches English at Mahamati Prannath Mahavidyalaya, Mau-Chitrakoot, Uttar Pradesh. Recent publications include *Gandhi and Tagore: Politics, Truth and Conscience* (2016) and (co-edited) *Exploring Agency in the Mahabharata: Ethical and Political Dimensions of Dharma* (2018).

Geetanjali Shree is a fiction writer in Hindi. Her works have been translated into various Indian and European languages. Her latest novel is *Ret-Samadhi* (2019).

Contributors

George Mathew is Chairman, Institute of Social Sciences, New Delhi. His publications include *Panchayati Raj: From Legislation to Movement* (1994) and *Status of Panchayats in the States and Union Territories of India* (2013).

Ghanshyam Shah is a former professor at JNU. Recent publications include *Democracy, Civil Society and Governance* (2019) and 'Education and Process of Inclusion under Neo-Liberal Political Economy' (2018), a contribution to the edited volume *The Legacy of Nehru* (2018).

Gillian Wright is a writer and translator based in New Delhi. She has translated *Raag Darbari* (2012) by Shrilal Shukla and *A Village Divided* (2003) by Rahi Masoom Reza. Other publications include *The Presidential Retreats of India* (2015) and *Mishti, The Mirzapuri Labrador* (2017) for young readers.

Gopal Guru is Editor of *Economic and Political Weekly* and former Professor at the Centre for Political Studies, JNU. Recent publications include *Atrophy of Dalit Politics* (2005) and *The Cracked Mirror* (co-authored with Sundar Sarukkai) (2012).

Gopal N. Raj is a senior science journalist who has written extensively about India's space programme. His publications include the book *Reach for the Stars: The Evolution of India's Rocket Programme* (2000).

Gopika Nath is a textile artist and writer. A Fulbright scholar, her stitch journal, www.gopikanathstitch-journal.blogspot.com, adds contemporary philosophy to an ancient craft.

Gurcharan Das is the author of a trilogy on life's goals: *India Unbound* (2000), *The Difficulty of Being Good* (2009) and *Kama, the Riddle of Desire* (2018). He studied philosophy at Harvard and was CEO of Proctor & Gamble, India, before he became a full-time writer. He is General Editor for Penguin's fourteen-volume 'Story of Indian Business'.

H. S. Shylendra is with the Institute of Rural Management Anand (IRMA). He is engaged in teaching, training and research in areas like rural livelihood and development, rural banking, microfinance and local governance.

Harish Trivedi is former Professor in the Department of English, Delhi University. He has authored *Colonial Transactions: English Literature and India* (1993) and has co-edited *The Nation across the World: Postcolonial Literary Representations* (2007) and *Literature and Nation: Britain and India 1800–1990* (2000), among other books.

Harsh Mander is Director of the Centre for Equity Studies. A former officer in the Indian Administrative Service, he is an activist who works with survivors of mass violence and hunger as well as homeless persons and street children.

Harsha V. Dehejia is a physician and professor of Indian Studies at Carleton University, Ottawa. His main area of interest is in aesthetics, especially *Krishna shringara*, and he has published over twenty-five books on this subject.

Contributors

Hemachandran Karah teaches English literature at the Humanities and Social sciences faculty at IIT Madras. His research is on issues of disability, health, the language question, literary criticism and musicology.

Hilal Ahmed is Associate Professor at Centre for the Study of Developing Societies (CSDS), New Delhi. His book *Muslim Political Discourse in Postcolonial India: Monuments, Memory, Contestation* (2014) attempts to make sense of the nature of contemporary Muslim political discourse.

Hoshang Netarwala is a retired chartered accountant who has worked across various industries, such as shipping, logistics, garments, market research, pharmaceuticals and sugar.

Ipshita Chanda teaches at the English and Foreign Languages University, Hyderabad. Her books include *Packaging Freedom: Feminism and Popular Culture* (2003) and *Tracing the Charit as a Genre* (2003). She translates between Hindi, Bangla, Urdu and English.

Ira Pande is a former university lecturer who was earlier chief editor of the Publications Department at the India International Centre. Her recent publications include translations of *Apradhini: Women without Men* (2010) and the Hindi novella, *T'ta Professor* (2006).

Irfanullah Farooqi teaches sociology at South Asian University. His areas of interest include Islam and Muslims in South Asia, the sociology of knowledge and literature and modern Indian social thought.

Irwin Allan Sealy is a writer. His publications include the verse novel *Zelaldinus* (2017), the novels *Trotter-nama* (1988) and *The Small Wild Goose Pagoda* (2014), the memoir *Red: An Alphabet* (2006) and the travelogue *From Yukon to Yucatan* (1994).

Iwan Pranoto teaches Mathematics at Bandung Institute of Technology, Bandung, Indonesia. He has been Cultural Attache at the Embassy of Indonesia, Delhi. His areas of interest include mathematics, education and culture.

Jaskiran K. Mathur teaches sociology at St Francis College, Brooklyn Heights, New York. Her research interests are in gender issues, rehabilitation, development and voluntary work.

Jasmine Anand teaches at the Postgraduate Department of English, Mehr Chand Mahajan DAV College for Women, Chandigarh. Her areas of research interest are postcolonial literatures, Indian writings in English, cinema and cultural studies. Her most recent publications are research papers in a book by Springer (2018) and the *Caesura Journal* (2019), Romania.

Jatindra Kumar Nayak is former Professor of English from Utkal University, Bhubaneswar. His English translation of the classic Odia novel *Yantrarudha* was published in 2003.

Contributors

Jean Drèze is Visiting Professor at the Department of Economics, Ranchi University. His recent books include *An Uncertain Glory: India and Its Contradictions* (co-authored with Amartya Sen) (2013) and *Sense and Solidarity: Jholawala Economics for Everyone* (2017).

Jeemol Unni is Professor of Economics at Ahmedabad University. Her areas of research interest are labour markets, the informalization of labour and the gender implications of this process. Her most recent publication is an article for *Journal of Global Entrepreneurship Research* (2016).

Jitender Parsad is former Professor of Sociology, M.D. University, Rohtak, Haryana. His books include *Tribal Movements in India* (2009), *Gandhi, Ambedkar and Dalit's Emancipation* (co-authored with Sangita Parsad) (2015).

K. Narayana Chandran is Professor of English in the School of Humanities, University of Hyderabad. A translator and writer in Malayalam, his recent publications include *Why Stories?* (2014).

Kaisser Rana is a teacher at the Shining Star School, Ramnagar, Uttarakhand. He is also a translator and social activist, who has translated the renowned investigative journalist, Rana Ayub's 'Gujarat Files'.

Karthika Sathyanathan has an MA in English studies from IIT Madras. She is working on the use of language in school education as a fellow at the Ministry of Human Resource Development in New Delhi.

Katyayani Dalmia is a postdoctoral researcher and lecturer at the Department of Social Anthropology and Cultural Studies (ISEK), University of Zurich. Her research investigates how people link bodily traits with caste, class, religion and gender in everyday life.

Kavery Nambisan is a novelist and surgeon, who has served as a member of the governing council of the Association of Rural Surgeons of India. Her recent novels include *The Story That Must Not Be Told* (2010) and *A Town Like Ours* (2014).

Kavita Panjabi is Professor of Comparative Literature, Jadavpur University, Kolkata. She has recently published *Unclaimed Harvest: An Oral History of the Tebhaga Women's Movement* (2016).

Keki N. Daruwalla is a poet and novelist and former IPS officer. He was member in the National Commission for Minorities between 2011 and 2014 and his latest novel is *Swerving to Solitude* (2018).

Lakshmi Subramanian is Professor, Humanities and Social Sciences, BITS, Pilani (Goa campus). She is currently Associate Fellow at the Institute of Advanced Studies, Nantes, and scholar-in-residence, Godrej Archives, Mumbai. Recent publications include *The Sovereign and the Pirate: Ordering Maritime Subjects in India's Western Littoral* (2017).

Contributors

Lallan S. Baghel teaches at the Department of Philosophy, Panjab University, Chandigarh. He has recently co-edited *Modernity and Changing Social Fabric of Punjab and Haryana* (2018).

Leela Samson is a dancer and choreographer. She headed Kalakshetra for seven years and was chairperson of the Central Board of Film Certification and Sangeet Natak Akademi, Delhi. Recent publications include *Rhythm in Joy* (1987) and *Rukmini Devi: A Life* (2010).

Madhavan K. Palat has been the editor of the *Selected Works of Jawaharlal Nehru*, published by the Jawaharlal Nehru Memorial Trust, New Delhi, since 2011. His most recent publication is the Russian Revolution Centenary Lecture, titled 'Utopia and Dystopia in Revolutionary Russia' (2017).

Madhulika Banerjee teaches political science at the University of Delhi and has researched knowledge systems for development on margins, focussing on medical knowledge in particular.

Mahmood Farooqui, a writer, is best known for reviving Dastangoi, the lost art of Urdu storytelling.

Maidul Islam is Assistant Professor of Political Science at the Centre for Studies in Social Sciences Calcutta. Recent publications include *Limits of Islamism* (2015) and *Indian Muslim(s) after Liberalization* (2019).

Malashri Lal is former Professor, Department of English, University of Delhi, and member, English Advisory Board of the Sahitya Akademi. She has written over fifteen books in the area of literature and gender studies.

Manas Ray is a retired professor of cultural studies at the Centre for Studies in Social Sciences, Calcutta (CSSSC). He is currently editing a two-volume collection of essays on the state of Indian democracy.

Manindra Thakur teaches at the Centre for Political Studies, JNU. His areas of interest include Indian intellectual traditions, Marxism, the philosophy of science, social science research methods, literature and politics.

Manish Thakur teaches sociology at the Indian Institute of Management, Calcutta. He is the co-editor of *Doing Theory: Locations, Hierarchies and Disjunctions* (2018).

Manisha Madhava is an Associate Professor at SNDT Women's University. Her recent publications include a contribution to the edited volume *The Indian Parliament and Democratic Transformation* (2018).

Maruthi P. Tangirala is a civil servant who has twice served in the Union Public Service Commission (UPSC). His recent book is titled *Telecom Sector Regulation in India: An Institutional Perspective* (2019).

Contributors

Mary E. John is Senior Fellow at the Centre for Women's Development Studies, New Delhi. Recent publications include *Women's Studies in India: A Reader* (2008) and *The Political and Social Economy of Sex Selection: Exploring Family Development Linkages* (2018).

Masood Ali Beg is Associate Professor, Department of Linguistics, Aligarh Muslim University. His research interests include socio-historical linguistics, pragmatics and discourse analysis.

Mazdoor Kisan Shakti Sangathan (Association for the Empowerment of Labourers and Farmers), MKSS, collective is an Indian social movement and grass-roots organization best known for its successful struggle and demand for the Right to Information Act (RTI).

Melvil Pereira has been the director of North-Eastern Social Research Centre since 2012. His specialization is Customary Laws of the Tribal Peoples of North East India.

Merdijana Kovacevic is a PhD candidate in clinical psychology, focusing on trauma-related assessment and treatment, at the University of Tulsa, Oklahoma.

Mohd. Sanjeer Alam is an Associate Professor at the Centre for the Study of Developing Societies (CSDS), Delhi. Recent publications include *Religion, Community, and Education: The Case of Rural Bihar* (2012) and *Fixing Electoral Boundaries in India: Processes, Outcomes and Implications for Political Representation* (co-edited with K. C. Sivaramakrishnan) (2015).

Mohini Mullick is former Professor of Philosophy at IIT Kanpur. Recent publications include *Classical Indian Thought and the English Language* (co-edited with Madhuri S. Sondhi) (2015).

Mona G. Mehta is Assistant Professor in Humanities and Social Sciences at the Indian Institute of Technology (IIT), Gandhinagar. Her research interests include democracy, urban transformations, remaking of city spaces and middle class politics and youth aspirations and skill development programs in urban and rural India. She has co-edited, *Gujarat Beyond Gandhi: Identity, Conflict and Society* (Routledge 2010) and authored several scholarly and research articles.

Montek Singh Ahluwalia is an economist and civil servant who was the deputy chairman of the Planning Commission of India and previously the first director of the Independent Evaluation Office at the International Monetary Fund.

Muzaffar Assadi is Special Officer, Raichur University, Karnataka. Recent publications include *Identity Politics and Fundamentalism: Some Thoughts* (2014).

N. Jayaram is Visiting Professor at the National Law School of India University, Bengaluru. Recent publications include three edited volumes: *Knowing the Social World* (2017), *Social Dynamics of the Urban* (2017) and *Democratisation in the Himalayas* (co-edited with Vibha Arora) (2017).

Contributors

N. Manu Chakravarthy teaches critical theory, postcolonialism and film theory at the National College Basavanagudi, Bengaluru. His publications include *Culture and Creativity* (2019), *Moving Images Multiple Realities* (2015) and *Conversations and Cultural Reflections* (1999).

Nalini Nayak taught economics at Miranda House and at PGDAV College, University of Delhi, from where she retired as reader in economics. She has co-authored *Microeconomic Theory* (2002).

Navprit Kaur is ICSSR Postdoctoral Fellow at the Department of Political Science, Panjab University, Chandigarh. Her areas of research include the politics of caste, childhood studies and urban studies.

Navroz K. Dubash is a professor at the Centre for Policy Research. His primary area of research is the politics of climate change, energy, water and regulation. Recent edited collections include *India in a Warming World: Integrating Climate Change and Development* and *Mapping Power: The Political Economy of Electricity in India's States*.

Nazima Parveen is ICSSR Postdoctoral Fellow at CSDS. She writes for *Seminar*, *Economic and Political Weekly* and *The Quint* on the rights of ethnic and religious minorities with special reference to urban transformation in postcolonial India.

Neera Chandhoke is former Professor of Political Science, Delhi University. Recent publications include *Democracy and Revolutionary Politics* (2015) and *Contested Secessions: Democracy, Rights, Self-Determination and Kashmir* (2012).

Neilabh Sinha a PhD candidate at the Institute of History, Leiden University. His project, 'Renaissance Kings between the Natural and the Supernatural: A Comparative Study of Nature and Kingship in Eurasian Visual Culture' studies ideas about Nature and kingship as they appear in the visual culture of the Mughal and Habsburg courts.

Nilanjan Mukhopadhyay is a journalist and host of the TV political talk show 'Present, Past and the Future'. His publications include *Narendra Modi: The Man, The Times* (2013) and *Sikhs: Untold Agony of 1984* (2015).

Om Prakash teaches at the Department of Humanities and Social Sciences, Gautam Buddha University. Recent publications include the edited volume *Linguistic Ecology of Mizoram* (2017) and *Linguistic Foundation of Identity* (co-edited with Rajesh Kumar) (2018).

P. Vigneswara Ilavarasan is a Professor at the Department of Management Studies, IIT Delhi. He researches the production and consumption of information and communication technologies (ICTs) with a special focus on development and India.

Pallavi Pant is a postdoctoral research associate with the Department of Environmental Health at the University of Massachusetts, Amherst. She is interested in public engagement on air quality and health and in increasing the participation of women in science.

Pamela Philipose, presently ombudsperson, *The Wire*, began with *The Times of India*. She has worked as an editor for several publications, including *The Indian Express*. A fellowship with the Indian Council of Social Science Research in 2014 saw her shift focus to media studies.

Paranjoy Guha Thakurta is an investigative journalist and former editor of the *Economic and Political Weekly*. He is also an author, publisher, documentary film-maker and teacher.

Parikshit Ghosh is an Associate Professor at the Delhi School of Economics. His publications include *Character Endorsements and Electoral Competition* (2016) and *Electoral Competition, Moderating Institutions and Political Extremism* (2002).

Partha Ghose is former Professor, S. N. Bose National Centre for Basic Sciences, Kolkata, and honourary scientist, Indian National Academy of Sciences. Recent publications include the edited volume *Einstein, Tagore and the Nature of Reality* (2017).

Paula Banerjee is the Vice Chancellor of The Sanskrit College and University, Kolkata, and editor of *Refugee Watch*. Her recent publications include *Statelessness in South Asia* (2016) and *Unstable Populations, Anxious States* (2013).

Paula Richman is Professor in the Humanities, Department of Religion, at Oberlin College, Ohio, United States. She has edited *Extraordinary Child: Poems from a South Indian Devotional Genre* (1997) and *Many Ramayanas: The Diversity of a Narrative Tradition in South Asia* (1991).

Pavan K. Varma is a former diplomat and currently national general secretary and national spokesman of the Janata Dal (United). Recent publications include *Chanakya's New Manifesto* (2013) and *Adi Shankaracharya: Hinduism's Greatest Thinker* (2018).

Peter Ronald deSouza is a Professor at CSDS and former Director of the Indian Institute of Advanced Study, Shimla. Recent publications include *In the Hall of Mirrors: Reflections on Indian Democracy* (2018) and the edited volume *At Home with Democracy: A Theory of Indian Politics*, the essays of D. L. Sheth (2017).

Poonam Muttreja is the Executive Director of Population Foundation of India. Her recent publications include a chapter in the edited volume *Seven Decades of Independent India: Ideas and Reflections* (2018) and in *A Roadmap to India's Health* (2018).

Pradip Phanjoubam is a senior journalist. He was a Fellow of the Indian Institute of Advanced Study, Shimla, during 2012–14, and is currently a fellow of the Nehru Memorial Museum and Library, New Delhi,. Recent publications include *The Northeast Question: Conflicts and Frontiers* (2016) and *Shadow and Light: A Kaleidoscope of Manipur* (2016).

Prakash Singh was former Police Chief of Uttar Pradesh and Assam and former director general of Border Security Force. Recent publications include *The Naxalite Movement in India* (2006).

Contributors

Pralay Kanungo is currently DAAD Guest Professor at South Asia Institute, University of Heidelberg. Recent publications include *RSS's Tryst with Politics* (2002) and the edited volume *The Algebra of Warfare-Welfare: A Long View of India's 2014 Elections* (2019).

Praveen Singh is doing a PhD in Linguistics at the Indian Institute of Technology, Madras. He is interested in theoretical linguistics, the Western and Indian grammatical traditions and the philosophy of language.

Pulapre Balakrishnan teaches at Ashoka University, Sonipat. His most recent publication, co-authored with Ashima Goyal, is a chapter in the edited volume *Handbook of the Indian Economy in the 21st Century* (2018).

Pulin B. Nayak is former Professor of Economics, Delhi School of Economics. He was Director, Delhi School of Economics, during 2005–8. His recent publications include the edited volume *Economic Development of India* (2015).

Punam Tripathi is an independent researcher in the area disaster studies and vulnerability. Her latest publication is *Vulnerable Andaman and Nicobar Islands: A Study of Disasters and Response* (2018).

Raghavendra Lal Das has worked at the Reserve Bank of India for thirty two years and has taught at Patna University.

Rahul Tripathi is Professor and Head, Department of Political Science, Goa University.

Rajat Subhra Banerjee is an architect and author in Bengali, who writes nonsense poetry and prose.

Rajeev Bhargava is a professor at CSDS and was the Director from 2007 to 2014. His recent publications include *What Is Political Theory and Why Do We Need It?* (2012) and *The Promise of India's Secular Democracy* (2010).

Rajesh Kumar is Professor of Linguistics at the Indian Institute of Technology Madras. His research interests include the study of the structure of Indian languages and multilingualism in education, human cognition and politics.

Rajni Palriwala is Professor, Department of Sociology, University of Delhi. Her recent publications include *Marrying in South Asia: Shifting Concepts, Changing Practices in a Globalised World* (co-edited by Ravinder Kaur) (2013).

Rama Kant Agnihotri is former Professor and Head, Department of Linguistics, Delhi University. His recent books include *Indian English: Towards a New Paradigm* (co-edited with Rajendra Singh) (2012) and *'Impure Languages': Linguistic and Literary Hybridity in Contemporary Cultures* (with C. Benthien and T. Oransakia) (2015).

Ramana Murthy V. Rupakula teaches at the School of Economics, University of Hyderabad. Recent publications include the edited volume *Agrarian Relations: The Long Debate* (2018)

Ramanjit Kaur Johal is a Professor of Public Administration and Public Policy at Panjab University, Chandigarh, and a Fulbright and Shastri scholar. Her recent publications include co-authored chapters in *Sustainable Waste Management: Policies & Case Studies* (2019) and the *Vision 2030 Document* of the Government of Punjab (2016–17).

Ranjeeta Dutta teaches at the Centre for Historical Studies, JNU. Her publications include *From Hagiographies to Biographies: Ramanuja in Tradition and History* (2014) and *Negotiating Religion: Perspectives from Indian History* (co-edited with Rameshwar Prasad Bahuguna and Farhat Nasreen) (2012). Ranjeeta is also the editor of *The Medieval History Journal*.

Ranjit Nair is the founding director of the Centre for Philosophy and Foundations of Science and president of the World Institute for Advanced Study under the aegis of CPFS, New Delhi. He is chief editor of a twelve-volume series entitled 'The Foundations of Philosophy in India'.

Ravi Vasudevan is at the Centre for the Study of Developing Societies and co-founder of CSDS's media research programme, Sarai and the screen studies journal *Bioscope*. His publications include *Making Meaning in Indian Cinema* (2000), *The Melodramatic Public: Film Form and Spectatorship in Indian Cinema* (2010), and the *Marg* special issue, *Documentary Now* (2018).

Ravinder Kaur is Professor of Sociology and Social Anthropology at the Department of Humanities and Social Sciences, IIT Delhi. Her recent publications include the edited volume *Too Many Men, Too Few Women: Social Consequences of Gender Imbalance in India and China* (2016).

Reetika Khera is Associate Professor of Economics and Public Systems Groups at the Indian Institute of Management, Ahmedabad. Recent publications include *Dissent on Aadhaar: Big Data Meets Big Brother* (2018).

Rita Kothari is a Gujarati, Sindhi and English language author and translator. She has authored *Memories and Movements* (2016) and has co-edited *Decentring Translation Studies: India and Beyond* (2009) with Judy Wakabayashi. She is currently associated with the English department, Ashoka University.

Ritajyoti Bandyopadhyay is Assistant Professor of History and Political economy at the Indian Institute of Science Education and Research (IISER), Mohali. Recent publications include a chapter (with Ranabir Samaddar) in the edited volume *Caste and the Frontiers of Postcolonial Accumulation* (2017) and an article in the journal *Modern Asian Studies* (2016).

Rochelle Pinto is a research fellow at the L'Institut des ÉtudesAvancées, Nantes. She has recently contributed a chapter to the edited volume *Commodities and Affect* (2017).

Contributors

Roma Chatterji is Professor and Head, Department of Sociology, Delhi School of Economics, Delhi University. She is the author of *Writing Identities: Folklore and Performance in Purulia, West Bengal* (2009) and *Speaking with Pictures: Folk Art and the Narrative Imagination in India* (2016).

Ronki Ram teaches political science at Panjab University, Chandigarh. His latest publications include a chapter in *Brill's Encyclopaedia of Sikhism* (2017) and articles in the journals *Contributions to Indian Sociology* (2017) and *Economic and Political Weekly* (2017).

Rudolf C. Heredia, S. J. was Director of Research and Editor of the institute's journal *Social Action* at the Indian Social Institute. His recent publications include *Changing Gods: Rethinking Conversion in India* (2007) and *Taking Sides, Reservations Quotas and Minority Rights in India* (2012).

Rukmini Bhaya Nair is Professor Emerita, Linguistics and English, at the Indian Institute of Technology Delhi. Recent publications include the critical work *Poetry in a Time of Terror: Essays in the Postcolonial Preternatural* (2009), the novel *Mad Girl's Love Song* (2013) and 'Epithymetics: the Psychology of Desire' in *Psychology: ICSSR Research Surveys and Explorations* ed. G. Misra (2019).

S. Imtiaz Hasnain is Professor of Sociolinguistics, Department of Linguistics, Aligarh Muslim University. He is currently working on the documentation of endangered languages and a collaborative multi-varsity project on linguistic activation and bidirectional reading.

Saba Sharma has recently completed a PhD at the Department of Geography in the University of Cambridge on citizenship in the Bodoland Territorial Area Districts of Western Assam.

Salil Misra teaches history at Ambedkar University, Delhi, where he is currently pro vice chancellor. His publications broadly centre on the themes of communal politics, nationalism, the politics of language and social science teaching.

Samir Kumar Das is Professor of Political Science at the University of Calcutta. His recent publications includes *Migrations, Identities and Democratic Practices in India* (2018) and *India: Democracy and Violence* (2015, edited).

Sandeep Mertia is a doctoral student at the Department of Media, Culture, and Communication, and Urban Doctoral Fellow at New York University. He is an ICT engineer by training, with research interests in software studies, science and technology studies and anthropology.

Sanjay Chaturvedi is Professor of International Relations at South Asian University, New Delhi. His recent publications include *Environmental Sustainability from Himalaya to the Ocean: Struggles and Innovations in China and India* (co-edited with Shikui Dong and Jayanta Bandyopadhyay) (2017) and *Climate Terror: A Critical Geopolitics of Climate Change* (co-authored with Timothy Doyle) (2015).

Sanjay Palshikar is Professor at the University of Hyderabad. Recent publications include *Evil and the Philosophy of Retribution: Modern Commentaries on the Bhagavad-Gita* (2014).

Sanjit Chakraborty teaches at Indian Institute of Management Indore and he has been a faculty member in the Department of Philosophy at University of Hyderabad. He has published articles in the journals *Philosophia, Philosophical Readings, APA Newsletters, ESEP* and *JICPR*. Book publications include *The Labyrinth of Mind and World* (2019) and *Understanding Meaning and World* (2016).

Sanjoy Hazarika is International Director, Commonwealth Human Rights Initiative. An activist, author, journalist and film-maker who specializes in understanding India's north-east, his most recent book is *Strangers No More: New Narratives from India's Northeast* (2018).

Santana Khanikar is a political scientist who teaches at JNU. Her recent book *State, Violence, and Legitimacy in India* (2018) draws on ethnographic fieldwork of policing practices in Delhi and anti-secessionist army operations in Assam.

Santosh Desai is a columnist, media critic and the author of *Mother Pious Lady: Making Sense of Everyday India* (2010). In his professional life, Santosh is the MD and CEO of Futurebrands, a brand and consumer consultancy company.

Sarojini Ganju Thakur is a former civil servant with the IAS (1977 batch). Recent publications include a manual for trainers on gender and governance and *Gender Responsive Planning and Budgeting in Bhutan: From Analysis to Action* (2016).

Sasheej Hegde teaches sociology at University of Hyderabad. His publications have been on the themes of law/ethics, the sociology of knowledge, and modern Indian political thought.

Satish C. Aikant is former Professor and Head, Department of English, H. N. B. Garhwal University, Uttarakhand. His publications include *Critical Spectrum: Essays on Literary Culture* (2004) and *Postcolonial Indian Literature: Toward a Critical Framework* (2018).

Satish Padmanabhan is a journalist and deputy editor with *Outlook* magazine. He has a special interest in theory, literature and the arts.

Savita Bhakhry retired as joint director (research), National Human Rights Commission of India. In 2016, she brought out a revised edition of her book *Children in India and Their Rights*.

Seema Khanwalkar is an adjunct professor (social sciences) at the Faculty of Design, CEPT University, Ahmedabad, and visiting faculty at the IIM Ahmedabad and NID Ahmedabad. Her research interests include applied semiotics, design semantics and cultural anthropology.

Shahzad Gani is a doctoral student in engineering at the University of Texas at Austin. His current research focus is on understanding the role that anthropogenic and natural processes play in driving air pollution, with a focus on India.

Contributors

Shail Mayaram is a Professor at the Centre for the Study of Developing Societies, Delhi. Her latest book is *The Secret Life of Indian Nationalism: Transitions from the Pax Britannica to the Pax Americana* (2019).

Shashi Tharoor currently serves as Member of Parliament from Thiruvananthapuram, Kerala. Former Under-Secretary General for Communications and Public Information at the UN, and a former Minister in the Government of India, he has authored nineteen books of fiction and non-fiction, most recently, *The Hindu Way* (2019).

Shiv Visvanathan teaches at O. P. Jindal University and is Director of the Centre for the Study of Knowledge systems. He is best known for his contributions to developing the field of science and technology studies and for the concept of "cognitive justice", a term he coined.

Shivangini Tandon is an Assistant Professor at the Centre for Women's Studies, Aligarh Muslim University. Currently visiting fellow at the Max Planck Institute for Human Development, Berlin, she is working on the representation of emotions in the literary cultures of early modern South Asia.

Shivani Chopra is Head, Department of Hindi, DAV College, Panjab University, Chandigarh. She has contributed several research articles to Hindi journals like *Samved*, *Samyantar* and *Naya Path* and to the *CSDS Social Sciences Encyclopedia* in Hindi.

Sibaji Bandyopadhyay is former Professor of Cultural Studies, Centre for Studies in Social Sciences, and former Professor of Comparative Literature, Jadavpur University. Recent publications include *Three Essays on the Mahābhārata* (2016) and the text of the graphic novel *Vyasa: The Beginning* (2017).

Sibesh Bhattacharya is a former professor of ancient history, culture and archaeology, Allahabad University, and former national fellow, Indian Institute of Advanced Study, Shimla. Recent publications include *Some Essays of Tagore: History, Politics, Society* (2018) and the co-edited volume *Exploring Agency in the Mahabharata* (2018).

Siddharth Peter De Souza is a doctoral candidate in Law at the Humboldt University of Berlin. He works on the role of indicators for measuring access to justice in plural justice systems and is the founder of Justice Adda, a legal design consultancy.

Souvik Naha is Marie Curie Postdoctoral Fellow at the Department of History, Durham University. Recent books include *Ethical Concerns in Sport Governance* (co-edited with David Hassan) (2019) and *FIFA World Cup and Beyond: Sport, Culture, Media and Governance* (co-edited with Kausik Bandyopadhyay and Shakya Mitra) (2018).

Souvik Mukherjee is an Assistant Professor and head of department at Presidency University, Calcutta. Recent publications include *Videogames and Storytelling: Reading Games and Playing Books* (2015) and *Videogames and Postcolonialism: Empire Plays Back* (2017).

Sudarsan Padmanabhan teaches at the Humanities and Social Sciences Faculty at IIT Madras. His interests are in social and political systems, Indian medical ethics and Indian philosophy.

Sudha Gopalakrishnan is one of the founders of Sahapedia. She has prepared successful nomination dossiers for the recognition of Kutiyattam, Vedic Chanting and Ramlila as UNESCO Masterpieces of the Oral and Intangible Heritage of Humanity.

Suhas Palshikar taught political science at Savitribai Phule Pune University, Pune. He is Chief Editor of the journal *Studies in Indian Politics*. His recent publications include *Indian Democracy* (2017).

Suhrud Dave has been a judge of the High Court of Gujarat and chairman, Gujarat State Law Commission and Gujarat Electricity Regulatory Commission. He has written on Indian personal law and is the author of the monograph *The Privy Council, The British Courts and the Personal Laws of India* (2014), *Nuclear India* (2017) *and The Supreme Court, The High Courts and the Personal Laws of India* (2018).

Supriya Chaudhuri is Professor Emerita in the Department of English, Jadavpur University, Kolkata. Her most recent publication is the co-edited *Commodities and Culture in the Colonial World* (2018).

Surinder S. Jodhka is Professor of Sociology, JNU. His publications include the edited volume *A Handbook of Rural India* (2018), *Caste in Contemporary India* (2018) and *Caste* (2012).

Susan Visvanathan is Professor of Sociology at JNU. She is a fiction writer, besides being an author of several sociological works, including *The Christians of Kerala* (1993) and *Adi Shankara and Other Stories* (2017).

Tabish Khair is an associate professor at Aarhus University, Denmark. His latest publications include the academic work *The New Xenophobia* (2016) and the novel *A Night of Happiness* (2018).

Taslima Nasrin is a writer, physician and human rights activist. She is the recipient of several international awards, including the European Parliament's Sakharov Prize for Freedom of Thought and the Kurt Tucholsky Award from Swedish PEN. She has written forty books in Bengali and her works have been translated into thirty different languages.

Thomas Abraham is a Bangalore-based author and former professor at the Journalism and Media Studies Centre, University of Hong Kong. He is the author of *Twentieth Century Plague: The Story of SARS* (2005) and *Polio: The Odyssey of Eradication* (2018).

Timeri N. Murari began his career writing for *The Guardian*. He has since written nineteen works of fiction, including a children's book, novels for young adults, stage and screenplays. His latest novel is *Chanakya Returns* (2014).

Contributors

Tista Bagchi is former Professor of Linguistics at Delhi University. Her professional interests are in semantic and syntactic theory, historical linguistics and bioethics. She is also an accomplished musician.

Tridip Suhrud is Professor and Director, Archives, CEPT University, and Director of the L D Institute of Indology, Ahmedabad. He has published the critical editions of M. K. Gandhi's *Hind Swaraj* (2018) and *An Autobiography or the Story of My Experiments with Truth* (2018).

TRS Sharma has worked in several universities and research centres. He was a fellow at the Indian Institute of Advanced Study. His recent publications include *Reading Alfred Korzybski Through Inter-Theoretic Explorations: Indian and Western* (2018) and *Dialogics of Cultures in Ancient Indian Literatures* (2014).

Ujjwal Kumar Singh is Professor, Department of Political Science, University of Delhi, and was ICCR Chair Professor in UTS, Australia. He is the author of *Political Prisoners in India* (1998), *The State, Democracy and Anti-Terror Laws in India* (2007) and *The Election Commission of India: Institutionalizing Democratic Uncertainties* (2019).

Ulka Anjaria is Professor of English at Brandeis University, Massachusetts. She is the author of *Reading India Now: Contemporary Formations in Literature and Popular Culture* (2019) and the editor of *A History of the Indian Novel in English* (2015).

Uma Chakravarti is an Indian historian and feminist who taught at the Miranda House, University of Delhi. An activist, she has authored several books including *Gendering Caste* (2003) and *Social Dimensions of Early Buddhism* (1988).

Uma Vangal is Visiting Professor of Film at Kenyon College, Ohio, and an adjunct faculty at Asian College of Journalism, Chennai. She writes 'The FitMuS Test', a column in *The News Minute* that analyses films from the gender perspective of popular Indian films.

Usha Mudiganti is an Assistant Professor, School of Letters, Ambedkar University, Delhi. Her research interests include gender stereotypes in India, constructions of childhoods in literature and society and the tropes of childhood in postcolonial literature.

V. Geetha is Editorial Director, Tara Books. A feminist historian who writes widely in Tamil and English, her most recent publication is *Undoing Impunity: Speech after Sexual Violence* (2016).

Valerian Rodrigues holds the Ambedkar Chair at Ambedkar University, Delhi. His recent publications include *Conversations with Ambedkar: 10 Ambedkar Memorial Lectures* (2019), *Speaking for Karnataka* (co-authored with Rajendra Chenni, Nataraj Huliyar and S. Japhet) (2018) and *The Indian Parliament: A Democracy at Work* (co-authored with B. L. Shankar) (2011).

Contributors

Vanamala Viswanatha is a Professor at Azim Premji University, Karnataka. Her recent work includes *The Life of Harishchandra*, the English translation of a medieval Kannada poetic text (2017) and *Indira Bai*, a collaborative translation of the first social novel in Kannada (2019).

Varsha Bhagat-Ganguly is a former professor at the Institute of Law, Nirma University and Centre for Rural Studies and the Lal Bahadur Shashtri National Academy of Administration (LBSNAA), Mussoorie. Her recent monograph on Gujarat's protest movements (2015) and edited volumes have been on land rights (2016, 2018), on land titling (2017), and on *India's Scheduled Areas: Untangling governance, law and politics* (2019).

Vibha Puri Das is a career civil servant who retired as Secretary to Government of India. Recent publications include short essays in *The Essential RS Tolia* (2017), *Uttarakhand @ 15* (2016) and a monograph on home-based workers for use in the Curriculum for Human Rights (2000).

Vijaya Singh teaches English literature in the Department of English at Post-Graduate Government College, Sector 11, Chandigarh. She has published *Level Crossing: Railway Journeys in Hindi Cinema* (2017). She is also a filmmaker and has made two short films: A documentary on railway stations: *Unscheduled Arrivals* (2015) and a fiction film: *Andhere Mein* (2016).

Vijayanka Nair is an A. W. Mellon Postdoctoral Fellow at the Center for the Humanities, University of Wisconsin-Madison and Scholar-Leader Fellow at The New School India China Institute. Recent publications include an article on India's Aadhaar initiative in *Contemporary South Asia* (2018) and the *South Asia: Journal of South Asian Studies* (2019).

Vimala Ramachandran was formerly Professor from the National Institute for Educational Planning and Administration. Her recent publications include *Inside Indian Schools: The Enigma of Equity and Quality* (2018) and *Getting the Right Teachers into Right Schools: Managing India's Teacher Workforce* (2018).

Vipul Mudgal is the Director of 'Common Cause'. He was a visiting senior fellow at CSDS and where he directed the 'Publics and Policies' Programme. He has published *Claiming India from Below: Activism and Democratic Transformation* (2016).

Virginius Xaxa is former Professor of Sociology, Delhi School of Economics and Tata Institute of Social Sciences Guwahati Campus. He has published *State, Society and Tribes: Issues in Post-Colonial India* (2008).

Vrinda Dalmiya is Professor of Philosophy, University of Hawaii, Manoa. She is the author of *Caring to Know: Comparative Care Ethics, Feminist Epistemology and the Mahābhārata* (2016) and co-editor of *Exploring Agency in the Mahābhārata: Ethical and Political Dimensions of Dharma* (2018).

Contributors

Yogendra Kumar has been the Indian ambassador in Tajikistan and the Philippines (concurrent accreditation to Palau, Micronesia and the Marshall Islands) and High Commissioner in Namibia. He has authored a book on diplomatic dimension of India's maritime challenges (2015) and edited and contributed to a book on maritime order in the Indian Ocean (2017).

Yogesh Snehi is an assistant professor of history at Ambedkar University, Delhi. His recent publications include the monograph *Spatializing Popular Sufi Shrines in Punjab: Dreams, Memories, Territoriality* (2019) and the co-edited volume *Modernity and Changing Social Fabric of Punjab and Haryana* (2018).

Yousuf Saeed is a Delhi-based independent film-maker and author who has produced documentaries such as *Inside Ladakh, Basant, Khayal Darpan, Khusrau Darya Prem Ka* and *Campus Rising*. His publications include the monograph *Muslim Devotional Art in India* (2012).

INDEX

Aadhaar (ādhār)   121, 122, 137, 162, 352
Aai   262
Aam aadmi   82, 382
Aam Aadmi Party   209, 291
aamchunaav   354
aatankwadi   377
aatmadarshana   19
aatmajnaanam   19
aatmanivedanam   19
aatmatattvam   19
aavaam   259
Aazadi Bachao Andolan   291
Abbas, Ghulam   156
    Aanandi   156
Abhinaya   26
Abraham, Thomas   132
Accredited social health activists (ASHAs)   240
acharyakoti   200
achhoot (the untouchable)   29
Act XXXV of 1860   226
adda (addā)   299, 300
Additional district magistrate (ADM)   363
Adigal, Ilango   106
    Silappadikaram   106, 318
Adim Jati Sevak Sangh   233
Adivasi (ādivāsī)   32, 93, 150, 233, 234, 235, 345, 398, 399, 402, 409, 417
    adimjati   233, 234
    anusuchit janjati   233
    janjati   233
    vanvasi   233
    vanyajati   233
adjust   149, 261, 301, 332, 419
Advaita   34, 57, 118, 333
Advaita Vedanta   118, 333
Advani, Lal Krishna   328, 373
aesculapius   123
African National Congress (ANC)   63
African Union   172
AFSPA (Armed Forces Special Powers Act)   12, 88, 343, 344, 391, 413
Against Corruption and Unabated Taxation (ACAUT)   180
Agarwal, Bina   144
Agnihotri, Rama Kant   48, 209, 258, 303, 324, 330
Agni Purana   333
agriculture   23, 129, 135, 150, 211, 256, 274, 297, 324, 364, 397, 398
ahamkara   57
ahimsa (ahinsā/hinsā/satya/asatya/śānti)   9, 12, 20, 21, 254, 285, 417

A-hinsā   20
Ahkam-al-khamsah   203
Ahluwalia, Montek S.   147
Ahmed, Hilal   181, 221
AIIMS   297
Aikant, Satish   245
Air (Prevention and Control of Pollution) Act of 1981   167
Akananuru   78
Akbar   69, 88, 246, 347
akhara   87
Akhil Bharatiya Vidhyarthi Parishad (ABVP)   372
Akhyayika akhyana (variant)   47
akshara (aksara)   8, 302
    yukta   302
Alam, Mohd. Sanjeer   264
Alankara (alankāra)   75, 76
    arthalamkara   75
    shabdalamkara   75
Alexander the Great   107, 352
Al-Hujweri, Ali   95
Ali, Amir   203, 421
Ali, Ghulam   114
All India Anna Dravida Munnetra Kazhagam (AIADMK)   185
All India Institute of Hygiene and Public Health   229
All Tripura Tiger Force (ATTF)   379
Alma-Ata World Conference   170
Altekar, Anant Sadashiv   70
Amarakośa   2
Ambedkar, Dr B. R.   5, 55, 84, 230, 235, 236, 237, 248, 256, 267, 325, 331, 370
    Mahad Satyagraha   55
Ambedkarism   235, 236, 237
Ambedkarite   84, 235, 236, 237, 249
    Buddhists   249
Amganavādī workers (AWWs)   240
Amir Gharib (amīr/gharīb)   237, 238, 239
amma   262
ammi   262
Anand, Dev   142
Anand, Jasmine   197
Anand, Mulk Raj   191
Anand, S.   83
ananda   108
anarthakah mantrah   54
anasakti   36
Andrews, Charles Freer   285
anekāntavāda   35
anganwadi (ānganavādī)   4, 239, 240
anirvacaniya   57

Index

Anjaria, Ulka   30, 60
antaraatman   19
antariya   105, 106
anti-Brahminism   55
anwikshki   195
aparigraha   285
Apte, V. S.   19
Aravindan, G.   112
Archaeological Survey of India (ASI)   42
arishadvarga   26
Aristotle   1, 140
Arnold, Matthew   11
    Culture and Anarchy   11
artha (artha)   22, 36
Arthashastra   21, 22, 182, 195, 410
Aryan (āryan)/Dravidian   23, 24, 69, 105, 112, 183, 188, 190, 210, 217, 255, 284, 302, 319, 325, 386
Arya Samāj   55, 273, 289
Arya Varna   23
asceticism   35
ashram/asram (asrama)   68, 118, 122, 201, 202, 254, 294, 334
asmita (asmitā)   24, 25, 417
Asmitadarsha   25
aspatre/haspatal (aspatre/haspatāl)   122, 123
Asram Vidyalaya   294. *See also* Vishwa Bharati (viśva-bhāratī)
Assadi, Muzaffar   397, 398
Astāngika mārga   34
asteya   285
Āstika   33
Atharva Veda   47, 333, 346
Atigal, Ilanko   318
    Silappadikaram   106, 318
atma (ātmā)   12, 19, 25, 37, 58, 59, 94, 118
atma gauravam   25
atmaparivartan   370
Atrocities Act   345
atrocity   12, 25, 234, 345, 346, 357, 388, 391
attuliyam   345
atyaachaara   345
Aurobindo   57
avidya   57
avihamsa   20
award-*wapsi*   94
Ayodhya (ayōdhyā)   69, 99, 202, 346, 347
Ayurveda   220, 241, 242, 244
AYUSH (āyūs)   241, 242, 243, 244, 245
Azad, Ghulam Nabi   330
Azad, Ismail   97
Azad, Maulana   218
Azad, Yusuf   97
azan (azān)   8, 181, 182
Azizun Bai   292

baat   303, 304, 418
baat-cheet (bātcīt)   303
Babri Masjid   70, 346, 347, 373

babu (bābū)   348, 349, 376, 382
babuness   349
Bachchan, Amitabh   88, 110, 146, 191, 264
badh (badh)   182, 183
badhna   182
badh peedit   183
badh rahat kosh   183
Bagchi, Tista   97
Baghel, Lallan   316
Bahujan Samaj   185, 236, 259, 296
Bahujan Samaj Party (BSP)   55, 185, 236, 296
Bajrang Dal   233
Balakrishnan, Pulapre   135, 151
balti (Balti)   4, 183, 184
Balzac   206
    Le Pere Goriot   206
BAMCEF (Backward and Minority Communities Employees Federation)   236
Banabhatta   106
    Kadambari   106
Banaji, Jairus   398
bandh (bandh)   362
Bandyopadhyay, Ritajyoti   228
Bandyopadhyay, Sibaji   51
Banerjea, Surendranath   290
Banerjee, Madhulika   241
Banerjee, Paula   171
Banerjee, Rajat Subhra   116, 432
Bangdu   322
Baniyas   259
Bappa, Thakkar   233
Bapu, Asaram   202
Baruah, Sanjib   180
bawla   251
Baxi, Upendra   383
BDO (block development officer)   4, 363, 364
Beatles   118, 201
beauty parlour   4, 5, 86
Beg, Masood Ali   64, 72, 237
begging   227, 257
Begum Hazrat Mahal   292
Behal, Vikas   81
behaviour   36, 69, 93, 131, 143, 161, 186, 200, 202, 205, 220, 222, 263, 281, 300, 323, 324, 325, 333, 355, 356, 405
    coalition   356
    ethical   131
    patterns of   300, 324
    righteous   36
    social   93
    spontaneous   323
behen   184, 313, 314
behenji. *See* Mayawati
behenji (bahanjī)   184, 185
belief   1, 22, 28, 29, 30, 37, 41, 44, 49, 52, 59, 66, 67, 79, 95, 116, 182, 205, 213, 243, 257, 281, 301, 357, 411, 419
    Islamic   67

Index

below the poverty line 148, 159, 364
benami 124
benamidar 124
Bengal Chowkidari Act 393
Bennett, Tony 12
Bernier, Francois 71
betas 154
betis 154, 185
bhaavana 26
Bhabha, Homi K. 32, 61, 348
bhadralok (bhadralōk) 15, 185, 186
Bhadra-samaj 186
bhadra-sampraday 186
Bhagalpur riots of 1989 60
bhagat 79
Bhagat, Chetan 132
Bhagat-Ganguly, Varsha 149
Bhagavad Gita/Bhagvad Gita 21, 26, 27, 34, 50, 57, 58, 66, 104, 118, 285, 288, 290, 331, 333
Bhagavata Purana 333
Bhagwati, Jagdish 154
Bhagwat Purana 223
bhagya 67
bhaichara (bhā'īcārā) 245, 246
bhailo 187, 188, 418
Bhairabi Kawali. *See* Quawali
bhaisaheb 184
bhaiya 187, 188
Bhakhry, Savita 374
bhakt 132, 133
bhakti (bhakti) 27, 28, 34, 44, 59, 69, 91, 108, 206, 208, 246, 251, 268
Bharadwaj, Vishal 81
Bharata 26, 108
    Natyashastra 26, 78, 108
Bharatamuni 78
Bharatananda, Swami 291
Bharatanātyam 78
Bharatha 102, 103
    Natyasastra 102, 106
Bharati, Sadhvi Uma 201
Bharati, Subramania 293
Bharatiya Janata Party (BJP) 70, 132, 133, 154, 166, 201, 259, 273, 356, 359, 373, 385, 399
Bharatiya Jan Sangh (BJS) 372, 373, 399
Bharatiya Mazdoor Sangh (BMS) 372
bharatnatyam 78
bharatnatyam (bharatanātyam) 77, 78
Bhargava, Rajeev 406
Bhartihari 324
Bhartiya Janata Party 259, 297
Bhartrhari 1, 6
bhasha (bhāsā) 303, 304, 305, 308, 309, 310, 322, 348. *See also* languages
Bhatia, Bela 388
Bhatkhande, Vishnu Narayan 98
Bhattacharya, Rakhee 179, 180
Bhattacharya, Sibesh 47

Bhaumik, Subir 180
bhava (bhāva) 26, 28, 78, 89, 108, 334
Bhavanrao 291
bhāva pradhan 108
Bhave, Vinoba 218, 291
    bhoodan ('land grant') movement 291
    Sarva Seva Sangh 291
bhed 195
bhentvaartaa 303
Bhindranwale, Jarnail Singh 39
Bhiwandi riots of 1984 60
Bhojpuri. *See* languages
bhola/bholi/bhondu 251
bhoot (bhūta) 79
Bhopal gas tragedy 291, 310
Bhopali, Shakila Bano 97
bhrunhatya 196
Bhukamp (bhūkamp)/Bhuchal/Bhuchalam/Bhudol/ Bhuinchalo/Bhuinkampa/Bhukampa/Bhukampamu 188
bhukh hartal 362
bhushan, Prashant 291
Bhushanabhatta 106
Bhutacaitanyavadin 35
bhutakhela 79
Bhutto, Zulfiqar 63
Bibek 90, 91, 168
Bin Laden, Osama 91
biradaari 382
biradri (birādarī). *See* Parivar/Samaj/Biradri (parivār/samāj/birādarī)
Birsa Munda rebellion 399
Bismil, Ram Prasad 290
black economy 125
blog 110, 130
Board of Control for Cricket in India (BCCI) 193
boli 304, 322. *See also* languages
Bollywood 2, 80, 81, 82, 112, 115, 137, 156, 199, 326, 327, 351, 410, 420
BOLT 175
Bombay Plan 297
Bombay riots of the 1990s 60
Bombay Stamp Act of 1958 226
border 29, 216, 344, 350, 351, 378
Boruah, Bijoy 35, 37
Bose, Ajoy 184
Bose, Buddhadev 299
Bose, Netaji Subhash Chandra 95, 293, 297, 327, 329, 386
Boulanger, Chantal 106
BPO (business process outsourcing) 130, 138, 164
Brahmanda 65
Brahma Sutras 34
Brahmasvarūpa-Svagata-bheda 34
Brahma Vidya 39, 40
Brahmin 29, 56, 85, 195, 230, 283, 284, 312, 395
Brahminism 55, 56

443

Index

Brahmo Samaj   273, 294
Brahmo school   294
Braj   322
Braj Bhasha   322
Brass, Tom   398
breaking news   126, 127
bribes   358
brideprice   252
Brihadaranyaka Upanishad   50
Brihatkalpa Bhasya   21
British East India Company   292, 348
Browning, Gary K.   4,
BSE   175
Buddha, Gautama   34, 74
Buddhism   21, 33, 34, 35, 36, 40, 44, 46, 57, 118, 201, 250, 370
Buddhists   28, 118, 248, 249, 318, 370, 408
   Ambedkarite   249
budwak   251
bureaucracy   4, 139, 242, 265, 311, 348, 351, 352, 364, 396
Bureau of Police Research and Development   410
Burnell, A. C.   12
Byrce, T. J.   398

Calcutta killings of 1946   60
Cama, Bhikaiji   63
Cama, Dr Shernaz   63
Cama, Madame   290
Campaign for Lesbian Rights (CALERI)   258
Camus, Albert   104
   Caligula   104
Canepari, Michela   205
Canet, C.   229
Canning riots of 2013   60
cappal   189, 190
carita   47
Cartagena Declaration   172
Cārvāka   33, 35
cashlessness   137
Castells, Manuel   164
castes   2, 5, 14, 24, 28, 29, 30, 38, 44, 55, 56, 69, 76, 77, 79, 84, 85, 86, 93, 96, 115, 139, 140, 141, 142, 143, 167, 170, 183, 185, 186, 187, 194, 195, 205, 206, 210, 216, 224, 225, 230, 233, 235, 236, 237, 246, 248, 249, 250, 252, 253, 256, 257, 258, 260, 261, 262, 267, 269, 270, 272, 273, 274, 275, 276, 282, 283, 284, 290, 294, 295, 296, 300, 312, 313, 330, 345, 346, 357, 360, 363, 365, 366, 374, 375, 382, 387, 389, 390, 393, 395, 396, 400, 403, 406, 408, 409, 411, 413
   association   382
   divisions   260, 282, 283
   dominant   236, 256, 261, 295, 346, 365, 366
   identity   77, 85, 270, 296
   lower   79, 93, 115, 230, 236, 275, 295, 408
   senas   389
   traditions   236
   upper   77, 141, 185, 186, 249, 257, 275, 284, 295, 296, 300, 390
Catyāri ārya satyāni   34
Cawasji Jahangir Gallery   63
Central Identities Data Repository (CIDR)   121
Césaire, Aimé   61
chai   2, 197, 198
chai nashta/nashto   197
chai pani   197
Chaitanya, Sri   90
chaiwala   194
Chakraborty, Sanjit   39
Chakravarthy, N. Manu   213, 224
Chakravarti, Uma   274
Chakravarty, I.   229
champalu   189
Champaran, Bardoli and Kheda satyagrahas   398
Chanda, Ipshita   222
Chandhoke, Neera   413
Chandra, Bankim   327
Chandra, Bipin   357
Chandran, K. Narayana   308
Chandrayaan   247
chaori   122
chapana   189
chapanhi   189
chappal (cappal)   4
chappala   189
chappien   189
charana-upanah   189
charan-panhi   189
charchaa   303
chastity   72, 205, 275, 318, 319
Chatterjee, Partha   230
Chatterji, Roma   90
Chaturvedi, Sanjay   45
Chaudhuri, Supriya   185
chaupal   156, 157
chawls   147, 203
cheruppu   189
chhota khayal   96
child   16, 79, 86, 88, 89, 91, 117, 156, 160, 163, 170, 196, 212, 217, 227, 228, 239, 240, 253, 262, 264, 290, 375
   vulnerability and innocence of a   228
children   69, 82, 89, 102, 115, 140, 154, 156, 157, 160, 170, 172, 191, 196, 200, 208, 209, 217, 227, 228, 236, 239, 240, 261, 263, 274, 286, 294, 308, 374, 375, 380, 412, 417
Chimni, B. S.   171
Chiranjeevi   112
chirharan līlā   92
chittavrittinirodha   50
choolah (cūl'hā)   190, 191, 198
Chopra, Shivani   183
choutti   189
Chowdhury, Prem   205
Christian missionaries   234

Index

Christians 28, 144, 186, 252, 315, 372, 375, 387, 408
chulha 4
chuli 190
Chunaavi jumlā 355
Chunav Ayog (Election Commission) 354
chunav (cunāv)/election 353, 354, 355
chunav prakriya 354
Churchill, Winston 63
    Poverty and Un-British Rule in India 63
cinema/film 7, 63, 80, 81, 83, 96, 97, 112, 115, 141, 192, 199, 202, 211, 221, 225, 246, 260, 268, 300, 334, 351, 369, 410
    Bengali 112
    Hindi 112
    Kannada 112
    Malayalam 112
    Soviet 112
    Telugu 112
citizenship 131, 151, 271, 310, 311
    global 271
civilization 1, 24, 31, 46, 58, 61, 74, 107, 117, 118, 182, 187, 214, 220, 250, 255, 264, 267, 271, 287, 288, 319, 409
    Islamic 264
civil society 157, 158, 180, 250, 350, 373, 375, 414
class struggles 186
climate change 46, 127, 128, 129, 150, 373
climate mitigation 128
Clive, Robert 359
coalition dharma 6, 355, 356
Codana lakshana 36
Cohen, Stephen 352
colonialism 30, 31, 32, 61, 242, 266, 269, 312, 316, 349, 359, 408
communal riot 356
communal solidarity 255
communal violence 356, 357, 385, 413
Communist Party of India (CPI) 388, 399
Communist Party of India (Marxist) (CPI[M]) 388
Communist Party of India (Marxist-Leninist) (CPI[ML]) 388, 389
Community Action for Health (CAH) 170
computer 129, 130, 227
conflicts 172, 270, 350, 378, 385, 389
    multiple 378
Congress Party 107, 116, 132, 139, 162, 165, 166, 213, 273, 295, 296, 297, 325, 368
conjugality 260, 287
Constitution of India 94, 153, 231, 234, 249, 267, 278, 282, 304, 305, 307, 354, 366, 374, 386, 387, 393, 405, 406, 408
    Article 14 278
    Article 19 278
    Article 21 168, 278
    Article 40 393
    Article 51-A 282, 374
    Article 352 366, 367, 401
    Article 371 231
    Article 371A 231
    Article 371G 231
    Directive Principles of State Policy 94, 374, 393
    Eighth Schedule 304, 305, 306, 307, 325, 405
    Forty-Second Amendment 282, 367
    Fundamental Duties 282, 374
Controversial New Religions 201, 202
conversation 2, 4, 5, 8, 10, 13, 14, 32, 116, 129, 130, 134, 161, 229, 232, 237, 251, 259, 261, 269, 284, 286, 303, 320, 321, 323, 325, 339, 358, 371, 411, 416, 418
Coolie 191, 192
Corporate social responsibility (CSR) 131
corruption 114, 121, 129, 147, 166, 177, 180, 279, 286, 291, 311, 317, 326, 339, 355, 358, 359, 360, 381, 396, 401, 412
    fight against 129
counterfeiting 134, 227
Craig, Jeffrey 12, 338
    Keywords for Modern India 12
cricket 31, 80, 111, 192, 193, 211, 330, 420
Crime and Criminal Tracking Network and Systems (CCTNS) 278
crimes 205, 206, 253, 402, 410
criminality 379
Criminal Procedure Code (CPC) 364
CSIR 297
cultural politics 213, 322
cultural practices 29, 45, 92, 93, 236, 260, 283, 314
cultural self-expression 287
culture 1, 3, 4, 6, 7, 8, 11, 12, 13, 23, 26, 28, 29, 41, 50, 66, 79, 83, 89, 93, 96, 97, 108, 110, 113, 118, 129, 130, 137, 141, 147, 152, 155, 191, 195, 198, 199, 206, 211, 212, 216, 220, 221, 231, 237, 245, 246, 250, 263, 267, 271, 272, 278, 279, 284, 291, 294, 299, 300, 301, 306, 307, 309, 312, 317, 319, 322, 323, 324, 325, 335, 359, 360, 361, 370, 371, 372, 377, 382, 387, 392, 409, 417, 418, 419
    elite 324
    Indian 28, 130, 195, 221, 359
    lal batti (VIP) 382
    local 272
    political and bureaucratic 317
customary law 231
cyber 1, 132, 192
cyberbhakt 132, 133, 418
cyberbhakti 132
cybercafe' 130
cyber fortifications 1
cybermohalla 130
cyberseva 132
cycle-wala (sā'ikilwālā) 193, 194
Cyprus the Great 107
Cyrus the Great 62

Daasya bhava 28
Dalal 156, 332
Dalal Street 175

445

Index

Dalit 3, 25, 32, 55, 56, 61, 77, 83, 85, 93, 185, 210, 223, 230, 235, 236, 248, 249, 267, 270, 273, 282, 295, 296, 338, 345, 346, 357, 370, 388, 389, 402, 409
Dalmia, Katyayani 76, 84
Dalmiya, Vrinda 280
dance 77, 78, 81, 90, 91, 92, 93, 96, 102, 106, 112, 115, 208, 220, 221, 224, 232, 295, 334, 340, 412
Danda (daṇḍā) 4, 194, 195, 211
Dandadhikari 195
dandamuor namaskaram 314
dandaniti 195
danda samhita 195
danda vidhan 195
Daridranarayana 285
dars-e-aliya 266
dars-e-nizami 265
darshana 33, 34, 35, 118
darshana (darśana) 33, 34, 35, 118
darshana marga 33
Darul Uloom Deoband 265
Daruwala, Keki 62
Das, Chitta Ranjan 290
Das, Gurcharan 49, 315
   A Fine Family 315
Das, Kamala 15
Das, Raghavendra Lal 172
Das, Samir Kumar 361
Dasa Varna 23
Dasgupta, Aditya 138
Dasgupta, Dipak 142
Dastan-e Amir Hamza 320
Dastangoi 320
Datta, Sudhin 24
Dave, Justice Suhrud 405
Dawkins, Richard 9
Dayabhaga 144, 145
Debroy, Bibek 168
Deccan Revolt of 1875 398
decency 205
deen bandhu 285
deepa gana 84
Dehejia, Harsha V. 75, 107
democracy 4, 5, 6, 21, 135, 235, 249, 250, 271, 279, 291, 296, 317, 318, 330, 340, 344, 352, 353, 354, 355, 363, 364, 366, 367, 380, 382, 393, 399, 401, 413, 414, 419
  direct 291
  Indian 4, 135, 250, 271, 317, 318, 353, 354, 413, 419
  majoritarian 271
demonetization 125, 133, 134, 173, 239
  process of 134
Dennett, Daniel 9
deprivation 140, 160, 227
Desai, Santosh 86, 301
Desani, G. V. 316
desh 255, 321, 328

desi 114, 360, 361
desivad (dēsīvād) 360, 361
DeSouza, Peter Ronald 4, 14, 249, 385
De Souza, Siddharth Peter 383, 436
destiny 50, 66, 67, 141, 291
  beliefs about 66
Deva, Acharya Narendra 55
devadasis 77
development 25, 42, 43, 55, 72, 73, 89, 94, 99, 103, 122, 127, 128, 129, 131, 133, 135, 136,137, 140, 141, 150, 151, 159, 164, 165, 167, 168, 170, 172, 173, 178, 179, 220, 221, 232, 234, 235, 239, 240, 241, 249, 254, 272, 274, 281, 286, 290, 291, 294, 297, 305, 306, 317, 347, 364, 369, 375, 391, 405, 406, 410
  early childhood 240
  economic 150, 254, 272, 297
  process 297
  state-funded 179
Devi, Rukmini 78
Devra, G. S. L. 71
dhaaranaa 37
dhani 255
dhansak 63
Dhar, P. N. 310
Dharampal-Frick, Gita 12
dharanā 250, 278
dharanikampa 188
dharatikampya 188
dharma (dharma) 2, 6, 12, 22, 34, 35, 36, 43, 48, 50, 51, 69, 94, 106, 108, 214, 283, 333, 355, 356, 361, 418
  coalition 6, 356
dharmasastra 106
Dharmashastra 22, 333
Dharma Sutras 333
dharmayuddha 66
dharmin 34
dharmshala 122
dharna (*dharnā*) 361, 362, 398, 417
Dhyana (Dhyāna) 37
dictionary 6, 10, 11, 12, 24, 82, 109, 129, 134, 167, 179, 182, 187, 212, 218, 224, 225, 269, 272, 335, 348, 380
didi 184
digi-naka 130
Digital India 136, 137, 138, 177
digital media 137, 138, 161
digital payments 134
dignity 123, 140, 192, 194, 214, 236, 248, 266, 346, 374, 380
diplomacy 46, 74, 330, 332, 377
disability 251, 252
disgrace 205
dishonour 68, 205
Divyang 251
Dixit, Rajiv 291
DM (district magistrate) 363, 364
D'monte, Darryl 145, 432

Index

Dom 223
dorai 312
dowry (dahēj) 184, 196, 252, 253, 261, 327
Dowry Prohibition Act, 1961 253
drama 72, 88, 89, 91, 100, 102, 103, 104, 115, 208, 287, 320, 334, 341, 343
Dravida Kazagham 399
Dravida Munnetra Kazhagam (DMK) 185, 319, 334, 399
Dravidar Kazhagam (DK) 284
Dravidian 23, 24, 69, 105, 112, 183, 188, 190, 210, 217, 284, 302, 319, 325, 386
Dravidian movement 112
Drèze, Jean 193
Dubash, Navroz K. 127
Dubey, Abhay Kumar 321
duragatam 345
Durant, Charles 155
Dutt, Sanjay 88
Dutta, Ranjeeta 220
dvaita 92
Dwyer, Rachel 12
dynasticism 273

early childhood care and education (ECCE) 240
East India Company 62, 110, 225, 226, 292, 308, 312, 348, 349
E-chaupal (E-caupāl). *See* Mandi, E-chaupal (mandī/E-caupāl)
Eco, Umberto 216
economic development 150, 254, 272, 297
economic policy 63, 151, 254
economic policymakers 133
economic recession 186
economic reforms 152, 165, 166, 297
Economic Survey of 2017–18 154
Economic Times 165
economy 7, 32, 45, 52, 80, 81, 104, 125, 134, 135, 136, 147, 149, 151, 152, 156, 172, 173, 175, 176, 187, 193, 214, 227, 228, 229, 235, 254, 256, 258, 261, 272, 297, 298, 341, 350, 378, 396, 397, 420
    black 125
    formalization of 134
    Indian 152, 175, 193, 227, 297, 298, 420
    political 214, 396, 397
    underdeveloped 297
    world 7, 152, 176
education 5, 14, 56, 122, 125, 131, 140, 149, 152, 154, 161, 163, 168, 170, 177, 186, 216, 230, 239, 240, 250, 251, 254, 261, 264, 265, 266, 281, 282, 286, 290, 294, 295, 297, 300, 302, 305, 308, 309, 319, 331, 337, 338, 349, 364, 365, 366, 369, 373, 374, 375, 392, 406, 412, 417
    bilingual 338
egalitarianism 38, 44
Eighth Schedule 304, 305, 306, 307, 325, 405
Ekal Vidyalaya 233
Election Commission of India 399

electoral calculations 229
electoral mobilization 229
electoral process 240, 354
Ellis, F. W. 24
Elmhirst, Leonard 294
emergency 140, 146, 160, 259, 282, 291, 328, 334, 366, 367, 368, 373, 389, 401, 408
    medical 140
    national 146, 160, 282, 366
Emergency of 1975 366, 367
Encyclopedia of Islam 66
English. *See also* languages
    adaptability of 309
    appropriation of 420
    Babu 348, 349
    imperialist 289
    Indian 130, 316, 355
    phrase 108, 338
    translation 35, 97, 205, 315
equality 20, 38, 140, 144, 145, 170, 213, 235, 236, 249, 250, 254, 262, 264, 267, 278, 283, 299, 302, 317, 330, 369, 374, 382, 413
EXCOM 172
exploitation 192, 227, 234, 236, 237, 248, 256, 274, 276, 345, 374, 398, 403, 413
extremism 21, 139

Facebook 130, 137, 176, 177, 415
Faiz, Faiz Ahmed 268
falak 66
famine 186
Fanon, Frantz 61
farmers' movement 398
Farooqi, Irfanullah 368
Farooqui, Mahmood 320
fatwa (fatvā) 181, 204, 368, 369, 370, 420
Fazl, Abul 347
    Ain-I Akbari 347
Federation of Indian Chambers of Commerce and Industry (FICCI) 80
female foeticide 196, 197, 253
fidelity 275, 318, 340
file 261, 279, 310, 311, 410
Finance Act of 1997, Clause 77A, Section 65 111
firangi/angrez (phirangī/angrēj) 311, 312
First War of Independence 289
Five-Year Plan 152, 297
    Second Plan 152, 297
Flaubert 61
folklore 57, 70, 79, 217, 221, 324, 326, 367
food 30, 114, 123, 128, 138, 139, 142, 143, 149, 150, 153, 154, 156, 167, 170, 177, 184, 198, 199, 200, 209, 210, 220, 222, 224, 227, 228, 229, 243, 244, 281, 287, 291, 328, 329, 365, 392
foreign direct investment (FDI) 155, 165
Foreign Exchange Regulation Act [FERA] 125
foto (phōtō) 82, 418
Foucault, Michel 10, 361

Index

FRAMES (Film Radio Audio-Visual Music Events Shows)   80
French, Patrick   15
   India: A Portrait   15
Freud, Sigmund   12
Friedman, Thomas   163
Frydman, Maurice   291
fundamental rights   234, 366, 367, 374
The Future of Knowledge and Culture: A Dictionary for the 21st Century   88

gaali (gālī)   312, 313, 314
gadya   322
Galeano, Eduardo   104
Galen   241
Gama   255
gana (gānā)   83, 84
Gandhi, Indira   39, 88, 160, 280, 282, 328, 352, 373
Gandhi, M. K.   5, 21, 39, 70, 94, 141, 162, 189, 191, 214, 218, 233, 246, 253, 254, 256, 267, 281, 282, 283, 285, 288, 290, 291, 325, 329, 334, 352, 362, 369, 372, 393, 398, 412
   Hind Svarāj   267, 288
Gandhi, Sanjay   146
Gandhi, Sonia   107
Gandhian   5, 21, 230, 233, 253, 254, 260, 291, 310, 327, 376, 383, 398
Ganesan, Sivaji   112
Ganga-Jamuni tehzib   246
Ganguly, Himika   115
   The Great Indian Matrimonial Tamasha   115
Gani, Shahzad   167, 190
gaon (gānv)   255, 256
garibi hatao   153, 328
garva   25
Gatha   47
gaunkaria   187
Gavaskar, Sunil   80
gavati chai   197
Geetha, V.   235, 267, 282
gender   14, 32, 41, 76, 86, 92, 140, 141, 144, 145, 159, 165, 170, 177, 186, 214, 216, 218, 223, 230, 236, 250, 254, 257, 265, 275, 283, 286, 292, 334, 357, 369, 385, 409
   discrimination   165, 254
   prejudices   230
ghanti   187, 188
Ghar Wapsi (ghar vāpsī)   370, 371
Ghatak, Ritwik   268
ghazal   96, 114
gherao (ghērāv)   362
Ghose, Partha   293
Ghose, Sagarika   132
Ghosh, Arjun   114
Ghosh, Parikshit   153
Ghosh, Parimal   186
Gilchrist, John   322

Gili Danda (gillī dandā). *See* Kabbadi, Gili Danda, Jallikatta (kabaddī, gillī dandā, jallikattū)
Ginwala, Frene   63
girmitiya   191
girmitiyas   191
global North   127
Global South   127, 244
godmen   44, 200, 201, 202
godrej almirah (godrej ālmirah)   202, 203
Goethe   361
gohand   255
Gokak, V. K.   315
Golden Temple   38, 39
Golwalkar, M. S.   372, 373, 387
   Bunch of Thoughts   372, 387
Gond revolt   399
Goods and Services Tax   116, 362
goods sector   297
Gopalakrishnan, Adoor   112
Gopalakrishnan, Sudha   98, 100
Gopani, Chandraiah   345
gopis   90, 91, 92
Gorapan (gōrāpan)   84, 85
Goswami, Rupa   28
Goswamy, B. N.   82
gourava   25
governance   21, 42, 69, 121, 129, 136, 137, 150, 167, 180, 227, 231, 234, 239, 266, 267, 278, 279, 290, 292, 310, 311, 352, 369, 373, 374, 393, 411, 412, 420
governmentality   137, 251, 396
Govinda   50, 59, 88, 92
Gowda, Chandan   217
gram sabha   249, 393
green revolution   281, 365, 397, 398
Grey, J. E. B   15
   Homo phoneticus indicus   15
Grhya Sutras   70, 333
Grossberg, Lawrence   12
gross domestic product (GDP)   125, 140, 148, 154, 165, 297
groupings   29, 256, 273, 296
   community   296
GST   180
guckkasten   82
Guha, Ranajit   296, 408, 409
Gujarati. *See* languages
Gujarat riots of 1969   60
Gujarat riots of 2002   60
gunas   33, 34, 220
Gupta, Abhinava   108
Gupta, Shekhar   154
Guptha, Abhinava   102
gurbani   207
guru (guru)   3, 25, 38, 39, 40, 44, 54, 79, 82, 200, 201, 202, 207, 246, 248, 257, 409
Guru, Gopal   248
Guru Amar Das   38
Guru Arjan Dev   38, 39

Index

Guru Granth Sahib 38, 39
gurukul 40
Guru Nanak 82, 246
guru *parampara* 40
gurupasadana 39
Guru Ram Das 38
Guru Ram Rahim 202
guru–shishya parampara 40
gym 5, 86, 87

Haasan, Kamal 112
haat 155, 156
hacker movement 138
Hadiths 266
hafta 359
haj 41, 42, 222
Halba rebellion 399
Haldar, Gopal 299, 300
Hamara Gaon Hamara Raj movement 291
Hand, Chris 130
handi 130
Hankin, Nigel 12
hannatala 362
haram/halal (harām/halāl) 203, 204
Hardin, G. 7
Harijan 248, 249, 346
Harimandir Sahib 38, 39
Harriss, John 12
hartal (hartāl) 362
Hasan, Zoya 398
Hasnain, Nadeem 77
    The Other Lucknow 77
Hasnain, S. Imtiaz 64, 66, 72, 237
Hawley, John 70
Hazare, Anna 291, 359
Hazarika, Sanjoy 377
health 87, 118, 119, 125, 131, 139, 140, 142, 150, 152, 154, 160, 161, 167, 169, 170, 171, 201, 234, 239, 240, 243, 244, 245, 253, 282, 297, 335, 336, 374, 386
    public 119, 169, 170, 171, 245, 374, 386
'Health for All by the Year 2000 A.D.' 170
Hedgewar, Dr K. B. 372, 373
Hegde, Sasheej 55
Hellenism 107
Hello-ji (hēlō jī) 314, 315
Herbert, George 27
Heredia, Rudolf C. 370
heritage sites 42, 43
Herodotus 47, 62
hero/heroine 28, 50, 68, 87, 88, 192, 326, 334, 349
hierarchy 28, 29, 30, 141, 187, 194, 195, 275, 295, 306, 365, 376, 382, 403, 409, 410, 413
    ascriptive 30
hijra (hijdā) 72, 232, 257
Hindi. *See also* languages
    colloquial 110, 316, 321
    development of 305, 405
    phrase 191, 293
    spoken 304
    spread of 405
Hindi–Urdu controversy 232
Hindu 9, 21, 25, 28–9, 40, 43–5, 56, 59–60, 62, 68–70, 77, 95, 106–7, 117–18, 132–3, 144, 147, 185–6, 201–2, 206–8, 220, 222, 233, 236, 246, 254, 258, 262, 270–1, 283, 290, 293, 312, 314, 327, 345, 350, 370, 372–3, 387, 408
    conservatives 290
    darsanas 118
    practice 222
Hinduism 6, 28, 29, 33, 35, 37, 40, 43, 44, 45, 46, 56, 223, 230, 235, 244, 332, 333, 370, 372
    practice of 230
Hindu–Muslim riots 60, 372
Hindu philosophy 44, 117, 118, 220
Hindu Rashtra (hindū rāstra) 372, 373
Hindu Succession Amendment Act (HSAA) 144
Hindutva 6, 59, 273, 372, 373
hinsā 20
Hippocrates 241
Hirsch, E. D. 11
    Cultural Literacy 11
Hitapodesha 289
Hitler 387
HIV/AIDS 258, 357
Hobson-Jobson 12, 331, 348
    A Glossary of Colloquial Anglo-Indian Words and Phrases, and of Kindred Terms, Etymological, Historical, Geographical and Discursive 12
Holkar, Ahilyabai 293
homeopathy 241
honour killing 205, 261
Hopkins, Gerard Manley 27
huccuhole 183
human development 136, 140, 159, 375
Human Development Index (HDI) 375
humanity 45, 60, 136, 267, 271, 294, 374
human rights 140, 170, 172, 278, 343, 374, 375
humiliation 106, 192, 205, 267, 345, 358, 413
The HUNGAMA Survey Report 2011 166
Husain, Intizar 321
    Kata Hua Dibba 321
Huxley, Aldous 281
huzoor 153
Hyderabad riots of the 1990s 60

ichha 57
identity 8, 15, 24, 25, 34, 44, 77, 85, 96, 107, 121, 122, 137, 160, 187, 188, 231, 234, 235, 241, 249, 255, 270, 272, 273, 280, 295, 296, 300, 304, 310, 348, 357, 372, 379, 387, 392, 399
    absolute 34
    biometrics-based 121
    foundational 372
    Goan 187

449

Index

individual   122
modern   241
politics   372, 379, 399
primordial   296
regional   25
unitary   273
universal   121
verbal   8
verification   121
xenophobic   188
ideological mockery   14
ideology   30, 81, 112, 267, 274, 275, 357, 369, 372, 373, 388
   fanatical   388
   political   112, 369, 372
   right-wing   372
IEL (Indian English Literature)   316
IFS (Indian Foreign Service)   375, 376, 377
iftar   60, 222
IIAS (Indian Institute of Advanced Study)   14
IIMs   297
Ilavarasan, P. Vigneswara   176
ILE (Indian Literature in English)   316
iman   41
immunization   170, 240
India
   Communist movement in   388
   economic policies in   389
   Nehruvian vision of   372
   outsourcing services in   164
India Against Corruption   177, 291, 359
India CSR Reporting Survey 2017   131
Indian Administrative Services (IAS)   352, 353, 363, 364, 375, 376, 377, 411, 412
Indian Civil Services (ICS)   290, 352, 353, 363, 376
Indian Council of Medical Research (ICMR)   167
Indian Institutes of Technology (IITs)   281, 297
Indian microfinance movement   157
Indian National Congress   283, 290, 329, 353, 354, 369, 394
Indianness   33, 94, 301, 318, 330, 377
Indian Ocean   45, 46
Indian Penal Code (IPC)   253, 258, 343, 345, 385, 402
   Article 377   385
Indian Railways   141
Indian Revolt of 1857   292
Indian Space Research Organisation's (ISRO)   247
Indian Statistical Institute   129, 138
Indian Succession Act of 1925   144
Indian writing in English (IWE)   315, 316
IndiaStack   137
industry   6, 77, 80, 81, 86, 88, 97, 111, 112, 126, 130, 141, 156, 164, 165, 180, 193, 224, 243, 297
Indus Valley civilization   24, 105, 107, 116, 117, 255
inequality   28, 29, 125, 139, 235, 282, 283, 298
inflation   125, 134, 142, 143, 175
information technology (IT)   130, 132, 138, 164, 179
inheritance systems   144, 145

injustice   48, 125, 236, 237, 246, 291, 413, 414
Institute for Health Metrics and Evaluation (IHME)   167
institutionalisation   274
insurgency   179, 180, 344, 378, 379, 390
insurgency/terrorist/jihādī/militant   39, 132, 179, 180, 229, 266, 344, 373, 377, 378, 379, 390
insurgent groups   179, 180
Integrated Child Development Services (ICDS)   239, 240
internalization   37
International Society for Krishna Consciousness (ISKCON)   60, 201
International Yoga Day   119
IPL   193
Iqbal   237, 238
Iqbal, Allama   67
   Kulliat-i-Iqbal   67
Ishq (iśq)   89
Islam   44, 46, 62, 66, 72, 96, 181, 204, 222, 223, 264, 265, 266, 369, 378, 387
Islam, Maidul   41, 314
isogamy   260
istifta   369
itihasa (itihāsa)   47, 48, 52, 53, 65
itihasika school   47
itivritta   47, 48
Iyengar, K. Srinivasa   315
Iyer, Justice Krishna   363, 383, 384
izzat   205, 417

Jaag   207
jabaan   304
Jabaladarshana Upanishad   20
Jaffrelot   296
Jagannath/Juggernaut (jagannāth/juggernaut)   206
jagat   34, 57
jagraata   207
jagran/kirtan/bhajan (jāgaran/kīrtan/bhajan)   207, 208
Jahangir   63, 199, 353
Jai Kisan Andolan   291
Jaimini   34, 36
   Mimamsa Sutra   36
Jain   20, 21, 28, 52, 58, 69, 105, 106, 206, 220, 259, 334, 346, 385, 408
Jainism   20, 33, 35, 40, 44
jajman   256
Jajmani   256
jallikatta (jallīkattū)   177. *See also* Kabbadi, Gili Danda, Jallikatta (kabaddī, gillī dandā, jallīkattū)
jal pralay   182
jal-vaayu parivartan   128
jamia   264, 265
Jan, Gauhar   96
janaaza   223
Janata Dal   259
Janata Party   259

Index

janmapatri 14, 48, 49
jan sunwai 278
janta (jantā)/public 4, 20, 21, 31, 32, 51, 55, 78, 80, 94, 96, 99, 111, 119, 121, 126, 128, 129, 130, 133, 134, 135, 137, 140, 143, 146, 148, 151, 152, 154, 155, 159, 160, 168, 169, 170, 171, 172, 174, 177, 181, 186, 195, 198, 225, 226, 228, 229, 230, 239, 242, 245, 247, 250, 254, 258, 259, 266, 267, 278, 279, 286, 290, 297, 299, 301, 306, 309, 317, 319, 327, 329, 330, 331, 343, 345, 346, 354, 358, 359, 360, 362, 373, 374, 376, 377, 379, 380, 381, 382, 383, 384, 385, 386, 390, 393, 396, 401, 402, 404, 407, 412, 418, 419
    aavaam 259
    figures 80
    interest 94
    logbaag 259
    memory 51
    party 139, 154, 259
    perception 412
    public sphere 404
    space 32
jantar mantars 55
jati 29, 55, 69, 233, 365, 366.
jatra (*jātrā*) 90
Jayadeva 50, 92
    Gita Govinda 50, 92
Jayalalithaa, J. 88, 112, 185, 334
Jayaram, N. 252
Jayasi, Malik Muhammed 71
jeernodharan 43
Jeffrey, Craig 12, 338
    Timepass 338
Jehad 261, 378
Jesudoss, Perianayagam 319
jharoo/teel jharoo/eerkali chool (jharu/teel jhādū/eerkali chool) 208, 209
jhuggi, jhopri, slum, chawl (jhuggī, jhōpdi, Slum, cāl) 145, 146, 147, 229, 317
jigil gana 84
jihadis 266
Jijabai 293
Jinnah, Mohammad Ali 238, 328, 394
Jīva 33
Jivātman 34
Jnāna 34, 35
jnanamarg 57
jobless growth 147, 148, 165
jobs 142, 148, 149, 153, 154, 194, 230, 296, 300, 358, 376
Jodhka, Surinder S. 28
Johal, Ramanjit Kaur 225
Johar, Karan 81
John, Mary E. 402
Jones, William 23, 61
jootha (jūthā) 209, 210
jugaad (jugād) 316, 317, 318, 415
ju'gāra 130, 154

jumla (jumlā) 355, 379, 380, 381
jumlanomics 381
jushth 209
Jussawalla, Adil 63
jutth 209
juuthan 210

kaanaaphuusi 303
kabbadi (kabaddī). *See* Kabbadi, Gili Danda, Jallikatta (kabaddī, gillī dandā, jallīkattū)
kabbadi, gili danda, jallikatta (kabaddī, gillī dandā, jallīkattū) 210, 211, 212
Kabir 6, 28, 246, 268, 289
Kadar, Mala 318
Kafka 310, 311, 326
kaharwanaach 92. *See also* Naach (nāc)
kā'ī 210
kai (*kāī*) 212, 213
kaibittaru 213
kaihididaru 213
Kaijodisu 213
Kaikelage 213
Kaikoosu 213
kaikottaru 213
kaitege 213
Kaivalya 118
Kaivalya padas 33
Kakar, Sudhir 15
    The Indian People 15
Kalam, A. P. J. Abdul 247
Kaliachak riots of 2016 60
Kalidasa 104
    Meghaduta 104
Kalinga War 246
Kalithogai 211
Kalpa Sutras 333
Kama and Kamasutra (kāma and kāmasūtra) 22, 26, 36, 49, 50, 51, 89, 108, 109
Kamagita 51
kamin 256
Kanāda 34
    Vaisheshika Sutra 36
Kannada 24, 69, 105, 109, 112, 164, 183, 188, 189, 212, 213, 218, 224, 302, 306, 314, 335, 338, 397
Kanthimathi 323
Kanungo, Pralay 372
kanya bhrunhatya 196
Karah, Hemachandran 102
karma 3, 34, 36, 57, 58, 67, 118, 220
karma marg 57
Karma Mīmāmsa 34
Karnad, Girish 268
karpazhippu 319
karpu 318, 319
kar seva 285
Karunanidhi, Muthuvel 319, 334
Karve, Iravati 256
Kasaravalli, Girsh 112

451

Index

Kashyap, Anurag 81
kassdmlik 66
katha, kahani, qissa, dastaan (kathā, kahānī, kis'sā, dāstān) 89, 293, 320, 321, 324
Katha *prabandh* 320
Katha *prasang* 320
Kathā Upanishad 19
katha *vartta* 320
kathopkathan 320
Katrak, Kersy 63
Kaur, Navprit 327
Kaur, Ravinder 196
Kautilya 21, 22, 47, 48, 182, 195, 410
    Arthashastra 21, 195, 410
Kawali 96. See also Qawwālī
kayaka (kayaka) 213
Kayasth/Kayastha 395, 405
Keats, John 104
    Ode on a Grecian Urn 104
Kejriwal, Arvind 291
Kelkar, Vijay 169
Kelkar Committee 169
Key Concepts for Modern Indian Studies 12
khadaun 189
khadava 189
khadi (khādī) 70, 322, 376
Khair, Tabish 348
Khakkar, Bhupen 284
Khalji, Ala-ud-Din 71
Khan, Ashfaq Ullah 290
Khan, Fahima Ayub 323
Khan, Kallan 96
Khan, Nusrat Fateh Ali 97, 351
Khan, Salman 88
khandaan 382
Khanikar, Santana 409
Khanwalkar, Seema 109
khap 246, 255, 257
kharī 190, 214
Khari Boli (khadī bōlī) 321, 322. See also languages
    Bambaia 321
    Braj Bhasha 322
    Dakhani 321
    Kalkatia 321
Khatoon, Rashida 97
Khera, Reetika 161, 255
khickhic 303
Khilafat Movement 369
Khilnani, Sunil 15
    The Idea of India 15
Khusrau, Amir 95, 98, 246, 268
Kipling, Rudyard 7, 349
Kirloskar-Steinbach, Monika 12
kisan satyagrahas 398
kismat (qismat). *See* kismat/takdir (qismat/takadir)
kismat/takdir (qismat/takadīr) 66, 67
Kittel, F. 212

kolam 100, 101
kolaveri (kōlāverī) 323
Koli uprising 399
Kollywood 80, 112
Kond tribal revolt 399
Konkani 187, 217, 224, 306
Koshi, Annie 251
Kothari, Rajni 295, 366
Kothari, Rita 339
Kovacevic, Merdijana 335
Koya tribal revolt 399
Krishna Iyer, E. 78
Krishnan, M. 312
    The Genus Feringhee 312
krodha 26
kroorata 345
Ksanika-vāda 34
Kshatriya 29, 30, 195, 230
kulhad chai 197
Kulkarni, Dipti 202, 230
Kumar, Arun M. 125, 131
Kumar, Ashutosh 399
Kumar, A. K. Shiva 140, 121
Kumar, Rajesh 303
Kumar, Yogendra 375
kundali 49

labour 87, 137, 141, 147, 148, 149, 165, 186, 191, 194, 213, 214, 233, 235, 252, 254, 266, 274, 345, 362, 369, 375, 396, 412, 413
Lakshman Rekha (laksman rēkhā) 215, 216
Lal, Lalluji 322
    Prem Sagar 322
Lal, Malashri 70
Lal, Shaikh 96
Lal, Vinay 12
lal batti (lāl battī) 381, 382
land 7, 38, 101, 117, 124, 129, 135, 139, 141, 144, 145, 146, 147, 149, 150, 151, 154, 162, 168, 182, 183, 187, 224, 225, 226, 234, 246, 254, 256, 263, 269, 271, 291, 294, 303, 320, 345, 347, 350, 353, 360, 363, 364, 366, 372, 378, 382, 383, 388, 389, 395, 396, 397, 398, 405, 406
    acquisitions 149, 150, 151
    administration 364
    agricultural 144, 145, 350, 396
    grabbing 149, 150, 151
    grant 291
    records 145, 364, 395, 396
    reform 396, 406
    transformations 149
langda 251
languages 1, 2, 3, 4, 5, 6, 8, 10, 11, 13, 15, 19, 22, 23, 24, 26, 29, 32, 34, 38, 40, 41, 43, 47, 56, 57, 60, 61, 62, 65, 68, 69, 71, 77, 78, 82, 84, 86, 88, 89, 91, 95, 96, 97, 99, 103, 104, 105, 107, 109, 110, 112, 115, 121, 123, 126, 128, 129, 130, 134, 164, 165, 176, 177, 183, 187, 188, 189, 197, 205, 210,

Index

212, 213, 216, 219, 220, 221, 224, 225, 229, 232, 237, 238, 242, 248, 249, 251, 258, 259, 263, 266, 268, 269, 273, 279, 280, 289, 294, 295, 296, 300, 302, 303, 304, 305, 306, 307, 308, 309, 311, 312, 313, 314, 315, 316, 320, 321, 322, 323, 324, 325, 328, 331, 337, 338, 339, 340, 345, 348, 349, 357, 360, 361, 372, 380, 386, 387, 394, 402, 404, 405, 406, 411, 415, 416, 417, 418, 419, 420
Aka-Bo 307
Angika 307
Apbhranshas 324
Assamese 69, 109, 188, 302, 306, 314, 324
Awadhi 322, 324, 325
Banjara 307
Bazika 307
Bengali (Bangla) 15, 24, 25, 28, 40, 53, 84, 90, 109, 112, 129, 142, 184, 185, 186, 188, 189, 205, 206, 210, 264, 266, 289, 299, 300, 302, 303, 304, 306, 312, 314, 324, 328, 362
Bhojpuri 191, 304, 307, 325, 416
Bhoti 251, 307
Bhotia 307
Bundelkhandi 307
Chhattisgarhi 307
Chinese 294
common 387
Coorg 307
Dhatki 307
endangered 103, 308
English 2, 3, 4, 5, 12, 15, 24, 32, 35, 40, 49, 56, 57, 61, 89, 91, 93, 97, 102, 108, 126, 128, 129, 130, 133, 164, 166, 167, 177, 182, 185, 187, 188, 191, 192, 199, 200, 205, 206, 211, 212, 215, 218, 220, 224, 232, 242, 254, 255, 259, 263, 269, 272, 278, 287, 289, 290, 294, 302, 304, 306, 307, 308, 309, 310, 311, 312, 315, 316, 323, 326, 327, 334, 335, 337, 338, 339, 348, 349, 355, 362, 380, 387, 402, 411, 417, 418, 419, 420
European 23, 24, 337
Garhwali 307
Gondi 307, 389
Greek 11, 47, 52, 72, 107, 324, 334
Gujarati 24, 25, 40, 62, 105, 109, 130, 183, 188, 189, 266, 287, 304, 306, 324, 339, 362, 379
Gujjar 307
Gujjari 307
Hindi 5, 40, 55, 64, 67, 69, 80, 84, 92, 95, 99, 100, 109, 110, 111, 112, 122, 126, 128, 129, 130, 133, 139, 142, 156, 157, 160, 161, 164, 165, 182, 183, 184, 187, 188, 189, 190, 191, 192, 194, 196, 198, 205, 208, 209, 225, 231, 232, 233, 238, 239, 245, 246, 249, 251, 252, 254, 255, 259, 266, 273, 278, 286, 289, 293, 302, 303, 304, 305, 306, 309, 311, 312, 313, 314, 316, 317, 320, 321, 322, 324, 325, 326, 327, 328, 331, 335, 337, 345, 348, 349, 350, 353, 361, 362, 372, 379, 381, 389, 400, 402, 405, 410
Ho 81, 307

Indian 11, 19, 22, 24, 29, 40, 47, 69, 89, 91, 97, 105, 109, 121, 123, 129, 130, 164, 189, 210, 212, 242, 249, 266, 289, 302, 304, 311, 316, 328, 339, 340, 345, 348, 360, 402, 419, 420
Indo-Āryan 188, 302, 324, 331
Indo-European 23, 61
Kachachhi 307
Kamtapuri 307
Kannada 24, 69, 105, 109, 112, 164, 183, 188, 189, 212, 213, 218, 224, 302, 306, 314, 335, 338, 397
(*see also* languages)
Karbi 307
Khasi 307
Kodagu 24
Kodava 307
Kok Barak 307
Kumaoni 307
Kurak 307
Kurmali 307
Latin 11, 29, 122, 134, 135, 167, 172, 179, 324, 334, 345, 378, 379, 387, 399, 405, 407, 408, 416
Lepcha 307
Limbu 307
Maithili 53, 98, 304, 306
Malayalam 24, 40, 47, 53, 84, 105, 109, 112, 183, 188, 189, 208, 210, 303, 304, 306, 314
Marathi 24, 63, 105, 110, 115, 130, 146, 147, 183, 187, 188, 189, 225, 304, 306, 324, 328, 335, 360, 397
Middle Eastern 61
mother 337
national 304, 325
native 15
Nepali 53, 304, 306
Nevari 304
non-trivial 15
Odia 105, 109, 302, 306, 314, 324
Pahari 163, 307
Pali 20, 105, 209, 248, 278, 307
Prakrit 69, 92, 105, 307, 322
precarity of 61
Punjabi 95, 130, 188, 189, 198, 199, 226, 306, 315, 322, 324, 326
regional 337, 338, 380
Sanskrit 10, 11, 12, 20, 23, 24, 25, 26, 28, 33, 35, 40, 44, 49, 50, 53, 56, 58, 65, 68, 70, 73, 89, 90, 91, 92, 97, 98, 99, 101, 105, 106, 108, 182, 185, 186, 188, 189, 190, 199, 209, 218, 222, 255, 262, 290, 292, 293, 302, 303, 304, 306, 316, 320, 322, 324, 328, 331, 332, 333, 348, 353, 355, 359, 361, 362, 386, 392, 410, 416
Sindhi 189, 306
South Asian 61
southern 337
Tamil 24, 27, 28, 47, 53, 69, 73, 78, 83, 84, 91, 105, 106, 109, 112, 183, 188, 189, 191, 210, 211, 212, 266, 284, 293, 304, 306, 311, 312, 314, 318, 319, 323, 334, 335, 339, 345, 386, 397

453

Index

Telugu 24, 25, 40, 53, 100, 102, 109, 112, 164, 183, 188, 202, 210, 289, 302, 304, 306, 314, 325, 345, 389, 397
Toda 24
Urdu 64, 82, 84, 94, 95, 96, 109, 110, 124, 130, 156, 181, 183, 205, 231, 232, 238, 239, 257, 259, 263, 269, 304, 306, 311, 314, 320, 321, 322, 328, 348, 349, 351, 379
laptop 129
lathi (lāthī) 195
law and order 231, 277, 352, 362, 363, 381, 395, 410
Law Commission of India 124
Lawrence, T. E 6
  Seven Pillars of Wisdom 6
Leela (līlā) 50, 56, 71, 77, 91, 92, 99, 100
Lenin 397
Lenin, Vladimir 397
Lerner, Gerda 274
lexicon 12, 13, 14, 15, 29, 43, 88, 94, 130, 133, 146, 173, 184, 225, 229, 233, 259, 262, 279, 308, 367, 385, 419, 420
LGBT 257, 258, 319, 375
LGBT movement 258
LGBT politics 258
LGBT rights 258
liberalism 152, 271
liberation 21, 22, 33, 34, 35, 36, 37, 51, 57, 59, 154, 180, 290, 334, 378, 379, 390, 415
licence raj 153
lilasakti 92
Lingayats 385
linguistic states 13, 325, 419
lobha 26
local self-government 270, 291, 364, 393
Lochana-Kavi. *See* Sharma, Lochana
Lochana-Pandita. *See* Sharma, Lochana
Lochtefeld 332, 333
logbaag 259
Lohia, Rammanohar 55
Lok adalat (lōk adālat) 383, 384
lokaparva 355
Lok Janshakti 259
Lōk Sabhā 132, 354
Lok Swaraj Abhiyan 291
Lollywood 80
loola 251
Lord Curzon 113, 352
Lord Dalhousie 292
  Doctrine of Lapse 292
Lord Mayo 393
  resolution of 1870 393
Lord Warren Hastings 363
Lord William Bentinck 71
lota (lota) 183, 184
love marriage 259, 260, 261, 262
LPG (Liberalization, Privatization and Globalization) 32, 46, 80, 81, 126, 129, 138, 147, 148, 149, 151, 152, 153, 155, 163, 164, 176, 184, 186, 193, 258, 316, 359
Lutyens, Edward 133

maa (*mām*) 262, 263, 264
maadar 262
maai 262
maanam 319
maat 262
maataa 262
maateshwari 262
maatri-bhasha 304
maatrikaa 262
maatsarya 26
maatu 262
mabuh 204
McAdam, Jane 172
McAdam, Marika 224
  Lonely Planet 224
Macaulay, Lord 294, 305, 309, 349
  Minute on Indian Education of February 1835 294
McDowell, Dr Ephraim 123
Machiavelli 326
māda (*mād*) 26. *See* mada, nall (*mād, nāl*)
mada, nall (*mād, nāl*) 217
Madhava, Manisha 295
Mādhava, Vedāntin 33
  Sarvadarśana Sangraha 33
madrasa (*madrasā*) 264, 265, 266
Madrasa Mazahirul Uloom 265
Maffei, Xavier 187
Mahābhārata 9, 21, 26, 47, 48, 50, 51, 52, 53, 65, 70, 104, 106, 118, 189, 195, 262, 292, 333
Mahadalit 249. *See also* Dalit
Mahadeva, Devanuru 338
  Odalaala 338
Mahalanobis, P. C. 138, 297
Maharaj, Swami Karpatri 201
Mahayana Buddhism 21, 33, 36, 118. *See also* Buddhism
  Mahaparinirvana Sutra 21
Maheshwari, S. R. 352
  Indian Administration 352
Mahesh Yogi, Maharishi 118
mahila 186, 232
mahtaari 262
mai 262
mai baap sarkaar 154
mai baap sarkaar (maim bāp sarkār) 153, 154
mai bap sarkaar 154
Maithili. *See* languages
maiya 262
Majumdar, Boria 192
makruh 204
maktab 264, 265
maktub 66
Malabar rebellion of 1921 60

Index

Malaviya, Madan Mohan   95
Malayalam. *See* languages
malik   153
mall   80, 155
  shopping   155
malnourishment   150
Malviya, Madan Mohan   327
manana   40
mandabuddhi   251
Mandal, Chedi   161
Mandal commission   296
mandana   101
Mander, Harsh   227, 356
Mandi (mandi). *See* Mandi, E-chaupal (mandī/E-caupāl)
Mandi, E-chaupal (mandī/E-caupāl)   156, 157
Manekshaw, General Sam   63
mangalmaya   75
Mann ki Baat   251
mansab   395
Mansingh, Raja Sawai   55
Mantena, Madhu   81
Mantra (mantra). *See* Mantra, Tantra, Yantra (mantra, tantra, yantra)
Mantra, Tantra, Yantra (mantra, tantra, yantra)   3, 40, 54, 55, 280, 333
Manu   29, 182, 213, 224, 333
manudharma   283
Manudharmashastra   283
Manuel, Thomas   83
Manusmriti   29, 55, 56, 195
Manuvadi (manuvādī)   55, 56
Maoist Communist Centre [MCC]   389
Mapilla rebellion   398
Marana Gana   84
Marathi. *See* languages
Mariaselvam, Abraham   318
Markandeyapurana   333
Marquez, Gabriel Garcia   104
  I Only Came to Use the Phone   104
marriages   14, 29, 48, 49, 50, 63, 68, 85, 86, 106, 144, 145, 199, 252, 253, 256, 258, 259, 260, 261, 262, 272, 283, 290, 313, 375
  arranged   259, 260, 261
  heteronormative   261
  inter-caste   260
  love   259, 260, 261, 262
  self-arranged   261
Marx, Karl   61, 140, 311, 397
Marxism   236, 388
masala chai   197
Massively multiplayer online roleplaying games (MMORPGs)   130
matahari   262
Mathew, George   386, 392
Mathur, Jaskiran K.   207
matka   184
Matlabi (matlabī)   326
matri   262

matsya   182
Matthew Arnold   11
Maya (māyā)   5, 56, 57, 58, 92
Mayaram, Shail   408
Mayawati   185
Mazdoor Kisan Shakti Sangathan (MKSS)   278
mazra   255
Mazumdar, Charu   388
Medhatithi   47
meditation   33, 35, 37, 40, 50, 72, 103, 118, 294, 332
Meera   28
Meerut riots of 1987   60
Mehta, Deepa   258
Mehta, Mona   353, 379
Mehta, Nalin   126
mela (*mēlā*)   217, 218, 219
memorialization   2
Menon, A. G. K.   42
Mertia, Sandeep   136
metaphor   5, 7, 19, 75, 104, 142, 215, 293, 339, 408
Metcalfe, Charles   255, 393
Meursault   104
MFI (Microfinance Institution)   157, 158
MGNREGA   162
mhangai   142
microcredit   158
microfinance   157, 158, 159
  impact of   158
microfinancing   159
microlending   158
middle class   32, 50, 115, 146, 159, 160, 186, 244, 296, 299, 300, 301, 309, 411
migration   23, 46, 186, 394
Mihira, Varaha   188
  Brihat Samhita   188
militancy   379
Millennium Development Goals (MDGs)   165
Mīmāmsa   33, 34
Minhaj-al-Shiraj   265
minorities   59, 60, 172, 235, 258, 270, 271, 304, 305, 358, 372, 374, 385, 387, 388, 394, 395, 409
  linguistic   305, 385
  non-Muslim   394
  oppression of   60
  policy of accommodation of   385
  religious   358, 385, 394
  sexual   258, 385
miqdar   67
Mir, Hazrat Sai Mian   38
misogyny   83
Misra, Salil   394
missed call   130, 219, 301, 420
Mistry, Cyrus   63
Mitaksara   144
Mitakshara   145
MKSS   278
mobile phones   129, 130, 178

455

Index

Model Police Act   277
modernity   14, 31, 32, 44, 87, 244, 261, 266, 267, 268, 299, 300, 310, 321, 418
modernization   30, 137, 242, 243, 266
  infrastructural   137
modesty   36, 69, 205, 215, 345, 402
Modi, Narendra   24, 119, 124, 132, 133, 136, 154, 166, 177, 251, 297, 368, 373, 388
  Mann ki Baat   251
Modi, Sohrab   63
Mody, Perveez   260
moha   26, 57
mohabbat   89
Mohalla (*mōhallā*)   269, 270, 291, 329
Mohammad, Wali   96
Mohani, Maulana Hasrat   328
moksha/nirvana (*mōksa/nirvāna*)   3, 21, 22, 34, 36, 51, 57, 58, 59, 118, 223
  conceptions of   59
Mokshya   33
Mollywood   112
monetization   62
Monier-Williams   200, 218, 220
Monopolistic and Restrictive Trade Practice [MRTP]   125
moral   12, 15, 21, 22, 26, 36, 47, 52, 87, 90, 94, 102, 108, 167, 186, 205, 208, 215, 222, 246, 248, 254, 288, 290, 291, 296, 317, 320, 330, 354, 359, 414
moral dilemmas   15
morality   21, 108, 204, 235, 288, 319
mornaacha   92. *See also* naach (nāc)
Mudgal, Vipul   165
Mudiganti, Usha   292
mudrasphiti   142
Muehlmann, Shaylih   8
Mueller, Max   24
mugga   183
muggu   101
Mughals   9, 62, 71, 96, 110, 111, 113, 153, 232, 245, 269, 270, 346, 347, 352, 353, 387, 393, 395, 396, 410
muhuurat   49
Mukherjee, Aditi   288, 302
Mukherjee, Souvik   129, 163, 178
Mukherjee, Sujit   315
Mukherji, Gangeya   20
Mukhim, Patricia   179
Mukhopadhyay, Nilanjan   272
Mukul, Akshaya   200
Müller, Max   24
Mullick, Mohini   22, 56
multilinguality   324, 325
Mundakopanishad   39
munshi   237, 348, 349
Munshi, K. M.   24
Murari, Timeri N.   113

Murdoch, Rupert   126
Murray, Padmini Ray   130
music   27, 40, 78, 80, 83, 84, 92, 95, 96, 97, 98, 102, 114, 178, 220, 221, 224, 232, 264, 283, 293, 294, 295, 300, 315, 334, 351, 369
  classical   27, 97, 98
  practices of   96
  qawwali   95
  Sūfī   97
Muslim League   385, 394, 395, 399
Muslim Personal Law (Shariat) Application Act of 1937   144
Muslims   28, 32, 38, 41, 42, 59, 60, 61, 73, 86, 132, 133, 144, 145, 147, 181, 182, 186, 191, 221, 222, 252, 262, 265, 270, 271, 296, 311, 315, 347, 365, 369, 372, 375, 385, 387, 388, 394, 395, 401, 408, 409
Mussalman (*musalmān*)   59. *See also* Muslims
mustafti   369
mustahab   203
Mutiny of 1857   289
Muttreja, Poonam   160, 169
Muzaffarnagar riots of 2013   60
myth   11, 35, 70, 161, 169, 172, 215, 216, 267, 268, 305, 325

naach (nāc)   92, 93
  chamaruanaach   93
  dhobiyanaacha   93
  gondnaach   93
  launda   92
  rautnaach   93
  traditions   93
naayaka-naayikaa bhava   28
Naga and Mizo Customary Law   231
Naga People's Movement for Human Rights (NPMHR)   344
nagar   255, 386
nagara palika   354
Nagara Raithara Dange   398
Nagarjuna   33, 58, 221
Nagar movement   398
nagar palika (*nagar pālikā*)   386
nagar palikas   386
Nagpur riots of 1927   60
Naha, Souvik   210
Naidu, Sarojini   5
Naik, M. K.   316
  History of Indian English Literature   316
Nai Kahani movement   321
Nair, P. T.   405
Nair, Ranjit   54, 58, 73, 117, 281
Nair, Rukmini Bhaya   9, 13, 14, 215, 250
Nair, Vijayanka   121
nairātmavāda   34
nakhra (*nakhrā*)   93
  Ruthna (sulking)   93

Index

nall (nāl). *See mada, nall (mād, nāl)*
Nāmalingānuśāsanam 2
nama-rupa 57
namaskar 314, 369
namaskaragalu 314
namaskaram 314
namaste 314, 315
namaz 181, 222
Nambisan, Kavery 122
Nandi Foundation 166
Nandy, Ashis 12, 192, 282
   Tao of Cricket 192
Naoroji, Dadabhai 63, 290
nara (nārā) 108, 327, 328
narasamsi 47
Narasimha Rao, P. V. 297
Narayan, Jayaprakash 291, 328, 373
   sampoorna kranti ('total revolution') 291
Narayan, Sunetra Sen 126
narratives 4, 12, 13, 24, 26, 44, 48, 52, 61, 65, 66, 68, 69, 71, 81, 90, 91, 99, 114, 115, 127, 129, 136, 138, 158, 210, 213, 216, 258, 260, 320
Nasbandi (nasbandī) 160, 161
nasib 66
Nasrin, Taslima 59
NASSCOM (National Association of Software and Services Companies) 164, 178
Nāstika 33
Nath, Gopika 105, 189
nathdwara/srinathji chai 197
national, anti-national 7, 21, 31, 32, 42, 69, 77, 94, 107, 112, 113, 121, 122, 127, 134, 138, 141, 145, 146, 150, 160, 166, 187, 189, 193, 199, 211, 228, 235, 250, 254, 259, 260, 271, 272, 278, 279, 281, 282, 291, 294, 295, 296, 297, 304, 325, 329, 347, 351, 352, 356, 359, 360, 366, 367, 369, 370, 375, 376, 382, 386, 388, 390, 393, 395, 399, 402, 412
National Action Plan on Climate Change 128
National Campaign for the People's Right to Information (NCPRI) 278, 279
National Conference 399
National Democratic Alliance (NDA) 356
National Front Government 296
National Health Mission 170
National Health Policy (NHP) 170
National Human Rights Commission (NHRC) 374, 375
National Informatics Centre (NIC) 137
nationalism 21, 31, 32, 94, 132, 133, 180, 267, 271, 272, 284, 372, 373, 387, 388
   Indian 267, 271
   Nehruvian 271
nationality 41, 171, 172, 187, 304
National Liberation Force of Tripura (NFLT) 379
national movement 21, 291, 393
National Planning Committee (NPC) 276, 297
National Police Commission (NPC) 276, 297
National Rural Employment Guarantee Act (NREGA) 161. *See also* NREGA (naregā)
   implementation of 162
National Rural Health Mission 240
National Sample Survey (NSS) 148
National Socialist Council of Nagalim (Isak-Muivah) (NSCN [I-M]) 180
nation-state 31, 32, 94, 241, 259, 316, 350, 351, 394
   postcolonial 241
nattuvanar 78
naturopathy 202, 241, 244
natya 92. *See also naach (nāc)*
navgrahas 49
Naxalism 21, 250, 378
Naxalite (nakslā'it) 132, 327, 388, 389, 390
   Maoist samarthak 390
   naxali dalal 390
Naxalite movement 327, 389, 390
nayak 76, 87
Nayak, Asawari 217, 224
Nayak, Jatindra Kumar 206, 307, 337
Nayak, Nalini 296, 430
Nayak, Pulin B. 296, 430
Nayaka, Bhatta 103
Nayudu, C. K. 192
Nazan, Aziz 97
Nazir, Prem 112
Nazism 387
Neelakantan, P. 319
Nehru 153, 214, 246, 256, 267, 271, 272, 281, 296, 297, 325, 385, 386, 391, 393
Nehru, Motilal 290
Nehru, Pandit Jawaharlal 214, 256, 271, 281, 296, 297, 325, 385, 386, 391, 393
   Discovery of India 281
Nehru Memorial Museum and Library (NMML) 14
Nehruvian 246, 271, 272, 291, 328, 372
   ideal 272
   nationalism 271
   socialism 291
   vision of India 372
Nehruvianism 271
Nellie massacre of 1983 60
Nemade, Bhalchandra 360
neoliberalism 32, 188
neoliberal moment 258
Neta (nētā)/netri 328, 329, 330
   mobilizational power of 329
Netaji 297, 328, 329. *See also* Yadav, Mulayam Singh
Netarwala, Hoshang 174
Neville, Pran 93
New Keywords: A Revised Vocabulary of Culture and Society 11
New Religious Movements (NRMs) 201, 202
NGOs 158, 258
niddidhyasana 40

457

Index

Nigel, Hanklyn 12
    Hanklyn-Janklin 12
nilatukkam 188
nirakshara 302
nirankar 38
nirvaachan 353
nishkama karma 36, 58, 118
niti 55, 354
NITI (National Institution for Transforming India) Aayog 297
nivrtti 34
niyama 37
Niyati 90, 91
Nizamuddin, Mullah 265
Nizamuddin Aulia 95
N. Murari, Timeri 113
Noakhali riots of 1946 60
nomoskar 314
non-Brahminism 55, 56
non-violence 12, 21, 35, 53, 254, 267, 285, 417
Northeast India 179, 180, 231, 233, 234, 275, 378, 379, 413
    tax in 180
notebandi 133
NREGA (naregā) 161, 162, 163
nutrition 227, 239, 240, 374
nyaaya vaisheshika school 19
Nyāya 33, 34
Nyāya prasthāna 34

OAU Convention 172
Obeyesekere, Gananath 318
Odia *See* languages
Official Language Resolution 1968 306
Official Secrets Act (OSA) of 1925 278
Ogden, C. K 4
ojha 79
Omprakash Valmiki
    Joothan 210
oppression 60, 67, 95, 236, 291, 385, 408
Organization of African Unity (OAU) Convention 171
orientalism 15, 32, 60, 61
    American 61
    Ottoman 61
    Zionist 61
Orsini, Francesca 89, 260
Orwell, George 104, 387
    Animal Farm 104
Other Backward Classes (OBCs) 296
Oudh peasant movement 398
outcastes 44
outsourcing 80, 130, 138, 163, 164
    IT 138
    powers of 163

paan-beedi 192
pachadi 102

padārtha 34
Padma Awards 94, 95
    Bharat Ratna 94, 95
    Padma Bhushan 94
    Padma Shree 94
    Padma Vibhushan 94
Padmanabhan, Satish 219
Padmanabhan, Sudarsan 253, 334
paduka 189
padya 322
Painter, Habeeb 97
paklo 187
palas 90
Palat, Madhavan 271
Palriwala, Rajni 259
Palshikar, Sanjay 24
Palshikar, Suhas 366
Panchayati Raj (pancāyatī rāj) 271, 364, 392, 393
Panchayati raj institutions 393
Pande, Ira 110
panhi 189
Panikkar, Raimon 371
Panjabi, Kavita 266
Pant, Pallavi 167, 190
paraamarsh 303
paraapara 280
parampara 40
parangi 311, 312
parayattam 83
paricharchaa 303
Parikh, Harivallabh 383
parivar (parivār). *See parivar/samaj/biradri (parivār/samāj/birādarī)*
parivar/samaj/biradri (parivār/samāj/birādarī) 55, 272, 273, 287, 288
parivarwad 273
Parsad, Jitender 255
Parsi (pārsī) 62, 63
Partition 32, 144, 186, 198, 229, 268, 290, 300, 344, 350, 354, 357, 372, 385, 394, 395, 408
Partition in 1947 198, 395
Partition of Bengal 290
Partition of India 385, 394
Partition of Punjab 350
Parveen, Nazima 231, 269
Pashupati seal 117
patangnaach 92. *See also naach (nāc)*
Patānjali 25, 33, 37, 50, 74, 118, 221
    yogaschittivrtiinirodhana 118
    Yōgasutra 25, 118
Patel, Aakar 351
Patel, Anushka Rajesh 335
Patel, Chimanbhai 24
Patel, Gieve 63
Patel, Sardar Vallabbhai 386
Patel, Vallabhbhai 256, 391
paternalism 274, 275, 276
Patha Bhavana. *See also* Vishwa Bharati (viśva-bhāratī)

Index

Pathalgadi movement   291
pativrata   275, 276
Patnaik, B. N.   65, 103
patri   48
patriarchy   161, 236, 274, 275, 276, 328
   Brahmanical   275, 276
patwari (patvārī)   395, 396, 397
Peare *sahib*   96
peasant movements   397, 398
peend   255
People's Liberation Guerrilla Army (PLGA)   390
Pereira, Melvil   231
Permanent Account Number (PAN)   121
Perna, Nick   147
Persian   43, 64, 66, 69, 82, 89, 95, 97, 110, 113, 114, 153, 205, 231, 238, 241, 265, 272, 311, 320, 322, 348, 349, 352, 353, 404, 405
Perutz, Max   281
   Is Science Necessary?   281
Phalke, Jahnavi   88
Phanjoubam, Pradip   390
Philipose, Pamela   126
Phule, Jyotirao   246
Phule-Ambedkarite-Marxism   236
phusphusaahat   303
pidi   210
Pillai, Satya   227
Pillai, Vedanayagam   83
Pinter, Harold   104
   Art, Truth and Politics   104
Pinto, Rochelle   187
pir/murid (pīr/murīd)   38, 64, 65, 89, 91
Planning Commission   297
planning process   297, 298
Plato   58
pluralism   1, 10, 35, 271, 360, 373, 408
poem   71, 92, 98, 100, 106, 181
poetry   15, 23, 24, 27, 50, 52, 66, 69, 75, 89, 95, 96, 97, 102, 103, 104, 106, 211, 238, 268, 320, 322, 334, 351
   Arabic   66
   Persian   66
   secular   95
   Turkish   66
police reforms   276, 278
policy deadlock   165
policy gridlock   165
policy paralysis   165, 166
political class   125, 382
political economy   214, 396, 397
political families   273
political identity   235
political ideology   112, 369, 372
political inclination   260
political independence   187, 327
political institutions   295
political mobilization   84, 327, 357

political movements   125, 235, 327
political parties   24, 48, 137, 142, 153, 154, 177, 206, 229, 259, 288, 295, 296, 317, 327, 329, 355, 359, 372, 385, 399, 401
political patronage   296
political power   5, 6, 139, 235, 236, 291, 365, 373, 380, 381, 396
political success   334
politicization   296, 399
politics   15, 21, 22, 25, 31, 56, 59, 83, 94, 107, 112, 128, 135, 137, 177, 201, 209, 213, 235, 236, 242, 246, 248, 249, 250, 253, 254, 257, 258, 267, 270, 273, 283, 284, 295, 296, 319, 322, 329, 334, 338, 343, 346, 355, 358, 366, 367, 368, 369, 370, 372, 373, 379, 380, 381, 385, 387, 394, 395, 399, 413, 414, 415, 417, 418, 420
   cultural   213, 322
   identity   372, 379, 399
   LGBT   258
   vote bank   295, 296
pollution   29, 30, 59, 128, 167, 170, 351
Polo, Marco   71
polyphony   14
poorna swaraj   290
Pope, Alexander   104
   An Essay on Criticism   104
Pope, G. V.   318
pornography   137, 176
postcolonialism   31, 32, 349
povertarianism   154
poverty   63, 69, 94, 125, 140, 148, 153, 154, 157, 159, 160, 165, 210, 214, 234, 237, 238, 254, 281, 285, 297, 328, 352, 358, 364, 375, 386, 396
   eradication   157, 297
PPP (Public private partnership)   168, 169
prabhat pheri   208
pragyachakshu   251
praja   55, 107
Prakash, Brahma   79, 92, 93
Prakash, Om   305
Prakrit. *See* languages
prakriti   57, 75, 76, 108, 218, 220
prakriti pradhan   108
Prakriti/Sanskriti (prakrti/sanskrti)   11, 33, 220, 221
pramā   34
pramana   35, 108
pranamamu   314
Pranoto, Iwan   73
Prasad, G. J. V.   315
Prasad, Leela   56
Prasad, Rajendra   256
Praśastapāda   34
Prasthānatrayi   34
Pratītyasamutpāda   34
pratyahara   37
pratyaksha   118
pravaahamu   183

459

Index

pravachan (*pravacan*)   330, 331
pravrtti   34
prayojana   107
prem   89, 259
Premchand, Munshi   348
prem vivah   259
prithvikampa   188
Progressive Writers Association   268
Progressive Writers' Movement   246
Prophet Ibrahim   41
Prophet Muhammad   41, 64, 96, 222, 368
prose   39, 89, 238, 268, 320, 322, 334, 339
proselytization   371
public distribution system (PDS)   143
public health   119, 169, 170, 171, 245, 374, 386
Public Health Foundation of India (PHFI)   167
Public Partnership Appraisal Committee (PPPAC)   168
public private partnership   168
public sector   152, 168, 169, 297, 412
puja pandal   111
Punjabi   95, 130, 188, 189, 198, 199, 226, 306, 315, 322, 324, 326
punyabhumi (holy land)   372
purana (*purāna*)   47, 48, 52, 65, 66, 223, 320, 333, 334
   rajasic   65
   satvik   65
   tamasic   65
puravritta   47
purdah   141, 232
Puri Das, Vibha   94
purnatva   76
purusartha/purushartha   22, 36, 48, 58, 75, 109
Pūrva Mīmāmsa   34
pyar (*pyār*)   89

qadr   67
qadrun   67
qawwālī (*qavvālī*)   95, 96, 97
Qubacha, Nasiruddeen   265
qudir   67
Quit India movement   291, 344, 354
Qur'an   41, 64, 66, 144, 222, 264, 265, 266

Radhakrishnan, S.   57
Rafi, Muhammad   96
raga (*rāga*)   78, 95, 97, 98, 208
   Asavari   98
   Bageshri   98
   Bhairav/Bhairon   98
   Bihag   98
   Bilawal   98
   Miyan ki Kanara   98
   Miyan ki Malhar   98
   Mukhari   98
   Multani   98
   Purva   98
   Purvi   98
   Todi   98

Raga-malika   98
Raga-Tarangini   98
Raghavan, Dr V.   78
   Bharatanātyam Classical Dance – The South Indian Nautch   78
rag-picking   227
Rai, Lala Lajpat   290
rail roko (*rēl rōkō*)   362
Raj, Gopal N.   247
Raj, Yash   81
Rajagopalachari, C.   70
Rajam, V. S.   318
Rajamouli   112
rajas   33, 220
Rajatarangani   189
Rajdharma   420
Rajeshwari, B.   356
Rajkumar   112
Rajneesh   58, 202
Rajnikanth   112, 334
Raju, Byrraju Ramalinga   124
Rajya Sabha, Lok Sabha (rājya sabhā, lōk sabhā)   367, 393, 400, 401
Ram, Ronki   38
Ramachandraiah, C.   155
Ramachandran, M. G. (MGR)   112, 334
Ramachandran, Vimala   286
Ramakrishnan, V.   83
Ramakrishnan Mission   285, 330, 331, 385
Rama Rao, N. T. (NTR)   25, 112
Ramasamy, E. V.   236, 267, 282, 283, 319
Ramayana (rāmāyana)   9, 65, 68, 69, 70, 98, 99, 105, 189, 215, 216, 333, 346
Ramcharitmanas   99
Ramdev   202
Ramjanmabhoomi   70, 373
Ramlila (rāmlīlā)   88, 99, 100
Ramzan (ramzān)   221, 222
Rana, Kaisser   387
Ranchi-Hatia riots of 1967   60
rangamandapa   75
rangoli (rangōlī)   100, 101, 102
   aipan   101
   alpana   100, 101
   aripana   101
   chowkpujan   101
   kalam   101
   kalamezhuttu   101
Rani Avantibai   292
Rani Lakshmibai   292, 293
Rani Padmini   71
ran-niti   354
Rao, Khasa Subba   291
   Swarajya   291
Rao, V. K. R. V.   310, 311
rape   202, 319, 331, 345, 358, 389, 402, 403
rasa (*rasa*)   9, 26, 28, 75, 91, 92, 102, 103, 108, 218
   adbhuta   102

Index

bhayaanaka 102, 103
bibhatsa 102
haasya 102
karuna 102
raudra 102
shringara/sringaara 102, 208
vira 102
rasa līlā 91, 92
rashtra-bhasha 304
Rashtriya Janata Dal (RJD) 259, 296
Rashtriya Swayamsevak Sangh (RSS) 132, 151, 233, 273, 372, 373, 387, 388
ratjagga 207
Ratnam, Mani 112
Ratnatraya 35
Ravidas 246
Ray, Debraj 153
Ray, Manas 299
Razzaq, Abdur 96
realism 31, 35, 50
Reddy, C. Rammanohar 133, 358
Redfield, Robert 256
Red Sari, The 107
refugees 3, 94, 171, 172, 198, 229
   climate 172
   de facto 172
   definition of 171, 172
   ecological 94
   humanitarian 172
   OAU and Cartagena-type 172
   problem 171
   Punjabi 198
Rehman, Waheeda 142
religion 1, 21, 27, 29, 31, 43, 44, 45, 58, 59, 60, 61, 67, 86, 107, 141, 144, 171, 187, 224, 246, 261, 267, 271, 273, 283, 284, 294, 295, 296, 313, 325, 357, 358, 361, 369, 370, 371, 372, 374, 387, 394, 407, 409, 420
religious efficacy 145
religious identity 270, 357
religious movement 294
   reformist 294
Reserve Bank of India (RBI) 135, 142, 143, 172, 173
Reserve Bank of India Act of 1934 173
Reuters Report 166
Revenue Officer (revenue officer) 349, 364
Revolt of 1857 292, 293
Richards, I. A. 4
Richman, Paula 68
rickshawwala 194
Right to Information (RTI) 4, 138, 278, 279, 310
Right to Information Act 279
Rig Veda 20, 23, 35, 50, 75, 189, 255, 293, 331, 332, 393
riots 60, 147, 151, 347, 356, 357, 372, 373, 398
   communal 356
   hindu–muslim 60, 372
rishis 200

rituals 23, 30, 34, 41, 44, 47, 54, 56, 66, 70, 79, 101, 132, 176, 200, 207, 212, 217, 223, 232, 245, 257, 269, 290, 295, 326, 332, 333, 340, 341, 343, 351, 365
   vedic 333
Rodrigues, Valerian 400
Roget's Thesaurus 2
Rohingyas 377, 379
Rohinton 63
Roop Kanwar 71
Roy, Dunu 289
Roy, M. N. 21
Roy, Rammohan 71, 273
Roychand, Premchand 175
roza 222
rozedar 222
rta 108
Rulli, Maria Cristina 149, 150
Rupakula, Ramana Murthy V. 395
Rushdie, Salman 309, 369, 417
Russell, Bertrand 281
Russian revolution 397
ryotwari settlements 395

saakshara 302
saandala 189
SAARC (South Asian Association for Regional Cooperation) 403, 404
Sabhawala, Jahangir 63
Sabri brothers 97
sabzi mandi 156, 157
Sadhana 33
Sadhukkari Bhasha 322
sadir 77, 78
Saeed, Yousuf 95
Sahasrabuddhe, Annasaheb 291
Sahitya (sāhitya) 103, 104, 316
Said, Edward 32, 61
   Orientalism 32, 61
sailab 182
sakthi 318
salat 41, 181, 222
Salwa Judum 389
sama 95, 96, 195
samaadhi 37, 331
Samāchār Chandrikā 185
Samāchār Darpan 185
samadharma 283
Samadhi 33
Samaj (samāj). *See* Parivar/Samaj/Biradri (parivār/samāj/birādarī)
Samajwadi Party (SP) 296
Sama Veda 333
samayojan 316
Samkhya 57, 118, 220
Samkhya school 118
sampoorna kranti ('total revolution') 291
sampoorna swaraj 290

461

Index

sampradayas 200
samsara 37, 57, 58, 108
Samson, Leela 77, 91
Samyak charitra 35
Samyak darshana 33, 35
Samyak jnāna 35
Sangam 78, 211, 318, 334
Sanjana, Behman Kaikobad 62
    Qisseh-i-Sanjan 62
Sankaracharya/Sankara, Adi 47, 57, 333
Sānkhya 33
sannidhya 75
Sanskrit. *See also* languages
    phrase 302
    pronunciation 259
    textual formations in 56
    theoretical and poetic usage 320
Santhal insurrection 399
Santhanam Committee 359
śānti 20–1
Santiniketan 293–4
sants 200, 201
sanyasa 285
sanysasis 200
sapinda 144
sarakāra 153, 317
Śaram 205
Saraswati, Dayananda 55, 289, 290
    Satyarth Prakash 290
Saree (sārī) 105, 106, 107, 156, 219
Sarkar (sarkār) 8, 153, 167, 348, 349, 404, 405, 418, 419, 420
Sarkar, Sir Jadunath 353
sarvarthasiddhi 22
Sarva Shiksha Abhiyan (sarva śiksā abhiyān) 286
Sat-cit-ānanda 34
Sathyanathan, Karthika 303
Sathya Sai Baba 202
Sati/Jauhar (satī/jauhar) 12, 32, 70, 71, 196, 267
sat sri akaal 314
sattva 33, 220
satya 20, 21, 254, 327
Satyagraha (civil disobedience) 230, 250, 267, 285, 362
Satyanarayana 285
saubhhagya 107
saundarya (saundarya) 107, 108, 109
Savarkar, V. D. 290, 372
    Hindutva 372
Sayanacharya 47
schedule 231, 304, 305, 306, 307, 325, 405, 406, 417
scheduled castes (SCs) 85, 248, 249, 296, 345, 346, 374, 375, 400, 406, 411, 413
Scheduled Castes and Scheduled Tribes (Prevention of Atrocities) Act of 1989 345
scheduled tribes (STs) 180, 345, 346, 400, 406
schelling 57
    Philosophy of Mythology 57

science and technology 267, 281, 297, 317, 337
scientific temper 281, 282
scripts 66, 67, 73, 112, 118, 302, 303, 304, 319, 325, 417
    Devanagari 302
SC-ST PoA Act 1989 345
Sealy, Irwin Allan 87
secular 20, 47, 59, 70, 78, 89, 95–6, 108, 133, 144, 145, 207, 246, 267–8, 271, 274, 287, 290, 370–3, 382, 387, 406–8
secularism 32, 271, 407, 408, 409
Securities Exchange Board of India (SEBI) 175
seedha 251
seedhi 251
sehri 222
self-examination 287
self-expression 287
self-government 95, 270, 291, 327, 364, 393
self-identity 234
selfie 13, 109, 110, 130, 420
self-interest 40
self-knowledge 19, 37
self-practices 287
self-protection 228
self-questioning 15
self-realization 40, 94, 290
self-respect 25, 106, 140, 248, 267, 282, 283, 290
self-respect movement 282, 283
self-responsibility 290
self-rule 5, 94, 283, 287, 288, 289, 290
self-sacrifice 70
self-sufficiency 211, 256, 297
self-sustainability 158
Sen, Amartya 15, 136, 140, 154, 196
    The Argumentative Indian 15
    Identity and Violence 12
sensex 174, 175, 176
settled 331
seva (sēvā) 55, 284, 285, 288, 291
Sevagram Ashram 218
sevayajna 285
Seventy-Third Amendment 291
Sewa Bharti 233
sexual 15, 50, 83, 93, 170, 184, 202, 218, 222, 227, 257, 258, 260, 274, 314, 344, 345, 358, 365, 385, 402
    assault 170, 344, 402
    behaviour 202
    crimes 402
    difference 257
    exploitation 227, 345
    fantasists 15
    innuendos 83
    intercourse 222
    minorities 258, 385
    morality 204
    pleasure 50
    union 218

Index

violence 170, 358, 402
Shabd kīrtan 207
Shah, Ghanshyam 345, 365
Shah, Sultan Hoshang 71
shahada 222
shaher 255
Shah Jahan 113, 312
Shaivism 108
Shakespeare, William 104, 361
    Macbeth 81, 104
shakti (śakti) 5, 223, 263, 278, 280, 328
shamiyana (śāmiyānā) 110, 111
shamshan (śmaśāna) 222, 223
Shankara 44, 54, 59, 118, 201
Shankar-Shambhu 97
Sharam 205
shariah 368, 369
Shariat Act 144
Sharma, Banwarilal 291
Sharma, Brahma Dev 291
Sharma, Dinesh 129
Sharma, Lochana 98
Sharma, Saba 179
Sharma, TRS 19, 26, 27
Sharmila, Irom 88, 343, 344
Shaw, Adrienne 130
shehar faseel (city wall) 270
Shenoy, B. R. 152
Shia 86, 144, 181, 222, 353
Shiromani Akali Dal 399
Shivaji 293
Shivaprakash, H. S. 79
Shiva Purana 333
Shiv Sena 25
Shourie, Arun 154
Shraddhanand 290
Shrauta Sutras 333
Shree, Geetanjali 262
Shri Krishna Chaitanya Bharati 293
Shrivastava, Deepti 227
shrngaara 28
shruti and smriti (śruti and smrti) 40, 332, 333
Shudra 29, 56, 230
Shylendra, H. S. 157
siddha 241, 244
Sikhs 28, 38, 39, 271, 285, 314, 350, 357, 408
Singh, Bhagat 328
Singh, Dr Manmohan 297
Singh, Khushwant 15
    We Indians 15
Singh, Maharaja Ranjit 39, 312
Singh, Manmohan 124, 165, 166, 297, 378
Singh, Prakash 276
Singh, Praveen 312, 332
Singh, Ujjwal Kumar 343
Singh, Vijaya 141
Singh, V. P. 296
Singh Sabha Movement 39

Sinha, Chandan 404
Sinha, Neilabh 404
Siqueira, Alito 217, 224
Sircar, Shoojit 81
sittlichkeit 36
Sixth Schedule 231, 406
Skype 130
slave 23
Slum Rehabilitation Authority (SRA) 146
smartphone 109, 110, 126, 130, 137, 194
Smriti 40
Smrti prasthāna 34
sneha 89
Snehi, Yogesh 350
Soares, Angela 15
social
    identity 272
    social inequality 283
    social interaction 30, 272
    social media 1, 97, 106, 109, 126, 130, 132, 133, 134, 137, 160, 176, 177, 178, 237, 300, 380
    social revolution 235, 283
    social security 145, 148, 162
    social stratification 382
socialism 235, 271, 272, 283, 284, 291
    Nehruvian 291
sociocultural life 255
socrates 241
soft power 74, 119
sogadu (*sogādū*) 224
solidarity 245, 246, 253, 255, 328, 356, 369, 393
    communal 255
Sorabjee Committee 277
soteriology 37
Southey, Robert 206
    The Curse of Kehama 206
    The Travels of Sir John Mandeville (1357–71) 206
South Indian AIDS Awareness Programme (SIAAP) 258
South Indian film/cinema 112
South Indian Gana Singers Association 84
sowa rigpa 241, 244
Spencer, J. W. 155
Spivak, Gayatri Chakravorty 32
sramana philosophy 334
sravana 40
Sridevi 112
Sridharan, E. 355
Srimad Bhagavata 65, 66
Srinivas, M. N. 295, 310, 311, 365
    The Social Structure of a Mysore Village 295
srishti 82
srngara 89
Śruti prasthāna 34
SSA (Sarva Shiksha Abhiyan) 286
stamp paper scam 225–7
stanapatta 105

463

Index

stanmasuka 105
start-ups 130, 137, 178, 179
state formation 21
State Human Rights Commissions (SHRC) 375
statelessness 172
State of Emergency in 1975 291
street children 227, 228
street vendors 228, 229
   hawker 229
   nationalization of 229
   peddler 229
   pheriwala (peddler) 229
   squatter 146, 229
Street Vendors (Protection of Livelihood and Regulation of Street Vending) Act 2014 (SVA) 228
subaltern 79, 360, 408, 409, 412
sub-divisional magistrate (SDM) 363
Subramaniam, Lakshmi 23
sudhar (sudhār) 287, 288
Sūfī 95, 96, 97, 238, 246, 268, 289
Sufi (sūfī) 38, 64, 65, 72, 73
Sūfī Nizamuddin Aulia 95
Sufism 2, 64, 72, 97, 238, 268
Suhrud, Tridip 214, 284, 287
sukh-dukh (sukh-dukh) 288, 289
Sulemani chai 197
Sundaram, Dr B. M. 78
Sunni 144, 181, 222, 347
supplementary nutrition (SN) 240
Surdas 28, 251
Suri, Sher Shah 395, 404
surma 87
surya namaskar 369
Susegad (sussegād) 224, 225
Sustainable Development Goals (SDGs) 170, 375
svabhaava 26
svadharma 27
svarāj 94, 283, 285, 287, 288
svarga 36
svarūpa 34
Svetlana, Alexievich 104
   Voices of Chernobyl 104
Swaminathan, Captain Lakshmi 293
Swaminathan, M. S. 139, 281
swamis 200
swaraj (svarāj) 5, 13, 289, 290, 291, 327, 417
Swaraj Party 290
Swarajya 291
syaandal 189
syādvāda 35

taaza Hindi *khabar* 126
Tagore, Maharshi Debendranath 294
Tagore, Rabindranath 21, 214, 256, 293, 294
Tājamahala 167
Taj Mahal 9, 113, 114

takdir (takadīr). *See* kismat/takdir (qismat/takadīr)
tamas 33
tamasha (tamāśā) 114, 115, 116
tamepas 338. *See also* time-pass
Tamil. *See* languages
Tana Bhagat struggle 399
Tandon, Shivangini 66, 89, 205
Tangirala, Maruthi Prasad 411
Tanglish 323
tantra (tantra). *See also* mantra, tantra, yantra (mantra, tantra, yantra)
taraweeh 222
tarayati 54
taswir 82
Tata Institute of Fundamental Research (TIFR) 129
tattva-darśana 33
Tavernier, Jean-Baptiste 71
tax 63, 111, 116, 125, 134, 135, 154, 179, 180, 225, 265, 362, 380, 395
   goods and services tax 116, 362
   grazing 63
   one-nation-one- 180
   rates 125
tehsildars 364
television rating points (TRPs) 126
Tellis, Ashley 257
Telugu. *See* Languages
temple entry 44, 230
   denial of, to outcastes 44
tension 30, 324, 335, 336, 337, 351, 412, 419
   causes of 336, 337
   cycles of 336
   feature of 336
   meaning of 335
   symptoms of 336
   use of 335
terrorism 21, 344, 378
   revolutionary 21
teva 48
Thakur, Ashok 363
Thakur, Manindra 194
Thakur, Manish 328, 381
Thakur, Sarojini Ganju 239
Thakurta, Paranjoy Guha 124
Thalaivar (talaivar) 334, 335
thana (thānā) 269, 409, 410, 411
Thapar, Romila 23, 248
thappaattam 83
Tharoor, Shashi 43
thirthankars 346
Thiruchandran, Dr Selvy 318
Three language formula 337
thumri 96
Tilak, Bal Gangadhar 290, 327
   Hind Swaraj 290
time-pass 338
Times of India 132
tip 45, 48, 190

Index

Tirukkural 318
Tiwari, Dr Bhola Nath 322
Todd, James, Lieutenant Colonel 71
   Annals and Antiquities of Rajasthan 71
Tolkappiyam (*karpiyalcutrams*) 318
Tollywood 112
Tolstoy 154, 281
trade unions 229
traditions 2, 10–11, 14–15, 20–2, 28–9, 35–6, 40–1, 43, 47, 50, 53–4, 56, 59, 64, 68–9, 71–2, 76, 79, 83, 89, 91–3, 96, 98–101, 106, 108, 114, 118, 189, 194–5, 198–9, 205, 208, 220, 232, 236, 238, 241–2, 244, 246, 252, 256–7, 260–1, 267–8, 271–2, 280–1, 287, 292, 302, 309, 320, 324–5, 351, 360–1, 370–1, 383, 407, 417
   anti-caste 236
   Brahmanical 56
   caste 236
   grammatical 54
   Indian 35, 91, 106, 189
   intellectual 194
   Islamic 41, 64
   naach 93
   Perso-Arabic 238
   philosophical 118, 417
   poetic 268
   saka 71
   vernacular 89
   warkari 324
Transcendental Meditation (TM) 201
transgender 257, 383
translation 2, 5, 14, 35, 42, 65, 69, 97, 99, 109, 129, 142, 164, 205, 242, 249, 263, 315–18, 332, 339–40, 409, 418–19
trayati 54
trayee 195
tribal customary law 231
tribalism 1
tribal movements 398
Tribal National Volunteers (TNV) 379
tribals 135, 231, 233, 234, 235, 273, 398
tribes 180, 233, 234, 235, 271, 296, 325, 345, 360, 374, 375, 391, 400, 406, 411, 413
Trinamool Congress 185
Tripathi, Govardhanram 287
Tripathi, Punam 182, 188
Tripathi, Rahul 403
Tripitakas 34
Trivedi, Harish 191, 340
trottinettes 194
Tully, Mark 15
   Non Stop India 15
Turing, Alan 13
   mind 13
Twitter 130, 133, 137

Uda Devi 292
ulema 181, 204, 265
ummah 41
Unani 241, 242, 243, 244
UN Convention Relating to the Status of Refugees 171
UNESCO 100, 119, 307, 308
UN General Assembly 119
UN Human Rights Council 375
UNICEF 240
Union Public Services Commission (UPSC) 277, 307, 363, 411, 412, 418
Unique Identification Authority of India (UIDAI) 121, 122, 162
United Liberation Front of Asom (ULFA) 180, 378
United Naga Council (UNC) 379
United Nations Centre for Human Settlements (Habitat) 227
   Strategies to Combat Homelessness 227
United Nations (UN) Framework Convention on Climate Change 127
United Nations High Commissioner for Refugees (UNHCR) 171
United Nations Organization (UNO) 127, 131, 135, 136, 157, 171, 227, 374, 391
United Progressive Alliance (UPA) 162, 165, 166, 359
Universal Declaration of Human Rights 374
unmaatha taandavam 91
Unni, Jeemol 156
untouchability 30, 235, 246, 254, 282
untouchables 16, 29, 30, 38, 56, 85, 210, 249, 267, 345, 365, 370
Upadhyay, A. 261, 378
   India's Fragile Borderlands 378
upanat 189
Upanishad 19, 20, 27, 40, 50, 57, 66, 118, 200, 333
Urdu. *See* languages
US–India Business Council (USIBC) 165
Uttaradhyayana Sutra 21
uttararūpam 40
uttsava 92

vaartaa 303
vaartaalaap 303
vaartaamaanam 303
Vaastu (vāstu) 116
Vaastu Shastra 116
Vaastu Vidya 116
vachic satya 20
Vaikom Satyagraha 230
Vaiśesika 33, 34
Vaiśesika Sūtra 33, 34
Vaishnavas 65
Vaishya 29, 30, 230
Vajpayee, Atal Bihari 238, 247, 328, 373
Valan, Antony Arul 83, 318
Valmiki 68, 98, 103, 105, 346
   Rāmāyana 105
Valmiki, Omprakash 210

Index

Vamana 65
Vamana Purana 65
vamsa 47
vamsanucarita 47
vanakkam 314
vanangu 314
vande mataram 327, 370
Vangal, Uma 112
vanpunarvu 319
Vanvasi Kalyan Ashram 233
vardhan 182
Varma, Pavan K. 16, 159
varna 29, 30, 38, 69, 230. *See also* caste
varnashrama dharma 22, 283
varnashramas 58, 117, 283
   brahmacharya 58
   grhastha 58
   sannyasa 58
   vanaprastha 58
varta 195
vastraharan 106
Vasubandhu 33
Vasudevan, Ravi 80
Veda 20, 23, 27, 33, 35, 36, 40, 47, 50, 52, 57, 58, 75, 118, 189, 255, 293, 302, 331, 332, 333, 346, 393
Vedanta 19, 33, 34, 57, 58, 118, 333
Vedānta 33, 34
Vedantic school 19
Veda Vyasa 47
veer 87
veganism 35
veliyerram 183
vellam 183
Verma, A. K. 346
Verma, Mahesh Prasad 201
Verma, Pavan 15
   Being Indian 15
very important person (VIP) 340, 341, 382, 419
Vetrimaraan 112
Viability Gap Funding Scheme 169
Vibhuti 33
vichaarvimarsh 303
Victoria and Albert Museum 107
videogame 130, 164
Vidhan Sabhā 354
Vikramaditya, King Chandra Gupta 81, 347
violence 12, 20, 21, 35, 53, 69, 170, 172, 177, 212, 254, 261, 266, 267, 268, 285, 311, 336, 345, 346, 356, 357, 358, 367, 368, 369, 371, 375, 378, 379, 383, 385, 389, 390, 394, 398, 402, 403, 407, 409, 410, 413, 414, 417
   concept of 12
   gendered 345
   genealogy of 12
   innate 21
   mental 20
   physical 170
   retributive 21

   sexual 170, 358, 402
   sexual hate 358
virangana (vīrānganā) 292, 293
Viśesa 34
Vishnu Purana 65, 333
vishranti 108
Vishwa Bharati (viśva-bhāratī) 293, 294, 295
   Cheena Bhavana 294
   Kala Bhavana 294
   Patha Bhavana 294
Vishwa Hindu Parishad (VHP) 201, 233, 293, 372, 373
Vishwa Katha Kosha 293
Visvanathan, Shiv 310, 326, 331, 340
Visvanathan, Susan 208
Viswanath, K. 112
Viswanatha, Vanamala 212, 338
Vivakjnānya 33
Vivekacudamani 59
Vivekananda, Swami 57, 58, 118, 233
Vivekananda Kendra 233
vote bank/vote banking 229, 295, 296
   politics of 295, 296
   urban 229
Vyāsa 33
   Yōga-Bhāsya 33

wadas 203
wage 148, 149, 162, 163, 236, 297, 380, 389
Walby, Sylvia 274
watandari 395, 396
Water (Prevention and Control of Pollution) Act of 1974 167
Water (Prevention and Control of Pollution) Cess Act of 1977 167
Weber, Max 381
Weiner, Myron 171
WFP 240
whataboutery 133
WhatsApp 130, 132, 137, 177
WHO (World Health Organization) 167, 169, 244, 245
Whorf, B. L. 13
Williams, Raymond 76, 78, 80, 81, 82, 84, 86, 87, 88, 300, 336, 340, 409
   Keywords: A Vocabulary of Culture and Society 1, 8
Wittgenstein, L. 1
women 15–16, 25–7, 32, 41, 50, 56, 61, 63, 69–71, 76–7, 79, 84–5, 87, 92, 96, 100–1, 105–7, 115, 133, 141, 144–5, 155, 157–62, 170, 178, 185–6, 190, 193, 196–8, 204–6, 210, 214, 222, 229–32, 236, 239–40, 253–4, 257, 261–4, 273–6, 282–3, 287, 290, 292–3, 300, 318–19, 328, 336, 343–4, 357, 365, 374–5, 382, 386, 388–9, 393–4, 401–3, 408, 411
   Ambedkarite 236
   lower-caste 236
   male dominance over 274

sexual control of   274
sexual violation of   402
World Bank (WB)   136, 157, 170, 240, 419
World Trade Organization (WTO)   152, 153
World War, Second   10, 42, 281, 297, 329, 354
worship   27, 44, 79, 82, 100, 189, 208, 223, 230, 264, 287, 290, 294, 361
Wright, Gilian   311

Xaxa, Virginius   233

Yadav, Lalu Prasad   330
Yadav, Mulayam Singh   328
Yadav, Yogendra   291
yajna   34, 285
Yajnavlakya Smriti   333
Yajur Veda   333
Yantra (yantra). *See* Mantra, Tantra, Yantra (mantra, tantra, yantra)
Yaska   54
  Nirukta   54
yatra   90, 206, 293

Yeats, W. B.   104
  Sailing to Byzantium   104
yoga (yōga)   2, 3, 9, 33, 37, 40, 50, 117, 118, 119, 202, 220, 221, 241, 244
  practice of   37, 118
  pranayama   37, 118
  yogic perception   118
  yogic posture   118
Yogi, Mahesh   118, 201, 202
  The Science of Being and the Art of Living   202
Yojana (yojanā)/Planning   296
YouTube   49, 166, 177, 415
yukti   316
Yule, Henry   88

zakat   41, 222, 265
zanana (zanānā)   231, 232
zero   9, 73, 74, 221, 401
Zila Parishad   364
Zoroaster   62
Zubaan   232
  Begmati   232
zuk-zii-skyon-ba   251

www.ingramcontent.com/pod-product-compliance
Lightning Source LLC
Chambersburg PA
CBHW081754300426
44116CB00014B/2119